Cash Pooling and Insolvency

A Practical Global Handbook

Consulting Editor **Marcel Willems**

Consulting editor
Marcel Willems

Publisher
Sian O'Neill

Editor
Carolyn Boyle

Production
Russell Anderson

Publishing directors
Guy Davis, Tony Harriss, Mark Lamb

Cash Pooling and Insolvency: A Practical Global Handbook
is published by
Globe Law and Business
Globe Business Publishing Ltd
New Hibernia House
Winchester Walk
London SE1 9AG
United Kingdom
Tel +44 20 7234 0606
Fax +44 20 7234 0808
Web www.globelawandbusiness.com

Printed and bound by CPI Group (UK) Ltd, Croydon, CR0 4YY

ISBN 978-1-905783-91-5

Table of contents

Introduction 5
Marcel Willems
Kennedy Van der Laan NV

Cash pooling and the EU Insolvency Regulation 13
Bart de Man
Kennedy Van der Laan NV

Austria 13
Arno Brauneis
Brauneis Klauser Prändl Rechtsanwälte GmbH

Australia 23
Ian Walker
Minter Ellison

Argentina 37
Tomás M Araya
Daniela A Bianchi
Mario Benjamín Terán
M&M Bomchil Abogados

Belgium 55
Tom Geudens
Yves Lenders
Lydian

Brazil 71
Celso Caldas Martins Xavier
Demarest e Almeida Advogados

Canada 75
Mary Arzoumanidis
Michael J MacNaughton
Borden Ladner Gervais LLP

China 89
Belinda Danqing Zhou
Hans Qizong Zhang
Tian Xu
Eiger Law

Cyprus 99
Venetia Argyropoulou
Alexandra Pelaghias-Christodoulou
Pelaghias, Christodoulou, Vrachas LLC

Czech Republic 111
Bill Finney
Ernst Giese
Giese & Partner, vos

Denmark 125
Carsten Ceutz
Morten Krogsgaard
Arne Riis
Bech-Bruun

England 139
Graeme Levy
Squire Sanders (UK) LLP

Finland 161
Pekka Jaatinen
Anna-Kaisa Remes
Castrén & Snellman Attorneys Ltd

France 173
Anja Droege Gagnier
BMH Avocats

Germany ____ 187
Daniela Mader
Kirsten Schümann-Kleber
GÖRG Partnerschaft von Rechtsanwälten

Greece ____ 203
Constantinos N Klissouras
Christina K Papachristopoulou
KP Law Firm

Hungary ____ 217
János Tóth
Wolf Theiss

Ireland ____ 231
Daragh Bohan
Frank Flanagan
Maurice Phelan
Mason Hayes & Curran

Italy ____ 251
Flavio Acerbi
Domenico Gioia
Paolo Manganelli
Cosimo Pennetta
Paul Hastings (Europe) LLP

Japan ____ 291
Naoya Ariyoshi
Maya Ito
Shinsuke Ushirobira
Nishimura & Asahi

Luxembourg ____ 307
Laurent Fisch
Molitor Avocats à la Cour

Mexico ____ 325
Darío U Oscós
Oscós Abogados

Netherlands ____ 333
Joris van Horzen
Kennedy van der Laan NV

Norway ____ 345
Borge Grottjord
Kari Amalie Pettersen
Grette DA

Portugal ____ 369
Miguel de Avillez Pereira
João Ochôa
Abreu Advogados

South Korea ____ 379
Sang-Jin Ahn
Keum-Ho Lee
Steve Sunghwa Song
Kim & Chang

Spain ____ 391
Luisa de Alarcón
Borja Pardo
Felipe Pineda
JAUSAS

Sweden ____ 411
Kristina Einarsson
Odd Swarting
Setterwalls Law Firm

Switzerland ____ 423
Benedict F Christ
David Jenny
Nadia Tarolli Schmidt
VISCHER Ltd

United States ____ 433
Judith Elkin
Kourtney P Lyda
Arsalan Muhammad
Kelli M Stephenson
Hayes and Boone LLP

About the authors ____ 455

Introduction

Marcel Willems
Kennedy Van der Laan NV

Some years ago, the International Bar Association Section on Insolvency, Restructuring and Creditors' Rights held a session on cash pooling at its annual spring meeting. The session was very interesting and generated a lively debate on the issues. This gave rise to the idea to publish a guide to cash pooling, discussing the legal and practical implications of the topic in various jurisdictions.

Careful consideration was given as to which jurisdictions to include in the guide. It was ultimately decided to include most EU countries, the United States, Canada and Australia, the BRICS (Brazil, Russia, India, China and South Africa) and certain other countries. Some jurisdictions were excluded because they do not recognise cash pooling; others because of difficulties in gathering the necessary information. We have attempted to make the guide as comprehensive and reader friendly as possible, given the complexities of the subject.

In today's globalised era, cash pooling is a hot topic. It is essential that corporate officers and directors, attorneys, insolvency practitioners, bankers and financial institutions understand how cash pooling works in their own jurisdictions, as well as in situations involving cross-border financial relationships This guide discusses the practical and legal aspects and effects of cash pooling agreements, as well as the implications of the insolvency of any of the parties involved in the relationship, giving insolvency practitioners and other interested parties concerned a clearer insight into the rights and obligations related to and resulting from cash pooling agreements.

In preparing this guide, we identified a number of questions which must be answered to understand how a cash pooling agreement works and the impact of insolvency on the agreement. Each contributor was asked the same questions, but was free to modify them in a way that allowed them to be answered as most appropriate to the relevant jurisdiction. In some instances, this resulted in the use of different terminology. For example, the terms 'bankruptcy' and 'insolvency' are both used, but may have different connotations; the same goes for the terms 'insolvency practitioner', 'insolvency administrator', 'trustee', 'liquidator' and so on. Contributors were free to use the terminology that is normally used in their own jurisdictions, allowing for a fluent discussion of the benefits and potential pitfalls of cash pooling agreements in each jurisdiction covered.

We have, however, defined some of the basic terms that are used in this guide, as follows:

- Group company – a company participating in a cash pooling agreement (not the master account holder).

- Master account holder – the company (usually the parent company or a special treasury entity) that enters into a cash pooling agreement with a bank.
- Liquidation event – the process by which a company either voluntarily or compulsory seeks (temporary) relief from its creditors or is wound up with the aim of selling its assets and distributing the proceeds of sale among its creditors. By way of example, liquidation events are set out in Chapter 7 and Chapter 11 of the US Bankruptcy Code, and insolvency proceedings are defined in Article 2 of the EU Insolvency Regulation.
- Master account – the main bank account used for the cash pooling scheme.
- Physical cash pooling – a cash pooling agreement that involves the physical movement of money between group company accounts and the master account. In practice, it is implemented through various different techniques, such as zero balancing and target balancing.
- Notional cash pooling – a cash pooling agreement in which a bank notionally combines the balances across several accounts and pays or charges interest (only) on the combined balance.
- Zero balancing – periodic transfers of credit amounts to the master account.
- Target balancing – periodic transfers of credit amounts to the master account followed by the retransfer of certain amounts, established in advance, from the master account to group company accounts.

We hope and believe that this guide will be a helpful tool in understanding the workings of cash pooling agreements, as well as the potential risks that may occur should one of the parties involved become insolvent.

Finally, we would like to express our gratitude to all those who have contributed to this guide. Without their time and effort, we could never have achieved this tremendous result.

Cash pooling and the EU Insolvency Regulation

Bart de Man
Kennedy Van der Laan NV

1. Introduction

A cash pooling agreement is often used in an international context, whereby the group of companies included in the arrangement are situated in different jurisdictions. In this chapter we expand on cross-border jurisdiction issues, when one or more participants to the cash pooling agreement are located in the European Union and become subject to insolvency proceedings.

2. EU Insolvency Regulation

On May 31 2002, the EU Insolvency Regulation came into force.[1] The regulation is applicable in all EU member states, except Denmark. The regulation is applicable only to insolvency proceedings whereby the centre of main interests of the debtor is located in the European Union.[2] The centre of main interests of a company is presumed to be located in the jurisdiction where that company has its registered office.[3] The regulation provides a set of rules for the competence of the courts, the recognition and execution of decisions and applicable law – all in the context of insolvency proceedings and actions that directly derive from insolvency proceedings and are closely linked to them.[4]

3. Relevance of the regulation for cash pooling agreements

If one or more of the companies participating in the cash pooling agreement have their centre of main interests in the European Union and become subject to insolvency proceedings opened in an EU member state, the insolvency proceedings will be recognised by all other EU member states from the time that it becomes effective in the state of the opening of proceedings.[5]

The law of the state of the opening of proceedings (the *lex concursus*) shall

1 Council Regulation (EC) No 1346/2000 of May 29 2000 on insolvency proceedings (*Official Journal of the European Union* June 30 2000, L160/1).
2 The various insolvency proceedings that fall under the scope of the regulation are listed in Annexes A and B, as referred to in respectively Article 2(a) and (c) of the regulation.
3 Article 3(1) of the regulation. The most significant European Court of Justice (ECJ) cases regarding determination of the centre of main interests to date are: judgment of May 2 2006 in *Eurofood IFSC Ltd* (C-341/04) [2006] ECR I-3813 and judgment of October 20 2011 in *Interedil Srl (in liquidation) v Fallimento Interedil Srl* (C-396/09).
4 See the judgment of the ECJ of February 12 in *Seagon v Deko Marty Belgium NV* (C-339/07) [2009] ECR I-767.
5 Article 16 of the regulation.

determine the conditions for the opening of those proceedings, their conduct and their closure.[6]

It is important to learn what laws govern the rights and obligations of the parties to the cash pooling agreement, the transactions performed under the arrangement and when and how to affect those rights, obligations and transactions.

Hereafter we describe the legal issues arising from application of the EU Insolvency Regulation in relation to:

- agreements in general;
- set-off;
- security rights;
- joint and several liability as well as (parent) guarantees;
- fraudulent conveyance;
- directors' and officers' liability;
- corporate matters such as *ultra vires*, financial assistance (maintenance of capital) and conflict of interests; and
- what will happen if the bank becomes subject to insolvency proceedings.

3.1 Agreements in general

A cash pooling agreement is a multi-party agreement between a bank and two or more companies belonging to the same group of companies. Article 4(2)(e) of the EU Insolvency Regulation provides that the law of the state of the opening of proceedings determines the effects of insolvency proceedings on current contracts to which the debtor is a party. The regulation does not define the term 'current contracts'.

The law of the state of the opening of proceedings therefore also determines whether and to what extent the bank (or any other party to the cash pooling agreement) has a right to terminate that agreement, even if such a right would be granted under the agreement if insolvency proceedings were opened.

How much the law of the state of the opening of proceedings will determine in relation to current contracts can differ substantially from jurisdiction to jurisdiction. Insofar as the law of the state of the opening of proceedings does not determine what the effects of the insolvency proceedings are, these will still be determined by the law applicable to the agreement (the *lex contractus*).

If one or more participating companies enter into insolvency proceedings, the consequence thereof could be that the cash pooling agreement is terminated by law (as a result of the law of the state of the opening of proceedings) or by the bank (or one of the remaining participating companies) using its contractual termination right. This could be a partial termination – that is, it is terminated only with regard to the participant in insolvency proceedings – or a full termination with regard to all parties to the agreement. The parties to the cash pooling agreement will have to take these possible consequences into account when concluding it, and may want to include an arrangement for the remaining participants that are not subject to insolvency proceedings.

---

6 Article 4(2) of the regulation.

3.2 Set-off

The basis of a cash pooling agreement is that claims and obligations of the participants towards the bank are offset. Article 4(2)(d) of the EU Insolvency Regulation says that the law of the state of the opening of proceedings determines the conditions under which a right of set-off may be invoked. It also determines the rights of creditors that have obtained partial satisfaction after the opening of insolvency proceedings through a set-off.[7] The opening of the insolvency proceedings does not affect the right of creditors to demand the set-off of their claims against the claims of the debtor, where such a set-off is permitted by the law applicable to the debtor's claim under Article 6 of the regulation.

Article 6 of the regulation is applicable only to set-off of mutual obligations which have been entered into prior to the opening of insolvency proceedings. After the opening of insolvency proceedings, Article 4 of the regulation is applicable. A set-off can still be void, voidable or unenforceable as referred to in Article 4(2)(m) of the regulation.[8]

One might think that Article 9 of the regulation is also applicable to cash pooling agreements, as it speaks of "payment or settlement systems". A cash pooling agreement can be considered to qualify as some kind of a settlement system. Nevertheless, Article 9 of the regulation is not intended to apply to cash pooling agreements. Paragraph 27 of the preamble to the regulation explains the rationale of Article 9, which is to be found in transactions as governed in particular by the EU Settlement Directive.[9] The payment systems referred to therein should be designated by the member states and notified to the European Commission.

3.3 Security rights

Security rights in favour of the bank usually form part of a cash pooling agreement, in particular – but not necessarily limited to – a security right over the credit balances of all accounts that are part of the arrangement.

Security rights of creditors over assets that, at the time of the opening of proceedings, are located in other EU member states are not affected by the opening of insolvency proceedings according to Article 5 of the EU Insolvency Regulation. More specifically, Article 5 of the regulation provides that the opening of insolvency proceedings shall not affect "rights *in rem*" of creditors in respect of assets belonging to the debtor, which are situated within the territory of another member state at the time of the opening of proceedings.

The regulation does not define what a "right *in rem*" is. It will be determined by the law applicable to the assets where they are located at the relevant time.[10] Where an asset is located will be determined by the private international law rules of each member state jurisdiction, including applicable EU rules.

---

7 Article 4(2)(i) of the regulation.

8 Article 6(2) of the regulation.

9 Directive 98/26/EC of the European Parliament and of the Council of May 19 1998 (*Official Journal of the European Union* June 11 1998 L166/50), amended by Directive 2009/44/EC of the European Parliament and of the Council of June 10 2009 (*Official Journal of the European Union* June 10, 2009 L146/37).

10 See Virgós and Schmit, *Report on the Convention on Insolvency Proceedings* dated July 8 1996 (6500/1/96 ANNEX).

Under Article 5(2) of the regulation, the 'rights *in rem*' referred to mean, in particular:

(a) *the right to dispose of assets or have them disposed of and to obtain satisfaction from the proceeds of or income from those assets, in particular by virtue of a lien or a mortgage;*

(b) *the exclusive right to have a claim met, in particular a right guaranteed by a lien in respect of the claim or by assignment of the claim by way of a guarantee;*

(c) *the right to demand the assets from, and/or to require restitution by, anyone having possession or use of them contrary to the wishes of the party so entitled;*

(d) *a right* in rem *to the beneficial use of assets.*

Article 5 of the regulation applies only to rights *in rem* created before the opening of proceedings. If the assets are situated in a non-EU member state, Article 5 of the regulation is not applicable.

Article 5(1) of the regulation does not preclude actions for voidness, voidability or unenforceability as referred to in Article 4(2)(m) of the regulation.[11]

3.4 Joint and several liability and (parent) guarantees

Most cash pooling agreements contain provisions to the effect that all participating companies are jointly and severally liable to the bank. Moreover, the agreement will usually contain a guarantee from the parent company and master account holder.

What the validity of these provisions will be after insolvency proceedings are opened against one or more of the participating companies is primarily a matter of the rule applicable to current contracts. This is discussed above at section 3.1.

If one of the participants makes a payment under the joint and several liability obligations, or as a guarantor, it will have a claim for compensation against the non-paying debtor and group company that is involved in the insolvency proceedings. The law of the state of the opening of proceedings will determine what rights this paying creditor has against the debtor/group company accordingly. Under Articles 4(2)(g) and (i) of the the EU Insolvency Regulation, the law of the state of the opening of proceedings determines:

- the claims which are to be lodged and the treatment of claims; and
- the rules governing the distribution of proceeds and the ranking of creditors.

3.5 Fraudulent conveyance

It may be argued that under certain circumstances a cash pooling agreement can be detrimental to the rights of other creditors of a participating company, in particular when this company becomes subject to insolvency proceedings. All EU jurisdictions have provisions of some sort regarding the voidance, avoidability or unenforceability of legal acts if they are or could be detrimental to the rights of other creditors ('fraudulent conveyance'). Reference is made to several chapters in this book in which this risk is recognised.

The EU Insolvency Regulation contains specific provisions regarding fraudulent conveyance.

---

11 Article 5(4) of the regulation.

The general rule is set out in Article 4(2)(m) of the regulation, which provides that the law of the state of the opening of proceedings determines rules relating to the voidness, voidability or unenforceability of legal acts that are detrimental to all creditors.

Article 4(2)(m) does not apply, however, if the person that benefited from such detrimental act provides proof that:

- the act is subject to the law of a member state other than that in which the insolvency proceedings were opened; and
- that law does not allow for any means of challenging the act in the relevant case.[12]

This is an important rule, providing a way out for the benefiting creditor if it succeeds in passing this double test.

3.6 Directors' and officers' liability

The EU Insolvency Regulation does not contain any specific rules regarding jurisdiction or applicable law in relation to directors' and officers' liability.

However, the courts of the member state within the territory of which insolvency proceedings have been opened have jurisdiction under Article 3(1) of the regulation to decide about actions that directly derive from insolvency proceedings and are closely linked to them, even if the defendant has its registered office in another member state.[13] This includes actions to set aside transactions by virtue of insolvency. It also includes claims that an administrator or liquidator in insolvency proceedings has against (former) directors and officers of a company that is subject to insolvency proceedings.[14] This jurisdiction seems to be exclusive.[15]

Under Article 25 of the regulation, the courts of other member states have to recognise such decisions of the courts of other member states.

The regulation does not contain any rules regarding the applicable law in relation to directors' and officers' liability. This will be determined by the private international law of each member state.

3.7 Corporate matters such as *ultra vires*, financial assistance (maintenance of capital) and conflict of interests

The EU Insolvency Regulation does not contain specific rules regarding jurisdiction or applicable law in relation to *ultra vires*, financial assistance (capitalisation requirements) and conflict of interests.

---

12 Article 13 of the regulation.

13 See European Court of Justice judgment of February 12 2009 in *Seagon v Deko Marty Belgium NV* (C-339/07) [2009] ECR I-767.

14 This can be derived from the *Seagon v Dekon Marty* case. It has been explicitly confirmed by the Netherlands Court of First Instance in Dordrecht in a judgment of February 3 2010 (*Gilhuis v X*), JOR 2010/90. This case was about insolvency proceedings opened in the Netherlands and the Belgian director being held liable in the Netherlands.

15 Again, although not explicitly stated, this can be derived from the judgment in *Seagon v Deko Marty*, and it was stated explicitly by the Netherlands Court of Appeal in Amsterdam in a judgment of November 3 2009 (*Groet Houdstermaatschappij v Conrads*), JOR 2010/244. This case concerned a German liquidator claiming exclusive jurisdiction for the courts of Germany where insolvency proceedings were opened in relation to a fraudulent conveyance action. The Amsterdam Court of Appeal decided that the German courts had exclusive jurisdiction.

It could be argued that claims of an administrator or liquidator to set aside transactions, based on *ultra vires*, capitalisation requirements or conflict of interests, are to be brought before the courts of the member state within the territory of which the insolvency proceedings have been opened. Such claims are directed at the same assets as, or assets additional to, those pursued by the claim arising from the right to seek to have a transaction set aside by virtue of insolvency (see paragraph 3.6 above). A question in relation to maintenance of capital has been referred to the European Court of Justice by the German Court of First Instance in Essen.[16] It is uncertain what will be decided by the European Court of Justice. An argument against what is proposed above could be that these actions do not derive from the insolvency proceedings and are not closely linked to them, since they derive from the corporate legal system in a country and do not have a direct link to the insolvency proceedings. Rather, these actions have only an indirect link with the insolvency proceedings, from the administrator or liquidator starting an action based thereon for the purpose of increasing the estate in the insolvency proceedings.

3.8 Bank becomes subject to insolvency proceedings

The EU Insolvency Regulation does not contain any rules regarding jurisdiction or applicable law in relation to insolvency proceedings of banks or other financial institutions.

The rules regarding the reorganisation and winding up of credit institutions have been incorporated in national legislation by the EU member states as a result of the Directive of the European Parliament and of the Council dated April 4 2001.[17]

---

16 Landgericht Essen November 25 2010, ZIP 2011, 875.

17 Directive 2001/24/EC of the European Parliament and of the Council of 4 April 2001 on the reorganisation and winding up of credit institutions (*Official Journal of the European Union* May 5 2001 L125/15).

Austria

Arno Brauneis
Brauneis Klauser Prändl Rechtsanwälte GmbH

1. Types of cash pooling agreement

Both physical and notional cash pooling agreements are well established in Austria. Austrian law does not in principle prohibit a corporation from entering into such an agreement, or a holding company from setting up such arrangements with its group members, regardless of whether any are foreign companies.

Regarding the basic cash pooling structure, the master account holder and the pool bank enter into a framework agreement to which the other pool companies then accede. This establishes legal relations between the pool bank and the master account holder, which then extend to and connect the separate pool companies. These legal relations differ depending on whether a physical or notional cash pooling system is in place.

In the case of a notional cash pooling agreement, a bank will notionally combine the balances across several accounts and pay or charge interest only on the combined balance. Notional cash pooling is based on the fictive consolidation of account balances; there is no real movement of funds between the relevant accounts. Credit and debit balances are notionally brought together and offset to establish a net position for the calculation of interest.

Because the funds never actually leave the group company accounts, such a notional cash pooling agreement is largely irrelevant with regard to Austrian capital maintenance rules and creditor protection rules, and thus is not discussed further in this chapter.

The legal relations regarding physical cash pooling concern services such as account management, the execution of transfers, the granting of credit lines, the acceptance of liabilities and the creation of collateral.

A cash pooling agreement usually has no direct legal consequences with regard to third parties and requires no loss-sharing agreement between the companies involved. Internally, a cash pooling agreement is subject to the general rules applicable to continuing obligations. Based on the autonomous nature of the agreement, restrictions mainly arise from corporate and tax laws.

2. Corporate law issues

2.1 Capital maintenance

Austrian corporate law requires adherence to a number of provisions regarding cash pooling agreements. The most important are the rules on capital maintenance.

According to Section 82 of the Limited Liability Companies Act and Section 52 of the Joint Stock Companies Act, no contributions may be repaid to the shareholders, because they are entitled only to net profits. Moreover, a company may make payments to shareholders beyond the distribution of net profits only if appropriate consideration on an arm's-length basis is granted for those payments.

In all other cases, a shareholder of a limited liability company can make no claims for payment and the company can make no payments to its shareholders.

Section 82 of the Limited Liabilities Companies Act is a mandatory provision aimed at maintaining the company's capital. The same holds true for Section 52 of the Joint Stock Companies Act.[1]

Whether a benefit granted to a shareholder[2] constitutes a return of equity is not purely a question of there being a disparity between the benefit granted and the benefit received. Any such disparity leads to an assumption that a forbidden return of equity has been made.[3] However, this may be rebutted if it can be proved that the transaction was entered into on an arm's-length basis[4] – in other words, that the company would also have entered into a similar transaction with an unrelated third party.[5] Any advantage granted to shareholders which would not have been available to an unrelated third party is thus void.[6]

A return of equity that is forbidden in principle may nonetheless be justified if there are special corporate reasons in the interests of the company – but here again, only in the case of an arm's-length transaction.[7] A forbidden return of equity may in particular be assumed if an interest-free or discounted loan has been issued to the shareholders of a limited liability company or a joint stock company.[8]

3. Liability issues

According to Section 70 of the Joint Stock Companies Act, the managing board of a joint stock company[9] shall be solely responsible for management. The introduction of cash pooling within a group generally constitutes a management measure within the managing board's decision-making powers. According to Section 81(1) of the Joint Stock Companies Act, the managing board shall immediately report to the supervisory board[10] all circumstances which may affect the company's liquidity.

The managing board may also be required to obtain the supervisory board's

1 *Koppensteiner/Rüffler, GmbHG-Kommentar,*[3] Section 82 marg note 12, *Artmann* in *Jabornegg/Strasser Aktiengesetz,*[5] Section 52 marg note 1 *et seq* – with respect to the relation to the Equity Replacement Act: marg note 50 *et seq.*

2 Not only upstream, but also sidestream benefits are subject to the rules on capital maintenance.

3 OGH, JBl 1996, 388.

4 Cf *Koppensteiner*, GmbHG[3], Section 82, marg note 16, cf Artmann, AktG5, Section 52 marg note 11 *et seq*, 29 *et seq.*

5 RS 0105540.

6 SZ 2003/133 with further notes.

7 See OGH JBl 2006, 288.

8 See OGH JBl 2006, 388.

9 The management of an Austrian joint stock company ('*Vorstand*') is best translated as 'managing board' (which consists of one or more members), whereas the management of a limited liability company ('*Geschäftsführer*') is best translated as 'managing directors'. While joint stock companies must also have a supervisory board ('*Aufsichtsrat*'), which must consist of at least three members, this is the case for limited liability companies only under certain special conditions.

10 See note 8.

consent before cash pooling is introduced, as certain activities that may significantly affect the company require the supervisory board's prior consent. Section 95 of the Joint Stock Companies Act lists those transactions which fall outside the ordinary course of business and thus require the supervisory board's prior consent.

According to Section 95(5) of the Joint Stock Companies Act, the raising and granting of major loans and credits are transactions that require prior approval. Since the raising and granting of a large number of intra-group loans is integral to physical cash pooling, this form of lending falls outside the ordinary course of business. Therefore, the introduction of physical cash pooling will normally require the supervisory board's prior consent. (No intra-group loans are made in connection with notional cash pooling, so the supervisory board's consent is not necessarily required. However, other instruments – such as the articles of association – may stipulate that all cash pooling requires such consent.)

According to Sections 20 and 25 of the Limited Liability Companies Act, the managing directors of a limited liability company[11] are generally responsible for the management of the company.

Section 25 of the act obliges the managing directors to act with the care and diligence of prudent managers. In case of violation, the managing directors will be liable to the company. In particular, a managing director might be held liable for agreements with the shareholders of the company, if such agreements are not at arm's length.

As a rule, the managing directors of a limited liability company must observe instructions issued by the general shareholders' meeting. The managing director, however, need not do so if such instructions violate the law (eg, if they violate the capital maintenance rules). Such a violation would result in the invalidity of the resolution itself.[12]

According to legal commentators, undertakings such as the raising or granting of intra-group loans or specific forms of investment fall outside the ordinary course of business.[13] Measures that fall outside the ordinary course of business further require the shareholders' prior consent.[14] The shareholders of a group company must therefore adopt a resolution instructing the managing directors to invest or lend.

According to legal doctrine and case law, the fact that managing directors are acting on the shareholders' instructions does not relieve them of their liability towards third parties (eg, creditors, in particular in case of insolvency). Such liability cannot be avoided by a binding instruction from the general shareholders' meeting.

A violation of the capital maintenance rules may also result in the personal liability of the supervisory board's members.

Furthermore, a company's managing directors and members of its managing board may be held personally liable in the event of criminal activities such as fraudulent insolvency,[15] preferential transfers,[16] gross negligence leading to

11 See note 8.
12 *Koppensteiner*, GmbHG^3 para 20 marg note 9.
13 *Koppensteiner* GmbHG 3rd ed Section 20 marg note 4.
14 *Koppensteiner*, as above.
15 See Section 156 of the Criminal Code.
16 See Section 158 of the Criminal Code.

insolvency,[17] misrepresentation of the company's financial situation[18] or failure to file for insolvency in due time.[19, 20]

3.1 Arm's-length principle

Any transfer of assets by a company to its shareholders which benefits the shareholders at the company's expense (other than a distribution of net profits) is not permitted. To ensure that cash pooling does not violate this principle, the cash pooling agreement and the resulting transactions must transparently observe the arm's-length principle.

The managing board or directors of a company must thus be satisfied that this is the case. If there is any violation of the principles set out below, the managing board and/or directors will likely be found to have failed in their duty to act with the care and diligence of prudent managers.

With respect to the arm's-length principle, just as in the case of any third-party transaction:

- reasonable interest must be charged for the provision of funds. A 'reasonable rate of interest' is often defined as one that is consistent with rates charged by commercial lenders (see, however, section 4 below);
- the risk arising from the loan transaction must be continuously evaluated and the company must be permitted to inspect its shareholders (ie, parent companies or affiliates) to evaluate that risk. In order to allow for proper risk assessment, the agreement must grant the company full rights of information. The company must be able to obtain a detailed account of the invested funds on a daily basis, as well as the lender/borrower status and economic situation of its shareholders. Any violation of such obligations will entitle the company to terminate the agreement and withdraw the funds;
- the economic risk to any company that has made a loan or invested funds with its shareholders (parent companies) or affiliates must further be evaluated. As with any other third-party borrower, suitable customary collateral (eg, bank guarantees or mortgages) must be granted by the borrowing shareholders; and
- the company must retain the right to terminate the agreement for the reasons set out above, as well as at any time.

Before a company joins a physical cash pooling system, it must therefore be considered, in addition to the rules above, whether appropriate consideration is being granted for accession to that system and whether the company will enjoy an economic benefit as a result.

According to recent case law and legal commentary, a group company's management may also consider existing group benefits when determining whether

---

17 See Section 159 of the Criminal Code.

18 For example, regarding information given to the certified public accountant or included in the financial statement.

19 See Section 26 of the Limited Liability Companies Act.

20 The same is true for public limited companies (Section 84 of the Joint Stock Company Act for directors) and the same holds true for supervisory directors (Section 99 of the Joint Stock Company Act).

participation in a cash pooling agreement is economically legitimate. However, the group company must also have relevant individual interests in participating in the pool.

3.2 Shareholders' liability

As a general principle, the corporate veil cannot be pierced under Austrian law. Neither the shareholders nor their managers are liable towards third parties for the liabilities of an Austrian limited liability company or joint stock company.

Only in exceptional cases do legal doctrine and case law provide for direct liability of a company's shareholders. This might apply, for instance, if:

- the company is actually being managed by its shareholders (eg, if the shareholders intervene in the company's daily business by giving specific instructions to the management);
- there is an under-capitalisation within the meaning of Section 22 of the Business Reorganisation Act from the start; or
- there is an abuse of corporate form.[21]

In such cases a company's shareholders might risk being directly liable to creditors or, in case of insolvency, the receiver.

Because the corporate veil cannot, as a rule, be pierced, it is difficult (but not impossible) to pursue other group companies for any losses suffered.

3. Banking issues

Any banking business conducted on a commercial basis requires a licence. In Austria, it is unclear whether the activities of an Austrian corporation that acts as master account holder are considered to constitute banking business and are thus governed by the Banking Act.

If a licence must be obtained, the Banking Act stipulates certain requirements (eg, minimum initial capital requirements for managers and owners, availability of adequate internal control systems and risk management procedures). In addition, all provisions of the Banking Act (eg, those on own funds and solvency, large exposures and liquidity) must be observed. If any banking business is conducted without authorisation, this constitutes an administrative offence for which the Financial Market Authority may impose a fine of up to €50,000, unless the scale of the offence is a matter for the courts.

According to Section 1(1) of the Banking Act, banking business which may be eligible for cash pooling includes (but is not limited to) chequing account business, deposit business and credit business. This is because in the course of physical cash pooling, the master account holder transfers payments between different group companies.

However, a licence under the Banking Act need be obtained only if these activities are carried out "on a commercial basis", as defined in Section 1(1) of the Banking Act, which bases its definition on the Value Added Tax (VAT) Act. This states

---

21 *Torggler*, 5 *(Anti-)Thesen zum Haftungsdurchgriff* in JBl (2006), 85 *et seq*; *Koppensteiner/Rüffler*, GmbHG[3], § 61 Rz 34 *et seq*.

that an activity is deemed to be carried out on a commercial basis if it is aimed at generating income and involves a certain degree of sustainability.

However, legal commentators have developed another definition, based on the supervisory objectives of the Banking Act, which holds that activities that may jeopardise the operability of the banking business or counteract the protection of investors are deemed to be carried out on a commercial basis. Thus, purely intra-group financing activities such as cash pooling need not be supervised, due to the restricted number of participants; and because such activities are not carried out on a commercial basis, no licence is required.

For example, the German Banking Act stipulates that companies that undertake banking business with group companies only are not considered credit institutions and therefore need not obtain a licence. No such provision exists in Austria, and in consequence the legal situation remains unclear.

Otherwise, there are no banking law regulations regarding cash pooling agreements in Austria. Further, if a bank in Austria enters into a cash pooling agreement with a corporate group, it need not meet specific requirements regarding regulatory capital and security structure.

4. Tax issues

From a tax perspective, an Austrian company is free to enter into a cash pooling agreement. There is no general requirement to inform the tax authorities of its implementation.

However, the tax authorities are entitled to demand any documentation that is relevant to determining a company's Austrian tax base. In practice, this means that the tax authorities will request the cash pooling agreement during a tax audit.

Pre-approval of the cash pooling agreement by the Austrian tax authorities is not necessary, although rulings may be obtained.

Generally speaking, interest payments from an Austrian participant to a non-resident company are not subject to withholding tax in Austria, so no specific declarations need be disclosed to the Austrian tax authorities in connection with the cash pooling agreement. However, interest derived by non-resident companies from loans secured by immovable property located in Austria is subject to non-resident taxation.

There are no specific regulations on interest rates for cash pooling agreements. However, the arm's-length principle again applies. And while normal market interest rates might appear acceptable, the Austrian tax authorities hold that such a 'simple' arm's-length test is insufficient for such purposes.

In determining the arm's-length interest rate, many other factors (eg, total funds needed, variable or fixed interest rates, risk, creditworthiness and collateral) should be considered. Appropriate documentation is required to prove that the charged interest complies with the arm's-length principle. Although no legal documentation conditions need be satisfied, the tax authorities usually request general transfer pricing documentation during an audit and often require documentation showing that no excessive residual profit is retained by the master account holder. Thus, it may be necessary to specifically document the risks and functions of this company.

The tax authorities rely on the Organisation for Economic Cooperation and Development (OECD) transfer pricing principles and the OECD documentation requirements are generally regarded as sufficient

Further, the tax authorities usually take the view that no excess residual profit should be retained by the master account holder; the interest spread should cover the costs. Consequently, a transfer pricing study is advisable in order to evaluate the accuracy of the interest rates.

As a rule, interest resulting from the crediting and debiting of balances to a master account would be subject to VAT;[22] but according to Section 6 of the VAT Act, such interest is exempt from VAT.[23] If the master account holder does not have a permanent establishment in Austria, then the majority of its foreign-based services might – if not tax exempt – be subject to the reverse charge mechanism (as a rule, the service provider is liable to pay VAT, but under special circumstances the service recipient may become liable instead).

In addition, the National Bank must be informed of all cross-border interest income and expenses. Should the total of all loans granted between the group companies (calculated on a worldwide basis) exceed €3 billion in any given month, the Austrian pool company must report the fact.

5. Insolvency issues

If a group company that participates in a cash pooling agreement is in crisis, a loan granted within the scope of the agreement may be considered an equity-replacing loan. An Austrian limited liability company or joint stock company is in crisis if it is insolvent or over-indebted, or if the company is in need of reorganisation. According to Section 22 of the Business Reorganisation Act, a company is presumed to be in need of reorganisation is if it is undercapitalised[24] and has a hypothetical redemption period[25] of more than 15 years. In such cases a claim for payment of the loan receivable would qualify as a subordinate claim against the company in the event of bankruptcy. A pro-rated payment in connection with that claim cannot be made before all other creditors have been satisfied in full. Even if the loan is constructed as a direct transaction between two group companies, it will still be viewed as an equity-replacing loan, even though the creditor is not legally a shareholder of the debtor.[26]

In addition, equity-replacing loans already redeemed may have to be repaid to the insolvent company, because such loans may not be redeemed during a crisis. So if such loans are repaid, it must be established that the borrowing company is not subject to a crisis as defined by the Equity Replacement Act. If an equity-replacing loan is given without shareholder approval or is against the law (eg, on grounds of unlawful distribution), the managing board/managing directors or the shareholders become personally liable.[27]

---

22 Sections 1 and 3a of the VAT Act.
23 Section 6 of the VAT Act.
24 Equity capital ratio of less than 8% (see Section 23 of the Business Reorganisation Act).
25 See Section 24 of the Business Reorganisation Act.
26 The reason for that is the legal fiction in Section 9 of the Equity Replacement Act.
27 Section 25 of the Limited Liability Companies Act and Section 84 of the Joint Stock Companies Act.

Even if a redeemed loan does not qualify as an equity-replacing loan, a judicially appointed bankruptcy trustee may challenge payments made by the insolvent company under the Bankruptcy Code (including, without limitation, based on the offences of fraudulent preference and knowledge or negligent lack of knowledge of inability to pay).

If a parent company is subject to insolvency proceedings, the subsidiaries' loan receivables will be satisfied only through a claim against the bankruptcy estate on a pro-rated basis.

On the other hand, if the parent company and master account holder become insolvent while in possession of a loan that does not adhere to the arm's-length principle (notably without collateral) and cannot be repaid, the managing board/managing directors of the group company may become personally liable to creditors or to the receiver, where applicable. It is irrelevant whether the group company or the parent company is listed, or whether the distressed parent company is registered in a foreign jurisdiction.

Austrian case law and legal doctrine have not yet touched on the question of whether the bank holding the master account may become liable to creditors should one of the companies (notably the master account holder) become insolvent. However, such liability might be argued if the bank managing the master account knows that the management practices of the master account holder do not adhere to the arm's-length principle or contravene the prohibition against return of equity.

Upon taking over the management of the company, the receiver is duty-bound to act with the care and diligence of an expert.[28] It has the authority to void suspect pre-petition transactions – specifically:

- those intended to put creditors at a disadvantage;[29]
- those without fair consideration;[30]
- those which provide security or settlement for a debt not yet due;[31] and
- those in which the other party knew or should have known of the insolvency.[32]

Except for transactions in which the insolvent company is the creditor, there is no right for early termination of the contract. If the insolvent company is the debtor, the receiver must notify the commencement of the insolvency proceedings publicly to give creditors the chance to file their claims.

Should the bank holding the master account become insolvent, any group company's claim remains a claim against the master account holder. The master account holder has an impaired claim against the bank.

The managing board and managing directors can be held liable in their relations with the insolvent company – often due to a failure on their part to file for

28 Section 1299 of the General Civil Code.
29 If the other party knew of the intent, up to 10 years; if the other party should have known, up to two years.
30 Up to two years.
31 Up to one year.
32 Up to six months.

insolvency in due time.[33] In such cases the claim is part of the estate, meaning that only the receiver can file it.[34, 35]

The conduct of the managing board and managing directors can also be punished under the Criminal Code.[36] In that case, third parties can base their claims on any such criminal conduct.

33 Sections 99 and 84 of the Joint Stock Companies Act.
34 Section 85 of the Joint Stock Companies Act.
35 RS0049479, 5 Ob 306/76.
36 Sections 156, 158 and 159 of the Criminal Code.

Australia

Ian Walker
Minter Ellison

1. Introduction

1.1 Admissibility of cash pooling agreements

There is no legal prohibition in Australia that prevents a corporation from entering into a cash pooling agreement, or that would operate to prevent its holding company from setting up a cash pooling agreement with its group members. It does not matter whether the type of cash pooling is notional or physical. The fact that the master account holder is a foreign corporation does not change this.

1.2 Types of cash pooling agreement

The cash pooling agreements used in Australia are often dictated by the jurisdiction of the master account holder, where an Australian subsidiary is involved in a global group. This tends to mean that cash pooling agreements that operate in Australia are often governed by English, US or other foreign law and take the form that operates in those jurisdictions.

1.3 Legal requirements from various perspectives

Australia does not have specific legal requirements with respect to cash pooling agreements. No practical distinction is made between physical and notional cash pooling. Normal corporate governance requirements must be observed in relation to entry into a cash pooling agreement.

In terms of banking law, the bank providing the banking service used in the provision of the cash pooling must take appropriate steps to ensure that the mechanism of a notional cash pooling agreement works in practice, by taking a guarantee from the participants. Otherwise, there is little in the way of specific legal requirements for a bank entering into a cash pooling agreement.

From an insolvency perspective, a cash pooling agreement can be terminated as far as an Australian company participant is concerned once a counterparty master account holder becomes insolvent. The operation of *ipso facto* clauses is not restricted under Australian insolvency law. Termination within the terms of the agreement remains a possibility if one of the parties becomes insolvent. Whether the insolvency of one party will cause the entire agreement to be terminated, as opposed to preventing the participation of one participant, will depend on its provisions.

Tax can be relevant to cash pooling agreements. No income tax, stamp duty or goods and services tax is payable on the transfer of cash from the subsidiary's bank account to the master account. If an Australian entity has to pay interest on advances it receives under the cash pooling agreement and it is liable to pay interest to the master account holder overseas, that payment will be subject to Australian interest withholding tax at the rate of 10%. Interest charged on intra-group loans under a cash pooling agreement must be fixed on an arm's-length basis. Failure to do so may attract the operation of the transfer pricing rules of the Australian Taxation Office. The extent of deductions claimed may also be affected by the thin capitalisation rules.

1.4 General legal requirements

The normal rules that govern the entry of companies into contracts under Australian company law will apply to entry into a cash pooling agreement. A company's legal capacity to enter into a transaction is governed by Section 124 of the Corporations Act 2001 and the company's constitution, if it has one. However, even if there is an express restriction on the exercise of a power in the constitution, an exercise of a power in contravention of that restriction is not necessarily invalid.[1]

A company can execute a document without using the company's common seal if it is signed by two directors or a director and the company secretary.[2] Where the common seal is used, the two directors and/or a director and the company secretary must witness the affixation of the seal.[3] The director of a single director proprietary company can execute the document or witness the affixation of the seal.[4] Where the document has been executed in accordance with these provisions, a party can assume that the company has duly executed a document.[5] If a person has knowledge or a suspicion that the assumption is incorrect, the person cannot safely assume that the document has been properly executed.[6]

A bank providing the master account facilities will commonly require evidence not just that the documents have been properly executed, but also that the directors have considered the transaction from the perspective of the benefit of the participating companies involved in the transaction. Under Australian law, directors are under a statutory obligation to exercise their powers and discharge their duties in good faith in the best interests of the company and for a proper purpose.[7]

In the case of insolvency of a party to a cash pooling agreement, a solvent party to the agreement will try to avoid continued performance of the agreement. Under Australian corporate insolvency law, there is nothing to prevent a solvent counterparty from ceasing to participate in the cash pooling agreement where continued participation would put its own assets at risk. The operation of *ipso facto* clauses is not prohibited in Australia. A solvent group entity will be at risk if it lends money to an insolvent master account holder that has no capacity to repay the loan or provide further drawdowns on the master account. Continued involvement in the cash pooling agreement exposes the solvent group company to potential damage, as

---

1 Section 125(1) of the Corporations Act 2001.
2 Section 127(1) of the Corporations Act 2001.
3 Section 127(2) of the Corporations Act 2001.
4 Sections 127(1)(c) and (2)(c) of the Corporations Act 2001.
5 Sections 129(5) and (6) of the Corporations Act 2001.
6 Section 128(4) of the Corporations Act 2001.
7 Section 181(1) of the Corporations Act 2001.

it could become an unsecured creditor of the insolvent master account company (if it is not already), and the likelihood of further drawdowns on the master account is limited. Where a group company has received money from an insolvent master account holder in repayment of a loan created through the cash pooling agreement, it may be liable to disgorge the payment as an unfair preference.

There are no regulatory requirements for a cash pooling agreement in Australia, although there may well be transfer pricing and thin capitalisation issues from a tax perspective, depending on the rate of interest being applied and the level of debt on which deductions are being claimed.

2. Specific questions

2.1 Perspective A: corporate group

(a) *Liability of group company and/or master account holder directors in the event of insolvency of a group company*

At the operational core of a physical cash pooling agreement will be a loan from the group company participant to the master account holder of money swept from the group company's account into the master account. The insolvency of a group company participating in a cash pooling agreement will lead to a focus on the legitimacy of the participation in the agreement, by reference to the duties of the directors of the insolvent group entity.

The conduct of the directors of a group company will be scrutinised where they allow the group company to participate in the cash pooling agreement once insolvency intervenes and it makes loans to the master account holder. The daily sweeping of the accounts of cash pool participants occurs automatically. However, most cash pooling agreements depend on the cash of group participants being deposited in specific accounts. This must leave open the option when insolvency threatens for a group participant to choose not to deposit money into the account from which the funds will be swept.

Where insolvency threatens a company, its directors must broaden the focus of their obligations to take into account the interests of company creditors. With insolvency threatening, the need to consider those interests suggests that it would be a questionable decision for the group company to continue participating in a cash pooling agreement that removes cash from the group company's bank accounts and replaces it with a loan to the master account holder. Among the elements of the transaction that might expose the directors to risk is the making of an unsecured loan to the master account holder. Unless the directors can be sure that the group company can draw down on the master account to recover the funds lent, the group company's cash resources will be depleted at a time when access to cash is likely to be critical. If the broader group is under financial stress, then making an unsecured loan to a related entity – even though it is under a pre-existing arrangement – is probably a breach of the directors' duties.[8]

8 *Walker v Wimborne* (1976) 137 CLR 1; *Kinsella v Russell Kinsella Pty Ltd (in liq)* (1986) 4 NSWLR 722; *Bell Group Ltd (in liq) v Westpac Banking Corporation [No.9]* [2008] WASC 239 at [4439] (2008) 39 WAR 1.

Another element of cash pooling agreements that may give rise to a potential liability of the directors for breach of duty arises out of a possible conflict. The conflict arises when the directors of the insolvent group company continue to favour the master account holder's interests over those of creditors of the group company, as they are providing cash to the master account holder, with the consequence that they have deprived the insolvent group company of access to its own cash. As soon as they allow the group company's cash to be transferred, they are potentially using their position to gain an advantage for the master account holder at the expense of the insolvent group company. In that case they may have breached Section 181 of the Corporations Act, in that they will not have exercised their powers or discharged their duties in good faith, in the best interests of the group company and for a proper purpose.

This potential liability is further highlighted by Section 187 of the Corporations Act, which enables a director of a wholly owned subsidiary to act in the interests of the holding company, provided that the constitution of the subsidiary authorises it and the subsidiary is not insolvent and does not become so as a result of the act of the director.

The insolvency of a group company participant in a cash pooling agreement must therefore act as a circuit breaker to prompt a group company director to reconsider the wisdom and viability of continuing to participate in the arrangement, particularly where there is a little or no prospect of recovering cash from the master account holder.

The directors in a corporate group must give consideration to the specific interests of the group company of which they are directors. Failure to do so could lead to them breaching their fiduciary duty to the company, which can also give rise to a risk of liability for the recipient of a benefit from the directors' wrongful exercise, or as a participant in their breach of duty, as a constructive trustee.[9] In this context, that could expose the master account holder to the risk of disgorgement of a payment made by a group company if the directors of the group company acted in breach of their fiduciary duty to the company. Liability as a constructive trustee means that the group company payment could be recoverable as trust property. Whether the remedial constructive trust has priority over other creditors of the master account holder when the master account holder is insolvent is not totally free from doubt.[10]

The operation of a physical cash pooling agreement may also deprive the company of funds to pay its creditors at a critical juncture, as cash is swept out of group companies' accounts on a daily basis. While a cash pooling agreement is operating normally, it may be possible for a further drawdown to be made from the master account by a group company. However, the likelihood is that once the group

---

9 *Barnes v Addy* (1874) LR 9 Ch App 244

10 *Crouch v Abell; Application of Crouch* [2005] NSWSC 1308. The decision is at odds with decisions from other jurisdictions – see *Re Goldcorp Exchange Ltd* [1995] 1 AC 74 and an Australian decision of *Re Australian Elizabethan Theatre Trust* (1991) 30 FCR 491 per Gummow J at 510, who warned against the use of remedial constructive trusts in insolvency cases. See "Remedial Constructive Trusts in Corporate Insolvency" by Dr David Morrison (2006) 14 Insolv LJ 50.

company's poor financial position is known within the group, draws will be stopped. Many cash pooling agreements make it clear that they are not to be used to prop up financially precarious entities in a corporate group and permit the giving of notice to bring participation to an end if one of the counterparties becomes insolvent.

The existence of the ability to draw on the cash pooling agreement may be used by the directors of the group company as comfort to support an opinion that the company will be in a position to pay its creditors as their claims fall due. If that is a reasonable expectation, the directors can use it as a defence to an insolvent trading claim.[11]

If the insolvent group company's account is not in debit with the master account holder and the payment creates a credit or a loan to the master account holder, then the payment at the time of the cash sweep is not in the nature of a payment to a creditor and is not an unfair preference under Section 588FA of the Corporations Act. However, that does not mean that there is no basis for a challenge by a liquidator of the group company to such a payment.[12] A possible challenge by a liquidator could be that such a payment is an uncommercial transaction under Section 588FB of the Corporations Act, where the transaction is assessed having regard to the benefits taken or the detriment suffered by the parties as result of the transaction. A less likely basis of challenge could be as an unfair loan under Section 588FD of the Corporations Act, if the interest or charges on the loan are extortionate when the loan was made, or become so. Whether the interest on the intercompany loan is extortionate for the purposes of Section 588FD(2) will be considered in light of the risk to the lender, the security given, the term and schedule and the amount of the loan.[13]

(b) Liability of group company and/ or master account holder directors in the event of insolvency of the master account holder

If the master account holder becomes insolvent, directors of the group company participants in the cash pooling agreement cannot ignore its insolvency and continue to participate in the arrangement. Continued participation means that a group company's credit balances are swept out of its account into the master account of the insolvent master account holder. Fundamentally, this equates to allowing an asset of the company – its cash – to be paid by way of loan to an insolvent party that has no ability to repay it or otherwise observe the terms of the cash pooling agreement. This could expose the group company's directors to a claim for breach of duty.[14]

Under Australian law, if the group company suffers a loss due to some negligence or default on the part of the directors, then the group company's creditors cannot sue the group company or the directors directly in negligence for the losses suffered

11 Section 588H(2) of the Corporations Act 2001.

12 In Australia, winding up when the company is insolvent, initiated either by the company or by order of the court, leads to the appointment of a liquidator, who has the power to recover voidable transactions. Another common form of insolvency is administration is under Part 5.3A of the Corporations Act. However administrators do not have the same power as liquidators to recover voidable transactions.

13 Section 588FD(2) of the Corporations Act 2001.

14 *Walker v Wimborne* (footnote 8 above).

by them as a result of the poor management decisions that led to the continuation of participation in the cash pooling agreement, when the master account holder was insolvent. The corporate veil is, generally speaking, still honoured in Australia. There are some limited exceptions – one of which is where directors breach their duty to prevent insolvent trading.

For the directors of the group company, if the master account holder becomes insolvent the issue will be whether they should have taken action to prevent the group company's continued participation in the cash pooling agreement. If they should have prevented further involvement and a reasonable director in their position would have done so, then they may be found to have breached the duty imposed on them under the Corporations Act,[15] which requires them to exercise their powers and discharge their duties with the degree of care and diligence that a reasonable director in a similar position in the company's circumstances would exercise.

Although in Australia the doctrine of *ultra vires* has been abolished since the mid-1980s, directors are entitled to exercise only the powers conferred by the company's constitution and the law. Directors are also constrained by the obligation to use their powers for a proper purpose and must not abuse their power.[16]

On the assumption that a group company's directors have breached their duty by allowing continued participation in the cash pooling agreement, the party with a claim against them is the group company itself. A creditor of the group company has no direct standing to sue. Where the group company remains under the control of the same directors, there is little or no chance that an action will be taken by the company against those directors. In those circumstances a third party may bring proceedings on behalf of the group company with leave of the court.[17] However, the only parties that can apply for leave to bring such derivative proceedings are a member, a former member, someone entitled to be registered as such or an officer or former officer of the company. Leave to bring these proceedings will be granted only if the court is satisfied that it is probable that the company will not bring the action itself and it is in the best interests of the company that the party, which must be acting in good faith, be granted leave.[18] Once the company goes into liquidation, the liquidator becomes responsible for taking action against the directors or other participants in the breach of duty. To that end, the question of the cost of bringing the action when measured against the benefits to be gained will be relevant. If the directors have no assets, then there is limited value in the claim.

Under Australian law, directors have a duty to prevent the company of which they are directors from incurring debts at a time when the company is insolvent.[19] Breach of the duty can lead to a piercing of the corporate veil, as the directors will be rendered liable for losses suffered by creditors whose debts are not paid by virtue of the company's insolvency.[20] This is known as insolvent trading. Section 95A of the

---

15 Section 180 of the Corporations Act 2001.
16 *The Bell Group Ltd (in liq) v Westpac Banking Corporation* [No.9] [2008] WASC 239 at [4457].
17 Sections 236 and 237 of the Corporations Act 2001.
18 Section 237(2) of the Corporations Act 2001.
19 Section 588G of the Corporations Act 2001.
20 Section 588M of the Corporations Act 2001.

Corporations Act 2001 provides that a company is solvent only if it is able to pay all its debts as they become due and is payable. Solvency or insolvency is largely determined on a cash-flow basis.[21] Accordingly, if participation in the cash pooling agreement occurs when the company is insolvent, participation in the cash pooling agreement exposes the directors of the master account holder to a risk of liability for breach of their duty to prevent insolvent trading, on the basis that the insolvent master account holder has incurred a debt – the intercompany loan from the group company – that does not get paid as result of the insolvency of the participant.

The directors of the master account holder are exposed to a variety of potential liabilities if it becomes insolvent. The initial and most obvious is the insolvent trading risk created by Section 588G of the Corporations Act in connection with debts incurred, including debts to the group company under the cash pooling agreement. As far as the directors of the insolvent master account holder are concerned, where the master account holder is treated as a debtor, one element of the cash pooling agreement that becomes relevant is when the debt owed by the master account holder to the group company payable. If the debt is repayable on demand, then during the currency of the debt the risk of insolvent trading liability heightens for the directors of the master account holder.

If the bank where the master account is held is based in a foreign jurisdiction, that probably heightens the care required of group company directors when entering the transaction to make sure that the elements of the transaction work effectively as far as group companies are concerned. The mechanics of the arrangement must not produce an impediment that prevents group companies from gaining access to their cash. Other than that, the Australian companies in the agreement must have determined that it is in their interests to participate in the cash pooling agreement, whether with a foreign bank or an Australian bank. Acts or omissions of directors of Australian companies that occur outside Australia can still give rise to liability. However, the Australian law does not apply to acts of directors of foreign companies.[22]

(c) *Liability of group companies in the event of insolvency of the master account holder*

The insolvency of the master account holder does not give a right to creditors of that company to hold other group companies liable for losses suffered by them as a result of the failure of the master account holder, unless a guarantee or indemnity is in place. In Australia, corporate group members can be required in certain circumstances to provide a cross-guarantee so that each entity in the corporate group guarantees payment of the creditors of every other entity in the corporate group. This cross-guarantee is a requirement of Australia's corporate regulator, the Australian Securities & Investment Commission (ASIC), where it provides relief from the reporting requirements of the Corporations Act and allows a corporate group to

21 *Brookes v Heritage Hotel Adelaide Pty Ltd* (1996) 20 ACSR 61 at 64.

22 *Ford's Principles of Corporations Law*, Dr RP Austin and Professor Ian Ramsay, paragraph 8.062, and CA 2001 s186.

file one set of accounts and avoid the need to file separate annual reports for each company in the group.[23]

The location of the creditor has no bearing on whether the creditor can take action against other Australian group companies for losses suffered.

(d) *Liability of master account holder in the event of insolvency of a group company*

The existence of the corporate veil means that if a group company in Australia goes into liquidation or otherwise becomes financially distressed, then creditors of that company cannot automatically look to other companies in the group for compensation. If a cross-group guarantee has been given by the Australian entity in relation to the liability of another company in the group, that will alter the position, but the claim exists because of the guarantor's obligations rather than as a function of the group relationship.

2.2 Perspective B: bank

(a) *Banking requirements*

There are no formal requirements for an Australian bank entering into a cash pooling agreement. If the cash pooling agreement is notional, then under Prudential Standard APS 112[24] an Australian bank is required to apply risk weights to its on-balance sheet assets in accordance with the risk classes in APS 112 for regulatory capital purposes. Risk weights are designed to reflect the risk of counterparty default. The bank will be permitted to use credit risk management techniques in determining the capital requirements for a particular exposure.[25] (See Attachment A to APS 112, where all claims on private sector counterparties can be given a 20% to 150% risk weight, depending on the rating of the counterparty.[26])

(b) *Liability of the bank in the event of insolvency of the master account holder or a group company*

The bank providing a physical cash pooling facility is unlikely to have any liability for losses merely as a result of the provision of banking services associated with the facility to the master account holder, or to the group of companies, should one or more of them become insolvent. If the master account holder becomes insolvent with a credit balance in the master account, that balance is a debt owed by the bank to the master account holder and is an asset that its liquidator would seek to recover. If, instead of the credit balance remaining on foot, the bank appropriated the balance in the master account due to the exercise of a right of set-off or combination of accounts, then questions may arise as to whether that appropriation of funds was proper. In the case of a notional cash pooling agreement, the bank will look to the

---

23 ASIC Class Order [CO 98/1418], www.asic.gov.au/asic/pdflib.nsf/LookupByFileName/co98-1418-co09-626.pdf/$file/co98-1418-co09-626.pdf.

24 Prudential Standard APS 112 *Capital Adequacy: Standardised Approach to Credit Risk*, Australian Prudential Regulatory Agency, December 2010, www.apra.gov.au/adi/Documents/APS_112_Dec%20_2010_Update_Final_reformatted_Jan2012.pdf.

25 APS 112 paragraphs 8 and 9.

26 APS112 paragraph 12.

guarantee it takes at the outset as the instrument to ensure that it can appropriate all credit balances it requires, but the continued existence of the original balances in the accounts under a notional pooling arrangement should mean that no payment to the bank has occurred to warrant the liquidator of an insolvent participant in a notional cash pooling agreement taking action against the bank.

Where an insolvent group company has made a payment under the cash pooling agreement to the master account, the fact that the bank provides the master account facilities for the cash pooling to occur should not expose the bank to a risk of liability. The bank that provides the account facilities for the master account holder is not receiving the payment as a creditor of the group company. Once the payment has been received in the master account, the bank owes the master account holder a debt represented by the credit constituted by the cash pooling payment coming from the insolvent group company. However, the bank is not responsible for losses suffered by the group company where the loan to the master account holder is not repaid.

In one scenario the bank providing a master account facility might be at risk of liability if it became aware of a breach of fiduciary duty being committed by the directors of a paying entity and even perhaps by the receiving entity, the master account holder. The circumstances where such a liability might arise will depend on the directors of the paying or receiving entity being engaged in a breach of their fiduciary duties as directors. If they are acting in breach of those duties when authorising or allowing payments to be made under a cash pooling agreement, then any party, such as a bank, that knowingly assists in that breach of duty can be liable as a constructive trustee under the principles of *Barnes v Addy*,[27] in which case they will be called upon to account for the property transferred in breach of trust.

2.3 Insolvency

(a) Cash pooling agreements from the insolvency practitioner's perspective

If a bank operating in Australia is providing the master account and goes into liquidation, then the Banking Act 1959 (Cth) offers some protection to depositors that have placed money on deposit with the bank. If the bank is an Australian authorised deposit-taking institution (ADI) under the Banking Act 1959 (ADI), then banking regulator the Australian Prudential Regulation Authority (APRA) has the power to appoint an ADI statutory manager to take control of the ADI's business or to investigate the ADI's affairs, or to appoint an administrator to take control of the ADI's business.[28]

Once APRA has applied for a winding-up order under Section 14F of the Banking Act, the minister may declare that account holders with the ADI which have a protected account[29] with a net credit balance when the declaration is made are entitled to be paid by APRA an amount (subject to the limit noted below) equal to

27 (1874) LR 9 Ch App 244; *Farah Constructions Pty Ltd v Say-Dee Pty Ltd* (2007) 236 ALR 209.
28 Section 13A(1) of the Banking Act 1959.
29 Protected accounts are defined in Sections 5 (4),(5),(6) and (7) of the Banking Act 1959.

the sum of the balance of the account, plus any interest accrued but not credited before the declaration.[30]

If the account is a protected account, it is the subject of the Financial Claims Scheme (FCS) for ADIs, whereby APRA will pay the account holder the amount on deposit up to the prescribed limit. The prescribed limit was originally A$1 million. That changed on February 1 2012 to A$250,000. The limit of A$250,000 applies per account holder, per ADI, and is aggregated across all eligible deposit accounts that the account holder has with a particular ADI.[31] Once APRA pays the account holder, APRA is given first priority for repayment of that sum in the winding-up of the ADI.[32] The customer's account with the ADI must be recorded in Australian currency if it is to receive protection.[33]

The FCS scheme extends to a foreign subsidiary bank – that is, where the bank is an Australian subsidiary of a foreign bank. However, it does not apply to branches of foreign banks. If the deposit is held with a branch of a foreign bank in Australia, it is not subject to the FCS scheme.

If the liquidator of the foreign bank applies for recognition in Australia under the United Nations Commission on International Trade Law Model Law under the Cross-Border Insolvency Act 2008 (Cth), then provided that the procedural steps are satisfied in the process of recognition, the foreign liquidator should be able to obtain recognition of the foreign insolvency as a foreign main proceeding. Once that has been obtained, the foreign liquidator can obtain approval to transfer the assets of the foreign bank to the country of the foreign main proceeding where the centre of main interests will be located.[34]

If the foreign liquidator chooses instead to seek the assistance of an Australian court via a letter of request from a foreign court for the return of the Australian assets into the pool of assets in the main liquidation, then that is likely to be permitted by an Australian court, provided that the court's jurisdiction is properly invoked under Section 581 of the Corporations Act. An Australian court is likely to recognise what Lord Hoffman described as the "golden thread" running through English insolvency law – the principle of modified universality as it affects a global insolvency – as a factor in ensuring that the assets in Australia are distributed to the main liquidation, wherever that might be.[35]

In case of the liquidation of the master account holder, the credit balance held in its account in Australia would no doubt be claimed by the liquidator in the first instance. The nature of a physical cash pooling agreement does not give rise to a trust arrangement, such that when it becomes insolvent the credit balance is being held on trust for the paying entities. The nature of most cash pooling agreements means that receipt by the master account holder gives rise not to a trust, but rather a loan.

---

30 Section 16AF of the Banking Act 1959.

31 APRA, *Financial Claims Scheme for Authorised Deposit Taking Institutions*, February 1 2012, page 3 www.apra.gov.au/CrossIndustry/Documents/ADI%20Financial%20Claims%20Scheme%20FAQ%2001%2002%2012.pdf.

32 Section 13A(3) of the Banking Act 1959.

33 Section 5(5) of the Banking Act 1959.

34 Article 20(2) of Schedule 1to the Cross Border Insolvency Act 2008.

35 *Re HIH Casualty & General Insurance Ltd* [2008] 1 WLR 852.

The master account holder would be the debtor, treated as borrowing from the group company the amount of the cash pooling payment made by the group company. In those circumstances the credit balance in the insolvent company's bank account would be an asset of the insolvent company. Whether it would be repaid would depend on the existence of other assets and the size of overall creditor claims, given that group companies rank *pari passu* with other unsecured creditors.

The obligations of the liquidator of the master account holder towards the bank, in the absence of the bank participating in a breach of a director's fiduciary duty, would be limited to securing the asset of the company constituted by the credit balance in the master account. Under the Corporations Act, where a company is being wound up in insolvency or by the court, the liquidator must take into his custody all property of the company.[36] Under the Corporations Regulations 2001, a liquidator must open a bank account known as the liquidator's general account and pay into that account all money received by the liquidator no later than seven days after it has been received.[37]

If the bank holding the master account is in another jurisdiction, that fact serves only to complicate the process of the Australian liquidator recovering the assets of an Australian group company.

Any claim by the liquidator of the master account holder against a group company that has received a transfer of money under a cash pooling agreement prior to insolvency of the master account holder would most likely be based on Part 5.7B of the Corporations Act, "Recovering Property or Compensation for the Benefit of Creditors of Insolvent Company". These provisions include voidable transactions such as unfair preferences, uncommercial transactions, unfair loans and unreasonable director-related transactions.[38] A payment out by the master account holder to a group company which is probably a creditor of the master account holder is most likely to be challenged as an unfair preference. If the group company becomes insolvent, then its liquidator has the same power to challenge payments made under the cash pooling agreement. The actual basis of the challenge will be different, however, given that the payment to the master account holder is not necessarily a payment made to a creditor. In that case the unfair preference provisions are not applicable. Unless the transaction is an uncommercial transaction or unfair loan, the liquidator of the group company will need to establish that the directors have breached their duty in allowing a payment to be made. This would necessitate using the principles in *Barnes v Addy*.[39] That is likely to be more difficult to establish than the burden of proof on the liquidator in an unfair preference claim.

(b) Special rules as regards other parties to the cash pooling agreement

In the event that one of the counterparties to the cash pooling agreement goes into liquidation, generally speaking, there are no special rules for dealing with obligations owed towards solvent counterparties in the same corporate group. Where only one

36 Section 474 of the Corporations Act 2001.

37 Regulation 5.6.06 of the Corporations Regulations 2001.

38 Sections 588FA,588FB, 588FD and588FDA of the Corporations Act 2001.

39 See footnote 9 above.

of the corporate group is insolvent, that will not necessarily lead to the insolvency of the entire corporate group. This might change where the remainder of the corporate group is liable for the insolvent entity's debts through the medium of a guarantee. A cash pooling agreement is no different from any other contract that operates on an intra-group basis. Where one of the group goes into liquidation, the remaining solvent entities will need to take care regarding the continued operation of the agreement, and certainly regarding any interaction under the agreement with the insolvent entity.

(c) Dissolution/termination of the cash pooling agreement in the event of liquidation of the master account holder or a group company

There is no constraint in Australia on the operation of clauses that permit one party to a contract to terminate the contract in the event of the insolvency of the other party. It is not unusual outside the United States for cash pooling agreements to contain provisions that permit a notice of termination to be given on the grounds of insolvency. Although there is stay on proceedings against the company in both administration under Part 5.3A of the Corporations Act and liquidation, nothing in Australian law prevents the termination of a contract on insolvency, such as exists under Section 365(e)(1) of the US Bankruptcy Code, which applies to executory contracts and leases and prevents a termination of the contract based on the insolvency of a counterparty.

2.4 Perspective D: regulatory

There are no obvious regulatory requirements that relate to cash pooling agreements in Australia.

2.5 Perspective E: tax

Both physical and notional cash pooling agreements can give rise to potential tax issues. We have already noted the need for withholding tax to be retained on interest payable to a foreign account holder under a physical cash pooling agreement.

In Australia, for cash pooling agreements there is an interaction between the thin capitalisation provisions contained in Division 820 of the Income Tax Assessment Act 1997 and the transfer pricing provisions. Transfer pricing methods in relation to debt arrangements are subject to Division 13 of Part III of the Income Tax Assessment Act 1936.

The transfer pricing provisions apply so as to require an arm's-length consideration for debt funding which is provided on a non-arm's-length basis.[40] If there is no consideration for the provision of the finance or it is less than an arm's-length consideration, the tax commissioner has the power to apply the level of consideration equal to an arm's-length consideration, with the consequence that the tax commissioner can disallow as a deduction an amount that is not charged on an arm's-length basis. However, that deduction may also be affected by the thin

---

40 Explanatory Memorandum to the Exposure Draft Stage One Transfer Pricing Reforms, www.treasury.gov.au/contentitem.asp?NavId=037&ContentID=2348.

capitalisation rules contained in Division 820 of the Income Tax Assessment Act 1997.

Thin capitalisation arises in the context of international transactions and can potentially limit the amount of debt deductions where a party's debt-to-equity ratio exceeds a certain limit. The thin capitalisation rules deny allowable deductions for an entity in the same proportion and to the extent that it has excess debt. Either a safe harbour or an arm's-length test will be used to set the maximum debt level. For outward and inward investing entities, the safe harbour gearing ratio of 3:1 applies.[41] Deductions that relate to a level of funding that exceeds the maximum level permitted under Division 820 will be disallowed. Generally, the transfer pricing provisions will be applied before the thin capitalisation provisions in determining allowable deductions for interest charged.[42]

Changes have been foreshadowed to the cross-border transfer pricing provisions that will ensure consistency in the application of Australia tax treaty pricing rules with the operation of the principles operating in Division 13. Accordingly, the transfer pricing articles contained in Australia's tax treaties are to apply and operate independently of Australia's unilateral transfer pricing provisions. To achieve that, the draft legislation proposes that the international treaty pricing rules be expressly incorporated into the Income Tax Assessment Act 1997 and the arm's-length principle be interpreted as far as is consistently possible with relevant Organisation for Economic Cooperation and Development guidance.

41 New Business Tax System (Tax Capitalisation Bill 2001), Explanatory Memorandum paragraphs 2.5 and 3.9.

42 Paragraph 4 of Taxation Ruling TR 2010/7 http://law.ato.gov.au/atolaw/view.htm?rank=find&criteria=AND~tr~basic~exact:::AND~2010%2F7~basic~exact&target=EA&style=java&sdocid=TXR/TR20107/NAT/ATO/00001&recStart=1&PiT=99991231235958&Archived=false&recnum=3&tot=7&pn=ALL:::ALL

Argentina

Tomás M Araya
Daniela A Bianchi
Mario Benjamín Terán
M&M Bomchil Abogados

1. Introduction

1.1 Admissibility of cash pooling agreements

Cash pooling in any of its forms is not specifically regulated under Argentine law. That notwithstanding, general provisions of corporate, bankruptcy, banking, foreign exchange and tax law are applicable to cash pooling involving Argentina.

Although none of those provisions expressly forbids cash pooling, several of them may limit the efficiency and effectiveness of this type of agreement and, in case of the insolvency of a group company, may expose the master account holder (usually the parent company) and/or other group companies and their directors to the risk of liability actions.

In a similar vein, the implementation of time and cost-effective multi-jurisdictional cash pooling agreements is severely curtailed by foreign exchange regulations on the inflow and outflow of funds, which apply to international transfers between the banking entity, the master account holder and group companies where one or more of the above is an Argentine resident and the other a non-resident.

Additionally, in the event of the insolvency of one or more group companies, transfers between the affiliates and the master account holder (whether for funding or zero or target balancing) prior to the group company's insolvency may serve as sufficient grounds for the initiation of liability or 'extension of bankruptcy' actions against the master account holder, through which compensation in the form of damages may be sought. To this end, the grounds for compensation would be that the insolvent group company was managed not in accordance with the company's best interests, but rather for the group's (or the master account holder's) best interests.

Finally, regardless of whether the cash pooling agreement involves one or more jurisdictions, cash pooling involving Argentina is made impractical and more costly by certain taxes that may be levied on transfers between the master account holder and group companies.

For these reasons, cash pooling is not currently used in Argentina; this situation is unlikely to change without material changes in legislation.

1.2 Types of cash pooling agreement

As mentioned above, cash pooling agreements are not currently used in Argentina.

1.3 Legal requirements from various perspectives

As cash pooling is not regulated in Argentina, there are no specific requirements with which compliance is required.

(a) *General legal requirements*

Regardless of whether cash pooling involves one or more jurisdictions, transfers between the banking entity, the master account holder and group companies under a physical cash pooling agreement that falls under the scope of Argentine law will typically be classified as loans regulated by the Commercial Code[1] and the Civil Code. Furthermore, in the absence of specific regulations, when dealing with notional cash pooling, the credit and debit positions assumed by the master account holder and group companies that are periodically offset would also typically fall under the scope of the provisions applicable to loans in Argentina.[2]

Accordingly, all transfers made by group companies to the master account holder and by the latter to the banking entity would typically be regarded as repayment of loans granted under the agreements. In addition, unless the cash pooling agreement provides otherwise, all repayments made thereunder will be allocated first towards the interest and then to the principal.[3]

In all cases such loans – even when entered into between affiliate parties such as the master account holder and group companies – should be made at arm's length, and the transfer of sums from the parties must be properly executed.

With regard to general corporate requirements, pursuant to Article 11(3) of the Commercial Companies Law (19,550[4], as amended) and Article 66 of Resolution 7/2005 of the Public Registry of Commerce of the City of Buenos Aires,[5] in order for the master account holder to grant a loan to a group company under the cash pooling agreement, its corporate purpose (reflected in its bylaws) must be broad enough to allow for the granting of financing.[6]

As is explained below, if the company's corporate purpose is not broad enough to allow for the granting of financing, and the board of directors nonetheless approves the execution of a cash pooling agreement by virtue of which financing is granted, then pursuant to Article 274 of the Commercial Companies Law, the directors shall be jointly and severally liable with regard to the company, shareholders and third parties for violation of the company bylaws and/or any other damage suffered as a result.

When dealing with multi-jurisdictional cash pooling agreements involving

---

1 Articles 558 to 571 of the Commercial Code.

2 However, as notional pooling structures are not used in Argentina and there are no legal precedents dealing with such matters, there is no definitive legal concept for this type of structure. Moreover, there are several aspects of notional cash pooling which, if implemented in Argentina, would have to be reviewed and specifically regulated in light of tax and accounting regulations, as many aspects of such arrangements could be classified as intercompany commingling and offsetting of funds.

3 Articles 776 and 777 of the Civil Code.

4 Published in the *Official Gazette* on April 25 1972.

5 Published in the *Official Gazette* on August 25 2005.

6 Although it is not a legal requirement, when the company's corporate purpose meets the requirement indicated above and there is no limit on granting financing in the company bylaws, it is common practice in Argentina for the board of directors to approve the decision to grant and/or take out financing.

Argentina, foreign exchange regulations[7] restrict the inflow and outflow of funds and the acquisition of foreign currency by Argentine residents and non-residents,[8] thus preventing the efficient implementation of such agreements.[9]

The first cardinal rule arising from the foreign exchange regulatory framework is that all funds entering and leaving Argentina must be settled and exchanged (ie, converted into local currency and vice versa) through the Argentine Single Free Exchange Market created by National Decree 260/2002,[10] as supplemented by several Central Bank regulations.[11] The settlement and exchange of funds must be executed in each case by banking or exchange entities authorised by the Central Bank to undertake foreign exchange operations at the exchange rate agreed upon with such entities. Therefore, the regulatory framework applies to the purchase of foreign currency and, in practice, to the performance of international transfers, since these are always preceded by the purchase of foreign currency, as foreign currency cannot be directly transferred and credited into a bank account in Argentina or to an offshore account from Argentina.

The rationale behind this regulatory framework is that no transaction can be executed if it is not expressly permitted by the regulations. Transactions which are not expressly permitted by the regulations can be executed only with the Central Bank's prior authorisation. As a consequence, before executing any transaction, its underlying nature must be disclosed and evidenced in order to allow the banking entity involved to verify that the transaction is permitted under the foreign exchange regulations and meets the requirements set out in the regulations.

National Decree 616/2005,[12] as extensively supplemented by the Ministry of Economy[13] and the Central Bank[14] regulations, establishes a general rule whereby all sums brought into Argentina by non-residents are subject to a mandatory deposit, pursuant to which 30% must be deposited with a local banking entity for 365 days. The deposit is non-transferable, accrues no interest and cannot be disposed of or used as collateral.

Furthermore, pursuant to that decree, as specifically supplemented by Communication A 4359 of the Central Bank[15] (as amended), all loans granted by non-residents to residents – even those between affiliate parties – must be exchanged

---

7 In Argentina, the foreign exchange regulatory framework is comprised of regulations issued by the National Congress, the National Executive Branch, the Ministry of Economy and the Central Bank.

8 The criterion for determining residence adopted by the foreign exchange regulations in Argentina is taken from the Balance of Payments Manual of the International Monetary Fund. Pursuant to the foreign exchange regulations, the Central Bank regulations provide that an entity shall be considered a resident of a given country when it has its centre of economic interest in that country. In this regard, an entity shall be deemed a resident upon engaging in economic activities and transactions on a significant scale for one year or more, or intending to do so.

9 Regardless of the obligations and restrictions set out in the foreign exchange regulations, residents are allowed to hold offshore banking accounts, in which only funds of "free availability" may be kept. As a general rule, loans received from third parties and received from the export of products or services must be brought into Argentina and converted into pesos within a short period of time.

10 Published in the *Official Gazette* on February 8 2002.

11 Including, but not limited to, Communications A 3471 and 3473, as amended and supplemented.

12 Published in the *Official Gazette* on June 10 2005.

13 Including Resolutions 365/2005, 637/2005, 731/2006, 1076/2006 and 280/2009, as amended.

14 Including Communications A 4359, 4762 and 4901, as amended

15 Published in the *Official Gazette* on June 30 2005.

for local currency within 30 days of disbursement, and 30% of the sum entering Argentina must be allocated to the mandatory deposit mentioned above.

Certain foreign loans are exempt from the mandatory deposit requirement, to the extent that the funds disbursed thereunder are specifically allocated in accordance with the foreign exchange regulations and this allocation is evidenced before the relevant banking or exchange entity. Among others, foreign loans allocated to the acquisition of non-financial assets, direct investments[16] by residents in foreign companies, repayments of outstanding debts to non-residents and financing of imports and exports by residents are exempt.

However, pursuant to the regulations, regardless of whether a foreign loan is exempt from the mandatory deposit, in all cases the principal of such loan can be repaid only provided that the funds disbursed thereunder have entered Argentina and been exchanged for local currency, and 365 days have elapsed since the disbursement. During this period, the regulations not only prevent residents from purchasing foreign currency for the purpose of repaying of the principal, but also restrict repayment of the principal at all. Moreover, foreign loans which are exempt from the mandatory deposit are subject to longer minimum terms, ranging from between two and 10 years (taking principal and interest for the calculation), during which repayment of the principal is restricted. In addition, pre-payment is not permitted unless the minimum applicable term has elapsed and the amount being pre-paid does not exceed the debt's present value at the time of pre-payment.[17] In all cases, interest payments can be made at any time in the five days prior to the scheduled due date or accrued during the current interest period of the loan.

These rules arising from the foreign exchange regulatory framework are highly relevant to a cross-border cash pooling agreement involving Argentina, since they will typically apply to international transfers between the master account holder and/or group companies, to the extent that one of these parties is an Argentine resident and the other a non-resident.

In this scenario – as they would qualify as foreign loans, and given the applicability of the foreign exchange regulations to such loans – transfers from a non-resident account holder to a resident account holder would have to be brought into Argentina within 30 days of disbursement. Unless an exemption applied by virtue of the allocation of the transfer, 30% of the funds would also be subject to the mandatory deposit for 365 days, during which such amounts could not be disposed. In turn, because of the restrictions imposed on repayment and pre-payment of the principal of foreign loans, the resident account holder receiving the funds transferred would typically be prevented from purchasing foreign currency and transferring the funds received to the non-resident account holder's offshore account for at least 365 days.

In all cases, the execution of transactions which do not comply with foreign

---

16 Pursuant to Communication A 4237 of the Central Bank, the direct investment is inclusive of stock purchases or capital contributions in companies that involve a contribution equal or greater than 10% of the company's stock capital.

17 The debt's present value for the stated purposes must be calculated pursuant to a formula set out in Communication A 4324 of the Central Bank.

exchange regulations in Argentina is subject to sanctions set out in the Criminal Exchange Law (19,539,[18] as amended), which provides for fines of up to 10 times the amount of the relevant transaction[19] in case of a first infringement.[20]

2. Specific questions

2.1 Perspective A: corporate group

(a) *Liability of group company and/or master account holder directors in the event of insolvency of a group company*

Under the Commercial Companies Law, companies are subject to a one-tier board structure, and the board may be composed of both executive and non-executive directors. However, the law does not distinguish between the types of function performed by the different members, imposing joint and several liability on all board members in case of mismanagement. Further, Articles 269 and 270 of the Commercial Companies Law provide for two forms of delegation of the board of directors' authority. The first involves the appointment by the board of an executive committee, which must be comprised solely of company directors and whose purpose shall be the administration of the company's ordinary business. The second involves the appointment of managers to perform tasks relating to the company's administration. Such managers need not be directors, but shall nonetheless be liable to the same extent as directors under the Commercial Companies Law.

Therefore, the discussion below regarding the liability of directors in Argentina applies to all board members, whether they are actively involved in the company's management or act only as non-executive or supervisory directors.

Generally, under Argentine law the directors (whether executive or non-executive) of a group company risk liability to the extent that they do not comply with the duties imposed upon them by the Commercial Companies Law. In the event of the company's distress or insolvency, liability actions can be initiated on the grounds that amounts transferred to the master account holder or other group companies constituted unlawful distributions which were not in the company's best interests, as they allegedly caused or aggravated its distress or insolvency status.

On the other hand, directors (whether executive or non-executive) of the master account holder and/or other group companies should not be liable to the extent that they are not considered *de facto* directors of the distressed entity, in which case they will be subject to the same duties with regard to the company as formally appointed directors.

---

18 Published in the *Official Gazette* on December 10 1971.

19 In case of multiple transactions, Article 3 of the Criminal Exchange Law provides that the fine will be of an amount equal to the sum of all fines that would be imposed for each transaction (which may, in each case, be up to 10 times the amount of each transaction). However, the amount of the fine cannot exceed an amount equal to 10 times the amount of the largest transaction involved.

20 This law also provides for fines of three to 10 times the amount of the transaction or imprisonment for one to four years in case of a first repeat offence, and imprisonment for one to eight years plus the maximum applicable fine in the case of a second repeat offence. Moreover, the directors, legal representatives, chief executives, managers and members of the surveillance committee who take part in the transaction are jointly and severally liable for the fines.

As a general rule, under Argentine law directors are not responsible for the company's debts and obligations; they will be held liable only upon a breach of their duties under the Commercial Companies Law. In practice, the risk of liability of the directors of a troubled company is directly connected to the amount of unpaid liabilities of that company.

Article 59 of the Commercial Companies Law sets out the standard to which directors must perform their duties, mandating that they act with loyalty and with the diligence of a good businessperson. As a consequence, the duty of loyalty and care applicable to directors requires them to prioritise the company's interests above any other interests, regardless of whether the company is part of a group. Accordingly, Article 8 of Transparency Decree 677/01,[21] which regulates listed companies, expressly provides that company directors must prioritise the corporate interests of the issuer and the common interests of all shareholders above any other interests, including their own or those of the controlling shareholders.

In case of a conflict of interests (whether actual or potential), the director must inform the board accordingly and must abstain from participating in the deliberation of the matter. In accordance with Article 274 of the Commercial Companies Law, directors shall be jointly and severally liable with regard to the company, shareholders and third parties for the wrongful exercise of their duties according to the standard stated in Article 59 of the Commercial Companies Law (ie, breach of the duties of loyalty and/or care), violation of the law and/or company bylaws and any other damages caused through malice,[22] abuse of power or gross negligence.

In case of financial distress or bankruptcy, Argentine law does not provide for the automatic liability of the directors of the troubled company. However, liability actions based either on the Commercial Companies Law or, if bankruptcy proceedings have been opened, on the Bankruptcy Law (24,522,[23] as amended) can be filed against them, as well as against the controlling shareholders.

Corporate liability actions (based on the Commercial Companies Law) aim to obtain redress for any damages suffered by the company itself, and may be filed by the company only with the approval of the shareholders' meeting. A corporate liability action may also be filed by individual shareholders representing the company:

- in the case of inaction on the part of the company board for at least three months, as from the date on which the shareholders' meeting approved the filing; or
- where dissenting shareholders representing at least 5% of the stock capital have voted against approving the performance of the board members as such.

In both cases, although the action may have been filed by an individual shareholder, any damages recovered will belong to the company.

Under the Commercial Companies Law, shareholders are not allowed to withdraw funds out of a company, except as distributions of net realised and liquid

21 Published in the *Official Gazette* on May 28 2001.
22 Malice in the sense of wilful misconduct
23 Published in the *Official Gazette* on August 9 1995.

profits,[24] as shown in the annual financial statements approved by the annual shareholders' meeting.[25] An unsatisfied creditor of a bankrupt group company may argue that by approving transfers to the master account holder or to other group companies under a cash pooling agreement, the directors breached their duties under Article 59 of the Commercial Companies Law, as such transfers constituted unlawful distributions which caused or aggravated the company's insolvency.

In addition, Article 54 of the Commercial Companies Law sets out two important rules applicable to companies which are taken into consideration when evaluating the board members' conduct, especially regarding transactions between group companies. Both rules aim to protect the company's corporate interests, considered individually and not as part of a corporate group.

The rationale underpinning these rules is that if a controlling shareholder takes advantage of assets or any corporate opportunity of the company for its own benefit, then any profits deriving therefrom belong to the company and, should the business fail, any losses must be borne exclusively by the controlling shareholder. Should the directors of the troubled entity permit, either expressly or implicitly, this kind of conduct by the controlling shareholder, they may be found liable with regard to the company.

Finally, directors of the master account holder and/or other group companies should not be held liable for liabilities of a troubled group company, to the extent that they are not considered *de facto* directors of such troubled group company.

Recently, the executive branch of the Argentine government presented to Congress a bill which proposes relevant amendments to the Civil and Commercial Codes and other legislation such as the Commercial Companies Law. One of these proposed amendments involves the inclusion of a corporate group interest in the legislation.[26] Pursuant to this amendment, in implementing a business policy in a group company's interest, it will be permissible to offset any damages caused by the policy against benefits received or envisaged from the policy over a reasonable term, as long as the disadvantages (or damages) to be offset do not threaten the company's solvency or viability. If enacted, the inclusion of this principle will be of great significance in interpreting transactions between group companies such as those typically performed under a cash pooling agreement, and in evaluating the conduct of group company directors and the controlling shareholder.

Listed versus private companies: In Argentina, listed companies are subject to a specific regulatory framework, comprising the Public Offering of Securities Law (17,811,[27] as amended), the Transparency Decree and National Securities Commission regulations. Unless otherwise stated within this regulatory framework,

24 Articles 68 and 224 of the the Commercial Companies Law.

25 Certain companies described in Article 299 of the Commercial Companies Law are allowed to distribute dividends in advance of the annual meeting which approves the annual financial statements.

26 Commentators have repeateadly noted that when a controlling company is incorporated within a group, it is inevitable that the administration of that company will be affected and/or oriented towards the interest of the group rather than its own individual corporate interest (Manóvil, Rafael, *Grupos de Sociedades*, Ed Abeledo Perrot, Buenos Aires, p 580).

27 Published in the *Official Gazette* on July 22 1968.

listed companies are also governed by the Commercial Companies Law and, upon the initiation of bankruptcy proceedings, by the Bankruptcy Law. Therefore, directors of listed companies can be subject to liability actions as outlined above.

Specifically, Article 73 of the Transparency Decree mandates that a certain procedure (involving the prior approval of the audit committee) must be followed in cases where a listed company executes certain acts or transactions with a related party, such as a controlling entity or an entity which is under the common control of a parent company. If a shareholder alleges that specific acts or transactions have caused damage to the company, and if this prior approval procedure was not followed for such acts or transactions, then it will be up to the board (on behalf of the company) to prove that the acts or transactions were performed in accordance with market conditions and caused no damage to the company.

In addition, Article 75 of the Transparency Decree provides that when filing a corporate liability action against controlling shareholders or directors, shareholders can seek compensation for indirect damages suffered, which are calculated by taking their percentage of stock ownership against the total alleged damages suffered by the company.

In the case of the insolvency of a listed company, the National Securities Commission will typically initiate an administrative proceeding in which the directors' conduct will be scrutinised. If the commission determines that an infringement has occurred, it may impose several sanctions, including fines of between Ps1,000 and Ps1.5 million – representing up to five times the amount of the benefit obtained or the damage suffered as a consequence of the unlawful conduct, whichever is higher – and suspension from acting as a director for up to five years.

Foreign registered companies: If the distressed group company is registered in a foreign jurisdiction, then the liability of its board members will be evaluated in accordance with the corporate and bankruptcy regimes (or such other applicable law) in effect in that foreign jurisdiction.

(b) Liability of group company and/or master account holder directors in the event of insolvency of the master account holder

As previously mentioned, there is no automatic or direct responsibility of the directors (whether executive or non-executive) of a bankrupt company for the company's obligations. Where the troubled company is the master account holder, its directors may be found liable only if it is proved that they did not comply with their duties under the Commercial Companies Law.

The conclusions set out in section 2.1(a) apply to the directors of both the master account holder and other group companies.

Where the master account holder enters into bankruptcy proceedings, the directors may be subject to a bankruptcy liability action, which can be filed by the receiver against directors, officers, administrators or agents of the debtor if they acted with wilful misconduct and thus "contributed to, facilitated, permitted or worsened the debtor's economic situation or its cessation of payment status", thereby causing prejudice to the creditors.

The conduct that is subject to such scrutiny is that performed up to one year before the initial date of cessation of payments, which is established by the court during the bankruptcy proceedings. The limitation period for filing a bankruptcy liability action is two years from the date of the bankruptcy order, and the bankruptcy court has jurisdiction to hear and decide such actions notwithstanding the domicile or place of incorporation of the defendant.

Prior to filing a bankruptcy liability action, the receiver must obtain the express authorisation of a majority of the unsecured admitted creditors.

(c) Liability of group companies in the event of insolvency of the master account holder

Under Argentine law, the members of a corporate group are not jointly liable for the obligations of one group company. Article 172 of the Bankruptcy Law ratifies this principle by stating that where two or more persons (normally, but not always, companies) are members of the same business group, even when there is a controlling relationship, the bankruptcy of one group member does not extend to the other group members, unless the requirements set out in Article 161 of the Bankruptcy Law are met. Legal commentators have emphasised that this also holds true outside the bankruptcy sphere and should be read as a general legal principle, allowing a corporate group to be established without risk of joint liability provided that all group entities are managed in accordance with the law (ie, without detriment to one company in favour of the controlling entity or other group affiliates).[28]

Generally, if the bankruptcy estate does not have sufficient assets to pay the admitted claims and the administrative expenses (ie, the receiver's fees), the receiver and/or an unsatisfied creditor of the distressed master account holder may seek compensation from third parties, as follows.

Controlling entity liability: Article 54 of the Commercial Companies Law sets out important principles that apply to all types of company.

Article 54 states that shareholders or controlling entities which cause damage to the company by acting with malice or negligence are jointly and severally liable to compensate such damage, and cannot argue that such losses are offset by profits generated by other businesses controlled by them.[29] It further provides that a shareholder or controlling entity which uses or applies the company's "funds or effects" for its own personal benefit, or that of a third party, is obliged to present the company with any profits resulting from such activity, while any losses are its exclusive responsibility.

Both of these rules are aimed at protecting the company's corporate interests, considered individually and not as part of a corporate group.[30] The rationale behind these provisions is that whenever a controlling entity takes advantage of its

---

28 Cabanellas de las Cuevas, Guillermo, "*Fusiones y otros actos de concentración societaria. Los grupos de sociedades*", in *Derecho Societario Parte General*, Volume 11, Ed Heliasta, Buenos Aires, p 548.

29 On the other hand, damages may be offset against the benefits or profits arising from the same act that caused such damages (Manóvil, Rafael, *Grupos de Sociedades*, Ed Abeledo Perrot, Buenos Aires, pp 690-691).

subsidiary's assets or any opportunity of the company for its own benefit, the profits deriving therefrom belong to the subsidiary and any losses must be borne exclusively by the controlling entity.

Representative liability and third-party liability: The Bankruptcy Law imposes liability on any third party that, acting with malice, participated in any action that was wilfully aimed at reducing the assets or increasing the liabilities of the bankrupt company, either before or after the bankruptcy order. Such parties are obliged to return the assets that are still in their possession and compensate any damages caused, and are barred from making any claims in the bankruptcy proceedings.

In addition, as mentioned, directors, officers, administrators or agents of the debtor that, acting with malice, have "contributed to, facilitated, permitted or worsened the debtor's economic situation or its cessation of payment status" can also be subject to liability should the requirements of the Bankruptcy Law[31] be met.

Extension of bankruptcy: This action foresees the extension of the bankruptcy proceedings to a third party, provided that certain requirements set out in Article 161 of the Bankruptcy Law are met. In the case of the commingling of assets and liabilities between the debtor and the third party, the extension of the bankruptcy proceedings will result in the consolidation of both proceedings. The circumstances in which a bankruptcy extension may be sought are as follows:

- The *'maitre d'affaire'* extension – a third party, under the appearance of the operation of the debtor, has executed acts in its personal interest and disposed of the debtor's assets as if they were its own, thereby defrauding the creditors.
- The abuse of dominance extension – a controlling entity has "unduly deviated" from the corporate interest of the debtor and has imposed on it a unified management for its own benefit or that of the economic group to which it belongs. In such cases, a 'controlling entity' is:
  - a company that, directly or indirectly, holds a participation interest which grants it the votes required to adopt corporate decisions; or
  - any entity that, acting jointly, holds a participation interest as defined above and is responsible for the relevant conduct.
- The commingling of assets and liabilities extension – there is a commingling of assets and liabilities between the debtor and the third party that impedes the clear delimitation of all or almost all assets and liabilities.

If the extension of bankruptcy is accepted by the court and there has been a commingling of assets and liabilities, then a single estate is formed comprising all assets and liabilities of both companies. Otherwise, two separate estates are formed, keeping a

30 Please see the comment above regarding the possible amendment of the Commercial Companies Law and the incorporation of the corporate group interest. If this bill is ultimately enacted, then the standard to evaluate the parent company's conduct will be modified, as it will be admissible to offset the damages suffered by such group business policy against the benefits received or foreseen out of the implementation of a corporate group policy over a reasonable term, as long as the disadvantages (or damages) to be compensated do not threaten the company's solvency or viability.

31 Article 173 of the Bankruptcy Law.

division between the different creditors of each debtor. These proceedings typically last for several years without increasing the distribution quota for the creditors.

Breach of legal entity doctrine: Finally, Article 54 of the Commercial Companies Law further provides that any activity of the company aimed at achieving extra-corporate goals that involve a violation of the law, public order or good faith, or that deceive third parties or frustrate their rights, will be directly attributed to the shareholders or controlling parties that made such activity possible. Such shareholders or controlling entities will be jointly and severally liable for all damages caused to the company and third parties as a result.

Thus, once certain acts or the whole activity of a subsidiary has been attributed to the controlling entity, this entity will be held responsible for all liabilities of the subsidiary to third parties.

The courts normally adopt a restrictive approach[32] in cases involving this doctrine, particularly when there are contractual creditors. In case of the insolvency of the master account holder, unpaid creditors may seek to attribute to the controlling entity the unpaid obligations of the master account holder by alleging that the subsidiary's activity was in fact only a means through which the controlling entity could frustrate the rights of third parties (ie, creditors). To a great extent, the likelihood of this kind of petition will depend on whether the defendant can convince the court that it has not influenced the subsidiary's decisions and that the subsidiary has always pursued its own corporate interest.

2.1.4 Liability of the master account holder in the event of insolvency of a group company

As mentioned above, as a general rule there is no joint liability of group companies (or of the master account holder) for the liabilities of a troubled group company. Therefore, creditors of the troubled entity are not entitled to hold other companies liable for losses suffered.

That notwithstanding, other group companies or the master account holder may be exposed to liability actions as outlined in section 2.3(c), to the extent that the requirements specified in each case are met. In case of bankruptcy, relevant elements in assessing the potential liability of other group companies (or, individually, the master account) holder will be whether:

- they can be considered a controlling entity of the troubled company; and
- there has been an "undue deviation" from the corporate interest of the troubled company, which has been managed according to the interests of either the controlling party or the economic group as a whole.

Generally, if the group company's domicile is located in Argentina, then the bankruptcy proceedings will be governed by Argentine law and will be heard by the Argentine courts. In this case, notwithstanding the domiciles of other group companies, Argentine law will apply. If, on the other hand, the group company's

32 Except in cases of unpaid labour creditors, where a broad approach is generally adopted.

domicile is located outside Argentina, then the bankruptcy proceedings will be governed by the applicable foreign law.

2.2 Perspective B: bank

(a) *Banking requirements*

Although there are no specific provisions under Argentine law applicable to cash pooling agreements, the Central Bank's general regulations on credit limits restrict the amount of credit that a banking entity may grant to the master account holder and/or group companies.

Under the Central Bank regulations, credit limits mainly depend on:

- the eligible regulatory capital[33] of the bank granting the loan;
- the eligible regulatory capital of the company receiving the financing; and
- risk concentration.

For credit limit purposes, groups or related entities in the private non-financial sector are considered to be a single client. The definition of 'related companies' is specifically set out in the Central Bank regulations and is based on control of the companies' affairs, which is determined by stock ownership, number of board members shared by the companies and actual or potential participation on governing bodies. Specifically, the Central Bank regulations[34] provide that one company has control over another if the former, directly or indirectly:

- owns or controls 25% or more of the votes in the company;
- owns or controls 50% or more of the votes at the shareholders' meetings at which directors are appointed; or
- owns or controls less than 25% of the votes, but nevertheless has control over third companies which in turn may influence the decisions of the company.

Under the Central Bank regulations, banking entities are subject to the following credit assistance limits with respect to companies or corporate groups:[35]

- 15% of the banking entity's eligible regulatory capital, considering only unsecured loans; and
- 25% of the banking entity's eligible regulatory capital, including secured loans.

Moreover, loans of over Ps750,000 to companies are subject to a general maximum credit limit of 100% of the eligible regulatory capital of the recipient. Provided that certain requirements are met, the Central Bank regulations

---

33 The 'eligible regulatory capital' of banks and financial institutions determines the number of assets and the percentage of their value that the banks and financial entities can consider in order to comply with their minimum capital requirements.

34 Specifically, Annex I of Communication A 2140 of the Central Bank, as amended and/or supplemented.

35 The Central Bank regulations distinguish between financing granted to affiliated companies, which is subject to close scrutiny and strict maximum percentages, and financing granted to non-affiliate parties. Limits to the amount of credit that a bank may grant to its affiliated companies are not included in our analysis.

additionally foresee a complementary limit of 200% of the company's eligible regulatory capital, as long as such limit does not exceed 2.5% of the eligible regulatory capital of the banking institution.

The Central Bank regulations also impose limits on risk concentration. Pursuant to Point 2.1, Annex II of Communication A 2140 of the Central Bank,[36] as amended, for the purpose of such regulations, there will be risk concentration when a bank grants loans to a company or corporate group which exceeds 10% of the bank's eligible regulatory capital. Accordingly, a bank's risk concentration typically cannot exceed three times its eligible regulatory capital in respect of transactions with companies or corporate groups (whether or not they are related), excluding loans granted to local banking entities, and five times its eligible regulatory capital when contemplating loans granted to local banking entities.

(b) *Liability of the bank in the event of insolvency of the master account holder or of a group company*

As a general rule, the bank involved in the cash pooling agreement will have no liabilities in the event that the master account holder or a group company becomes distressed. That notwithstanding, provided that certain conditions are met, the bank might be subject to liability actions if large sums of credit have been granted to the master account or group company in distress.

In such a scenario, the bank might be classed as a controlling entity of the master account holder or group company under Article 33 of the Commercial Companies Law, which acknowledges two types of control: *de jure* (legal control) and *de facto* (actual control). The bank might be regarded as a *de facto* controlling entity of the master account holder or group company under Article 33 of the Commercial Companies Law if, based on its predominant position as creditor, it has direct or indirect influence over the company and its decisions. If the bank is deemed a *de facto* controlling entity, then the provisions detailed in sections 2.1(c) and 2.1(d) above on controlling entity liability will apply.

Additionally, the bank might be held liable for negligently granting credit to the master account holder or group company under Article 1109 of the Civil Code, which provides that anyone that causes harm to a third party due to its personal fault or negligence when performing an act is obliged to remedy the damage. In order to consider a bank liable under Article 1109, the court must accept that the bank was negligent in providing credit to the troubled entity at times when there were signals of financial distress, and that by such conduct it allowed the distressed entity to appear solvent, thus frustrating third parties' rights.

The rationale for imposing this liability is that by granting credit, the bank has given the distressed company a false appearance of financial stability which may result in prejudice or damage to creditors, whether they have engaged in business with the company before, during or after the credit was granted. By negligently granting credit, the bank may also have enabled the distressed company to delay filing for bankruptcy.

---

36 Issued on September 15 1993.

2.3 Insolvency

(a) *Cash pooling agreements from the insolvency practitioner's perspective*

Article 130 of the Bankruptcy Law provides that obligations between third parties and the bankrupt company may be offset only when they arose prior to the bankruptcy order.[37]

Therefore, upon the opening of bankruptcy proceedings involving either the master account holder or a group company, the counterparties to the cash pooling agreement cannot offset their mutual obligations arising after the issuance of the bankruptcy order. Therefore, if at the time the bankruptcy order is issued, the bankrupt company is a creditor of other group companies, those companies must pay it the sums owed. Alternatively, if the bankrupt company is a debtor of other group companies, then the latter must file a proof of claim to be accepted by the court as an admitted creditor in the bankruptcy proceedings.

Foreign bankruptcy proceedings: On the subject of cross-border insolvency, the Bankruptcy Law is still influenced by the outdated 'territorialist approach' and, as a consequence thereof, there are no general provisions recognising the faculties and powers of receivers appointed in foreign bankruptcy proceedings.

In this regard, Argentina has ratified only the Montevideo Treaties on International Commercial Law of February 12 1889 and March 19 1940, respectively, which recognise the power of receivers appointed in any of the ratifying countries; but this is an exception to the general regime.[38] Argentina has not adopted the United Nations Commission on International Trade Law Model Law on Cross-Border Insolvency.

Recognition of a foreign proceeding (and therefore of the foreign appointed receiver) may be problematic if there are local creditors that claim rights over the debtor's assets located in Argentina, as Article 4 of the Bankruptcy Law provides that, unless otherwise stated in a treaty, a foreign bankruptcy proceeding may not be invoked to dispute the rights of local creditors over assets located in Argentina.

Bank, master account holder or group company enters into liquidation: In all these situations, and depending on the special characteristics of the cash pooling agreement, the insolvency administrator will have similar rights and obligations as regards the bankruptcy estate and the counterparties. Generally, if the administrator concludes that the cash pooling agreement has been detrimental to the debtor, it must immediately stop transfers to third parties and may even decide to launch avoidance actions to obtain reimbursement of any funds which took place during the suspect period prior to the declaration of bankruptcy.

---

37 Although this rule is included in the bankruptcy regulations of the Bankruptcy Law, scholars and case law have concluded that it must also be applicable in a reorganisation proceeding. This criterion was recently ratified by Panel D of the National Commercial Court of Appeals (*In re Metrogas SA s/concurso preventivo s/incidente de restitución de fondos*, August 18 2011, La Ley, January 17 2012).

38 The Montevideo Treaty on International Commercial Law of February 12 1889 has been ratified by Argentina, Bolivia, Colombia, Paraguay, Peru and Uruguay, while the Montevideo Treaty of March 19 1940 has been ratified by Argentina, Paraguay and Uruguay. Neither Brazil – Argentina's main commercial partner – nor Chile has ratified these treaties.

If any of the counterparties are located in a foreign jurisdiction, the applicable foreign laws will determine the faculties and rights of a foreign-appointed insolvency administrator.

Transfers to group companies or master account holder prior to bankruptcy: The transfer of funds between the master account holder and/or group companies within a certain period prior to the bankruptcy of either party may be subject to avoidance (clawback) actions, to the extent that certain requirements set out in the Bankruptcy Law are met.

These clawback actions may be filed by the receiver or by any admitted creditor, upon the receiver's failure to act. The suspect period cannot exceed two years prior to the bankruptcy order.

The following acts are considered as acts of avoidance as a matter of law, without any evidentiary requirements:

- any gratuitous act performed by the debtor;
- advance payments of debts scheduled to mature on the date of the bankruptcy order or thereafter; and
- the granting of mortgages, pledges or any other kind of priority right as security for non-due obligations which originally were not entitled to such priority right.

Any other transaction executed by the debtor within the suspect period may be declared void by the court if the following conditions are met:

- At the time that the act was executed, the third party was (or should have been) aware that the debtor was in cessation of payments; and
- The act is detrimental to the debtor's creditors.

The defendant bears the burden of proving that the act caused no prejudice to the creditors, which is normally difficult when registered assets or funds deposited in a bank are transferred to a third party without sufficient consideration.

In the case of a cash pooling agreement, the matter must be decided under the normal avoidance procedure, which requires that the plaintiff prove that the defendant knew (or should have known) that the debtor was insolvent at the time that the funds were transferred. In this case, if the debtor's participation in a cash pooling agreement ended up being detrimental to the company (and therefore to its creditors), the likelihood that most of these transfers will be considered void is high.

As mentioned, if the administrator is appointed in a foreign country, Article 4 of the Bankruptcy Law states that unless otherwise provided in a treaty,[39] foreign bankruptcy proceedings may not be invoked either to dispute the rights of local creditors over assets located in Argentina or to nullify acts performed by them with a local debtor. Under this rule, therefore, local creditors will have sufficient grounds to reject the avoidance powers of a foreign-appointed administrator.

---

39 As to the treaties currently ratified by Argentina, please see footnote 38 above.

(b) *Special rules as regards other parties to the cash pooling agreement*

Upon the opening of bankruptcy proceedings, third parties with a pre-petition claim against the debtor must file individual proof of claims within the term stated in the bankruptcy order. Only labour creditors are entitled to a faster (and more favourable) admittance process.

This general rule does not apply in the event of an extension of bankruptcy (eg, if bankruptcy proceedings involving the master account holder are extended to a group company). In this case, Article 170 of the Bankruptcy Law provides that all creditors shall, if applicable, be admitted by a joint report of the receivers appointed in the different bankruptcy proceedings, without the need to file separate proofs of claim. Further, in the event of an extension of bankruptcy due to the commingling of assets and liabilities, claims which the debtors hold against each other shall not form part of the bankruptcy estate.

(c) *Dissolution/termination of the cash pooling agreement in the event of liquidation of the master account holder or of a group company*

Under Argentine law, if any party to a cash pooling agreement (the master account holder, one or more group companies or even the banking entity) goes into liquidation, the cash pooling agreement will typically be deemed to be an executory agreement, in which both parties have pending obligations to be executed.

Generally, the Bankruptcy Law provides that:

- if the obligation with which the debtor is charged has been fulfilled, then the counterparty must comply with its obligations in due time;
- if the obligation with which the third party is charged has been fulfilled, then the latter must file proof of its claim in the bankruptcy proceedings; and
- if both parties have pending obligations, then the third party has the right to terminate the agreement (Article 143 of the Bankruptcy Law).

The continuation or termination of an executory agreement is subject to a complex procedure set out in Article 144 of the Bankruptcy Law, under which the court must decide either to terminate or to continue the executory contract after the receiver has issued its opinion on the convenience of the contract for the estate.

In the event of liquidation of the master account holder, the cash pooling agreement will normally be terminated, as it would be risky for group companies to continue transferring funds to an insolvent entity. This will also be the result in the case of liquidation of a group company.

In either case, the solvent entity must request from the court termination of the cash pooling agreement under the procedure set out in Article 144 of the Bankruptcy Law. Pursuant to this procedure, the third party has 20 days from publication of the last notice[40] in the *Official Gazette* in order to inform the court of its intention. Normally, the parties' obligations under the contract will be suspended until the bankruptcy court has issued its decision.

---

40 Once the bankruptcy order has been issued, the court overseeing the proceedings must order the publication of notices in the *Official Gazette*, and in a newspaper if the estate has sufficient funds.

2.4 Perspective D: regulatory

As mentioned above, there are no specific provisions under Argentine law specifically governing cash pooling agreements and therefore no regulatory requirements are applicable.

2.5 Perspective E: tax[41]

Although cash pooling agreements involving Argentina will typically be subject to taxes generally levied in Argentina, taxes specifically imposed on bank debits and credits and on transfers of funds between companies which do not involve market-value interest rates make cash pooling costly and impractical.

In Argentina, cash pooling agreements will typically be subject to the general tax implications regarding transfer pricing, income tax withholding and value added tax (VAT).

The transfer pricing regulations apply the arm's-length principle to transactions between related parties, such as the master account holder and group companies. Accordingly, parties must prepare and submit a transfer pricing report, periodically file transfer pricing tax returns and maintain supporting documentation. The purpose of this regime is to ensure that all transactions between related parties are performed on arm's-length terms. In addition, interest on transfers between group companies that qualify as loans will typically be subject to income tax withholding at a 35% effective tax rate; and VAT at a rate of 21%.

In addition, transfers between the master account holder and group companies will typically be subject to the tax on bank debits and credits established by Law 25,413[42], as amended, and levied at a general rate of 0.6% of the sum involved. This tax alone makes cash pooling agreements extremely costly, due to the number of transfers that such structures involve on a regular basis.

Transfers between the master account holder and group companies under a cash pooling agreement may also be regarded as taxable income under Article 73 of the Income Tax Law (20,628,[43] as regulated by Decree 649/97,[44] as amended and/or supplemented), to the extent that they do not meet the requirements set out therein.

In this regard, Article 73 of the Income Tax Law sets out an assumption whereby funds transferred by one company to a third party where the transfer is not performed in the interests of the company shall be deemed taxable income under the law at a rate equal to the interest rate established by the Banco de la Nación Argentina for commercial discounts or to the rate of inflation plus 8%, whichever is higher. This assumption will apply – and therefore the transfer will be taxable – if any interest rate agreed between the parties is lower than the rate foreseen in Article 73 by 20% or more.[45]

The following requirements must be met in order for the assumption to apply:

---

41 The authors would like to thank Ariadna Artopoulos for her valuable comments regarding the tax implications of cash pooling agreements.

42 Published in the *Official Gazette* on March 26 2001.

43 Published in the *Official Gazette* on December 31 1973.

44 Published in the *Official Gazette* on August 6 1997.

45 Article 103 of the Income Tax Law Regulatory Decree.

- The funds must be transferred between a company and another third party;
- The recipient must be a 'third party'; and
- The transfer must not be in the interests of the company transferring the funds.

The applicability of this assumption to fund transfers between companies that are part of the same group has been thoroughly discussed in case law regarding the interpretation of what constitutes a 'third party' pursuant to the Income Tax Law. Two interpretations have been put forward. The first – the 'formal' interpretation – disregards the fact that the transfer is between companies that belong to the same corporate group, on the grounds that both companies are separate legal entities and as such are third parties in relation to one another. The second – the 'realist' interpretation – argues that the fact that both companies belong to the same corporate group cannot be disregarded even though they are separate legal entities, and thus they do not strictly constitute third parties in relation to each other.

The Supreme Court of Justice recently upheld the formal interpretation in two precedents dated March 6 2012, by virtue of which group companies were considered as third parties under Article 73 of the Income Tax Law.[46]

46 Supreme Court of Justice, *In re Fiat Concord SA TF* (16.778-I) c/ DGI, June 3 2012, Ruling No F 260 XLIII, elDial.com – AA743D and *BJ Services SRL (TF 22.638-I) c/ DGI*, Ruling No B 824 XLIII RO.

Belgium

Tom Geudens
Yves Lenders
Lydian

1. Introduction

1.1 Admissibility of cash pooling agreements

In Belgium, it is neither explicitly nor implicitly forbidden by law for corporations to enter into a cash pooling agreement and/or for holding companies to set up a cash pooling agreement with group members. In respect of their admissibility, notional cash pooling and physical cash pooling are not regarded differently. Further, it also makes no difference from the point of view of Belgian law if one of the group companies or the master account holder is a foreign company.

1.2 Types of cash pooling agreement

Cash pooling agreements in Belgium are typically one of three types: target balancing, notional interest pooling and real interest pooling. Target balancing is a type of physical cash pooling, while notional interest pooling and real interest pooling are both types of notional cash pooling.

(a) Target balancing

According to Belgian legal doctrine, target balancing involves the effective, periodical (monthly, weekly, daily) transfer of credit amounts from the accounts of the group companies to the master account held by the master account holder. Credit amounts are transferred by means of a standing order to the master account, while debit amounts are credited by transfers from this master account. In that way, a type of current account relation is created between the group companies and the master account holder, which acts as a sort of intra-group financing company.

The master account holder pays to, or receives from, the bank interest on the global balance of the master account, with the effect that higher debit interest will be charged only insofar as the global balance is in debit. As such, higher debit interest linked to the individual debit balances is often avoided.

The main goal is to achieve a profit on interest at a group level, which will be settled between the master account holder and the group companies. The group companies having a credit balance will receive higher interest, while the group companies having a debit balance will pay lower interest compared to what the banks would pay or retain.

From the point of view of Belgian law, corporate groups are free to determine the terms and conditions of the target balancing arrangement. It is possible, for instance, to provide that only credit amounts above a certain minimum will be transferred. However, in practice, a zero balancing system is usually used, whereby balances are always brought back to zero.

Target balancing is the most far-reaching form of cash pooling, as it is the only form where there is an actual pooling of accounts.

(b) *Notional interest pooling*

In notional interest pooling, there is no actual transfer of credit amounts. It is merely a method of calculating interest. Each group company pays to, or receives from, the bank interest based on the credit or debit balance of its own account. Subsequently, the different individual account balances are combined. but only to the extent of calculating the interest on that global balance. Any positive difference between the combined individual interest amounts and the interest on the global balance will be paid to the master account holder as a bonus, which can be divided partially or fully between the group companies.

(c) *Real interest pooling*

As with notional interest pooling, real interest pooling is also a form of global recalculation of interest achieved without actually transferring amounts or effectively pooling accounts. However, in contrast to notional interest compensation, here the actual debit interest amounts to be paid to the bank are offset against the credit interest amounts to be received. As such, the group companies having a credit balance do not receive interest payments, while group companies having a debit balance do not have to pay interest. If the group has a global credit balance, then the bank will pay interest on this credit position to the master account holder. If the group has a global debit balance, then the master account holder will pay interest to the bank.

1.3 Specific legal requirements from various perspectives

Under Belgian corporate, insolvency and tax laws, there are no specific legal provisions governing cash pooling agreements. Nor are there any specific banking laws or regulatory provisions applicable to banks entering into a cash pooling agreement. In addition, the activities of a group company acting as master account holder under a cash pooling agreement will in principle not trigger any banking licence or regulatory requirements.

However, as transfers and draw-downs of funds to and from the master account under physical cash pooling have the nature of the grant and repayment of intra-group loans, the following requirements must be taken into account.

(a) *Thin capitalisation rule*

Belgian tax law includes a specific 7:1 debt-to-equity ratio rule aimed at avoiding thin capitalisation, which may have an impact on cash pooling agreements. According to this rule, interest payments, other than those on bonds or similar publicly issued debt securities, to beneficiaries that are not subject to income tax or which benefit from a substantially more favourable tax regime in respect of such interest income compared to the normal tax treatment in Belgium are not tax deductible to the extent that they relate to that part of the loans granted by such beneficiaries which exceeds seven times the sum of the taxed reserves (at the beginning of the taxable period) and the issued and paid-up capital (at the end of the taxable period) of the Belgian borrowing company.

By the programme law of March 29 2012 the 7:1 thin capitalisation rule has been replaced by a general 5:1 debt-to-equity ratio, and its scope has been widened to encompass all intra-group loans. The new 5:1 rule entered into force as of July 1 2012, which should enable the Belgian government to work out a budget-neutral and legally and technically solid solution for the potentially adverse consequences of this new rule on cash pooling agreements and group structures centralising certain financing activities in Belgium. In particular, US-based companies with a subsidiary in Belgium have threatened to transfer their activities to other countries, as they believe that this new rule is likely to make it unattractive for companies to engage in cash pooling agreements, inter-company netting and inter-company financing from Belgium.

This thin capitalisation rule is also applicable to cross-border interest payments, where its compatibility with both the 'arm's-length' principle in the relevant bilateral tax treaty and EU law needs further attention.

(b) Capital maintenance rules

According to Article 633 of the Companies Code, directors of a company must convene a shareholders' meeting within two months of the moment the directors know that the company's net assets have dropped under half of its share capital, in order to decide whether the company should be put into liquidation. Article 634 of the Companies Code applies when the net assets drop under the minimum share capital as set by the Companies Code. In that event, any interested third party can file a petition with the courts, seeking the dissolution of the company.

If a Belgian company finds itself in one of these situations, it is unlikely that entering into a cash pooling agreement will be considered to be in the interest of that company, which may lead to nullity of the cash pooling agreement in respect of that company and may also trigger directors' liability.

(c) Commingling of assets

The cash pooling agreement and the various transfers of moneys under it should be well documented and/or structured in order to ensure that any bankruptcy of a participating Belgian company does not expand to other group companies.

When it is unclear which assets belong to the bankrupt company and its group companies, legal scholars have questioned whether the bankruptcy of one company should not lead to the bankruptcy of the others with which the assets are commingled. The Belgian Supreme Court has ruled that even in such a case, each company should be considered separate from the other, each with its own assets. The assets which are commingled are then part of the asset base of each separate company, but held in co-ownership. Only in very exceptional circumstances, where there is no alternative but to conclude that the assets are completely commingled between the bankruptcy company and its group companies, may the bankruptcy of one company lead to the bankruptcy of the others in order to have one single bankruptcy estate.

1.4 General legal requirements

Although no specific rules or requirements in respect of cash pooling agreements exist under Belgian law, the following general legal principles and requirements should be taken into account when entering into a cash pooling agreement.

(a) *Corporate purpose*

Any transaction, including a cash pooling agreement, entered into by a Belgian company must be within its corporate purpose. The corporate purpose is laid down in the articles of association of the company and describes the scope of activities which the company can or cannot undertake. Therefore, it always has to be checked whether the corporate purpose of the company as described in its articles of association allows the company to enter into a cash pooling agreement and, if so, whether there requirements regarding guarantees and/or security. Cash pooling agreements are not always explicitly mentioned in the purpose clause of the articles of association. There is, however, often general language in the articles of association that states that the Belgian company may do everything in order to achieve its corporate purpose.

If a transaction is considered to be outside the corporate purpose of the company (ie, *ultra vires*), it may be declared null and void and, provided that certain conditions are met, the creditors of the Belgian company may be entitled to act directly against the company in respect of the acts performed outside the corporate purpose. Furthermore, as directors of a Belgian company may act on behalf of the company only insofar as the transactions fall within the corporate purpose of the company, the directors can be held liable to the company and third parties if they take actions which fall outside the scope of the company's corporate purpose.

(b) *Corporate interest*

The entry into and performance of cash pooling agreements must also be in the corporate interest of the Belgian company. However, this point can never be settled beyond doubt, as it will mainly depend on the factual situation, such as the benefit that the Belgian company may derive out of the whole transaction. Moreover, the lack of a definition of 'corporate interest' in the Companies Code has generated much discussion, controversy and legal theory.

In considering the corporate interest of a company which enters into intra-group transactions, it is necessary:

- on a primary level, to take into account any direct benefits that the Belgian company will receive from the transaction(s); and
- only on a secondary level, to take into account any indirect benefits, such as the benefit of the group.

Lacking any conclusive case law in this respect, the majority of Belgian legal writers have always argued that a direct corporate benefit for a Belgian company that enters into a transaction is of utmost importance. However, jurisprudence has over time accepted the idea of a 'group interest' (ie, indirect benefit), which has already been recognised for some time in other European legal systems, under which it is a legitimate interest for a Belgian company to contribute and, to a certain extent and under certain conditions, to make certain sacrifices to the benefit of the group. On this point, some Belgian legal writers argue that the transaction may not be exclusively for the benefit of one group company, but should also be for the benefit of the group as a whole. A mere indirect, group benefit alone will most probably not satisfy the corporate interest test for a Belgian company, it being understood that there should be at least some form of tangible direct benefit, such as better financing conditions or the receipt of a guarantee fee or higher interest payments.

The main criterion for assessing the level of risk which can be incurred by a Belgian company, and consequently the (potential) financial or commercial solidarity which it should be willing to enter into with the group, is proportionality. The risk or potential loss which could be incurred by the company may not be disproportionate when compared with the benefits it expects to receive out of the envisaged transaction. As each transaction creates its own risk/benefit balance, no clear definition of proportionality has been developed in case law.

It is important to note that:

- the ultimate decision as to whether a transaction is within the corporate interest of a Belgian company, lies with the board of directors of that company; and
- certain mechanisms exist that may enhance either the direct corporate benefit to the Belgian company, or the risk/benefit balance (ie, the proportionality test).

(c) Misuse of company assets

It is necessary to be conscious of potential misuse of company assets in intra-group transactions such as cash pooling agreements. In an intra-group context, misuse of company assets occurs where a director (eg, another group company) or a *de facto* director directly or indirectly applies the assets or the credit of the company to its own benefit, knowing that such application would have a material adverse effect on the company itself and its creditors or shareholders.

Misuse of company assets is a criminal offence under Belgian law.

(d) Insolvency: termination of contracts

As a rule, all transactions entered into with a company in financial difficulties prior to the initiation of any liquidation event remain valid during any such subsequent liquidation event.

However, Belgian bankruptcy law specifically provides that certain transactions entered into with a bankrupt company during the so-called 'hardening period' may be declared by the court to be unenforceable against the bankruptcy estate. The hardening period is a period of a maximum of six months prior to the declaration of bankruptcy by the commercial court. A hardening period, which is the exception and not the rule, can be put in place by a court decision only when there are clear indications that the company was virtually bankrupt before the date of the court decision declaring the company bankrupt. Actions entered into during the hardening period that can be declared unenforceable against the bankruptcy estate include:

- transactions entered into without compensation, or entered into on extremely beneficial terms;
- payments other than in money for debts due, or payments for debts that are not due; and
- security provided for debts existing prior to the date on which the court declares the company bankrupt.

All other payments for outstanding debts and all acts for valuable consideration that took place during the hardening period can be declared unenforceable by the commercial court if the other party to the agreement knew of the suspension of payment. Moreover, acts or payments at any time made by the debtor with the intention to cause damage to creditors are unenforceable.

(e) Transfer pricing

According to Belgian tax law, companies of the same group must perform their transactions at arm's length – that is, a company must be able to demonstrate that the prices at which it trades with affiliated companies are comparable to the prices and terms that would prevail in similar transactions between unrelated parties.

If a transaction is found not to be performed at arm's length, the Belgian tax authorities can:

- add the advantage granted to the tax base; and
- challenge the deductibility of tax losses (or other deductions) up to the amount of abnormal or gratuitous benefits received from an affiliated company.

The Belgian federal tax authorities have adopted the transfer pricing guidelines published by the Organisation for Economic Cooperation and Development and recommend that taxpayers maintain documentation supporting their transfer pricing policy.

Further, taxpayers can apply for a unilateral, bilateral or multilateral advance transfer pricing agreement or ruling from the federal tax authorities respecting the arm's-length nature of a pricing agreement.

The federal tax authorities have a special transfer pricing audit department, which has grown over the past few years leading to an increase of audit file investigations and adjustments. The audit activity of the special transfer pricing audit department and the level of transfer pricing adjustments will certainly increase in 2012 and onwards.

2. Specific questions

2.1 Perspective A: corporate group

(a) Liability of group company and/or master account holder directors in the event of insolvency of a group company

Directors' liability under Belgian law applies only to directors of a Belgian company. Therefore, liability of the directors of the group company or the master account holder will kick in only insofar as such companies are incorporated under Belgian law. With regard to possible liability, Belgian law does distinguish between whether the troubled company is a listed corporation or a privately held corporation, or if the bank or the distressed group company is registered in a foreign jurisdiction.

In Belgium, in addition to the concept of 'directors', who are appointed by the shareholders of a company in accordance with its articles of association and the Companies Code, the concepts of '*de facto*' directors and 'shadow' directors are also recognised. However, there is no such concept as 'supervisory' directors.

Directors: Under Belgian law, directors of a company can incur both civil and criminal liability.

With respect to civil liability, as a general rule, a director validly representing a company is not personally liable for the undertakings he makes in the name of that company. A director will be personally liable only if he has committed a fault, a third party has incurred losses and there is a causal connection between the fault and the losses. Fault can also consist of negligence or inaction. Belgian courts do not have the power to assess decisions taken by a director. A court may perform only a limited judicial review, and may impose sanctions only on actions that flagrantly involve fault. Therefore, bad decisions do not of themselves constitute fault. Furthermore, a court may judge only *a priori*, – that is, based on the knowledge and facts known at the time the director made the decision.

With respect to criminal liability, a director will be liable only if the action he took constitutes a criminal offence.

Belgian law recognises various grounds for director's liability:

- Companies Code – the Companies Code describes various situations which may lead to civil liability of the directors of a Belgian company. As a general rule, directors are liable for any shortcomings in the performance of their duties. Only the company itself can invoke such liability.

  Directors may be further held jointly and severally liable for all damages caused by a breach of the Companies Code or the articles of association of the company (*ultra vires* actions). Such liability may be invoked by the company and any third party.

  The entering of a Belgian company into an agreement without sufficient corporate interest may also incur civil and criminal liabilities for the directors of that company. It may furthermore lead to the nullity or unenforceability of any guarantee or security and any related agreements.

  In cases of bankruptcy, the directors may be held personally liable for all or part of the debt of the company which exceeds the asset value, if the directors have committed a serious default that contributed to such bankruptcy. The Companies Code explicitly states that tax fraud, for instance, is to be considered as a serious default.
- Unpaid taxes and social security contributions – directors' of a Belgian company are under certain circumstances liable for unpaid taxes and social security contributions.
- Criminal liability – a director may be held criminally liable for criminal

offences committed in the performance of his duties (eg, misuse of company assets), but may also be held criminally liable for offences committed by the company itself (eg, environmental or accounting offences).

Bankruptcy law also provides a series of criminal offences, which may lead to disqualification of a director for three to 10 years.

***De facto* directors:** In Belgian law, the concept of *de facto* directors is not defined as such, but if has been developed by case law and legal writers. A *de facto* director is basically a person that has not been formally appointed as a director, but is nonetheless treated as such.

Three criteria determine whether a person qualifies as a *de facto* director:

- He performs a positive act of management;
- His actions qualify as real acts of management that can lead to liability – such acts of management are decisions that affect the commercial and financial position of the company; and
- He perform the act of management in total independence and freedom.

The consequences of being a *de facto* director are diverse.

First, a criminal judge may choose who he holds responsible for a criminal act committed by a company from among the appointed directors and/or the *de facto* director(s).

Second, the Companies Code provides that *de facto* directors are personally liable for the debts, and personally and severally liable for the outstanding social security contributions, of the company in cases of bankruptcy where the debts exceed the profits and it is proven that the *de facto* director committed a serious fault that contributed to the bankruptcy.

Further, *de facto* directors may also be held liable towards the company and third parties for damage caused by their faults (tort liability).

Shadow directors: In addition to *de facto* directors, Belgian law recognises the concept of shadow directors, based on the general law principle of sham representation. Where a person acts as if he is the representative of a company towards a third party, that third party, acting in good faith, may hold the company liable for the acts committed by the sham representative, provided that the following conditions are met:

- The person does not have any power to represent the company, or exceeds his power of representation;
- The third party acts in good faith;
- The sham causes damage to the third party; and
- The act can be attributed to the company.

Piercing the corporate veil: Notwithstanding the fact that a shareholder under Belgian law can be held liable only for its investment in a Belgian company, there are nevertheless situations whereby the corporate veil of a company can be pierced and shareholders can face personal liability.

The conditions for courts to impose personal liability on shareholders are strict, and arise only in exceptional circumstances. These are assessed on a case-by-case basis by Belgian courts, mainly based on the general principles of tort law. It is highly exceptional and there is very little case law on this matter, but what there is can be summarised as follows:

- In the event of bankruptcy, if the company's debt is greater than the company's assets, liability can be imposed on the shareholders in case of a fault committed by a shareholder which could have had an impact on the bankruptcy of the company;
- Shareholders can be held personal liable, in the event of bankruptcy, if abuse of law can be demonstrated. This would include a situation where the company is used by the shareholder only in order to benefit from limited liability; and
- A parent company is liable towards its subsidiaries (eg, if there has been undercapitalisation of the subsidiary).

(b) Liability of group company and/or the master account holder director in the event of insolvency of the master account holder

The discussion at point (a) above applies to this situation as well, with the necessary changes being read in as to which party is which.

(c) Liability of group companies in the event of insolvency of the master account holder

There is no specific law, statute or regulation in Belgium that deals with, or provides for specific regulations applicable to, a group of companies. Although specific areas of law refer to the concept of a group (eg, accounting law and certain provisions of financial law) and Belgian legal writers, backed by limited case law, have developed the 'group' concept in specific circumstances (eg, the group benefit relevant for Belgian companies in international financing transactions), Belgian law will always assess each group company as a separate legal entity, and does not recognise the group as a legal vehicle with its own set of rights and obligations. The Belgian Supreme Court has confirmed in many cases that the independence of each company as a separate legal entity is one of the cornerstones of Belgian company law.

Claims of one member of a corporate group against other members of that group are as a rule valid and enforceable, as all members of the group are to be considered as separate legal entities with their own set of rights and obligations.

Belgian law does not recognise the pooling of assets and liabilities in such a way that the creditor of one company becomes a creditor of all members (other than in contractual pooling arrangements). Each Belgian company that forms part of a group will be seen as a separate legal entity with its own asset base that serves as general collateral for its creditors. It has been confirmed on many occasions by the Belgian Supreme Court that an obligation entered into by one company remains an obligation of that company and not of the group as a whole.

When it is unclear which assets belong to the bankrupt company and which to another company within the group, legal scholars have questioned whether the bankruptcy of the one company should not lead to the bankruptcy of the other with whose assets the bankrupt company's assets are commingled. The Belgian Supreme Court has ruled that even in such case, each company should be considered separate from the other, each with its own assets. The assets which are mingled are then part of the asset base of each separate company, but held in co-ownership. Only in very exceptional circumstances, where the conclusion that the assets are completely commingled between the bankrupt company and the other company cannot be avoided, can the bankruptcy of one company lead to the bankruptcy of the other, in order to have one single bankruptcy estate.

Further, and despite the clear view of the Belgian Supreme Court, insolvency case law shows a very diverse landscape of tools and techniques used to extend obligations entered into by one group company to the other group companies. Such techniques consist of damages payable by group companies for obligations entered into by one group company, subordination of intra-group claims in more fraudulent circumstances and so on. However, as the case law is so diverse, and given the clear view of the Belgian Supreme Court in this respect, it cannot be concluded that there is a clear rule in pooling assets and liabilities of group companies; but it must be mentioned that it is possible.

(d) Liability of the master account holder in the event of insolvency of a group company

The discussion at point (c) above applies to this situation as well, with the necessary changes being read in as to which party is which.

2.2 Perspective B: bank

(a) Banking requirements

As cash pooling agreements as such are not separately regulated under Belgian law, there are also no specific regulatory requirements for banks providing cash pooling services. Of course, banks established in Belgium have to meet general requirements in respect of minimum capital, solvency and liquidity. The supervising authority here is the National Bank of Belgium.

As Belgium is an EU member state, the Belgian requirements in respect of minimum capital, solvency and liquidity are basically implementations of EU directives. Current banking requirements, and those foreseeable in the near future, are a consequence of the global financial crisis, which has pointed up the need to harmonise banking requirements throughout the European Union and to reinforce the structure of EU financial supervision. Therefore, Belgium will have to implement the Basel III standards in its national laws and regulations by January 1 2013. In the context of the new European supervisory system, the envisaged goal is to be able to detect any risks to stability and to set up an efficient alert system. Moreover, the new structure meets the objective of a single, stable market for financial services, bringing together all of the national supervisory authorities within a European operational network which has shared and mutually reinforcing responsibilities.

(b) ***Liability of the bank in the event of insolvency of the master account holder or a group company***

In principle, the bank involved in the cash pooling agreement will not be held liable for any losses in the event that the master account holder or a group company goes into distress. The only situations where the bank could be held liable is when the losses are the consequence of its own fraud, wilful misconduct or gross negligence.

2.3 Insolvency

(a) ***Cash pooling agreements from the insolvency practitioner's perspective***

Belgian law distinguishes two main types of insolvency procedures: judicial reorganisation and bankruptcy.

Judicial reorganisation: The commercial court can grant judicial reorganisation to any Belgian company whose continuity is threatened, whether immediately or in the future. If the net assets of the company have fallen to under 50% of its share capital, the continuity of the company is always presumed to be at risk. A company that is theoretically bankrupt can also be the subject of, and be protected from its creditors under, a judicial reorganisation. The judicial reorganisation aims to preserve the continuity of a company as a going concern and can be qualified as a Chapter 11/administration-like procedure.

After a petition has been filed with the competent commercial court to implement judicial reorganisation, the president of the commercial court appoints a delegated judge. The delegated judge reports to the court on the admissibility of the request. In this role, the delegated judge may hear the company and any other relevant person he deems necessary, and request all necessary information.

If the request for judicial reorganisation is approved, the delegated judge remains in place. He has an advisory role towards the court and a supervisory role over the company during the whole of the judicial reorganisation procedure.

Within 10 days of the date of filing the petition, a formal court hearing behind closed doors will be organised, in which only the company and the delegated judge will be heard, unless the company has expressly requested a public hearing. The company need not pre-notify creditors of the filing of the petition, but in practice the most important creditors (eg, the banks) will be informed by the company of its intention to file a judicial reorganisation petition (the reason for this being that the creditors have to approve the reorganisation plan by simple majority vote). The company and its creditors (or at least the heavyweight ones) may even negotiate a pre-packaged agreement before filing of the petition with the commercial court. If creditors are informed of the judicial reorganisation petition, they may provide the court with information and any views they have on the petition and/or the proposed reorganisation.

During a judicial reorganisation procedure, the directors and shareholders of the company stay in charge, but the company or a stakeholder (eg, a creditor) may request the appointment of a mediator in order to assist the company during its reorganisation process. The mediator must be an independent person with experience in managing companies and accountancy.

Bankruptcy: The conditions for a bankruptcy order are that a company which pursues commercial activities must be in a situation of cessation of payments and be unable to obtain further credit. 'Cessation of payments' is generally accepted to mean that the company is unable to pay its debts as they fall due. Such situation must be persistent and not merely temporary. A bankruptcy procedure may be initiated by the company, by unpaid creditors or upon the initiative of the Public Prosecutor's Office.

If a bankruptcy petition is filed, a formal court hearing will be organised in which all parties concerned, and especially the company, will be summoned and heard, and the court will assess whether the insolvency conditions are met. If the commercial court decides that the insolvency conditions are met, the bankruptcy order appoints a supervising judge and a receiver. Receivers are lawyers chosen from a list drawn up by the commercial court. The receivers are appointed by the commercial court and cannot be chosen by the bankrupt company. There is, as a rule, no debate on the appointment of the receiver. Any interested third party can appeal the decision of the commercial court, including the appointment of the receiver, within 15 days of the publication of the bankruptcy decision in the *State Gazette*. However, it is rather uncommon to appeal against the appointment of a particular receiver.

The receiver takes full control over the company in respect of collecting outstanding debts, realising the assets of the bankruptcy estate and distributing the proceeds to the creditors. The receiver has the obligation to act in the interest of the bankruptcy estate and the interests of the creditors.

The costs of bankruptcy (essentially, the fees of the receiver) are costs of the bankruptcy estate and rank as privileged debts. The fees of the receiver are determined in a royal decree.

Belgian bankruptcy law specifically provides that certain transactions entered into with a bankrupt company during the hardening period may be declared unenforceable against the bankruptcy estate. The hardening period is a period of a maximum of six months prior to the declaration of bankruptcy. A hardening period, which is the exception and not the rule, can be put in place by a court decision only when there are clear indications that the company was virtually bankrupt before the date of the court decision declaring the company bankrupt. The actions entered into during the hardening period which can be declared unenforceable against the bankrupt estate are:

- transactions entered into with no compensation, or entered into on extremely beneficial terms,
- payments other than in money for debts due, or payments for debts that are not due; and
- the provision of security for debts existing prior to the insolvency date.

All other payments for outstanding debts and all acts for valuable consideration that took place during the hardening period can be declared unenforceable if the other party to the agreement knew of the suspension of payments.

Moreover, acts or payments made by the debtor at any time with the intention to cause damage to creditors are unenforceable.

(b) ***Special rules as regards creditors of other parties to the cash pooling agreement***
As a general rule, the receiver has to act in the interest of the bankruptcy estate and the interests of the creditors, including the other parties to the cash pooling agreement. The rights of the creditors of the other parties to the cash pooling agreement need not, as such, be taken into account by the receiver.

(c) ***Dissolution/termination of the cash pooling agreement in the event of liquidation of the master account holder or a group company***
As there are no specific Belgian law provisions regarding cash pooling agreements, general Belgian contract law applies. Under Belgian contract law, the general principle is that contracting parties are free to determine the content of a legally binding agreement – in other words, there is freedom of contract. The freedom of contract is restricted only by legal provisions of public order and mandatory law, and by the principles of fraud and wilful misconduct.

It is market practice to provide for the termination of a contract in the event of insolvency proceedings (bankruptcy and judicial reorganisation).

However, the Belgian Law on the Continuity of Companies of January 31 2009, regulating the judicial reorganisation, procedure, is a public order measure and provides that ongoing contracts cannot be terminated as a consequence of the initiation of a judicial reorganisation as it aims to preserve the continuity of a company in difficulties. Termination of the cash pooling agreement based on events of default other than the initiation of a judicial reorganisation can still be invoked by the other parties to the agreement.

In the event of bankruptcy, all ongoing contracts (ie, the contracts existing before the commencement of the bankruptcy procedure) continue to exist as a general rule notwithstanding the initiation of the bankruptcy procedure. It will be up to the receiver to terminate the ongoing contracts, in accordance with their terms and conditions. The receiver may even choose to continue the business of the debtor with a view to a possible sale of part or whole of the business, and as a consequence not to terminate the contracts, provided that he receives the authorisation of the court and the continuation of the business causes no prejudice to the creditors. The other parties to the cash pooling agreement remain entitled to terminate that agreement.

A liquidation procedure does not terminate ongoing contracts. Parties can, however, contractually agree that a liquidation constitutes a termination event. As is the case under bankruptcy, a right of set-off is enforceable during liquidation.

2.4 Perspective D: regulatory

Belgium has no regulatory requirements regarding cash pooling agreements.

2.5 Perspective E: tax

For transfer pricing issues in respect of cash pooling agreements, please refer to section 1.4 above.

With regard to withholding taxes, a distinction should be made between physical cash pooling and notional cash pooling.

(a) Physical cash pooling

In the event of physical cash pooling between group companies, the cash pooling results in a series of loan and interest payments between the master account holder and the group companies.

Belgian tax law qualifies payments from the bank to the master account holder and from the master account holder to group companies as interest. The Belgian withholding tax rate on interest payments increased from 15% to 21% as of January 1 2012. Many other EU member states also levy a deduction at source on inter-company loans, applying various rates.

Belgium has implemented the EU Interest and Royalties Directive establishing a common system for the payment of interest and charges between affiliated companies domiciled in various member states. Such interest payments are no longer subject to deduction at source. However, this exemption is restricted to loans between a parent company and direct subsidiaries, or between directly affiliated companies without any intermediary.

Given the various tax regulations of the EU member states and non-EU states, in combination with international treaties, it is key when structuring international cash pooling agreements to optimise the cash pooling agreement from a tax point of view in order to extend the scope of the exemption – for instance, by setting up a series of direct target balancing transactions between parent companies and subsidiaries or between affiliated companies. Also, the master account should be located in a country where credit interest paid by banks is not subject to deduction at source, or in a country that does apply deduction at source, but where the master account holder is exempt from withholding tax on interest it receives when investing the group's surpluses or when borrowing from a bank. Further, the country of domicile of the master account holder also plays a role here, since it is better if interest on lending and borrowing between the master account holder and group companies is not subject to deduction at source.

(b) Notional cash pooling

Under the system of notional pooling, taxation is less important, but is still a delicate issue. The service provided by the bank consists of optimising the terms for the accounts involved (by reducing the debit interest rates and increasing the credit interest rates), without generating new financial transactions. No new loans or deposits are set up.

There is no change to the tax treatment as a result of the cash pooling agreement. The tax status of a company does not change: if the bank is subject to deduction at source when there is no pool, it is also subject to such deduction within the pool.

With notional pooling, the basic aim as regards tax is to ensure that the improved financial terms do not give rise to a transfer of profit among the members of a pool or among the participating banking establishments. Accordingly, where the pools have an international dimension, it is advantageous to reduce the taxable profit in one country by transferring all or part of that profit to another country.

Therefore, often a method is set up for calculating interest that spreads the profit resulting from the notional pooling system on the basis of the contribution by each participant to the generation of a profit margin for each of the banking units involved.

Notional pooling ultimately provides each party with more advantageous credit or debit interest. This amount is communicated to the local accounting units to be applied to the respective accounts, on the basis of the tax status of each participant in the notional pooling scheme.

Brazil

Celso Caldas Martins Xavier
Demarest e Almeida Advogados

1. Introduction

Cash pooling has been a useful tool in many countries to improve cash management among companies of the same group. By entering into a cash pooling agreement, a group of companies can benefit from better interest rates and, in some cases, improve the cash needs of other group members.

In Brazil, the concept of cash pooling lacks specific regulation. There is no specific law that governs this kind of agreement. As a consequence, if a cash pooling agreement were to be executed, it would be governed by general principles of corporate, civil, tax, regulatory and insolvency law, since its complex nature involves all such fields.

2. Physical cash pooling

From a practical standpoint, a cross-border cash pooling agreement is not a feasible tool for Brazilian companies. Brazilian exchange regulations are complex and the inflow and outflow of money – where there is a cross-border physical cash pooling agreement – will involve bureaucracy and taxes that will prevent the cash pooling agreement from achieving its main target – that is, serving as a cost-effective tool to improve management and group members' financial needs.

In addition, any inflow into or outflow of money from Brazil must be effected through foreign exchange contracts, which are under the supervision of the Brazilian Central Bank. Depending on the nature of the transaction, the foreign exchange contract will trigger different accounting and tax consequences.

For reasons explained below in more detail, the lack of specific regulation governing cash pooling agreements creates difficulties in classifying the transfer of money under such an agreement in the required foreign exchange contracts. This is a hurdle that a company wishing to establish a cash pooling agreement will have difficulties in overcoming, if it manages to at all.

In the case of a very active cash pooling agreement, the transactions conducted under its umbrella would require several foreign exchange contracts, in respect of which there is no specific category into which the cash pooling agreement would fit. Hence, the tax and accounting treatment to which such transactions would be subject and how they would impact on Brazilian group members is highly debatable.

For domestic cash pooling agreements the situation is not that different with regard to physical cash pooling. Although there is no prohibition as such, the transfer of money between different group members, despite any actual underlying transaction, will be seen as a loan and will trigger the payment of taxes. If it is not classified as a loan, it will be seen as a inter-company loan and will trigger other important tax and accounting issues, which will likewise cause the cash pooling agreement not to be an effective option for cash management.

In summary, it could be said that there is no specific category for the actual transfer of money among companies under a cash pooling agreement which would exempt them from tax and accounting issues. Therefore, even though Brazilian law does not prohibit a physical cash pooling agreement, the issues related to the transfer of money are likely to cause it to be unfeasible from a financial standpoint. This conclusion will prevail until Brazil passes a law that could exempt transactions under cash pooling agreements from the common taxes and accounting restrictions, and that is the main reason why physical cash pooling is not used in Brazil.

The other reasons is the same as those related to the risks associated with a notional cash pooling agreement, as explained below, but to a greater degree. For example, the risks of having the corporate veil pierced in relation to a cash pooling agreement are outlined below. Because physical cash pooling involves the actual transfer of money, for the reasons explained below the risk of this doctrine being applied to a physical cash pooling agreement is much greater than in the case of notional cash pooling. In other words, group members may be held liable for the debts of another group member under a financial distress procedure.

2.1 Liability in the event of insolvency

From a group member management standpoint, a financial crisis in any group member would be unlikely to harm the management of the other group members, unless they have behaved unlawfully in any way. As for the master account holder, however, its management may be involved in judicial discussions, since it is in charge of controlling the group members' activities. It is hard to foresee the degree to which the master account holder's managers would be involved in a potential lawsuit, but this is a risk that should be borne in mind before entering into such a transaction.

In the event of the master account holder's being under a financial distress procedure, this is likely to affect the group members, unless the cash pooling agreement contains specific provisions that would set aside the bank account in an insolvency scenario. Even in this case, however, Brazilian labour courts tend not to respect such provisions and may order the seizure of the master account regardless of whether the money deposited in it belongs exclusively to the account holder.

These conclusions are the same whether the group members are listed companies or not, and whether they are located in Brazil or abroad.

Taking the above into account, it could concluded that only a domestic notional cash pooling agreement could theoretically be viable from a purely financial point of view. Even in this case, however, the structure of the cash pooling agreement should be carefully designed by the participants, which should be aware that legal risks will arise, particularly in a bankruptcy scenario, as explained below.

3. Notional cash pooling

Unlike physical cash pooling, in notional cash pooling there is no actual transfer of money, which means that there will be no inflow and outflow of money into and out of any of the group members' accounts. The cash pooling agreement, then, will be mostly an agreement between a bank and a group of companies which are members of the same economic group. The goal will be the improvement of the rate of interest paid on investments and avoidance of interest where one of the group members has a negative balance in its bank account, while another member has a positive balance.

For these reasons, the questions are more of a contractual nature and will be related to the bank's willingness to accept the arrangements outlined above and any others that could be included in a notional cash pooling agreement. Theoretically speaking, a notional cash pooling agreement could be designed in such a way that there would be no tax or accounting restrictions, which, as explained above, are the main reasons why a physical cash pooling agreement would not be viable.

Before entering into a notional cash pooling agreement, however, companies should assess the risks arising from it with regard to third parties. In summary, Brazil adopts the notion that shareholders should held liable for their company's liabilities only in very few cases. Piercing of the corporate veil is permitted in cases related to consumer law and when the corporate veil has been used for fraudulent purposes – although the word 'fraudulent' is a vague concept that may give rise to some uncertainty.

However, case law has been broadening the concept, under the theory of the 'economic group'. This theory allows shareholders and, in a few cases, sister companies, to be held liable whenever the company actually holding the liability does not have sufficient funds to pay off its debt.

This theory is commonly used in labour cases to pierce the corporate veil and hold shareholders liable. In civil cases and insolvency cases, its application is more narrow and will depend on the way that the assets of the company are actually managed. There are precedents in civil cases for holding shareholders liable whenever it is found that the shareholders' and company's assets are managed as if they were mixed. In this case, precisely because of the lack of a clear separation between the shareholders' assets and those of the company, Brazilian courts have a tendency to pierce the corporate veil, even if fraud is not found. This is why it is concluded above that a physical cash pooling agreement has a greater risk of having the corporate veil piercing and economic group doctrines applied than a notional cash pooling agreement.

The concept of the economic group is also used in bankruptcy scenarios, particularly in liquidation cases. In any liquidation there will be an investigation to determine the causes of the liquidation. It will be investigated whether the liquidation has been caused by an ordinary market reason, mismanagement, fraud and so on. This investigation will be decisive in determining the extent to which shareholders may be held liable (ie, if mismanagement or fraud is found, shareholders and directors may be held liable for the company's debts).

It is very likely that a cash pooling agreement will be used to hold the parties to it liable for any liability of any group member. Because a cash pooling agreement involves actual or notional transfer of funds among the group members, this will be an important piece of evidence to trigger the economic group concept and, eventually, hold the group members of the cash pooling agreement liable. A cash pooling agreement is likely to show that the assets of the group members are somehow mixed, even if there is strict control of credits and debts among the group members and contractual terms making such assets distinct.

Therefore, when entering into cash pooling agreements in Brazil, companies should be aware that in the event of liquidation of any group members, liabilities may arise for all of them. The extent of the risks will depend on the type of cash pooling agreement and the circumstances of the case. In any event, the cash pooling agreement should be considered a risk for financially healthier group members, and this fact should given serious consideration.

The bank where the master account is held has no reason to be held liable, since it is only the place where the bank accounts of the group members are held. The master account holder for the cash pooling agreement, however – particularly if it is a group member – is likely to be held liable for any of the group members' debts if the economic group concept is applied. From an individual perspective, neither the directors or supervisory directors of the master account holder nor the directors or supervisory directors of the group company would be held liable in event of the liquidation of any group member. Liability will attach to such individuals only if mismanagement or fraud is found.

As to the relationship among group members, any credit arising between them will be deemed a subordinated claim under the Bankruptcy Law. Such claims have no priority in a liquidation scenario and, in the event of a court-supervised restructuring, the creditors will not have voting rights in the approval of any restructuring plan.

As a consequence of the issues outlined above, although a notional cash pooling agreement could theoretically be used in Brazil, the potential liabilities arising from it – and, perhaps, the banks' lack of willingness to enter into such agreements, may be the reason why cash pooling agreements are not a common practice in Brazil.

Cash pooling agreements might start being more commonly used if a specific law was passed to govern their use and to address the current risks associated with them. Obviously, if the intention of a cash pooling agreement is to boost group companies' finances, it is clear that its application will be restricted in any country where taxes, accounting and regulatory hurdles are found. For logical reasons, no cash pooling agreement will be executed if the liquidation of a group member, for instance, may harm the other group members or their shareholders, which is a real threat in Brazil.

Canada

Mary Arzoumanidis
Michael J MacNaughton
Borden Ladner Gervais LLP

1. Introduction

A critical aspect of managing a corporate group is the optimal management of liquidity and cash flow. Cash management systems are precisely designed to enable this. Principally, cash management systems allow a corporate group to know its cash position at any given time. Other benefits of a cash management system include the maximum utilisation of internal liquidity before using external sources, minimising interest expenditure while maximising interest income and controlling cash. It is common practice in Canada for cash management systems to be implemented among a corporate group. However, there may be some restrictions on the implementation of a cash management system depending on the nature of the group's business or because of trust accounting obligations.[1]

1.1 Pooling mechanics

While a distinction is typically made in most jurisdictions between physical cash pooling (which involves the actual transfer of funds between accounts) and notional cash pooling (which involves, as the name implies, a notional transfer of funds between accounts), that line is somewhat blurred in Canada. A typical cash pooling agreement in Canada involves elements of both physical and notional cash pooling structures. This practice is likely attributable to a decision of the Ontario Court of Appeal wherein the transfers of funds under an arrangement that was intended to be structured as notional pooling in that case were held to be actual transfers, thus taking on the flavour of physical cash pooling.[2]

(a) Physical cash pooling

Physical cash pooling, often referred to as cash sweeping or zero balancing, involves the actual transfer of funds between the bank accounts of a corporate group. Typically, a 'zero balancing agreement' is entered into between the bank and the cash pool participants. In this type of arrangement, each pool participant maintains its own separate operating bank account (the designated account) at the same or different bank branch. At the close of each business day, each designated account

---

1 For example, Ontario case law suggests that a banker that provides cash management services to customers involved in the construction industry or whose business involved the receipt and use of trust funds may be at risk to trust claimants in certain circumstances. See *Arthur Anderson Inc v Toronto-Dominion Bank*, [1994] 17 OR (3d) 363 (Ont CA).

2 See *Arthur Anderson, ibid.*

with a credit balance is automatically 'swept' to create a zero balance. Credit balances in designated accounts are physically transferred to a master or concentration account usually maintained in the name of the corporate parent. Debit balances in designated accounts are eliminated by the transfer of funds from the concentration account to the designated account which is in overdraft. From a cash management perspective, this type of cash pooling agreement is attractive since the true financial picture of each designated account can be determined at any given point in time. The bank statements of each account show the daily movement of funds to and from the concentration account. Further, the transfers to and from the designated accounts and the concentration account represent actual movement of funds and are generally treated as inter-company loans to or from the master account holder (typically, the parent company). At any given point in time, a transfer may result in a loan or a repayment of a loan. Further, since there is an actual transfer of funds, there are also transaction costs associated with each such transfer.

(b) Notional cash pooling

Unlike physical cash pooling, notional cash pooling does not involve real transfers of funds across accounts. Typically, a 'mirror accounting' agreement is entered into between the bank and the cash pool participants. In this type of cash pooling agreement, the transfer of funds occurs notionally through the use of 'mirror' accounts. A mirror account is created for each designated account in the same currency as the designated account. Pool participants do not have access to the mirror accounts and cannot therefore make deposits or withdrawals from those accounts. A separate concentration account is also created, typically in the name of the parent company.

At the end of each business day, the bank transfers the balance in each designated account, whether debit or credit, to the concentration account. The transfers are made by posting entries in each mirror account in an amount equal but opposite in value to the closing balance of the designated account. In effect, the credit or debit balance in each designated account is 'swept' out to create a zero balance. The corresponding debits or credits are then transferred to the concentration account. No entries are posted in the designated accounts, which leaves their bank statements free of multiple journal entries (but can lead to a misrepresentation of the true financial position of the company). The concentration account shows the single net position (whether in credit or debit) of all pool participants. As a result, the bank can pay or charge interest on the combined balance only.

Although this kind of pooling can be said to be notional only, as a result of the decision of the Ontario Court of Appeal in *Arthur Anderson*, it would appear that courts – in Ontario at least – would view transfers made in a notional pooling structure to be actual transfers. From this perspective, there does not appear to be a real difference between physical and notional cash pooling.

(c) Features common to both physical and notional cash pooling structures

Typically, cash pooling agreements will require that steps be taken to eliminate any overdraft, whether in the concentration account or in each individual designated account. For example, if there is a debit balance in a designated account, a transfer of funds from the concentration account to the designated account may be made to eliminate the overdraft. Further, since pool participants typically have credit facilities with the bank, which would include an authorised credit limit, under the cash pooling agreement the bank is given the power to refuse to honour any drawing upon a designated account which would cause the concentration account to be overdrawn over and above its credit limit, or would cause the designated account to be overdrawn beyond any credit limit that applies to it.

(d) ***Cash pooling agreements***

Canadian banks offer different types of cash pooling agreement depending on the type of arrangement that the corporate group wishes to establish (either physical or notional pooling). Cash pooling agreements do not need to be structured in any specific form, as there are no specific legislative requirements in that respect. Generally, the cash pooling agreements, as with all agreements that banks have with their customers for all their services and product offerings, are governed by the law of the province in which the account is located. At a minimum, the mechanics and the nature and effect of the pooling mechanism between the bank and the participants to the cash pool, and as between the participants themselves, must be clearly set out in any cash pooling agreement, so that there is no question about the nature and effect of the cash pooling agreements in the future.

2. Legal considerations for cash pooling agreements

There is no specific statutory framework that applies to the implementation and maintenance of cash pooling agreements in Canada. The rules applicable to cash pooling agreements are based on general law pertaining to the areas of corporate law, banking law, insolvency law, regulatory law and tax law.

2.1 Corporate law

(a) ***Internal approvals for cash pooling agreements***

There are no specific corporate law requirements that apply to cash pooling agreements. Most jurisdictions in Canada do not require that lending and borrowing from affiliates (as occurs in cash pooling) be listed as a specific corporate object in the articles of incorporation; however, corporations are permitted to include restrictions on the conduct of the corporation or its activities in its articles. In any event, it is good practice for each participating group company to obtain the prior authorisation of its board of directors before putting in place a cash management system. Further, while corporations are not required to obtain shareholder approval, unless otherwise required in accordance with the provisions of a shareholders' agreement, a shareholders' resolution approving the cash pooling agreements should also be considered.

(b) ***Financial assistance***

In certain provinces and territories in Canada, the issue of related-party financial assistance to insiders or others may arise in connection with cash pooling agreements. Generally, the corporate statutes in these jurisdictions impose extensive limitations with respect to the provision of financial assistance (directly or indirectly, by way of loan, guarantee or other otherwise) by one member of a corporate group to another, unless the corporation can satisfy certain tests to ensure that the transaction would not negatively impact on the solvency of the corporation.[3] Generally, contracts made in contravention of the financial assistance prohibition are void and of no effect, and the transaction that constitutes the financial assistance would likely be unenforceable. However, the legislation typically allows the corporation that made the contract in violation of the financial assistance provisions or a "lender for value in good faith without notice of the contravention" to enforce the contract.

2.2 Banking law

While there are no specific banking laws that apply to cash pooling agreements, given certain legislative limitations on deposit-taking in Canada only federal banks and certain other provincial financial institutions can provide cash pooling facilities. For the purposes herein, only federally regulated financial institutions, such as banks, are considered.

2.3 Insolvency

(a) *Overview of insolvency proceedings in Canada*

Canada's insolvency rules stem from two principal pieces of federal legislation: the Bankruptcy and Insolvency Act[4] and the Companies' Creditors Arrangement Act.[5] The federal statutory insolvency regimes are supplemented with provincial legislation dealing with creditor rights. Additionally, the Winding-Up and Restructuring Act[6] governs the liquidation of insolvent banks and other financial institutions.

Bankruptcy proceedings (which are analogous to Chapter 7 proceedings in the United States) are governed solely by the Bankruptcy and Insolvency Act. Upon bankruptcy, all property of the corporate debtor is transferred by operation of law to a licensed trustee in bankruptcy who is charged, under the Bankruptcy and Insolvency Act, with the disposition of the corporate debtor's property, its conversion to cash and the distribution of the proceeds in accordance with the priority regime contained in the act.

Restructuring proceedings (which are analogous to Chapter 11 proceedings in

3 The corporate statutes of New Brunswick, Prince Edward Island, the Northwest Territories, Nunavut and the Yukon require compliance with solvency tests prior to the provision of any related-party financial assistance, subject to certain exceptions. Federally incorporated corporations, and corporations incorporated in Ontario, Manitoba, Nova Scotia and Quebec are no longer subject to any statutory obligations relating to financial assistance, while corporations in Alberta, British Columbia and Saskatchewan are permitted to provide related-party financial assistance provided that disclosure is made of the transaction.

4 Bankruptcy and Insolvency Act, RSC 1985, c B-3, as amended.

5 Companies' Creditors Arrangement Act, RSC 1985, c C-36, as amended.

6 Winding-Up and Restructuring Act, RSC, 1985, c W-11, as amended.

the United States) are governed by both the Bankruptcy and Insolvency Act and the Companies' Creditors Arrangement Act. If the insolvent company's liabilities are less than C$5 million, the restructuring must take place under the Bankruptcy and Insolvency Act; where the liabilities are more than C$5 million, the restructuring is typically undertaken pursuant to the Companies' Creditors Arrangement Act. In either case, the debtor remains in possession of its assets and business and an independent officer of the court is appointed to monitor the business and financial affairs of the company (a 'proposal trustee' under the Bankruptcy and Insolvency Act; a 'monitor' under the Companies' Creditors Arrangement Act). Both the acts' restructuring provisions have a stay of proceedings which comes into effect once the restructuring process has formally begun.

The Winding-Up and Restructuring Act governs the liquidation of insolvent banks and other financial institutions, and provides a mechanism for the orderly gathering and realisation of assets and the rateable distribution of those assets among creditors under the supervision of the court. A liquidator (analogous to a trustee in bankruptcy) is appointed by the court to take custody or control of all of the property of the insolvent company and to wind up the business of the company.

(b) Relevant considerations in the event of an insolvency of a group company or the master account holder

Canada has a statutory and common law framework in which directors can be held personally liable for decisions made by the corporation they serve. Any action or decision of the directors to move assets out of the corporation that renders a corporation insolvent or near insolvent will be scrutinised to ensure that the directors' actions or decisions did not precipitate the insolvency. Although courts have imposed liability on directors where they have continued to operate the business knowing of the company's inability to pay its debts, the circumstances in which they have done so are relatively narrow. Generally, 'insolvency' occurs when a corporation is unable to pay its liabilities as they become due.[7]

The Canada Business Corporations Act[8] establishes two main duties to be discharged by directors in managing a corporation. The first duty is referred to as the statutory fiduciary duty, which requires directors to act honestly and in good faith with a view to the best interests of the corporation.[9] Insolvency of the corporation does not shift a director's focus away from the corporation.[10] In the context of cash pooling, the fiduciary duty must be exercised with respect to the company itself and not the corporate group as a whole. Therefore, even if a company's participation in a cash pooling agreement benefits all participants, a director will incur liability if he has not fulfilled his duty with regard solely to the company that he serves.

A director's fiduciary duty also requires the director not to place himself in a

7 Bankruptcy and Insolvency Act, Section 2.

8 Canada Business Corporations Act, RSC, 1985, c C-44, as amended (and corresponding provisions across provinces and territories; provincial corporate statutes may differ in both the wording of the duties and also as to the minimum standard required).

9 Canada Business Corporations Act, Section 122(1)(a).

10 *Re People's Department Stores Ltd (1992) Inc, 2004* SCC 68 (SCC); see also *Re BCE Inc*, 2008 SCC 69 (SCC).

position where the duty to act in the best interests of the corporation conflicts with his personal interests. If a director acts in breach of any fiduciary duty to the company in entering into the cash pooling agreement, will not only the director be liable for any loss that the company suffers as a result, but will be liable to account to the company for any profit he makes. For example, a conflict of interest can arise if a director sits on the board of directors of more than one group company and one group company stands to benefit more than the other. Directors can avoid liability here if a shareholders' resolution is obtained authorising the director to participate despite the conflict of interest.

The second duty established by the Canada Business Corporations Act is a duty of care, which requires directors to "exercise the care, diligence and skill that a reasonably prudent person would exercise in comparable circumstances".[11] This duty of care is owed to all stakeholders of the company, including shareholders and creditors.[12] In the context of cash pooling, this duty will be met if a director takes adequate steps to ensure that the cash pooling agreement does not contains terms that may adversely affect the company or the company's liquidity. Failure to do so may result in the director being liable for losses that the corporation suffers at the instance of shareholders or creditors or any other stakeholder.

If the business decision to enter into the cash pooling agreement was made honestly, prudently, in good faith and on reasonable grounds, taking into account all relevant information, and the interests of different stakeholders of the corporation, the court will defer to the business judgement of directors (known as the 'business judgement rule') when assessing whether there has been a breach of duty.[13]

Further, when a corporation faces insolvency or is insolvent, there is potential for oppressive or unfair prejudice to the interests of any security holder, creditor, director or officer on the part of the company.[14] If directors fail to give appropriate consideration to those interests, they could be found responsible under the oppression remedy or pursuant to a derivative action. The oppression remedy gives the court broad powers to impose any remedy it sees fit, including the varying or setting aside of a transaction or contract (eg, a cash pooling agreement) or compensating any aggrieved person. Creditors of a corporation whose "finances deteriorate" may have a case to bring a derivative action on behalf of the company.[15]

Directors may also face personal liability arising for operating a company while in a state of insolvency where there is a finding of negligent misrepresentation. In *NBD Bank, Canada v Dofasco Inc*,[16] the director of a company was held personally liable to creditors for making negligent misrepresentations to creditors regarding the financial position of the company which creditors relied on in advancing new credit to the company. In that

11 Canada Business Corporations Act, Section 122(1)(b) (and corresponding provisions across provinces and territories; provincial corporate statutes may differ in both the wording of the duties and the minimum standard required).

12 *People's Department Stores*, cited above in note 12, at paragraph 57.

13 *Ibid*, paragraph 67.

14 Canada Business Corporations Act, Section 241.

15 Canada Business Corporations Act, Section 239 (and corresponding provisions across provinces and territories).

16 *NDB Bank, Canada v Dofasco*, (1999) 46 OR (3d) 514 (Ont CA).

same case, it was deemed to be a fraudulent act for a board of directors to permit a company to continue in business, incurring liabilities, when there is little or no reasonable basis to expect that these incremental liabilities will be satisfied.

Directors may also be personally liable where a court determines that the director was privy to a transfer at undervalue under the Bankruptcy and Insolvency Act.[17] In the cash pooling context, transfers made in a cash pooling setting might be argued to be a disposition of property by a pool participant where the consideration received by the other pool participant is the creation and offset of an overdraft or debt within the corporate group. If that argument succeeded, a court could order the director to pay the difference between the value of the consideration given and received by the insolvent pool participant.

If a group company actually becomes bankrupt,[18] and has committed offences under the Bankruptcy and Insolvency Act, a director may be found a party to and guilty of the offence and held liable to pay a fine of up to C$10,000 (or can even be imprisoned, or both) whether or not the bankrupt corporate has been prosecuted or convicted of the offence, if the director "directed, authorized, assented to, acquiesced in or participated in the commission of the offence".[19] For example, if the transfers under the cash pooling agreement are set aside under the fraudulent preference provisions of the Bankruptcy and Insolvency Act,[20] the bankrupt corporation and its directors could be found guilty of making a fraudulent disposition of property before the bankruptcy. In addition, where the director has been convicted of an offence under the Bankruptcy and Insolvency Act, the court may make an order compensating any person for the loss or damage caused as a result of the commission of the offence.[21] Having said that, prosecution of persons for bankruptcy offences is relatively unusual, especially in this kind of context.

It is unlikely that directors of the parent corporation can be held liable for losses suffered by an insolvent subsidiary as a result of the cash pooling agreement unless the parent's corporate veil is lifted. Canadian courts respect the separate legal personality of each corporation and refuse to ignore it, except in exceptional circumstances. For example, the corporate veil has been lifted where:

- the subsidiary is formed for a fraudulent or improper purpose;
- the subsidiary acts as an agent or puppet of the parent;
- the subsidiary is under the parent's control to the extent that they constitute one enterprise; or
- the subsidiary is a mere sham or alter ego of the parent.[22]

---

17 Bankruptcy and Insolvency Act, Section 96. A transfer at undervalue refers to a disposition of property or provision of services for which no consideration is received by the debtor, or for which the consideration received is conspicuously less than fair market value of the consideration given by the debtor.

18 A corporate debtor can become bankrupt under the Bankruptcy and Insolvency Act through a voluntary assignment in bankruptcy, through involuntary creditor initiated bankruptcy proceedings, or as a consequence of failed reorganisation proceedings under the act.

19 Bankruptcy and Insolvency Act, Sections 198 and 204.

20 Bankruptcy and Insolvency Act, Section 95.

21 Bankruptcy and Insolvency Act, s. 204.3(1).

22 *Transamerica Life Insurance Co of Canada v Canada Life Assurance Co* (1996), 28 OR (3d) 423 (Ont Gen Div), affirmed [1997] OJ No 3754 (Ont CA); see also *Graci v New Steel Roofers Inc*, 2011 ONSC 2384 (Ont Sup Ct J), paragraphs 71-76.

It is doubtful that a valid cash pooling agreement would justify the lifting of the corporate veil of the parent corporation, as holder of the master or concentration account.

The same considerations set out above apply to directors in the event of an insolvency of the parent company, as holder of the master or concentration account.

(c) *Liability of pool participants in the event of insolvency of another pool participant*

In the event of the insolvency of a pool participant – either of the parent company as holder of the master or concentration account, or of a subsidiary as pool participant – creditors may seek to hold other pool participants liable for losses suffered by the insolvent pool member. Creditors of an insolvent pool member looking to enhance their recoveries should consider the doctrine of substantive consolidation, which enables creditors of one insolvent company in a corporate group to assert claims against another member company. Substantive consolidation treats affiliated companies as a single entity by combining their unsecured assets and liabilities to form a common asset pool out of which the claims of creditors of all the companies in the group can be satisfied.

Canadian courts have recognised substantive consolidation under both the Bankruptcy and Insolvency Act and the Companies' Creditors Arrangement Act, although neither act expressly authorises substantive consolidation. It is generally very difficult to obtain a substantive consolidation order in Canada, since it essentially requires dismantling of the walls separating the members of the corporate group and putting all of their assets and liabilities into one common pool. Accordingly, there have been very few cases in which substantive consolidation has been applied in Canada and even fewer that provide guidance on its application.

Generally, the remedy will be granted where:

- there is evidence of intertwined assets and liabilities, integrated administrative functions and operations, a perception by creditors that they are dealing with an integrated entity and common control and governance structures;
- it would be impracticable to separate the affairs of related entities;
- it is more cost effective and beneficial to creditors to have the proceedings administered as a single estate; and
- it would result in an expeditious and administratively efficient administration of the proceeding.[23]

In at least one reported decision in the context of proceedings under the Companies' Creditors Arrangement Act, the existence of a centralised cash management system (as well as inter-company debt, cross-default provisions and cross-guarantees) was a factor taken into account by the court when deciding whether to authorise substantive consolidation.[24]

---

23 Janis Sarra, *Corporate Group Insolvencies: Seeing the Forest and the Trees* (Toronto: Thomson Reuters, 2008) (WL).

24 *Re Lehndorff General Partner Ltd* (1993), 17 CBR (3d) 24 (Ont Gen Div [Commercial List]).

It is doubtful whether the bank in a cash pooling agreement can be held liable for the losses suffered by a pool participant, unless the transfer of funds was challenged as a fraudulent preference under the Bankruptcy and Insolvency Act (discussed below) and the bank was required to account for any benefit it received from the transfer.

(d) The insolvency practitioner's perspective

The insolvency practitioner and the insolvency of a bank: Generally, all funds received by a bank for deposit to the account of a customer become the property of the bank. The balance of an account owing to the customer from time to time is a simple contract debt. In the insolvency of a bank, moneys on deposit will form part of the general pot of money available to pay the all of the bank's creditors. Moneys deposited with the bank would rank as ordinary unsecured claims. A pool participant would be entitled to prove the principal amount of a credit balance together with interest accrued to the date of the winding-up and take its *pro rata* share on a distribution of the bank's assets by the liquidator. In the event there are insufficient funds available for distribution to cover the amount of the pool participant's claim, the Canada Deposit Insurance Corporation (which provides deposit insurance to a bank's depositors) will pay out a maximum of C$100,000 (principal and interest combined) on each eligible deposit held by a bank (provided that the bank is a member of the Canada Deposit Insurance Corporation).

Additionally, under the Winding-Up and Restructuring Act, the law of set-off applies to all claims against the bank and to proceedings for the recovery of debts due or accruing due to the bank as though the bank were not being wound up.[25] Cash pooling agreements typically contain provisions permitting the bank to combine or consolidate accounts of pool participants (including operating accounts, designated accounts and mirror accounts) and apply any net credit balances resulting therefrom, including any credit balance in the concentration account towards the payment of any indebtedness or liabilities of the pool participants to the bank upon the occurrence of certain events. Accordingly, provided that the conditions for set-off have been met under the agreement, the bank's liquidator would be entitled to assert rights to set-off against the credit balances of pool participants.

While the Winding-Up and Restructuring Act contains a number of extremely intricate provisions that permit a liquidator to attack a range of pre-liquidation transactions which the liquidator can use to claim a credit balance of a pool participant for the benefit of the insolvent bank's creditors,[26] it is unlikely that a liquidator could successfully rely on its avoidance powers to claim funds on behalf of the bank in a legitimate cash pooling agreement.

The insolvency practitioner and the insolvency of a group company or master account holder: A trustee in bankruptcy or monitor may attempt to challenge the

25 Winding-Up and Restructuring Act, Section 73.
26 Winding-Up and Restructuring Act, Sections 96-99.

transfer of funds in a cash pool arrangement between pool participants as a fraudulent preference.[27] A preference occurs when an insolvent debtor pays one or more creditors at the expense of other creditors. In order to challenge any such transaction, the following three factors must be established:

- The transferor was insolvent at the time of the transfer;
- A transfer of property made, provision of services made, charge on property made, payment made, obligation incurred or a judicial proceeding taken or suffered in favour of a creditor occurred during the applicable statutory review period; and
- The transaction was taken with a view to giving that transferee a preference over other creditors.

If the court concludes that there has been a fraudulent preference, the transaction will be void as against the trustee or monitor and the transfer of property (or other relevant transaction) can be set aside with the effect that the funds paid out by the transferee would flow back into the estate of the insolvent pool participant.

A trustee or monitor may challenge any transactions creating a preference that occur three months prior to the initial bankruptcy event (typically being the date of bankruptcy, proposal proceedings under the Bankruptcy and Insolvency Act or proceedings under the Companies' Creditors Arrangement Act, as applicable) and ending on the date of bankruptcy or the date that the initial order under the Companies' Creditors Arrangement Act is made, provided the transferee is at arms' length with the transferor. This time is extended to one year prior to the initial bankruptcy event if the transferee is not at arms' length with the transferor. If there is no evidence to the contrary, related persons are deemed not to be dealing at arm's length with one another.

Where the transfer of property (or other relevant transaction) was made to an arm's-length party, if the transaction has the effect of giving a creditor a preference during the review period, then in the absence of evidence to the contrary, the transaction is presumed to have been made with a view to giving such creditor a preference. The transferee can rebut that presumption by showing there was no fraudulent intent on the part of the debtor to prefer one creditor over another. While the transfer of funds to the bank could give rise to this presumption, an argument can be made that the intent of the cash pooling agreement was not to give a preference to the bank if the arrangement was entered into in the ordinary course of business in order to take advantage of the benefits of a cash management system.

Where the transfer of property (or other relevant transaction) was made to a non-arm's-length party (eg, between the parent and a subsidiary), there is no requirement to show that the transferor had the requisite fraudulent intent. Instead, the impugned transaction need only have the effect of giving the transferee a preference over other creditors.

A critical element in a successful fraudulent preference attack is that the transfer of property (or other relevant transaction) have been made to a person that was a

27 Bankruptcy and Insolvency A, Section 95; Companies' Creditors Arrangement Act, Section 36.1.

creditor or to a person in trust for a creditor. Accordingly, the transfer of funds must be made to a pool participant in its capacity as creditor of the transferor. If there is no such debtor-creditor relationship, there is no basis for attacking a transfer of funds as a fraudulent preference.

As between the master account holder and a group company, there is an argument to be made that cash pool arrangements give rise to a debtor-creditor relationship. Since cash pool transfers may be treated as inter-company loans, on any given day, depending on whether the balance transferred from the group company's designated account to the master account holder is a credit or debit balance, the debtor-creditor relationship likely can be established. Further, since the master account holder and a group company (eg, parent and subsidiary) would be considered to operate as non-arm's length parties, a transfer between them need only have the effect of giving a preference to the non-insolvent pool participant. There is no requirement to show that either had the requisite fraudulent intent. Accordingly, a trustee or monitor on behalf of creditors of the insolvent master account holder can likely challenge a transfer of funds made to a group company, and vice versa.

As between one group company and another group company, it is unlikely that a successful fraudulent preference claim can be made by a trustee or monitor appointed over one of the group companies. It is doubtful that a creditor-debtor relationship would arise as between group companies, since there is no direct transfer of funds made between designated accounts in the cash pool arrangement.

Transfers at undervalue: A transfer of funds between pool participants may also be attacked as a transfer at undervalue by a trustee or monitor of an insolvent pool participant. A transfer at undervalue is a disposition of property or provision of services for which no consideration is received by the debtor or for which the consideration received is conspicuously less than the fair market value of the consideration given by the debtor.

On the application of a trustee or monitor, a court may declare that a transfer at undervalue is void against the trustee or monitor and may make an order that a party to the transfer or any other person that is privy to the transfer, or all of those persons, pay to the estate the difference between the value of the consideration received by the debtor and the value of the consideration given by the debtor.[28] Transfers made in a cash pooling setting may be considered a disposition of property by a pool participant where the consideration received by another party is the creation and offset of an overdraft or debt within the corporate group.

A 'person that is privy' to a transfer means a person that is not dealing at arm's length with a party to a transfer and by reason of the transfer, directly or indirectly, receives a benefit or causes a benefit to be received by another person. Since cash pool participants are part of a corporate group and hence related, a court will likely find that they are to be considered privy to each other. It is unlikely that the court would find the bank as privy to a transfer between the bank and a pool participant, since the transfer will typically be at arm's length.

28 Bankruptcy and Insolvency Act, Section 96; Companies' Creditors Arrangement Act, Section 36.1.

If the parties are dealing at arm's length, a transfer of funds could be found void if the transfer occurred one year before the date of the initial bankruptcy event, the debtor was insolvent at the time of the transfer and the debtor intended to defraud, delay or defeat its creditors. Related persons are deemed not to deal at arm's length, unless there is evidence to the contrary.

If the parties are not dealing at arm's length, a transfer could be found void if it was completed in the year prior to the date of the initial bankruptcy event, or if the transfer occurred between five years and one year before the initial bankruptcy event, the debtor was insolvent at the time of the transfer (or was rendered insolvent by it) or the debtor intended to defraud, delay or defeat its creditors.

Fraudulent conveyances: Conveyances made by a debtor with the intent to defeat, hinder, delay or defraud creditors may also be challenged under provincial legislation such as Ontario's Fraudulent Conveyances Act.[29]

A conveyance found within the scope of the Fraudulent Conveyances Act is valid as between the parties to the conveyance, but it is voidable at the instance or creditors or others. The usual remedy is a court order directing the transferee to make the property available to satisfy the claims of creditors. Where the property is more than sufficient to satisfy the claims of creditors, the surplus remains with the transferee.

Where the debtor is not insolvent, a creditor may bring an action itself to attack a fraudulent conveyance. Where the debtor is insolvent, it is open to the trustee in bankruptcy appointed over the creditor to attack the conveyance under the Fraudulent Conveyances Act.

For a conveyance to be found voidable under the Fraudulent Conveyances Act, a conveyance of real or personal property must be made with the intent to defeat, hinder, delay or defraud creditors or others. The words 'creditors or others' have been interpreted broadly to include judgment creditors, secured creditors, creditors with liquidated claims and even persons with contingent or unliquidated claims, whether the claims of these persons arose before, at or after the time of the transaction being attacked.

Although proof of the debtor's intent to defeat creditors is required, proof that the debtor was insolvent at the time the property was conveyed is not required; nor is proof that creditors were actually defeated by the conveyance. However, if the conveyance was made for good consideration, it is necessary to show the fraudulent intent of both parties to the conveyance to defeat creditors in order to render the transaction void.

(e) Termination of a cash pooling agreement in the insolvency context

In general, the insolvency of a company participating in a cash pooling agreement will not automatically terminate the cash pooling agreement. A reorganising debtor under the Bankruptcy and Insolvency Act or the Companies' Creditors Arrangement Act may disclaim a contract with the consent of the trustee or monitor.[30] If the trustee

29 Fraudulent Conveyances Act, RSO 1990, c F.29.
30 Bankruptcy and Insolvency Act, Section 65.11; Companies' Creditors Arrangement Act, Section 32.

or monitor does not consent to the disclaimer, the debtor can apply for a court order to disclaim the agreement on notice to counterparties. Counterparties that suffer a loss as a result of disclaimer have a provable claim against the debtor. A trustee or monitor will typically consent to their termination. As a result of the stay of proceedings that is typically in place during reorganisation proceedings, counterparties would be prevented from taking any steps towards terminating the cash pooling agreement (without obtaining court approval).

Bankruptcy itself will not terminate a cash pooling agreement entered into by the bankrupt company. The trustee in bankruptcy may terminate a contract entered into by the bankrupt, which would entitle the other party to treat the contract as broken and assert a claim for damages. In a cash pooling agreement, it would be open to a pool participant or the bank to assert a claim for breach of contract, provided it could quantify and support its claim.

2.4 Regulatory law

The federal government regulates the Canadian banking sector under the auspices of the Office of the Superintendent of Financial Institutions, which regulates federally regulated financial institutions such as banks, insurance companies, trust and loan companies and credit unions. Many financial institutions (not including banks) that are incorporated at the provincial or territorial level have ceded jurisdiction to the Office of the Superintendent of Financial Institutions as well, in order to avoid regulation by two levels of government. The Office of the Superintendent of Financial Institutions works in conjunction with the Bank of Canada (Canada's central bank), the Canada Deposit Insurance Corporation (which provides deposit insurance for member banks' depositors) and the Financial Consumer Agency of Canada (which monitors banks to ensure that they comply with consumer protection measures).

At present, there is no law, regulation or direction that pertains to cash pooling agreements, other than complying with general reporting requirements to the Office of the Superintendent of Financial Institutions, the Bank of Canada and the Canaa Deposit Insurance Corporation in relation to deposit accounts.

2.5 Tax law

Where all of the participants in the cash pooling agreement are Canadian, there are typically very few Canadian tax considerations. A Canadian-resident creditor will be taxable on any interest income receivable. Interest owing by a Canadian-resident debtor will generally be deductible in computing the debtor's income for Canadian tax purposes, so long as:

- the debt on which the interest accrues was used for an income-earning purpose (eg, in the debtor's business);
- the debtor has a legal obligation to pay the interest; and
- the rate of interest is commercially reasonable.

As a general rule, there is no obligation on the part of one Canadian corporation to charge interest on loans made to a related Canadian corporation (ie, low or no-interest loans are permissible).

Where a Canadian corporation lends money to a related non-resident person, the Canadian tax rules generally require that at least a certain amount of interest be charged, failing which interest income may be imputed to the Canadian creditor or a benefit may be considered to have been conferred on the shareholder of the Canadian corporation (giving rise to an income inclusion for Canadian residents or 25% non-resident withholding tax for non-residents, subject to reduction under any applicable tax treaty). As a general rule, a downstream loan by a Canadian corporation to a controlled foreign subsidiary is excluded from these adverse provisions.

If an amount owing to a Canadian corporation by a related non-resident either remains outstanding one year after the end of the taxation year of the Canadian corporation in which the debt arose or is part of a series of loans and repayments, that amount may be included in the debtor's income for Canadian tax purposes (and, in the case of a non-resident made subject to Canadian dividend withholding tax). Again, downstream loans to a foreign affiliate of the Canadian creditor are generally exempt.

Conversely, where a foreign subsidiary of a Canadian corporation lends money to the Canadian corporation, any interest income earned by the foreign creditor may be included in its foreign accrual property income. Foreign accrual property income earned by a controlled foreign affiliate of a Canadian corporation is imputed to, and taxed in the hands of, the Canadian corporation, as a way of preventing Canadians from avoiding Canadian tax on passive, investment-type income earned through a foreign subsidiary.

Under new rules announced in 2011, an amount loaned to a Canadian corporation by one of its foreign subsidiaries will be included in the Canadian corporation's income for tax purposes in some circumstances (generally where the loan is outstanding for more than two years or is part of a series of loans and repayments).

Foreign exchange gains (relative to the Canadian dollar) on debts and receivables may be taxable in the hands of Canadian residents (or included in the foreign accrual property income earned by a controlled foreign affiliate of a Canadian resident).

If the foreign participant is not a subsidiary of one of the Canadian members of the corporate group, the Canadian tax implications of a cash pooling agreement can become quite complicated.

The authors are especially grateful to Kevin McGrath, a partner with the Toronto office of Borden Ladner Gervais LLP and a member of the firm's financial services group, and Steve Suarez, a partner with the Toronto office of Borden Ladner Gervais LLP and a member of the firm's tax group, for constructive comments and useful discussions.

China

Belinda Danqing Zhou
Hans Qizong Zhang
Tian Xu
Eiger Law

1. Introduction

1.1 Admissibility of cash pooling agreements

Cash pooling, as an effective liquidity management tool, has now become essential for the optimisation and use of a business entity's excessive cash. Companies within a corporate group transfer their surplus cash into a master account and draw funds to satisfy their own cash-flow requirements. This benefits companies through improved visibility and control of cash, as well as reduced interest. With the development of globalisation and Chinese policies of economic reform and liberalisation, this popular instrument has also garnered the attention of numerous local and international corporations that intend to extend, or have already extended, their business in the country. However, for a long time, because of traditionally strict controls on inter-company lending and foreign exchange, cash pooling agreements – especially foreign currency cash pooling – were rarely utilised because of a lack of clear policies and legal framework. Fortunately, China has issued several regulations regarding cash pooling agreements in recent years, and it is now possible for companies to adopt this advantageous tool.

In China, direct lending between different legal entities is not allowed.[1] As a consequence, physically pooling funds from group entities into a central pool cannot be facilitated using traditional techniques found in other countries. Instead, entrusted loans[2] have now become a method of accommodating commercial needs within existing lending rules. Under the entrusted loan structure, a bank serves as an intermediary between the lending and borrowing parties, where the money is provided by the trustor, not the bank. Entrusted loans were initially not available in foreign currencies, but only in the local currency, the renminbi. In order to enable

---

1 Under Article 61 of the General Rules of Loans, direct lending and borrowing among legal entities is not allowed.

2 Entrusted loans were allowed by the People's Bank of China in 2000, via the 'Circular on the Related Matters Concerning the Initiation of Entrusted Loans Business by Commercial Banks (*Yin Ban fa* [2000] 100)'. However this circular became invalid in 2007, according to relevant notices from the China Banking Regulatory Commission. Currently, the legal basis is Article 7 of the General Rules of Loans, which states:

> *Entrusted loans shall refer to loans funded by such entrusting parties as governmental departments, enterprises and institutions or individuals, disbursed and supervised by lenders (ie, the entrusted parties) on behalf thereof according to the loan object, purpose, amount and term, and interest rate determined by the entrusting parties, and recovered with the assistance of the lenders. The lenders (the entrusted parties) shall only charge handling fees, and shall not bear any loan risks.*

Under the entrusted loan framework, the banks charge only a service commission, taking no credit risk on the transaction.

multinational corporations to optimise the use of foreign currency capital, the State Administration of Foreign Exchange began issuing a series of policies and measures. The first step came in 2004, when a circular[3] was introduced to give qualified foreign companies the possibility of transferring cash overseas to their headquarters or to related companies through entrusted loans.[4] In August 2005, the first foreign currency cash pooling project was approved by the State Administration of Foreign Exchange.[5] The same year, the State Administration of Foreign Exchange and Shanghai Pudong district government launched a pilot programme (the so-called 'Pudong Nine Measures'), providing the possibility for multinational corporations with regional headquarters in the Pudong New Area of Shanghai to conduct the centralised management of foreign currency more effectively. In 2008, an enterprise group's[6] finance companies[7] gained explicit policy support from the State Administration of Foreign Exchange[8] for the spot sale and purchase of foreign currency, giving multinational corporations more choices in utilising their foreign currency funds. Compared with the rapid economic development in China, however, these changes still seem to be one step behind. In 2009, another circular[9] (Circular 49) was enacted to lower the threshold applicable to centralised management of foreign currencies.

1.2 Types of cash pooling agreement

(a) Physical cash pooling

Under China's current cash pooling structure, capital movement between legal entities is regarded as a physical flow, whereby capital funds are transferred from the participating accounts into the master account through a physical sweeping method –

3 Notice of the State Administration of Foreign Exchange on Issues Concerning the Management of Foreign Exchange Funds Used for Internal Operations of Transnational Corporations, *Huifa* [2004] No.104, which came into force on November 1 2004, has been superseded by *Huifa* [2009] No. 49.

4 This regulation allows subsidiaries of selected local and foreign multinational corporations temporarily to lend excess foreign currency funds to related group entities domestically within China or overseas prior to formal declaration and payment of dividends. However, multinational corporations must meet certain requirements – for example, a foreign-currency entrusted loan can be arranged only when principal and interest for the last entrusted lending in foreign currency between the entrusted lender and the borrower concerned have been recovered within the agreed time limit. Foreign multinational corporations must have at least three subsidiaries in China, while Chinese multinational corporations must have at least three subsidiaries overseas.

5 In 2005, US company General Electric and China Merchant Bank came to an agreement that the bank would provide US dollar cash pooling services for General Electric.

6 'Enterprise groups' refers to conglomerates which:
- are registered under applicable laws within the territory of China;
- have capital as a link, parent companies and subsidiaries as major members, and the group's articles of association as the common code of conduct;
- are composed of parent companies, subsidiaries, non-controlling companies and other member enterprises or institutions; and
- are enterprise legal persons.

7 'Enterprise group's financial company' refers to financial companies that are established by an enterprise group. Thus international financial companies are excluded.

8 Circular of the State Administration of Foreign Exchange Regarding the Administration of the Business of Spot Sale and Purchase of Foreign Exchange of an Enterprise Group's Financial Company, *Huifa* [2008], 68, came into force on December 6 2008, and has been superseded by *Huifa* [2009] 49.

9 Notice of the State Administration of Foreign Exchange on the Issuance of Regulations on Centralised Management of Foreign Exchange Funds by Core Members of Domestic Enterprise Groups, *Huifa* [2009], 49, came into force on November 1 2009.

the entrusted loan. The most common forms of physical cash pooling in practice are zero balancing and target balancing. In a zero balancing structure, all of the funds in a participating account are swept and concentrated to the master account on a regular basis[10] (eg, at a particular point during the day). In a target balancing structure, a particular amount is set and only money exceeding the particular level is transferred.

(b) *Notional cash pooling*

Unlike the physical cash pooling structure, notional cash pooling[11] is not permitted in China, under either a renminbi or a foreign currency cash pooling agreement. The biggest obstacle to this is the strict interest rate regulations in China. In the case of notional cash pooling, there is no actual transfer of cash, and credit and debit balances are offset without any cash movements. The bank only pays or charges interest only on the net balance. The interest that should be calculated by a single entrusted loan is therefore neglected, which means that the lender does not charge interest for the debt and the borrower does not have to pay interest. This kind of operation could be considered as circumventing prevailing interest rate policies. Tax problems are another barrier that should be taken into consideration. Normally, each entrusted loan is subject to the payment of stamp duty, which is payable by all parties involved in the cash pooling agreement: the entrusted bank, the concentration leader and the participating enterprise. By using notional cash pooling, however, the stamp duty is easily evaded because there are no inter-company loans.

1.3 Master account holder

Under the current cash pooling structure (using either renminbi or a foreign currency), any participating company of an enterprise group can take the lead and actively manage the foreign currency funds of all members of a group.[12] In other words, not only the parent company but also its subsidiaries are allowed to act as the master account holder.

As far as the nationality of the companies is concerned, foreign companies are not allowed to take part in renminbi or foreign currency-based cash pooling agreements; only domestic companies[13] can engage in cash pooling activities.

1.4 Legal requirements and restrictions for cash pooling agreements

(a) *Foreign currency cash pooling*

With the introduction of Circular 49 in 2009, banks and enterprises finally received a comprehensive guide in respect to the operation of foreign currency cash pooling.

---

10 For example, in the well-known GE cash pooling scheme, the bank system automatically scans the accounts of the group at 4:00 pm every afternoon. The exact time for sweeping can be negotiated between the bank and enterprises.

11 Capital funds are not really transferred under notional cash pooling. Each company maintains its own account. The bank offsets debit balances of the participating accounts with credit balances in the pool, and either pays or charges interest on the net balance.

12 For foreign currency cash pooling agreements, see Article 15 of Circular 49; there is no explicit regulation for renminbi cash pooling agreements, but in practice this is the same as a foreign currency cash pooling agreement.

13 Domestic companies refer to companies which are set up in China, including wholly foreign owned enterprises, equity joint ventures and cooperative joint ventures.

Companies considering arranging a foreign currency cash pooling agreement must meet the following requirements:

- To engage in a foreign currency cash pooling agreement a company must be:
  - a parent company;
  - a subsidiary in which the parent company holds more than 51% of the shares;
  - a company in which the parent company and subsidiaries hold more than 20% of the shares either respectively or jointly, or hold the largest portion of the shares if less than 20% of the total; or
  - an affiliate company of the parent company or subsidiaries that is an institutional legal entity or society legal entity.[14] This provision is also applicable to domestic enterprises controlled by the same overseas parent company.[15]
- When loaning foreign currency funds to one another and engaging in foreign currency capital pool management activities, the internal members must use only self-owned foreign currency in their foreign currency capital accounts and foreign currency current accounts.[16]
- Companies intending to engage in foreign currency cash pooling activities must be legally registered and established. The registered capital must be paid up in full and on time. In addition, there should be no record of breaching any foreign exchange regulations over the past two years.[17]

Moreover, there are some restrictions, to which the participants in the agreements should pay attention:

- When conducting foreign currency cash pooling, activities shall be handled in compliance with the rule of settling all payable and receivable accounts in full as is, and there must be no settling of accounts by offsetting payables against receivables without prior permission.[18] The loan rates must be set in line with the level of commercial loan rates on the international financial market during the same period and must not be abnormally high or abnormally low.[19]
- Funds under an entrusted loan structure may not be used in foreign settlement or foreign currency pledged loans. Where such settlement is required, domestic enterprises must have the funds transferred back to the foreign currency capital accounts or foreign currency current accounts from where they were originally taken, along the original route, before proceeding to such settlement, according to relevant regulations.[20]
- When banks and participating members have negotiated and agreed on a daily overdraft limit that allows the latter to run overdrafts from their entrusted loan accounts in order to make payments, the overdrafts must be

14 Article 2 of Circular 49.
15 Article 28 of Circular 49.
16 Article 5 of Circular 49.
17 Article 14 of Circular 49.
18 If companies attempt to settle accounts by offsetting payables against receivables, they have to apply to the State Administration of Foreign Exchange or its sub-bureau for approval.
19 Article 5 of Circular 49.
20 Article 6 of Circular 49.

repaid on the same day using funds from the foreign currency capital accounts and foreign currency current accounts of the participating members, or the entrusted loan funds repaid to (or borrowed by or transferred into its account by) the master account holder. Delay of the repayment of the overdraft beyond the same day is not allowed.[21]

- When banks and the master account holder have set an overnight overdraft limit for master accounts, the master account holder shall repay the overdrafts with entrusted loan funds repaid to (or borrowed by or transferred into their accounts by) the participating members, or with funds in their own foreign currency capital accounts and foreign currency current accounts.[22]

Because of their impact on the market, listed companies are prohibited from directly or indirectly providing funds to controlling shareholders and their affiliates by either lending or entrusted loans via banks or non-banking financial institutions.[23]

In accordance with Circular 49, foreign currency cash pooling agreements can be organised by both banks and financial corporations. However, not every bank is qualified to deal with this kind of business – only designated foreign exchange banks are allowed to do so. Designated foreign exchange banks are those banks that have obtained permission from the People's Bank of China to deal with foreign exchange transactions, including buying and selling foreign currency from and to their customers. Designated foreign exchange banks include Chinese-funded banks[24] and foreign-funded banks.[25] As with designated foreign exchange banks, financial corporations must also meet certain conditions, such as having:

- approved qualifications for conducting the relevant financial services and foreign exchange services;
- a complete internal management system concerning foreign exchange trade and settlement businesses;
- full technical capacity and an infrastructure for foreign exchange trade and settlement transactions; and
- had no breaches of the foreign exchange regulations in the previous two years.[26]

(b) Renminbi cash pooling

In contrast to the position with foreign currency cash pooling agreements, there are no regulations or laws that specify policies and requirements for renminbi-based

---

21 Article 17 of Circular 49. Unlike with foreign currency cash pooling agreements, there are no such requirements for participating members of renminbi cash pooling agreements to repay an overdraft on the same day.

22 Article 17 of Circular 49.

23 In 2003, a regulation was introduced by the China Securities Supervision and Regulation Commission and State owned Assets Supervision and Administration Commission for the purpose of controlling risks involved in listed companies providing external guarantee and lending.

24 'Chinese-funded banks' are policy banks, wholly state-owned commercial banks, joint-stock commercial banks and the branch offices thereof, urban and rural commercial banks and other approved banks.

25 'Foreign-funded banks' are foreign-funded banks, branch offices of overseas banks, joint-venture banks and other approved banks that are incorporated and engaged in business operations within Chinese territory.

26 Article 21 of Circular 49.

cash pooling agreements. The establishment of a renminbi-based cash pooling agreement does not need approval from the competent authorities. Once a bank and enterprise reach an agreement, a cash pooling structure can be set up and operated. The arrangement of a renminbi-based cash pooling agreement is easier and faster than that of a foreign currency cash pooling agreement. In fact, a number of commercial banks are developing this service in China, with major players including the Bank of Communication, China Merchants Bank and China Everbright Bank.[27] As the cash pooling business expands and matures, renminbi-based cash pooling agreements are destined to become more and more popular.

2. Specific questions

2.1 Perspective A: corporate group

(a) Directors' liabilities

China's Company Law states in Article 21 that directors, supervisors and senior managers[28] shall not take advantage of their affiliated relations to damage the interests of a company. If they violate these duties, directors and supervisors who are in charge shall be liable for losses caused to the company. Where a director, supervisor or senior manager violates laws, administrative regulations or the company's articles of association while performing his or her duties for the company, and thereby causes losses to the company, he shall be liable for compensation. If unlawful distribution, *ultra vires* or conflicts of interest are involved, then the person in question shall have personal liability, unless the company's articles of association exempt him from such duties. A similar provision can be found in the Enterprise Bankruptcy Law:[29] where a director, supervisor or senior manager violates the obligation to be honest and practise due diligence, which leads to the insolvency of an enterprise, he shall have responsibility for the losses incurred. In relation to cash pooling, the obligation of honesty and due diligence requires the directors and supervisors of the group company to make efforts to ensure the proper functioning of the cash pool. For example, if another group company faces financial distress, the directors and supervisors of a group company have the obligation to find solutions to ensure that the company's liquidity will not be influenced by its involvement and the funds transferred will be repaid. When directors and supervisors fail to perform their obligations and that failure leads to the bankruptcy of an enterprise participating in a cash pooling agreement, it is possible that they will be personally

---

27 Among these banks, China Everbright Bank takes the lead in operating cross-bank cash pooling, which means that the master accounts and participating accounts can be opened in different banks, and the sweeping will be conducted on a cross-bank platform. However this kind of cash pooling agreement is not yet mature and no successful cases have appeared.

28 'Senior managers' refers to the general manager (CEO), deputy general manager and the person in charge of financial affairs (CFO) of a company, the secretary of a board of directors of a listed company and the other persons specified in a company's articles of association. Their function is stipulated in the company's articles of association. In general, their basic functions are: to take charge of production by, and the operation and management of, the company; and to organise implementation of the resolutions of the board of directors.

29 The Enterprise Bankruptcy Law of the People's Republic of China came into effect on June 1 2007.

liable for the losses.[30] However the provisions in the company and bankruptcy laws specify neither the extent of the liabilities nor any imputation principles and exceptions, which gives rise to difficulty in dealing with such cases.

(b) *Group companies' liability*

In the event that the master account holder goes into liquidation, the group companies will have to repay the loans they got from the master account holder under the cash pooling agreement. However, the creditors of the master account holder are not entitled to hold other group companies liable for losses suffered. This is because, legally, the group companies are considered normal debtors of the master account holder (if there is a negative balance). As a debtor, the duties of a group company are the clearance of its own debt, not including the debts of its creditor – the master account holder.

(c) *Master account holder's liabilities*

In principle, a parent company and its subsidiaries are separate legal entities; the obligations of one are independent from those of the others. Nevertheless, under exceptional circumstances, the parent company will be held liable for the payment of sums owed to creditors of the subsidiary, if the master account holder is proved to have abused its rights as a shareholder and thereby caused losses to the company and other shareholders.[31]

In the event that the master account holder falls into distress, a group company has a right to get back the money it lent, if it is a creditor of the distressed master account holder. If such a group company is indolent in exercising its matured creditor's rights and thereby causes losses to creditors, then those creditors may petition a court to subrogate the group company's creditor's rights and exercise them.

2.2 Perspective B: bank

Because of the neutral role that a bank plays in a cash pooling agreement, it will bear no substantial liability for any losses arising from the insolvency of the master account holder or a group company.

2.3 Insolvency

(a) *Cash pooling agreements from the insolvency practitioner's perspective*

In the event of the liquidation of the master account holder or the group company, the insolvency administrator will claim any credit balance against the other party, if that credit balance is a result of a cash pooling agreement. If a liquidated company

30 Article 125 of the Enterprise Bankruptcy Law.

31 Like many other countries, China has also incorporated the theory of piercing the corporate veil as stated in Article 20 of the Company Law, under which shareholders of a limited liability company are required to bear the liabilities incurred in the name of the limited liability company in certain strictly defined circumstances, often involving shareholders using the corporate veil as a sham or alter ego to defraud a company's creditors.

has a debit balance against the other party, the insolvency administrator will repay it.[32] By contrast, in the event of liquidation of the bank, the insolvency administrator has no grounds to claim credit against the master account holder or the group companies with regard to the amounts that the bank lends to the two other parties based on an entrusted loan, because it is not an actual creditor to either party.

(b) Special rules as regards creditors of other parties to the cash pooling agreement

In the event that either the bank, the master account holder or a group company goes into liquidation, the administrator need not observe any special rules or obligations in regards to creditors of the other parties to the cash pooling agreement.

(c) Dissolution/termination of the cash pooling agreement in the event of liquidation of the master account holder or a group company

When a group company goes into a bankruptcy procedure, there may be two major situations regarding claims or debt:

- The group company has a claim against the master account holder; or
- The group company has a debt owing to the master account holder.

If the group company has a claim against the master account holder, the claim then belongs in the bankruptcy proceedings and will be allocated among creditors if the company is declared bankrupt. By contrast, if the group company has a debt against the master account holder, this debt – as well as all other debts of the bankrupt group company – will be immediately due as a general result of the starting of the bankruptcy procedures under Chinese law. The debt will be allocated in the third and last class of creditors' claims, unless the claim is guaranteed by collateral. In addition, interest ceases to accrue.[33] With respect to the operation of the cash pooling agreement, the master account holder may invoke the 'right of unassured pleadings',[34] thereby suspending the further performance of the cash pooling agreement between the master account holder and the distressed company. If the distressed company is declared bankrupt, it will lose the capacity to invoke civil rights and the capacity for civil conduct, leading to the consequence of termination of all signed contracts, including the cash pooling agreement insofar as concerns that company's rights and obligations.

When the master account holder goes into bankruptcy, there will be similar situations as for a group company. However, if the distressed holder of a master account is declared bankrupt, then the whole cash pooling agreement must be terminated, because of the closing of the master account holder.

If the bankrupt entity is a bank, then the whole cash pooling agreement must also be terminated. This is because the bankrupt bank will no longer be allowed to conduct cash pooling agreement transactions. Both the master account holder and the group company will become creditors of the bank if there is a positive balance,

32 Article 113 of the Enterprise Bankruptcy Law.
33 Article 46 of the Enterprise Bankruptcy Law.
34 Article 68 of the Contract Law of the People's Republic of China, effective as of 1999.

or debtors, if there is a negative balance. The money that a bank lends to other parties by the means of an entrusted loan is not deemed to be a debt owed to the bank by the parties. Rather, only the money that a bank lends to other parties by means other than an entrusted loan is a debt owed to the bank by the loanee.

2.4 Perspective D: tax

When multinational corporations operate cash pooling structures in China, tax implications are significant for the determination of liquidity management techniques. Depending on the operation framework of the cash pooling, a range of tax issues should be considered.

(a) Stamp duty

In China, entrusted loan agreements are subject to stamp duty under the relevant regulations.[35] A one-off payment of 0.005% of the value of the agreement must be paid for each original copy of the agreement. Considering the frequent transfer of capital, the corporation and the bank can agree on a total amount of the entrusted loan and register the amount with the responsible tax authorities. It is common practice for the bank to estimate the maximum amount of the daily loan upon conclusion of the agreement and to pay stamp duty on this basis. If it turns out later that the total amount of the entrusted loan exceeds this estimate, extra stamp duty payments will be required.

(b) Business tax

Interest income resulting from an inter-company entrusted loan is subject to business tax. In a cash pooling structure, business tax is incurred when the surplus funds of the participants sweep to the master account and when the funds sweep from the master account to the participants. Currently, business tax is payable at a rate of 5% of the interest income.

3. Conclusion

With the development of cash pooling all over the world, China has recognised the rationality and necessity of establishing a facility for cash pooling by large companies. With a general legal framework in place since 2009, Chinese local banks are collecting experience with setting up and operating both renminbi and foreign currency cash pooling agreements. However, in practice, cash pooling is available only for Chinese companies, which means that for a foreign investor to be able to benefit from this structure, it needs to set up a commercial presence in China. Companies interested in participating in a cash pooling agreement need to be aware of the relevant requirements, restrictions and liabilities. Further improvement is needed and expected to enhance the practicability of the Chinese framework.

35 Article 2 of the Interim Regulations of the People's Republic of China on Stamp Tax, effective as of 1988.

Cyprus

Venetia Argyropoulou
Alexandra Pelaghias-Christodoulou
Pelaghias, Christodoulou, Vrachas LLC

1. Introduction

1.1 Admissibility of cash pooling agreements

Cyprus does not have a specific legal framework for cash pooling. Under common law, the terms of a valid contract are enforceable insofar as they are not specifically prohibited or illegal.

That said, a cash pooling agreement may be affected by several legislative provisions, especially with regard to liquidation. Cypriot companies may participate in cash pooling agreements with non-Cypriot inter-group companies and banking institutions, or even with Cypriot banking institutions, which sometimes offer cash pooling schemes to attract clients.

Before Cyprus joined the European Union, the distinction between physical and notional cash pooling was very important for Cypriot resident corporations. Physical cash pooling was regarded as extending credit abroad and was prohibited under the Exchange Control Rules, unless a relevant permit was obtained from the Central Bank of Cyprus. Different standards applied for foreign companies (ex IBCs[1]), for which the transfer of funds was not restricted. In addition, the legislation did not prevent notional cash pooling where there was no physical transfer of funds. The law was partly changed on October 1 2004, when the Cyprus government lifted all restrictions on foreign direct investment from non-EU countries. After Cyprus's accession to the European Union, all exchange control restrictions were lifted and physical cash pooling was no longer prohibited.

1.2 Types of cash pooling agreement

Two types of physical cash pooling agreements are available:

- zero balancing agreements, whereby the cash pool members may transfer their entire cash surplus; and
- target balancing agreements, whereby a certain cash surplus threshold cash surplus must be reached before any remaining surplus can be transferred into the master account.

1 Legal entities whose beneficial ownership and business activities lie outside the country of incorporation and:
- whose shares belong directly or indirectly exclusively to aliens; and
- whose income is derived from sources abroad and business conducted outside the country of registration. However, if the shareholder of the company is a European citizen, then the company is also allowed to conduct its activities within Cyprus.

The latter allow the cash pool members to better regulate their solvency and liquidity. In both account types, cash pool members are jointly liable for any negative balance on the master account. In either case, transfers to the master accounts are not usually completed automatically by the bank, but are effected by each individual cash pool member.

1.3 Legal requirements from various perspectives

Although Cyprus as yet has no specific legal requirements with respect to cash pooling agreements, the participation of a Cypriot company or bank in such a scheme will trigger various elements of domestic legislation.

The Companies Law (CAP 113) regulates all domestically registered companies and governs all permissible actions and relevant procedures. Together with the company's memorandum and articles of association, it contains all provisions with which a Cypriot company must comply – not least when entering into a cash pooling agreement.

In particular, the memorandum of a Cypriot company specifies all of its permitted objects. The authority of the company's board of directors is limited by such corporate objects; any act outside the scope of the company's memorandum is considered *ultra vires* and may be annulled as void if no innocent/*bona fide* third parties are involved. The board of directors is therefore bound by the company's memorandum; if it takes any action that is outside the scope of the company's objects, then the directors may be held liable to the company and third parties.

As such, the question arises as to whether a company may engage in cash pooling agreements if these are not mentioned in the company's memorandum. Although, as mentioned, the company may engage only in such activities as are mentioned in its memorandum, the latter is intended only to offer a guide to permitted activities, and a specific reference to each and every possible activity need not be included. As such, cash pooling activities need not be expressly included in the company's objects; it is sufficient that the memorandum allows the company to lend and borrow moneys to and from other companies, and to grant guarantees.

Whether a cash pooling agreement is *ultra vires* will depend on the construction of the memorandum and the circumstances of the case, and specifically on whether relevance to the company's permitted business scope can be proved. Even if this is the case, the company will be bound with regard to third parties by the actions or transactions of its directors, even though these may not fall within the objects of the company, unless:

- such actions or transactions exceed the powers granted or permitted to those officials by law; or
- the company can prove that the third party knew that those actions or transactions did not fall within the company's objects; or
- it would have been impossible to ignore this taking into consideration all of the relevant circumstances.

---

2 Section 33A of the law.

Publication of the company memorandum and articles of association does not in itself constitute sufficient proof of knowledge by a third party.[2]

The Companies Law contains various capital maintenance rules with which a company must comply before taking any action that may impact on its own finances. Thus, a company may not purchase its own shares or redeem its own preference shares except in certain specific cases. It may reduce its share capital only according to the conditions set out by the law and it may distribute dividends only out of its distributable profits. However, the Companies Law does not specifically regulate a Cypriot company's indebtedness, unless it is a public company (see section 2.1). Therefore, a company may enter into both physical and notional cash pooling agreements without limitations.

That said, one cannot overlook the directors' long-established common law duty – reiterated many times in case law – to act in the company's best interests. In order for directors to avoid liability, they must carefully consider all relevant parameters and risks of the special cash pooling agreement.

The Companies Law also describes the process and rights of all parties involved in the event of a Cypriot company's insolvency. It outlines the circumstances in which agreements or transfers of funds effected prior to the insolvency of a cash pool member may be cancelled.

Tax law is also relevant to a cash pooling agreement, especially in relation to physical cash pooling.

2. Specific questions

2.1 Perspective A: corporate group

(a) Liability of group company or master account holder directors in the event of insolvency of a group company

Mismanagement: Under the Companies Law, the board of directors may exercise all powers of the company, except for those specifically reserved to its shareholders. However, the company's articles of association may confer additional powers on the shareholders. In most cases companies follow the sample articles of association provided in Appendix A of the Companies Law, which state that "the business of the Company shall be managed by the Directors, who.... may exercise all such powers of the Company as are not, by the Law or by these Articles, required to be exercised by the Company in general meeting". This basically precludes shareholders from dictating to the directors how the company is to be managed and from overruling any decision taken by the board in the legitimate exercise of their powers.

If the board acts beyond its powers, the company or its shareholders may request compensation from the directors if the company is damaged as a result. The directors have an overriding duty to act in the company's best interests. This duty does not extend to the shareholders (either collectively or individually), to other companies with which the company is associated, to creditors or to parties with which the company has a fiduciary relationship. Certain exceptions to this rule apply, especially when the company is insolvent and the creditor's rights take precedence; but the general rule remains that the directors are obliged to act solely for the benefit of the company.

As such, the directors must ensure that entering into a cash pooling agreement will be of net benefit to the company. Otherwise, they may be held personally liable. And although there are no thin capitalisation rules restricting the extent of a Cypriot company's exposure to indebtedness, the directors have a specific duty to preserve the company's assets and to refrain from entering into transactions that may adversely affect its financial viability. They must therefore carefully evaluate all possible consequences of the company's participation in a cash pooling agreement.

Physical and notional cash pooling involves several main risks. If funds are physically transferred from the company's account to the master account, the main risk is that the pool leader may be unable to repay the transfer in full, because of either its own cash shortages or those of other pool members. In physical cash pooling, the weak financial position of the pool leader and/or other pool members may prevent the company from drawing on the master account. That said, physical cash pooling does also offer benefits to the company, as pooled funds can return a higher rate of interest than any that might be held in a separate account. Also, the company may be able to use funds from other pool members in the event of financial jeopardy.

In the case of notional cash pooling, where no funds are actually transferred but the company is asked by the bank to guarantee the liabilities of other pool members, the main risk is that the company may be called upon to pay debts that are not its own, and for which it will not be reimbursed, while the benefits remain the same. A side benefit of both physical and notional cash pooling is the potential reduction of administrative costs through the centralisation of cash management – for example, lower treasury and back office costs, lower overdraft fees or lower interest charges on debit balances.

Ultimately, there is no general rule as to whether it is in a Cypriot company's best interests to enter into a cash pooling agreement. A director must balance all the above elements, weigh up the circumstances and decide accordingly.

Should the worst happen and a company become insolvent because of its involvement in a cash pooling agreement, a director may be held personally liable for mismanagement if he failed to act prudently in the company's best interests.

Fraudulent preference: Participation in a cash pooling agreement while the company is insolvent may trigger the fraudulent preference provisions of the Companies Law. In investigating a case of (usually involuntary) winding up, the official receiver will also examine any civil or criminal liability of the company's directors. The directors may be found guilty if any misapplication of property, misfeasance or breach of trust has taken place. If found guilty, they may be ordered by the court to compensate the company for any consequential loss out of their own personal property. The company's directors may also be found guilty of criminal offences. These include:

- failing to make full disclosure of property to the liquidator;
- concealing property;

- making any material omissions in the books of the company or in the statement of affairs;
- fraudulently alienating the property of the company before winding up; and
- falsely inducing any person to give credit to the company.

Directors who are suspected of any criminal offence are liable to prosecution by the attorney general. If, in the event of a cash pooling agreement, it can be shown that the disposition of any of the company's property or funds took place in order purposely to damage the creditors' rights, not only will such disposition be cancelled, but the company's directors may also be found civil and criminally liable.

Conflicts of interest: In a cash pooling agreement, the members and/or directors of the participating companies are commonly interlinked. Generally speaking, it is the duty of a director to avoid any conflict of interests between him and the company. Any director who is either directly or indirectly interested in a contract or proposed contract with the company must declare the nature of his interest at a directors' meeting – either when the relevant contract is first under consideration or (if the director concerned was unable to attend) at the next directors' meeting. Should a director become interested in a contract after it has been executed, he must declare his interest at the next directors' meeting.

In addition, the Companies Law specifically provides that where a director is a member of another company, he is to be regarded as an interested party where any contract is concluded with that company. General notification that he is a member of such a company shall suffice. Upon receipt of such notice, the company may then decide to exclude the director in question from the decision process. Any director who fails to comply with his section shall be liable to a fine of up to €855.

Piercing the corporate veil: A fundamental rule of Cypriot law is that in the case of companies limited by shares, the liability of each member is limited to the nominal value of the shares held. When this value is fully paid up, the member's liability for the company's debts is extinguished. Cypriot law thus does not allow for the corporate veil to be pierced in the strict sense, although it does allow for some form of unlimited liability in the event of fraud in accordance with Section 311 of the Companies Law or the Fradulent Transfers Avoidance Law (CAP 62). According to the former, "if in the course of the winding up of the Company it appears that any business of the Company has been carried on with the intent to defraud creditors of the Company, or any other person, or for any other fraudulent purpose, the Court, on the application of the official receiver, or the liquidator or any creditor or contributor in the company, may, if it thinks it would be proper, declare that any persons, who are knowingly parties to the carrying on of the business in a fraudulent manner, shall be personally responsible, without any limitation of liability, for all or any of the debts or other liabilities of the Company as the Court may direct."

Such a declaration is usually accompanied by instructions providing more detail as to how it may best be realised. In particular, the court may direct that the liability of any such person under the declaration be made a charge on any debt or obligation due to him from the company; or on any mortgage or charge or any interest in any mortgage or charge on any assets of the company held by or vested in him or any company or person on his behalf, or any person claiming as assignee from or through the person liable, or any company or person acting on his behalf. The court may also, from time to time, make such further order as may be necessary for the purpose of enforcing any charge imposed under Section 311. The Companies Law also provides for fines of up to €2,565 and the imprisonment of responsible parties.

If a company's directors and/or shareholders have entered into or acted on a cash pooling agreement with the intent to defraud creditors and jeopardise their rights, then they may be held personally responsible for all of the company's debts under the Fradulent Transfers Avoidance Law.

(b) Liability of group company and/or master account holder directors in the event of insolvency of the master account holder

Public companies in Cyprus need not be listed on the stock exchange, but they must fulfil certain prerequisites, which include a requirement to have at least seven members and a fully paid-up share capital of €24,000. In the case of a public company, Section 169F of the Companies Law provides as follows:

- In the case of a loss of the subscribed capital by 50% or at a figure which, in the directors' opinion, creates doubts as to the ability to reach the aims of the company, such loss emanating from past financial years or from other reasons, an extraordinary general meeting shall be convened immediately and in any event not 28 days from the time that the directors became aware of the reduction; such meeting shall be convened not later than 56 days from the day of taking the decision to convene the meeting for the purpose of considering whether the company should be wound up or any other measures taken.
- The directors of the company shall be guilty of a civil offence if they fail to take the aforementioned actions, and they shall be made liable to pay compensation. They shall be liable in person, without limitation, and shall be jointly and severally liable.

This obligation is a significant risk that the directors need to consider prior to entering into a cash pooling agreement. They will need to implement effective regulatory/supervisory mechanisms to ensure the solvency of the master account holder. Section 169F does not oblige the directors to take positive steps to check at any particular time whether the net assets of the company have fallen below the relevant thresholds But when entering into a cash pooling agreement, the directors a Cypriot company will need to ensure that a balance is maintained between the interests of the company and those of the group. These interests will not be balanced if the company finds itself in the situation referred to in Section 169F (even if it is not a public company).

Furthermore, a company has the right to opt out of the cash pooling agreement, even if it is still solvent and the master account requires funds. However, its ability to do so will hinge on the wording of the agreement. Agreements commonly contain clauses stating that a member is allowed not only to terminate the cash pool agreement, but also to recover all funds ceded to the master account.

Such clauses are advisable, as they protect the company from unlimited liability and the risk of insolvency. It is also advisable to implement an early warning system that provides the directors with adequate financial information about a master account to which they have either loaned money or acted as guarantors, and to include early termination rights in case their own company's financial standing would deteriorate after drawdown. Failure to include such clauses might expose the directors to charges of mismanagement, according to the provisions mentioned above.

The above rules apply even if the bank or its counterparties do not reside in Cyprus.

(c) Liability of group companies in the event of insolvency of the master account holder

If the requirements of Section 311 of the Companies Law are fulfilled, then action may be taken against anyone who is knowingly party to the business's continued trading. This does not exclusively apply to directors; the prospect of criminal liability may also arise for other parties that collude in sustaining the business of a company in distress. This is one of the few circumstances in which the corporate veil can be pierced, and the only circumstance in which creditors of a company may hold third parties liable for loss of property.

Should any of the involved parties (master account holder, claiming creditor, group company) be located outside Cyprus, this will not jeopardise their substantive rights or their defences, but procedural rules may differ if a suit is brought in the Cypriot courts (eg, more time may be needed to serve petitions on parties located outside Cyprus).

2.2 Perspective B: bank

(a) Banking requirements

According to Section 11 of the Banking Services Law, a bank must not be financially exposed to the same person or a group of related persons in an amount that exceeds 25% of the bank's own funds (or €150 million, whichever is the smaller), taking into account the effect of credit risk mitigation tactics specified in the instructions of the Central Bank on the calculation of capital requirements and large exposures. The above law defines 'exposure' as, among other things, "the administration of any loan or opening of a current debit account, or the granting of any lease (financial leasing), or the provision of bank guaranties or other endorsements". Each bank must have sound administrative and accounting procedures and adequate internal control mechanisms for identifying and recording all large exposures and subsequent changes in accordance with the law and EU directives. The aforementioned law grants the Central Bank the authority and obligation to monitor banking institutions within Cyprus in collaboration with an external credit assessment institution that meets the conditions set out in the EU Credit Rating Regulation (1060/2009), and to ensure that such institutions meet the capital adequacy requirements and maintain liquidity.

Apart from the above, Cypriot law imposes no specific regulatory requirements on banks when entering into a cash pooling agreement.

As a rule, a bank involved in running a cash pooling agreement will not be liable for any losses incurred should the master account holder or a group company become distressed. A bank may be held liable only if it is directly implicated under Section 311 of the Companies Law.

2.3 Insolvency

(a) *Insolvency practitioner's perspective*

According to Section 232 of the Companies Law, "where a company is being wound up by the Court, the Court may on the application of the liquidator, by order direct that all or any part of the property of whatsoever description and wherever located belonging to the company or held by trustees on its behalf shall vest in the liquidator by his official name, and thereupon the property to which the order relates shall vest accordingly, and the liquidator may, after giving such indemnity, if any, as the Court may direct, bring or defend in his official name any action or other legal proceeding which relates to that property or which it is necessary to bring or defend for the purpose of effectually winding up the company and recovering its property". Therefore, the liquidator may, by court order, claim either all or part of the company's credit balance.

If the insolvent entity is a Cypriot company, the administrator must be appointed by the Cypriot courts and must be a Cyprus resident. According to Section 209, "the competent Courts are those where the insolvent entity had its registered seat".

If the bank involved in the cash pooling agreement goes into liquidation, then Article 33 of the Banking Services Law states that "the sections of Companies Law, Cap.113 vis a vis the procedure and the effects of the liquidation will also be applicable for the liquidation of banking institutions".

The Companies Law does not provide for the automatic termination of all existing agreements when a company is declared insolvent. Section 233 allows the liquidator to continue the business of the company if doing so would benefit the winding-up process. If the liquidator does not do so, then existing contracts are terminated and the counterparties are treated as creditors of the company. In addition, the liquidator may disclaim unprofitable and onerous contracts that burden the company.[3]

It is standard practice that all contracts – especially if a bank is a counterparty – contain relevant provisions granting the counterparty an unconditional right to terminate or accelerate the contract in the event of insolvency proceedings. Such clauses have been upheld by the court in many cases and would in this case allow both the master account holder and the group company to terminate the cash pooling agreement. The lack of any such clause may render the directors of both the master account holder and the group company liable for mismanagement.

---

3 Section 304 of the Companies Law.

Regarding the liquidator's obligations with regard to both the master account holder and the group company, its primary duty is to notify them of the insolvency and advise whether it will be terminating the cash pooling agreement. It is irrelevant whether either the master account holder or the group company is a resident business, although different procedural rules will apply.

The liquidator's duties will be largely the same should the master account holder go into liquidation. The question of whether the group company should be included in the list of creditors will depend on the nature of its claim against the master account holder (ie, whether it is rightfully a debt or a trust claim). The law states that "the contributories (all past and present members) will be called to pay to the extent that any part of the nominal value of the shares they possess remain due, in the manner directed by the Court; and only when all the creditors are paid in full, will any money due to a contributory from the company may be allowed to him by way of set-off against any subsequent call".

The insolvency of a Cypriot company involved in a cash pooling agreement will not automatically result in the early termination of the agreement. This creates a question around any transactions made after the commencement of winding-up proceedings, but before the court issues a winding-up order.

In order to protect creditors from any action that might jeopardise their claims, the Companies Law includes various provisions that may invalidate any such transaction or debt incurred by the company in question. Section 301 provides that "any conveyance, mortgage, delivery of goods, payment, execution or other act relating to property made or done by or against a company within six months before the commencement of its winding-up shall, in the event of the company being wound up, be deemed a fraudulent preference against its creditors and be invalid accordingly".

To determine whether a fraudulent preference exists, the court will focus on any intention of the company to defraud creditors, and not on the result. The burden of proof rests with those claiming fraudulent preference to prove that that the debtor's real intention was to place the creditors in a prejudicial position. Only if the court is satisfied that this is the case will the charge be invalidated.

Section 303 of the Companies Law further provides that "when a company is being wound up, a floating charge on the undertaking or property of the company created within 12 months of the commencement of the winding-up shall, unless it is proved that, immediately after the creation of the charge, the company was solvent, be invalid, except to the extent of any cash paid to the company at the time of or subsequently to the creation of and in consideration of the charge". In this case the burden of proof is reversed – the debenture holder must prove that the floating charge is valid and provide evidence of the company's solvency.

Any transactions that are proven to have been carried out at an undervalue in order to put the company's assets beyond the reach of creditors will be classed as transactions carried out with the intention to defraud. Any such transaction may well be declared null and void by the court.

Lastly, according to Section 3 of the Fradulent Transfers Avoidance Law (CAP 62), "every pledge, mortgage, gift, sale or other transfer or disposal of a movable or immovable property made by any person with the intent to hinder or delay his creditors or any of them in recovering their debts from him will be deemed to be fraudulent and will be invalid against such creditors. In such case that the Court finds that a Fraudulent Transfer has taken place, the property or asset may be seized and sold to satisfy any judgment debt due from the person who made the pledge, mortgage, gift, sale or other attempted or actual transfer or disposal."[4] A transaction that constitutes fraudulent transfer avoidance may thus lead to the piercing of the corporate veil.

In summary, a cash pooling agreement and/or any disposition of property occurring in these circumstances may be invalidated if:

- the requirements set out in Sections 301 and 303 are met;
- any such disposition was made at an undervalue; or
- the requirements of Section 3 of the Fradulent Transfers Avoidance Law are satisfied.

Once a liquidator has been appointed, all powers of the directors cease, except insofar as the company (in a general shareholders' meeting)[5] or the liquidator sanctions their continuance. The liquidator assumes the directors' powers, and similarly owes a duty to the company as a whole rather than to individual shareholders or creditors (although their rights are taken into consideration for the purposes of the winding-up). In the event of insolvency of either the bank, the master account holder or the group company, the liquidator owes a primary duty towards the insolvent company and must take into consideration the rights of its creditors alone. That said, Section 233 of the Companies Law further grants to the liquidator "the right to make any compromise or arrangement with creditors or persons claiming to be creditors, or having or alleging themselves to have any claim, present or future, certain or contingent, ascertained or sounding only in damages against the company, or whereby the company may be rendered liable and to compromise all calls and liabilities to calls, debts and liabilities capable of resulting in debts, and all claims, present or future, certain or contingent, ascertained or sounding only in damages, subsisting or supposed to subsist between the company and a contributory or alleged contributory or other debtor or person apprehending liability to the company". If the creditors of other parties to the arrangement have a possible claim against the insolvent company, the liquidator is thus free to negotiate with them in order to mitigate any potential liability.

(b) Dissolution/termination of the cash pooling agreement in the event of liquidation of the master account holder or of a group company

If the master account holder goes into liquidation, a participating group company is entitled to terminate the arrangement; as can the master account holder if the group company goes into liquidation. Either can terminate the arrangement in the event of the bank going into liquidation. As previously explained, most cash pooling agreements contain clauses allowing one member to terminate the arrangement if

4 *Adamou v Kitchiou* (1978) 1 JSC 12 and *Lymperopoulou v Christodoulou* (1957) 22 CLR 184.
5 In the event of a voluntary liquidation.

another member becomes insolvent. Even if no such clause exists, case law has upheld that the insolvency of one party allows the remaining parties to terminate the agreement.

2.4 Perspective D: regulatory

Aside from those discussed, there are no further banking regulatory mechanisms concerning cash pooling agreements in Cyprus. That said, notional cash pooling may require additional formalities. Specifically, participating companies may be asked to sign cross-pool guaranties. The Companies Law provides that "any changes over any assets of a Cypriot company, need to be registered with the Registrar of Companies or otherwise, these charges (and any amen dements or assignments thereto) will be void towards the liquidator and the creditors of the company." This basically means that a cross-pool guarantee is valid only if registered with the registrar of companies. In addition, both physical and notional cash pooling may be subject to stamp duty.

2.5 Perspective E: tax

According to Section 39 of the Income Tax Law, "whenever a company, controlled by not more than five persons, grants a loan or any other financial facility to any of its directors or shareholders or, in case such directors or shareholders are individuals, to their relatives up to the second degree of kindred, the Commissioner may deem that interest at the rate of eight per cent (8%) per annum is payable to the company on the amount of the loan. Such interest is subject to special defence contribution[6] ('defence tax') at the rate of 10%."

On January 1 2011 Section 39 was amended so that no speculated interest would apply if the shareholder was a corporation, whereas the interest rate for individuals was raised to to 9%. That said, under Article 33 of the Income Tax Law, such loans were still required to be granted at an interest rate based on prevailing market conditions. If a company granted a loan interest free or at a preferential rate, then the income tax authority had the right to impose the market interest rate.

As of the 2012 tax year, Section 39 has been abolished and individual directors or shareholders (including spouses and second-degree relatives) who receive financial assistance from a Cypriot company are deemed to have received a monthly benefit in kind of 9% per annum. This is taxed under the pay as you earn system. Fifty percent of the amount is exempt and the remainder is taxed at 10% income tax, while the full sum is subject to a 10% defence tax. Interest on shareholder loans or bank loans cannot be offset against interest income for income tax and defence tax purposes.

Withholding tax incurred abroad on income which is also subject to domestic taxation will be credited against payable Cypriot tax, irrespective of any applicable double tax treaty. In addition, interest payments from Cypriot tax residents to non-residents are exempt from Cypriot withholding tax.

---

6 The special contribution for defence tax is another form of taxation targeting specific types of income and applies to Cyprus tax residents only.

Czech Republic

Bill Finney
Ernst Giese
Giese & Partner, vos

1. Introduction

1.1 Admissibility of cash pooling agreements

As in most European countries, the use of cash pooling in the Czech Republic follows the global standard for concentrating cash into a master account. In recent years it has quickly grown to become a common practice. Larger companies are now more reliant on direct financing for their short and long-term needs, rather than financing provided by banks. Local companies, and often their parent companies that may be located in foreign jurisdictions, seek to maximise liquidity and control cash flows while minimising the cost of funds.

Generally, cash pooling is available to companies which are part of a group of parties that are economically related through share ownership. This requirement is justified by the fact that the mechanism used for managing the cash pool structure needs a level of implementation that is basically available only to companies with unified control.

While certain jurisdictions use the term 'concern' to describe the related entities, the Czech Commercial Code (Act 513/1991 Coll. as amended) recognises this word in a stricter legal sense.[1] For a cash pooling transaction, it is therefore preferable to work with a concept of 'related' (or 'affiliated') entities, which also includes directors, members of the board and their related persons. In practice, a controlling share of the Czech company concerned is necessary to implement a cash pooling agreement, since the cash pooling mechanism needs, in general, consent of the general meeting to become a member of the pool.

No local law explicitly or implicitly forbids corporations to enter into a cash pooling agreement or prevents holding companies from setting up such an agreement with group members, although certain restrictions apply in the Czech context as described in this chapter. As a matter of fact, Czech law fails explicitly to regulate or even mention the concept of cash pooling.[2] Therefore, the nature of cash pooling needs to be examined in the first place from the perspective of general Czech legislation in order to determine which rules apply.

Nevertheless, given the international origin of cash pooling mechanisms, the

1 See Section 66a of the Czech Commercial Code

2 With a single exception of Czech National Bank Decree 34/2003, as amended, concerning a duty to notify cross-border transactions to the regulator. However, this decree has already been cancelled by Czech National Bank Decree 33/2006, as amended, which fails to provide any references to cash pooling.

possible solutions for cash pooling in the Czech Republic are similar to those in the rest of Europe and differences arise due to the specific requirements of each country.

As mentioned above, the Commercial Code does not directly refer to the concept of cash pooling as such; however, it may be perceived as providing the most important set of rules that impact on cash pooling activities. Consequently, careful consideration should be given to the structure and mechanisms in order to avoid any company law problems that may arise as a result of the invalidity of transactions within the cash pooling agreement, and which would impose liability on the directors of the companies involved in the arrangement for breaching their fiduciary duties to the company. As a final resort, criminal liability of company directors might be invoked as well.

Furthermore, the Commercial Code provides rules for a number of related issues, such as transfers of profit, reporting to minority shareholders, transfer pricing and the liquidation process.

Other Czech laws also impose certain obligations concerning cash pooling activities, such as the Income Tax Act (586/1992 Coll, as amended) which regulates tax issues related to cash pooling.

From an insolvency practitioner's point of view, the Insolvency Act (Act 182/2006 Coll, as amended) should be taken as a crucial statute, as it is a major piece of legislation thoroughly regulating the prerequisites for insolvency and bankruptcy proceedings as well as the entire process, the powers of the receiver (the insolvency administrator under Czech law), courts, creditors, and the rights and obligations of a bankrupt.

Further statutes indirectly provide for certain obligations which apply to relations arising within a cash pooling agreement; in particular:

- the Foreign Exchange Act (219/1995 Coll, as amended) which deals with cross-border aspects of cash pooling transfers;
- the Payment Systems Act (284/2009 Coll, as amended) which imposes a number of duties on banks with regard to electronic transfers and the administration of funds;
- the Banking Act (21/1992 Coll, as amended) which regulates certain aspect of capital adequacy; and
- the Accounting Act (Act 563/1991 Coll, as amended) which is very important for correct bookkeeping and book records regarding transactions within the cash pool.

Regarding the most common types of cash pooling mechanism, the following major principles and issues regarding Czech jurisdiction should be noted.

As for notional pooling, in which a bank will notionally combine the balances across several accounts and pay or charge interest only on the combined balance, there are practically no limitations whatsoever, since there is no transfer of funds between the related entities. Notional pooling is therefore the easiest way to implement a cash pooling agreement. Of course, certain issues may arise in this connection anyway, the most important being distribution of interest. The interest may either be credited or debited only to a master account, or be distributed among or charged to all members of the pool. In the former case, certain issues should be taken into account, especially whether the master account holder actually enjoys an unjustified benefit.

The situation is much more difficult under Czech law when physical cash pooling is used and funds are physically moved between the group's company accounts and the master account, involving techniques such as zero balancing and target balancing. From the point of view of Czech law, physical cash pooling is to be perceived as the provision of loans, where the master account holder has, in general, the position of a borrower and the other group companies transferring funds to the master account serve as lenders to the master account holder. Depending on the type of cash pooling, particular participants may play both roles, typically in the event of reverse/two-way pooling.

In the case of physical cash pooling, certain restrictions imposed mainly by the Commercial Code apply to these transactions, in particular in terms of the affiliated companies.

The transactions must be carried out based on arm's-length conditions to comply with Section 196a[3] of the Commercial Code. This provision has become a significant piece of law which needs to be kept in mind in most transactions concerning related entities.

In addition, in the event of an upstream loan, prior approval of the general shareholders' meeting of the group company is required (in the case of a company with one shareholder, it may exercise the powers of the general meeting without certain notice requirements). Depending on the particular bank providing cash pooling agreements and the wording of the memorandum of association or bylaws of the company in question, other consents (eg, those of the board of directors or the company's executives) may be required.

Finally, with regard to cross-border physical pooling, there is a duty of notification[4] to the Czech National Bank regarding the general fact of the cross-border transfer of funds. However, reporting on a daily basis concerning each transaction is not required.

1.2 Types of cash pooling agreement

There are no standard contractual forms for cash pooling provided under Czech law; therefore, all cash pooling agreements are basically so-called 'innominate agreements.' According to the civil law tradition, such contracts are not classifiable under any

3 Section 196a (1) of the Commercial Code provides that a company may conclude a credit or loan contract with a member of its board of directors, supervisory board, procurator or another person authorised to act in the name of the company, or with persons close to them, or a contract on securing the obligations (debts) of these persons, or a contract for free-of-charge transfer of property from the company, only with the prior approval of the general meeting and only under the terms customary in business transactions.
Section 196a (2) of the Commercial Code provides that should the persons under Section 196c (1) also be authorised to act in the name of another person, the provisions of Section 196c (1) shall apply, as appropriate, to any performance (payments) stipulated therein in favour of such persons. Approval by the general meeting is not required if a credit or loan is granted by the controlling person to the controlled person, or if the controlling person is to secure obligations (debts) of the controlled person.

4 The Foreign Exchange Act, as amended.

particular name. As innominate agreements concluded by business professionals, they are governed by the Commercial Code, which provides for a rather broad discretion of the parties to stipulate the terms and conditions of the transaction.

The particular types of cash pooling agreement are distinguished according to their content. In general, all classic forms of cash pooling are used on the local market – that is, physical and notional cash pooling providing for zero balancing or target balancing, with one-way or reverse flow of funds. Cross-border pooling and multi-level pooling are also commonly used in the Czech Republic, in particular by large multinational corporations with a number of local subsidiaries or branches.

The underlying documentation differs substantially between notional pooling and physical pooling, as the latter requires a more extensive set of agreements. Notional pooling may be concluded solely between the bank and the group companies, and, in certain cases, merely between the master account holder and the bank, as long as the bank can exercise control over or access the accounts of the other participants for the purpose of determining the balances in their accounts.

In practice, the bank will only artificially put all the funds together for the purposes of calculating the interest. Such artificial (virtual) transfers and calculation do not commonly require approval by the other members of the pool, so there is usually no need to enter into an agreement regarding the intra-group lending. The benefit of this structure may be seen in the fact that such a scheme does not necessarily require a joint guarantee from all members of the pool for potential liabilities against the bank providing the cash pool. Of course, banks commonly request a joint guarantee to be provided; however, in case of notional pooling there is more scope for the pool members to negotiate with the bank about the possibility of waiving such a requirement.

In this context, cash pooling is commonly used not only by multinational corporations, but also by multinational providers of utilities, as it allows effective cash collection from various jurisdictions. Since cash pooling is of foreign origin, a number of Czech banks use standard templates for cash pooling agreements provided by their parent companies. Such agreements are adapted to local regulations; however, from time to time concepts imported from foreign jurisdictions which are not explicitly prohibited under Czech law are reflected in the forms of cash pooling agreement used on the local market.

In addition, a cash management agreement, treasury management agreement or similar type of agreement (hereinafter referred to as a 'management agreement') is usually concluded between the participants in the cash pool.

Such management agreements are also innominate agreements under Czech law. The purpose of the management agreement is to describe and regulate the structure of the group that is subject to cash pooling, the relationships between particular members of the pool, the distribution of benefits and an outline of the arrangement and credit facilities and remuneration for intra-group loans.

Management agreements govern intra-group corporate relations, in particular the terms of the relationships between the master account and other accounts. The content of the management agreements is usually subject to approval by the general meeting of the companies, though this depends not only on the articles of association of the companies involved, but also on the exact terms of the management agreement, which may trigger a statutory requirement for approval by the general meeting regardless of the wording of the articles of association. The management agreement may also set out a framework for the provision of loans between the pool members; alternatively, a separate framework agreement regarding intra-group loans can be concluded.

Although it is not a type of cash pooling agreement, a controlling agreement under Sections 66a (7) and 190b of the Commercial Code should at least be mentioned among agreements applicable to cash pooling, as it regulates the relationship between the controlling and controlled entities and provides for compensation for any damage incurred by the controlled entity due to acts of the controlling entity. Based on the controlling agreement, the controlled entity undertakes to submit to the management (control) of the controlling entity. The controlling agreement may include an obligation on the controlled entity to transfer profits to the controlling entity. Furthermore, the controlling entity may give orders to the controlled entity which may even be detrimental to the controlled entity. Since a cash pooling mechanism may result in certain adverse effects on its participants, regulation of such adverse effects may be contained in the controlling agreement.

1.3 Legal requirements from various perspectives

There are no specific requirements set out by the Commercial Code for notional cash pooling, as there is no actual transfer of assets between affiliated companies. In terms of notional pooling, funds are merely artificially (virtually) put together, most commonly for the purpose of calculating interest.

For physical pooling, however, general regulations regarding transactions between affiliated companies and relationships between controlling and controlled entities apply.

Since physical pooling is generally perceived as the provision of loans under Czech law, the law focuses on the conditions applying to such loans – in particular, satisfaction of the arm's-length condition and, as the case may be, compensation for any detriment caused to controlled companies by companies which exercise control over them.

The major obligation under the Commercial Code is the requirement for prior written approval of the transaction by the general meeting of the company granting the loan within the cash pooling agreement where it is provided between related entities. This is required for upstream loans.

If no controlling agreement is concluded between the controlling and controlled entities, under Czech law, physical cash pooling agreements must be described in an annual report on the relationship between interconnected entities. Furthermore, if damage is incurred by the controlled company due to influence exercised over the controlled entity by the controlling entity, the controlling entity will be liable to compensate the controlled entity and its shareholders for that damage. The law provides that the members of the statutory body of the controlling entity are jointly and severally liable as guarantors for that compensation.

In some instances the memorandum of association or articles of association of the participating Czech company may need to be adapted to allow physical cash pooling. There may be additional restrictions in the memorandum or articles going beyond the statutory requirements regarding transfer of assets.

Cross-indemnity provisions are typically included in cash pooling agreements in the form of cross-guarantees provided by the participants of the cash pool. Often these participants are jointly and severally liable for liabilities of any member of the pool against the provider of the cash pooling.

Such security granted to affiliated companies is subject to approval by the general meeting. Since Czech law does not provide for any standard indemnity instruments which may be directly used for the purposes of cash pooling agreements, it is common for indemnification clauses from other jurisdictions to be restated and adapted in cash pooling agreements.

Instruments of Czech law which may be effectively used in order to secure obligations arising from the cash pooling agreement are either guarantees from other members of the pool and/or a third party in line with Sections 303 and following of the Commercial Code, or a bank guarantee provided by a bank under Section 313 of the Commercial Code. For the avoidance of any doubt, the bank providing such a guarantee will not be the bank maintaining the cash pool.

(a) *Banking law requirements*

In the event that an intra-group bank is established[5] for the purpose of management of cash flow and particular accounts, a standard banking licence is required by Czech law under the Banking Act.

Such a licence is granted by the Czech National Bank after satisfaction of a great number of conditions. In practice, an intra-group bank is set up only by large multinational corporations that often provide other financial services to the public where a banking licence is also a prerequisite for other business activities.

Such activities may be pursued based on a single banking licence issued in compliance with the applicable EU legislation (Directive 2000/12/EC), which has been implemented by the Banking Act. In such case, an organisational unit (branch) of a foreign bank should be established in the Czech Republic.

The Czech Payment Systems Act imposes a number of duties on cash pooling providers. However, except for consumers and small businesses, parties may exclude application of the provisions regarding the bank's disclosure duties and certain cases of liability. The majority of cash pooling providers exclude application of these provisions in their cash pooling agreements or in their cash pooling terms and conditions, as they are viewed as rather onerous since they impose on banks a number of obligations resulting in increased paperwork and liability.

(b) *Termination in the event of insolvency*

Although the applicable law does not explicitly require that a cash pooling

5 Under Czech law it is possible that a corporation itself can establish a bank for the purpose of the cash pooling agreement, although such a scenario is extremely rare and practically feasible only for large companies which would otherwise seek to be active in financial markets and financial services (they would need the banking licence for their usual scope of business).

agreement be automatically terminated in the event of insolvency of any member of the pool, cash pooling agreements themselves commonly provide for instant termination of the agreement in the event that insolvency proceedings are commenced against any member of the pool or, as the case may be, grant participants in the pool a right to withdraw from the cash pooling agreement.

This applies to both notional and physical cash pooling. Furthermore, in most cases, the cash pooling provider (ie, the bank) is secured by way of cross-indemnity provided by other participants in the cash pooling agreement. Such cross-indemnity is usually based on joint and several guarantees from the participants in the pool securing liabilities of any member of the pool.

Therefore, in the event of insolvency of any member of the pool, it is only reasonable for the members of the pool, (ie, the guarantors) to terminate their participation in the pool as well as related indemnification obligations arising in this connection. Otherwise, directors of the guarantor(s) may be held responsible for remaining in the pool with a bankrupt.[6]

(c) ***Banking notification requirements***

As mentioned earlier, in case of cross-border physical pooling, there is a duty of notification to the Czech National Bank regarding the general fact of cross-border transfers of funds. However, reporting on a daily basis is not required.

(d) ***Tax law issues***

Regulations regarding thin capitalisation apply. Under the Income Tax (586/1992 Coll, as amended), all expenses incurred for the purpose of generating, assuring or maintaining taxable income of a company are deductible. This includes interest payments on loans under a physical cash pooling agreement. However, only interest payments up to four times the company's equity (which generally means the total of share capital, other capital reserves, contributions of the shareholders beyond the share capital and retained profit) are tax deductible. In the case of banks, interest payments of up to six times the bank's equity are deductible.

The interest accrued within the cash pooling structure is included in the tax base of tax residents in the Czech Republic (each group company is taxed only on actual interest accrued in its account). For foreign entities, if the interest is to be paid abroad, the interest is subject to a withholding tax. The actual tax always depends on applicable double taxation treaties concluded between the Czech Republic and the relevant foreign state.

1.4 General legal requirements

As already pointed out above, general rules regarding transactions between affiliated

6 Termination of the cash pooling agreement in general does not automatically terminate a guarantee previously given. However, it depends on the wording of the guarantee as to which claims arising after termination of the cash pooling agreement will be secured. Banks usually structure the guarantees so as to cover as many claims as possible. Still, it depends on the negotiating power of the particular cash pooling participants (eg, large multinationals) which may substantially limit the guarantee in terms of future claims.

companies[7] and relationships between controlling and controlled entities apply to physical cash pooling, as it represents, in the view of Czech law, a loan between the companies.

According to the Commercial Code, a company may conclude a loan agreement with a member of the board and/or a director, holder of procurement and/or any other person that may conclude such agreement on behalf of the company, and/or affiliated persons, only with the prior written approval of the general meeting of the company and based on arm's-length conditions. If such persons are entitled to represent any other entity, the above applies to transactions with that entity as well. This is very common for a holding structure where the same persons serve as directors or members of the board for multiple concerns, which can present a conflict of interest.

A downstream loan between the controlling entity as lender and controlled entity as borrower is allowed under Czech law without requesting the approval of the general meeting of either company involved. With regard to cross-border cash pooling agreements, withholding tax issues and treaties on double taxation need to be taken into account.

2. Specific questions

2.1 Perspective A: corporate group

(a) *Liability of group company and/or master account holder directors in the event of insolvency of a group company*

If a group company is no longer able to meet its payment obligations, but is still a party to the cash pooling agreement, it is uncommon for there to be a risk of liability on the part of the directors of the group company or the directors of the master account holder. It is a market standard that cash pooling agreements provide for their termination as of the moment of commencement of insolvency proceedings against any participant in the cash pooling agreement in order to limit their liability.

However, in the event that physical pooling remains in place after the commencement of insolvency proceedings, the debtor is obliged not to dispose of its assets.[8] A transfer of funds based on a physical cash pooling agreement may be perceived as such a disposition of assets. Failure to comply with the statutory prohibition results in ineffectiveness of the disposition as regards creditors of the debtor, which may trigger an action against the other party involved in the transaction for return of the assets. Furthermore, the directors are liable for any loss and, in addition, their criminal liability under the Criminal Code might be invoked. In particular, the criminal offence of damaging a creditor and the offence of preference of a creditor should be taken into account in this connection.

The directors of the master account holder could be held liable in the event that

---

7 Section 196a of the Commercial Code.

8 However, this is not a case when a reorganisation under the Insolvency Act is approved. In such a case, the disposition right of the debtor is not suspended.

they refuse to comply with their obligations under the Insolvency Act. Furthermore, the directors might be held liable for any loss if they breach their fiduciary duties to the master account holder; for instance if, in the event of two-way pooling, they allow (due to their failure to comply with the obligation to exercise their authority with the due care of a prudent businessman) the funds in the master account to be transferred (as a loan) to the account of an insolvent group company and such funds are not recovered afterwards by the master account holder due to the insolvency of the group company which received the funds.

Regarding the liability of members of the supervisory board, it should be noted in the first place that a supervisory board is mandatory only for joint stock companies in the Czech Republic. Therefore, limited liability companies, which make up more than 90% of the companies established under Czech law, have the option to establish a supervisory board. As a result, a supervisory board is established by only a very small percentage of limited liability companies, and their practical role is therefore marginal. The members of the supervisory board are primarily liable for losses caused to a company (and, as the case may be, indirectly to third parties in the following place) based on the same principles as the directors of the company – that is, the possibility of liability for a breach of their fiduciary duties (exercising the due care of a prudent businessman) applies to them as well. However, since the nature of the supervisory board is mostly limited to exercising control over the directors, the liability of members of the supervisory board may be invoked against them only in the event of a breach of their statutory duties – that is, in the event that they failed to exercise the prescribed control over the directors of a company and that company or its creditors incurred a loss as a result of that failure. However, in the majority of cases, the control exercised by the supervisory member is based on an assessment of the actions of the directors subsequent to their occurrence. As such, the supervisory board has very limited powers in terms of preventing particular actions of the directors being taken where they could lead to immediate or future damage.

Furthermore, under the Commercial Code,[9] the members of the supervisory board who are liable for any loss must jointly and severally guarantee any liabilities of the company if the liable member of the supervisory board fails to make good such loss and the creditors cannot satisfy their claims against the company from its assets in insolvency. Nevertheless, the liability of the members of the supervisory board is an additional liability supplementary to that of the directors. The liability of the members of the supervisory board is also commonly more difficult to prove, as it derives from a harmful act of the directors and the incapability of the members of the supervisory board to prevent that act or to make the directors compensate the loss.

Finally, the Insolvency Act applies both to privately held and listed companies.

(b) *Liability of group company and/or master account holder directors in the event of insolvency of the master account holder*

In terms of physical cash pooling with one-way transfer of funds, in the event that the master account holder is declared bankrupt, the other group companies, being

9 Section 194(6) read together with Sections 138(2) and 200(3) of the Commercial Code.

virtual lenders of the master account holder, can invoke their debts against the master account holder only by way of application for payment through the insolvency proceedings. Their debts will be treated as standard unsecured liabilities and as such are subordinated to priority liabilities within the meaning of the Insolvency Act.

The directors of group companies may be liable for any loss if they have breached their fiduciary duty to exercise the care and diligence of a prudent businessman, which is understood as an objective liability.

Such liability could arise in the event that the master account holder is declared bankrupt and the other group companies continue to transfer funds to that account. A similar situation might occur when the inability of the master account holder to repay its debts was foreseeable at the time of conclusion of the cash pooling agreement.

The directors might argue a lack of liability on the basis that the cash pooling agreement was approved by the general meetings of the companies involved. Nevertheless, should the behaviour of the directors constitute a gross breach of the standard of care outlined above, which is set by the applicable legislation, the directors will not escape liability even if they acted upon the instructions of the general meeting of the company. Similarly, liability could arise in two-way cash pooling where the controlling entity returns funds to the controlled entity.

(c) Liability of the master account holder in the event of insolvency of a group company

In the event that a group company is in distress or goes into liquidation, Czech law does not give creditors of that company the legal right to hold other group companies or the master account holder liable for losses suffered unless there is evidence of their exercising substantial influence over the company, according to the Commercial Code. Of course, criminal liability of such persons may be invoked if their acts could be deemed criminal offences.

In addition, the general regulation of liability of a controlling entity for damage or detriment caused to a controlled entity may be considered in this respect; however, such liability arises only in respect of damage caused to the controlled entity and/or its shareholders. It cannot be simply extended to creditors of the company.

Finally, as there are commonly cross-indemnity clauses in cash pooling agreements, it is possible that without termination of the agreement in time – in other words, as long as there are no outstanding liabilities from the pooling arrangement in the event of a group company being insolvent – the group companies may be held liable for the debts of the bankrupt company, on the basis of the cross-guarantee provided under the cash pooling agreement.

2.2 Perspective B: bank

(a) Banking requirements

If a bank enters into a cash pooling agreement, it will have to meet requirements set out by the EU Basel II Directive and implemented by the applicable Czech banking legislation, which imposes an obligation on banks to hold sufficient capital against certain risks stated therein. These regulations also impose on the bank an obligation to undertake an internal credit analysis of every borrower, to provide every borrower with an individual credit line and to assess credit risks within a borrower's structure, especially with regard to required security.

Additionally, banks in the Czech Republic are required to pay contributions to the Deposit Insurance Fund. This obligation also applies to funds within a cash pooling structure insofar as the group companies are Czech companies or branches of foreign banks registered to do business in the Czech Republic.

(b) Liability of the bank in the event of insolvency of the master account holder or of a group company

According to the Payment Systems Act, a bank may be held liable for operating an incorrect payment service or unauthorised payment transactions. However, such liability is commonly excluded by banks in cash pooling agreements, unless there is gross negligence or intentional damage, which is possible as long as the other parties to the agreement are not consumers or small businesses.

In the event of insolvency of the master account holder or the group company, there is no particular liability attaching to the bank unless the bank has breached its obligations arising under applicable laws or under the cash pooling agreement.

In addition, since the bank will not be a party to any management agreement, the liability arising thereupon may be invoked only between its parties – that is, between the group members (including the master account holder).

2.3 Insolvency

Different scenarios may arise between the bank, the master account holder and the group company. In the event of the insolvency of a bank maintaining an account, there is no need for creditors to file an application registering their claims under the insolvency proceedings, since all liabilities against the bank are registered by operation of law.[10]

The debts may be claimed to their full extent. Nevertheless, they are ranked among standard unsecured liabilities, which are satisfied after satisfaction of priority liabilities and secured creditors. Therefore, such debts are likely to be satisfied only in part. The assets of an insolvent company commonly suffice to satisfy only a very small part of the liabilities.

Regarding transfers of funds prior to the insolvency of a master account holder or a group company, any creditor may challenge such transfers if they have an impact on its enforceable claims and were carried out within three years preceding the insolvency of the debtor, as long as it is an affiliated company. Upon a successful challenge, such transactions are ineffective as regards the creditor. If the counterparties to such transactions could not have foreseen, exercising due care and diligence, that the actions of the debtor would cause damage to its creditors, then the transaction in question is rather hard to challenge.

---

10 Every holder of an account is a creditor of the bank in respect to the funds in the account. Of course, if the bank goes bankrupt immediately after a clean sweep of the funds to the master account and before any new funds arrive to the account, there will be no debts to claim against the bank.

As for the governing law, the above applies only to insolvent Czech entities. In such case, domestic and foreign creditors need to comply with the Insolvency Act and will have basically the same legal position as local entities. Most commonly, Czech legal entities would be in the position of creditor.

Unfortunately, we cannot comment on cases where an insolvency administrator is appointed abroad, as such cases are not subject to Czech law. Unless there is a special provision regarding a conflict of laws, an insolvency administrator appointed abroad normally follows its own insolvency rules and Czech entities must comply with them.

(a) Special rules as regards creditors of other parties to the cash pooling agreement

In the event that either the bank, the master account holder, or a group company goes into insolvency in the Czech Republic, the insolvency administrator does not have to observe any special rules or obligations as regards the creditors of other parties to the cash pooling agreement.

The insolvency administrator should, of course, always review whether there are any liabilities secured by a cross-indemnity mechanism which it could invoke against the guarantors. Nevertheless, since such a cross-indemnity mechanism is designed in the first place to protect the interest of the bank providing the cash pooling, it is unlikely that any other creditors could successfully invoke their claims taking the advantage of cross-indemnity. Such a situation would be uncommon indeed.

The relationships based on cash pooling agreements establish standard lender-creditor obligations between the companies concerned in the case of physical pooling. In the case of notional pooling, there are virtually no relationships between the companies which should be taken into consideration if the insolvency of any member of the pool occurs. One exception would be regarding unsettled interest to be distributed among the members of the pool in accordance with the management agreement and the relevant cash pooling agreement.

(b) Dissolution/termination of the cash pooling agreement in the event of liquidation of the master account holder or of a group company

Depending on the exact terms and conditions of the particular cash pooling agreement, in the event that the master account holder goes into insolvency, the group company that is a party to the cash pooling agreement may dissolve or terminate the agreement (as may the master account holder in respect of an insolvent group company). Such situations are commonly regulated by cash pooling agreements and present grounds for instant termination of the agreement by the bank or the master account holder. In some instances, the bank has a right under a cash pooling agreement to block any credit balances on any accounts within the pool pending the exercise of any rights of set-off that the bank may have in respect of those balances. Of course, this depends not only on the wording of the cash pooling agreement but also on the provisions of other bank documentation, such as the agreement on opening of an account, applicable overdraft agreements and related agreements.

Directors of the companies involved in the pooling arrangement should always analyse the risks associated with any cross-indemnity or cross-guarantee provisions of a cash pooling agreement and exit the pool before the companies they manage incur any loss based on payment obligations arising from the cross-indemnity provisions due to default by an affiliated company going into insolvency.

2.4 Perspective D: regulatory

As mentioned above, in the event of cross-border physical pooling, the Czech National Bank must be notified of the general facts regarding cross-border physical cash pooling. However, reporting of each transaction arising from daily management of the pool is not subject to any duty of notification.

2.5 Perspective E: tax

As mentioned earlier, under Czech income tax legislation, all expenses incurred for the purpose of generating, assuring or maintaining taxable income of a company are deductible. This includes interest payments on loans under a physical cash pooling agreement. However, only interest payments up to four times of the company's equity, or six times in case of banks, are tax deductible (as a result of the thin capitalisation rules). As for notional pooling, no restriction applies from the tax perspective.

In terms of affiliated companies, standard market interest rates should apply to physical pooling between such companies and transfer pricing documentation must be prepared for this purpose. Auditors are generally very sensitive to the issues regarding proper transfer pricing, as the companies may be subject to investigation and significant penalties imposed by the relevant Tax Office should there be any breach of statutory duties in this respect.

Regarding physical pooling, interest paid to entities outside the Czech Republic is subject to an automatic withholding tax equivalent to 15% of the interest paid under the Income Tax Act. The provisions of any applicable double taxation treaties need to be considered when determining the actual tax burden.

Denmark

Carsten Ceutz
Morten Krogsgaard
Arne Riis
Bech-Bruun

1. Introduction

1.1 Admissibility of cash pooling agreements

The entering into a cash pooling agreement by Danish companies is neither explicitly nor implicitly forbidden by statutory Danish law, and Danish holding companies may set up a cash pooling agreement with group members.

Under Danish law, a group cash pooling system employing physical cash pooling is considered a lending and borrowing arrangement among the participants and is subject to the Danish statutory legal regime regulating financial assistance.

In respect of this regime, where the master account holder is incorporated and which jurisdictions govern the other companies participating in a multi-jurisdictional cash pooling agreement are of importance, as the exemptions applicable to shareholder lending are dependent on the corporate form of the parent in the jurisdiction of its incorporation, as further described below.

Notional cash pooling is not considered a lending and borrowing arrangement among the participants and is therefore not subject to the Danish statutory regime regulating financial assistance.

1.2 Types of cash pooling agreement

In Denmark, as in many other jurisdictions, corporate treasury management focuses on managing the group's liquidity, including utilisation of internal liquidity before external liquidity, ensuring that the required cash resources are available at the right time, in the right place and in the right currency. The goal is not only to minimise the cost of financing or to maximise the return on surplus cash, but also to reduce financial risks such as interest and currency rate fluctuations.

Consequently, many banks operating within the Danish market offer wide varieties of cash pooling systems. Some banks have developed and established frequently used systems for either physical cash pooling, including cash concentration such as zero balancing and target balancing, or national cash pooling.

As an effective cash pooling agreement takes into consideration tax efficiency, costs and the regulatory regime of the jurisdiction involved, as well as the reduction of financial risks, other banks have specialised in providing custom-made cash pooling solutions which may be in the form of hybrid cash pooling systems combining cash concentration at a local level and notional cash pools.

1.3 Legal requirements from various perspectives

In Denmark, there are no specific mandatory legal requirements applicable only to cash pooling agreements.

However, general legal requirements are in many areas of law relevant in respect of cash pooling agreements involving Danish group companies.

(a) *Company law*

As stated above, under Danish law, a group cash pooling agreement employing physical cash pooling is considered a lending and borrowing arrangement among the participants and is subject to the Danish statutory legal regime regulating financial assistance.

The Danish legal regime on financial assistance is divided into two sub-regimes:

- The financial assistance regime reflects the implementation in Danish law of EU Council Directive 77/91/EEC (as amended), which sets out (on an objective basis) the persons and liabilities to which the provision of shareholder loans and financial assistance by a Danish company are not permitted; and
- The corporate benefit regime reflects the limits within which the management of a Danish company may, in specific circumstances, provide loans and financial assistance with due consideration of the risk of incurring personal liability.

Under the financial assistance regime, a Danish company is prohibited from providing financial assistance in whatever form (lending or providing security, including guarantees and indemnities) for the indebtedness of a shareholder (whether natural or corporate) in that Danish company or in any of its direct or indirect parents.

By exception, this does not apply to financial assistance for the indebtedness of parent companies covered by an executive order issued by the Danish Business Authority, which at the date of writing includes any entity in the corporate form of:

- a public limited company (*aktieselskab*);
- a limited partnership company (*partnerselskab*);
- a private limited company (*anpartsselskab*) (as such terms are defined in the Danish Companies Act); or
- a company with an equivalent corporate form, having its registered office in Denmark or in any other country which is a member state of the European Union or the European Economic Area, or in Switzerland, Australia, Canada, Hong Kong, Japan, South Korea, New Zealand, Singapore, Taiwan or the United States.

The provision of financial assistance to, or for the indebtedness of, related companies of the Danish company (cross-stream and downstream assistance) is not subject to the statutory legal regime regulating financial assistance.

The above exceptions do not apply to a potential abuse of the exception, such as lending to an affiliate for the purpose of such person then passing on the benefit of the financial assistance to another person not qualified to benefit from the exception.

A Danish company is not precluded entirely from participating in a cash pooling system even though the other participants do not qualify under the above exceptions. It is the practice of the Danish Business Authority that a Danish company in such a case may participate in a cash pooling system if:

- participation in the cash pooling system is an ordinary business transaction;
- there is corporate benefit to the Danish company – which includes that the Danish company will be entitled to withdraw amounts from the cash pool comparable to the amounts which it may contribute, that the risk assumed by the Danish company is reasonably balanced against the benefit it obtains from participating in the cash pool, and that the group benefit from the cash pooling system is distributed in a reasonable manner between the cash pool participants; and
- the Danish company from time to time has the right to withdraw from the cash pooling system or the right to limit deposits if the risk assumed by the Danish company is deemed to be unacceptable in the then-existing circumstances.

Assessment of the criteria will be made on a case-by-case basis looking at the specific circumstances.

Under the corporate benefit regime, the board of directors is under an obligation to consider from time to time whether the financial position of the company is sound in context of the company's operations. This obligation entails, among other things, that:

- the board of directors (and each director) must at all times consider whether the company is adequately capitalised in relation to the business operations of the company and the commercial and financial obligations which the company undertakes; and
- in relation to participation in a cash pooling agreement, the board of directors must consider whether the risk assumed thereby is proportionate to the financial capacity of the company in the light of its business operations and other commercial and financial obligations.

In relation to risk taking, it is primarily a financial and commercial decision. The perspective from which the matter will be considered is based on the company's ability to discharge its commercial and financial obligations towards its stakeholders. The board of directors' assessment must include an analysis on the basis of the company's financial conditions at the time of provision of the assistance, but must also include a forward-looking analysis.

Notional cash pooling (in its cleanest form) is not considered a lending and borrowing arrangement among the participants and is therefore not subject to the Danish statutory legal regime regulating financial assistance.

(b) *Banking law*

Danish banks are subject to the regulation set out in the Financial Business Act and executive orders issued under it. The Financial Business Act and the related executive orders implement pertinent EU legislation, including the Capital Requirements Directive.

The Danish banking regime does not impose specific requirements in respect of cash pooling systems. Amounts standing to the credit of a cash pool participant will have an impact on the bank's liquidity requirements. In respect of credit facilities related to a cash pooling agreement, the bank will be subject to capital requirements in respect of any loans made.

(c) *Insolvency law*

The Danish insolvency regime does not impose specific requirements in respect of cash pooling systems. Once formal insolvency proceedings have been initiated and acknowledged by the bankruptcy courts, a cash pooling system has to be considered as payables and receivables between independent parties, equivalent to inter-company accounts.

In terms of perfection of a security interest, Danish bankruptcy law does not provide for the choice of any other governing law but Danish. Denmark has entered into binding conventions only with the other Scandinavian countries with regard to recognition of foreign bankruptcy proceedings.

(d) *Regulatory*

There is no general requirement that the master account holder be licensed as a credit institution under the Danish implementation of the EU Credit Institutions Directive. In Denmark, regulated banking activity involves the taking of deposits and other repayable funds from the general public. Accepting loans from one or more group companies will not constitute the taking of deposits and other repayable funds from the general public.

Similarly, there is no general requirement that the master account holder be licensed as a payment service provider under the Danish implementation of the EU Payment Services Directive, as the provision of payment services to group companies is exempt from the Danish payment service rules.

(e) *Tax law*

From a Danish tax perspective, cash pooling is considered as a borrowing and lending transaction, provided that the debtor company has a legal obligation to repay a debt to the creditor company.

This has the consequence that the borrower and the lender may realise gains and losses on receivables or payables, respectively, which would generally be recognised for Danish tax purposes. Further, a Danish borrower would at the outset be entitled to make a tax deduction for interest paid or accrued on its debt in the cash pool and a Danish cash pool lender would be taxable on interest received.

However, as cash pool borrowers and lenders are normally group related, also for Danish tax purposes, specific rules apply which may subject the parties to different tax treatment in Denmark than when Danish companies use third-party bank finance.

Main rule – tax deductibility: As a general rule, interest is a tax-deductible cost under Danish tax law. For Danish corporate entities, interest is deductible on an annual accrual basis.

Deductibility of interest may be subject to limitations under various rules in Danish tax law.

Thin capitalisation: As a general rule, interest paid by a Danish company is tax deductible. The deductibility of interest and capital losses on debt owed to a related legal entity ('controlled debt') may, however, be restricted under the Danish thin capitalisation regime (and the interest deduction limitations described below).

The thin capitalisation regime applies to entities which are subject to full Danish tax liability (Danish resident companies) or limited Danish tax liability (due to a permanent establishment). In the following, both types of entities are referred to as the 'Danish debtor'.

Thin capitalisation restrictions will apply if all of the following four conditions are met:

- The Danish debtor has controlled debt;
- The controlled debt exceeds a threshold of Dkr10 million;
- The Danish debtor's debt-to-equity ratio exceeds 4:1 at the end of the tax year; and
- The Danish debtor cannot prove that a similar debt would be available from an unrelated party (market terms).

If the Danish debtor is thinly capitalised and unable to demonstrate that unsecured third-party debt is available on similar terms, the Danish debtor will be subject to deductibility limitations. Thus, if the cash pool offers the Danish borrowing company a lower interest rate than would be available from a bank, the rules will apply.

The deductibility limitations will apply to interest payments and capital losses on controlled debt. Interest payments and capital losses on unsecured third-party debt are not affected. The restriction of deductibility applies to the portion of the controlled debt which should be converted into equity in order to avoid the limitation of deductibility.

Irrespective of the 4:1 debt-to-equity ratio being exceeded, the thin capitalisation restrictions would not apply to interest payments which are subject to Danish withholding tax (which applies to interest payments to a related party resident offshore, meaning a jurisdiction outside the European Union which does not have a tax treaty with Denmark).

Assets and earnings before income and taxes imitation: In addition to the thin capitalisation rules, Denmark applies limitations to the tax deductibility of net financing expenses on the basis of the tax value of the company assets, as well as on the basis of earnings before income and taxes. Accordingly, under the so-called asset limitation, tax deductibility of net financing expenses will be limited to an amount corresponding to 3.5% (2012) of certain qualifying assets. The rate of 3.5% will be adjusted annually. The limitation applies only if the net financing expenses exceed Dkr21.3 million (approx €2.86 million).

Under the earnings before income and taxes limitation, net financing expenses cannot be deducted for tax purposes to the extent that such expenses exceed 80% of earnings before income and taxes. The limitation applies only if the net financing expenses exceed Dkr21.3 million (approx €2.86 million).

In contrast to the thin capitalisation rules, the asset and earnings before income and taxes limitations also apply to debt owed to unrelated parties.

Transfer pricing: Under Danish law, transactions between related parties must be carried out in accordance with the arm's-length principle. This requirement would therefore generally also apply to a cash pooling agreement. Danish law includes special rules on transfer pricing corresponding to the Organisation for Economic Cooperation and Development (OECD) guidelines.

The arm's-length principle is defined in accordance with OECD guidelines, and the Danish tax authorities recognise the methods set out in the guidelines.

When filing its tax returns, a company must report the type and scope of inter-company transactions and demonstrate the transfer pricing method applied and conditions applicable to inter-company transactions.

Danish withholding tax regime: No Danish withholding tax will apply to interest paid by a Danish corporate entity to a person or entity which does not qualify as a foreign controlling or group-related entity lender (the definition of which is given below).

Interest paid by a Danish corporate entity to a foreign controlling or group-related entity lender will be subject to Danish withholding tax, unless:

- the foreign controlling or group-related lender has a permanent establishment in Denmark to which such interest income is attributed;
- the foreign controlling or group-related lender is entitled to claim reduction or elimination of Danish withholding tax under the EU Interest and Royalty Payments Directive (2003/49/EU) (no tax is levied and no withholding tax applies) and the relationship with the Danish borrower is upheld for a minimum period of one year;
- the foreign controlling or group related lender is protected under a tax treaty with Denmark (irrespective of the treaty rate) and the relationship with the Danish borrower is upheld for a minimum period of one year, or
- the foreign controlling or group-related lender is controlled (as defined under the Danish tax consolidation rules) by a Danish entity;
- the foreign controlling or group-related lender is controlled by a party resident in a country that has concluded a tax treaty with Denmark, and that country may further tax the related foreign lender on the interest payments under the controlled foreign corporation taxation rules of that country; or
- the foreign controlling or group related lender can demonstrate that it has paid foreign income tax on the interest received at a rate of at least 18.75%

(as of 2012) and has not entered into a back-to-back loan with an entity that has paid foreign income tax on the interest received at a rate of less than 18.75%.

For purposes of the Danish interest withholding tax rules, 'control' means direct or indirect legal ownership of more than 50% of the shares, or legal control over more than 50% of the voting rights. Ownership or control is not conferred from a pledgor to a pledgee solely as a result of a pledge over shares.

When determining whether the lender controls the Danish borrower (or vice versa), votes and shares held by group-related entities are considered. Votes and shares held by non-related shareholders may also be considered if an agreement has been made between the lender and the non-related shareholders for the purpose of exercising a common controlling influence over the Danish borrower. A shareholders' agreement may constitute an agreement to exercise common controlling influence over the Danish borrower.

Not only taxable legal entities are considered entities for the purposes of control; fiscally transparent entities may also be considered if they are governed by rules of corporate law, a corporate law agreement or articles of association.

'Group related' means two or more entities which are directly or indirectly controlled by the same group of shareholders, or under common management.

The very broad definition of 'group' means that a Danish borrower in a cash pooling agreement would need to consider Danish withholding tax exposure and whether it is entitled to claim one of the exemptions outlined above. In practice, the most relevant exemptions would be the second or third listed above.

The Danish tax authorities have tightened the interpretation of the rules, with the result that foreign recipients of dividends and interest from Danish companies must now satisfy a beneficial ownership requirement in order to qualify for exemption from Danish withholding tax according to either the EU Interest and Royalty Payments Directive or a Danish tax treaty. This also means that Danish companies will have a withholding tax obligation more often than previously when paying out dividends and interest to foreign investors.

It is the opinion of the Danish tax authorities that a company will not qualify as beneficial owner if the company has the characteristics of a conduit company – that is, a company which is interposed strictly for tax purposes, but which does not have any decision-making power with respect to the income received. In determining whether a foreign holding company should be considered a conduit company, it appears that the Danish tax authorities will in particular consider:

- the right of the foreign holding company to dispose of the funds received;
- the flow of funds (ie, how payments to and from the foreign holding company are structured and the timing of inbound and outbound payments); and
- the substance of the foreign holding company – that is, the physical presence of the holding company in the jurisdiction of incorporation and the extent of work carried out in and from the holding company in the jurisdiction of incorporation.

It will therefore be important, for Danish withholding tax purposes, to examine the cash pooling agreement on a case-by-case basis to assess who will qualify as the beneficial owner of the interest paid under the arrangement and whether Danish withholding tax may apply

2. Specific questions

2.1 Perspective A: corporate group

(a) Liability of group company and/or master account holder directors in the event of insolvency of a group company

Although the requirements for having boards of directors, the managing directors or accountants held liable according to Danish law are quite hard to meet, there is a risk of liability once the point beyond which there can be no successful restructuring has been passed.

The most commonly used legal doctrine is unjustified continuation after the point beyond which there can be no successful restructuring, causing a loss for providers of more cash on unsecured terms as well as unsecured deliveries. The standard of proof is lower where the body taking the actions is acting outside the scope of the business purpose (*ultra vires*) but being out of the scope of business purposes alone is not enough; loss must be realised too.

It makes no difference what kind of company is doing the business, or in which jurisdiction the bank is located; but it is usually more expensive and troublesome for a foreign bank to initiate court proceedings outside its domestic jurisdiction.

With regard to lenders' and/or management liability, there is no specific statutory or common law regulation of cash pooling. Mismanagement of cash pooling is considered – together with unlawful distribution, conflicts of interest, mismanagement and piercing the corporate veil – as part of the same doctrine under which lenders' and/or management liability might arise, the main rule of which is that the lender and/or management can be held liable only if it is shown that the lender's or management's actions led to a loss and that the loss was foreseeable at the time of the action.

(b) Liability of group company and/or the master account holder directors in the event of insolvency of the master account holder

The discussion above is equally applicable if the situation is seen from the point of view of the master account holder.

(c) Liability of group companies in the event of insolvency of the master account holder

If a creditor can show an independent legal basis of liability against another group company it can hold that company liable. There is no automatic liability for other group companies if the agreements entered into do not justify such liability.

With reference to the discussion above, it makes no difference as to in which jurisdiction the bank is located.

(d) *Liability of the master account holder in the event of the insolvency of a group company*

The discussion under paragraph (c) is equally applicable if the situation is seen rom the point of view of the group company.

2.2 Perspective B: bank

(a) *Banking requirements*

As stated above, Danish banks are subject to the regulation set out in the Financial Business Act and executive orders issued under it. The Financial Business Act and related executive orders implement pertinent EU legislation, including the Capital Requirement Directive.

The Danish legal regime does not set up specific requirements in respect of cash pooling systems. Amounts standing to the credit of a cash pool participant will have an impact on the bank's liquidity requirements. In respect of credit facilities related to a cash pooling agreement, the bank will be subject to capital requirements in respect of loan granted.

It is notable that the Danish legal regime has very little scope for credit risk mitigation in respect of cash pooling agreements, such as capital relief by way of netting, guarantees and security.

Nevertheless, in respect of cash pooling agreements, whether physical or notional, with a related credit facility, it is often the case that cross-guarantees and/or cross-collateral is requested. While banks frequently include in their standard terms and conditions a right of set-off enabling the bank to offset a group company's debit balance in one account against funds held in other accounts with the bank, it is not common for a bank to seek set-off rights with respect to accounts held by affilitates or in other jurisdictions. It may be argued that such right of set-off constitutes a security right which should be executed in accordance with the applicable law.

(b) *Liability of the bank in the event of insolvency of the master account holder or of a group company*

Apart from avoidance claims or claims based on wrongful perfection of a security interest, lenders' liability is very rare, though not entirely unknown, in Danish law. There is no distinction as regards from whom or where a claim derives.

2.3 Insolvency

(a) *Insolvency of the bank*

According to the Guarantee Fund for Depositors and Investors Act, a depositor is guaranteed up to €100,000 in the event of a bank's insolvency.

If the account is set up using the master account holder's value added tax or other identification number, which depends on the agreement with the bank, the entire cash pooling agreement is regarded as one deposit (this would be the case with physical cash pooling). This means that only the master account holder is guaranteed €100,000.

In contrast, up to €100,000 on each individual deposit is guaranteed from the

Guarantee Fund for Depositors and Investors if deposits and loans by the individual group companies are made into separate accounts subject to an overall framework agreement with the bank (as happens with notional cash pooling).

Amounts exceeding the guaranteed €100,000 are not covered by the Guarantee Fund for Depositors and Investors. Any unguaranteed amounts in the cash pooling accounts must therefore be recovered from the funds of the bankruptcy estate. The group must therefore settle for proving its outstanding account with the bank as an unsecured claim against the estate.

Any interest accrued to the cash pooling account until the date of the bankruptcy order is covered by the guarantee scheme. In contrast, interest accrued after the date of the bankruptcy order is not covered by the guarantee scheme. Such claims must be proved against the estate as secured claims.

The guarantee fund scheme is a result of EU Directive 94/19/EC. The deposit-guarantee scheme is based on the home member state principle, whereby deposits made to a branch located in Denmark, stemming from another EU member state, are covered by the home member state's deposit-guarantee scheme and not by the Danish deposit-guarantee scheme. However, the amount of cover of €100,000 has been fixed in the directive and it is therefore in reality irrelevant whether the bank has its head office in Denmark or is registered in another member state.

(b) Insolvency of the master account holder

As a general rule, payments made by group companies into the cash pooling account are included in the account holder's assets and are therefore covered by the latter's bankruptcy estate.

Third-party property, on the other hand, is not covered by the assets of the bankruptcy estate. However, this applies only if the payments made by group companies may be unconditionally appropriated in the cash pooling account.

In connection with unconditional appropriation, it is easy to determine which deposits belong to which group companies. In addition, if the payments have been appropriated unconditionally, the master account holder will be acting unlawfully if its effects a transaction contrary to the agreement with the contributing company, such as lending the amount paid to another group company despite an agreement to the contrary.

In relation to physical cash pooling where the contributing group companies pay into and withdraw from a joint cash pooling account, the individual payments will not be appropriated to such extent that appropriation may be considered unconditional. The reason is that loans from the cash pooling account are not conditional upon the contributing companies' acceptance (thus, loans from the account are not unlawful), and deposits are in general not earmarked for particular group companies. Consequently, the bankruptcy estate may in such cases demand that an amount be paid into the cash pooling account.

The contributing group company must therefore, in such case, settle for filing an unsecured claim against the estate.

In the case of notional cash pooling, where the different group companies keep separate accounts, the issue of appropriation is not relevant. In this event, it is clear which accounts belong to which company and consequently, payments to the cash pooling account appear as secured claims. In this case, the trustee cannot demand that the payments accrue to the estate.

(c) *Insolvency of a group company*

As a general rule, consolidated enterprises are not liable for each other's debts. However, in one Supreme Court judgment from 1997 (*The Midtfyn Festival*), a consolidated enterprise and a spouse retaining undivided possession of the estate of the bankrupt company's managing director were held liable for the bankrupt company's debt. The reasoning of the court was that the commingling of the companies' finances and activities resulted in identification between the companies, and consequently the other company was liable for the debts of the bankrupt company.

If, in respect of cash pooling, the participating companies' identities are respected, the cash pooling factor alone cannot lead to the other group companies' being liable for a company's bankruptcy. This means that the group company's estate cannot demand that deposits made to the master account be returned to the estate.

The schemes concluded between the group and the bank may, however, differ. Some schemes entail that the group companies are liable only for their contributions or deposits, whereas under other schemes the companies are jointly liable with the other group companies for the bank's net liability. Such an agreement between the bank and the group concerns only the relationship between the group companies and the banker.

The fact that the companies have concluded an agreement with their banker on joint liability with respect to loans from the cash pooling account cannot entail that the other group companies are held liable in the event that one of the companies participating in the scheme goes bankrupt. This would require that the identity between the companies be similar to that existing between the companies referred to in the Supreme Court judgment noted above. Similarly, it may be concluded that if the companies are not identical, the other group companies will not be affected by the bankruptcy of a group company. This means that the trustee of a bankrupt company cannot demand that deposits made to a cash pooling account be returned to the estate.

In the event that the bank, the master account holder or another group company goes into liquidation, the following is relevant as regards the position of the administrator.

The trustee is responsible for protecting the assets of the bankruptcy estate. This duty of protection requires the trustee to ensure that the assets of the estate are stored at a safe location, insured, registered and evaluated.

The obligation to protect the estate's assets also requires that the trustee ensure that all accounts of the bankrupt company are frozen. In relation to cash pooling, this means that a bankrupt company involved in a cash pooling agreement cannot make any payments to or take any loans from the account. The trustee is therefore obliged to ensure that the balances owed to and owned by the bankrupt company are terminated on the date of the bankruptcy order

Other obligations include the trustee's obligation to notify the bankrupt party's creditors of the bankruptcy order immediately after it is issued.

The trustee is moreover obliged to keep the creditors of the estate informed on an ongoing basis. Creditors are to be provided with a list of the estate's assets and liabilities, and a statement of affairs accompanied by a summary of the most important financial accounting figures every six months.

With regard to the trustee's obligation towards the creditors, it is irrelevant in which jurisdiction the creditors are registered, as their nationalities are not taken into consideration under the Bankruptcy Act.

If the bankrupt master account holder has transferred money to a group company prior to its bankruptcy, the loan prohibition laid down in the Companies Act applies. This provides that a limited liability company may not, directly or indirectly, advance funds, make loans or provide security for shareholders or the management of the companies. This also applies to shareholders or the management of the company's parent company, and to businesses other than parent companies having control over the company. However, the Companies Act stipulates that a limited liability company may, directly or indirectly, advance funds, make loans or provide security to a specific group of persons for the purpose of usual business transactions.

If a group company goes bankrupt, the question arises of whether avoidance is possible in relation to companies having benefited from payments from the company through cash pooling.

The application of the avoidance rules to the bankruptcy of a contributing company was considered by the Supreme Court in a judgment from 2000 (*Klinge*).

In that case, Company S acted as administration company to all companies in a group, including Subsidiary D. According to an agreement between the group companies, all payments to them were made in US dollars into S's US dollar account with Bank B, with the effect that S's managing director could control the amounts deposited in the account and could also decide to which companies the amounts were to be transferred. The individual companies in the group had inter-company balances. Payments to D were usually made to S's account and expenses concerning D were also paid from this account. When S and D were declared bankrupt, the bankruptcy estate initiated bankruptcy proceedings against B claiming payment of approximately Dkr43 million with reference to B having in fact managed the group's liquidity and controlled invoice payments to the effect that these had been received for the purpose of covering S's debt to B.

Since the administration scheme had to be regarded as concluded for commercial purposes, there were no grounds for disregarding the scheme or avoiding payments to S's account. Further, the capital transfers between the group companies were not gifts, not in relation to B either, and consequently avoidance was not possible. An invoice discounting scheme could not be avoided either, and since there were no grounds for assuming that a guarantee scheme's validity could be affected by claims for avoidance against B, judgment was delivered in favour of B on all points.

The possibility of avoiding payments made under a group account scheme must, in accordance with the Bankruptcy Act and this Supreme Court judgment, be considered limited to transactions that are undue or characterised as gifts or extraordinary payments.

Section 64 of the Bankruptcy Act provides that gifts may be avoided if effected later than six months prior to the date of filing for bankruptcy (usually earlier than the date of the bankruptcy adjudication order), while Section 67 of the act stipulates that payment of debt effected later than three months prior to the reference date may be avoided where such payment has been effected by unusual means of payment, before the due date for payment or in amounts which have substantially impaired the debtor's ability to pay its debts, provided that such payment did not appear ordinary under the circumstances. Section 70 of the act concerns charges for old debt. Section 74 of the act concerns transactions that are voidable if the debtor gives preference in an improper manner to a creditor at the expense of any other creditors, or if the debtor's property is withheld from creditors, or the debtor's debts are increased to the detriment of the creditors if the debtor was, or through the transaction became, insolvent and the preferred party knew or had reason to know this and the circumstances make the transaction improper.

(d) Insolvency administrators licensed abroad

A number of inter-state organisations are focusing on the possibilities for harmonising international insolvency law through the drafting of new international trade law conventions containing insolvency provisions, and through the adoption of uniform laws and common principles in the area.

The United Nations Commission for International Trade Law has drafted a model law which was adopted in 1997 and which aims to promote the adoption of modern and fair legislation to be applied when an insolvent debtor holds assets in more than one state.

This model law lays down the conditions, in connection with foreign insolvency proceedings, for granting permission to a trustee of the courts of a member state that has adopted the model law and the conditions for recognising foreign insolvency proceedings and protective remedies to the benefit of the foreign trustee. Moreover, the model law enables the courts and trustees of the various countries to cooperate more efficiently, and contains provisions harmonising insolvency proceedings taking place at the same time in different states.

In addition, the EU Insolvency Regulation (1346/2000) has been in effect from May 31 2002. This regulation was adopted with a view to introducing uniform rules in the European Union. Under this regulation, provisions definitively determine the consequences of a bankruptcy abroad and the powers of a foreign trustee in the home country.

However, these new and clear rules of the regulation do not apply between Denmark and the other EU member states, since Denmark, through its opt-outs from the Maastricht Treaty, so far does not participate in such measures of legal cooperation. Denmark has tried to negotiate a solution, a so-called parallel agreement, but the Council has not allowed the European Commission to commence negotiations with Denmark on such an agreement.

Nonetheless, the situation is now that Denmark (and Norway, as a non-member state) applies the same principles for mutual recognition of other EU member states' procedures. Under these principles, a bankruptcy and the consequences thereof must, under the Bankruptcy Act, be settled in accordance with the laws of the country where the insolvency proceedings are commenced. This means that, in connection with a Danish insolvency process, Danish bankruptcy provisions must be applied in relation to the trustees.

(e) Cash pooling agreements from the insolvency practitioner's perspective

The administrator's task is to preserve all values of the insolvent entity. Therefore, if the cash pooling agreements continue in relation to a continuing business the administrator has the obligation to separate the cash so that the inter-company accounts frozen at the date of initiation of the formal insolvency proceedings do not lead to further lending on unsecured terms to other group companies.

(f) Disssolution/termination of cash pooling agreement in the event of liquidation of the holder of the master acount or of a group company

Initiating formal insolvency proceedings in Denmark not considered as a defaulting event under Danish law. Under formal restructuring and bankruptcy proceedings, the debtor has the right to enter into or continue the existing agreements (in terms of restructuring, even if the agreement has already been subject to default) on the original terms, provided that the debtor can fulfil the debtor's obligations going forward. This goes for all parties to a cash pooling agreement, whether bank, master account holder or group company.

2.4 Perspective D: regulatory

(a) Regulatory requirements as regards cash pooling agreements

In Denmark, regulated banking activity involves the taking of deposits and other repayable funds from the general public. Accepting loans from one or more group companies will not constitute the taking of deposits and other repayable funds from the general public.

However, particular caution is advised when the master account holder is a special treasury entity which has funded itself through the issue of corporate bond or notes. Such corporate bonds constitute other repayable funds under Danish law. If such corporate bonds have been sold to the general public and more than 25% of the balance sheet constitutes "other repayable funds", a Danish licensing requirement may be triggered. As the special treasury entity also undertakes the activity of funding the group companies, a full banking licence is likely to be required.

2.5 Perspective E: tax

Tax issues relating to cash pooling agreements are discussed under section 1.4(e) above.

England

Graeme Levy
Squire Sanders (UK) LLP

---

1. Introduction

1.1 Admissibility of cash pooling agreements

English law provides no express or implied prohibitions on the creation or implementation of cash pooling agreements.

1.2 Types of cash pooling agreement

English law gives considerable freedom of contract, and cash pooling agreements can be constructed as physical pooling or notional pooling.

(a) *Physical cash pooling*

Accounts are opened by the master account holder and the group companies at a bank. A sweep mechanism is agreed whereby, on a regular basis (often daily at a set time), credit balances then held by the group companies are swept into a master account. The sweep can be arranged to sweep all credit balances (zero balancing) or can be set at specific levels (target balancing, which can also be capable of variation from time to time). Accounts held by group companies which are then in debit receive transfers of funds from the master account to reduce or clear the overdraft. Such arrangements give rise to inter-company debts between the relevant group company and the master account holder. Service or other fees may be levied. Interest is generally credited by the bank to the master account and may from there be paid down to group companies, usually proportionately.

(b) *Notional cash pooling*

Accounts are opened by the master account holder and the group companies at a bank. The bank and the group companies agree that the credit and debit balances of each relevant account be notionally consolidated, and interest (and sometimes fees) are paid or charged on the net balance from time to time. To give effect to this, a master account is established to which the consolidated interest is debited or credited. The bank may agree to act on the instructions of the master account holder in the distribution of interest credited to the master account. Save for the crediting or debiting of interest and sometimes fees, usually to the master account alone, the accounts are operated by the group companies as their own accounts under their own control and no physical sweep takes place.

(c) *Common features*

Commonly, the bank requires each participant to indemnify the bank, and/or to provide a guarantee to like effect, against any other participant's default (eg, if a participant becomes insolvent while its balance is in debit), though such liability may be limited to amounts standing to the credit of that participant's own account. The bank is usually given express authority to apply credits of any company against debits of any other (netting and set-off rights). While technically, in the context of a notional cash pooling agreement at least, it may be argued that the need for such indemnities or cross-guarantees should be limited to any fees or interest payable to the bank where there are insufficient funds in the master account, it is rare to see the indemnities or guarantees so limited.

English law has no general restriction or maximum limits as to the amount that may be guaranteed, though a guarantor company's constitution documents will need to be checked and consideration given to whether it is appropriate that shareholder resolutions be passed in addition.

Cash pooling agreements can operate in a multi-currency environment. In such circumstances the various accounts are usually pooled by currency and a master account established for each currency. Foreign exchange controls may operate from time to time or in relation to particular currencies which may need to be taken into account.

Under English law, the relationship between a bank and its customer is one of debtor/creditor.

Almost invariably the relationships created between the master account holder and each group company in a physical cash pooling agreement would be analysed as debtor/creditor relationships as well, but the position should be analysed (and drafted for) in each case.

In a notional cash pooling agreement, there is no physical sweep mechanism, but the arrangements will result in interest and possibly fees being received or incurred by the master account holder at the expense of (or possibly to the benefit of) participant companies. As between themselves, the participants and master account holder should determine how the resulting benefits and costs are attributed and accounted for.

Generally in this chapter, it is assumed that all companies party to the relevant cash pooling agreement are members of the same group of companies and that the relevant agreement is governed by English law. No account is taken of the judicial, administrative and legislative variations encountered in Scotland and Northern Ireland.

1.3 Legal requirements from various perspectives

Cash pooling arrangements are not identified as such by rules of law relating specifically to them in company, banking, insolvency, regulatory or tax law.

However, numerous different legal principles can come into play in the context of any cash pooling agreement and the most significant of these are touched on below.

(a) *Company law*

Although there are no specific requirements in English company law with respect to cash pooling agreements, such agreements constitute a bundle of contractual rights and obligations, the principal elements of which are that a participant will in all probability be lending and borrowing moneys and guaranteeing the obligations of other (group) companies. Each participant company's directors should take into account the relevant general legal and regulatory requirements before the company enters into such arrangements. These include the following.

Directors' duties: The Companies Act 2006 contains a codified statement of the general duties of directors.

English law makes no distinction between executive and non-executive directors. It does, however, recognise, and generally attach liability to, shadow directors (persons in accordance with whose directions or instructions the directors of the company are accustomed to act) in the same way as to other directors. In addition, *de facto* directors (ie, persons who are treated by the company and its directors as directors, but whose particulars have not been filed with the English Companies Registry) will be treated in the same way. English law does not recognise the concept of a supervisory director and English companies have a single board: the board of directors.

The Companies Act 2006 contains seven statutory duties which are owed by the directors to the company (Sections 170(1) and following of the act). In general terms, only the company can enforce these duties although, in certain limited circumstances, the shareholders may bring an action (known as a derivative action) against directors who are in breach. (In a liquidation, the company will be represented by the insolvency practitioner and these duties may be enforced by him on behalf of the company; there are also provisions under the Insolvency Act 1986 enabling a liquidator to pursue directors for misfeasance and breach of duty.) There are seven duties under the Companies Act.

First, a director must act in accordance with the company's constitution and must exercise his powers only for their proper purpose. There are protections for a third party dealing with a company in good faith: the power of the directors to bind the company (or authorise others to do so) is deemed not to be limited by the company's constitution. Moreover, a third party is not bound to enquire whether there are any limitations on the power of the directors. These protections do not, however, affect any liability incurred by the directors by reason of exceeding their powers.

Second, a director must act in the way he considers, in good faith, would be most likely to promote the success of the company for the benefit of its shareholders (which are also called members) as a whole. In so doing, the director must have regard (among other matters) to:

- the likely consequences of any decision in the long term;
- the interests of the company's employees;
- the need to foster the company's business relationships with suppliers, customers and others;

- the impact of the company's operations on the community and the environment;
- the desirability of the company maintaining a reputation for high standards of business conduct; and
- the need to act fairly as between the members of the company.

The duty is subject to any enactment or rule of law requiring directors in certain circumstances to consider or act in the interests of the creditors of the company, and accordingly the duty is displaced when the company is insolvent, and may be modified by an obligation to have regard to the interests of creditors as the company nears insolvency.

Third, a director must exercise independent judgement. The duty will not be infringed by a director acting in accordance with an agreement entered into by the company that restricts the future exercise of the directors' discretion or in a way authorised by the company's constitution.

Fourth, a director must exercise the care, skill and diligence that would be exercised by a reasonably diligent person with both:

- the general knowledge, skill and experience that may reasonably be expected of a person carrying out the functions of the director in relation to the company; and
- the general knowledge, skill and experience that the director actually has.

Fifth, a director must avoid a situation in which he has, or can have, a direct or indirect interest that conflicts, or possibly may conflict, with the interests of the company. The disinterested directors of the company may, however, authorise the conflict by board resolution, provided that certain conditions are met. In the context of a cash pooling agreement, where the participants are a group of companies, the likelihood is that there will be some common directors. Directors should ensure that their determinations as to any particular company within the cash pooling agreement are by reference to the position of that company alone.

Sixth, a director must not accept any benefit from a third party which is conferred because of his being a director, or his doing or not doing anything as a director.

Finally, a director has a duty to declare any interest in a proposed transaction or arrangement with the company.

Maintenance of capital: English law imposes capital maintenance rules on English companies. The rules contain a number of restrictions on public companies not likely to be relevant for cash pooling agreements, but do regulate for all companies – whether public or private – the circumstances in which dividends or distributions may be paid. A company (whether public or private) may make distributions to its members only out of distributable profits (defined and circumscribed in the Companies Act). Additional requirements apply to distributions by a public company (ie, a company which is named as a public limited company or plc in its name, which does not necessarily betoken that its shares are publicly listed or traded on any recognised exchange): the amount of its net assets must be not less than the aggregate of its called-up share capital and its undistributable reserves, and the distribution must not reduce the amount of its net assets to less than that aggregate sum. A distribution made in contravention of the rules is unlawful. Consequently, parties to a cash pooling agreement where moneys are passing between group companies will want to ensure that the status of these transmissions (and their categorisation, which is usually as creating, or constituting repayment of, intra-group loans) is clear so that they are not construed as potentially unlawful distributions.

Corporate governance; risk management; internal control and reporting requirements: Companies (whether incorporated in the United Kingdom or elsewhere) which have a premium listing of equity shares on the Main Market of the London Stock Exchange (ie, the form of listing with more stringent requirements than those applicable to the standard listing on this market) are subject to the 'comply or explain' regime of the UK Corporate Governance Code. The code contains principles of good governance relating to a number of areas, including (in Section C) principles relating to risk management and internal control. The Listing Rules (LR 9.8.7R and LR TR 4) require companies covered by the code to state, in their annual financial reports, whether they have complied with the code and, if not, to explain their reasons for non-compliance. Directors of the relevant category of companies considering entering into a cash pooling agreement should consider the impact of the requirements of the code. The code does not apply to companies with a standard listing of equity shares on the Main Market of the London Stock Exchange or to companies traded on any of the other London exchanges, such as AIM.

Formalities: Cash pooling agreements are contractual arrangements and English law requires, in order for there to be a valid contract, that there be offer, acceptance, consideration and an intention to create legal relations. Cash pooling agreements will usually include guarantees, and guarantees are required under the Statute of Frauds 1677 to be made in writing and signed by or on behalf of the guarantor. The Companies Act also legislates for the manner in which contracts or deeds (as the case may be) are executed.[1] Although not a statutory requirement, guarantees (and indemnities too) are often entered into as deeds. More stringent signatory requirements will apply than for a simple contract, but the use of a deed will avoid any questions regarding the presence or (from the perspective of legal formalities only) sufficiency of consideration. For the protection of the directors of the company giving the guarantee and indemnity, as well as for the benefit of the counterparty, a shareholders' resolution approving the arrangements should be passed. Unless the arrangements give rise to the creation of security, however, there should be no public registry registration requirements. (Banks' rights of set-off would not generally be regarded or framed as security rights requiring registration, even were such rights to constitute security, registration at the English Companies Registry would not be likely to be required by virtue of the Financial Collateral Arrangements (No 2) Regulations 2003.)

(b) ***General contract law***

Cash pooling agreements drafted under English law may rely on protective provisions (depending on the perspective of the draftsmen – usually the bank's lawyers – and often completed and agreed by the customers without the benefit of legal input) designed to protect the bank. As previously noted, participants may be required to provide guarantees and indemnities, but banks may also include express rights of set-off (to bolster bank rights of set-off, a special right recognised as a matter of common law), and flawed asset clauses (clauses which provide that title to a particular right or asset is conditional in some way – for example, that a depositor has no right to its deposit back unless certain liabilities have been discharged).

(c) ***Insolvency law***

The main circumstance where a cash pooling agreement is likely to be reviewed, or possibly challenged, is in the context of the insolvency of one or more parties to it.

English insolvency law – basics and applicable legislation: English insolvency law (excluding laws relating specifically to special categories of company such as banks and insurance undertakings) is encompassed in the following legislation (and, in the context of cross-border matters, in the following order of precedence):

- the EU Insolvency Regulation (1346/2000);
- the Cross-Border Insolvency Regulations 2006 (which represent the UK enactment of the UNCITRAL Model Law on Cross-Border Insolvency); and
- the Insolvency Act 1986.

In a purely domestic (English) context, the Insolvency Act is the principal relevant legislation. The EU Insolvency Regulation and the Cross-Border Insolvency Regulations are important in a cross-border context and are dealt with below in that context.

In addition to the statutory regime, over the years the English courts have developed extra-statutory (common law) principles of comity, whereby English courts will assist foreign courts and their officers, and in the context of insolvency, principles of universality (ie, that there is benefit in one insolvency process and law governing the entire insolvency of any given entity). Where none of the EU Insolvency Regulation, the Cross-Border Insolvency Regulations or the Insolvency Act provides assistance, foreign insolvency officials may consider asking for assistance under these common law principles.

---

1 Deeds differ from contracts mainly in that contracts may be oral (though some types of contract are required to be in writing, such as guarantees), and require, in order to be binding:
- an offer;
- acceptance of that offer;
- that a *quid pro quo*, or consideration, pass from the promisee; and
- the intention to create legal relations.

Where made in writing, the form of execution requires little in the way of formality. Deeds, on the other hand, can bind parties without there being an offer, or acceptance, or the passing of consideration. Deeds must be in writing must make clear that a deed is intended, and must be validly executed and delivered; the execution formalities are thus greater than for any type of contract. Some documents must be made by way of deed, such as land transfers and powers of attorney.

Processes available: The principal insolvency processes generally available in relation to bodies corporate under domestic insolvency legislation are as follows:

- Administration – this is a process which may be used for rehabilitative purposes, but is used more often in terminal situations where ultimately (and sometimes after a sale of the business as a going concern) the company will be liquidated and finally dissolved. One of its main attributes is that it provides the debtor with the benefit of a moratorium on creditor actions.
- Liquidation (also referred to as winding-up) – this is a process whereby assets are realised for the benefit of stakeholders, often by way of break-up rather than through a sale on a going-concern basis, At the end of this process, the company will cease to exist (being dissolved by striking the name from the official register of companies in England). A winding-up can be voluntary (solvent or insolvent) if commenced by appropriate resolutions, or can be compulsory (otherwise known as a winding-up by the court) commenced by a petition to court.

English insolvency processes are not 'debtor-in-possession' processes: Administrations and liquidations (save for some compulsory liquidations where a governmental agency, known as the Official Receiver, will act as liquidator) are run, managed and controlled by licensed insolvency practitioners. As a matter of English law, such practitioners are deemed court officers and therefore the English court has general jurisdiction over them and the processes that they supervise.

Other processes – such as company voluntary arrangements and schemes of arrangement (essentially, consensual compromise arrangements binding on all creditors if a required percentage of them agree) and receivership (a private remedy available to holders of fixed charge security) – exist, but are not dealt with in this chapter.

Broadly, in a cross-border context:

- English companies with a centre of main interests in England would be subject to insolvency proceedings in England, under English law, as 'main' proceedings. 'Secondary' or 'territorial' (using the terminology of the EU Insolvency Regulation) or 'non-main' (using the terminology of the Cross-Border Insolvency Regulations) proceedings might be commenced elsewhere if appropriate under local laws;
- English companies with a centre of main interests other than in England would usually be subjected to main proceedings in, and under the laws of, the state where the centre of main interests is located. Secondary or territorial, or non-main, proceedings might be started in England under English law in certain conditions, and recognition of the validity and effect of the foreign main proceedings may also be granted (either separately or with an English insolvency process co-existing). Where the foreign proceedings are the main proceedings, local (English) secondary or non-main proceedings would be limited to substantive winding-up proceedings relating to local assets;
- foreign incorporated companies with their centre of main interests in England can be subjected to English insolvency processes, and English insolvency law would then be applied; and

- foreign companies with their centre of main interests other than in England can be the subject of English law compulsory (but not voluntary) winding-up. Usually, main proceedings would be commenced elsewhere and the English proceedings would be territorial, secondary or non-main.

Banks: Banks are subject to special rules in the context of English insolvency law. These are complex, and detailed analysis is beyond the scope of this chapter. There are different rules for English banks (banks formed and registered in the United Kingdom), banks incorporated within the European Economic Area and banks incorporated elsewhere. Wherever incorporated, credit institutions are excluded from the ambit of the EU Insolvency Regulation and the Cross-Border Insolvency Regulations.

Principles of English insolvency law which may be relevant in the context of a cash pooling agreement: The following principles of English law will be among those taken into account in any insolvency which applies English law:

- Creditors of a company in an insolvency process should be paid *pari passu* (equally and rateably), unless they are secured or have preferential status as a matter of law. The obligations to pay creditors are enshrined in the Insolvency Act (Section 127) and in case law (*British Eagle*). Provisions that subvert this rule will be struck down.
- English law recognises the concept of trusts and equity. Where an asset is held on trust for one party by another, the relevant assets will fall outside the estate of the insolvent and an insolvency official dealing with the estate will be bound to account for the asset to the beneficiary of the trust. That asset will therefore not be available for distribution to creditors of the trustee/debtor. For this reason, any accounts operated by any group company on any form of trust basis should be excluded from any cash pooling agreement (and a bank may require warranties from participants to this effect). The relationships created between participants in a cash pooling agreement will almost invariably give rise to inter-company debt positions and not trust arrangements.
- English law has mandatory rules of set-off applicable in insolvency (though not necessarily to the exclusion of other contractually agreed set-off rights). These provide that mutual debts and dealings between two companies prior to the insolvency be offset and only the balance due from one to the other then be payable. The provisions are set out in the Insolvency Rules 1986, in Rules 2.85 and following (for administrations) and 4.90 (for liquidations). There is extensive case law on mutuality in this context and there are some exclusions to prevent trading in debts prior to insolvency to obtain an unfair advantage. Some practical effects of set-off are pointed out in the discussion under section 2.3 (a) below.
- English law provides that transactions at an undervalue and preferences may be set aside if they are entered into within certain periods before the onset of insolvency; the discussion under section 2.3 (a) below gives further detail on these topics. Accordingly, in the context of a cash pooling agreement, where

one group company goes into insolvency, payments made or the reduction of inter-company loans previously effected by netting and set-off, or pooling, under the agreement may be the subject of review to determine whether the agreement has given rise to preferences or transactions at an undervalue. Questions arising from this can be very complex.

- English law has no general principle allowing or requiring groups of companies, or their assets and liabilities, to be dealt with in any insolvency process as one amorphous whole.
- English law does not (unlike the position in some other jurisdictions) generally prohibit the exercise of contractual termination rights on an insolvency. Termination rights which go beyond mere termination and have the effect of depriving a company of its assets upon its insolvency may be subject to challenge, however, though this is unlikely to be relevant in a cash pooling agreement.

(d) *Banking/regulatory law*

Anti-money laundering: Account establishment processes typically raise 'know-your-customer' and anti-money laundering issues. The United Kingdom has implemented the EU Third Money Laundering Directive in the Money Laundering Regulations 2007. Proposals for a Fourth Money Laundering Directive are likely to appear in Autumn 2012, following the European Commission's review of the implementation of the Third Directive. Different anti-money laundering and know-your-customer arrangements will apply in different countries. The Money Laundering Regulations require identification of beneficial owners in certain circumstances. Where a global cash pooling agreement is to be put in place, it would be practical to adopt a single standard approach. It is generally considered that the EU regime is the highest common denominator and an approach which provides 'know-your- customer' and anti-money laundering information to EU standards (ie, Money Laundering Regulations standards) ought to satisfy global banks.

Financial Services and Markets Act 2000: The Financial Services and Markets Act is the principal legislation in the United Kingdom governing bank establishment and operation. It is heavily influenced by EU directives, many of which are implemented under the Financial Services and Markets Act or statutory instruments made under it.

In a physical cash pooling agreement involving cash sweeps resulting in inter-group company loan balances, circumstances may arise in which it might be argued that one member of a group is accepting deposits from other companies within the cash pooling agreement. Under Article 5 of the Financial Services and Markets Act (Regulated Activities) Order 2001, accepting deposits is a regulated activity. Performing regulated activities without authorisation constitutes a criminal offence, unless for some reason the test is not met or an exclusion is available. Under Article 6 of the order (exclusions), sums "paid by one company to another at a time when both are members of the same group or when the same individual is a majority shareholder controller of both of them" will be excluded. Therefore, when setting up physical cash pooling agreements, attention ought to be paid to group structures to ensure that only group companies (as above) are involved. If the group exclusion in Article 6 of the order is not available, there may be other, more difficult arguments available which are beyond the scope of this chapter.

This deposit-taking issue does not seem to arise in the case of notional cash pooling because no physical transfer of moneys takes place.

Cash management and payment services: Cash pooling agreements may be arranged alongside a number of other banking products and services, including hedging services and custody services. One area of services which has relatively recently become regulated for the first time is that of payment services. The EU Payment Services Directive (2007/64/EC) was implemented with effect from November 1 2009 in the United Kingdom by the Payment Services Regulations 2009 (SI 2009/209). The regime falls outside the Financial Services and Markets Act, but the Financial Services Authority is the competent authority for regulated payment services activities in the United Kingdom.

Where banks provide money remittance, cash transfer, electronic payment facilities and similar services related to payment accounts, they will usually be caught by the Payment Services Regulations. Although banks did not need to apply for authorisation as payment institutions (where they were already authorised as deposit-taking banks), they did become subject to some detailed conduct of business obligations. In relation to cash pooling agreements, it is likely that a corporate putting cash pooling in place will fall outside of the more consumer-focused conduct of business aspects of the Payment Services Regulations. As such, it is open to the bank to contract out by agreement with its customer if the customer is not a consumer, micro-enterprise (an entity employing fewer than 10 persons and with a turnover of less than €2 million) or a charity. If banks deal with both consumers and corporates within the same division, they may decide not to opt out at all on the basis that it is more straightforward for them to operate a single Payment Services Regulations-compliant approach.

Corporates provided with payment services will typically be provided with an annex or schedule to their bank mandate documentation containing Payment Services Regulations-compliant disclosures and service levels. One interesting aspect of the Payment Services Regulations is that they include mandatory liability provisions on payment services providers (eg, Regulation 61 on a payment service provider's liability for unauthorised payment transactions and Regulation 76 on non-execution or defective execution of payment transactions initiated by the payee). Attempts to exclude liability for such provisions contractually will fail.

Regulatory capital requirements: There are a number of consequences arising from a bank's decision to offer cash pooling agreements which impact on bank capital adequacy, liquidity requirements and risk management. These requirements may in turn impact on the availability of cash pooling agreements and the pricing at which they may be offered.

Broadly, from January 1 2007, Basel II implemented changes to the way in which regulatory capital had to be calculated. In the United Kingdom, implementation of Basel II was through changes to the Financial Services Authority's Prudential Sourcebooks, BIPRU and GENPRU.

Whereas Basel I required risk weightings of 100% on all balance-sheet exposures, Basel II provided banks with greater flexibility where they were in a position to assess the credit quality of the counterparty. Using the basic standardised approach to credit risk assessment under Basel II (and BIPRU in the United Kingdom), risk weights are assessed on the basis of external ratings. Unrated corporates have 100% risk weights, but external ratings can lead to lower risk weightings and hence to lower capital requirements for banks. In addition, BIPRU 5 allows banks to carry out on-balance sheet netting, and thus for net customer account balances to determine the associated bank capital requirement, provided that the bank ensures that exposures are properly monitored and (through legal opinions) that the netting arrangements are legally effective and enforceable in all relevant jurisdictions.

As discussed above, banks offering cash pooling are likely to require cross-guarantees or netting and set-off agreements from all participants. In the event that one company in a group becomes insolvent, these should enable the bank to recover against other group companies on a joint and several basis. The impact in terms of regulatory capital is likely, therefore, to be the same for both notional and physical cash pooling agreements – if the bank is able to net the positions across the participant group, the bank will be able to calculate its regulatory capital on the basis of a lower (ie, net) exposure.

With the advent of Basel III over the next few years, the expectation is that many banks will be required to increase their regulatory capital. Although the Basel II provisions and BIPRU 5 provisions do not seem likely to be affected (and so balance-sheet netting will still be effective potentially to reduce capital requirements), changes to the counterparty credit risk framework will likely see banks having to improve substantially their ability to measure exposure.

In addition, new liquidity requirements under Basel III will likely impact on banks offering cash pooling agreements. A new liquidity-coverage ratio will require banks to have up to 30 days' liquidity to withstand a 30 day net cash outflow. Basel III does not detail liquidity coverage ratios, but it is expected that measures will be adopted which mean that liquidity coverage ratios for bank and non-public debt will be treated less favourably.

Overall, the impact of Basel III could result in higher cost and lower availability. It may also mean that banks are more keen to offer their own money market fund alternatives to corporate treasurers (avoiding any capital requirement on the bank).

(e) *Tax law*

The relevant tax issues will depend to some extent on the type of cash pooling used. In particular, a physical cash pooling agreement may create an intra-group loan relationship subject to very detailed UK tax legislation.

Broadly, the main tax implications are as follows:

- Withholding tax may need to be applied on intra-group interest payments, though it is likely that the group will be able to benefit from a reduction/elimination of this under a double tax treaty. Where interest is paid to a UK bank, there is no withholding tax.

- Her Majesty's Revenue and Customs (HMRC), the UK revenue authority, is increasingly concerned that a master account holder may be thinly capitalised and unable to substantiate the return on capital that it earns. At the same time, group members that bear the credit risk receive low interest returns. It is possible to enter into advance thin capitalisation agreements with HMRC.
- The UK debt cap rules prevent excessive interest deductions in the United Kingdom in respect of excessive debt owed by UK members of a large group. To determine the disallowed amount, a comparison is made between the net borrowing costs of the UK members of the group and the gross borrowing costs of the group as a whole. The worldwide debt cap legislation contains a number of exclusions for particular types of company, including financial service companies and, on an elect-out basis, group treasury companies. Most large groups will have a group treasury company operating a similar function to that of a bank – managing cash and making loans and investments. The activities of this type of company would not fit in well with these rules, so the legislation allows the company to exclude its interest and expenses from the figures of the overall group.
- Group companies must take an arm's-length approach to costs of the transactions, such as the appropriate interest rate to be applied to intra-group balances, how any guarantee is priced and how the master account holder is remunerated. These values are not always easy to determine, particularly given the credit risk of the loans, but it is possible to enter into advance pricing agreements with HMRC. Any transfer pricing decisions must be adequately documented.
- It is unlikely that a UK group treasury company would, merely by holding and operating the master account, be deemed to have a taxable permanent establishment in the United Kingdom, but groups should be aware of the risk.
- Any UK member of the group must notify HMRC of the arrangement in order to fall outside the scope of the international movement of capital reporting obligations.

2. Specific questions

2.1 Perspective A: corporate group

(a) Liability of group company and/or master account holder directors in the event of insolvency of a group company

English law recognises the principle of separate legal personality for companies. Directors will attract potential liability in respect only of the group company (or companies) of which they are directors, shadow directors or *de facto* directors. The directors of the troubled company could have potential liability under English company law provisions (see below in relation to insolvency law provisions) only if they were in breach of their duties as directors, failed to uphold the capital maintenance requirements in breach of their duties or did not comply with the 'comply or explain' regime of the Corporate Governance Code (if applicable), all as described in section 1.4 above.

If the distressed group company is incorporated in a foreign law jurisdiction, the English company law provisions relating to directors' duties and capital maintenance will not apply, although the company may still be subject to the 'comply or explain' regime of the Corporate Governance Code, if applicable.

In practical terms, though English law does provide circumstances where a company may be regarded as a sham and the corporate veil pierced, examples of this are very rare indeed. Provided that the parties were all solvent at the time that the cash pooling agreement was commenced, due consideration was given to the agreement at its inception, and the resulting effects and incidents of the agreement (eg, any guarantees and resulting intra-group indebtedness issues) were considered and duly approved by the directors, it is unlikely that issues will later arise in respect of corporate law formality or capital maintenance issues, or as to whether the directors were in breach of their duties.

Should the relevant company's distress lead to the commencement of English insolvency law proceedings, personal liability can accrue to the directors of a company under the Insolvency Act 1986 where there has been 'wrongful trading'. If a company goes into an insolvent liquidation and at some time before then the directors knew or ought reasonably to have concluded that there was no reasonable prospect of avoiding the insolvency, they may be made liable to contribute to the assets of the company. A director will have a defence if, after having concluded that the insolvency was not reasonably avoidable (or after he ought to have come to that conclusion), he takes all appropriate steps to minimise potential losses to creditors. Allowing the continuation of a cash pooling agreement (and consequent movement in inter-company balances) during the relevant period may be a factor that influences losses, and may affect any quantum of liability under this head. At the onset of any distress within the group, each participant in the cash pooling agreement would be well advised to consider the implications for itself.

As would be expected, should fraud be involved in any aspect of a company's trading or affairs, a raft of additional and separate offences and remedies may apply; these are not considered in this chapter.

English law does not (with minor exclusions in relation to money laundering and financial sanctions legislation) generally discriminate in relation to the identity or location of creditors or contractual counterparties that have claims against companies in English insolvency proceedings, so the location or place of incorporation of the bank is unlikely to be of relevance.

(b) Liability of directors of the group company and/or the master account holder in the event of insolvency of the master account holder

This is dealt with in the discussion under paragraph (a) above.

(c) *Liability of group companies in the event of insolvency of the master account holder*

There is no general principle whereby, on the insolvency of one company (the first company), another group company (the second company) can be made liable for the defaults of the first company or (in the absence of an appropriately crafted and approved arrangement such as an English law scheme of arrangement or company voluntary arrangement to which all relevant companies are party) whereby assets of a group of companies are pooled together and applied for the benefit of creditors of more than one entity. Thus, if the master account holder were to go into insolvency, its creditors would themselves generally have no direct right of action against a participant company. However, there are exceptions:

- If a participant company is found to be a shadow director or *de facto* director of the master account holder, under English law there are circumstances whereby directors can be made personally liable for some or all of the debts of the master account holder (for wrongful trading); and where directors can be made liable, generally so too can shadow directors and *de facto* directors. Shadow directorship and wrongful trading are dealt with in more detail in the discussion in section 2.2 (b) below. Any claims under this head would, however, be made by the liquidator of the master account holder; no rights under this head are given directly to creditors of the master account holder.
- If a participant company had itself incurred liability direct to the relevant creditor of the master account holder – for example, by way of guarantee – or (with or without a payment covenant) had granted security in respect of the relevant obligations, such creditor would itself have a claim under that guarantee, covenant or security.

The above assumes an English law insolvency of the master account holder. If that company were placed into a foreign insolvency, claims against it would be governed by the applicable law of the insolvency. Claims by creditors of the master account holder against entities (eg, a participating company) that are not in an insolvency process would be governed by normal litigation principles (including as to the appropriate forum).

(d) *Liability of the master account holder in the event of insolvency of a group company*

See paragraph (c) above, which applies equally here from the perspective of an insolvency of the master account holder (though clearly there must be a greater likelihood that the master account holder would be seen to be a shadow director of a participating company than vice versa). Specifically, there is no general principle that makes a parent entity liable for the financial liabilities of its subsidiaries or implements a pooling of group assets and liabilities.

2.2 Perspective B: bank

(a) *Banking requirements*

Banking requirements are discussed in section 1.4.

(b) *Liability of the bank in the event of insolvency of the master account holder or of a group company*

There is no principle of English law that, of itself, would render the bank liable to creditors of the master account holder or of a participating group company, save in the possible following circumstances:

- The bank is regarded as a shadow director or *de facto* director of master account holder or of a group company in circumstances where directors of either of those companies have been found liable for the debts of the company (the company having gone into liquidation in an English liquidation process). English insolvency law provides that directors can be made liable to contribute to the assets of a company where they are found liable for wrongful trading under Section 214 of the Insolvency Act 1986. This provides that where a company goes into liquidation and at some time before then the directors knew or ought reasonably to have concluded that there was no reasonable prospect of avoiding the insolvency, then they may be made liable personally to contribute to the assets of the company. Such liability may attach to *de facto* directors (persons who are regarded as directors but whose details have never been registered as such at the English Registrar of Companies) or shadow directors (persons in accordance with whose instructions or directions the directors are accustomed to act). If the banking relationship is a usual relationship, these provisions would not apply. Shadow directors and *de facto* directors can be liable for a number of other liabilities in the same way as directors. It is unlikely that any of these would apply in the absence of unusual circumstances, and they are not discussed further here. Any claim based on wrongful trading/shadow directorship would be a claim brought by a liquidator in an insolvent liquidation (and no other process), and is not a claim open to third parties to bring directly. A liquidator would (assuming that funds are available and there is an appropriate likelihood of success) be the only person able to bring the claim. The location or residence of the creditor is of no relevance.
- The bank has issued references or by its conduct led third parties to believe that it was somehow underwriting the relevant liabilities. Banks are now very circumspect in references or representations that they are willing to give, and it would be most unusual for the bank to have exposed itself to liability under this head.
- The bank has issued guarantees, assurances of payment, letters of credit or other instruments under which it has itself taken on liability. This is mentioned for completeness only, as clearly these would constitute a liability for the bank as principal and not constitute liability for the account holder's debts.

The above assumes that English law is applicable: any claim by the third party against the bank would need to be analysed to see what law might apply. If the master account holder or the participating company is located abroad, then whether there is a cause for commercial litigation by the creditor against the bank may not necessarily be a matter of English law; the location of the bank, the creditor and any other relevant factors would need to be taken into account.

2.3 Insolvency

(a) *Cash pooling agreements from the insolvency practitioner's perspective*

In the following references to there being an English insolvency official are taken to predicate an English insolvency process.

In considering the various scenarios outlined below, unless otherwise indicated, the analysis for a notional cash pooling agreement is the same as for a physical cash pooling agreement. The main practical difference will be that in physical cash pooling the balances held by a participating company are more likely to be nil, depending on the nature and timing of the sweep, than in notional cash pooling.

Insolvency of the bank: Credit balances represent a debt owed by the bank to the master account holder (in respect of that company's credit balances) and a participating company (in respect of its credit balances). If the master account holder also has debit balances, the credits and debits will (assuming that the debts are mutual) be offset against each other and only the net amount will be due (either way). The same goes for a participating company.

The master account holder and a participating company may each hold more than one account, and some may be in credit and some in debit. This position is more likely to be encountered in a notional cash pooling agreement than in physical cash pooling (because in notional cash pooling actual balances are left untouched, whereas in a physical cash pooling balances are – at least in zero balancing cash pooling agreements – likely to be cleared down on a regular basis and there may not, at the time of insolvency, be a nexus of credits and debits).

The concern from the master account holder's and the participating company's perspective will be that if the bank goes into insolvency, not only will they lose some or all of their credit balances, but the question will arise as to whether debit balances can be offset against the credit balances. If they cannot be offset, the companies may have to pay the amount of the debit balances as well, without taking into account the credit balances. The issue can be demonstrated by considering the position where one participating company (C1) holds (only) credit balances and a second participating company (C2) holds (only) debit balances at the date of the commencement of the insolvency. In that circumstance, the question will arise as to whether C2 can offset its liability to the bank against the credit balance held by C1. Whether set-off is available to C2 (under English law) will depend on detailed construction of the contractual terms of the cash pooling agreement and analysis of the true relationship between the parties, as well as English principles of mandatory set-off. The issue has been the subject of judicial consideration in England (*Re BCCI No 8* in 1998 and *MS Fashions v BCCI* in 1993). In these cases relating to BCCI, the failed bank, depositors wanted to have their deposits offset against debts owed to BCCI by a different company. In *MS Fashions*, the depositor was expressed as a 'principal debtor' (along with the other company), and accordingly set-off was allowed. This of course meant that the other company had no further debt to pay to BCCI to the extent of the amount of the deposit. In *BCCI No 8*, on the other hand, the depositor was not expressed as (primarily or otherwise) liable for the third party's debt; it had merely granted security to BCCI for it over the deposit. Accordingly (and perhaps harshly), the debt owed by BCCI to the depositor was not matched by any debt owed by the depositor to BCCI and there were therefore no mutual claims which could give rise to statutory set-off. As a result, in this case the depositor lost its deposit (but had a claim in the liquidation of the bank as a result) and, because the amount of the deposit was not offset against the principal obligor's debt, the principal obligor had to pay its debt to BCCI quite separately out of its own, and other, resources.

Foreign banks are likely to be put into a process under their domestic laws and the relevant insolvency official may then make applications for recognition to local courts in other jurisdictions (eg, England) for recognition of the process.

If the bank is subject to a foreign insolvency process, the process of determining the status of claims in respect of credit balances will be governed by the applicable law of the insolvency; usually, that will be the law of the jurisdiction under which the insolvency official was appointed. In some circumstances a foreign insolvency official will want or require English judicial recognition of his status and of the applicability in England of such insolvency laws, and machinery is available, depending on the circumstances, to enable English courts to provide that support (which may include giving effect to any applicable moratorium or stay on actions against assets situated in England). Even where the bank's centre of main interests is within the European Union, the relevant machinery is likely to be under general laws of comity. It is unlikely that the EU Insolvency Regulation or the Cross-Border Insolvency Regulations will apply, as both exclude from their ambit of operation the insolvency of credit institutions. Section 426 of the Insolvency Act 1986, which provides that courts in the United Kingdom shall cooperate with courts in any other part of the United Kingdom and certain other specified territories (generally members or former members of the Commonwealth) may apply.

Insolvency of the master account holder: English law contemplates a number of different insolvency processes. Each process has different specific rules of notification and consultation with creditors, and in addition English insolvency officials are licensed by various regulatory authorities and expected to adhere to the rules of their licensing body. They are also officers of the English courts and have duties accordingly. Their powers and functions are circumscribed broadly (and without detailed codification) by statute and regulation, and statute also provides remedies for their breach.

The duties of the insolvency official are not constrained or affected by the location of creditors. If the master account holder and participating companies are (after application of any applicable set-off or netting arrangement) creditors, they should be sent notices and other communications just as local creditors. If they are (after operation of any applicable set-off or netting arrangement) debtors, they may be pursued in the name of the bank, which will act through the insolvency official (who, in foreign territories, may require local court assistance in recognising his authority).

English law does not, in the insolvency of banks, recognise any priority for customers' claims relating to their deposits as against other categories or types of creditor. There is a statutory scheme (the Financial Services Compensation Scheme) which provides some protection for some depositors where their bank fails, but in relation to corporate depositors, only smaller companies (as defined in Section 382 of the Companies Act 2006) will be covered, and then in an amount capped at £85,000.

If the master account holder goes into insolvency, the credit balance remains an asset of that company and its powers to deal with it remain vested in it acting through its insolvency official. If the bank is situated abroad, local advice may be necessary to determine whether the applicable insolvency practitioner's authority will be recognised by the bank and local court recognition proceedings may be necessary. Where the bank is an English bank or operated though an English branch, upon the bank becoming aware of master account holder's insolvency or imminent insolvency (eg, becoming aware that a creditor has issued a winding-up petition against the company), the bank is likely to freeze any credit accounts (and usually it will have contractual authority to do this) in England until:

- (if the insolvency is a compulsory winding-up) a court order, known as a validating order is made under Section 127 of the Insolvency Act 1986, which allows or requires the account to be unfrozen; or
- the later of:
  - the bank's having satisfied itself that no accounts against which it may exercise rights of set-off are in debit (in which case it may wish to exercise rights of set-off before remitting any balance); and
  - the company's having been placed into liquidation or administration and instructions for transfer have been received by a duly appointed insolvency official.

The same principles apply as in the case of an English insolvency official where a foreign insolvency official is appointed, save that the effect of the appointment of the foreign insolvency official (which predicates a foreign insolvency process) will be a matter of the relevant foreign law, and (consequently) the status of the foreign insolvency official, and the effect of the relevant process into which it has been placed, may not be understood by the bank, in which case the insolvency official may require UK court assistance or a recognition order, or the commencement of an English (possibly secondary or non-main) insolvency process.

With regards to the insolvency official's obligations to the bank and participating companies, please see the observations above regarding obligations in the event of the bank's insolvency (though the Financial Services Compensation Scheme will be an irrelevance in the insolvency of the master account holder). The master account holder could be either a debtor or creditor of the bank and/or participating companies depending on the circumstances. Mandatory set-off will be applied and the bank may be entitled to contractual or banker's rights of set-off or other contractual netting arrangements under the cash pooling agreement, or to enforce guarantees given by participating companies. The master account holder will be entitled to any residual credit balances held by the bank or to discharge any liability to the bank. Liabilities to the bank may be either secured or unsecured. Claims against participating companies will be capable of being pursued in the ordinary course. Claims by participating companies against the master account holder will, if they are unsecured claims, be proved as debts in the insolvency (subject to any restriction placed on a participating company by the terms of any guarantee that it has given to the bank; see below). If a participating company holds security for any claims, its position will be different and its claims as a secured creditor will rank largely or entirely ahead of unsecured creditors.

Under the cash pooling agreement the master account holder and a participating company may each have guaranteed the obligations of the other to the bank (though as mentioned above, the guarantee may have been limited to the extent of credit balances held at the bank). The participating company may have agreed that some or all of its claims against the master account holder will not be pursued until any amounts owed by the master account holder to the bank have been paid in full. There may also be suspense clauses, which entitle a creditor with claims against multiple parties to place any recoveries into a suspense account, so that repayment of the relevant debt is technically not then made, enabling the creditor to maximise claims against other debtors before applying the amounts received against the debt (though recovery is limited overall to the amount of the debt). The operation and effect of suspense clauses may be affected by mandatory set-off requirements of English law where a formal insolvency has begun (see *MS Fashions v BCCI* in 1993).

Can the (English or foreign) insolvency official set aside transfers made to a participating group company before the onset of the master account holder's insolvency?: Transfers made by a company to another person may, where English law applies to the insolvency, fall into the ambit of one or more of the following:

- Transaction at an undervalue – Sections 238 and following of the Insolvency Act 1986 provide that a transaction at an undervalue (ie, where the value to the transferor of what, if anything, is received in return for the transfer is significantly less than the worth of what is transferred by it) may be set aside, or subject to other appropriate court order, if the transferor (here the master account holder) goes into liquidation or administration within two years of that transaction. There is a statutory 'good faith' defence. The transaction can be set aside under these provisions if the transferor (the master account holder) was insolvent (on a cash-flow or net-assets basis) at the time of the transfer, but this requirement is rebuttably presumed satisfied where the transferee (here, the participating company) is a connected person (it would be expected that the participating company and the master account holder would be connected if they are participants in the same cash pooling agreement);
- Preference – Sections 239 and following of the Insolvency Act provide that where a company (here, the master account holder) goes into liquidation or administration and within a period (two years for connected persons) before then, the company has done anything which has the effect of putting a

creditor (eg, a participating company) into a better position than it would have been otherwise in the event of the company's insolvency, the transaction can be set aside as a preference by the company (here the master account holder). There must be a desire to produce the preference effect for the transaction to be capable of being attacked under this provision, but that desire is rebuttably presumed where the parties are connected.

- There are also provisions (Sections 423 and following of the Insolvency Act) designed to deal with (in effect) fraudulent transfers at an undervalue designed to put assets beyond the reach of creditors. These provisions are somewhat unusual, as they allow action to be taken not only by an administrator or liquidator, but also in some cases by any victim. The 'look-back' period is theoretically unlimited.

Insolvency of a participating group company: The issues and answers above in relation to the master account holder are equally applicable in relation to insolvency of a participating company. The company's relationships and claims against, or by the master account holder (or indeed other group companies) are therefore as set out in the section on insolvency of the master account holder above (with party references to the master account holder and the participating company being reversed and read and construed accordingly).

(b) Special rules as regards creditors of other parties to the cash pooling agreement

An insolvency official appointed to any of the bank, the master account holder or a participating group company has no direct obligations or duties other than to the creditors of the company over which he is appointed. Thus, for example, an administrator of the bank has obligations to the master account holder and the participating companies (if they are creditors of the bank) but has no direct obligations to creditors of those companies.

(c) Dissolution/termination of the cash pooling agreement in the event of liquidation of the master account holder or of a group company

There is no preclusion on the exercise of contractual termination rights under English law, even during the existence of insolvency proceedings. Practically, any insolvency official appointed over the master account holder or a group company will take steps as soon as appointed to prevent further moneys being credited to bank accounts where the receiving bank might exercise rights of set-off (also not precluded), since the insolvency official will want to ensure that the bank does not get given an inadvertent advantage by the ability to reduce its own exposure by set-off at the expense of other creditors. The possible practical effect of that may be that the bank may freeze the bank accounts of other members of a cash pooling agreement, or suspend or terminate the cash pooling agreements (hopefully with contractual provisions allowing it to do so), while the bank seeks to work out its own possible exposure.

2.4 Perspective D: regulatory

Please see the banking/regulatory law section of the discussion in section 1.4 above.

2.5 Perspective E: tax authority

See the tax law section of the discussion in section 1.4 above.

Finland

Pekka Jaatinen
Anna-Kaisa Remes
Castrén & Snellman Attorneys Ltd

---

1. Introduction

1.1 Admissibility of cash pooling agreements

Cash pooling agreements are permitted in Finland, regardless of whether the arrangement is notional or physical or whether the participants are Finnish or foreign. The only difference regarding foreign participants is that the Bank of Finland requires reporting on any cash pooling agreements between residents and non-residents.

1.1 Types of cash pooling agreement

In terms of products and services, the major Finnish banks offer a wide variety of cash pooling alternatives. The most common is single legal account pooling, in which all physical payments are channelled through one external bank account, usually held by the parent company or a group treasury company. Other group companies participating in the arrangement have individual virtual reference accounts (transaction accounts). The group account holder authorises the other group companies to deposit assets into and withdraw assets from the group account through these transaction accounts. In single legal account pooling, the arrangement is viewed as though each group company had its own physical account, even though the transaction accounts are not real bank accounts in a legal sense. Since the group account holder alone has a physical bank account (which the transaction accounts merely adjust), the group account holder is legally the only debtor towards the bank. The balance of an individual transaction account reflects the debt relationship between the group account holder and the transaction account holder. Single legal account pooling is a simple form of cash pooling, as it provides for one net balance for all participants and allows for the use of a collective credit limit for all group companies.

Zero balancing is another form of cash pooling used in Finland. In contrast to single legal account pooling, in zero balancing every participant has a physical bank account with the bank. One of the bank accounts is the top account and the rest are considered sub-accounts. At the end of each day, the sub-accounts are zero-balanced against the top account, so that their net balance will be zero. This form of cash pooling is most commonly used in cross-border arrangements and is particularly popular when central European countries are involved. Conversely, zero-balancing is rare in arrangements between Finnish and Nordic companies.

For purely domestic arrangements, all major Finnish banks can also offer notional cash pooling, as long as each participant has its own individual account with the bank. Instead of being zero-balanced, the assets stay in the individual accounts. The bank calculates the interest for the assets by notionally netting the balances of all participating accounts. In order to avoid the commingling of funds, the banks offer additional solutions such as interest enhancement, interest apportionment and pure interest netting.

Finnish banks also offer a form of cash pooling called top sweeping, which is mainly used in cross-border transactions. In top sweeping, funds are transferred between the top account and sub-accounts in accordance with different pre-determined sweeping parameters. Whenever these parameters are realised, a transfer is triggered. In cross-border arrangements, the major Finnish banks offer this solution in association with their foreign cooperation banks.

1.2 Legal requirements from various perspectives

There is no specific legislation concerning cash pooling agreements in Finland. Cash pooling transactions between group companies are considered to be intercompany loans. Thus, a group company transferring funds to the master account is a creditor to the master account holder, and a group company withdrawing funds from the master account is a debtor.

As previously mentioned, the Bank of Finland requires reporting on cash pooling transactions between residents and non-residents. Its authority in this respect is based on the Bank of Finland Act (214/1998) and EU Regulation 2533/98 (as amended by EU Regulation 951/2009) on the collection of statistical information by the European Central Bank (ECB). Data on foreign assets and liabilities is gathered monthly from select Finnish resident companies, financial institutions and insurance institutions, as well as from central and local government. The reporting duty concerns only cross-border cash pooling transactions, because the Bank of Finland requires reporting only on loan transactions between residents and non-residents.

The Bank of Finland collects monthly payment statistics by issuing questionnaires to roughly 500 resident companies, which are required every month to inform the bank of their foreign assets and liabilities. All other resident companies provide information once a year, with the exception of a few that report every quarter. In a group of companies, each company will usually submit its own report.

Furthermore, the Bank of Finland can oblige any entity to supply information for the compilation of balance of payments statistics, and can fine any that does not comply. In addition, the ECB has the power to impose sanctions on companies that infringe its reporting obligations – for example, by providing incorrect or incomplete information, or impeding the collection or verification of information. Such infringements incur a fine of up to €200,000.

Corporate law requirements: The granting of loans in favour of a group company (or another closely related person) is governed by the general principles of the Limited Liability Companies Act (624/2006). There are no express provisions on the acceptability of such credit arrangements in the act, except that the principal terms of the debt must appear in the company's annual accounts.

Since no express provisions exist, the acceptability of any cash pooling agreement depends on the general principles and rules of the Companies Act – that is, the principle of corporate benefit, the rules on creditor protection and the specific prohibition against financing the acquisition of a company's own shares.

The principle of corporate benefit consists of two main elements. First, the purpose of the company is to generate profits to the shareholders (Chapter 1(5) of the Companies Act). Second, the management of the company has a duty to act with due care and promote the interests of the company (Chapter 1(8) of the Companies Act). Corporate benefit is also expressed in Chapter 13(1)(3) of the Companies Act, which states that a transaction that reduces the assets of the company or increases its liabilities without a sound business reason shall constitute an unlawful distribution of assets. Overall, a cash pooling agreement is not acceptable if it contradicts the principle of corporate benefit.

Whether a sound business reason exists for a cash pooling agreement is assessed on the basis of the information available at the time when the funds are transferred to the cash pool – mainly that contained in the latest financial statement. However, changes in the company's financial position must be taken into account even after the conclusion of the financial statements. Whether the transaction subsequently proves to be unprofitable to the subsidiary is not relevant. The key point is whether the company's management should have known at the time of granting the loan that it was not in the interests of the subsidiary.

Corporate benefit must be taken into account in all corporate operations that aim to maximise profits. A loan arrangement that takes the form of cash pooling must conform to this aim. The Companies Act states that granting loans or securities in favour of a company's inner circle is not usually in the company's interests. It may, however, be acceptable if it benefits the company – for example, by creating future financing possibilities or reorganising the financing of the group. Since cash pooling can achieve reduced financing costs, more efficient use of liquid assets and enhanced financing opportunities, it usually complies with the principle of corporate benefit. Cash pooling is widely used in Finland – and in the government's proposed revision of the Companies Act, is specifically mentioned as an example of an inter-company loan that can generally be considered acceptable.

With regard to the principle of corporate benefit, there is no concept of group interest in Finnish law. Every group company should act for its own benefit, and not for the benefit of the group as a whole. The cash pooling agreement must thus benefit every participant involved in the arrangement. When considering corporate benefit for an individual company, the assessment should focus on the interests of that company alone. Those of the parent company or other group companies are irrelevant.

The principle of corporate benefit can be violated when one company enters into in a cash pooling agreement with another which is financially unstable. Cash pooling may contradict the solvent company's interests, particularly if it was known at the time of the transfer that the other participant could not pay back the loan.

Technically, the principle of corporate benefit can be disregarded by unanimous decision of the company's shareholders. If not specifically prohibited in the articles of association, the shareholders can unanimously decide to distribute assets even if this would not seem to be in the company's interest. This would enable the company to participate in a cash pooling agreement in a situation where the corporate benefit requirement was not met. The only limitations on such an act are the amount of the company's unrestricted equity and the rules governing creditor protection, since not even a unanimous shareholders' decision can jeopardise the company's solvency. Nonetheless, such arrangements bear the risk that the company's creditors would consider the loan transactions to be unlawful, as it lacked a sound business reason. This could lead to the company and all or any members of the management (ie, members of the board directors, the managing director or members of the supervisory board) being held liable for any damages. Therefore, engaging in a cash pooling agreement is not recommended if it is not beneficial to the company.

Protection of creditors is the second relevant general principle from the Companies Act that applies to cash pooling. It states that a company may not distribute assets in an amount that exceeds its unrestricted equity reserves, less the assets that are to be left undistributed under the articles of association. It also specifically states that a company may not distribute assets if it is known (or should have been known) at the time of deciding to do so that the company is insolvent or that the distribution will cause insolvency (Chapter 13, Section 2).

Whether a company's financial standing is sufficient to grant a loan without the risk of insolvency shall be assessed on the basis of the latest financial statements and other available information. In making such an assessment, the company's management will need to consider various aspects. The Companies Act does not automatically prevent the distribution of assets, even in poorly performing companies. So even if the company becomes insolvent relatively shortly after the distribution of assets, the act will not necessarily have been violated.

With regard to creditor protection, the management's awareness of the company's insolvency is critical. If the management was (or should have been) aware of the company's insolvency, the transaction will constitute an unlawful distribution of assets. When evaluating the company's solvency, future receivables should be taken into account and present and future liabilities should be compared against the present and future revenue and the possibility of receiving credit funds. Unreasonable requirements should not be imposed on the management. In particular, the solvency of small companies is often rather low, and the distribution of assets should not be made impossible for them.

The general prohibition of financing the acquisition of a company's own shares is expressed in Chapter 13(10) of the Companies Act. It prohibits a company from providing loans, assets or security for the purpose of a third party acquiring shares in the company or its parent. However, a company can finance the acquisition of its shares by its employees, or by employees of group companies, provided that the financing is done within the limits of the distributable assets.

This prohibition is especially relevant in situations where the acquirer and the target will participate in the same cash pooling agreement after the acquisition. The prohibition may be breached if the acquirer pays off the acquisition debt with the money that it has received from the target through cash pooling. However, engaging in a cash pooling agreement after an acquisition is not categorically prohibited, since the transferred funds can be used for a wide range of purposes other than repayment of the acquisition debt.

In addition to these principles and requirements, all cash pooling agreements should be reported in the company's annual report or financial statements. According to the Companies Act, all loans, liabilities and commitments (including their principal terms) to related parties should be separately stated in the annual report, if their total exceeds either €20,000 or 5% of the equity capital of the company's balance sheet.

Insolvency law requirements: According to the Act on Recovery of Assets to a Bankruptcy Estate (758/1991), a transaction that improperly favours one creditor to the detriment of others, puts assets beyond creditors' reach or increases the liabilities of the debtor to the detriment of the creditors is to be reversed, provided that the debtor was insolvent at the time or that the transaction itself caused the insolvency. To reverse such a transaction, the receiving party must also have been aware (or should have been aware) of the counterparty's insolvency. As established by the Supreme Court, group companies are considered to be related parties and are thus assumed to be aware of such insolvencies unless proven otherwise. In such instances, it is up to the participants in the cash pooling agreement to prove that they were unaware of the insolvency. A transaction can be reversed only if it has somehow damaged the creditors – for instance, if it worsens the financial state of the debtor and thus reduces the assets available for distribution in a bankruptcy.

In insolvency situations, the lack of group interest should also be taken into account. Since each group company is considered to have its own assets and liabilities, they will also be seen as separate debtors or creditors if one of the group companies becomes insolvent.

According to the Bankruptcy Act (120/2004), the opening of bankruptcy proceedings does not terminate the company's existing contracts. The administrator can have the company fulfil them if this is deemed profitable, and thus continue trading. A cash pooling agreement can also be continued if it complies with the principle of corporate benefit for the participating companies.

2. Specific questions

2.1 Perspective A: corporate group

(a) Liability of group company and/or master account holder directors in the event of insolvency of a group company

Whether a company is privately held or listed has no bearing on the liability of the supervising directors – the provisions and principles of the Companies Act apply equally in either case. A bank or a group company's nationality has no relevance either. Finnish law includes no specific provisions on companies registered in a foreign jurisdiction. Nationality matters only if Finnish law is deemed inapplicable, by virtue of a cash pooling agreement's international connections.

As provided in Chapter 1(8) of the Companies Act, the company's management shall act with due care and promote the interests of the company. The company must be organised and managed appropriately and in compliance with the law. The management must keep track of the company's situation and make sure that its business arrangements are working to its benefit. A member of the board of directors, the managing director or a member of the supervisory board exercising such a duty of care may be held liable for any damage that he or she causes to the company, whether intentionally or through negligence (Chapter 22(1)). The management is also liable for damage caused to shareholders or other persons if this results from an intentional or negligent violation of the articles of association or of the provisions of the Companies Act other than Chapter 1(8) (Chapter 22(2)). If the damage is due to a violation of the articles of association or the Companies Act, the management must prove that it acted with due care.

The first consequence of any such unlawful distribution of assets is that the transaction will be deemed invalid and will not bind the company. If a transaction is not permitted under the Companies Act, the good faith of the counterparty is not protected, since the counterparty is expected to be aware of the mandatory provisions of the Companies Act. Also, an unlawful distribution can lead to the imposition of a restoration obligation on the receiver. As regulated in the Companies Act (Chapter 13(4)), assets that are unlawfully distributed should be restored to the company if their recipient either knew or should have known that their distribution was unlawful. These two factors can restrict the damage caused to the company or other persons, and thus limit the compensation payable.

It is similarly unlawful for a loan transaction to be made by a representative who has no authority to do so. According to the Companies Act, if a company representative performs a transaction that is against the competence limitations set out in the Companies Act, the transaction will not bind the company. If the assets transferred cannot be recovered, the representative can be held liable for any damages caused.

As described earlier, the managers of each participant company in a cash pooling agreement need to satisfy themselves from the outset that the arrangement is beneficial to their company's interests. Managers can be held liable if the prerequisites for the acceptability of the arrangement are not met. Since all cash pooling agreements must be beneficial to the participating company in order to be acceptable, there can be no internal conflict of interest within a group company that would result in liability of the management, provided that participating in the cash pooling agreement is in line with the principle of corporate benefit.

Since cash pooling agreements are typically automated, the fund transfers (which are technically considered loans) are effected without the management making individual decisions. Thus, the passive act of remaining in a cash pooling agreement can give rise to liability if it no longer meets the principles of corporate benefit or creditor protection. The company's management might be obligated to exit the arrangement if circumstances change to such an extent that remaining in the arrangement is no longer in the company's interests or is otherwise against the principles and provisions of the Companies Act.

The Companies Act contains no specific provisions on piercing the corporate veil, and the separation of legal entities has primacy. Any assessment of the possibility of piercing the corporate veil must consider the behaviour and express commitments, as well as the factual ownership and authority, of the companies involved. Piercing the corporate veil would require that the different legal entities in reality constitute one functional entity. The Supreme Court of Finland is reluctant to set precedent in this regard. Exceptions are scarce and, when it comes to cash pooling agreements, largely irrelevant.

If a group company is no longer able to meet its payments, participation in a cash pooling agreement can result in the liability of its management. Companies must not distribute their assets if it is (or should have been) known at the time that the company was insolvent or that such distribution would cause its insolvency (Chapter 13(2) of the Companies Act). Loans made within a cash pooling agreement can constitute an unlawful distribution and thus result in management liability. As the arrangement in these situations is in breach of a specific provision of the Companies Act, the management can be liable not only for damage caused to the company itself, but also for that caused to shareholders, creditors and others. The question of whether the company's management should have known that distribution would result in insolvency requires case-by-case analysis, taking into consideration the duty of care and the information that was available to management at the time of the decision. The management will not be held liable if it is considered to have acted with due care.

As for the possible liability of the master account holder's management, transferring assets to a group company that no longer can meet its payments can create a serious credit risk and thus contradict the principle of corporate benefit. Such a transaction may be considered to reduce the company's assets without a sound business reason and may thus constitute an unlawful distribution of assets (Chapter 13(1)(3) of the Companies Act).

The management is liable for any damage it causes if it acts against the duty of care set out in Chapter 1(8) of the Companies Act, and it is considered that the management should have been aware that its actions were not in the company's interests or lacked a sound business reason. In assessing the latter, the recipient's lack of solvency is an important factor. In deciding whether the management has violated the duty of care, the management's awareness of the recipient's financial situation plays a central role. Although closely related, group companies are nonetheless separate entities with their own interests. Therefore, the management cannot automatically be expected to be fully acquainted with the financial situation of other group companies. If, however, the management is considered to have violated the duty of care, it becomes liable towards the company. If the transaction is considered to have reduced the company's assets without a sound business reason, then the management will be liable towards other persons as well, since the transaction is in violation of Chapter 13(1)(3) of the Companies Act.

(b) Liability of group company and/or master account holder directors in the event of insolvency of the master account holder

The management of a group company can be held liable for damage caused by a cash pooling agreement if it should have been aware that the master account holder might have been be unable to repay. As mentioned above, the decision to remain in a cash pooling agreement that is not in the interests of the company (or, more specifically, the lack of a decision to disengage) can be considered a negligent violation of the duty of care under the Companies Act. Any transactions in these circumstances can constitute an unlawful distribution of assets if they lack a sound business reason. The management can thus be held liable towards the company and other persons.

On the other hand, the management of the master account holder can be primarily held liable if the arrangement violates the principle of creditor protection. Basically, if the arrangement leads to the insolvency of the master account holder, the management can be held liable if it should have been aware of this potential consequence. In such a situation, the management will be liable not only towards the company itself, but also towards shareholders and other persons, since this constitutes a breach of Chapter 13(2) of the Companies Act.

(c) Liability of group companies in the event of insolvency of the master account holder

In such a situation, a group company probably cannot be held liable towards other companies. If, for example, assets are transferred from the master account holder in violation of the principle of creditor protection (and thus in violation of Chapter 13(2) of the Companies Act), then the company distributing the assets or the management responsible for the unlawful distribution will be held liable instead of the recipient company.

Group companies can be held liable towards the master account holder only if they violate the restoration obligation set out in Chapter 13(4) of the Companies Act. This states that the recipient of an unlawful distribution must return the assets if it either knew or should have known that the transaction was unlawful. This might happen if, for example, the master account holder violates Chapter 13(2) of the Companies Act by distributing assets when insolvent. Should the recipient fail to restore the assets, even though it was aware that the transaction was unlawful, it may be held liable. If the recipient no longer has possession of the assets and the creditors are unable to recover them, the recipient company – and possibly its management – may have to pay damages.

In such instances, group companies are considered to be closely related parties, whose knowledge of each other's financial standing and decision making will probably be better than that of outsider companies. On the other hand, the participants in a cash pooling agreement are separate entities with separate interests, and the loans in an ongoing cash pooling agreement can be transferred without any decisions being made by the participating the companies. Unreasonable requirements to monitor the lawfulness of other participants' transactions should not be imposed on the recipient company. When considering creditors' options for protecting their interests in the described situation, the most viable is usually under the Recovery Act.

(d) Liability of the master account holder in the event of insolvency of a group company

This situation is very similar to that described in section 2.1(d), and creditors would again be best protected by the Recovery Act. Nonetheless, there could be a change in the liability of the account holder if it is also the parent company. If the parent company somehow used its authority to transfer funds from the insolvent subsidiary through cash pooling, the transaction would be considered an unlawful distribution (ie, in violation of the principle of creditor protection or corporate benefit), and the parent company could be held liable. However, such liability could not be based directly on the Companies Act provisions on unlawful distribution. Due to the separation of legal entities, it is the group company that would technically be considered to have distributed the assets unlawfully, even though the decision would have been made under the parent company's influence.

Nonetheless, the parent company could possibly be found liable under the general rules of the Tort Liability Act (412/1974). The parent company could be seen to have acted intentionally, or at least negligently, since it used its authority to make a decision that violated the Companies Act. Under the Tort Liability Act, an economic loss that is not connected with a personal injury or damage to property can be recovered only if it has been caused by an act that is punishable by law, in the exercise of public authority or in other cases where there are especially weighty reasons for compensation. Since there are such strict prerequisites for the recovery of economic damages in the Tort Liability Act, the parent company would not necessarily be found liable even if the transaction violated the Companies Act.

2.2 Perspective B: bank

(a) Banking requirements

In Finland, cash pooling accounts maintained outside the group (eg, with a bank or another financial institution) are regarded as deposit accounts. To maintain such accounts, a financial institution must have a deposit bank licence. There are no specific banking law provisions regarding the implementation of a cash pooling agreement, but general provisions on deposit banking should nevertheless be observed. Deposit bank licences are granted by the Financial Supervisory Authority (FSA) upon application.

The terms and conditions of deposit accounts are no longer approved in advance by the FSA, since the relevant legislation – Section 10(3) of the Credit Institutions Act (121/2007) – was repealed by amendment (1357/2010) on December 31 2010. Nowadays the FSA undertakes retrospective supervision, and will intervene in cases where terms and conditions are deemed unreasonable to the customer, as defined in Section 126(1) of the Credit Institutions Act.

The capital adequacy rules form the cornerstone of credit institution regulation in Finland. This is determined as the ratio of the bank's capital to risk-weighted assets such as lending, investments and off-balance sheet commitments. Depending on the underlying risk, each asset item is given its own minimum capital requirement. As a result of the global financial crisis, new bank capital requirements have been established in the form of the Basel III reform. These cover the quality of capital required to be held by banks, the minimum level of core bank capital, separate capital conservation and countercyclical buffers, and non-risk based leverage ratios. Due to their strong financial standing, Finnish banks generally satisfy the new requirements.

(b) ***Liability of the bank in the event of insolvency of the master account holder or of a group company***

In cash pooling agreements the bank merely provides banking services to the company group and is not considered an actual participant in the arrangement. The bank thus cannot be held liable if any company becomes distressed or enters into liquidation. Depending on the form of the arrangement, the bank may possibly be a creditor or debtor in a company's insolvency proceedings, but it will not be liable for any damage caused by the company s financial distress.

2.3 Insolvency

(a) ***Cash pooling agreements from the insolvency practitioner's perspective***

The money transfers in a cash pooling agreement are treated as loans for the purposes of bankruptcy proceedings. When a company is declared bankrupt, the bankruptcy administrator claims its property and assets, including the entire credit balance. All claims existing before the commencement of bankruptcy proceedings are considered bankruptcy claims. Assets transferred to the bankrupt company after proceedings have commenced are not considered part of the bankruptcy estate.

In single legal account pooling, the question of who owes what to whom depends on whether the bankrupt company is the master account holder or a sub-account holder, and whether the account balance is positive or negative. If a sub-account holder is bankrupt, the master account holder has a claim against the bankruptcy estate should the balance of the sub-account be negative. If it is positive, the bankruptcy estate of the sub-account holder will be owed assets by the master account holder. The sub-account holder is never owed assets directly by the bank.

If the master account holder is bankrupt, a negative balance in the master account constitutes the master account holder's debt to the bank. If the sub-account is in credit, the sub-account holder has a claim against the master account holder (the bankruptcy estate), but never against the bank. If the sub-account has a negative balance, the sub-account holder owes debt to the master account holder.

If the master account holder faces bankruptcy, the bank will terminate the cash pooling agreement – at least in the case of single legal account pooling. The sub-account holders (usually subsidiaries) may be held liable towards the bank if they have given guarantees on behalf of the master account holder.

If the bankruptcy is declared in a foreign jurisdiction, it will not be recognised in Finland. Only bankruptcies that fall within the scope of the EU Insolvency Regulation (1346/2000) or the Bankruptcy Convention between Denmark, Finland, Iceland, Norway and Sweden (which entered into force on November 7 1933) are recognised in Finland. Thus, only bankruptcy judgments handed down in EU member states, Iceland or Norway are automatically enforceable upon being recognised by a Finnish court. Foreign administrators have the same rights as Finnish administrators in Finnish bankruptcies.

To recover assets situated in Finland, an administrator representing the estate of a company that has been declared bankrupt in a jurisdiction outside the European Union, Iceland or Norway needs an enforcement decision from a Finnish court. In order to extend the effects of the bankruptcy to Finland, the administrator must obtain a declaration of bankruptcy in Finland as well. However, even if a foreign bankruptcy is not recognised in Finland, the bankruptcy estate has the right to seize any of the bankrupt company's assets situated in Finland.

The applicable form of cash pooling has a bearing on the rights of any companies involved in insolvency proceedings. In single legal account pooling, the master account holder holds the only physical bank account and thus is the only participant that can be regarded as a creditor in the event of the bankruptcy of the bank (or a debtor, if the situation is reversed). In zero balancing and top sweeping, all group companies have physical accounts with the bank and can therefore be regarded as either creditors or debtors.

According to Chapter 12(1) of the Bankruptcy Act, all creditors – regardless of nationality – have the right to secure their claims, receive satisfaction of their claims and exercise other rights granted by the act. Although the act does not expressly state that all creditors are equal, this basic principle is generally accepted in bankruptcy proceedings. In practice, this means that all creditors shall be given an equal part of the proceeds, treated even-handedly and given an opportunity to participate in the bankruptcy estate's decision making. The administrator has a duty to be impartial and to ensure that the principle of equality is observed.

If money is transferred from a master account to a group company (or vice versa) prior to the transferring company becoming bankrupt, then the transfer may be invalid and the sums involved may be restored the transferring company. If the management of the company transferring the money knew, or should have known, that the company as insolvent at the time, or that the transaction would cause its insolvency, the transfer of assets could be considered to violate the principle of creditor protection as set out under Chapter 13(2) of the Companies Act. As a result, the transaction will not bind the company, since it will be considered an unlawful distribution and thus invalid. Furthermore, the administrator can demand the restoration of the assets under the Recovery Act if the transaction transferred money out of the creditors' reach or favoured certain creditors.

There are no special obligations concerning the bankruptcy of a company involved in a cash pooling agreement. The participants are to be treated in the same way as all other creditors, since all creditors must be treated equally.

However, as subsidiary and parent companies are considered closely related, transactions between them can be more easily reversed. The administrator must ensure that no creditors or debtors are favoured to the detriment of others. This involves assessing the bankrupt company's recent transaction history for any transactions that may fall under the Recovery Act. The administrator must ensure that assets transferred out of the bankrupt company against the creditor protection rules are restored to the bankruptcy estate. If the cash pool arrangement continues after the declaration of bankruptcy, the administrator must ensure that subsequent transactions are kept separate from the bankruptcy receivables.

(b) Dissolution/termination of the cash pooling agreement in the event of liquidation of the master account holder or of a group company

The Bankruptcy Act specifically states that the opening of bankruptcy proceedings does not terminate existing contracts. The administrator can thus continue to run the debtor's business by requiring the debtor to fulfil its contractual obligations, if this is considered beneficial. In other words, the debtor's contractual counterparts cannot terminate contracts simply due to the debtor's insolvency.

If any participant enters into liquidation, remaining in the cash pooling agreement could constitute a credit risk for the other participants. In such a situation, the arrangement will no longer be in the other companies' interests and its continuation will most likely violate the corporate benefit principle. Therefore, each company's management would have to reassess the arrangement and withdraw if there were no longer any benefit in participating. However, the bankruptcy of a cash pooling participant does not necessarily constitute a risk to the other group companies, which is why the management is not automatically obliged to terminate the arrangement. But in most insolvency cases (and certainly in any case of a bankrupt master account holder), banks have in practice required that the cash pooling agreement be terminated.

2.4 Perspective D: regulatory

There is no specific regulation on cash pooling in Finland. However, reporting to the Bank of Finland is necessary if the arrangement is between residents and non-residents. For more details, please see section 1.

2.5 Perspective E: tax

With regard to tax law, the terms and conditions of cash pooling agreements should comply with the arm's-length principle. The main tax issue involved is the question of transfer pricing. According to the Tax Procedure Act (1558/1995), the interest on loan transactions in a cash pooling agreement should reflect fair market interest rates (Section 31). If the interest rate does not do so, the tax authorities can challenge the transactions and the companies will be taxed as if the interest rate had been set at the right level.

France

Anja Droege Gagnier
BMH Avocats

1. Introduction

Many corporate groups have entered (or wish to enter) into a cash pooling agreement with a bank. Cash pooling agreements provide an opportunity for corporate groups to efficiently manage their liquidity, benefit from improved interest rates and improve their internal financial management. However, the legal framework governing a cash pooling agreement can be complex, especially if the entities within the corporate group are spread out over multiple jurisdictions.

Setting up a multi-jurisdictional cash pooling scheme usually proves to be a complicated undertaking, since many legal aspects need to be considered. In some jurisdictions (eg, Germany and Austria), specific laws and regulations on capital maintenance have a direct influence on the participating companies. Other jurisdictions (eg, the Netherlands and Spain) lack specific rules, but in these jurisdictions general principles of corporate law play an important role. Foreign currency regulation, reporting duties, transfer pricing issues, (withholding) tax issues, restrictions on intra-group loans and even corporate governance codes could lead to further complications.

Local and global banking regulations also need to be considered. In some jurisdictions (eg, Russia), placing intra-group loans on a regular basis can be considered a banking activity which might be restricted by law. The Basel II (and upcoming Basel III) regulatory framework and EU legislation (eg, the Capital Requirements Directive) must be observed by banks when setting up cash pooling agreements with corporate groups. Risk coverage, management and capital requirements have been tightened and may influence current and future cash pooling agreements.

And since cash pooling agreements have a considerable impact on the financial condition of the participating companies, various liabilities may arise in the event of financial distress or even insolvency of one of the participating companies, or the bank.

1.1 Admissibility of cash pooling agreements

Under French law, cash pooling agreements constitute a lawful corporate practice as long as they comply with the requirements imposed by various legal branches.

One such requirement is the banking monopoly provision of the Financial and Monetary Code.[1] This rule makes it unlawful for anyone other than a credit institution

1 Article L515-5 of the Financial and Monetary Code

to routinely carry out banking operations. In other words, granting loans to and regularly receiving public money from various persons is forbidden unless the lender has been granted a banking licence. However, Article L511-7 para 3 of the code sets out an exception to this rule by stating that a company can "undertake cash transactions with companies which have, directly or indirectly, ties by way of share capital which confer to one of the affiliated company an effective power of control over the others".

This provision, which basically allows cash pooling agreements, has been interpreted rather generously by the French courts and very few agreements have been declared contrary to the banking monopoly provision. For example, it was ruled that sister companies, in circumstances where one is fully owned and another managed and partially owned by the same individual, could lend money to each other without breaching the above provisions.

Cash pooling agreements are also subject to provisions in corporate law, most of which rely on the corporate interest concept. Under these regulations, a cash pooling agreement must be in the corporate interest of any company that is a party to it.

Notional cash pooling agreements are not subject to these requirements, as they generally do not involve any actual transfer of funds between the participant companies.

If the master account holder is a foreign company, then any group companies with headquarters registered in France generally need to comply with French law regarding the banking monopoly, corporate law (corporate interest), insolvency law and tax law (eg, transfer pricing). In general, a cash pool connecting a corporate group across national borders must comply with the laws of the relevant jurisdictions.

2.1 Types of cash pooling agreement

French law does not favour any specific form of cash pooling – both physical and notional variations are lawful. The French economic and regulatory context, however, favours notional over physical cash pooling among French companies.

(a) Physical cash pooling

In French business practice, physical cash pooling is achieved through either direct or indirect account balancing. Direct account balancing means that the sweeping of funds between the master account and the group companies' accounts takes place instantly and without any intermediate accounts. Conversely, indirect balancing is implemented with the help of secondary 'mirror' accounts that reflect the balances of each account, just as if direct balancing had actually occurred. In this case, the group companies' accounts are not affected by the cash pooling agreement until the set periodic transfer of positions actually takes place. This indirect or postponed balancing has proved problematic, as some group companies believed they had entered a notional cash pooling agreement when in fact their balance had actually been reduced to a zero position, leading in some cases to insolvency proceedings.

(b) Notional cash pooling

Notional cash pooling agreements are often referred to as an interest optimisation mechanism. They are legally simpler and subject to less scrutiny than their physical counterpart, mainly because they generally do not involve group companies in any actual money lending and so do not require complex intra-group agreements. They are therefore subject to less scrutiny from a corporate law point of view. A notional cash pooling system is possible in practice only if the interest optimisation for the master account holder and the group companies is carried out by the same bank. Notional pooling is also less problematic from both an insolvency law and a tax law perspective, as the participant companies maintain legal and fiscal separation. Also, notional cash pooling is simpler from an administrative standpoint, and therefore more economic. These advantages make notional pooling attractive for French companies – but the practice itself has only come recently to France, as remuneration of sight deposits[2] was not allowed until 2005.

2.2 Specific legal requirements from various perspectives

Under French law, cash pooling agreements are not governed by a general regulation. They are therefore subject to multiple rules, including corporate law, tax law and insolvency law.

Under French corporate law, cash pooling agreements executed between a joint stock company (*société anonyme*) and its parent are considered to be regulated contracts that may trigger conflicts of interest. Consequently, they require the prior approval of the companies' boards of directors, or else the subsequent approval of a shareholders' meeting (based on a report drafted by the company's chartered accountant). Occasionally, contracts entered into under normal conditions are not subject to these requirements. French courts have ruled that 'normal conditions' were met in cases where participating companies received interest at the market rate on money that they transferred to the pool, and when transactions made under the agreement did not exceed the companies' financial capacities.

A cash pooling agreement could be considered null and void in any case of 'abuse of majority' exercised by a majority of a company's shareholders. A corporate decision is considered an abuse of majority when it is deemed contrary to the company's interest. In taking such a decision, a majority of shareholders or the board of directors will be judged to have acted in their own personal interest and at the expense of the shareholder minority. In practice, examples of abuses of majority in cash pooling are few and far between.

French law requires that cash pooling agreements respect the corporate interests of each participating company. This requirement has been eased by the French Supreme Court, which – in a famous corporate criminal case – relied upon the 'group interest' argument. The court ruled that an inter-company agreement could be detrimental to one group company and beneficial to another if it is entered into and executed in the corporate interest of the group as a whole. This means that inter-company cash pool loans or advance payments must be remunerated with a sufficient interest rate, and must not financially jeopardise the existence of the disadvantaged group company. In general, group interest must translate into economic, corporate and financial terms.

---

2 Cash deposits on accounts that can be withdrawn at any time.

In circumstances of acquisition, other special provisions may apply to cash pooling agreements, such as the prohibition of financial assistance (Article L225-216 of the Commercial Code). This states that the cash of the target (eg, a loan to the holding company, which is the purchaser) must not be used to finance its own acquisition (eg, should not be used to reimburse the external loan financing the purchase price).

In French criminal law, directors[3] of participant companies can be held liable under the 'abuse of corporate property' offence.[4] This ruling prohibits using corporate property or funds in bad faith, in a way that is known to be contrary to the company's corporate interest but instead satisfies a personal interest or favours another company in which a director has direct or indirect interests. In a cash pooling agreement, both the directors of the master account holder and the directors of the relevant group companies can be held criminally liable on this basis. However, directors can circumvent this liability if they can prove that they acted in the interest of the group as a whole. In order for the group interest condition to be accepted, the three requirements outlined above must demonstrably be met.

Should a group company or the master account holder become insolvent, cash pooling agreements (eg, upstream payments) may allow insolvency proceedings to extend to another (supposedly healthy) parent company. They may also lead to liability of the directors and officers on both criminal and civil grounds (see below).

French insolvency law offers different tools for the reorganisation of companies, whether voluntary or involuntary. The last major insolvency reform (Law 2005-845 of July 26 2005)[5] introduced new voluntary proceedings, supposed to prevent insolvency, called safeguard proceedings. These are available to companies that are not yet insolvent under the French insolvency test[6] and therefore can be filed only by the debtor in question. The reorganisation proceedings and liquidation proceedings are mandatory proceedings that are triggered when the insolvency test is met.

Liquidation proceedings aim to liquidate all of a debtor's assets through a court-appointed liquidator,[7] whereas reorganisation proceedings aim to rescue the company and to save jobs. In practice, the court opens reorganisation proceedings if the company has employees to consider. All insolvency proceedings (whether safeguard, reorganisation or liquidation proceedings) imply a moratorium in favor of the debtor. The court appoints a *mandataire judiciaire* called a creditors'

---

3 The term 'directors' is a general term. Under the abuse of corporate property offence, it has the following meanings:
- If the company is a *société anonyme*, the term can cover the president, the members of the board or the general managers.
- If the company is a *société à responabilité limitée*, the term is limited to the general manager.
- If a person is convicted for having acted as *de facto* manager, he or she could also be held liable under the different criminal offences applicable to directors.
- In general corporate law, it can also comprise the supervisory directors. The criminal law offence 'abuse of corporate property' does not list the supervisory directors.

4 Article L242-6 3° of the Commercial Code

5 In force since January 1 2006, amended several times.

6 *Cessation des paiements* means if the debtor is unable to pay its debts as they fall due with its available assets.

7 Who is a *mandataire judiciaire* (see below).

representative, who acts for the creditors and collects, accepts or rejects their claims. The court appoints an administrator if the size of the debtor[8] meets certain thresholds. In general, the administrator acts to assist the debtor over an observation period of up to 18 months, during which the possibility of reorganisation of the business is analysed, a reorganisation plan is set up which is to be submitted to the court and/or a partial or total asset sale is considered. In some cases, the administrator is appointed to replace the debtor's manager. The creditors can file for the appointment of a representative controller,[9] to be chosen from among their number. The controller represents them collectively, collects information about the proceedings and must be consulted by the court on all major decisions (eg, should the business be put up for sale, the controller must be consulted with respect to the different offers, although the final decision will be taken by the court). In practice, the ability to appoint a controller is useful for creditors, which do not enjoy extensive rights within France's largely debtor-driven insolvency proceedings.

2. Specific questions

2.1 Perspective A: corporate group

(a) Liability of group company and/or master account holder directors in the event of insolvency of a group company

French law provides various grounds for holding directors liable in insolvency procedures.

The Commercial Code lists three types of offence:

- civil liability for excess of liabilities over assets (also called shortfall in assets);
- personal bankruptcy and other restraining orders; and
- the so-called *banqueroute* and other criminal offences.

These apply both to *de jure* and *de facto* directors. In addition to the *de jure* directors of the insolvent group company, the directors of the master account holder (*de facto* directors) can, provided that there is evidence of a *de facto* directorship (eg, heavy interference in the group company's management and business), be held liable on these grounds if the group company becomes insolvent. These are general offences, not specific to cash pooling. However, a cash pooling agreement with abnormal streams (eg, upstream and streams between sister companies) can be considered as a contributing factor to an insolvency situation.

In a case of mismanagement, *de jure* or *de facto* directors can be held liable for excess of liabilities over assets (*action en responsabilité pour insuffisance d'actif*, better known as *action en comblement de passif*). Section L651-2 of the Commercial Code states:

> *Where the rescission of a safeguard plan or of a reorganization plan or the liquidation of a legal entity reveals an excess of liabilities over assets, the Court may, in instances where management fault has contributed to the excess of liabilities over assets, decide*

---

8 Turnover at least €3 million (excl. taxes) and 20 employees or more.

9 *Contrôleur.*

that the debts of the legal entity will be borne, in whole or in part, by all or some of the de jure or de facto managers who have contributed to the management fault...

This claim can be brought only by the creditors' representative (*mandataire judiciaire*), the creditors' controller or, if the latter does not act, the liquidator or the public prosecutor. It only applies to faults committed before the opening of the insolvency proceedings. A successful claim requires three conditions: a fault committed by the manager (*de jure* or *de facto*), a loss suffered by the insolvent company and a causal relationship between the two. Managerial faults can range from criminal offences listed in Sections L654-1 to L654-15 of the Commercial Code (see below) to conduct reflecting manifest incompetence in managing the insolvent company (eg, starting a business without proper equity, setting a disproportionate payroll) or the granting of advantages to a sole creditor which is aware of the debtor's distressed situation.

The injury suffered by the company consists in its insolvency, and is appreciated on the day of the court's ruling. The management fault must have contributed to the excess of liabilities over assets, but need not be its exclusive or main cause. In most cases, the director bears only part of the debt, because the court considers that the director's fault has contributed to the insolvency of the company, but was not the exclusive cause. In the presence of more than one director, the court may decide joint and several liability.

Another civil offence is the personal bankruptcy of the manager. This is a non-pecuniary sanction that results in "prohibition from running, managing, administrating or controlling, directly or indirectly, any commercial or craftsman's business, any agricultural activity or any business operating any other independent activity and any legal entity".

The misconduct that may lead to personal bankruptcy includes embezzling or concealing all or part of the company's assets or fraudulently increasing its liabilities, paying a creditor after cessation of payments and while being aware of this to the prejudice of other creditors, and not keeping accounts as required. Making personal use of the company's assets is also misconduct under this provision, and has been cited in cases of unbalanced cash pooling to the benefit of the master account holder.

Finally, the Commercial Code sets out the criminal offences which allow directors to be held liable. The most important is *banqueroute*, for which the penalty is up to five years' imprisonment and a fine up to €75,000. A director who has embezzled or concealed all or part of the debtor's assets, or has fraudulently increased the debtor's liabilities, is guilty of *banqueroute*. So is any director of an insolvent company who has kept accounts that are manifestly incomplete, irregular or false, or who has destroyed accounting documents belonging to the business. In order for the *banqueroute* offence to apply, the above acts must have been committed once the company was insolvent. This requirement makes it impossible to incriminate a director whose company is going through safeguard proceedings (since the company still meets its payment obligations). Finally, unlike the abuse of corporate property offence, *banqueroute* does not require proof that the manager was putting his own interests first, and he cannot escape conviction by claiming that his actions benefited the whole group.

If the insolvent company is a listed corporation, the directors' legal and regulatory obligations are generally more demanding, providing more grounds for the managers' liability to be incurred, especially in case of insolvency. Managers of listed corporations also face administrative sanctions set by capital market law. For example, it has been ruled that the managers of a publicly held company had failed in their duty to provide exact, precise and sincere information to the markets by not disclosing the situation of a subsidiary kept under its parent's dependence, as this situation had been hidden by the cash pooling agreement.

If the distressed group company is registered in a foreign jurisdiction, the directors' liability falls under the local law of that country. That said, French law may apply in any case of faults committed by the foreign directors of the French company (eg, interference in its management or abuse of corporate property), although the likelihood is fairly remote.

(b) *Liability of group company and/or master account holder directors in the event of insolvency of the master account holder*

If the master account holder is no longer able to meet its payment obligations and goes into insolvency proceedings, then its directors might, as outlined previously, face a risk of liability. However, as the master account holder is often the parent company, it seems unlikely that the directors of the group company (if different from the directors of the master account holder) would be held liable as *de facto* directors of the insolvent master account holder and parent company, since they would have to be convicted as having interfered heavily in the business of the parent company.

(c) *Liability of group companies in the event of insolvency of the master account holder*

Under French law, insolvency proceedings can be extended to a group company if it demonstrably has no distinct existence from the insolvent master account holder (insolvency proceedings extension, covered in detail below). In theory, a group company may be held liable for the losses suffered by the master account holder if, in the case of a *de facto* directorship, the offence of 'excess of liabilities over assets' (see above) can be proved.

In practice however, liability of a group company in the case of the master account holder's insolvency is unlikely, unless that group company is also the parent company.

In any case, a creditor is not authorised by law to bring such an action of extension to court. Only the administrator, the creditors' representative (*mandataire judiciare*) and the public prosecutor can do that.

If the group company is located in another EU member state, French insolvency proceedings can apply only if it demonstrably has no distinct existence from the insolvent master account holder, and (according to the EU Insolvency Regulation) the centre of its main interests is located in France. When this is the case, a company with its head office in another European jurisdiction can fall within the competence of the French insolvency courts. For example, a group company with its head office in Italy will be considered to have its main interests in France when strategic decisions are taken in France, or when most of its assets and employees are located there.

The same ruling applies if the insolvent master account holder is located in another

EU jurisdiction. Again, it must be shown that the centre of its main interests is located in France and that the French group company has no distinct separate existence.

(d) *Liability of the master account holder in the event of insolvency of a group company*

Cash pooling agreements, when centralised by the parent company, might at very least have the effect of challenging the financial independence of the group companies. However, this fact alone is not enough to make the master account holder liable for any losses suffered by the group company in distress. It is only one of a number of criteria by which the potential liability of the master account holder is adjudged. For example, the master account holder, in case it is convicted as *de facto* manager having mismanaged a group company, can be held liable for the offence called 'excess of liabilities over assets' (*insuffisance d'actifs/action en comblement de passif*) suffered by the group company. Moreover, if it can be proven that the group company is a 'sham' or if its assets are intermingled with those of the parent company, French law provides for an extension of the insolvency proceedings opened against a group company to the parent company master account holder. Obviously, such extension is interesting in the event that the latter is healthy. However, French case law imposes strict conditions for the piercing of the corporate veil, since the legal independence of corporations is one of the characteristics of French corporate law.

Section L621-2 of the Commercial Code states that: "the commenced proceedings may be extended to one or more other persons where their assets are intermingled with those of the debtor or where the legal entity is a sham."

Important case law has been established in this provision, in order to determine what 'intermingled' and 'sham' actually imply. The insolvent group company is considered a sham when it has no distinct existence from the parent company. The sharing of common directors, head offices and commercial purposes does not make the group company a sham, as long as it retains independent activity and accountability. Intermingling of assets is proved by showing either that the two companies' liabilities and assets cannot be distinguished, or that there have been abnormal transactions between the pair. The latter scenario is more frequent, but courts have been very rigorous in recognising the existence of abnormal transactions. Transactions between parent and group companies are considered abnormal when they do not involve any compensation, are not recorded in the companies' balance sheets and take place on a systematic basis. Cumulative fulfilment of these conditions is very unlikely within a formalised cash pool. According to this case law, abnormal transactions within cash pools should be sought only if there is no formalised agreement, or in the case of breach of any such agreement by the participant companies. Neither creditors nor the insolvent group company can bring this claim. Only the administrator, the creditors' representative and the public prosecutor can do so.

If the extending of insolvency proceedings from the group company to the parent company requires numerous facts to be established (see above), then the latter is more likely to be held responsible for the former's insolvency (*action en comblement de passif*) in case of liquidation or rehabilitation. It has famously been pointed out by the French Supreme Court (*Metaleurop*, April 19 2005) that bringing action on the grounds of the parent company's liability could be effective even where the extending of the proceeding ground was inappropriate. In order to be held responsible for the group company's insolvency, the parent company must be shown to have acted as the *de facto* director of the group company – and so must have taken 'positive direction acts' in complete independence from the *de jure* director. For example, *de facto* direction from the parent company is established when *de jure* directors of the group company receives all of their instructions from the parent company. After the *de facto* direction is established, it must be shown that the parent company mismanaged the group company and that its mismanagement helped to cause the insolvency. The parent company could also be held liable for the group company's insolvency if it can be shown to have been impetuously intrusive in the latter's direction, to the point where creditors are confused about the debtor's identity. As stated earlier, the claim for *action en comblement de passif* is brought before the court either by the liquidator, the creditors' representative (*mandataire judiciare*) or the public prosecutor. Creditors cannot act singly and, if the creditors' representative does not act, can only bring such action to court via their controller.

2.2 Perspective B: bank

(a) *Banking requirements*

General rules apply when a bank enters into cash pooling agreement with a corporate group. French law does not provide for specific requirements regarding regulatory capital and security structure. Basel II has been implemented in French law via two European directives (the EU Capital Requirement Directives), which have themselves now been introduced into French law.

Credit institutions must therefore comply with the Basel II solvency ratio, which (contrary to the Basel I solvency ratio) takes into account the level of credit risk attached to each different granted loan, thus leading to further individual evaluation of potential borrowers' soundness by the banks. Some have asserted that this would lead to a rise in prices charged by banks and therefore prove harmful to cash pooling agreements. Others argue that it would only harm small banks and would matter less to large banks, whose calculation of credit risk depends on many factors other than regulatory solvency ratios. The new ratios set by Basel III will progressively be implemented in France between 2013 and 2019.

(b) *Liability of the bank in the event of insolvency of the master account holder or of a group company*

If the master account holder or one of the group companies goes into distress, the bank can be held liable on the ground of granted financial support only in the following cases:

- fraud;
- indisputable interference in the management of the debtor; or
- if guarantees obtained for the loans are disproportionate.

This non-liability principle set forth in Article L650-1 of the Commercial Code aims at stimulating credit activity towards struggling companies. It goes against numerous former judgments, which held the banks liable either for unreasonable financial support or sudden termination of credit supply. This case law obviously created legal insecurity and led in practice to reduced credit supply to troubled companies.

The claim provided in Article L650-1 Commercial Code against creditors is not admissible outside insolvency proceedings. It can, however, be brought against any creditor (not only banks) of the insolvent company by the creditors' representative (*mandataire judiciaire*), the administrator, or the debtor itself when no administrator has been commissioned to represent it.

Fraud implies that the bank breached a rule or failed to observe rights protected by law. The aim of this provision is to prevent the bank from granting loans for any purpose other than maintaining the borrowing company's activity or ensuring its sustainability. For example, if the bank uses fraudulent means with the aim of giving a biased image of its debtor's situation, it can be held liable for irregular grant of loans.

Indisputable interference includes, but is not limited to, *de facto* managing (see above). It also involves excessive influence of the bank over the debtor, without the bank acting as *de facto* manager, and to the point where decisions made by the debtor company would not have been taken without the bank's involvement. Courts do not easily recognize the bank as interfering, as it must have been doing so 'indisputably'. For example, a bank is not necessarily interfering in the debtor's management when it asks for reorganisation measures as a condition for the granting of the loan.

Lastly, the disproportionate guarantees exception aims at sanctioning any bank which, while being aware of the debtor's troubled situation, asks for excessive guarantees at the expense of the debtor and other creditors. The amount is considered disproportionate when it prevents other creditors from obtaining sufficient guarantees themselves.

2.3 Insolvency

(a) *Cash pooling agreement's from the insolvency practitioner's perspective*

Should the bank itself become insolvent, French insolvency law in principle provides grounds for individual property claims (*action en revendication*). These allow the owner of assets retained by the debtor to ask for their restitution, thus avoiding them becoming part of the common estate of the collective insolvency proceedings. However, cash deposits become the property of the bank from the moment of deposit. The French *Cour de Cassation* considers that individual property claims of funds cannot take place under the *action en revendication*, and that the creditor's only option is to file a claim, like other non-secured creditors, within the collective insolvency proceedings. However, if the bank goes into liquidation, both depositor and creditor (ie, master account holder and group company) may be exempted from filing claims for the amount covered by the *fond de garantie des depots* (deposit guarantee funds), although any such exemption is capped at €100,000.

Should the master account holder become insolvent, the appointed administrator for the insolvency proceedings could introduce French civil law claims against any other participating company that does not appear to be meeting its contractual obligations towards the cash pooling agreement. In certain circumstances, the administrator may also take action based on claw-back provisions (see below). Claims arising out of inter-company loans must be declared. They are ordinary claims (unsecured). To some extent, set-offs are allowed if the reciprocal claims both are due and arise out of the same contract or contractual chain (so-called *dettes connexes*). For foreign creditors, the law sets out a longer timeframe for the declaration of claims (four months as from publication of the opening judgment).

Should one of the group companies become insolvent, exactly the same rulings apply.

In French insolvency law, an administrator is appointed in judicial reorganisation and safeguard proceedings, provided that the thresholds are met.[10] He is required to represent, monitor or assist the management of the troubled company. As such, his duties towards the creditors require him to act with diligence and prudence.

For example, the administrator is the only person entitled to decide whether a debtor's contract involving sequential performances should proceed or not, notwithstanding the non-performance by the debtor of its contractual obligations prior to the opening judgment.[11] However, the administrator must ascertain that the troubled company is now able to pay the contracting party according to the contractual provisions. Otherwise, he may be held liable for any damage suffered by the contracting party through not being paid.

In France, communication to creditors is generally conducted not by the administrator but by a creditors' representative (*mandataire judiciaire*), appointed in all insolvency proceedings notwithstanding the size of the debtor. The creditors' representative notifies the known creditors and collects the creditors' claims.

In the event of either master account holder or a group company becoming insolvent, any transfers of money between the two can be subject to claw-back if they took place during the 'hardening period' (*période suspecte*). This runs from the date of insolvency (as determined by the court) to the opening judgment date, and cannot be longer than 18 months. Transactions that took place during this period may be either found mandatorily void or declared so by the court. Mandatory voidance applies to a number of financial transactions listed in the Commercial Code. For example, donations, unbalanced contracts, abnormal payments and payments of debts that are not yet due shall be declared void if they took place during this period, because they will be considered by their nature to have disadvantaged other creditors while reducing the estate.

The court can also declare such transactions void if it is proved that at the time of the payment by the insolvent company, the contracting party knew or was in a position to know of the other company's insolvency. Cash pooling agreements do not prevent courts from declaring void transactions made during the hardening period. When dealing with intra-group transactions, French courts assume that the

10 Turnover of at least €3 million (excl. taxes) and 20 employees or more.
11 Article L622-13 para. 2 of the Commercial Code.

contracting party is aware of the insolvent company's situation. In such circumstances, the court action can be introduced only by the administrator, the creditors' representative (*mandataire judiciaire*) or the public prosecutor, or maybe (the law is unclear) by the controllers if the creditors' representative does not act. However, the administrator himself is not allowed to declare void any such transactions; the court has exclusive competence to rule on claw-back actions.

Administrators licensed abroad (ie, appointed to a company whose registered seat is outside France) have no other functional rights in France other than acting on behalf of the insolvent foreign company that they represent (ie, as a creditor). They may cooperate with French administrators in French insolvency cases.

As outlined above, the administrator has only indirect obligations towards the creditors of the insolvent company. If the creditors of the other (healthy) participatory companies are not direct creditors of the company undergoing insolvency proceedings, then the administrator has no special duties towards them.

(b) Dissolution/termination of the cash pooling agreement in the event of liquidation of the master account holder or of a group company

If either the bank, the master account holder or a group company enters insolvency proceedings (whether safeguard, reorganisation or liquidation), all dissolution clauses due to insolvency are considered null and void.[12] Insolvency proceedings either suspend or forbid financial claims for breach of contracts from creditors whose credit originates from before the opening insolvency judgment. Those provisions are meant to protect the debtor while there is still hope it can recover (safeguard and reorganisation), and to preserve common estate and equality among creditors if it cannot.

However, a creditor of an insolvent company under a cash pooling agreement can require the administrator to decide whether to terminate the contract. If the creditor's demand is unanswered after one month, then the contract shall be terminated. However, as stated above, the administrator can decide to continue the contract, in which case the debtor must perform. That said, it is very unlikely in practice for a cash pooling agreement to be continued if one of the participating companies is undergoing insolvency proceedings.

2.4 Perspective D: regulatory

There are no regulatory requirements specific to cash pooling agreements in France. However, the banks are subject to oversight by the *Autorité de Contrôle Prudentiel* (the French banking and insurance regulator).

The regulator aims to protect banks from insolvency and systemic risks by monitoring their compliance with rules on liquidity and solvency ratios (as covered in 'banking requirements'). Financial institutions and banks must have an appropriate internal control system measuring their risks and profitability. The *Autorité* can order a credit institution to take any measure in order to recover its

---

12 Article L622-13 Commercial Code (safeguard); Article L 631-14 of the Commercial Code (reorganisation); Article L. 641-11-1 I, para.1 of the Commercial Code.

financial situation, and can even instruct an institution to hold a higher amount of equity than is required by applicable ratios. Such controls can add to the growing capital requirements faced by banks participating in cash pooling agreements.

2.5 Perspective E: tax

From a tax law perspective, implementing a cash pooling agreement in France requires three sets of rules to be considered:

- transfer pricing issues;
- thin capitalisation rules; and
- depending on the countries involved, withholding tax issues.

Regarding transfer pricing issues, interest benefits or costs of intra-group loans might be set to an arbitrary level in order to avoid or reduce taxation in one jurisdiction. The French tax authorities may challenge interest rates that do not correspond to market standards (Article 57 of the *Code Général des Impôts*). However, the interest rates applied to loans in a cash pooling agreement may exceptionally be set below market price, if it can justified by the company's commercial interest (ie, the lender takes advantage from a commercial point of view).

Rules on thin capitalisation impose limits on tax deductions allowable against interest rates paid by an under-capitalised company to other group companies.

Withholding tax should not be a real concern for cash pooling agreements, as long as participant companies are resident in the European Union. Under certain conditions, cross-border interest payments between EU resident companies of the same group are exempt from withholding tax. As for interest paid to group companies residing outside the European Union, withholding tax is governed by double taxation treaties, and there are no withholding taxes between Organisation for Economic Cooperation and Development member states. In general, withholding tax of 50% shall only apply to payments made to blacklisted tax havens.

Germany

Daniela Mader
Kirsten Schümann-Kleber
GÖRG Partnerschaft von Rechtsanwälten

1. Introduction

1.1 Admissibility of cash pooling agreements

Holding companies and their group members are freely permitted to set up and enter into cash pooling agreements. However, there are restrictions on individual cash flows, especially with regard to capital maintenance and liquidity protection. Physical cash pooling poses one of the biggest problems, since money actually changes hands. On the other hand, notional cash pooling requires merely a theoretical combination and allocation of balances across several accounts – no actual payments are made. So capital maintenance and company liquidity can generally be affected only by physical cash pooling.[1] Whether substantive law applies to foreign companies depends on the applicable conflict of laws rules. German substantive law itself principally covers German and foreign companies alike.

1.2 Types of cash pooling agreement

Physical cash pooling is much more common than notional cash pooling, especially in multinational corporate groups. This is because some jurisdictions have imposed strict restrictions on notional cash pooling, while others prohibit it altogether.[2] Target balancing is the most frequently employed cash pooling model, as it combines the aim of optimising interest rates with reasonable liquidity control by each participating group company.[3] Since a typical cash pooling system does not exist, agreements differ greatly.[4]

1.3 Legal requirements from various perspectives

The admissibility of cash pooling agreements is primarily determined by the Act on the Modernisation of the Limited Liability Companies Act and on the Prevention of Abuses.[5] This statute mainly affects the Limited Liability Companies Act, the Stock Corporations Act and the Insolvency Act.

---

1 In contrast, the legal relevance of notional cash pooling under German law is generally limited, provided that no other actions occur, such as the granting of upstream securities. If that is the case, notional cash pooling involves comparable legal problems – see Kai Zahrte, *Finanzierung durch Cash Pooling im internationalen mehrstufigen Konzern*, 2010, p49.

2 Stefan Waldens, *Grenzüberschreitedes Cash Pooling im Spannungsfeld sich ändernder Rahmenbedingungen – Eine ertragsteuerliche Analyse*, Internationales Steuerrecht, 497, 498 (2003).

3 Ronald Sieder, *Cash Pooling im GmbH-Konzern*, 2011, p40.

4 Sieder, supranote 3, p 52.

(a) *Company law*

Most legal requirements for operating a cash pooling agreement stem from company law. Depending on the direction of the flow of the funds, agreements can raise various legal concerns. As notional cash pooling involves no actual payments, the following relates to physical cash pooling between private limited companies (GmbHs) and/or stock corporations (AGs).

Upstream loans and capital maintenance: Upstream funds qualify as upstream loans and may particularly raise concerns in view of capital maintenance rules (stated in Sections 30 and 31 of the Limited Liability Companies and Sections 57 to 62 of the Stock Corporations Act).

According to Section 30 of the Limited Liability Companies Act, company assets required to preserve the stated share capital may not be distributed to the shareholders. Any loan granted by a GmbH to a shareholder or affiliate must generally be limited to the amount by which the net assets exceed its registered share capital.[6] According to Section 57 of the Stock Corporations Act, capital contributions to an AG may not be returned to the shareholders at all.

However, both provisions contain exceptions to the definition of 'unlawful distribution', which may be significant in cash pooling agreements. First, Section 30 of the Limited Liability Companies Act and Section 57 of the Stock Corporations Act do not apply to benefits granted while a domination or profit-and-loss transfer agreement is in place. Second, the provisions do not apply to any benefits covered by a fully valuable counterclaim or retransfer claim against the recipient shareholder.

This latter exception has particular relevance, as it marks the return of the balance-sheet test.[7] In principle, any violation by an upstream loan of the capital maintenance rules need be tested only at the time of drawdown. If it becomes unfeasible for the shareholder to repay the loan, this does not retrospectively mean that the drawdown was illegal. However, such circumstances may oblige the management of the group company under its fiduciary duties to terminate the loan and enforce a repayment claim.[8] A prudent managing director should avoid long-term upstream loan agreements if they cannot readily be terminated. It is advisable to set up an early warning system and to include a respective termination right in the agreement. Some legal authors also apply the requirement of feasibility to a loss

---

5 *Bundesgesetzblatt* (BGBl. – *Federal Law Gazette*) 2008 I, p 2026. The act came into force on November 1 2008 and resolved significant controversy concerning the legal framework for cash pooling agreements which was especially caused by the November 24 2003 decision of the Federal Court of Justice, BGHZ 157, 52.

6 Relevant for the test as to whether a payment or other financial advantage by a GmbH results in a breach of Section 30 of the Limited Liability Companies Act is the equity of the GmbH as reported in its balance sheet, established in accordance with German generally accepted accounting principles.

7 The balance-sheet test was the prevailing view in case law and literature prior to the November 24 2003 decision of the Federal Court of Justice, and was questioned by the court; see Jochen Vetter & Christian Schwandtner, "Cash Pooling under the Revised German Private Limited Companies Act (GmbHG)", 9 *German Law Journal* (2008), 1155, 1161 *et seq*. According to the Federal Court of Justice (December 1 2008, BGHZ 179, 71), the exceptions shall apply regardless of whether the upstream loans were granted before or after November 1 2008; see Goetz Hueck & Lorenz Fastrich, "§ 30 GmbHG", *in GmbH-Gesetz* (Adolf Baumbach & Alfred Hueck eds, 19th ed, 2010), margin number 46.

8 BGHZ 179, 71, 79, margin number 14.

compensation claim (Section 302 of the Stock Corporations Act) arising from a domination or profit-and-loss transfer agreement.[9] No case law exists as yet, but it cannot be excluded that any payments made under a domination or profit-and-loss transfer agreement could be subject to the same strict balance-sheet test as other payments (even though the wordings of Section 30 of the Limited Liability Companies Act and Section 57 of the Stock Corporations Act indicate otherwise). As a result, upstream loans made within a cash pooling system do not conflict with capital maintenance rules if the repayment claim (or the loss compensation claim) of the group company against the parent company appears to be fully realisable at the time.

The consequences of any distribution not meeting the requirements of Section 30 of the Limited Liability Companies Act (or Section 57 of the Stock Corporations Act) are laid down in Section 31 of the Limited Liability Companies Act (or Section 62 of the Stock Corporations Act). In case of a breach, the company must first be reimbursed for any unlawful distributions by the recipients.[10] However, not only recipients, but also the shareholders, are liable in accordance with Section 31 of the Limited Liability Companies Act (or Section 62 of the Stock Corporations Act). The managing directors can also be held liable for unlawful distributions in accordance with Section 43 of the Limited Liability Companies Act or Section 93 of the Stock Corporations Act. A violation of the capital maintenance rules may also constitute a criminal offence by the managing directors of the company and by the managing directors of the shareholder that initiated the distribution, according to Section 266 of the Penal Code.

Downstream loans: Downstream funds qualify as downstream loans and may raise particular concerns in view of the rules on the subordination of shareholder loans. However, these rules are relevant in the event of insolvency of the recipient company only, and are therefore subject to insolvency law (see below).

Liquidity protection and destructive intervention: Transferring funds to a shareholder or affiliate – whether by way of an upstream loan or repayment of a downstream loan – may conflict with the rules and principles on liquidity protection.

Generally, managing directors cannot make any payment after the company has become illiquid or over-indebted (Section 64 of the Limited Liability Companies Act and Section 92 of the Stock Corporations Act). The prohibitions on shareholder payments are even stricter: it is forbidden to make shareholder payments that lead to the illiquidity of the company (Section 64 of the Limited Liability Companies Act and Section 92 of the Stock Corporations Act). Such acts are considered comparable to wrongful trading under common law.[11]

9 Hueck & Fastrich, supranote 7, margin number 45; Vetter & Schwandtner, supra note 7, p 1169.

10 *Bona fide* recipients are partly protected if the reimbursement is less than the amount required to satisfy the creditors. A specialised liability in accordance with Sections 311 to 317 of the Stock Corporations Act applies only if the controlled entity is an AG and no domination agreement is in place; see Uwe Hüffer, "§ 311 AktG", in *Aktiengesetz* (Uwe Hüffer ed, 9th ed, 2010), margin number 49 *et seq*.

11 See Ulrich Haas, "§ 64 GmbHG", in *GmbH-Gesetz* (Adolf Baumbach & Alfred Hueck eds, 19th ed, 2010), margin number 2.

In both cases managing directors are liable to the company for the full amount of the payment, unless they have demonstrably acted with appropriate prudence and diligence. In order to prevent such liability, the managing directors must constantly control the liquidity of the company, and must refuse any payments to shareholders that might lead to its insolvency.[12] No case law as yet exists to determine how far this clause can be interpreted. If the payment cannot be refused (eg, in the case of payments on security provided to a third-party creditor at the bank implementing the agreement),[13] the managing directors should provide other liquidity protection. The implementation of termination rights, limitation language in the finance documents and target balancing can all be crucial in this regard.

In exceptional cases, a shareholder that receives such a payment can also be held liable. Under German law, the transfer of assets to a shareholder is prohibited if doing so could render the company unable to fulfil its payment obligations when due. This liability is based, according to recent court rulings, on Section 826 of the Civil Code, a provision of tort law. It triggers an internal liability towards the company, and so can only partly be compared to piercing the corporate veil under common law. Hitherto, so-called 'destructive intervention' has been particularly relevant in cases where the GmbH is the group company. Comparable compensation for AGs is provided by Section 117 of the Stock Corporations Act.

Effective raising of capital: Under German law, cash pooling agreements can also be at risk from capital increases against cash contributions.[14] Here again, a distinction is made between upstream and downstream loans. Upstream loans made at the same time as a capital increase are qualified as 'back-and-forth payments'. Downstream loans are qualified as 'hidden contributions in kind'.[15]

These differ in the following respects:

- If a shareholder's cash contribution is assessed as being to any extent a hidden contribution in kind, the shareholder is not released from its contribution obligation. The relevant contracts and the legal acts concerned remain effective. However, the value of the asset will be deducted from the shareholder's obligation when the capital increase is registered in the Commercial Register (Section 19 of the Limited Liability Companies Act and Section 27 of the Stock Corporations Act).
- If a shareholder's cash contribution is assessed as a back-and-forth payment, then the shareholder is released from its contribution obligation – provided that the payment is:

---

12 According to the prevailing view, Section 64 of the Limited Liability Companies Act (or Section 92 of the Stock Corporations Act) not only regulates the managing directors' liability, but also allows the respective managing director to refuse payment to the shareholder. This, however, refers to payments to shareholders only and does not apply to payment obligations towards third-party creditors.

13 Upstream securities create payment obligations towards third-party creditors.

14 Here, the Act on the Modernisation of the Limited Liability Companies Act and on the Prevention of Abuses (implemented in Section 19 of the Limited Liability Companies Act) and the Act on the Implementation of the Shareholders' Rights Directive, BGBl. 2009 I, p2479 (implemented in Section 27 of the Stock Corporations Act) also provides some relief. The 'new' provisions apply to contributions provided both before and after November 1 2008 and September 1 2009 respectively.

15 BGHZ 182, 103.

- covered by a fully realisable repayment claim against the shareholder (which is due at any time or may become due through termination without notice by the company); and
- disclosed to the Commercial Register (Section 19 of the Limited Liability Companies Act and Section 27 of the Stock Corporations Act).

The different legal consequences require that a precise distinction be drawn between hidden contributions in kind and back-and-forth payments. To avoid this requirement, cash contributions must be diverted from the cash pooling system into a single deposit account.[16]

(b) *Banking law*

Alongside corporate relationships within the group of companies, there are separate contractual relationships between the group and the bank organising the cash pooling system. The following refers to both physical and notional cash pooling.

First, the master account holder, the group companies and the bank enter into a cash pooling agreement, which qualifies as a management service agreement according to Section 675 of the Civil Code.[17] This contains the framework arrangements with the bank, including balance details, interest rates, costs, technical proceedings and termination rights. Second, the master account holder and the group companies each have payment services contracts with the bank for the technical operation of cash pooling, according to Section 675f of the Civil Code. If a credit line is granted, the master account holder and the bank additionally enter into a credit agreement according to Section 488 of the Civil Code and Section 355 of the Commercial Code. Given that centralisation is the main purpose of cash pooling, no other credit lines will normally be provided.

All contractual relationships involve a duty to fulfil mutual obligations, which include informing, warning and protecting the other participants. This is the same as the usual contractual relationship that a bank has with its clients. So cash pooling agreements raise no other concerns on top of those arising from usual banking relationships. Similarly, there are no specific regulatory requirements with which the bank must comply.

(c) *Insolvency law*

Insolvency law is second only to company law as a source of legal issues concerning cash pooling systems. (Since notional cash pooling does not involve actual payments, the following refers to physical cash pooling only.)

As discussed, the managing directors are prohibited from making payments after the company has become illiquid or over-indebted (Section 64 of the Limited Liability Companies Act and Section 92 of the Stock Corporations Act). They must apply for the opening of insolvency proceedings without culpable delay (Section 15a

---

16 Daniel Komo, *Kapitalaufbringung im Cash Pool – aktuelle Entwicklungen in Rechtsprechung und Literatur*, Betriebs-Berater, 2307, 2313 (2011).

17 If the group companies do not sign individually, the master account holder normally acts on their behalf according to a power of attorney, or the group companies declare their assumption of debt later.

of the Insolvency Act). Otherwise, they will be held liable towards the company's creditors and will face criminal law liability risks. If, during this time, payments are made to the creditors' detriment, the law allows for the right to contest such payments (Sections 129 and following of the Insolvency Act). The insolvency administrator is more likely to contest any payments made in the three months immediately before or after an insolvency application[18] – especially where upstream loans are concerned. With respect to repayments of downstream loans, the suspect period can be even longer – the administrator may contest any repayments made a full year prior to an insolvency application (Section 135 of the Insolvency Act). Security provided for such loans within the preceding 10 years is subject to avoidance rights. The party in receipt of contested payments must refund the full sum to the insolvency estate.[19]

Claims under shareholder loans made once insolvency proceedings are underway are subordinate to the claims of all other creditors (Section 39 of the Insolvency Act). In view of these potentially harsh consequences for company groups, some authors argue that upstream funds which qualify as repayments of shareholder loans are really cash transactions (according to Section 142 of the Insolvency Act), and can be contested only in case of wilful disadvantage.[20] However, since no case law yet exists, a court may still strictly apply Sections 135 and 39 of the Insolvency Act. It is therefore strongly recommended to provide for constant control of the status of group companies and to suspend their participation in the cash pooling agreement at the first sign of a crisis that could lead to insolvency. To enable group companies to do this, respective termination rights should be included in the agreement.

(d) *Regulatory*

Companies conducting banking business or providing financial or payment services are usually subject to regulatory requirements set out in the Banking Act and the Payment Services Regulation Act. However, this does not apply if the services are provided to affiliated companies only.[21] Even though the master account holder may serve as a credit institution or payment service provider within the company group, it is exempt from the respective regulatory requirements (this applies to physical and notional cash pooling alike).

---

18 If the payment was made with the intention to disadvantage the creditors and the recipient was aware of that intention, the right to contest can also go back up to 10 years – Section 133 of the Insolvency Act.

19 Sections 39 and 135 of the Insolvency Act (new version) apply in any case in which both the repayment was effected and the insolvency proceedings were opened after November 1 2008. These provisions do not apply to shareholder loans for the purpose of the company's reorganisation and loans by minority shareholders.

20 Heribert Hirte, "§ 356 InsO", in *InsO* (Wilhelm Uhlenbruck, Heribert Hirte & Heinz Vallender eds, 13th ed, 2010), margin number 10; for details see Alexander Reuter, *"Die Anfechtbarkeit der Rückzahlung von Gesellschafterdarlehen im Cash-Pool: Explosive Massevermehrung nach § 135 InsO?", Neue Zeitschrift für das Recht der Insolvenz und Sanierung*, 921 (2011).

21 The exemptions according to Section 2 of the Banking Act apply to affiliated companies referred to in Section 290 of the Commercial Code); see Sven Schneider, *"Nichtanwendbarkeit des KWG bzw. WpHG trotz Erbringung regulierter Tätigkeiteni", Wertpapiermitteilungen*, 285, 288 (2008). The exemption according to Section 1 of the Payment Services Act has a narrower scope, as it refers to corporate groups, generally defined in Section 18 of the Stock Corporations Act. Neither applies if the respective service is provided to third parties, such as companies in which the parent company has a minority shareholding only.

(e) *Tax law*

Tax law exerts considerable influence on the implementation of cash pooling agreements. Inter-company claims and liabilities resulting from physical cash pooling can have a particular tax impact. (Unless otherwise indicated, the following refers to physical cash pooling only.)

Deemed dividends and transfer prices: Considerable tax benefits can be gained by upstream funds being qualified as deemed dividends. Such dividends are treated as usual dividend distributions according to Section 8 of the Corporate Income Tax. Their amount is added back to the taxable profit of the company, submitted to corporate taxation and subsequently attributed to shareholders as a dividend. The Federal Court of Finance views deemed dividends as either a decrease or a prevention of increase in wealth of the company, which:

- is caused by the company's relationship to its shareholders;
- affects the level of income; and
- is not connected to a profit distribution in accordance with company law for the distribution of profits.[22]

To avoid this qualification within cash pooling systems, the cash pooling agreement must meet arm's-length standards and should be implemented according to the terms of a clear-cut prior written contract.[23] If group companies assume joint and several liability to the bank, they should receive appropriate remuneration in return. The arm's-length requirements also apply to international cash pooling systems according to Section 1 of the Foreign Tax Act,[24] and are relevant to both physical and notional schemes.[25]

International cash pooling agreements can also be subject to imputational taxation according to Sections 7 and following of the Foreign Tax Act. However, the European Court of Justice (ECJ) has ruled that such taxation need not apply when profits are derived by a controlled EU foreign company, if it can be proven that the company is actually established in the host member state and carries on genuine economic activities there.[26] Thus, imputational taxation is rather restricted within the European Union.

---

22 BFHE 223, 131; Jutta Rengers, "§ 8 KStG", in *Blümich – EStG, KStG, GewStG* (Bernd Heuermann & Peter Brandis eds, 2011), margin number 235 *et seq.*

23 According to Section 90 of the General Tax Code, cross-border relationships are subject to increased documentation requirements anyway.

24 For details see BMF, "The Principles for the Examination of Income Allocation between Internationally Associated Enterprises (1983 Transfer Pricing Regulations)", BStBl II 1983, 218, Sec 4.2.1: "Where a person extends credit to a related party (eg, loans, mortgages, merchandise purchase credit, current account credit), the arm's length price is the interest that unrelated parties would have charged in extending credit in comparable circumstances on the money or credit market". More recently cf BMF, "The Principles for the Examination of Income Allocation between Internationally Associated Enterprises by Means of Cost Sharing Agreements", BStBl I 2005, 570; both in *Deutsches Außensteuerrecht – German International Taxation* (KPMG ed, 1st ed, 2010).

25 Wolfgang Oho, "§ 10 Finanzströme", *in Konzernsteuerrecht* (Wolfgang Kessler, Michael Kröner & Stefan Köhler eds, 2nd ed, 2008), margin number 135 *et seq.*

26 ECJ Case C-196/04 of September 12 2006, ECR 2006, I-7995 (*Cadbury Schweppes*); also cf BMF, *Imputational Taxation under the Foreign Transactions Tax Law*, BStBl I 2007, 99, in *Deutsches Außensteuerrecht* – German International Taxation (KPMG ed, 1st ed, 2010).

Withholding tax: Withholding tax is levied on interest income, such as the interest accrued in a German bank account.[27] In cash pooling agreements, it is triggered as soon as the master account is set up. In contrast, interest allocated between group companies and the master account holder is not taxed. According to Section 43a of the Income Tax Act, the withholding tax amounts to 25% of the capital income (plus a 5.5% solidarity surcharge). Any withholding tax actually paid on interest payments can be credited against the recipient's corporate income tax, provided that the recipient is located in Germany.

Thin capitalisation rules: German thin capitalisation rules restrict the deductibility of interest paid on liabilities. Even though legitimate business expenses are generally deductible for corporate income tax and trade tax purposes, the deductibility of interest expenses is limited. As from fiscal year 2008, GmbH and AG taxpayers may immediately deduct only net interest expenses up to 30% of taxable earnings before interest, tax, depreciation and amortisation (EBITDA), according to Section 8a of the Corporate Tax Act.[28] The interest deduction rule applies to all interest paid, regardless of whether to a shareholder, a related party or a third party. However, it does not apply where the annual net interest burden is less than €3 million or the taxpayer can demonstrate that the German borrower's equity borrower does not fall below the worldwide group's equity ratio by more than two percentage points (the so-called 'group clause').[29] The details are complex and must be assessed by a specialised legal adviser or a tax adviser.

Permanent debts: Interest expenses are subject to further deductibility restrictions with respect to trade tax. According to Section 8 of the Trade Tax Act, 25% of all remunerations for permanent debts must be added back to any profit from commercial business activity if they:

- were deducted for the purpose of determining taxable profits (ie, if they were not subject to the interest deduction rule mentioned above); and
- exceed €100,000 (together with other comparable payments, such as pensions and continuing loans, profit shares of silent partners and lease instalments).

Inter-company liabilities (eg, liabilities towards third parties) qualify as permanent debts if they exist to a minimum amount throughout the whole financial year.

---

27 Withholding tax is levied by paying agents only. According to Section 43 of the Income Tax Act, the functions of paying agents are exercised by German credit institutions or financial services institutions (Section 1 of the Banking Act) and/or German branches of foreign credit institutions or financial services institutions (Sections 53 and 53b of the Banking Act).

28 EBITDA is determined based on financial statements prepared using German accounting principles, with adjustments for additions and deductions made in computing German taxable income, such as non-taxable dividends. A tax group for German tax purposes is treated as one business.

29 The group clause test is based on financial statements for the German business at the end of the previous financial year. A uniform accounting standard must be used for the German business and the group financial statements (primarily International Financial Reporting Standards, or alternatively using any European or US generally accepted accounting principles as a last resort).

To avoid additional tax burdens stemming from thin capitalisation rules and permanent debts, a company group may be well advised to create a fiscal unit for corporate income tax and trade tax purposes.

Value added tax: Turnover tax is generally not triggered within cash pooling agreements. The services provided between group companies, the master account holder and the bank are exempt as 'other services', according to Section 4 of the Value Added Tax Act.

(f) General legal requirements

Statutory law also addresses the specific issues raised by cross-border agreements. Depending on the relevant conflict of laws rules, German substantive law may not be applicable to foreign companies.

German company law cannot be applied to EU companies, even when their actual centre of administration is in Germany. This is due to several landmark ECJ decisions rejecting the 'real seat' theory for inbound cases.[30] Therefore, an EU company located in Germany is to be respected in law as a foreign company, subject to the company law of its state of incorporation. Similarly, according to the German/US Treaty of Friendship, Commerce and Navigation, US companies are subject to US company law only.[31]

However, the situation is different as regards insolvency law. German courts can open insolvency proceedings if the centre of a debtor's main interests[32] is located in Germany (Article 3 of the EU Insolvency Regulation (1346/2000)).[33] If the centre of main interests is located in another member state, the German courts can open secondary insolvency proceedings with respect to German-based assets.[34] As soon as the German courts have jurisdiction, the insolvency proceedings and their effects are automatically subject to German insolvency law, regardless of whether the debtor is a German company.[35]

As regards non-contractual obligations arising out of a tort/delict, the applicable

30 ECJ Case C-212/97 of March 9 1999, ECR 1999, I-1459 (Centros); ECJ Case C-208/00 of November 5 2002, ECR 2002, I-9919 (*Überseering*); ECJ Case C-167/01 of September 30 2003, ECR 2003, I-10155 (*Inspire Art*); differently on outbound – see ECJ Case 81/87 of September 27 1988, ECR 1988, 5483 (*Daily Mail*); ECJ Case 210/06 of December 16 2008, ECR 2008, I-9641 (*Cartesio*). Companies from outside the European Union, except US companies, can be subject to German company law if their actual centre of administration (ie, headquarters) is located in Germany; see Marc-Philippe Weller, *Einleitung*, in *Münchener Kommentar zum GmbHG* (Holger Fleischer & Wulf Goette eds, 1st ed, 2010), margin number 350 *et seq.*

31 Article XXV of the German/US Treaty of Friendship, Commerce and Navigation of October 29 1954, BGBl 1956 II, p. 488; cf Weller, *supra* note 30, margin number 369, 370.

32 The centre of main interests is the place where the debtor conducts the administration of its interests on a regular basis and is therefore ascertainable by third parties; see Recital 13 of the EU Insolvency Regulation and ECJ Case C-341/04 of May 2 2006, ECR 2006, I-3813 (*Eurofood*); ECJ Case C-369/09 of October 20 2011, *Official Journal of the European Union* of December 10 2011, C 362/3 *et seq* (*Interedil Srl*). In the absence of proof to the contrary, the centre of main interests shall be presumed to be the place of the registered office – Article 3 of the EU Insolvency Regulation.

33 According to Article 1 of the EU Insolvency Regulation, the regulation shall not apply to insolvency proceedings concerning credit institutions; they are therefore subject to Sections 3, 335 and 356 of the Insolvency Act.

34 See Article 27 of the EU Insolvency Regulation and Section 356 of the Insolvency Act.

35 See Articles 4 and 28 of the EU Insolvency Regulation and Section 335 of the Insolvency Act.

law is generally that of the country in which the damage occurs (Article 4 of EU Regulation 864/2007 on the law applicable to non-contractual obligations).[36] Deviations are possible in circumstances where the party claimed to be liable and the injured party were both living in the same country at the time, or where it is otherwise manifest that the tort/delict is more closely connected with another country.[37] In essence, whether German substantive law applies depends solely on whether the respective provisions are subject to company, insolvency or tort/delict law.

2. Specific questions

2.1 Perspective A: corporate group

(a) *Liability of group company and/or master account holder directors in the event of insolvency of a group company*

Should a group company become illiquid or over-indebted, the managing directors risk personal liability[38] if they allow payments to continue (Section 64 of the Limited Liability Companies Act and Section 92 of the Stock Corporations Act). The same applies to payments to shareholders that lead to illiquidity (Section 64 of the Limited Liability Companies Act and Section 92 of the Stock Corporations Act), as well as payments that qualify as unlawful distributions according to Sections 43 and 30 of the Limited Liability Companies Act (or Sections 93 and 57 of the Stock Corporations Act).[39] This is covered in detail earlier in this chapter.

The managing directors therefore should stop making upstream or downstream loans as soon as (or, better still, before) the group company becomes insolvent. They will need to take care that they are not forced into making unlawful payments by the routine operations of the cash pooling agreement.

The specific role of supervisory directors exposes them to different risks of liability towards the group company. First, not every GmbH is obliged to establish a supervisory board. Where a company has done so voluntarily or due to a legal obligation (and with respect to the supervisory board of an AG), a liability towards group companies can arise only if the supervisory board violates one of its specific duties. The supervisory board must minimise any obvious disadvantages arising from commercially unreasonable behaviour by the managing directors (especially regarding the supervision of the credit risk management).[40] If they neglect their

36 This applies irrespective of the country in which the event occasioning the damage occurred and irrespective of the country or countries in which the indirect consequences of that event occur.

37 A manifestly closer connection with another country might be based in particular on a pre-existing relationship between the parties, such as a contract, that is closely connected with the tort/delict in question.

38 The right to claim such compensation generally rests with the company itself; but in an AG compensation can also be claimed by the creditors, provided that their claims have not yet been satisfied – Section 93 of the Stock Corporations Act.

39 Managing directors can also be held liable as criminal offenders according to Section 266 of the Criminal Code (Section 823 of the Civil Code), and/or as accessories to a destructive intervention by the shareholder of the group company (Sections 826 and 830 of the Civil Code).

40 Federal Court of Justice, decision of December 1 2008 – II ZR 102/07.

supervisory role, they can be held liable towards the company according to Sections 116 and 93 of the Stock Corporations Act in case of an AG; or Section 52 of the Limited Liability Companies Act, in conjunction with Sections 116 and 93 of the Stock Corporations Act, in case of a GmbH.[41]

Liability of managing directors and supervisory directors towards creditors or other third parties can arise only under the specifics of tort law – for example, if there is a deliberate violation of criminal law (eg, fraud) or deliberate immoral violation.[42]

Managing directors can, however, be held liable towards both company and creditors – and can also face criminal liability risks – if they breach their obligation to file for the opening of insolvency proceedings without culpable delay. Where a group company lacks a management body, the shareholders (in case of a GmbH) or the members of the supervisory board (in case of an AG) can also be obliged to file for insolvency and can therefore be held liable in case of breach (Section 15a of the Insolvency Act). Based on decisions of the Federal Court of Justice regarding predecessor provisions, the prevailing view in legal commentary is that a violation of this duty can lead to a director's personal liability. That aside, the members of the supervisory board have no personal duty to file for insolvency, but should at least use all of their influence to ensure that the management fulfils its responsibility to do so.

Insofar as liability claims are subject to insolvency or tort law, they apply to German and foreign companies alike. This especially refers to the civil and criminal law risks if an application for insolvency is not filed in time. Some legal authors maintain that this also applies to directors' liability (according to Section 64 of the Limited Liability Companies Act and Section 92 of the Stock Corporations Act).[43] The remaining claims are subject to company law and apply to managing and supervisory directors of German companies only.

The master account holder and its managing directors risk liability towards the group company for unlawful distributions (according to Section 31 of the Limited Liability Companies Act and Section 62 of the Stock Corporations Act), and for destructive intervention (according to Section 826 of the Civil Code). While the former is clearly a matter of company law, liability for destructive intervention cannot easily be attributed to company, insolvency or tort law. As the prevailing view is that it qualifies as insolvency or tort law,[44] liability may also extend to shareholders of a foreign distressed group company.

In view of the significant liability risks, a pre-warning system should be installed and a distressed group company should be excluded from the cash pooling agreement as soon as possible.

---

41 Federal Court of Justice, *Wertpapiermitteilungen*, 851 (2009).

42 Düsseldorf Higher Regional Court, decision dated June 23 2008 – 9 U 22/08.

43 KG, *Zeitschrift für Wirtschaftsrecht*, 2156 (2009); Haas, *supra*, note 11, margin number 21 *et seq*.

44 Cf Alexander Ego & Holger Altmeppen, *B. Europäische Niederlassungsfreiheit*, in *Münchener Kommentar zum* AktG (Wulf Goette, Mathias Habersack & Susanne Kalss eds, 3rd ed, 2012) margin number 416 *et seq*, 429 *et seq*; Klaus J Hopt, *Anhang nach § 177a*, in HGB-Gesetz (Adolf Baumbach & Klaus J Hopt eds, 35th ed, 2012), margin number 51e ; Peter Kindler, "Art. 4 VO (EG) 1346/2000", in *Münchener Kommentar zum BGB* (Franz Jürgen Säcker & Roland Rixecker eds, 5th ed, 2010), margin number 13; Hans-Friedrich Müller, "*Internationales Gesellschaftsrecht*", in *Aktiengesetz* (Gerald Spindler & Eberhard Stilz eds, 2nd ed, 2010), margin number 35.

(b) *Liability of group company and/or master account holder directors in the event of insolvency of the master account holder*

Should the master account holder become insolvent, the liability risks for the supervisory directors are essentially the same as those outlined above. The managing directors of a distressed company (whether a group company or master account holder) can similarly be held liable if they breach their obligation to file for insolvency without culpable delay (Section 823 of the Civil Code and Section 15a of the Insolvency Act), and/or if they allow payments to be made after the company has become illiquid or over-indebted (Section 64 of the Limited Liability Companies Act and Section 92 of the Stock Corporations Act). Again, these liabilities may also apply to managing directors of foreign companies.

Additionally, the managing directors of the group company can be held liable for unlawful distributions (Sections 43 and 30 of the Limited Liability Companies Act and Sections 93 and 57 of the Stock Corporations Act) and payments to shareholders that lead to the illiquidity of the group company (Section 64 of the Limited Liability Companies Act and Section 92 of the Stock Corporations Act). As some legal commentators attribute this liability to insolvency law, it also applies to managing directors of foreign companies. As the repayment claim is no longer valid, further payments to the master account are inadmissible. To avoid such liability risks, the master account holder must immediately be replaced by a healthy company.

Once again, if supervisory directors neglect their specific responsibilities, they can be held liable towards the company according to Sections 116 and 93 of the Stock Corporations Act in the case of an AG; or Section 52 of the Limited Liability Companies Act, in conjunction with Sections 116 and 93 of the Stock Corporations Act, in the case of a GmbH. The liability of supervisory directors towards creditors or other third parties can arise only under the specifics of tort law.

(c) *Liability of group companies in the event of insolvency of the master account holder*

In general, creditors of a distressed company have no legal right to hold other group companies liable for any losses suffered. Such liability claims as described above apply only to the distressed company.[45] If the distressed company becomes insolvent, the insolvency administrator will assert the claims in the interests of the creditors (Sections 80 and 85 of the Insolvency Act). The administrator can contest any group company payments that are detrimental to other creditors (Sections 129 *et seq* of the Insolvency Act). The group company that received such payment must refund the insolvent company, not the individual creditors. This applies regardless of whether the claiming creditors and/or the group companies are located in Germany, provided that the insolvent master account holder has its centre of main interests in Germany and German insolvency law applies (see above).

Outside insolvency proceedings, creditors can, under special circumstances,

45 Today, this also refers to the liability for destructive intervention; cf BGHZ 173, 246 (*TRIHOTEL)*. Before, the Federal Court of Justice understood the so-called '*existenzvernichtender Eingriff*' as an external liability towards creditors; BGHZ 149, 10 (*Bremer Vulkan*); BGHZ 151, 181 (KBV).

contest payments made to other creditors by raising a defence under Section 9 of the Act on Contestation or by bringing a lawsuit under Section 13 of the act. The right to contest ends immediately upon the opening of insolvency proceedings (Section 16 of the Act on Contestation). Moreover, since the Act on Contestation applies only if the payment concerned is subject to German law (Section 19 of the of the Act on Contestation), its practical relevance is limited.

(d) Liability of master account holder in the event of insolvency of a group company

The legal situation is the same if a group company either gets into distress or enters into liquidation. Once again, creditors of a distressed company generally have no legal right to hold other group companies or the master account holder liable for their losses, and must instead rely on the intervention of the insolvency administrator. According to the Act on Contestation, creditors themselves can in some cases contest payments made to other creditors outside insolvency proceedings.

2.2 Perspective B: bank

(a) Banking requirements

A bank that enters into a cash pooling agreement is subject to no regulatory requirements beyond those that normally apply to its contractual client relationships (see above).

(b) Bank's liability in the event of insolvency of master account holder or a group company

Any bank involved in a cash pooling agreement can be held liable only under special circumstances. All contractual relationships between the bank, the master account holder and group companies involve a duty to fulfil mutual obligations, such as informing, warning and protecting the other parties; and the bank can be held liable if it fails in this regard. However, the bank does not automatically owe comprehensive legal advice to its customers. It generally need do no more than highlight any economic and legal risks, and advise the company group to seek independent legal assistance as appropriate.[46] Apart from that, default and/or liability risks fall within the scope of risk of the master account holder and the group companies.

The above applies under German contract law, which will normally be applicable if a German bank is involved.[47] The location of the master account holder, the claiming creditor and/or the group company then becomes irrelevant.[48]

---

46 Nils-Christian Wunderlich, *Warnpflichten der Bank beim Cash-Management, Zeitschrift für Bank- und Kapitalmarktrecht*, 387, 394 (2005).

47 See No 6 para. 1 AGB-Banken (Banks' Standard Terms and Conditions).

48 Restrictions apply, for example, with respect to mandatory provisions of a member state and public policy, Articles 9 and 21 *Verordnung Nr 593/2008 über das auf vertragliche Schuldverhältnisse anzuwendende Recht* (Rom I VO – Regulation 593/2008 on the law applicable to contractual obligations).

2.3 Insolvency

(a) *Cash pooling agreements from the insolvency practitioner's perspective*

Should the master account holder transfer funds to a group company (or vice versa) prior to insolvency, then the insolvency administrator can claim the credit balance as soon as it forms part of the insolvency estate (Section 148 of the Insolvency Act). This applies when either the account forms part of the debtor's assets on the date that proceedings commence or the credit balance is subsequently acquired during proceedings, possibly due to contestation (Section 35 of the Insolvency Act). Thus, the insolvency administrator can assume immediate possession of the credit balance only if the master account holder becomes insolvent. If the bank or a group company becomes insolvent, the insolvency administrator is initially limited to compensation claims and contestation rights. Once it holds the assets, it must adjust the estate with respect to rights to separation and claims to separate satisfaction (Sections 47 *et seq* of the Insolvency Act). The latter can be based on pledge agreements and security assignments, provided mainly to the bank and partly to group companies.

Apart from that, all insolvency creditors must be treated equally by the insolvency administrator. The law does not distinguish between German and foreign creditors. If a member bank of the German Banking Association (BdB) becomes insolvent, the credit balance is protected not only by the statutory deposit insurance scheme,[50] but also by the deposit protection fund of the BdB.[51] The general effects of insolvency proceedings against the master account holder or a group company – including avoidance risks – have already been described above.

This situation refers to German insolvency law only, which is applicable if the German courts have jurisdiction to open insolvency proceedings. This will be the case when the debtor's centre of main interests is located in Germany or when the German courts open secondary insolvency proceedings limited to assets situated in Germany (as discussed earlier).

If either the bank, the master account holder or a group company goes into liquidation, then apart from rights to separation of assets not belonging to the estate and claims to separate satisfaction, no special rules apply to the creditors of the other parties to the agreement. All insolvency creditors must be treated strictly equally – the only exception being shareholder claims, which are subordinate.

(b) *Dissolution/termination of the cash pooling agreement in the event of liquidation of the master account holder or a group company*

Should the master account holder become insolvent, the group companies may immediately terminate any upstream loans either according to Section 490 of the Civil Code or if individual termination rights have been stipulated in the agreement. Apart from that, group companies can terminate the agreement with the master account holder without notice only if individual termination rights have been

49 See EU Directive 94/14/EC on deposit guarantee schemes, as most recently amended by Directive 2009/14/EC, and implemented into German law by the Deposit Guarantee and Investor Compensation Act.

50 For more information see www.germanbanks.org/.

stipulated in the agreement. In contrast, the management service agreement between the master account holder and the bank (according to Section 675 of the Civil Code) is not terminated by notice, but expires automatically upon the opening of insolvency proceedings (Section 116 of the Insolvency Act). The same applies to the payment services contract between the master account holder and the bank (according to Section 675f of the Civil Code) and any eventual credit agreement (according to Section 488 of the Civil Code and Section 355 of the Commercial Code).[51] Individual payment orders placed before the opening of insolvency proceedings continue to exist and can be executed by the bank (Section 116 of the Insolvency Act).

Essentially, the same legal situation applies if a group company becomes insolvent. The master account holder may give notice of immediate termination of downstream loans (according to Section 490 of the Civil Code), but otherwise may terminate the agreement without complying with a notice period only if individual termination rights have been stipulated. Again, the payment services contract with the bank expires automatically with the opening of the insolvency proceedings (Section 116 of the Insolvency Act). Individual payment orders placed before insolvency proceedings commenced continue to exist and can be executed by the bank (Section 116 of the Insolvency Act).

Other group companies may terminate the cash pooling agreement only if individual termination rights have been stipulated. In the event that the bank becomes insolvent, the master account holder and the group companies can terminate the payment services contracts.[52]

Since statutory termination rights do not necessarily exist for every insolvency event, cash pooling agreement should provide for additional contractual termination rights where the contracting parties become distressed.[53]

51 Ralf Sinz, "§ 116 InsO", in *InsO* (Wilhelm Uhlenbruck, Heribert Hirte & Heinz Vallender eds, 13th ed, 2010), margin number 16 *et seq.*

52 BGH, *Wertpapiermitteilungen*, 317 (1991); OLG Köln, *Wertpapiermitteilungen*, 504 (2001); Martin Henssler, *§ 627*, in *Münchener Kommentar zum BGB* (Franz Jürgen Säcker & Roland Rixecker ed., 5th ed, 2009), margin number 20.

53 Cf Sieder, supranote 3, p 63 *et seq.*

Greece

Constantinos N Klissouras
Christina Papachristopoulou
KP Law Firm

---

1. Introduction

1.1 Admissibility of cash pooling agreements

The concept of cash pooling as a specific legal and contractual concept is not expressly addressed by Greek law. It is certainly not forbidden, given the constitutionally protected right of freedom of economic activity (Article 5 of the Constitution) and the fundamental private law rule of freedom of contract (Article 361 of the Civil Code).

The institution of cash pooling agreements has historically given considerable headaches to multinational corporations active in Greece, both from a company law and from a tax law perspective. However, the economic reality of complex and extensive dealings between the affiliates of multinational groups active in Greece, which these days routinely involve cash pooling agreements, prompted the recent amendment (by Law 4013/2011) of domestic law, in the direction of relaxing the outright prohibition of upstream loans and security, and instead regulating them and the conditions of credit and other contracts between affiliated entities. This recent reform was effected by way of amendment of the law that implemented the rules related to directors' dealings and transactions between affiliated companies set out in the Second EU Company Law Directive (Article 23a of Codified Law 2190/1920, the Companies Law).

Despite the equivalence, in large measure, of the economic results of physical and notional cash pooling agreements, they remain conceptually quite distinct in the eyes of Greek law. The agreements concluded and performances exchanged in the course of physical cash pooling agreements remain standalone company-level transactions, and must therefore be individually assessed against the relevant company, tax and related considerations. Notional cash pooling, by contrast, may be treated in much greater measure as a contractual matter for the pool leader (the master account holder).

Save in exceptional circumstances, the nationality of the pool leader and/ or the pool members does not affect the general permissibility of cash pooling agreements. However, nationality may give rise to particular structuring considerations. As regards EU companies, this is self-evident by reason of the fundamental European freedoms of free movement of capital, freedom of cross-border provision of services and freedom of establishment. In addition, national law awards to aliens the civil and economic rights of nationals (Article 4 of the Civil Code), and, therefore, non-EU entities are equally at liberty to participate in cash pooling agreements.

1.2 Types of cash pooling agreement

Cash pooling is a relatively recent addition to the cash management techniques used in Greece, mainly as a result of:

- the outright prohibition of upstream credit and security; and
- uncertainty as to its treatment from a tax law perspective.

It is characteristic that, at present, only two domestic commercial banks openly offer cash pooling agreements as a specific financial product, although it is likely that the financing structures in place at many corporate groups contain at least notional cash pooling elements, which are not advertised as such. Cash pooling arrangements are fairly common for multinationals operating in Greece, and non-Greek financial institutions offer such products to multinational and domestic clients.

There is no published precedent from the litigation of cash pooling-related matters before the Greek courts and, to the best of our knowledge, no unpublished precedent either. Limited consideration has been given to the consequences of cash pooling agreements in the course of shareholder dispute arbitration, but we do not believe that this type of limited precedent foreshadows the positions which the Greek courts and administrative authorities are likely to adopt on matters related to cash pooling.

1.3 Legal requirements from various perspectives

(a) Company law

While Greek company law does provide for minimum regulatory capital, the requirement is sufficiently low to be irrelevant for cash pooling considerations (for the most relevant company type – the corporation limited by shares, or *société anonyme* – the minimum regulatory capital is €60,000 (Article 8 of the Companies Law)).

The principle that only actual realised profits may be distributed to shareholders, and the prohibition of distributions in the event that the company's own funds (equity plus profit/loss plus reserves) are or will become, as a result of such distribution, less than the company's paid-up share capital (plus non-distributable reserves), may interfere to a greater extent with the operation of cash pooling agreements. This means that cash pooling agreements may need to be revisited and possibly revised at least annually, to the extent they may result in payments to a pool member that is also a shareholder.

Of central significance for all forms of transaction in general, and for financial transactions in particular, between affiliated companies are the rules set out in Article 23a of the Companies Law, governing director dealings and transactions between affiliates.

Until 2007, Article 23a set out:

- an outright prohibition of financial transactions with the effect of upstream credit or security; and
- a requirement for a prior shareholders' resolution approving the conclusion and amendment of all other transactions between affiliates that could be deemed to be outside the ordinary course of business.

Both rules made cash pooling in both physical and notional form highly impracticable, if not impossible.

Two significant amendments (first by Law 3604/2007, and most recently by Law 4013/2011) opened the way for cash pooling agreements between affiliates. The law as currently in force retains the principle of prohibition of upstream credit and security, but does provide for broad carve-outs which permit both notional and physical cash pooling agreements subject to general principles of corporate action and transparency of accounting and financial statements.

Under the first general carve-out, cash pooling is allowed between entities that are subject to consolidation. Consolidation is an accounting obligation applicable only to capital companies (corporations), and therefore partnerships and unincorporated businesses do not benefit from the exception to the general prohibition. Minority shareholder minorities have considerable veto powers: cash pooling agreements must be sanctioned by majority shareholder vote, but one-third of the shareholders may veto the decision.

There is some dispute as to whether cash pooling may benefit from the second carve-out, which concerns transactions effected at arm's length in the ordinary course of business. In practice, most movements of funds under a cash-pool are usually well below the ceiling allowing standard authorisation by management. However, it is debatable whether credit transactions qualify conceptually as transactions in the ordinary course of business (since neither borrowing nor lending is usually the business of any undertaking outside the financial sector), and this theoretical objection is amplified if the terms of the cash pool and/or the aggregate actual movements of funds have a significant upstream credit or security effect.

Company law prohibitions of the distribution of corporate funds may also interfere with the permissible structures and proper operation of cash pools. Prohibited distributions include:

- distributions to shareholders of funds that do not represent net profit;
- distributions of reserves set aside by statute for specific designated uses; and
- distributions of dividends without due process (publication, auditing and shareholder approval of financial statements).

This may prevent companies from putting all their cash in the pool, or require diligent pool structuring so as to avoid cash movements which violate any of these rules.

Conversely, there is nothing to prevent downstream credit and security, and this is a focal point of departure in the structuring considerations for designing a cash pool. In such scenarios, subordination risks become highly relevant: although there is no general rule of subordination of shareholder loans and advances, several doctrines with the effect of subordination arise derivatively in circumstances of director liability, veil-lifting and insolvency, especially in cases of late filing and voidable contracts, such as transactions at an undervalue, continuation of trade by destructive means, and speculative and generally risky transactions. It follows that putting the pool leader towards the bottom of the tree is a common first idea, though not a panacea, in the structuring of an efficient pool.

Upstream security, real and personal (but not direct credit), is now generally permitted under a general carve-out, provided that:

- the granting of security is in furtherance of the company's (grantor's) interests;
- the company (grantor) retains full recourse against the debtor of the secured obligation;
- the secured creditor agrees in writing to subordinate the claim under the security to all other creditor claims at the time of creation of the security interest[1], or all such creditors agree in writing to waive such subordination; and
- the board of directors of the grantor delivers a written report to the shareholders, setting out the essential elements of the security interest, and procures a specific shareholders' resolution approving the conclusion of the corresponding agreements, which can be vetoed by shareholders representing 10% of the company's share capital, or 5% in the case of listed companies.

This resolution is subsequently subject to publication, and the security interest is perfected and becomes effective only after completion of publication formalities.

As a consequence of the combination of new rules outlined above, both physical and notional cash pooling are allowed under Greek law between corporations subject to consolidation of financial statements. The same rules and principles facilitate the design and contractual implementation of the cross-collateralisation techniques which customarily secure cash pools, especially if the pool funds represent credit extended under working capital credit lines.

Certain further rules of company law have the effect of limiting the exception in favour of cash pooling, however. To the extent that they constitute an upstream guarantee or credit, pool funds may not be used for the acquisition of shares of the pool member that is the borrower for the amount of that credit (Article 16a of Law 2190/20, which prohibits all borrowing for the purpose of acquiring own shares), unless:

- the terms of the relevant credit are at arm's length;
- the transaction has been approved with by a majority of two-thirds of the shareholders; and
- the provision of the credit does not result in the reduction of the company's own funds to an amount less than the sum of equity plus statutory reserves.

(b) *Banking regulation*

On the prudential regulation side, capital adequacy of credit institutions operating in Greece is governed by the combination of EU Directives 2006/48/EC relating to the taking up and pursuit of the business of credit institutions and 2006/49/EC on the capital adequacy of investment firms and credit institutions.

The impact of cash pooling agreements on the capital adequacy of banks is obviously too broad a topic to be addressed here, but evidently there is both a

---

1 In effect, it is a secured creditor in respect of claims arising after the granting of such security, but not claims which have arisen before, in respect of which the creditor is not even on an equal footing, but subordinate.

quantitative impact, associated with such considerations as on-balance-sheet netting of opposite direction transactions between the affiliated companies, and a qualitative impact, such as in cases of exposures and large exposures to affiliates or cross-collateralisation and cross-guarantees, which become particularly relevant when the pool funds are derived from credit extended under working capital, overdraft or other lending facilities (Bank of Greece Regulation 2635/2010).

As regards permissibility of cash pooling from a prudential regulation perspective, Law 3601/2007 explicitly excludes intra-group financing schemes from the general prohibition on the provision of financial services by any person other than a licensed financial institution. For the purposes of the exception, such intra-group financing includes affiliates within the meaning of the Company Law Directives (enacted as Article 42e, pargraph 5 of Law 2190/1920).

(c) Insolvency law

The scenarios where the insolvency of a pool member may affect the pool defy exhaustive enumeration, but the following general principles can generally serve as a point of departure for analysing specific contractual arrangements.

As from the occurrence of insolvency, all assets of a debtor form part of the insolvency estate and are subject to administration by the liquidator (Article 17 of the Insolvency Code).

As a rule, current contracts are not terminated automatically (Article 29 of the Insolvency Code), except where the Insolvency Code specifically provides otherwise. No such provision is relevant for cash pooling agreements, but contractual clauses providing for the termination of contracts on the occurrence of insolvency, whether automatically or following notice, are valid (Articles 31, paragraph 1 and 32, paragraph 1 of the Insolvency Code). The liquidator has cherry-picking powers and may elect which current contracts to terminate (Article 29, paragraph 1 of the Insolvency Code).

Set-off is permitted, provided that the legal and contractual conditions for set-off (mutuality of claims, certainty of amounts and payment dates) have occurred before the opening of insolvency proceedings. In addition, the opening of insolvency proceedings does not affect set-offs effected in regulated payment and clearing systems, or related to agreements for the provision of financial security (Article 36 of the Insolvency Code).

Transactions effected in the so-called 'suspect period' – a period of up to two years between the time of opening of insolvency proceedings and the time at which the court determines that the debtor was in fact insolvent (ceased to be in a position to pay obligations as they fell due) – may be void or voidable, if and to the extent that they prejudice the general pool of creditors. Absolutely void are:

- transactions at an undervalue or without adequate consideration, the payment of monetary obligations that are not yet due according to the applicable terms of the individual agreement;
- payments of obligations other than in cash; and
- the creation of real security interests for pre-existing debt, unless the obligation to provide such security also pre-exists (Articles 40 and 41 of the Insolvency Code).

All other transactions (those not void by law as outlined in the preceding paragraph) effected during the suspect period that prejudice the interests of the general pool of creditors are voidable, subject to proof that the counterparty was aware of the suspension of payments by the debtor and of the harm caused to the general pool of creditors by the transaction at issue. Subject to the additional element of intent to prejudice creditors, transactions are voidable as a fraudulent conveyance for a period of up to five years preceding their conclusion, irrespective of insolvency.

One further consideration relates to the issue of lender liability in the event of insolvency, in two distinct varieties.

- excessive (or imprudent) lending to an otherwise insolvent debtor, which creates the false appearance of solvency to the detriment of subsequent creditors, which are thereby induced to enter into transactions that they would not have entered into with a financially weaker counterparty; and
- unwarranted termination of credit, which the debtor for a legitimate reason routinely factored into its business calculations, when this precipitates an otherwise avoidable insolvency. To complicate matters, this source of liability is possible in respect both of the calling in of loans before maturity and the refusal to extend additional credit by the debtor's main and/or habitual lender.

A significant number of cases have been, and are being, litigated, but the courts have so far declined to pronounce any general extra-statutory principles of lender liability, electing instead to emphasise the special circumstances of each case. In conceptualising some of the problems of lender liability, the courts have been cognisant of the fact that lender liability is inherently reactive – in the sense of being a retrospective remedy to the failure of instruments and processes regulated elsewhere in law, such as financial reporting and disclosure rules – and have shown reluctance to pass on the resultant loss to lenders dealing with the debtor at arm's length.

On the other hand, the active fostering of a false appearance of solvency – for instance, through intra-group lending or the debtor's effective management by its main lender – can generally provide a foundation for lender liability under general tort law, as well as significant grounds for piercing the corporate veil. Such scenarios are highly relevant for the design and the actual day-to-day operation of cash pooling structures.

(d) Tax law

Transfer pricing is mainly addressed in the Income Tax Code (Article 39 of Law 2238/1994) and in trade regulations governing the formulation and transparency of intra-group transaction prices. It has been argued for some time that, unlike Article 9 of the Organisation for Economic Cooperation and Development Model Law, Article 39 of the Income Tax Code does not apply to plain loans and pure credit agreements in general. The legislation governing the recent private sector involvement programme for the exchange of Greek government bonds specifically ruled out the applicability of transfer pricing rules to all related transactions. However, legislative instruments of lesser authority (Ministerial Decisions A2-

8092/2008 and A2-1225/2010) have declared Article 39 of the Income Tax Code applicable to all intra-group transactions. As a result, to the extent that such transactions are not at arm's length, but give rise to a net benefit for one affiliate and a net loss for the other, they are most likely to be deemed as giving rise to taxable profit, without necessarily providing an offsetting tax-deductible loss for the counterparty.

All interest earned by and/or paid to pool members under a cash pooling agreement, as under any other agreement, constitutes taxable income under the Income Tax Code, and all interest paid on the underlying overdrafts or other lending facilities is deductible as a financial expense. In addition, interest paid to pool members is subject to a withholding tax of 20% if paid to a Greek pool member by a non-Greek financial institution, but 40% if paid by any Greek entity to a non-Greek one. Such withholding tax may be avoided under general double taxation principles, in accordance with the particular terms of the double tax treaty applicable to the particular transaction. Accrued interest on loans paid or credited to affiliated companies can be deducted if the ratio of such loans or credits to the net assets of the company does not exceed 3:1 on average in the fiscal year.

A significant debate surrounds the applicability of stamp duty rules to cash pools. As a general rule, credit agreements between corporations that are not financial institutions are subject to stamp duty of 2.4%, which makes such transactions simply uneconomical. Theory and practice have therefore developed techniques for legally avoiding this cost through executing the credit agreements or taking performance of the relevant obligations of payment and repayment outside the Greek territory. In such scenarios, stamp duty issues may be resurrected if there is repatriation of the resultant funds or cash flows.

Instead of stamp duty, credit agreements entered into with financial institutions are subject to a special transaction tax of 0.6%, which in the case of credit lines is payable on the upper limit of the facility. This obviously lowers the cost of pools where the pool funds represent financial credit extended by a bank, but requires meticulous structuring to avert the risk of such pools being found in violation of stamp duty law.

2. Specific questions

2.1 Perspective A: corporate group

Participation in a cash pooling agreement poses no special problems as regards the liability of directors, but the continuing operation of the pool (certainly a physical pool, and arguably also a notional pool) after the onset of economic insolvency does increase the chances of the commission of special insolvency torts, as well as general torts, that are attributable to the directors.

Directors are under the obligation to file for the opening of insolvency proceedings within 30 days of the onset of economic insolvency, and directors are personally liable (in tort) for loss to creditors resulting from the creation of new obligations in the period between the date on which insolvency ought to have been declared and the date on which it is actually declared (Article 98. paragraph 1 of the Insolvency

Code). Directors who are accessories to this special tort, such as directors of a corporate parent who induce or direct the debtor's board of directors to delay an insolvency filing when it is mandatory under the law, have identical liability.

In cash pooling scenarios, this means that directors of a pool member with significant surpluses, and therefore with claims on the pool, might in principle be personally liable for the amount of those claims. However, if the pool clears frequently or if such claims are payable and paid back to the pool member even after the filing, director's liability becomes a merely theoretical prospect.

As the probability of a pool actually functioning so as to cause insolvency is infinitesimal in all but the most peculiar circumstances, so too is the prospect of directors' joint and several liability for causing insolvency through gross negligence or intent (Article 98, paragraph 2 of the Insolvency Code) in connection with the conclusion and operation of the cash pool.

To the extent that a cash pool may result in unlawful distributions in the form described above, directors may be held personally liable in tort to the general pool of creditors.

Directors will usually be personally implicated in claims based on lender liability (in tort), and therefore the risk is heightened if the pool operates so as to create the false appearance of the solvency of a pool member. On the other hand, cash pools that cease to fill cash deficits rapidly – for instance, because of material adverse change clauses – may in theory give rise to claims in tort for causing or precipitating insolvency. As already noted, however, most lender liability claims are more a matter of theoretical debate than a real risk based on consistent precedent, so long as the courts continue to decline to pronounce general rules and principles of lender liability.

Ultra vires in the strict common law sense is unknown in Greek law; in principle, contracts will be valid and binding on a corporation even if their subject matter is not specifically set out in the objects clause of its articles of association. However, defects in the authority of directors who enter into cash pooling agreements may render such agreements generally null and void, and because of the requirement for shareholder approval, defects in the relevant shareholders' resolution may render the cash pooling agreement void or voidable in the same manner as any other contract (Articles 35(a)to (c) of the Companies Law).

Veil-piercing scenarios may interact with cash pooling schemes in circumstances where the legal seat of a pool member is not a given, but rather a factual and legal issue to be determined. Under Article 10 of the Civil Code, all elements of form and substance affecting the creation and existence of legal persons are governed by the laws of the state of their actual seat (which can be compared with *Sitztheorie* in Germany, *sièze reel/siège social* in France and *sede dell' administarzione centrale* in Italy). The concept is akin to the concept of centre of main interests set out in the EU Insolvency Regulation, but the dominant criterion is different: it is not just the place where a company maintains an establishment observable by third parties, but primarily the place where management truly operates. Failing this central criterion, further criteria, such as the place where the results (profit and loss) of the company's business activity are concentrated, serve as additional indicators of the company's real seat, and therefore of the applicable company law.

This is relevant in the context of cash pooling for several reasons. A cash pool located in Greece may well serve to support a finding that pool members that are holding companies with no real establishment whatsoever (eg, offshore companies) are in fact seated in Greece, if this is the real seat of the operating companies that are members of the pool, and/or the seat of the pool leader (the master account holder). It is invariably the practice that such entities are created in accordance with the laws of their registered seat, and never re-incorporate in accordance with any other laws. Therefore, such entities will normally not have complied with domestic incorporation requirements and procedures. As a result, which follows directly from the adoption by Greek law of the real seat doctrine, such entities are recognised not as foreign corporate entities, but by legal fiction treated as constructive *de facto* unlimited liability (general) partnerships between their purported shareholders and board members. Provided that such entities engage by profession in commercial activity, they are deemed to be merchants, and the constructive general partners incur unlimited personal liability and automatically join the partnership in bankruptcy.

Further veil-piercing scenarios may be relevant in the context of cash pooling schemes supporting centralised cash management and pool member funding on a 'need-to-spend' basis. These are common in several cross-border service providers, including providers of e-services such as global computer reservations systems, travel and tourism groups, and various types of brokerage business. With the aid of Article 281 of the Civil Code, which prohibits the abusive invocation and exercise of private rights, the courts have expounded the concept of veil piercing for over 50 years, and have rarely shied away from attributing liability for the obligations of one corporation to the natural or legal persons that own, control and support it in such a manner that the corporation's existence depends on their continued control and support. Amalgamation of parent and subsidiary assets, dependence on parent guarantees for obtaining trade or financial credit and identity of interests are all useful red flags for scenarios where one pool member may be at risk of being found liable for the obligations of another. The issue is ultimately a factual one, but the terms of the cash pooling agreement do require scrutiny from this angle.

The actual seat doctrine is inapplicable in respect of EU-incorporated entities, after the famous *Überseering* judgment of the European Court of Justice[2], which pronounced the doctrine contrary to fundamental EU freedoms. However, the doctrine is arguably fully applicable to non-EU entities and merits serious consideration in the design of cross-border cash pools involving non-EU pool members.

Mismanagement and breach of fiduciary duties are lesser issues in the context of cash pooling, since the valid conclusion of related agreements requires a direct shareholder vote. However, other types of director action, such as failure to exit the pool upon the occurrence of insolvency, may result in general and special liability in tort, as noted.

---

2 *Überseering BV v Nordic Construction Co Baumanagement GmbH* (C-208/00), [2002] ECR I-09919, on referral by the German Federal Supreme Court, decision of March 30 2000, VII ZR 370/98.

There is no difference in the general principles of director liability and veil-piercing risks associated with cash pooling depending on whether the corporation at issue is listed or privately held, and whether the distressed pool member is a foreign legal entity. The obstacles to successful litigation against foreign parents and their directors are such that no significant precedent informs academic debate on these issues.

The insolvency of the pool leader while the master account is in funds is bad news for creditors of the pool members, since their cash is trapped in the insolvency estate. The principles of director liability and veil piercing do not change for this reason alone, but the absence of legal segregation of pool member funds within the master account can materially increase the risks of director liability for mismanagement. Director liability thus becomes a question intimately linked to the terms of the pool agreements.

Conversely, the insolvency of the pool leader while the master account is out of the money potentially creates a series of voidable transactions and raises the risk of director liability across the pool for transactions prejudicial to the other creditors of the pool leader, since it will normally be the case that all pool member directors are aware of the financial position of other pool members (see the discussion of the insolvency aspects of cash pooling schemes above).

Cross-collateralisation between the pool members may complicate things further, since the creditors of the pool leader will then have direct recourse to the pool members' assets. However, as a rule, cross-collateralisation will not significantly impact on directors' liability, provided that the cash pool is generally valid.

Greek law recognises the concept of distinct legal personalities, and the liability of one pool member might spread to other members of the pool only under the veil-piercing principles outlined above.

2.2 Perspective B: bank

(a) *Banking requirements*

Cash pools generally are relevant for prudential regulation to the extent that the pool funds represent credit to the pool members. In such scenarios, EU Directives 2006/48/EC and 2006/49/EC apply in the same manner as everywhere else within the European Union.

Domestic regulation requires that credit extended to related clients be treated as a single exposure or large exposure (Bank of Greece Regulation 2635/2010). 'Related clients', within the meaning of this regulation, are two or more persons that represent a single credit risk to the bank by reason of the manner in which they are contractually or legally related, so that the inability of one of these persons to meet payment obligations as they fall due is likely to cause the other person also to become unable to meet its own payment obligations.

A 'large exposure' is a credit exposure amounting to 10% or more of the bank's equity (without regard for currency and market risk factors). A single credit risk may not exceed 25% of the bank's total equity, while the bank may assess secured exposures on a largely discretionary basis. This means that the bank has discretion to add further credit to the amounts comprising a large exposure and a single credit risk on the basis of a qualitative assessment of the security given to the bank for that credit. In other words, the 10% and 25% limits apply in principle only to unsecured credit and credit secured by 'soft security', such as personal guarantees that are not further secured by real security. On the other hand, credit secured by mortgages or liens on real property may be treated with discretion.

(b) Liability of the bank in the event of insolvency of the master account holder or a group company

Bank liability is a theoretical possibility and follows general principles regarding being an accessory to torts where torts are alleged against the pool members and their directors. Banks owe no fiduciary or legal duties to creditors of their clients, and therefore have no liability in their own right for losses suffered by such creditors from the actions of the pool members. In general, the operation of a cash pool according to its terms, under agreements previously approved by shareholder vote and subject to publicity, practically excludes the possibility of bank liability, save in the most exceptional of circumstances.

2.3 Insolvency

(a) Cash pooling agreements from the insolvency practitioner's perspective

Banks are, and have always been, exempt from the application of general insolvency law. At present, this results from operation of the national law (Law 3601/2007) implementing the EU Credit Institutions Winding-Up Directive (2001/24/EC), and Greece has never seen a bank failure resulting in the final seizing and/or loss of deposits (rather, 'good bank, bad bank' scenarios have been implemented by the liquidators, which are, and have always been, appointed by the Bank of Greece).

Having said this, the power of liquidators extends to all assets belonging to the insolvency estate including cash, but not claims for credit advances under current financing contracts, which are customarily terminated – either automatically or on notice – upon the occurrence of insolvency. Therefore, the insolvency of any party involved in a cash pool is relevant from a specific cash pooling perspective only insofar as the pool consists of pool member funds.

In such scenarios, disregarding the impact of EU Directive 94/19/EC on deposit-guarantee schemes, from the viewpoint of Greek law, it matters not whether a party is a financial institution: unlike securities, cash deposits are not assets subject to legal segregation or eligible for separation from the insolvency estate, and therefore simply form part of it, while claims to the portion of cash in the pool belonging to a pool member are, respectively, claims of or against the insolvency estate. The law of the centre of the distressed entity's main interests governs its insolvency, and therefore effects of insolvency will vary depending on the substantive rules of that system of laws.

The topic of reorganisation and winding-up of credit institutions is too broad to be addressed here. Again setting aside the consequences from the application of EU Directive 94/19/EC, the duties of the special liquidator of a Greek bank are no different from those of any liquidator: the duty to inventory assets and liabilities, collect claims and pay obligations according to the statutory order of preference for each class of creditor (generally preferred, secured, unsecured and subordinated). However, thanks to various combinations of reorganisation measures, quite apart from deposit guarantee schemes, in no case of a Greek bank failure have deposits actually been lost.

As already noted, the administrator's duties do not change by reason of the existence of a cash pooling agreement: he must inventory assets and liabilities, collect claims and pay obligations according to the statutory order of preference for each class of creditors.

(b) *Dissolution/termination of the cash pooling agreement in the event of liquidation of the master account holder or of a group company*

Void or voidable transactions are not declared by the liquidator, but recognised as void (in terms of declaratory relief) or avoided on the application of the liquidator, always by judgment of the insolvency court, provided that one or more of the general conditions of voidability are present. The law of the centre of the insolvent company's main interests determines the substantive rules applicable in insolvency, but other than that, the jurisdiction of debtors or creditors to a Greek insolvency estate makes no difference.

A cash pooling agreement, like any other contract, is a current contract for purposes of insolvency law. As already noted, current contracts are not terminated automatically (Article 29 of the Insolvency Code), except where the Insolvency Code specifically provides otherwise. No such provision is relevant for cash pooling agreements, but contractual clauses providing for the termination of contracts on the occurrence of insolvency, whether automatically or following notice, are valid (Articles 31, paragraph 1 and 32, paragraph 1 of the Insolvency Code). The liquidator has cherry-picking powers and may elect which current contracts to terminate (Article 29, paragraph 1 of the Insolvency Code).

The law on the reorganisation and winding-up of credit institutions contains no rules on the treatment of current contracts, which in principle remain unaffected, precisely because it is geared towards the preservation of all types of banking contract through restructuring measures, rather than the liquidation of assets for the purpose of meeting deposit repayment obligations. However, all contracts may be terminated for cause under general principles of the law of obligations, while general insolvency law principles may have analogous application to the termination of current contracts with banks.

2.4 Perspective D: regulatory

As indicated above, listed companies are under the obligation to disclose new loan agreements and any guarantees where they could be significant transactions for the financial state of the company, as knowledge of their existence could have an impact on the market price of the shares (Law 3340/2005). From this perspective, cash pooling agreements with a significant credit aspect should be disclosed.

Furthermore, to the extent that a cash pooling agreement constitutes transfer pricing under Article 39 of Law 2238/1994, and/or if the master account holder is deemed to provide a service to the other pool members by way of fund transfers to or from their accounts, for which a fee would be applicable under arm's-length principles in the open market, the cash pooling agreement must be disclosed to the competent ministry under Article 26 of Law 3728/2008 and Article 39 of Law 2238/1994, together with general information concerning the group and its activities (failure to disclose giving rise to administrative penalties).

2.5 Perspective E: tax

The tax implications of cash pooling agreements have been outlined above, at section 1.3(d).

Hungary

János Tóth
Wolf Theiss

1. Introduction

1.1 Admissibility of cash pooling agreements

There is no specific legislation governing cash pooling in Hungary and hence no specific rules restricting local companies from entering into different cash pooling structures. The possibility for a group of companies or a master account holder to implement a cash pooling agreement is governed by the general principles and provisions of Hungarian civil and corporate law. Since the relaxation of regulations on foreign currency transactions, local and international banks have been offering different cash concentration techniques for domestic or international group companies seeking to minimise their credit charges and optimise their liquidity. A decree of the Hungarian National Bank clearly defines and implicitly acknowledges the two basic cash pooling structures available: physical and notional cash pooling.

1.2 Types of cash pooling agreement

The Hungarian National Bank decree serves as a general guideline for differentiating between physical and notional cash pooling, and implicitly allows practitioners to employ variations on either structure. Physical cash pooling is further categorised by different techniques used to concentrate cash (ie, zero balancing and target balancing). Otherwise, parties may specify the details of their desired concentration structure, provided that the general principles and mandatory laws and regulations (in particular, those of civil and company law) are observed. Companies can and do utilise every recognised variation of cash pooling, with agreements most frequently implemented between affiliated group companies. Less frequently, cash pooling agreements are implemented between unaffiliated companies with independent capital, which cooperate in order to minimise credit charges and optimise liquidity.

1.3 Legal requirements from various perspectives

Although cash pooling agreements are not specifically regulated under civil law, various specific requirements apply under different areas of local law.

(a) Company law

Capital maintenance rules: Hungarian law includes stringent rules requiring companies to maintain sufficient equity capital. The general capital maintenance rules of the Companies and Accountancy Act require a company to possess sufficient assets for its day-to-day operations. Their main purpose is to ensure that a company's equity is not significantly or permanently less than its registered capital and does not fall below the relevant minimum capital requirement (this applies to both limited liability companies and public or private limited companies). If a company fails to meet the relevant capital maintenance rules, its shareholders must either inject more capital within a set timeframe to forestall the prospect of negative equity or decide on an appropriate decrease in registered capital (if possible). Alternatively, the shareholders can agree to transform the company into another form that is subject to a lower minimum (or zero) capital requirement, or to terminate the company without legal succession.

The Companies Act also includes strict dividend payment provisions, which specify the circumstances under which any amounts can be distributed to shareholders. These provisions must equally be observed when launching and operating a cash pooling structure (ie, when making withdrawals from or payments to the master account), in order to avoid the risk of invalid distributions.

Corporate governance/risk management: Capital maintenance rules have a direct effect on corporate governance and risk management. According to the Companies Act, company directors have a duty to act fully in the company's interests when managing its everyday business. If the company concerned is at risk of insolvency or bankruptcy (ie, if there is a risk of non-compliance with its payment obligations), the directors are legally obliged to act with special regard to the interests of creditors. Failure to do so may result in the directors' personal liability (or collective liability in the case of the board directors) for claims that cannot be satisfied in the liquidation proceedings. These provisions may call into question any cash pooling transactions concluded prior to liquidation. Directors must ensure that transfers to the master account (in case of physical cash pooling) do not trigger a negative equity situation.

(b) General legal requirements

As there are no specific regulations governing cash pooling agreements, Hungarian registered companies are free to set up any kind of agreement that they wish. However, when a company does so, its shareholders and directors must abide by general rules and principles of civil and corporate law, and of the Banking Act.

The same applies when joining or entering into an established cash pooling agreement. Thus, Hungarian registered companies need take no specific actions or measures in order to join a domestic or cross-border cash pooling structure. In certain cases, however, the approval of the shareholders' meeting may be required under the Companies Act. This is the case, for example, with limited liability companies, where any agreement between a group company and the master account holder requires approval by the highest corporate body.

Under the financial assistance restriction, a limited company is further prohibited from providing any loan that might assist a third party (ie, the master account holder or another group company) in buying its shares. Therefore, a Hungarian group company's contributions to the master account must not be used to acquire its own shares, whether by the master account holder or another group company. Doing so risks rendering the acquisition invalid, since contributions made under a cash pooling agreement qualify legally as intra-group loans.

2. Specific questions

2.1 Perspective A: corporate group

(a) Liability of group company and/or master account holder directors in the event of insolvency of a group company

Under company law, all supervisory directors must ensure that the company complies with certain legal requirements (eg, corporate governance and capital maintenance rules) relating to its business. Failure to comply may expose the directors to unlimited and joint liability.

(b) Liability of group company directors

The directors are responsible for a company's proper operation and management. They must abide by the law and regulations, the company's articles of association and the resolutions of the shareholders, and must act with a level of care and diligence befitting their position. Directors are legally obliged to put the interests of their company first (which, in the case of a cash pooling agreement, means optimising liquidity and thus prosperity) – but not to the extent of intentionally damaging third parties.

Liability for debts: If a company is at risk of failing to meet its payment obligations, the directors must do everything possible to remedy the situation. Specific provisions relating to limited liability companies and companies limited by shares require the directors to convene an extraordinary general meeting if it comes to their attention that:

- the equity capital has dropped to half (or, in the case of share-limited companies, two-thirds) of the issued capital, due to losses; or
- the company is on the brink of insolvency or has stopped making payments and its assets do not cover its liabilities. From this point onwards, the directors should act with special regard to the interests of creditors and not to those of the company.

If the directors fail to meet their obligations and the company goes into liquidation, the court may establish their unlimited liability for claims that could not be settled in the insolvency proceedings. However, the directors will not be held liable if they can prove that at the time, they did all that could be expected of them to remedy the situation and reduce the creditors' losses.

Directors must therefore ensure that they do everything necessary if they discover that continued participation in a cash pooling agreement may threaten the company's solvency (eg, due to the insolvency of another participant), and thus the interests of both the company and its creditors.

Liability for damages: Again, directors must comply with the relevant laws and regulations, the articles of association and shareholders' resolutions. They will generally be held liable to the company for any damage suffered as a result of their failure to comply with these provisions. Damage resulting from a breach of the directors' executive duties may also include damage caused indirectly to the company (ie, where the directors cause damage to third parties, which the company must then compensate).

Therefore, when entering into, setting up or maintaining a cash pooling agreement, the directors must act within the remit assigned to them by the relevant laws and the company's articles of association, or else risk personal liability. In this respect, they must do their utmost to ensure that the cash pooling agreement poses a minimal threat to the company's equity status.

However, directors may exculpate themselves if they can prove that they took all measures expected of their position and paid special regard to the interests of the company (except in the specific instance described above).

Managing directors or members of the board of directors (or chief executive officers): Generally, the same rules apply to directors irrespective of company form, subject to minor differences outlined above (ie, the obligation to take remediation measures).

Bank or distressed group company registered in foreign jurisdiction: Once the directors of a Hungarian registered group company become aware that another group company or the bank has liquidity problems, they must act diligently and give priority to the interests of the company and its shareholders when considering either leaving or renegotiating the terms of a cash pooling agreement. This is especially the case with physical cash pooling, or if the agreement contains no provisions that specifically address the repayment of contributions made by group companies. Non-compliance with the directors' corporate governance and liability obligations as set out above could trigger the unlimited personal liability of the directors concerned.

Liability of supervisory directors: Only in special cases is it mandatory for a Hungarian registered company to set up a supervisory board (eg, if it averages an annual headcount of over 200 employees). Members of the supervisory board (including the supervisory director, as the board's appointed head) are granted specific information rights in connection with the company's business and corporate governance (eg, they may consult the company books and request information relating to its business from the directors).

Supervisory board members are required by law to call an extraordinary shareholders' meeting if they discover that the directors' activities do not comply with the applicable laws and regulations, the company's articles of association or shareholders' resolutions, or are otherwise against the interests of the company and its shareholders. They must take necessary steps (eg, proposing remediation measures) if they conclude that entering into, maintaining or participating in a cash pooling agreement may harm the company's equity situation or even trigger its insolvency.

If a breach of the above supervisory obligations causes damage to the company (eg, pushing it into liquidation), the supervisory board members may also have unlimited and joint liability for such damage.

Liability of master account holder directors: The same rules apply to directors of the master account holder if a group company's financial distress threatens the solvency of the master account holder.

If the directors of the master account holder are aware that a group company is experiencing solvency difficulties that may threaten the liquidity of the master account holder itself, they must notify both the shareholders of the distressed group company and (if applicable) those of the master account holder of the need for remediation measures. This is very important if the master account holder is the parent of the distressed group company, as it risks unlimited liability for unsatisfied claims of the creditors of group companies in the event of liquidation. Directors of either a group company or the master account holder must generally act with special regard to that company's interests. Should the company be threatened with insolvency, the directors must give priority to the interests of creditors. Such a shift in obligations requires the directors to notify the relevant shareholders of the need to take remediation measures. They need not address the company's creditors directly, especially if it is still possible to remedy the company's financial situation.

As the potential insolvency or bankruptcy of a group company could put the whole cash pooling agreement at risk, the company should be either isolated or excluded from the agreement in order to minimise any possible loss to the master account holder, the other group companies and creditors.

Foreign jurisdiction: The above summary is based on the assumption that the group company and master account holder are both Hungarian registered companies. In the case of a foreign-registered company or bank, the liability and corporate governance of the directors may be subject to the rules of other jurisdictions.

(b) Liability of group company and/or master account holder directors in the event of insolvency of the master account holder

Liability of master account holder directors: If the master account holder is unable to meet its payment obligations or is otherwise at risk of insolvency, its supervisory directors are subject to the same rules concerning liability as outlined in the previous section.

Liability of group company directors: In this situation, the same liability rules as outlined above apply to the supervisory directors of the group company, especially if the distressed master account holder is also the parent company.

Liability of group companies in the event of insolvency of the master account holder: Creditors of the master account holder have no special right to hold other group companies liable for losses suffered due to its insolvency. Nevertheless, the

Insolvency Act asserts that all assets owned or controlled by the master account holder that are recoverable at the point of opening proceedings, as well as all assets acquired thereafter, are subject to the proceedings and hence may be used to satisfy creditors' claims.

Should the master account holder become distressed or enter into liquidation, any funds withdrawn from or transferred to the group company may be reclaimed directly by the creditors of the master account holder. If a beneficiary company is unable or unwilling to repay the creditors, then its directors may be held liable for such claims.

Master account holder is foreign registered company: If the master account holder is a foreign-registered company, the proceedings are subject to the insolvency and liability provisions of the jurisdiction where the company has its registered seat.

In addition, if the master account holder is registered in another EU member state, the EU Insolvency Regulation will apply.

Claiming creditor is foreign resident or registered company: Under the Insolvency Act, in the case of bankruptcy or insolvency proceedings foreign creditors can report their claims against a Hungarian-registered master account holder to the court-appointed administrator. The act also assigns specific obligations to a Hungarian-registered master account holder (eg, notification of known creditors), which helps creditors to pursue their claims successfully.

In addition, the EU Insolvency Regulation sets out certain creditor protection rules (eg, notification of known creditors by the court or the administrator), provided that the relevant company (ie, the group company or master account holder) is registered in the European Union. These can help creditors to pursue their claims should the master account holder become insolvent or bankrupt.

Group company is a foreign registered company: Generally, all assets of a Hungarian-registered master account holder (ie, its shareholdings in foreign-registered companies) are subject to bankruptcy or insolvency proceedings. Once again, however, the extent to which either creditors or the administrator can lay claim to such assets depends on the regulations of the jurisdiction in question.

(c) ***Liability of master account holder in the event of insolvency of a group company***

Both the directors and the shareholders of a company must abide by the statutory provisions and general principles of civil and company law. Should a group company get into distress or enter into liquidation because the shareholders failed in this regard, the creditors may request that the courts establish unlimited and joint shareholder liability for any claims left unsatisfied in the insolvency proceedings.

Liability of master account holder: Both the directors and the shareholders may be held liable for creditors' claims if they fail to comply with the general requirements of Hungarian law (eg, corporate governance or capital maintenance rules).

Under the creditor protection provisions of company law, if a limited liability company or company limited by shares is terminated without legal succession, a shareholder may hold unlimited and joint liability for any creditors' claims left unsatisfied in the insolvency proceedings. The corporate veil will be pierced if the shareholder in question has misused its limited liability to the detriment of the company's creditors. This may well be the case if the shareholder disposed of company assets as if they were its own, or if it reduced those assets (for its own benefit or the benefit of others) while in a position to know that doing so would put the company in distress. Non-compliance with the capital maintenance rules (as discussed earlier) can also trigger the shareholders' unlimited liability.

The same applies if a shareholder (ie, a master account holder) with at least 75% of the voting rights in the company concerned fails to comply with the general rules and standards outlined above and hence exposes the company to substantial strain in meeting its liabilities. If the company enters into liquidation, its creditors may request the court to declare that the majority shareholder holds unlimited liability for any claims left unsatisfied in the proceedings.

Master account holder is a foreign registered company: General liability provisions apply with respect to the shareholders of any Hungarian-registered company, irrespective of its parent's home jurisdiction. However, if the master account holder is a foreign-registered company, cross-border enforcement of Hungarian liability provisions could prove both difficult and expensive.

That said, if the master account holder owns a further establishment within the Hungarian territory (ie, a subsidiary separate from the cash pooling agreement), then under the terms of the EU Insolvency Regulation, any such assets may be forfeited to settle creditors' claims left unsatisfied by the insolvency proceedings.

Claiming creditor is a foreign resident or registered company: In the above situation, foreign creditors are equally entitled to request that the courts establish the master account holder's unlimited liability.

Group company is a foreign registered company: If the distressed group company is itself foreign-registered, the liability provisions of its home jurisdiction will determine whether any liability attaches to the master account holder.

Liability of holder of other group companies: Unless another group company is a shareholder of the distressed group company (or the terms of the cash pooling agreement stipulate otherwise), its creditors have no special rights to hold other group companies liable for any losses that may ensue.

2.2 Perspective B: bank

(a) *Banking requirements*

Requirements regarding regulatory capital and security structure are set out in the Banking Act, in line with the Capital Requirements Directive. Generally, banks must hold a minimum capital requirement of at least 8% of the risk-weighted assets. No additional rules apply to banks in relation to their cash pooling activities.

Liability of the bank in the event of insolvency of the master account holder or a group company: Should a Hungarian-registered master account holder or group company go into distress, the bank administering the cash pooling agreement may be held liable for losses if it fails to meet obligations set out in local law (eg, the Insolvency Act).

According to the Insolvency Act, directors of a company that files for bankruptcy or insolvency must notify any Hungarian bank or financial institution with which it maintains an account. Any financial institution thus notified may not enforce any claim of its own by debiting the company's account, or do anything that would give preferential treatment to certain creditors or to the bank itself. Once notification has been issued, any transfers from the affected accounts generally require prior approval by the court administrator. Failure to follow these restrictions may expose the bank to liability for creditors' unsatisfied claims.

If either the distressed company or the bank in question is registered abroad, the rules of its home jurisdiction may apply as to its notification obligations and the rights of its creditors.

2.3 Insolvency

If a group company becomes insolvent, a cash pooling agreement is of concern only if it physically transfers money from the bank account of one company to that of another. In the following analysis, it may generally be assumed that both the master account holder and the group company have a liability to repay any transactions conducted between themselves. However, as cash pooling agreements can be regulated under different legal frameworks (depending on the requirements of the participants and the services offered by the bank), the specific legal treatment may differ.

If a credit institution becomes insolvent, it can be wound up only through administered liquidation, and not through bankruptcy proceedings. The administrator in bankruptcy proceedings is the asset supervisor, and in liquidation proceedings the liquidator.

(a) Insolvency of the bank

Right of administrator of the bank to claim the credit balance: The credit balance of any bank account qualifies as a deposit under the Banking Act, and the credit institution holding the bank account is entitled to dispose of it. If the bank were to become insolvent, it follows that its entire credit balance would be included in its liquidation assets.

However, if the bank qualifies by regulation not as a bank, but as a payment service provider, it will not be entitled to use such assets to provide payment services for its clients or for other payment service providers. By law, such assets would fall outside the bank's insolvency assets. The liquidator thus could not claim either all or part of the entire credit balance attributed to the master account.

Provided that the bank has its seat in Hungary, a special banking liquidator may be appointed to proceed with the liquidation.

If the Hungarian branch of a credit institution seated within a different EEA member state becomes insolvent, the foreign administrator appointed by that state may proceed with liquidation and may claim any existing credit balance.

Obligations of administrator of the bank as regards the master account holder and group companies: The liquidator of the bank has obligations towards the master account holder or a group company only if either qualifies as a creditor through the Insolvency Act. (A 'creditor' is defined as a person that, at the commencement of the liquidation proceedings, has a claim against the debtor which is undisputed or acknowledged by the debtor, or is based on a final and binding court decision or any other enforceable resolution). Whether any parties to the cash pooling agreement qualify as creditors will be determined by the agreement's provisions. In most instances, the master account holder will qualify as a creditor and a group company probably will not.

However, if both the master account holder and the group companies qualify as creditors, the bank's liquidator is generally obliged to:

- register their claims;
- invite them to the creditors' committee; and
- provide them with information.

The fact that both are counterparties to a cash pooling agreement triggers no further obligations on the part of the liquidator.

If both the master account holder and the group companies are seated in another EEA member state, but qualify as creditors of a Hungarian credit institution engaged in EEA cross-border activity, then the bank's liquidator must inform them of the content of the court's orders (including the order for liquidation) and the legal consequences of missing any deadline set out therein.

(b) *Insolvency of the master account holder*

Right of administrator of master account holder to claim the credit balance: Should the master account holder enter into liquidation, the asset supervisor may not claim the credit balance and can only supervise the operations of the debtor. In doing so, the supervisor may instruct the debtor to collect any claims arising from the cash pooling agreement.

According to the Insolvency Act, a 'creditor' in these circumstances is any person that:

- at the start of the bankruptcy proceedings, has a claim against the debtor which is undisputed or acknowledged by the debtor or is based on a final and binding court decision or any other enforceable resolution;
- has a monetary claim against the debtor which is disputed at the start of the bankruptcy proceedings or becomes due during the bankruptcy proceedings, where the asset supervisor has registered such claim; or
- has an existing monetary claim arising from any agreement, falling due in the future or relating to the performance of the creditor on the basis of such agreement – again, where the asset supervisor has registered such claim.

Whether the bank or any group companies qualify as creditors is determined by the provisions of the cash pooling agreement.

When a master account holder enters into liquidation proceedings, the master account's credit balance forms part of the account holder's liquidation assets (as bank account receivables qualify as working capital). The liquidator of the master account holder may dispose of the entire credit balance.

However, as physical cash pooling is regarded as a lending activity, there may also be liabilities towards group companies (and towards the bank, depending on the terms of the agreement). The assets of the master account holder may be viewed as a liability originating in the cash pooling agreement and repayable to the group company (or similarly, a liability of the bank under the bank account agreement).

Place of the administrator's appointment: With respect to the administrator appointed in either bankruptcy or liquidation proceedings:

- if appointed in another EU member state, the administrator may act in Hungary in accordance with the EU Insolvency Regulation, provided that no secondary proceedings are underway; or
- if appointed in Hungary, the administrator may proceed in any other cases.

Obligations of administrator of the master account holder as regards the bank and the group company: In the case of bankruptcy proceedings, the asset supervisor has no specific obligations towards the bank or any group companies involved in the cash pooling agreement. However, the master account holder cannot pay any creditors – including participants in the cash pooling agreement – without the asset supervisor's approval.

In liquidation proceedings, the general obligations of the liquidator towards any agreement participants that qualify as creditors through the Insolvency Act are outlined earlier in this section.

Administrator's right to disregard/declare void money transfers from the master account holder to a group company: From the commencement date of bankruptcy proceedings, the asset supervisor may:

- challenge in court any agreement or legal statement issued without the asset supervisor's prior approval; and
- initiate court proceedings to reclaim any payment made to creditors contrary to the rules of the Insolvency Act.

In the case of liquidation proceedings, following publication of the liquidation order, the liquidator may generally, within 90 days (and in no case later than one year), challenge on the debtor's behalf any agreement or transaction made within:

- the five years preceding the filing of the liquidation petition by the debtor, if:
  - the outcome was a reduction in the debtor's assets; or
  - the debtor's intention was to defraud other creditors and the counterparty was in a position to know this;

- the two years preceding filing, if the subject was the sale of part or all of the debtor's entire assets, a commitment at the expense of such assets without consideration or any third-party transaction where the consideration paid to the debtor was at a gross undervalue; or
- the 90 days prior to filing, if the subject was to favour a particular creditor (especially if this involves the amendment of an existing contract or the provision of security in favour of an unsecured creditor).

In case of the first two points above, absence of consideration and bad faith must be presumed if the agreement was concluded with a party which either controls or is controlled by the debtor. The same is true of an agreement between two parties that are controlled or influenced by the same person.

If the liquidator's challenge is successful, the agreement or transaction will be invalidated and the original state restored.

Following publication of the liquidation order, the liquidator may generally, within 90 days (and in no case later than one year), reclaim on the debtor's behalf any act or service provided within the 60 days preceding filing of the petition, if the result has favoured a particular creditor outside of the ordinary course of business.

The liquidator may also terminate immediately any agreement concluded by the debtor. In this case the cash pooling agreement will immediately cease to exist and the participating bank and/or group companies will be entitled to exercise their claims as creditors.

Therefore, subject to a cash pooling agreement's specific provisions, the liquidator may challenge any of its activities or terminate its existence at any time.

Place of the administrator's appointment: If main proceedings are initiated in another EU member state, then in accordance with the EU Insolvency Regulation, the administrator may challenge any agreement or transaction only to the extent allowed by the laws of that state. If both main and secondary proceedings are initiated in Hungary, the respective Hungarian administrator exercises such rights respectively.

(c) *Insolvency of the group company*

Right of administrator of the group company to claim the credit balance: Should a group company become insolvent, the rights of the asset supervisor are the same as those outlined earlier in relation to the master account holder.

While the administrator in liquidation proceedings is not entitled to claim the entire credit balance, a group company's liquidation assets will partly consist of its claim against the master account holder concerning transfers into the master account. Such assets may therefore be claimed by the administrator in the course of collecting the group company's receivables. This may not apply if the group company has received more money out of the credit balance than it has in fact contributed (ie, if the company has been financed by the master account holder).

Administrator's right to disregard/declare void money transfers from the group company to the master account holder: The asset supervisor's obligations towards both the bank and the master account holder (including the right to void transfers between agreement participants) are identical to those which apply in the case of a bankrupt master account holder, as outlined earlier.

(d) ***Dissolution/termination of the cash pooling agreement in the event of liquidation of the master account holder or a group company***

Should the master account holder, a group company or the bank become insolvent, the authority of the surviving parties to dissolve the cash pooling agreement will depend on the type of insolvency proceedings underway.

Bankruptcy proceedings: Because the debtor company initiated bankruptcy proceedings against itself, none of the parties can terminate the arrangement during the payment moratorium, provided that the debtor continues to perform its obligations under the agreement. If the debtor fails to do so, the agreement can be terminated.

Liquidation proceedings: As they are not statutorily prohibited from doing so, the counterparties of a company under liquidation proceedings may terminate the cash pooling agreement if its provisions so allow (ie, if they contain an appropriate event of default clause). Once again, the liquidator may at any time terminate any agreement concluded by the debtor.

2.4 Perspective D: regulatory

The regulatory requirements regarding cash pooling agreements are relevant only with respect to physical cash pooling and depend on whether such cash pooling is a group financing (as set out below). A notification obligation also applies to banks providing cash pooling services.

For the purposes of the Banking Act, an agreement that provides for physical cash pooling is normally treated as a regulated lending activity between the master account holder and the companies transferring money into the account. Notional cash pooling is not regulated under the Banking Act.

Lending activity includes any financial transaction entered into jointly, either by a parent company and its subsidiaries or between the subsidiaries themselves, for the purposes of ensuring liquidity within the company group.

Lending activity is regulated by the Banking Act if it is provided as a business activity, and is subject to the appropriate licence granted by the Financial Supervisory Authority. In the case of an agreement involving cross-border activity, such licence will be granted by the service provider's home EU member state. According to the Banking Act, 'business activity' means any regular economic activity carried out for consideration in order to realise profit and by entering into transactions not specified in advance. If any of these attributes is missing, then the activity in question does not qualify as business activity.

However, under the Banking Act, a licence to lend is not required, provided that the cash pooling agreement operates within a group financing framework and neither the parent nor any subsidiary company qualifies as a financial institution (ie, a credit institution that collects deposits and provides credit and loan facilities) or a financial enterprise (which may provide limited financial services only). A 'subsidiary' is a company over which the parent company effectively exercises a controlling influence (eg, sole control of the majority of owner/shareholder votes through owning an equity interest, or control over the company's operations without having such an interest).

The bank providing cash pooling services must be appropriately licensed for all financial services it provides. It is also required by the Hungarian National Bank to make monthly reports of its cash pooling transactions.

2.5 Perspective E: tax

The Ministry for National Economy (formerly the Ministry of Finance) has issued a guideline regarding the tax treatment of cash pooling agreements. This states that cash transfers from group company accounts to the master account qualify as neither lending nor borrowing from a tax perspective. Therefore, neither the group companies nor the master account holder should pay or receive interest.

Interest and service fee payments made or received under cash pooling could be recognised for Hungarian corporate income tax purposes, insofar as these costs and expenditures are in line with the group companies' business purposes, the respective transfer pricing regulation and the thin capitalisation rules (see below).

Provided that the master account holder and the group companies qualify as related parties for tax purposes, the prevailing transfer pricing rules will apply to cash pooling. This means that a mark-up should be charged, based on the arm's-length price of such services (the amount will be specific to each case). The service fee and interest should be treated separately, with special regard to the transfer pricing rules.

Regarding documentation requirements, interest and service fees paid to any related parties should usually be supported by an appropriate transfer pricing study.

Further to the respective thin capitalisation rules, and in line with the cash pooling guideline, the group companies will be deemed to have borrowed cash from the bank, not from the master account holder. Thus, any interest paid on loans provided by the bank is not subject to the thin capitalisation rules.

Withholding tax is not payable on interest and service fee payments made to any corporate entity, regardless of its tax status or country of residence.

In respect of services, the general rules of the EU Value Added Tax (VAT) Directive and the Hungarian rules on its implementation state that services between taxable entities are subject to VAT in the country where the service purchaser (eg, the group company) is established for business purposes, or where its principal permanent establishment is located. However, financial services are exempt from VAT in Hungary and services provided by the master account holder may also be VAT exempt if they fall into this category.

Ireland

Daragh Bohan
Frank Flanagan
Maurice Phelan
Mason Hayes & Curran

1. Introduction

1.1 Admissibility of cash pooling agreements

Ireland has a liberal legal environment for treasury management and is regarded as an excellent location for a group treasury centre and for setting up regional or global cash pools.

Subject to compliance with general legal principles, as set out in this chapter, Irish law does not prohibit the use of cash pooling agreements, in the form of either notional cash pooling or physical cash pooling. The use of cross-border cash pooling agreements is permissible.

1.2 Types of cash pooling agreement

Both cash sweeping and cash pooling structures are used in Ireland.

Cash sweeping involves the physical movement of money between the bank accounts of group companies participating in a cash pool. The participating entities may transfer either their whole cash surplus (zero balancing) or cash above a particular excess level (target balancing). Generally, all companies contributing to the cash pool will be responsible for any negative balance on the master account, regardless of the amount that they have put into the cash pool. The system of transferring monies to and from the master account is comparable to the grant and repayment of intra-group loans.

As well as physical cash pooling, there is also notional or virtual cash pooling, whereby funds are not physically transferred. Instead, balances of different companies within the group are offset so that bank interest is on the group's net cash balance. This improves the group's status in terms of interest payments, but does not result in each group member attaining optimal distribution of liquid funds. Notional cash pooling generally does not result in the creation of intra-group loans because there is no physical movement of funds.

In terms of structure, both notional and physical cash pooling involve each group entity and the master account holder adhering to a facility agreement with the bank. In addition, the various group companies will enter into a cash pooling agreement. This agreement will address matters such as the availability of funds, interest payments, conditions precedent, warranties and undertakings. The agreement must be carefully structured to minimise the possibility of civil or criminal liability of the various group companies and their officers.

For a notional cash pooling agreement to work, the bank needs to have a legal right of set-off against a company's credit balances to clear the debit position of the other companies in the pool. Essentially, this means that each company in the pool must agree to guarantee the liabilities of the other companies to the bank. Although a cross-guarantee structure is not normally essential in the case of physical cash pooling, intra-group guarantees may also be put in place.

In Ireland, the actual transfer of funds from the group companies to the master accounts can take place in one of two ways. Either each individual group company individually transfers the funds to the master account or the bank is given a power of attorney entitling it to sweep the funds automatically.

1.3 Legal requirements from various perspectives

With the exception of regulated industries, Irish law contains no specific legal provisions governing cash pooling agreements. Similarly, Irish tax legislation contains no specific provisions governing cash pooling agreements. However, there are a number of general provisions governing interest deductibility, interest withholding tax, transfer pricing and taxation of foreign exchange gains and losses which should be considered in determining the optimum structure from an Irish tax perspective. These are discussed in more detail in section 2.5 below. Cash pooling agreements are governed by general principles of finance, insolvency and corporate law.

Specific requirements have been imposed in the case of regulated industries by the Central Bank of Ireland. By way of example, pursuant to a letter dated April 4/5 2011,[1] addressed to the chief executives of each of the insurance companies, the Central Bank of Ireland required regulated insurance businesses to undertake not to engage in lending except on the basis set out in that letter. In particular, that letter provided that all cash pooling agreements fall to be classified as "inter-group loans"[2] and provides in respect of such loans that:

> *Prior notification must be given to the CBI [Central Bank of Ireland] of "any transaction of a material nature" with a related company or companies. For clarification purposes, the CBI considers a "material transaction" as:*
>
> > *"any transaction or series of transactions between the same parties, the total of which, in the course of a financial year, exceeds 5% of the available solvency margin or €1m, whichever is lower".*

Before entering into a cash pooling agreement, certain due diligence needs to take place to ensure that the specific structure of the transaction:

- is not *ultra vires* the company;
- will not lead to a breach of existing contracts that the company has entered into (particularly banking covenants);
- is in the interest of each of the participating companies; and
- does not fall foul of certain restrictions on related party transactions under Irish corporate law.

---

1 www.centralbank.ie/regulation/industry-sectors/insurance-companies/Documents/Lending%20Letter%20for%20website_RINSandWINS.pdf.

2 We are of the view that this should read 'intra-group' and is a typographical error.

(a) ***Ultra vires***

An Irish company should not enter into a cash pooling agreement until the directors have satisfied themselves that the company has the requisite capacity and has been properly authorised to proceed. Specifically, the entry into the cash pooling agreement must fall within the powers of the company, as set out in its constitution (memorandum and articles of association) – preferably as an enumerated power, although a so-called 'Bell Houses' clause[3] may suffice. If there is any doubt on this point, the shareholders should pass a resolution to amend the constitution to grant the necessary power.

(b) ***Existing contracts***

The execution of the cash pooling agreement, and any required guarantees and facility agreements, could cause the company to breach existing banking covenants. Contracts may already exist which could limit the power of the company to incur financial indebtedness, make loans or grant guarantees. Thorough due diligence of existing contracts, particularly banking facilities, should be carried out. Where such restrictions are in place, the company should obtain waivers or consents before entering into the cash pooling agreement. Failure to obtain such consents will not threaten the validity of pooling structures, unless the cash pooling agreement violates a covenant which the other parties to the cash pooling agreement would be deemed to have notice of (eg, a negative pledge clause which would typically be apparent from an inspection of the filings in the Companies Registration Office). Moreover, entering into a cash pooling agreement in breach of covenant could constitute an event of default under existing banking facilities and expose the company to the risk of an action for breach of contract or loss of its existing facility.

(c) ***Restrictions on related party transactions***

Irish company law imposes certain limitations on related party transactions. These restrictions must be considered before entering into any cash pooling agreement, either physical or notional, involving Irish companies.

Section 31 of the Companies Act 1990 provides, insofar as material, that:

Except as provided by sections 32 to 37, a company shall not:

(a) make a loan or a quasi-loan to a director of the company or of its holding company or to a person connected with such a director;

(b) enter into a credit transaction as creditor for such a director or a person so connected; and

(c) enter into a guarantee or provide any security in connection with a loan, quasi-loan or credit transaction made by any other person for such a director or a person so connected.

---

3 A clause permitting the company to carry on any other business which can in the opinion of the board of directors be advantageously carried on in conjunction with or as ancillary to any of the above businesses or the general business of the company, or further any of its objectives. Named after the case of *Bell Houses v City Wall Properties Ltd* [1966] 2 All ER 674.

The transfer of funds within the group as part of a cash pooling agreement may constitute an intra-group loan and, as noted above, guarantees are usually required as part of a cash pooling agreement. In addition, it is common for the same executives to be directors of more than one group company. Consequently, in many cases, a cash pooling agreement may *prima facie* be caught by Section 31.

However, in most cases a cash pooling agreement benefits from the group exemption in Section 35 of the Companies Act 1990, as amended by the Company Law Enforcement Act 2001, which provides that:

Section 31 shall not prohibit a company from:

(a) making a loan or quasi-loan to any company which is its holding company, subsidiary or a subsidiary of its holding company or entering into a guarantee or providing any security in connection with a loan or quasi-loan made by any person to any company which is its holding company, subsidiary or a subsidiary of its holdings company; and

(b) entering into a credit transaction as creditor for any company which is its holding company, subsidiary or a subsidiary of its holding company or entering into a guarantee or providing any security in connection with any credit transaction made by any other person for any company which is its holding company, subsidiary or a subsidiary of tis holding company.

As originally drafted, Section 35 operated only to exempt from the provisions of Section 31 transactions or arrangements made by a subsidiary company in favour of its holding company. Consequently, there was a risk that transfers made by a parent company in favour of its subsidiaries, or between sister-subsidiaries, could still be caught by Section 31.

This risk was reduced by Section 79 of the Company Law Enforcement Act 2001, which extended this exemption to transactions or arrangements made by a holding company in favour of "any company which is its holding company, subsidiary or a subsidiary of its holding company". In terms of both physical and notional cash pooling, this was a significant development, as both intra-company loans and guarantees among all members of the group were now permitted.

Section 155 of the Companies Act 1963 defines one company as being a subsidiary of another company[4] (the parent or holding company) if, but only if:

(a) that other –

(i) is a member of it and controls the composition of its board of directors,[5] *or*

(ii) holds more than half in nominal value of its equity share capital, or

(iii) holds more than half in nominal value of its shares carrying voting rights (other than voting rights which arise only in specified circumstances); or

(b) the first-mentioned company is a subsidiary of any company which is that other's subsidiary.

---

4 Subject to some restrictions set out in Section 155(3) relating to fiduciary and nominee relationships.

5 It is not uncommon for a single so-called 'golden share', which carries the right to appoint the members of the board of directors, to provide the requisite control.

The scope of the parent-subsidiary relationship is quite broad. It is important to appreciate that one company can be the parent of another in circumstances where it holds only a small number of shares, but where it exercises effective control over board composition. When evaluating whether a parent-subsidiary structure is in place, one needs to look further than the mere percentage shareholding and also consider the control afforded by those shares.

While this point remains untested, there is a residual risk that cross-border cash pooling structures may not in fact come within the Section 35 exemption. This risk flows from the fact that Section 79 of the Companies Act 2001 applies the exemption to any 'company' in a group, rather than any 'body corporate'. While this is likely a drafting oversight, the term 'company' for the purposes of the Irish Companies Acts is defined as being an Irish company.[6] As against this reading, it is possible that a court would interpret the phrase 'company' in this context in a broader sense, as encompassing foreign entities. The plausibility of this reading is strengthened by Section 155(5) of the Companies Act 1963, which defines 'company' for the purposes of Section 155, which defines the meaning of 'holding company' and 'subsidiary' as including 'any body corporate'.

(d) Financial assistance

Section 60 of the Irish Companies Act 1963 imposes certain restrictions on the extent to which a company can provide financial assistance in the purchase of its own shares. There is a risk that the putting in place of a cash pooling agreement close to the time of an acquisition could constitute financial assistance (to the extent that it could smooth the path of any takeover). Take, for example, the situation where a target or acquired company is required by the buyer's lending bank to enter into a cash pooling agreement that will reduce the buyer's liability to that bank. To the extent that this arrangement makes it easier, or less costly, for the purchaser to acquire the funds to complete the acquisition, this agreement could be seen as constituting financial assistance.

Section 60 is a broadly drafted prohibition that provides that it is unlawful for a company to give financial assistance – whether directly or indirectly, or whether by means of loan, guarantee, provision of security or otherwise – for the purpose of or in connection with a purchase or subscription made or to be made by any person of or for any shares in the company or, where the company is a subsidiary company, in its holding company. Section 60(2) provides that a private company may give such financial assistance subject to it following a strict compliance process, known as the 'whitewash procedure', which requires the directors, among other things, to swear a declaration of solvency noting the form of the assistance to take, to whom the assistance is to be given, the purpose for which the company intends those person(s) to use such assistance and that the directors have made a full inquiry into the company's affairs.

A public limited company may not avail of the whitewash procedure, but may, along with private companies, avail of certain limited exemptions to Section 60.

6 In contrast, a 'body corporate' is generally understood as including both Irish and foreign entities.

(e) *Capital maintenance*

Companies in the cash pool, particularly the parent or treasury entity holding the master account, should also be mindful of rules in relation to the maintenance of share capital, such as rules regarding the payment of dividends. A company is permitted to declare a dividend only where it has sufficient distributable profits and reserves; it cannot use funds received under a cash pooling agreement to declare a dividend where it does not have adequate distributable profits to make such distribution.

Dividends, for the purposes of Irish company law, are different from circumstances in which Irish tax law may deem payments of interest over market rates to be distributions for tax purposes, considered below.

(f) *Transaction in the interests of the company*

The personal risks for directors authorising a cash pooling agreement are considered in more depth below. However, from a corporate governance perspective, Irish corporate law requires that the directors form a view that any transaction entered into is for the benefit of the company.[7] Consequently, to ensure the validity of a cash pooling agreement, it is important for the directors – and ideally the shareholders – to consider whether the transaction is in the interests of the company and, if so, to pass a resolution to that effect.

When considering the benefits of participating in a cash pooling agreement, the directors of a group company should not confine their consideration to the group-wide advantages of the arrangement. While a cash pool may be advantageous for the group as a whole, it may not be beneficial for an individual company.[8]

The board minutes recording the directors' approval of the transaction should specify the perceived benefits for the company (whether tangible or intangible) and should outline the board's evaluation of the solvency of the company and other companies within the group.

The board should also receive regular updates in relation to any risks or benefits of the cash pooling agreement. One of the directors should monitor the financial position of the companies within the group. If the board determines that the risk of participating in the arrangement is greater than the benefit, the arrangement should be terminated.

In order to avoid any future challenges to the validity of the cash pooling agreement on the basis that it was not for the benefit of the company, a shareholders' resolution may also be necessary. This is particularly the case if the company intends to guarantee the liabilities of its parent or sister companies. Any such resolution may be void if the company is insolvent, or in danger of becoming insolvent, at the time of passing the resolution. It does, however, provide comfort from the lender's perspective, as it will be more difficult to argue for the invalidity of a cash pooling agreement where board and shareholders' resolutions have approved the transaction.

---

7 *Hutton v West Cork Railway* (1883) 23 Ch D 654.

8 *PLC* November 2009: "Cash Pooling – Cascading Cost-efficiency and Control" (Louise Webb, Caroline Long, Mathew Padian and Rodger Burnett of Baker & McKenzie).

(g) ***Cross-border considerations***

As noted above, cross-border transactions may give rise to specific challenges with regard to the prohibition on related party transactions. More generally, however, if a transaction involves multiple jurisdictions, it is important to consider the enforceability of the arrangements in different jurisdictions, the legal regime applicable to insolvency in the participating jurisdictions, what assets and liabilities are in the arrangement and what happens on termination of the arrangement. Cross-border tax considerations are discussed at section 2.5 below.

2. Specific questions

2.1 Perspective A: corporate group

(a) ***Liability of group company and/or master account holder directors in the event of insolvency of a group company***

The rules governing directors'[9] obligations in these circumstances would broadly apply in the same way to listed and unlisted entities and would not appear to vary with the jurisdiction of the counterparty. However, it may well be that the standard of knowledge and expertise required of a director of a listed company may be higher.

Liability of group company directors: Directors owe a common law fiduciary duty to act in the interests of the company, not the corporate group. Once a company becomes insolvent, the duties of the directors are effectively owed to the creditors of the company. The key personal risk lies with the fact that the director may have approved, or presided over, an arrangement which may be rendering the company insolvent, for the purposes of benefiting other entities within a corporate group.

A limited form of indemnity for directors from negligence is available if Model Regulation 138 of Table A to the Companies Act 1963[10] is incorporated into its articles of association or if an equivalent provision is directly incorporated. Directors and their advisers should check carefully for the existence of such a provision.

The degree of diligence required of a director in performing his fiduciary duties is dependent on his ability[11] but in the context of cash pooling agreements, it appears

---

9 Ireland does not have a statutory concept of a supervisory director or a supervisory board. In practice, there are executive directors (essentially, those who are employees the company/group) and non-executive directors (essentially those who are members of the board but not employees). While the courts have made some allowances for the fact that non-executive directors cannot be expected to have intimate knowledge of the day-to-day affairs of the company (*Re Tralee Beef & Lamb Ltd* July 20 1994, unreported, High Court, Finlay Geoghegan J.), there is no significant distinction in the duties owed by executive and non-executive directors. Many of the obligations imposed on directors are imposed equally on:
- shadow directors – persons in accordance with whose instructions the directors are accustomed to acting; and
- *de facto* directors – persons who have a title or behave in a manner that indicates they are a director, even if not so formally appointed.

10 "Every director, managing director, agent, auditor, secretary and other officer for the time being of the company shall be indemnified out of the assets of the company against any liability incurred by him in defending any proceedings, whether civil or criminal, in relation to his acts while acting in such office, in which judgment is given in his favour or in which he is acquired or in connection with any application under section 391 of the Act in which relief is granted to him by the court."

probable that a director would be expected to be concerned, on an ongoing basis, with the solvency of all of the bodies corporate contributing to, and entitled to distributions from, the cash pool.

If the cash pooling agreement is for the commercial benefit of the company and the shareholders have approved it, this should mean that the risks for the directors are minimised. However, this may be a question of fact that could be determined before a court with the benefit of hindsight. For this reason, the directors should keep minutes of their meetings and the decisions reached and the reasons for entering into such arrangements. Of course, this is best practice in any event.

The failure of a director to act in accordance with his common law duties could result in personal liability for some or all losses of the company. A director may also be held to account for any profit he makes as a result of such breach of duty.

In a cash pooling agreement, it is probable that an individual director may sit on the boards of multiple group entities. This can give rise to conflicts of interest. Such a director may, in approving the cash pooling agreement, find himself in a position where his duties to one entity conflict with his duties to another. This risk is particularly acute in circumstances where one group company is likely to derive a greater benefit from the cash pooling agreement than the other. From a practical perspective, this conflict does not pose a challenge where the constitution of each company allows the relevant director to participate in the process of approving the arrangement. However, if a company's constitution does not permit such a scenario, the director should absent himself from each company's approval process.

Over and above common law duties, the Companies Acts impose certain obligations on directors that are relevant in a cash pooling context. In particular, Section 297A of the Companies Act 1963 provides that where a person, while an officer of a company, was knowingly a party to carrying on its business in a reckless manner, the court may declare such person personally liable for the debts of the company. It would appear that if directors allowed the cash balances of a company to be swept into a cash pool where one or more members of the cash pool were insolvent, and the directors should have known that the funds might not be returned, this could constitute reckless trading within the meaning of this section. Directors should be mindful of this when a company is party to such arrangement. Failure to monitor closely the operation of the arrangement could lead to the piercing of the corporate veil with the imposition of liability on the directors.

It is also important for the directors of companies contemplating entering into cash pooling agreements to be confident that the proposed agreement does not fall foul of Section 31 of the Companies Act 1990, as there are both civil and criminal penalties for breaches of this section, including the possible imposition of personal liability for the debts of the company on directors.

Liability of the master account holder directors: The directors of the master account holder fall under the same obligations as those of the group companies. In

---

11 And arguably the skills that the director held him out as having in support of his appointment to the board: *Daniels v Anderson* (1995) 16 ACSR 607 at 668.

circumstances where a group company is becoming insolvent, the master account holder will need to consider the probity of continuing to transfer funds to this entity. In circumstances where the directors of the master account holder authorise the transfer of pooled moneys to the insolvent entity, with little or no prospect of return, doubts may be raised about the extent to which such directors are properly exercising their duties to safeguard corporate assets. This consideration will, however, need to be weighed against any claim which the group company in difficulties may have on the pooled moneys.

(b) Liability of group company and/or master account holder directors in the event of insolvency of the master account holder

It is likely that, in practice, the master account holder will be either the parent entity or a group treasury entity. If this entity has become insolvent, it will most likely be due to adverse trading conditions or some similar challenge. To this extent, this position can be contrasted with the insolvency of a group company, where such insolvency could be the result of the removal of capital from the company by way of the cash pooling agreement.

As the master account holder is primarily a beneficiary of the cash pooling agreement, it is difficult to see how the presence of such an arrangement could lead to increased liability on the part of its directors in the event of insolvency.

However, the insolvency of the master account holder could lead to liability for the directors of group companies. Such an insolvency could prevent group companies from utilising funds which have been swept into the master account under the cash pooling agreement. Consequently, the existence of a cash pooling agreement creates the risk that the insolvency of the master account holder could choke the supply of working capital to group companies, which could in turn lead to their insolvency This may lead to allegations that the directors of the group companies breached their fiduciary duties by approving the cash pooling agreement or by failing to monitor its implementation.

To limit such risk, the directors of a group company should, before putting in place a cash pooling agreement, seek a declaration of solvency from the board of the company which is to hold the master account. In addition, the directors of a group companies should continue to monitor the solvency of the master account holder and, to the extent this is permissible under the agreement, should seek to prevent transfers up to the master account holder in the event of doubt as to its solvency.

In addition, in both the negotiation and implementation of the cash pooling agreement, it is important that the directors of the group companies consider and monitor the purposes to which the pooled moneys may be put. There may be a temptation for the master account holder to engage in treasury management activities which incur, rather than mitigate, risk. For example, it would be entirely proper for the treasury company to trade currency futures to hedge group currency risk, but it may stray beyond this and speculate on currency futures. Activities such as these should be closely monitored to ensure that the pooled funds are not exposed to undue risk.

(c) ***Liability of group companies in the event of insolvency of the master account holder***

In this situation, it may possible that the assets of the master account holder were wrongly transferred down to the various group companies under the cash pooling agreement. In the event that certain transfers made under the cash pooling agreement can be unwound, it may be possible to make certain assets that would otherwise have been dissipated available for creditors.

Where an Irish incorporated company enters into an insolvency process, those running the process are under a duty to maximise the assets of the company for the benefit of creditors. This is commonly done by seeking to impose personal liability on those involved in the operation of the company or by seeking to set aside transactions entered into before the insolvency. In practice, these claims will not be directly made by creditors, but will be made by a liquidator or receiver appointed to the company on behalf of the creditors.

These processes are based on the fact that the insolvent entity (here, the account holder) is located in Ireland. As a general matter, the jurisdiction of the claiming creditor should not be directly relevant to the evaluation of the legal claim. However, some of the statutory rules allowing for the piercing of a corporate veil following insolvency are drafted in a manner which suggests that they can apply only where all the various companies are Irish.

In addition, if the group company against which a contribution is sought is not located in Ireland, the liquidator of the account holder will likely need to seek to enforce any Irish court order before the courts of the relevant jurisdiction. Depending on the jurisdiction where the group company is located, this could prove to be a challenge.

***Ultra vires* transfers:** Where an Irish company becomes insolvent, it has been held that: "Where, as here, a company's situation was such that any creditor could have caused it to be wound up on the ground of insolvency, I consider that it can equally well be said that the company had ceased to be the beneficial owner of its assets with the result that the directors would have had no power to use the company's assets to discharge the liabilities of other [group] companies."[12]

Accordingly, any transfer by an insolvent company (be it the master account holder or a subsidiary) in favour of a group company, whether arising from an automatic sweeping arrangement or otherwise, could be argued to be *ultra vires* the company and invalid. As a result, inter-company payments cannot be made after the company becomes insolvent, and all the more so after the commencement of a winding-up procedure.[13]

If a winding-up resolution is passed by the company or a winding-up petition is presented to the court, the cash pooling agreement can be relied on only in relation to inter-company payments made before the company became insolvent, or in relation to debts incurred in favour of the bank before that time. Any netting of

---

12 *Re Fredreick Inns Ltd*, [1994] 1 ILRM 387.

13 Most powers of attorney terminate automatically on the commencement of a winding up of the grantor. Accordingly, the power usually relied on by a bank to sweep cash will likely terminate.

moneys which had actually been completed by the time the company became insolvent (such completion being evidenced by the substitution of one debt owed by one entity for several debts owed by and to several entities) would survive. However, any transfers made after this point would arguably be *ultra vires* the insolvent company and could be clawed back by a liquidator.

Contribution and pooling orders: Section 140 of the Companies Act 1990 provides that if a company is being wound up, the High Court may, if it is satisfied that it is just and equitable to do so, order any company which is related to the insolvent company to pay all or part of the debts of the company that is being wound up. This is usually termed a 'contribution order'.

Similarly, Section 141 of the Companies Acts 1990 stipulates that if two or more related companies are being wound up, the court may, if it is satisfied that it is just and equitable to do so, make an order that, subject to such terms and conditions as the court may impose, the companies should be wound up together as if they were one company. This is usually termed a 'pooling order'.

In making such orders, the court is obliged to look at the extent to which the insolvency of the first company is attributable to the actions of the second company and the extent to which the assets of the companies are intermingled.

Sections 140 and 141 allow the Irish courts to make pooling and contribution orders against 'companies'. As noted above, 'companies' is a defined term under Irish law and means 'Irish companies'. Consequently, it would appear that, in cases of a transnational cash pooling agreement, it would be difficult to obtain a pooling or contribution order against any non-Irish entities in the group. However, as with the arguments set out in relation to Section 35 of the Companies Act 1990 above, a court could find that the word 'company' in these sections should be construed as 'body corporate'.

Statutory grounds for setting aside transactions: There are a number of statutory provisions under which transactions may be set aside. In such cases, a liquidator may be able to seek the return of moneys transferred under a cash pooling agreement:

- Section 139 of the Companies Act 1990 (fraud on the company) – the court may order the return of assets where it is satisfied that the effect of the transfer of such assets was to perpetrate a fraud on the company, its creditors or members. This situation might occur, in the context of a cash pooling agreement, where an Irish company with large cash balances becomes insolvent in circumstances where its cash has been swept into a cash pool and dissipated to discharge the debts of insolvent members of the cash pooling agreement.
- Section 74 of the Land and Conveyancing Law Reform Act 2009 (fraudulent transfer) – any conveyance (transfer) of real or personal property made with the intention of defrauding a creditor or other person is voidable by any person prejudiced by the transaction. 'Intention' is broadly interpreted and includes the natural and probable effects of a transaction.[14] Consequently,

14 *Keegan Quarries v McGuinness* [2011] IEHC 453.

any sweeping of cash which would seem after the event to have had the natural and probable effect of defrauding a creditor may be set aside.

- Section 286 of the Companies Act 1963 (fraudulent preference) – where a company that is unable to pay its debts as they fall due makes a payment in favour of a connected person (which would include a group company) within two years of the date of the commencement of the company being wound up, that payment is deemed to be a fraudulent preference and to have been made with a view to giving a preference to the recipient over other creditors, unless the contrary is shown. Accordingly, in such circumstances the burden of proof is on the party seeking to uphold the transaction. In the context of a cash pooling agreement, it is possible to envisage a situation in which an Irish company was indebted to the cash pool over a significant period of time and made contributions to the cash pool in the two year period before the commencement of its winding-up. Such transactions are potentially at risk of being unwound.
- Section 211 of the National Asset Management Agency Act 2009 – the National Asset Management Agency was established by the Irish government following the 2008 financial crisis, to take over the administration of potentially problematic loans and remove them from the balance sheets of other banks. In circumstances where the debts of a company (which may include obligations under a cash pooling agreement) have been transferred by a financial institution to the National Asset Management Agency, that agency is entitled to apply to court to seek the setting aside of any disposition which has the effect of defeating, delaying or hindering the acquisition of an asset, or which reduced the value of that asset. A court may declare such a disposition void if it believes that it is just and equitable to do so.

(d) Liability of the master account holder in the event of insolvency of a group company

If it is arguable that the insolvency may have resulted from the sweeping of cash out of the group company to the master account, it is possible that the transfer of assets out of the insolvent company could be impugned as being improper, with the consequence that the moneys could be clawed back and made available to the creditors of the insolvent company.

The legal basis of such an application is as set out at section 2.1(c) above.

2.2 Perspective B: bank

(a) Banking requirements

For any notional cash pooling agreement operating in Ireland, certain requirements must be satisfied to enable the bank to report net exposure to the Central Bank. All on-balance sheet netting arrangements must be legally effective and enforceable in all relevant jurisdictions, including in the event of insolvency or bankruptcy of a counterparty. In addition, the bank must, at any time, be able to determine the assets and liabilities that are subject to the agreement. Finally, the bank must monitor and control the risks associated with termination of the arrangement.

The Basel II standards apply in Ireland. In addition, following the financial crisis, the Central Bank undertook a review of liquidity requirements and, among other things, has introduced a liquidity cover ratio in line with that proposed by Basel III.[15]

(b) Liability of the bank in the event of insolvency of the master account holder or a group company

If the master account holder or a group company becomes insolvent due to the negligence of the bank in implementing the cash pooling agreement (eg, failing to transfer funds across the group as required), it may be theoretically possible to bring a case against the bank in negligence for any resulting damage suffered. However, any action of this sort would be very much a test case. To bring a successful action for negligence, it would be necessary to show that the bank owed a duty of care to the affected person. It would be difficult for a creditor to show that the bank owed the creditor a duty of care due to the lack of proximity in the relationship. However, it is conceivable that a bank could be said to owe its customers (and, by extension, any liquidator appointed over them) a duty of care.

Whether such a case could be brought in Ireland would likely turn on any choice of law and jurisdiction provisions in the underlying facility agreement between the group entities and the bank.

2.3 Insolvency

Bank goes into liquidation: There is no precedent for an Irish bank entering into an insolvency process. At present, this is unlikely, as Irish banks[16] are supported by sovereign guarantees. In particular, deposits are guaranteed pursuant to the Credit Institutions (Eligible Liabilities Guarantee) Scheme 2009.[17] Accordingly, there is limited risk in relation to the insolvency of an Irish bank.

The situation should, however, be kept under review, as the Irish government has the right to terminate the guarantees, without prejudice to the applicability of the guarantees to the deposits on the date of such cancellation.

In the wake of the financial crisis, the Irish government has introduced a range of complex legislation relating to the stability of financial institutions, which is not feasible to cover in a single chapter.

If the institution used is not an Irish bank, then general principles of insolvency law will apply subject to EU derived law and, in particular, the European Communities (Reorganisation and Winding-up of Credit Institutions) Regulations 2011[18] and, in respect of moneys in transit when the proceedings are commenced, the European Communities (Settlement Finality) Regulations 2008.[19]

---

15 www.centralbank.ie/regulation/poldocs/dispapers/Pages/home.aspx.aspx.

16 Those banks which have been the subject of an order rendering them 'covered institutions' under SI 411/2008 – Credit Institutions (Financial Support) Scheme 2008.

17 SI 490/2009 as amended by SI 634/2011 – Credit Institutions (Eligible Liabilities Guarantee) (Amendment) Scheme 2011.

18 SI 48/2011, which implements EU Directive 2001/24/EC of the European Parliament and of the Council of April 4 2001 on the reorganisation and winding up of credit institutions.

19 SI 88/2008, which implements EU Directive 98/26/EC, the Settlement Finality Directive.

Ignoring the sovereign guarantees, as a matter of Irish law, a bank account is essentially an (unsecured) contractual claim by a depositor against the bank. In the event of insolvency, any cash held by the bank would fall within the pool of assets available for distribution to creditors. The master account holder would be a depositor, and therefore an unsecured creditor. The holder of that account would be entitled to prove a claim for the full balance in the account as at the date of the bank's insolvency. However, in practice, it would likely receive only a fraction of the value of the account in cash (if anything at all), as the bank's assets will be applied, in the first instance, in the satisfaction of secured and senior creditors.

If the bank that has become insolvent is based outside of Ireland, the manner in which its assets will be distributed would be a matter for the applicable local law.

Master account holder goes into liquidation: In this case, the balance in the account would fall, in the first instance, within the pool of assets available for distribution to the creditors of the account holder (a group which may, depending on the drafting of the cash pooling agreement, include group companies). In such an instance, the group companies would have no specific claim on the moneys.

To obtain priority over the other creditors, it may be possible for the group companies to assert that the moneys held by the master account holder were held on trust for the various group entities and, as such, should be returned to the group entities and should not form part of the general pool of assets available to the creditors. The success or otherwise of this argument would turn on the specific facts of the case and the drafting of the cash pooling agreement.[20]

Group company goes into liquidation: In the absence of some special trust arrangement, it would appear that the group company generally has no direct claim on the moneys in the pooled account. However, depending on the terms of the cash pooling agreement, it may be open to the liquidator of the group company to seek the return of certain assets transferred into the cash pool in reliance on the legal doctrines set out above.

Bank goes into liquidation: The liquidator's obligation where the bank goes into liquidation is to gather up, to the maximum extent possible, the assets of the insolvent entity and then to distribute those assets among the various creditors of the company, in accordance with law. The fact that potential creditors are located in another jurisdiction is not relevant from an Irish law perspective.

As noted above, to the extent that master account holder is a creditor of the bank, the liquidator has a duty to return to the master account holder such share of the bank's assets to which it is entitled under general principles of insolvency law. Leaving aside the possibility that group companies may have other accounts with the

---

20 Enhanced clarity in this regard may emerge from the recent application by a number of companies within the eircom Group (which provides fixed-line and mobile telecommunications services in Ireland) for the appointment of an examiner (similar to Chapter 11 in the United States). One of the companies that successfully applied for the appointment of an examiner was the group treasury company, while the English registered parent public limited company remained outside the process.

bank, the bank's liquidator would have no direct obligations to the group companies, as the master account, and therefore the claim in liquidation lies with the master account holder.

Master account holder goes into liquidation: The liquidator's obligation where the master account holder goes into liquidation is to gather up, to the maximum extent possible, the assets of the insolvent entity and then to distribute those assets among the various creditors of the company, in accordance with law. The fact that potential creditors are located in another jurisdiction is not relevant from an Irish law perspective.

If the bank has an outstanding claim against the master account holder, then depending on the agreements in place, it may seek to offset this claim against the moneys held in the master account.

Whether the master account holder's liquidator has any duties to the bank and the group companies will depend upon the agreement in place between the various entities – in particular, whether the bank or the group company could have a claim, provable in liquidation, against the master account holder.

Section 290 of the Companies Act 1963 allows a liquidator to apply to court to disclaim any onerous or unprofitable contracts. In such an application, the exclusive concern of the court is the interests of all persons interested in the liquidation.[21] A liquidator of the account holder may, in reliance on this provision, seek to disclaim the cash pooling agreement.

Group company goes into liquidation: The liquidator's obligation where a group company goes into liquidation is to gather up, to the maximum extent possible, the assets of the insolvent entity and then to distribute those assets among the various creditors of the company, in accordance with insolvency law. The fact that potential creditors are located in another jurisdiction is not relevant from an Irish law perspective.

Whether the liquidator of a group company will have any duties to the bank and the master account holder will depend upon the agreement in place between the various entities, and, in particular, whether the bank or the master account holder could have a claim, provable in liquidation, against the group company.

In the case of a group company, regard should be paid to the possibility that a liquidator may seek to disclaim the cash pooling agreement under Section 290 of the Companies Act 1963, as discussed above.

Voidability of transactions: If the bankrupt master account holder has transferred money to group companies prior to its bankruptcy or a group company has transferred money to the master account holder prior to the bankruptcy of that group company, Irish law provides a number of ways in which the administrator in the insolvency of the relevant company may have declared void those transactions and claim the amounts as part of the bankrupt estate. These are discussed at length in section 2.1(c) above.

21 *Tempany v Royal Liver Trustees Limited* [1984] ILRM 273.

There is no provision for 'licenced administrators' in Irish law. In practice, the liquidator of an Irish company will be an Irish accountant. However, there does not appear to an obvious reason why a non-Irish liquidator would be unable to seek the return of the moneys.

(b) ***Special rules as regards creditors of other parties to the cash pooling agreement***

In the event of insolvency of any one of the bank, the master account holder or a group company, the creditors of the other parties to the cash pooling agreement would, in effect, be creditors of the creditors of the insolvent entity. Liquidators do not generally owe duties to parties that are so remotely connected to the insolvency process.

(c) ***Dissolution/termination of the cash pooling agreement in the event of liquidation of the master account holder or a group company***

Irish law is liberal with regard to the contents of commercial agreements, including terms which regulate how those agreements can be terminated. Consequently, the ability to terminate the cash pooling agreement in the event of insolvency of the master account holder or a group company will turn on whether there is a provision in the cash pooling agreement allowing for such termination. This should be carefully considered during drafting.

2.3 Insolvency

Reporting obligations may arise during the existence of a cash pooling agreement, depending on the amounts periodically transferred between the participant's source account and the target account.

It may also be necessary to comply with rules relating to the reporting of cross-border financial transactions that apply to cross-border pooling scenarios.

Deposits should not be accepted by a person in the course of carrying out a deposit-taking business, unless authorised to do so or exempt from authorisation. To ensure that the borrowing of inter-company loans by any company under a cash pooling agreement does not result in the taking of deposits, it has been suggested that the inter-company loans should always be provided by a company within the same group.[22]

2.5 Perspective E: tax

Ireland is a popular choice for multinational groups as a location for group cash pooling operations, not least because of its favourable tax environment for treasury and cash management activities. Benefits include:

- no thin capitalisation rules restricting debt to equity ratios;
- a wide range of withholding tax exemptions in respect of cross-border interest payments;
- availability of a 12.5% rate of corporation tax in respect of profits arising from the carrying on in Ireland of a trade of financing and lending;
- extensive and expanding network of double tax agreements reducing or

---

22 *PLC* November 2009: "Cash Pooling – Cascading Cost-efficiency and Control" (Louise Webb, Caroline Long, Mathew Padian and Rodger Burnett of Baker & McKenzie).

eliminating withholding tax on cross-border payments to and from treaty partner jurisdictions;[23]

- limited transfer pricing provisions; and
- no controlled foreign company legislation.

From a tax perspective, the distinction between physical and notional pooling is highly relevant. As notional pooling does not typically involve the creation of intra-group loans or intra-group payments, it may often be achieved without significant tax implications. Transfer pricing may be relevant in terms of intra-group guarantees and interest rates; however, factors such as withholding tax, interest deductibility and taxation of interest receipts should not be of relevance where loans are not entered into. Accordingly, the factors highlighted below will be of relevance primarily in relation to physical pooling.

(a) Interest deductibility

Ireland has no thin capitalisation rules as such, and interest incurred wholly and exclusively for the purposes of a trade or business will normally be deductible for tax purposes. However, under Section 130 of the Taxes Consolidation Act 1997, certain interest may be treated as a distribution resulting in denial of a corporation tax deduction for the Irish paying company and potential imposition of Irish dividend withholding tax. Interest paid in respect of borrowings from a 75% non-resident group company may be treated as a distribution under Section 130(2)(d)(iv) of the Taxes Consolidation Act. This provision is, however, subject to a number of exceptions in circumstances where interest is:

- paid to a company which is a resident for tax purposes in an EU member state other than Ireland (Section 130(2B) of the Taxes Consolidation Act);
- paid by a company in the ordinary course of its trade to a company that is resident in the European Union or a country with which Ireland has executed a double tax agreement and the paying company has made an election in accordance with Section 452 of the Taxes Consolidation Act; or
- paid to a group company that is resident outside the European Union in a non-treaty jurisdiction, provided that that jurisdiction taxes such foreign source interest income at a rate equal to or greater than the Irish corporation tax rate of 12.5%.

In addition, Section 130(2)(d)(iii)(II) provides that where the interest rate paid represents more than a reasonable commercial return for the use of the principal, the excess will be treated as a deemed distribution. Accordingly, it is important that cash pooling agreements be entered into on an arm's-length basis. This will be relevant in an international transfer pricing context also.

(b) Withholding tax

Withholding tax applies at a current rate of 20% where yearly interest deriving from

---

23 Ireland has signed comprehensive double tax agreements with 65 countries, 59 of which are in effect.

an Irish source is paid by a company to a person whose usual place of abode is outside the state. This charging provision is subject to a wide range of exemptions and to the provisions of Ireland's double tax agreements, such that the withholding tax charge is largely disapplied in most situations. For example, interest paid by a company in the ordinary course of its trade or business is exempt from withholding tax where:

- the interest is paid to a company that is resident for tax purposes in an EU or tax treaty country which imposes a tax that generally applies to interest receivable in that territory by companies from sources outside that territory; or
- where the interest is exempted from the charge to income tax under the provisions of a double tax agreement, or would be so exempted if the double tax agreement had taken effect in accordance with the entry into force provisions set out therein when the interest was paid.

However, the exemptions do not appy where such interest is paid to that company in connection with a trade or business carried on in Ireland by the receiving company through a branch or agency.

In addition, Ireland's withholding tax provisions apply only in respect of payments of yearly interest. The term 'yearly interest' is not defined in statute; however, case law indicates that yearly interest is taken to be interest on a loan which runs or is capable of running for a period of a year or more. Short loans, on the other hand, are described as loans made for a period of less than of one year that do not allow for a revolving facility, and loans that are not intended to be continued, and are not continued, for a longer period.[24] In many cases, cash pooling agreements are structured so as to fall outside Irish interest withholding tax provisions through the use of short loans.

(c) *Trading activities*

One of the key considerations in structuring treasury and cash management activities in Ireland is the availability of the 12.5% rate of corporation tax, particularly where the master account holder is an Irish entity. Companies carrying on a trade in Ireland are subject to corporation tax at a rate of 12.5% in respect of profits arising from that trade. The existence or otherwise of a trade depends on a variety of factors, including the number and frequency of loans entered into by the Irish entity and the substance in terms of physical presence, senior Irish-based employees engaged by the company and composition of the board of directors of the company. The trading status of the company is also relevant in determining the treatment of foreign exchange gains and losses of the Irish entity.

The Irish Revenue Commissioners have issued guidance clarifying their position regarding the taxation of deposit interest arising to companies,[25] which is of particular relevance to Irish companies engaged in treasury and cash management operations. While the general position expressed by the Revenue Commissioners is that deposit interest is *prima facie* passive income (assessable to corporation tax at a rate of 25%), it is accepted that exceptions apply in the case of:

---

24 *Goslings & Sharpe v Blake* 2 TC 450.

25 Revenue Information Notice: "Deposit Interest – Whether a Trading Receipt?"

- deposit interest derived from investment of capital required to be held as a result of regulatory requirements; and
- deposit interest derived from investment of capital which is integral to the trade, such as in the case of standalone treasury companies or captive finance companies.

In these instances, deposit interest would typically be taxable at the 12.5% rate of corporation tax.

Finally, the use of tax losses is often relevant, particularly where multinational groups have existing Irish trading activities. Ireland's flexibility in terms of carry-forward of losses, group relief of excess losses and charges and carry-back of losses on cessation of a trade provides significant advantages, particularly in terms of the winding down of the structure.

(d) *Transfer pricing*

Limited transfer pricing rules were introduced in Ireland and took effect in respect of chargeable periods beginning on or after January 1 2011 in relation to arrangements whose terms were not agreed in advance of July 1 2010. The transfer pricing provisions enable the Irish Revenue Commissioners to apply arm's-length terms in computing the taxable profits or gains arising in respect of arrangements (including arrangements involving the supply and acquisition of money) between associated persons. Accordingly, where arrangements fall within the terms of Ireland's transfer pricing regime, group companies may need to consider appropriate arm's-length terms in respect of intra-group interest payments, guarantee fees and fees for cash management services provided by the master account holder. Appropriate transfer pricing documentation should be maintained supporting the arm's-length nature of these arrangements.

In addition to grandfathering of existing arrangements, there are a number of exemptions from the application of Ireland's transfer pricing provisions. The rules are subject to a minimum threshold and do not apply in computing the profits, gains or losses of small or medium-sized enterprises.[26] In addition, the transfer pricing provisions apply only to trading transactions, and therefore many holding companies do not typically fall within the new regime. Accordingly, certain Irish companies may still engage in interest-free lending as non-trading transactions.

(e) *Other taxes*

Although intra-group lending is typically treated as an exempt financial service for Irish value added tax (VAT) purposes, associated supplies such as management fees charged to group companies by the master account holder may be liable to Irish VAT (at a current rate of 23%). The VAT recovery position of each group company should be considered in this regard.

Irish stamp duty is not currently chargeable on documents evidencing the creation of a loan.

---

26 Within the meaning of Commission Recommendation 2003/361 of May 6 2003.

Italy

Flavio Acerbi
Domenico Gioia
Paolo Manganelli
Cosimo Pennetta
Paul Hastings (Europe) LLP

1. Introduction

1.1 Admissibility of cash pooling agreements

Italy has no specific legislation that governs cash pooling in full. The English term 'cash pooling' is therefore used to define any arrangement providing for a centralised management of the financial resources in a group of companies. Although certain legal scholars have in the past raised some concerns as to the lawfulness of cash pooling agreements[1], today such arrangements are considered fully valid under Italian law.

This opinion – which is in line with that expressed by a large majority of scholars[2] – has been confirmed by a number of acknowledgments of cash pooling in case law[3] and in rulings and circulars issued by several administrative authorities,[4] as well as more recently in certain regulatory measures[5] that make some reference to cash pooling (without, however, providing for full regulation thereof). For these reasons,

1 Reference is to E Gliozzi, *"Direzione unitaria di un gruppo di società e confusione di patrimoni"*, published in *Giur It*, 1996, I, 2, page 536 *et seq*; see also E Gliozzi, *L'imprenditore commerciale. Saggio sui limiti del formalismo giuridico*, Bologna, 1998, page 146, footnote 22.

2 Among others, M Tidona, *"Il cash pooling tra le società appartenenti ad un gruppo"*, in *www.magistra.com*, 2000; A Daccò, *L'accentramento della tesoreria nei gruppi di società*, Milano, 2002; M Castiglioni, *"Il contratto di tesoreria accentrata (cd cash pooling). I requisiti della società capogruppo nel Testo Unico Bancario"*, in *www.tidona.com*, 2002; F Baggio and G Rebecca, *"Tesoreria accentrata e finanziamenti infragruppo con società non residenti. Aspetti tributari"*, in *Il Fisco* 2003, n 43, page 23 *et seq*; R Moro Visconti, "Impresa commerciale e industriale", in *Impr. comm. ind.*, 2004, page 395 *et seq*; A Rittatore Vonwiller and M Ippolito, *I gruppi societari*, Milano, 2005, page 442 *et seq*; F Bencivegna and L Galeotti Flori, *"Il contratto di cash pooling"*, in *Il Foro Toscano*, 2007, page 251 *et seq*; SA Dalla Riva, *Cash pooling. Il governo centrale della liquidità nei gruppi societari. La gestione in azienda, la normativa, il fisco*, Milano, 2008, page 143 *et seq*; S Colombi, *Le holding e il gruppo di imprese*, Bologna, 2010; A Dragonetti, V Piacentini and A Sfondrini, *Manuale di fiscalità internazionale*, Milano, 2010, page 618 *et seq*; M Peverelli and A Francioso, *"Contratti di cash pooling: deducibilità degli interessi passivi e applicazione delle ritenute"*, in *Fiscalità e Commercio internazionale*, 2011, page 57 *et seq*; L Ruggeri, *"Brevi Note circa il cash pooling"*, in *Nuova Giurisprudenza Civile Commentata*, 2011, I, page 206 *et seq*; M Miola, *"Tesoreria accentrata nei gruppi di società e capitale sociale"*, in VVAA, *La struttura finanziaria e i bilanci delle società di capitali, Studi in onore di Giovanni E. Colombo*, Torino, 2011, page 36 *et seq*; L Gambini and G Battaglia, *"Section on Italy"* in J Jensen, *International Cash Pooling. Cross-border Cash Management Systems and Intra-group Financing*, Munich, 2011, page 201 *et seq*.

3 Courts of Forlì, Civil Division, Decision of June 30 2008, in *dejure.giuffre.it*; Supreme Court, Tax Division, Decision 14730 of June 23 2009, in *dejure.giuffre.it*; Regional Tax Courts of Turin, Division XXV, Decision 16 of March 17 2010, in *dejure.giuffre.it*; Courts of Pistoia, Civil Division, Decision of February 17 2010 in NGCC, 2011, I, page 202 *et seq*.

4 See Revenue Agency Ruling 58/E of February 27 2002; Revenue Agency Ruling 194/E of October 8 2003; Revenue Agency Circular 47/E of November 2 2005; Revenue Agency Circular 19/E of April 21 2009; Revenue Agency Ruling 131/E of May 27 2009; Ministry of Economy and Finance Circular 51/E of October 6 2010.

despite the lack of a complete and specific regulatory framework for cash pooling agreements, we are of the opinion that cash pooling is fully valid under Italian law.[6]

In light of the above, it is important to understand how a cash pooling agreement is classified under Italian law.

Technically speaking, a cash pooling agreement should be considered as a contract mentioned (but not specifically provided for) by law. Despite this, it can still be considered an irregular contract because, as noted above, there is currently no Italian law that provides for complete regulation of cash pooling.

Under Italian law, an irregular contract is fully valid and binding as long as it aims to generate interests worthy of protection according to the laws in force.[7] In order to assess the worthiness of protection, the reasons behind each party entering into a cash pooling agreement need to be verified, just as they would for any other irregular contract.

In almost all cases, the main objective of entering into a cash pooling agreement is to optimise the management of a corporate group's liquidity. This goal is entirely lawful and legitimate under Italian law, and compliant with the principles underlying applicable Italian corporate laws.

Therefore, it should be considered perfectly legitimate for corporations or entities to enter into a cash pooling agreement and for holding companies to set up a cash pooling agreement with group members.

1.2 Types of cash pooling agreement

The objective of optimising a corporate group's liquidity could be reached through different contractual schemes and, as a result, a cash pooling agreement in Italy may be structured in different ways. However, an initial general distinction must be made between physical cash pooling and notional cash pooling (the latter can also be referred to as virtual cash pooling).

A physical cash pooling scheme provides for actual movements of cash from each secondary account[8] to the master account[9] and vice versa. Periodically (usually at the close of business of each business day), the balance of each secondary account is

---

5 See Regulation of the Authority for the Supervisory over Public Contracts, Services, and Supplies 4/2011 of July 7 2011 (in *Official Gazette of the Republic of Italy* 171/2011 of July 25 2011) providing for Guidelines on traceability of financial transactions pursuant Article 3 of Italian Law 136/2010 of August 13 2010; Regulation of the Authority for the Supervisory over Public Contracts, Services, and Supplies 10/2010 of December 22 2010 (in *Official Gazette of the Republic of Italy* 4/2011 of January 7 2011) providing for additional instructions on traceability of financial transactions; Bank of Italy Regulation of July 5 2011 implementing Title II of Italian Legislative Decree 11/2010 of January 27 2010 regarding payment services; Regulation containing implementation rules of Italian Legislative Decree 58/98 of February 24 1998 on markets, adopted by the Italian Market Authority (CONSOB) with Resolution 16191 of October 29 2007, later amended by Resolution 16530 of June 25 2008, Resolution 16850 of April 1 2009, Resolution 17221 of March 12 2010, Resolution 17389 of June 23 2010 and Resolution 18079 of January 20 2012.

6 Given the absence of significant case law in respect of the validity of cash pooling agreements, all of the opinions expressed in this chapter reflect current common practice adopted in Italian cash pooling transactions according to the authors' experience and interpretation, taking into account, among other things, the views expressed by the Revenue Agency, the Bank of Italy and CONSOB, and the authors' interpretation thereof. However, the authors cannot exclude the possibility that judicial, tax and/or regulatory authorities may, in the future, reach conclusions in respect of the matters falling within the scope of this chapter that differ, even substantially, from the opinions expressed here.

7 Article 1322 of the Code.

transferred to the master account in order to accumulate the liquidity belonging to all group companies[10] into one single account (ie, the master account). Equally, if and when the balance of a secondary account falls below zero, then the master account holder[11] will debit the master account for an amount equal to the negative balance and credit such amount to the relevant secondary account so that the balance of that secondary account is no longer negative. The most frequent types of physical cash pooling are zero balancing and account sweeping.

In contrast to what occurs with physical cash pooling, a notional cash pooling scheme does not provide for any actual transfer of cash between the different accounts. The funds standing to the credit of the master account (if any) and those standing to the credit of the secondary accounts are not transferred and, essentially, remain untouched. The cash pool is obtained through a virtual netting of credits and debits resulting from the positive and negative balances of all relevant accounts. Then, the applicable interest rate is calculated on the aggregate balance of all participating accounts. This type of cash pooling is rarely employed in Italy because the Italian Revenue Agency has provided for the application of a tax regime less favourable than that applicable to physical cash pooling, due to a different classification of this type of cash pooling agreement from that applicable to the zero balancing system.[12]

Given the general distinction above, we analyse the different types of cash pooling that could be potentially implemented in Italy in more detail, in particular:

- the zero balancing system;
- the account sweeping system; and
- notional cash pooling.

For the sake of clarity, it is appropriate to specify that the only type of cash pooling that may be implemented in Italy without any particular concern is zero balancing.[13]

---

8 In the context of this chapter, 'secondary account' means each account belonging to a participating group company other than the master account holder.

9 In the context of this chapter, 'master account' means the main bank account used for the cash pooling scheme and managed by the master account holder.

10 In the context of this chapter, 'Group company' means a company participating in a cash pooling agreement.

11 In the context of this chapter, 'master account holder' means the company (usually the parent company or a special treasury entity) that enters into a cash pooling agreement with a bank.

12 For further details, see the section on tax law below, at section1.3(c).

13 This is due to the tax regime applicable to notional cash pooling under Revenue Agency Ruling 58/E of February 27 2002 and Ruling 194/E of October 8 2003, but also due to some uncertainties as to the compliance of notional cash pooling with certain Italian laws and regulations (eg, Ministry of Economy and Finance Ruling 8/1605 of December 21 1976; and Articles 26 and 26-*bis* of the Italian Presidential Decree 600/73 of September 29 1973); in this respect, see also F Bencivenga and L Galeotti Flori, "*Il contratto di cash pooling*", in *Il Foro Toscano*, 2007, page 253; S Colombi, *Le holding e il gruppo di imprese*, page 106 *et seq.*; A Dragonetti, V Piacentini and A Sfondrini, *Manuale di fiscalità internazionale*, page 618 *et seq.*; M Peverelli and A Francioso, "*Contratti di cash pooling: deducibilità degli interessi passivi e applicazione delle ritenute*", in *Fiscalità e Commercio internazionale*, 2011, page 57 *et seq*; R Moro Visconti, "*Impresa commerciale e industriale*", in *Impr comm ind*, 2004, page 395 *et seq*; A Rittatore Vonwiller and M Ippolito, *I gruppi societari*, page 442 *et seq*; SA Dalla Riva, *Cash pooling. Il governo centrale della liquidità nei gruppi societari*, page 144 *et seq*.

(a) *Zero balancing*

Zero balancing involves the physical movement of money between the master account and the secondary accounts. At the close of business of any business day, each secondary account is swept to create a zero balance and all the funds standing to the credit thereof are credited to the master account. In addition to sweeping positive balances in the secondary accounts up to the master account, a debit balance on any secondary account is cancelled by means of a mirrored sweep from the master account. Following any money transfer, the master account holder becomes either a creditor or a debtor in respect of each group company. As a consequence of each transfer, an intra-group relationship is created and is recorded (ie, accounted for) by both the master account holder and the relevant group company in an *ad hoc* accountability statement. Any entry in the master account accountability statements must be followed by an equivalent (inverse) entry in the relevant secondary account accountability statements. Interest accrued on the sums standing to the credit of the master account is paid down at pre-agreed rates to each group company on a *pro rata* basis.[14] In the absence of specific regulation, this type of contractual scheme – although not clearly identifiable either as a regular inter-company loan agreement[15] or as a regular non-bank current account agreement[16] – has been classified as an irregular inter-company loan agreement for tax purposes.[17] This legal classification must be taken into account in determining the rules applicable to a zero balancing cash pooling agreement.

(b) *Account sweeping*

As with the zero balancing system, the account sweeping system involves the physical movement of sums between the group companies' accounts. However, unlike zero balancing and notional cash pooling, the account sweeping system does not provide for any automatic transfer of sums on pre-agreed terms: each transfer is made upon instruction of the master account holder. Each instruction may be given from time to time with or without a framework agreement. This type of cash pooling is rarely used in Italy, probably as a result of the uncertainties created by the lack of decisions concerning this type of arrangement.[18]

---

14 For the avoidance of doubt, this is not a legal obligation and the interest accrued on the sums standing to the credit of the master account may be paid down to the group companies on a bullet basis.

15 A cash remittance under a cash pooling agreement may not qualify as a loan because the underlying rationale of a cash pooling agreement differs from the underlying rationale of a loan agreement. In a cash pooling agreement, the rationale is the best management of a group's liquidity, while in a loan agreement the rationale is obtaining immediate availability of money or other fungible goods with the obligation to reimburse the same amount of money or goods (plus interest, if any). In Italy, loan agreements are regulated under Article 1813 of the Civil Code.

16 Cash remittances may not qualify as a non-bank current account agreement mainly because of the unavailability of sums until the account is closed. Non-bank current account agreements are regulated under Article 1823 of the Civil Code, and their underlying rationale is the reciprocal granting of credit.

17 Revenue Agency Rulings 58/E of February 27 2002 and 194/E of October 8 2003.

18 The account sweeping system may sometimes be adopted by groups of micro and small enterprises. See L Del Federico, "*La gestione della tesoreria e del corporate financing attraverso holding di diritto estero*", in *Il Fisco*, No 7, February 13 2006, page 965 *et seq.*

(c) *Notional cash pooling*

Unlike zero balancing and account sweeping, notional cash pooling system does not involve the physical transfer of moneys between the master accounts (if any) and the secondary accounts. Nonetheless, under a notional cash pooling agreement, interest accrues on the aggregate amount determined as the sum of the balance of the master account (if any) and the balances of all secondary accounts. The operating bank[19] will notionally calculate the aggregate balance across several accounts and pay or charge interest on the combined balance only. The main feature of a notional cash pooling system is the absence of any actual physical transfer of moneys between the current accounts. This system is almost never used in Italy because the set-off of a credit on one account against a debt on another account is not permitted under Italian law.[20] Another obstacle to notional cash pooling under Italian law is the obligation to calculate positive and negative interest on the balance of each account on a daily basis.[21]

(d) *Target pooling, reverse pooling and margin pooling*

Hybrid forms of cash pooling, such as a combination of physical pooling and notional pooling, are also possible. However, these are less likely to be used in Italy than zero balancing (if at all), because they are also still virtually untested in the Italian courts. The main hybrid types of cash pooling agreements are as follows.

Target balance cash pooling: This is very similar to the zero balancing system, as it involves the physical movement of money between the master account and the secondary accounts, but at the close of business of any business day, each secondary account is not swept to create a zero balance. Instead, all accounts are pooled to ensure a pre-set balance. The extrapolated value date balance on the pooling day is transferred (ie, back values and same-day values are transferred with value date of the pooling day). Target balancing works by means of exchanging SWIFT messages (executing: MT101/103; reporting: MT940/942).[22]

---

19 In the context of this chapter, 'operating bank' means the bank providing for banking and payment services to the master account holder (if any) and the group companies in the context of a cash pooling agreement.

20 See F Bencivenga and L Galeotti Flori, *"Il contratto di cash pooling"*, in *Il Foro Toscano*, 2007 page 254; S Colombi, *Le holding e il gruppo di imprese*, page 120. See also SA Dalla Riva, *Cash pooling. Il governo centrale della liquidità nei gruppi societari*, page 144 *et seq* and, in particular, pages148 and 152, where the author states that "under the Italian Civil Code there is not an express prohibition against notional cash pooling" (page 148) but "the legal issues [underlying to a notional cash pooling] … represent an obstacle that is very hard to overcome despite the best treasurer's will and, as a matter of fact, represent an implicit prohibition against notional cash pooling in Italy" (page 152). On this subject, note Article 1252 of the Civil Code allowing voluntary compensation by agreement of the parties even in the absence of the conditions provided for by the law.

21 See Article 89, seventh paragraph, of Presidential Decree 917/86 of December 22 1986, which states that: "in relation to current account contracts, and banking transactions settled through current accounts, including reciprocal current accounts for services rendered between businesses and financial institutions, interest is treated as accrued also where the interest has been offset, whether that has occurred by law or by contract."
Therefore, the set-off mechanism underlying a notional cash pooling scheme must be disregarded for tax purposes because the lower tax base that results may theoretically be considered to be tax evasion.

22 SA Dalla Riva, *Cash pooling. Il governo centrale della liquidità nei gruppi societari*, page 97 *et seq.*

Reverse pooling: This is a merger between physical and notional cash pooling where balances remain on the secondary accounts while interest accrued thereon is credited to the master account. At the end of each business day, all amounts standing to the credit of the secondary accounts are transferred to the master account, but one minute after midnight (ie, at the start of the following business day), all amounts are credited back to the relevant secondary account. This may be the best way to get a 'notional pooling effect' in Italy, avoiding the downside of notional pooling.[23]

Margin pooling (also known as 'interest enhancement'): This is a variation of notional cash pooling under which margin compensation or interest offsetting is credited to all group companies' linked accounts, regardless of the currency in which they are denominated. The bonus paid is computed on the basis of offsetting carried out for all accounts involved in the pooling process. The advantage of this form of pooling is that interest is first levied on the accounts, as is customary, and bonus interest is subsequently applied. As far as we know, this form of pooling has never been used in Italy.[24]

(d) Cross-border issues

Particular attention to the structuring of a cash pooling agreement should be paid when one of the group companies participating in the agreement is not resident in Italy. As a matter of law, there are specific tax issues concerning the master account holder, with regard to the rate of interest and the fees payable to it, and any group company participating in the cash pooling agreement (including the master account holder), with regard to the effects of value added tax and the taxation of corporate incomes.[25]

1.3 Specific legal requirements from various perspectives

(a) Company law

Italian corporate law provides no specific provisions with respect to cash pooling agreements. However, the decision to enter into a cash pooling agreement would be subject to the general principles of Italian corporate law. Please see section 2.1 below with respect to, among other things, intra-group relationships, undercapitalisation, financial assistance, conflict of interests and selected aspects of the regulation of listed companies.

(b) Banking regulation

Italian banking regulation, as it affects cash pooling agreements, must be analysed at three different levels:

- the master account holder level;

---

23 *Ibid*, page 115 *et seq.*
24 *Ibid*, page 119 *et seq.*
25 For further details, see the section on tax law below, at section 1.3(c).

- the group companies level; and
- the operating bank level.

Master account holder: Uuntil September 19 2010,[26] the master account holder would have had to have been expressly licensed and authorised in advance by the Bank of Italy to carry out any cash pooling activity, if such activity was its main or sole activity.[27] In fact, until that date (ie, until the entry into force of the 2010 financial intermediaries reform),[28] cash pooling was a restricted activity due to the fact that any financial activity conducted on a professional basis was at the time deemed to be potentially exposed to a systemic risk.

The 2010 reform introduced a new approach to systemic risk in the financial sector. The new list of restricted activities as a result of exposure to systemic risk does not include the acquisition and management of participations in other entities, or trade in currencies and/or any other document representing currencies or intermediary currency. Such activities are now unrestricted (since they are not carried out as services offered to the public), and may be conducted without any prior authorisation or licence. This principle applies also to the master account holder's activity in cash pooling agreements.[29]

Consequently, as of September 19 2010, intra-group financing is no longer a restricted activity limited to licensed to authorised financial intermediaries, and there should no longer be any need to obtain third-party consent or approval to enable either a company to act as master account holder or another group company to participate in a cash pooling agreement. Thus, no special permission is required to set up a cash pooling agreement, provided that the financing activity under the cash pooling agreement is carried out only between group companies (ie, companies that belong to the same corporate group). This has been explicitly confirmed by the Bank of Italy.[30]

---

26 September 19 2010 is the date on which the register of financial intermediaries kept by the Bank of Italy under Article 113 of Legislative Decree 385/93 of September 1 1993 (the Consolidated Banking Act) was repealed, as a consequence of the coming into force of Italian Legislative Decree 141/2010 of August 13 2010, which reformed the regulation of entities working in the financial sector and credit brokers, amending, among other things, Article 106 *et seq* of the Consolidated Banking Act.

27 To determine whether the pooling activity was the main activity of the master account holder, the Bank of Italy took into account data such as the incomes and profits arising out of the pooling activity compared to the aggregate of incomes and profits made by the master account holder and other indices of the balance of its business. The treasury function could be entrusted to a company (not necessarily the parent company), but that company had to be enrolled on a special register kept by the then existing Italian Exchange Office (*Ufficio Italiano Cambi*, which in 2008 merged by way of incorporation into the Bank of Italy and has consequently been renamed the Financial Intelligence Unit. In order to obtain such registration, the master account holder had to comply with a regulatory regime that was less stringent than that applicable to the other financial intermediaries offering services to the public, but still satisfying general requirements as regards shareholders and company representatives, among other things.

28 Legislative Decree 141/2010 of August 13 2010. As at the date of writing this chapter, the relevant implementing regulation has not yet been issued, although the Bank of Italy, in January 2012, released a consultation paper on which experts have been invited to comment. On the 2010 reform of financial intermediaries, see MA Goffredo and F Berneri, "*La revisione della disciplina dei soggetti operati nel settore finanziario*", in *Le Società*, 2010, 12, page 1491 *et seq*; G De Gennaro, "*L'impatto delle modifiche introdotte dal D.Lgs. 141/2010 sui soggetti operanti nel settore finanziario*", on *www.tidona.com*, 2010.

29 S Colombi, *Le holding e il gruppo di imprese*, page 124 *et seq*.

No minimum share capital and no particular corporate form is required to act as master account holder in the context of a cash pooling agreement (nor was it even before the 2010 reform). The master account holder could also be a limited liability company with the minimum paid-up capital. In any case, in order to determine the minimum capital requirement, the thin capitalisation rules, undercapitalisation issues and fair value requirements should also be considered.

Before the entry into force of the 2010 reform, the master account holder was subject to regulations on the integrity of shareholders and independence of company representatives. Now, these obligations have been repealed (together with the dissolution of the register of companies offering financial activities within the corporate group).

The master account holder, as with any other Italian company, is subject to the general regulations on money laundering and the identification, registration and notification obligations provided for therein.

Usury: As mentioned above, a physical cash pooling agreement qualifies as an inter-company loan. Therefore, it is subject to the rules governing loans, including laws and regulations on usury. If an Italian court rules that the levels of interest due on borrowings made under a cash pooling agreement are usurious (ie, in excess of the applicable threshold rate set out quarterly by a decree of the Italian Ministry of Economy and Finance), the relevant borrowers will be entitled to a number of solutions, including the full discharge of their obligation to pay interest (including the reimbursement of any usurious interests previously paid), and various types of damages. Additionally, the lender may be criminally liable for usury as a result of the transfers of funds.

As a matter of Italian criminal law, the crime of usury occurs only if the alleged offender, acting wilfully, has agreed or received a payment of usurious interest from a borrower. Apart from constituting a criminal offence, lending at usurious interest rates has certain implications on the cash flows generated by the financing transaction. Among other consequences, an arrangement stipulating usurious interest is null and void and no interest is due,[31] and as a result, the relevant loan is automatically converted into a gratuitous loan. Italian law provides for two forms of the crime of usury:[32]

- a general usury crime, in which the interest rate agreed with the borrower

30 See Bank of Italy Regulation of July 5 2011 implementing Title II of Italian Legislative Decree 11/2010 of January 27 2010 regarding payment services. Article 2, Paragraph 2, Point (p) of Decree 11/2010 implementing the Payments Services Directive excludes intra-group activities from the scope of the regulation of payment services. Paragraph 2.2.2, Section II, of the Bank of Italy Regulation of July 5 2011 excludes from the exemption above "the execution of transfers of funds on behalf of companies belonging to the same group from and towards persons or entities external to the group". The Bank of Italy has clarified that intra-group operations are excluded from the scope of the regulation of payment services (ie, they do not require the intervention of a third-party payments services provider), since operating within restricted perimeters mitigates the need for protection of the entity making the payment and the entity in receipt of the payment, both of which have very secure (participative and/or contractual) relationships between each other. For further details, see the discussion of payment services below.

31 Article 1815, second paragraph of the Civil Code.

32 Article 644 of the Criminal Code.

(the 'contractual rate') exceeds the applicable threshold rate set out by law; or

- a special usury crime, in which the agreed contractual rate does not exceed the applicable threshold rate, but the interest is nevertheless disproportionate to the amount lent, and the borrower is in a situation of financial or economic difficulty.

Under the Usury Law,[33] the threshold rates are determined on a quarterly basis by the Ministry of Economy and Finance, in consultation with the Bank of Italy as follows:

- up until May 2011, 150% of the average percentage rate (APR) of charge per annum of the interest applied during the preceding quarter as quoted by banks and other financial intermediaries for each type of homogeneous transaction identified by the ministry; and
- as of May 14 2011, 125% of the relevant APR increased by 400 basis points – provided, however, that the threshold rate does not exceed the underlying APR by more than 800 basis points.[34]

In order to assess whether a contractual rate is usurious:

- according to a first line of interpretation, the contractual rate must be compared to the threshold rate applicable at the time of the stipulation of the underlying loan agreement; and
- according to a second line of interpretation, the contractual rate must be compared to the threshold rate applicable at the time of each payment; in this sense the threshold rate would be a moving target.

Following an interpretative statute enacted by the Italian legislature in 2001, the general position is that the first line of interpretation should be followed. Nevertheless, certain case law has maintained that this interpretative statute is limited in its scope and does not apply to floating rate loans. This means that if the relevant floating interest rate exceeds the applicable threshold rate over time, such excess will not be due to the lender. Under Italian law,[35] the contractual rate includes, in addition to interest, all fees, remuneration, costs and expenses connected with the advance of credit (excluding only taxes). In implementing this provision, regulations issued by the Ministry of the Economy and Finance and the Bank of Italy have instructed banks and financial intermediaries to deduct certain items from the calculation of both the APR and the contractual rates (the Bank of Italy calculation method).

More recently, adhering to a literal interpretation of Article 644 of the Criminal Code, the Second Criminal Division of the Italian Supreme Court[36] expressed a

---

33 Italian Law 108/96 of March 7 1996.

34 The reform of the threshold rates was introduced by Legislative Decree 70/2011, converted into Law 106/2011 of July 12 2011, amending Article 2, Paragraph 4 of Law 108/96.

35 Article 644 of the Criminal Code.

36 Second Criminal Division of the Italian Supreme Court, Decision 12028 of February 19 2010 and Decision 28743 of May 14 2010.

principle according to which contractual rates are determined so as to include all types of fees, remuneration, costs and expenses connected with the advance of credit (excluding only taxes), irrespective of whether these items were to be excluded from the calculation according to the Bank of Italy calculation method. In these judgments, the Supreme Court decided on usury cases involving the assessment of whether a specific type of expense, the overdraft commission fee had to be included in the calculation of the contractual rate. Nevertheless, it cannot be excluded that the Supreme Court has expressed a principle which may apply to any other expenses or costs which could be excluded from the calculation of the contractual rate based on the Bank of Italy calculation method. As a consequence, there may be a risk that, by including such other costs and expenses in the calculation, the relevant contractual rate may be higher than the figure resulting from the original calculation made by the relevant lender, and possibly higher than the applicable threshold rate.[37]

In a physical cash pooling agreement, if an interest rate proves to be usurious, the main consequences for the lending company (ie, the group company, which may be the master account holder, receiving usurious interest) could include the following:

- Automatic discharge of obligation to pay interest – under Article 1815, second paragraph of the Civil Code, if the parties agree to usurious interest, the clause is rendered null and void and no interest is due. According to scholars, loans affected by usury are automatically converted into gratuitous loans. Therefore, such loans will remain valid in accordance with their original terms (including the amortisation plan), with the one crucial difference that no interest is due from the borrower. In addition, lenders that have received usurious interest are obliged to refund interest unduly received from the borrowers. As a result, borrowers could in principle offset the lenders' obligation to reimburse usurious interest against their obligation to repay a corresponding amount of the principal.
- Damages – lenders charging usurious interest may be held liable for damages suffered by the borrower as a consequence of the usury.
- Criminal liability – in the event of a conviction for usury, the offender may be punished with imprisonment of between two and 10 years. In the event of aggravating circumstances, the term of imprisonment may be increased by half.

In order to mitigate the risk arising from the rules on usury, it is advisable to insert a clause in the cash pooling agreement providing that, should the interest rate result prove to be usurious, the interest rate is automatically lowered to the extent necessary in order to comply with applicable laws and regulations.

---

37 This seems to be the case with a decision of the Court of Alba of December 18 2010. By applying the principle stated by the Italian Supreme Court to life insurance policy costs connected to a loan, the Court of Alba recalculated the relevant contractual rate and found that it was higher than the applicable threshold rate. As a consequence, the borrower was discharged from its obligation to pay interest on the loan, as provided for by Article 1815 of the Civil Code.

Group companies: Each company participating in the cash pool (including the master account holder) must keep accurate accounting records and ensure full compliance with all laws and regulations mentioned above. There are no particular concerns with regard to banking laws and regulations, other than those outlined above.

Operating bank: The operating bank (the bank that provides banking services to the master account holder) will be required to comply with all applicable Italian laws and regulations (including those issued by the Bank of Italy, which cover, among other things, anti-money laundering, reporting duties related to cross-border payments, currency laws and supervisory instructions). There is no special section governing cash pooling, so general provisions and principles apply.[38]

Banking licence: In any type of cash pooling, each group company, including the master account holder, must open one or more accounts with the operating bank, into which corporate funds will be deposited and from which they can be managed. Such activity may qualify as fund-raising from the public which, together with the granting of credit, constitutes a banking activity – that is, an activity restricted to banks under Italian laws.[39] Neither the master account holder nor any group company needs to obtain a banking licence. Instead, they need only enter into a banking or payment servicing agreement with a bank or a payment institution.[40] The Bank of Italy keeps a register of the banks authorised in Italy and Italian branches of banks registered elsewhere in the European Union,[41] and grants authorisation to engage in banking where the following conditions are met:

- The corporate form adopted is that of joint stock company (*società per azioni*) or cooperative joint stock company with limited liability (*società cooperativa per azioni a responsabilità limitata*);
- The registered office and head office are located in Italy;
- The paid-up capital is not lower than that established by the Bank of Italy (currently €6.3 million when a bank is incorporated as a joint stock company or as a cooperative bank; €2 million when a bank is incorporated as a cooperative credit bank);[42]
- A programme of operations has been submitted together with the instrument of incorporation and bylaws;
- The owners of significant holdings satisfy certain integrity requirements, and certain additional conditions for a sound and prudent management are met;

38 See discussion below for further details.

39 Article 10 of the Consolidated Banking Act.

40 As a consequence, the master account holder and the group companies are not considered to be banks or payment institutions to the extent that they do not provide any banking or payment services to the public (which are restricted activities under Italian law).

41 Article 13 of the Consolidated Banking Act.

42 Cooperative banks (*banche popolari*) and cooperative credit banks (*banche di credito cooperativo*) are banks that satisfy certain mutual aid requirements and other additional requirements. They are regulated under Article 28 *et seq* of the Consolidated Banking Act. Minimum capital requirements are set out in Supervisory Instructions issued by the Bank of Italy, Title I, Chapter I, Section II.

- The persons performing administrative, managerial or control roles satisfy certain experience, integrity and independence requirements; and
- There are no close links between the bank or the components of the group to which it belongs and other persons preventing the effective employment of supervisory functions.[43]

EU banks may carry out activities subject to mutual recognition in Italy without establishing branches in Italy after the Bank of Italy has been informed by the competent authorities of the home member state non EU banks, on the other hand, may operate in Italy without establishing branches in Italy only upon authorisation by the Bank of Italy which is subject to consultation with the Italian Market Authority (CONSOB) in the case of securities business.

All banks operating in Italy must comply with all oBank of Italys and Ministry of the Economy and Finance circulars and regulations with regard, among other things, to capital adequacy requirements, the assessment process in respect of capital adequacy, disclosure requirements, anti-money laundering obligations and anti-usury measures.

Risk coverage and management/liquidity ratio: Italy has fully implemented the regulatory capital framework published by the Basel Committee on Banking Supervision in 2006 (the Basel II framework).[44] Basel II improves upon Basel I through the 'three pillars' concept:

- minimum capital requirements;
- supervisory review and monitoring obligations; and
- market discipline and disclosure obligations.

Under the first pillar (addressing risk), the risk weight to be applied to the operating bank's exposure under the cash pooling agreement depends on the securities and guarantees that the bank has obtained as collateral in entering into the relevant agreement. Banks adopting one of the ratings-based approaches must rely on the ratings generated by external agencies, while banks adopting the standardised approach must usually treat exposures to the group companies involved in a cash pooling agreement as unsecured. In such case, the standard risk weight is 100%, but it could also be a 150% weighting for borrowers with lower credit ratings. As elsewhere in the European Union, the minimum capital required is equal to at least 8% of risk weighted assets, with Tier 1 capital making up not less than half of this amount (4%). At an operational level, in order to mitigate the underlying risk, banks offering cash pooling agreements may require cross-collateralisation or other guarantees and/or the insertion in the relevant agreements to be entered into with the master account holder and the group companies of close-out netting and set-off clauses. The Basel Committee has approved significant changes to the Basel II

43 Article 14 of the Consolidated Banking Act.

44 The implementing regulation is provided for by the Consolidated Banking Act and the New Regulations for Prudential Supervision of Banks issued by the Bank of Italy in Circular 263 of December 27 2006 (last amended on January 31 2012).

framework. These changes are commonly referred to as Basel III, and include new capital and liquidity requirements intended to strengthen capital standards and to establish minimum liquidity standards for credit institutions. In particular, the changes refer to, among other things, new requirements for the capital base, measures to strengthen the capital requirements for counterparty credit exposures arising out of certain transactions and the introduction of a leverage ratio, as well as short-term and longer-term standards for funding liquidity (referred to as the liquidity coverage ratio and the net stable funding ratio). Member countries will be required to implement the new capital standards from January 2013, the new liquidity coverage ratio from January 2015 and the net stable funding ratio from January 2018. The European authorities have indicated that they support the work of the Basel Committee on the approved changes in general and the European Commission's corresponding proposals to implement such changes (through amendments to the Capital Requirements Directive) were presented on July 20 2011. With regard to the status of Basel III adoption, a draft regulation has been published and is currently under consideration by the Italian Chamber of Deputies.[45] In any event, no particular obligation in terms of risk coverage and management or liquidity ratio is required in respect of cash pooling.

Anti-money laundering: Since 1991[46] banks have been required to adopt certain measures for the prevention of money laundering. Such measures were strengthened in 2007[47] and are based on the following obligations:

- customer due diligence, which is mandatory when the transaction value is higher than €15,000 or where there are two or more transactions which the bank believes are linked and which together would amount to €15,000 or more;
- record-keeping requirements concerning business relationships and occasional transactions;
- adoption of adequate organisational procedures and internal control measures; and
- reporting of suspicious transactions.[48]

---

45 This corresponds to Level 2 in the Basel Committee's assessment of domestic rules in the European Union (ensuring regulatory consistency with Basel III). In particular, this status corresponds to cases where a draft law, regulation or other official document is already publicly available, for example for public consultation or legislative deliberation. The content of the document must be specific enough to be implemented when adopted.

46 Law 197/91 of July 5 1991.

47 Legislative Decrees 231/2007 and 109/2007, implementing EU Directive 2005/60/EC (also known as the Third Money Laundering Directive), supplemented by EU Directive 2006/70/EC. Anti-money laundering provisions are also contained in both international and European law, as well as in domestic primary and secondary sources. A fundamental contribution to legislative harmonisation was provided by the Financial Action Task Force, which is the main international body entrusted with the countering of money laundering and terrorist financing. The Financial Action Task Force has drawn up internationally recognised standards, which are not legally binding but exert moral force, known as the 40 recommendations, subsequently supplemented by the nine special recommendations on countering international terrorist financing. Other international sources consist of conventions drawn up by the main competent international organisations (the United Nations and the Council of Europe). The Egmont Group, entrusted with the development and strengthening of cooperation among financial intelligence units, has defined such units' core functions. International cooperation among financial intelligence units was later formalised at EU level by EU Council Decision 2000/642/JHA.

The Italian anti-money laundering legislation requires banks, financial intermediaries and non-financial businesses and professions to cooperate with the Financial Intelligence Unit. Banks are required retrospectively to verify the identity of customers in the case of transactions, a new relationship or as soon as they come into contact with the customer. The Italian system provides strict and detailed provisions on anti-money laundering and terrorist financing requirements. In general, it is possible to assign these obligations on the basis of risk (the risk-based approach became effective in December 2007). Account establishment processes typically raise 'know-your-customer' and anti-money laundering issues.

In relation to a cash pooling agreement, the operating bank should obtain evidence of identity of each group company, as well as the identity of the person physically present at the transaction, including the company name, registered office, tax code and evidence of the identity of the ultimate beneficial owner of the transaction. For correspondent banking relationships, the operating bank must perform enhanced due diligence and acquire information as provided by the public register. Where possible, it must evaluate the internal control system of the correspondent bank, and can start a business relationship only with the authorisation and under the responsibility of top management.[49]

Cross-border payments: The operating bank also has the burden of monitoring the compliance of each transfer carried out in the context of cross-border cash pooling with EU Regulation 2009/924 on cross-border payments. As from May 1 2012, the regulation applies to all payments made in euros in all EU member states.[50] The basic principle is that the charges for payment transactions offered by a payment service provider (eg, the operating bank) have to be the same whether the payment is domestic or cross-border. This regulation applies to all electronically processed payments, including credit transfers, direct debits, cash withdrawals, payments by debit and credit cards and money remittances (including those made in the context of a cash pooling agreement). Some conditions may apply depending on the type of payment transaction. Payment service providers shall levy identical charges for cross-border payments and electronically processed payment transactions where the payer's payment service provider and the payee's payment service provider are

48 Article 41 of Legislative Decree 231/2007 requires banks, financial intermediaries and non-financial businesses and professions to notify the Financial Intelligence Unit of all transactions deemed to be suspicious. In addition, Article 40 of Legislative Decree 231/2007 requires banks, post offices, financial intermediaries and auditing firms to send data to the Financial Intelligence Unit (so-called aggregate anti-money laundering reports), which can be done by direct access to the financial transactions database (*Archivio Unico Informatico*). The Financial Intelligence Unit carries out analyses aimed at identifying cases of money laundering and terrorist financing with reference to specific territorial areas.

49 Specific provisions prohibit banks and financial institutions from entering into or continuing correspondent banking relationships with shell banks. Moreover, there are specific provisions that prohibit banks and financial institutions from establishing relations with correspondent foreign financial institutions that permit their accounts to be used by shell banks.

50 EU Regulation 260/2012 of establishing technical and business requirements for credit transfers and direct debits in euros has amended, among other provisions, Article 3(1) of EU Regulation 924/2009, removing the words "up to the value of EUR 50,000". The new Article 3(1) provides that: "Charges levied by a payment service provider on a payment service user in respect of cross-border payments shall be the same as the charges levied by that payment service provider on payment service users for corresponding national payments of the same value and in the same currency."

located in different states and domestic payments and electronically processed payment transactions where the two service providers are located in the same state. The operating bank must also give each group company an international bank account number and communicate the relevant bank identifier code. These codes must be indicated by the relevant group company when making cross-border transactions. The group company may incur additional charges if it fails to do this. In this respect, the operating bank must inform the group company of the amount of additional charges before a transaction takes place. If there is an infringement of the provisions by the operating bank, each group company or any interested party may submit claims to the Bank of Italy.

There are also some additional obligations regarding the balance of payments and the international investment position.[51] In particular, every bank and every other financial intermediary must periodically file with the Bank of Italy a communication in respect of any cash transaction carried out on behalf of clients involving an Italian company and a foreign counterparty.[52] Additional communication is required by the Bank of Italy from a number of companies selected randomly among those companies carrying out cross-border transactions. Failure to provide such information is punishable by a fine of between €500 and €10,000.[53]

Payment services: Italy has implemented the EU Payment Services Directive[54] with effect as from March 1 2010.[55] At present, the rendering of payment services in Italy is reserved to banks, e-money institutions and payment institutions.[56] Banking and payment services rendered in connection with a cash pooling agreement are relevant under the Payment Services Directive and its implementing regulation. When providing money remittance, cash transfer, electronic payment facilities and similar services relating to payment accounts, the operating bank must, among other things:

- make sure that the personalised security features of the payment instrument are not accessible to parties other than the payment service user entitled to use the payment instrument (in the case of a cash pooling agreement, usually the group companies);
- refrain from sending an unsolicited payment instrument, except where a payment instrument already given to the payment service user is to be replaced;
- ensure that appropriate means are available at all times to enable the payment

51 See Bank of Italy Regulation of December 16 2009 providing for rules on the collection of statistical information on the balance of payments and the international investment position.

52 Article 6 of Bank of Italy Regulation of December 16 2009.

53 Article 7 of Bank of Italy Regulation of December 16 2009.

54 Directive 2007/64/EC of the European Parliament and of the Council on payment services in the internal market amending Directives 97/7/EC, 2002/65/EC, 2005/60/EC and 2006/48/EC and repealing Directive 97/5/EC.

55 The regulation implementing the Payment Service Directive in Italy is provided for in Legislative Decree 11/2010 of January 27 2010, which also amended Articles 114-*bis* to 114-*sexiesdecies* of the Consolidated Banking Act. Note also the Bank of Italy Regulation of July 5 2011 implementing Title II of Legislative Decree 11/2010.

56 Article 114-*sexies* of the Consolidated Banking Act.

service user to report the loss, theft or misappropriation of the payment instrument or its unauthorised use, reactivation request or issue of a new payment service, where the payment service provider has not provided it; and
- prevent all use of the payment instrument once notification of loss, theft or misappropriation of the payment instrument or its unauthorised use has been made.[57]

With particular regard to cash pooling agreements, the payment services regulation does not apply to payment transactions between group companies (ie, transfers between a parent and its subsidiary or between subsidiaries of the same parent, without any intermediary intervention by a payment service provider),[58] but only to those payment transactions between a group company and a company not belonging to the group. When explicitly questioned about the matter,[59] the Bank of Italy clarified that intra-group operations are excluded from the scope of the payment services regulation. The reason for this exclusion is that operating within a confined perimeter mitigates the protection needs of the ordering and beneficiary entities that have very close (participative and/or contractual) relationships between each other. The protection needs are, however, not mitigated when the ordering and/or the beneficiary entities of a payment are external to the companies' group. This means that payments to external entities should be ordered or received on accounts opened with a payment service provider in compliance with the transparency regulation and the payment services regulation. Hence, in order to make a payment to an external entity, the master account holder is not required to be a licensed payment service provider, but may otherwise avail itself of a licensed payment service provider (eg, the operating bank) to keep and manage the accounts to be operated in the name and on behalf of the group companies. In the latter case, the third-party payment service provider (the operating bank) will be responsible for complying with the transparency and payment services regulations in respect of any money transfer made to parties external to the group under the cash pooling agreement.

Transparency of contractual conditions and correctness of relations with customers: Italian law provides protection to customers of banks and financial intermediaries. This protection is granted by the rules on the transparency of contractual conditions and correct relations with customers,[60] which have the right to know what their entitlements and obligations are when they acquire banking and financial products (current accounts and other types of account, loans and payment instruments). Obviously, many of these banking and financial products are frequently used in the context of cash pooling agreements. The operating bank must, among other things:
- make the group companies aware of the features and costs of the services

57 Article 8 of Legislative Decree 11/2010 of January 27 2010.
58 Article 2, Paragraph 2, Point (p) of Italian Legislative Decree 11/2010 of January 27 2010.
59 See *www.bancaditalia.it/sispaga/sms/strupag/quesiti/faq;internal&action=_setlanguage.action#cap1*.
60 Article 115 *et seq* of the Consolidated Banking Act.

before they enter into the relevant service agreements;[61]
- ensure that the conditions applied correspond with those advertised;[62] and
- send periodic communications on contractual relationships and, in particular, on the actual amounts of lines of credit available.[63]

Any service contract between the operating bank, the master account holder and/or the group companies must be in writing and the group companies must be given a copy. Failure to comply with the prescribed form renders the contract null and void. Contracts must state the rate of interest and any other price and condition to be applied, including, in the case of credit agreements, any increase in charges in respect of arrears. Clauses which refer to usage for the determination of interest rates or any other price or condition to be applied are invalid and deemed not to form part of the contract, as are those which provide for rates, prices or conditions less favourable to the group companies than those made public.[64]

Where a contract is continuing (as is usually the case with cash pooling agreements), the operating bank must provide the group companies with a clear and comprehensive written report on the relationship at the expiry of the contract and at least once a year.[65] In particular, for current accounts, the statement of account must be sent to the group companies annually or, at the group companies' request, half-yearly, quarterly or monthly. In the absence of a written objection by the group companies within 60 days of receipt, statements of account and other periodic notifications to customers are deemed to be approved. Each group company is entitled to receive, at its own expense, within a reasonable time and in any event within 90 days, a copy of the documentation regarding individual transactions made over the last 10 years. In this respect, the operating bank must keep accurate records of any transfer and current account operation for at least 10 years.

The most recent provisions introduced in respect of transparency obligations concern:

- information to be provided to retail customers (including micro-enterprises with less than 10 employees and with an annual turnover of less than €2 million, which may theoretically participate in a cash pooling agreement); and
- organisational measures that guarantee compliance with the rules on the transparency of contractual conditions and correct relations with customers, such as those governing the handling of complaints and the use of transparent documentation for the marketing of banking and financial products.

The Bank of Italy supervises compliance with transparency and correctness

---

61 Article 116 of the Consolidated Banking Act.
62 Article 117, sixth paragraph of the Consolidated Banking Act.
63 Article 119 of the Consolidated Banking Act.
64 Article 117 of the Consolidated Banking Act.
65 The content and form of such report are established by the Credit Committee under Article 119 of the Consolidated Banking Act.

obligations by inspecting banks' and intermediaries' premises and organisation, and checking the effectiveness of internal procedures. During these inspections, provided for by the law on usury, each bank checks its compliance with the threshold rates on loans and other forms of financing.[66] If the Bank of Italy deems there to have been any anomalous or incorrect conduct, it will intervene with measures that will depend on the type and importance of the anomalies and will request intermediaries to:

- adjust their contracts in line with the relevant legal or regulatory provisions, reimburse customers that have had conditions applied that are more onerous than those advertised; or
- in the event of changes having been made with retroactive effects unfavourable to customers and about which they were not informed in the manner prescribed by law, restore the conditions that were agreed on.

(c) *Insolvency law*

The provisions applying to insolvencies of parties of a cash pooling agreement vary according to the status of the entities involved. Insolvency of the operating bank is treated very differently from that of the master account holder or any other group company. Please see the discussion regarding insolvency law at Section 2.3 below with regard to, among other things, the possibility of termination of the agreement in the event of insolvency and the obligation to repay cash received from a member of the cash pooling agreement in the event of its insolvency.

(d) *Tax law*

There is no law or regulation that specifically addresses the taxation of cash pooling agreements. As a result, discussion on the possible tax consequences of such transactions must involve consideration of those aspects with which the Italian tax authorities might take issue.

For tax purposes, the following may be relevant in respect of cash pooling agreements:

- taxation of corporate income (IRES);
- tax treatment of interest income and expenses for both the master account holder and each group company;
- withholding tax on interest paid in connection with a cash pooling agreement;
- tax treatment of interest and fees payable to the master account holder;
- local income tax on productive activities (IRAP); and
- indirect taxes.

Taxation of corporate income: With regard to the effects of the cash pooling agreement in terms of corporate income tax,[67] the consolidated legislation on income taxation[68] provides that in relation to current account contracts and banking transactions settled through current accounts, including reciprocal current accounts for services rendered between businesses and financial institutions, interest is treated

66 These threshold rates are the same rates referred to in the discussion on usury above.

as accrued also where the interest has been offset, whether that has occurred by law or by contract.[69]

Interest income and expenses must be charged for tax purposes by each group company on an accrual basis in the year of their accrual.[70] As a result of this provision, a group company (including the master account holder) must, in its income tax return, introduce an increase where interest income has been offset with interest expense and a decrease where interest expense has been offset with interest income, since those sums (having been offset) will not have been reported in the income statement.[71]

Since January 1 2008, Italian legislation has had less favourable thin capitalisation rules as a result of measures introduced under the 2008 Italian budget law[72] in relation to the deductibility of interest expense and similar charges.[73] Under the revised system,[74] interest expenses and similar charges are deductible in each tax period up to the amount of interest income and similar income. Interest expense over and above that amount is deductible only up to a maximum of 30% of earnings before interest, tax, depreciation and amortisation.[75]

Withholding tax: Whether interest paid in connection with cash pooling agreements is subject to withholding tax must be assessed in relation to both the location of the payer and the payee and the particular type of cash pooling

---

67 It may be appropriate to clarify that the following categories are liable to pay corporate income tax:
- companies, cooperative firms, and mutual insurance companies resident within Italy;
- public and private corporate bodies (other than companies) and trusts that are resident in Italy and whose sole or principal scope is the conduct of commercial operations;
- public and private corporate bodies (other than companies) and trusts that are resident in Italy and whose scope is not the conduct of commercial operations; and
- companies and corporate bodies of any kind, including trusts, whether or not they have distinct legal personality, that are not resident in Italy.

68 Presidential Decree 917/86 of December 22 1986, published in the *Official Gazette*, 302/86 of December 31 1986.

69 Article 89, seventh paragraph of the Consolidated Income Tax Legislation.

70 See M Peverelli and A Francioso, "*Contratti di cash pooling: deducibilità degli interessi passivi e applicazione delle ritenute*", in *Fiscalità e Commercio internazionale*, 2011, page 59.

71 In that regard, S Colombi has pointed out: "the information related to those amounts is provided by the master account holder, which must be in a position contractually to provide each company participating in the procedure with details of interest accrued and offset in each tax period." See S Colombi, *Le holding e il gruppo di imprese*, page 259.

72 Law 244/2007 of December 24 2007, published in the *Official Gazette*, 300/2007 of December 28 2007. The 2008 Italian budget legislation abolished Article 98 of the Consolidated Income Tax Legislation, which had governed thinly capitalised companies, and established that interest would not be deductible where it exceeded the ratio between the shareholders' loan amount and the equity invested by the same shareholder that granted the referred shareholders' loans (and/or its connected parties). Loans arising out of the grant of mortgage loans, contracts for the deposit of money and any other relationship of a financial nature that could constitute a loan would all be subject to tax for these purposes. In that light, the provision in question had been considered to apply to notional cash pooling, which the Revenues Agency treated as a loan agreement guaranteed by the pooler, capable of generating interest expenses for the associate companies.

73 See A Dragonetti, V Piacentini and A Sfondrini, *Manuale di fiscalità internazionale*, page 620, note 272.

74 Article 96 of the Consolidated Income Tax Legislation.

75 The difference between the value and the costs of production, after depreciation and finance lease fees. This provision is considered less favourable since it allows deductions to be made only by those companies with a particularly high gross operating profit, and where groups of companies have decided to make use of cash pooling agreements, the pool companies generally have no gross operating profit, with their income mostly deriving from financial transactions. See M Camerino, "*Cash pooling: aspetti contrattuali e fiscali e nuovi limiti di deduzione degli interessi*", in *Il Fisco*, 2009, pages 3057 *et seq.*

agreement that is being used (ie, whether it operates a zero balance system or as notional cash pooling).

In the event that the group companies are resident in Italy, interest paid to a master account holder also resident in Italy is not subject to withholding tax, under the principle that interest arising from funds granted as loans cannot be considered capital gains because they increase business income, qualifying as an income component.[76]

Nonetheless, cash pooling agreements are often structured by multinational groups in order to locate the master account holder in a country with lower taxation or, in some cases, where there is some form of overall exemption.

Assuming that the company contributing cash to the pool is resident in Italy and the company receiving the interest is resident abroad, interest income will be treated differently depending on the location of the recipient of that income.

If the recipient resides in a country that is not included in a list set out by a decree of the Italian Ministry for Economy and Finance identifying those countries that have entered into a treaty to prevent double tax and tax evasion,[77] a withholding tax of 20% will be applied.[78] Otherwise, Italian law provides for exemption from withholding tax for capital gains other than those arising out of deposits, bank accounts or interest and other proceeds arising out of money loans.[79]

It is therefore important to ensure that the movement of money is not seen as akin to movement regarding loans between the associate companies. In fact, only if the cash pooling agreement operates in a manner akin to that of a non-bank current account may the exemption properly be applied.[80]

If the nature of the contractual arrangements between the parties is instead considered to be a type of loan, then withholding tax will come back into

---

76 Article 48, second paragraph of the Consolidated Income Tax Legislation states that: "The income referred to in the first paragraph [interest, profit, and other income specified therein], when not subject to withholding at source by way of tax or substitutive tax, forms part of the aggregate income, as a component of business income."

77 Ministerial Decree of September 4 1996. The following countries are included in the list: Albania, Algeria, Argentina, Armenia, Australia, Austria, Azerbaijan, Bangladesh, Belgium, Brazil, Bulgaria, Belarus, Canada, China, Croatia, Cyprus, Czech Republic, Denmark, Ecuador, Egypt, Estonia, Finland, France, Georgia, Germany, Greece, Hungary, India, Indonesia, Ireland, Israel, Ivory Coast, Japan, Kazakhstan, Kuwait, Kyrgyzstan, Latvia, Lithuania, Luxembourg, Macedonia, Malta, Mauritius, Mexico, Morocco, New Zealand, Norway, Pakistan, Philippines, Poland, Portugal, Romania, Russia, Singapore, Slovakia, Slovenia, South Africa, South Korea, Spain, Sri Lanka, Sweden, Tajikistan, Tanzania, Thailand, the Netherlands, Trinidad and Tobago, Tunisia, Turkey, Turkmenistan, Ukraine, United Arab Emirates, United Kingdom, United States, Uzbekistan, Venezuela, Vietnam, Yugoslavia and Zambia.

78 Article 26, fifth paragraph of the Presidential Decree 600/73 of September 29 1973, published in the *Official Gazette*, 268/73 of October 16 1973.

79 Article 26-*bis* of Presidential Decree 600/73.

80 The Revenues Agency has identified zero balancing as the only form of centralised treasury management under which income from capital may be considered not taxable under Article 26-*bis* of Presidential Decree 600/73. Under its Ruling 58/E of February 27 2002, the Agency treated a cash pooling agreement that had been structured as a zero balancing system as a non bank current account, since:

- the relationship between the master account holder and the other group companies comprised reciprocal crediting and debiting of sums of money that had their origin in the group companies turning over their account balances to the master account holder on a daily basis;
- interest was calculated daily on the amount of the debit or credit in the client's account on each occasion, and was recorded at the end of each month;
- the remittances by the group companies did not imply an obligation to return those sums;
- there was reciprocity in the remittances; and
- the balance was irrecoverable and unavailable until the current account was closed.

application, at a rate of 20%. That will be the case, for example, with notional cash pooling.

This conclusion arises from the interpretation that the Revenues Agency provided in its Ruling 194/E of October 8 2003, and confirmed in its Circular 19/E of April 21 2009. It was made clear therein that notional cash pooling would be considered to be a loan of money and, as such, subject to withholding tax.

Where that withholding tax has been applied, it may be that interest paid to a company resident in an EU member state could be treated as non-taxable.[81] That exemption may apply only, however, when certain conditions and requirements relating to both the interest and its recipients are met.[82]

If interest is paid by a non-Italian resident company to an Italian-resident recipient, then the rules of the country in which the payer company resides will apply, subject to any applicable double tax treaties. The Italian entity should be able to claim credit for taxes paid abroad, provided that certain conditions are satisfied.[83]

Interest rates and fees payable to the master account holder: Where the cash pooling agreement involves group companies (including the master account holder) resident both in Italy and elsewhere, the rules on transfer pricing should be taken into account in determining the amount of fees.[84]

The transfer pricing legislation provides that components of income arising out of transactions with companies not resident in Italy that the Italian company controls, by which the Italian company is directly or indirectly controlled, or that are subject to control by the same company are measured on the basis of the normal value[85] of the assets transferred, the services supplied or the goods or services received, if an increase in income derives therefrom.[86]

Accordingly, in a cash pooling agreement, the interest rate and the fees agreed between the parties must satisfy this normal value test; if they do not, the appropriate changes will have to be made when preparing the tax return, in accordance with the tax legislation in force.[87]

It follows that the fees must be set at an appropriate amount – one that is proportional to the actual advantage from which each group company benefits, and the rate at which interest expenses accrue must be determined on an arm's-length

81 Article 26-*quater* of Presidential Decree 600/73.

82 For an explanatory (but not extensive) discussion on those conditions and requirements, please see the section 2.5.

83 Article 165 of the Consolidated Income Tax Legislation.

84 Article 110, seventh paragraph of the Consolidated Income Tax Legislation.

85 'Normal value' means, under Article 9, third paragraph of the Consolidated Income Tax Legislation:

The price or consideration applied on average for goods and services of the same or similar kind, upon arm's length terms and at the same stage of commercialisation, at the time and in the place in which the goods or services were acquired or provided, and, otherwise at the time and in the place nearest thereto. In determining normal value, reference shall be made where possible to the price lists and tariffs of the person that provided the goods or services, or otherwise, to the market reports or price lists of chambers of commerce and professional tariffs, bearing in mind such discounts as are usual. For goods and services whose prices are regulated, reference shall be made to the regulations currently in force.

86 If the master account holder is located in a country not on the list of countries with which Italy has a double tax treaty, the fees paid to it by the group companies will be subject to the limits on the deductibility of costs under the rules on controlled foreign companies.

87 See F Bencivegna and L Galeotti Flori, "*Il contratto di cash pooling*", in *Il Foro Toscano*, 2007, page 261.

basis, (ie, in light of what would have been agreed for a similar arrangement made between independent companies).[88]

Local income tax on productive activities: With respect to the effects of local income tax on productive activities (IRAP),[89] interest income and expense from a cash pooling transaction are not included within the taxable base for IRAP,[90] since these are amounts that would be reported in the income statement under "Financial income and expense".[91]

Indirect taxes: In terms of the value added tax (VAT) effects of a cash pooling agreement, a distinction must be drawn between those circumstances in which the master account holder and the group companies are both resident in Italy and those in which one of the two is not.

In the first case, transactions implemented in connection with cash pooling would be subject to VAT, but may qualify as exempt transactions.[92]

If the master account holder or the group company is a non-resident entity, then under the territoriality rules,[93] the supplies in question are deemed to be made in Italy where they are made to persons established in the country. If, on the other hand, the person supplied is not established in Italy, then for VAT purposes, the territoriality test fails.[94]

If the master account holder is resident in Italy and provides its services to a non-Italian group company, then the remuneration due to the master account holder from each group company for the services supplied will be outside the scope of VAT.[95] In such a situation, what is subject to VAT is the interest accrued upon the deposits the group companies make with the master account holder. Given that the group companies are non-Italian resident entities which, in this case, are supplying services, the master account holder is obliged to account for the transaction under a reverse-charge procedure.[96]

Alternatively, where the services are supplied to Italian-resident group companies by a non-Italian resident master account holder, the remuneration the latter receives in return for those services will be subject to VAT. Since the master account holder is supplying the service and is a non-Italian resident entity, the group companies account for the transaction under a reverse-charge procedure and the interest

---

88 *Ibid*, page 261.

89 *Imposta regionale sulle attività produttive*, hence the acronym.

90 Article 5 of Legislative Decree 446/97.

91 See S Colombi, *Le holding e il gruppo di imprese*, page 262.

92 Article 10(1) of Presidential Decree 633/72 of October 26 1972, published in the *Official Gazette*, 292/72 of November 11 1972. This provision expressly covers current account transactions, and also governs all financial transactions based upon lending practice.

93 Article 7-*ter*, of Presidential Decree 633/72.

94 G Paudice, "Le implicazioni iva delle operazioni finanziarie nell'ambito del «cash pool»", in *L'IVA*, 2010, page 17 *et seq*.

95 *Ibid*, page 19. The author points out how in any event the master account holder should issue an invoice without VAT, under Article 7-*ter* of Italian Presidential Decree 633/72, where the associate is resident in another EU member state (see Article 21, second paragraph, part (f-*bis*) of Presidential Decree 633/72).

96 Pursuant to and for the purposes of Article 17 of Presidential Decree 633/72.

accrued on the deposits made by the group companies into the master account will be outside the scope of VAT.[97]

Finally, with reference to registration tax, this will be payable in a fixed amount equal to €168 upon the cash pooling agreement's presentation for registration, should the need arise.[98]

2. Specific questions

2.1 Perspective A: corporate group

Italian corporate law includes no specific provisions with respect to cash pooling agreements. However, the decision to enter into a cash pooling agreement should be made taking account of the general principles of Italian corporate law, such as the directors' general fiduciary duty of care and loyalty to the company and its shareholders, the autonomy of a company and its corporate purpose (regardless of its nature as a subsidiary) and the duty of vigilance of the members of the supervisory board.[99] In the following paragraphs, we focus on some of those areas of Italian corporate law which are mostly relevant in a cash pooling agreement.

In particular, we discuss:

- the relationship between a subsidiary and its controlling entity;
- the risks of undercapitalisation of a company entering into a cash pooling agreement;
- the risk that a cash pooling agreement may be treated as a form of financial assistance from the controlling entity;
- the risks associated with directors' conflicts of interest; and
- special procedural and disclosure provisions applicable to listed companies.

(a) Relationship between a subsidiary and its controlling entity

A set of provisions of Italian law regulates certain specific issues regarding the relationship between a company and the entity that exercises direction and coordination powers over it. Arguably, this set of provisions constitutes the core of Italian corporate law on corporate groups.

Although the notion of exercise of direction and coordination powers is not

---

97 The considerations set out in note 27 equally apply here.

98 Under Italian law, a deed or an agreement may be subject to registration tax (which varies from a fixed amount of €168 to a rate of up to 3% of the value of the deed/agreement, depending on the nature of the deed/agreement), in the event of *caso d'uso* or *enunciazione*. '*Caso d'uso*' means the filing of a deed/agreement with an Italian court in the course of any administrative or judicial proceedings (unless the filing is compulsory as a matter of law or regulation). '*Enunciazione*' means the situation in which a deed/agreement, which was not filed, is referred to (eg, by way of a cross-reference) by another deed/agreement which was entered into by the same parties and was filed with the Italian tax office. If a deed/agreement falls within the scope of VAT (even if exempt or zero rated), registration tax applies at the referred fixed amount (see Article 40 of Presidential Decree 131/86 of April 26 1986, published in the *Official Gazette*, 99/86 of April 30 1986). A cash pooling agreement is considered to fall within the scope of VAT; therefore – should one of the events outlined above occur – a fixed rate registration tax applies (€168).

99 For the sake of simplicity, we refer in this contribution to the most common corporate governance structure among Italian limited liability companies (srl) and joint stock companies (SpA), which is based on a board of directors (or a sole director) and a supervisory board (the board of statutory auditors), both appointed by the shareholders. Other governance structures are feasible under Italian law.

clear-cut, Italian law provides certain presumptions whereby a company is considered subject to the direction and coordination powers of another entity. In particular, a company is presumed – unless the presumption is proved to be false, to exercise direction and coordination powers over another entity – where the controlling entity:

- is required by law to consolidate the financial statements of the subsidiary; and/or
- controls the subsidiary.[100]

Liability regime: Italian law sets out a specific liability regime applicable to a controlling entity, the so-called abuse of direction and coordination powers. In particular, a controlling entity that, in exercising its direction and coordination powers, acts in its own interests or in the interests of other third parties in violation of principles of good management may be held directly liable to:

- the subsidiary's shareholders, for any loss of profits or loss of value of the subsidiary's shares; and
- the subsidiary's creditors, for any adverse effects on the solvency of the subsidiary.

Liability for an abuse of direction and coordination powers may also extend to any person that either:

- participated in the abuse, in which case the liability is several and joint with the controlling entity; or
- was aware of the abuse and benefited therefrom, in which case the liability is limited to the aggregate amount of the benefit gained.[101]

Liability for an abuse of direction and coordination powers is excluded if:

- the ensuing damage is fully eliminated through subsequent transactions; or
- the damage is effectively offset by the global benefits derived by the relevant subsidiary from the continuing exercise of the direction and coordination powers by the controlling entity (so-called compensating benefits).

Therefore, the board of directors of the relevant subsidiary, as well as the

---

100 Under Article 2359 of the Civil Code, one company (A) is controlled by another company (B), either directly or indirectly, where:
- B is entitled to exercise the majority of the voting rights in the ordinary shareholders' meetings of A;
- B is entitled to exercise a number of voting rights that entitles it to have a dominant influence on the ordinary shareholders' meetings of A; or
- A is subject to the dominant influence of B because of particular contractual undertakings.

101 In the event of an abuse of direction and coordination powers, any enforcement action has to be filed first against the subsidiary. If the enforcement action against the subsidiary does not result in compensation being obtained, only then can enforcement action be taken against the controlling entity (see Article 2497, third paragraph of the Civil Code). According to several legal scholars, this provision is contradictory, since an enforcement action against the subsidiary may potentially negatively affect the profitability and value of the subsidiary's shares, contrary to the interests of the subsidiary's shareholders. See, among others, G Scognamiglio, "*Danno Sociale e azione individuale nella disciplina della responsabilità da direzione e coordinamento*", in *Il Nuovo Diritto delle Società*, III, Torino, 2007, page 947 *et seq.*

management that was actively involved in the transaction, may be held liable for an abuse of direction and coordination powers if a decision to enter into a cash pooling agreement was taken contrary to the subsidiary's interests or in violation of the principles of good management, unless the damage is offset through subsequent transactions or by the global benefits experienced by the subsidiary from its participation in the group.

A subsidiary may not be admitted to listings if it is party to an intra-group cash pool which is not consistent with the company's corporate interests.[102]

Requirement for a resolution to enter into a cash pooling agreement: Any decision by the board of directors of a subsidiary taken upon the instructions[103] of the controlling entity must explain analytically the rationale for, and indicate the reasons and interests behind, the decision being taken.[104]

Frequently, the board of directors of a company resolves to enter into a cash pooling agreement as a result of the group's strategy and, thus, under the influence of the controlling entity. The subsidiary's board should therefore carefully assess the advantages and disadvantages of a decision to enter into a cash pooling agreement. The advantages may consist of a good return on the sums transferred to the master account holder, compared to the interest rates attainable on bank deposits, better access to credit facilities, centralisation of treasury activities and consequent cost savings.

The subsidiary's board of directors should carefully consider the solidity and liquidity of the master account holder and the group. In fact, if an event of default on the part of the master account holder and/or one or more of the participating companies occurs, the sums transferred by a subsidiary to the holder of a master account under the cash pooling agreement may be subject to claw-back.

The cost/benefit analysis of the board of directors is an ongoing process. In fact, the subsidiary's board of directors is responsible for ascertaining that the cash pooling agreement is in the best interest of the company for the entire duration of the agreement.

A subsidiary considering joining a cash pooling agreement should carefully negotiate the terms of the agreement in light of the fiduciary duties of the directors and the doctrine on the abuse of direction and coordination powers. In particular, the terms of the cash pooling agreement should ideally provide that the subsidiary's board of directors will receive regular update reports on the economic and financial

---

102 Article 37, Section 1, Point (c) of the CONSOB Regulation 16191/2007 of October 29 2007, as amended and restated, provides for:

the shares of subsidiaries subject to management and coordination by another company or entity may not be admitted to trading on an Italian regulated market if the subsidiaries:

...

(c) have a centralised treasury, with the company exercising sole control or another company of the group, that is not consistent with the interests of the company. The consistency with the interests of the company should be confirmed by the board of directors in an analytically motivated written statement, subject to the supervision of the board of statutory auditors.

103 Literally, under the influence of the controlling entity (Article 2497-*ter* of the Civil Code).

104 Under Article 2362 of the Civil Code, any agreement entered into by a company with its 100% controlling entity that could prejudice the company's creditors is not enforceable unless it is documented in the book of resolutions of the managing body of the company, or it bears a certified date.

situation of the master account holder, the controlling entity and the other group companies participating in the cash pooling agreement. In addition to receiving regular reports, the board of directors should be immediately made aware of any default or breach of financial covenants by a contracting company under any group facility agreement, cash shortages and insolvency events of any company participating in the cash pooling agreement.

The board of directors should also ideally reserve the right to drop out of the cash pooling agreement at any time and for any reason, especially if one of the companies participating to the cash pooling agreement defaults on its obligations.

As a safeguard against possible shortages of cash and defaults, the cash pooling agreement may provide that the master account holder has easy access to external financing resources, such as revolving credit facilities, or that sufficient cash reserves exist for an amount equal to the cash transferred by the participating companies.

(b) *Risks of undercapitalisation*

Through a cash pooling agreement, a company may have access to external financial resources at a convenient price, possibly limiting the need for shareholders' contributions and allowing shareholders to keep a company undercapitalised. In broad terms, there is an undercapitalisation whenever a company's corporate capital is excessively low compared to its business activity.

The risks of an undercapitalisation of the companies participating in a cash pool are partially mitigated by the Italian regulations on financing arrangements between a controlled entity and its subsidiaries, and between subsidiaries of the same group.[105] In fact, according to legal scholars, a cash pool structure may be interpreted as an intra-group financing arrangement whereby cash transfers from the master account holder to an undercapitalised subsidiary may qualify as a form of financing. Under Italian law, the repayment of financing granted to an undercapitalised company by a controlling entity or any other subsidiary of the same group is subordinated to the satisfaction in full of the other creditors of the company in the event of liquidation of the company.[106] Moreover, repayment of intra-group financing to an undercapitalised subsidiary is subject to a form of claw-back, in the event that the company is made bankrupt within the same year.

(c) *Financial assistance*

Under Italian law, a joint stock corporation may grant, either directly or indirectly, funds, loans or security to a third party for the subscription or purchase of its shares (so-called financial assistance) only through a special procedure and within certain limitations.[107] On the other hand, a limited liability company (*società a responsabilità limitata*) may not grant any form of financial assistance for the subscription or purchase of its corporate capital.[108]

There is a possibility that upstream transfers by a subsidiary to the controlling

---

105 See L Ruggeri, *"Brevi Note circa il Cash Pooling"*, in *Nuova Giurisprudenza Civile Commentata*, 2011, I, page 206 *et seq.*

106 See Article 2497-*quinquies* and Article 2467 of the Civil Code. The criteria referred to by the Italian legislature are quite generic and open to different interpretations.

entity under a cash pooling agreement could qualify as a form of financial assistance.

For instance, if a company which has recently been acquired by a controlling entity enters into a cash pooling agreement, upstream cash transfers from the subsidiary to the controlling entity under the cash pooling agreement may be viewed as a form of financing by the subsidiary for the acquisition of its shares by the controlling entity. This risk, however, should not raise particular concerns where a cash pooling agreement is based on a solid business logic, since upstream cash transfers would not be linked to the acquisition (or subscription) of the subsidiary's shares by the controlling entity.

(d) Directors' private interests

The board of directors of a company proposing to enter into a cash pooling agreement should carefully consider the implications of Italian law on conflicts of interest and private interests of directors.

In particular, where a director has a personal interest (or an interest on behalf of a third party) in a transaction:[109]

- the interested director must disclose his interest in the transaction to the board of directors and the supervisory board, and the resolution of the board of directors must show adequate reasoning;
- if the interested director has delegated powers and authority (eg, if he is the chief executive) he may not proceed with the transaction and must refer the decision to the board of directors; and
- if the interested director is a sole director (and there is no board of directors), he may proceed with the transaction, giving prior notice of his interest in the transaction to the supervisory board. He will also have to make appropriate disclosure of his interest to the shareholders in the first meeting of shareholders following the transaction.[110]

A resolution of the board of directors which has been taken either in violation of Italian law on private interests of directors or through a decisive vote by an interested director (ie, where the resolution would not have been passed without the favourable vote of an interested director) may be challenged by a director or a member of the supervisory board in the event that it is potentially harmful for the company.[111]

Intra-group transactions, such as a transaction between a controlling entity and

---

107 In general, a joint stock corporation may grant financial assistance upon authorisation by a special meeting of shareholders, convened by the board of directors. The board of directors must prepare a report describing the transaction and explaining, among other things, the business rationale, why the result is in the company's interests, the risks to the liquidity and solvency of the company and the consideration being received. The aggregate amount of the funds or security granted by the company should not exceed its disposable reserves and distributable profits as shown in the last annual financial statement. See Article 2358 of the Civil Code for more details and exceptions.

108 Article 2474 of the Civil Code.

109 Article 2391 of the Civil Code.

110 M Venturuzzo, "Comment to Article 2391 of the Italian Civil Code", in *Amministratori (artt 2380-2396 cc)*, edited by F Ghezzi, Volume 4 of *Commentario alla riforma delle società*, supervisory editors P Marchetti, LA Bianchi, F Ghezzi and M Notari, Milano, 2005, page 474 *et seq.*

111 A director who voted in favour of the transaction may not challenge the resolution, provided that the interested director had duly disclosed its private interest in the transaction.

its subsidiary, may give rise to a conflict of interest, especially in the event of an interlocking directorate, where a director of a subsidiary also serves as director of the controlling entity.[112] Such a director would be in a position where he has a conflict of interest (or would, in any event, have a private interest) with respect to a resolution to enter into a cash pooling agreement, since he serves as director in both the subsidiary and the controlling entity. In this situation, both the rules on conflicts of interest and the rules on the relationship between a subsidiary and its controlling entity would apply (although these rules have areas in which they overlap). Therefore, in such a situation a director with a conflict of interest should:

- disclose to the board of directors and supervisory board his interest in the transaction (ie, the fact that he is also a director of the controlling entity);
- in the event that he has delegated powers (eg, as chief executive), refer the decision on the cash pooling agreement to the board of directors; and
- at the relevant board meeting, abstain from voting or make sure his vote is not decisive.

The relevant resolution of the board of directors should set out in a clear and coherent way the motivations for and benefits to the company entering into a cash pooling agreement, also taking into consideration any compensating benefits arising from the subsidiary's participation in the group.[113]

(e) Listed companies

The Civil Code[114] requires every listed company to adopt an internal regulation on transacttions with related parties aimed at ensuring the transparency and procedural and substantial fairness of such transactions. The Italian Market Authority (CONSOB) has issued a set of principles that listed companies[115] must comply with in their internal regulations and procedural requirements for any resolution to enter into a transaction with a related party.[116]

The decision of a listed company to enter into a cash pooling agreement would qualify as a transaction[117] with a related party[118] and should, therefore, also comply with the company's internal regulations on such transactions.

---

112 Some scholars argue that the rules on directors' private interests are in fact superseded by the rules on transactions between a controlling company and its subsidiaries (as described above). See Pennisi, "*La Disciplina delle Società soggette a direzione unitaria ed il recesso nei gruppi*", in VVAA, *Il Nuovo Diritto delle Società*, III, Torino, 2007, page 889 *et seq.*

113 See M Ventoruzzo, "Comment to Article 2391 of the Italian Civil Code", in *Amministratori (artt 2380-2396 cc)*, Volume 4 of *Commentario alla riforma delle società*, page 472 *et seq.*

114 Article 2391-*bis* of the Civil Code.

115 The rules on transactions with related parties also applies to non-listed companies with dispersed ownership (*società con azioni diffuse tra il publico in misura rilevante*). See Article 2 of CONSOB Regulation 17221 of March 12 2010 (the Related Party Transaction Regulation) and Article 2-*bis* of CONSOB Regulation 11971 of May 14 1999.

116 The regime is based on a flexible approach, with the scale of the procedural and disclosure obligations required varying according to the magnitude of the transaction (which is assessed on the basis of a number of different factors), with a simplified regime for newly listed companies, smaller listed companies (and non-listed companies with a dispersed shareholding).

2.2 Perspective B: bank

(a) Regulatory capital and security structure

As already mentioned above,[119] although there are no specific regulatory provisions governing cash pooling under Italian law, any bank in Italy (including any bank offering cash pooling agreements) must comply with stringent regulation, including provisions and duties regarding banking licence requirements, supervisory and prudential rules, anti-money laundering, usury, cross-border payments, payment services and the transparency of contractual conditions and of correct relations with customers.

With regard to regulatory capital requirements, general provisions also apply.[120] Therefore, cash pooling is relevant for prudential regulation to the extent that an operating bank will have exposures to the master account holder and/or the group companies under one or more agreements entered into in the context of a cash pooling transaction.[121] Of course, this issue becomes more important the greater the operating bank's exposure to the group companies is. From an operational viewpoint, the main difference for the operating bank in weighting the risks underlying a cash pooling agreement (when compared to weighting the risks underlying any other financing) is that in a cash pooling agreement there are as many counterparties as there are companies participating in the cash pooling agreement. This means that the operating bank must weight its exposure arising out of the cash pooling agreement taking into account the credit rating (or worthiness) of each group company participating in the cash pooling agreement.

---

117 Under Annex 1 to the Related Party Transaction Regulation, a transaction with a related party shall be understood as any transfer of resources, services or obligations between related parties, regardless of whether transferred for valuable consideration and shall include:
- merger transactions, spin-offs by incorporation or strictly non-proportional spin-offs, if carried out with related parties; and
- any decision on the allocation of wages and economic benefits, in whatever form, for members of the administrative and control bodies and management personnel with strategic responsibilities.

118 CONSOB's definition of 'related parties' substantially mirrors the definition of related parties under IAS 24 of the International Accounting Standards Board. In particular, under Annex 1 to the Related Party Transaction Regulation, an entity is a related party to a company if it:
- directly or indirectly, through subsidiaries, trustees or an intermediary:
  - controls the company, is controlled by or is under common control;
  - holds a stake in the company to exert significant influence over the entity;
  - exercises control over the company jointly with others;
- is an associate of the company;
- is a joint venture in which the company is a participant;
- is one of the key management personnel of the company or its parent;
- is a close relative of a person referred to in the first and fourth points above;
- is an entity in which a person referred to in pthe fourth or fifth points above exercises control, joint control or significant influence, or owns, directly or indirectly, a significant portion, but not less than 20% of the voting rights; or
- a supplementary pension fund, collective or individual, Italian or foreign, established for the employees of the company, or any other entity associated with it.

119 See the discussion under "Operating bank" in section 1.3(a) above.

120 Italy has transposed EU Directive 2006/48 relating to the implementation and pursuit of the business of credit institutions and EU Directive 2006/49 on the capital adequacy of investment firms and credit institutions and, therefore, the national provisions have been harmonised to the EU legal framework.

121 In fact, the operating bank usually acts in both capacities as banking services provider and as lender to the master account holder and/or one or more group companies, and the relevant loan amounts stand to the credit of the accounts under the cash pooling agreement. Therefore, the discussion relating to the weighting of the risk should be applied to the overall exposure of the operating bank to the master account holder and the group companies.

With respect to the credit risk capital calculations, there are three aspects to consider:[122]

- the assessment of counterparty risk (in the case of cash pooling this must be undertaken in respect of all group companies participating in the cash pooling agreement);
- the assessment of credit conversion factors for non-utilised commitments on overdraft facilities; and
- the assessment of risk mitigation (ie, the effect of reducing the effective exposure to a borrower through the use of collateral or other risk mitigation techniques). The main method of mitigating risk used in cash pooling transactions is the practice of on-balance-sheet netting, used in addition to the more traditional pledge of cash collateral, which is acceptable under Basel II.

Most, if not all, cash pooling schemes currently offered require a pledge of deposits or cash collateral in order to mitigate the risk for the purposes of regulatory capital calculations. In addition, banks are required to ensure that their documentation is binding on all parties and legally enforceable in all relevant jurisdictions. Pledges used in current cash pooling agreements will generally meet these requirements. No mandatory security structure is required in any case.

(b) Liability of the bank in connection with cash pooling agreements

Bank liability is a theoretical possibility and would follow general principles regarding being an accessory to wrongdoing if such were alleged against the group companies and their directors. Banks owe no fiduciary or legal duties to the creditors of their clients, and, therefore, are not liable for losses suffered by such creditors resulting from the actions of the group companies. In general, the operation of a cash pool according to the terms of agreements previously approved by shareholder vote and subject to publicity would in practice give rise to no possibility of liability on the part of the bank, save in the most exceptional of circumstances.

2.3 Insolvency

This section discusses the going into liquidation of:

- the operating bank;
- the master account holder; and
- a group company (the complications of simultaneous liquidations are not considered).

Any reference in this section to insolvency proceedings in Italy of anyone of an operating bank, a master account holder or a group company will assume the involvement of Italian insolvency officials.

A preliminary distinction must be made between a notional cash pooling agreement and a zero balancing cash pooling agreement. The two types of agreement

---

122 M Mars, "The impact of Basel II on the pricing of cash pooling", at *www.gtnewsstage.afponline.org*, 2005.

are treated differently under Italian insolvency law, since only the zero balancing cash pooling agreement involves actual transfers of funds from one entity to another within a group. A notional cash pooling agreement, in fact, as already noted in the introduction to this chapter, does not trigger any transfer of funds and works only as a set-off mechanism aimed at reducing the interest to be paid by each company of the group.

Bearing this in mind, we now analyse the consequences on cash pooling agreements in the event of the insolvency of the operating bank, the master account holder or any group company.

(a) *Operating bank's insolvency*

The insolvency of Italian banks is regulated by the Consolidated Banking Act, which provides for a special procedure[123] outside the ordinary bankruptcy procedures provided in the Bankruptcy Act (Royal Decree 267/42 of March 16 1942). Article 83 of the Consolidated Banking Act, however, provides for the application of certain articles of the Bankruptcy Act, including Article 78, which governs the effects of insolvency proceedings on pending contractual relationships.

Article 78 of the Bankruptcy Act states that bank account agreements are automatically terminated upon the insolvency of one of the parties, including banks.

Also, the bank's insolvency administrator has the duty to protect the interests of all creditors of the insolvency estate and, therefore, all payments owed by the bank are stayed.[124]

Bearing this in mind, should the operating bank be made insolvent, the following cases can be distinguished:

- Any credit balance in the cash pooling accounts represents a debt owed by the operating bank to the master account holder (in respect of the master account's credit balance) and the group companies (in respect of their credit balances). In such case the consequences of the operating bank's insolvency is that any bank account to which the cash pooling agreement is linked is frozen and the underlying agreement terminated. The master account holder and/or the group companies will have to file their proofs of claim with the bank's insolvency estate and will receive the relevant payment, in whole or in part, along with any other creditor of the operating bank after the completion and verification of the final list of creditors.
- If the cash pooling accounts are in debit, they represent a debt owed by the master account holder or the group companies to the operating bank, the bank accounts to which the cash pooling agreement is linked is frozen and the underlying agreement terminated, and the master account holder and/or the group companies must pay the amount due to the operating bank.

If the master account holder and the group companies have both credit and debit

123 The Consolidated Banking Act also provides for a pre-insolvency procedure, the *amministrazione straordinaria*, which, however, is not a liquidation process and is therefore not discussed here.

124 Article 83 of the Consolidated Banking Act.

balances, the credits and debits are offset against each other and only the net amount will be due (either way).[125]

It may also be the case that the master account holder and/or a group company have more than one account which may be either in credit or in debit (which would more likely occur in a notional cash pooling agreement rather than a zero balance cash pooling agreement). In this situation, Italian law provides that payables and receivables between two parties can always be offset to the extent that they are due and relate to cash to be paid. Therefore, notwithstanding the existence of more than one account, as long as the parties are the same (ie, the group company and the operating bank, or the master account holder and the operating bank), the relevant credit and debit position can always be offset to the extent permitted by law.[126]

Foreign banks are likely to be subject to insolvency procedures in their own jurisdiction and the relevant insolvency official may then apply to local courts for recognition in other jurisdictions (eg, Italy) of the process.

If the operating bank is subject to foreign insolvency proceedings, the process of determining the status of claims in respect of credit balances is normally governed by the law of the jurisdiction in which the insolvency procedure has been opened.

In this regard, an insolvency process opened in an EU member state is automatically recognised in Italy without the need for a court order or any other procedure. The insolvency process is governed by the laws of the member state in which the insolvency procedure has been opened.[127]

As to foreign jurisdictions outside the European Union, it should be verified on a case-by-case basis whether specific bilateral or multilateral treaties are in place concerning the reciprocal recognition of insolvency proceedings.

Bank's insolvency administrator's obligations to the master account holder and group companies: In the case of a bank's insolvency in Italy, the insolvency official is appointed by the Bank of Italy, along with a supervisory committee. The Italian insolvency official is a public official whose main duty is to manage the liquidation of the bank, protecting the interests of all of its creditors, under the supervision of the Bank of Italy.

The insolvency official, among other things:

- prepares the inventory of the bank's assets;
- draws up a list of creditors according to their respective priorities;
- assumes the obligations of or terminates any ongoing contracts;
- initiates any necessary lawsuits (eg, claw-back actions or damages actions

125 See Article 56 of the Bankruptcy Act.

126 Please note that generally offset among more than two parties is not allowed in Italy, although certain exceptions apply. In particular, a guarantor (including a third-party pledgor or mortgagor) may offset against its debts to the the creditor any amount due from the same creditor to the guaranteed debtor. See Article 1247 of the Civil Code.

127 See Article 95-*bis* of the Consolidated Banking Act implementing EU Directive 2001/24 of the European Parliament and of the Council dated April 4 2001 on the reorganisation and winding up of credit institutions, which came into force on May 5 2001 (and Article 95-*ter* which provides for exceptions to the general provision set out in Article 95-*bis*). For the avoidance of doubt, please note that the EU Insolvency Regulation (1346/2000) does not apply, as it excludes the insolvency of credit institutions from its scope.

against former directors and auditors);

- informs public prosecutors of any potential criminal liability related to the bankruptcy; and,
- drafts the liquidation plan, liquidates the assets and repays creditors in accordance with their respective priorities.

The duties of the insolvency official are not affected by the location of creditors or of their seat. If the master account holder and the group companies are creditors, they should receive a formal notice and other communications from the insolvency official just as any other creditor would (whether or not they are in Italy). If the master account holder and the group company are debtors, they may be pursued by the insolvency official (who, in foreign territories, may require local court assistance in recognising his authority).

Italian banks – and Italian branches of foreign banks, unless these have similar provisions in their home jurisdictions – must be covered by to a specific fund aimed at guaranteeing depositors within certain limits.[128] The maximum amount guaranteed to each depositor is €100,000.[129]

(b) *Master account holder's insolvency*

If the master account holder goes into insolvency under ordinary bankruptcy proceedings provided for in the Bankruptcy Act, the consequences mainly depend on the type of cash pooling agreement in place. With notional cash pooling, in the absence of any actual transfer of funds, any credit balance in favour of the master account holder would remain with the master account holder's insolvency estate, while the underlying agreement, although difficult to classify under Italian law, would very likely be automatically terminated under Article 78 of the Bankruptcy Act and the account frozen.

On the other hand, zero balancing cash pooling certainly creates more complexities in the event of the master account holder's insolvency. As mentioned, zero balancing cash pooling is characterised by actual transfers of funds between the master account holder and its subsidiaries. In the event that there is a credit balance in favour of the master account holder, those funds will remain with the assets of the insolvency estate. Also, given that upon a declaration of insolvency the account is frozen and no longer operating, any possible transfer due from the master account holder to a group company would be stayed, and the group company would be requested to file its proof of claims. If any amount is still owed to the group company after application of possible set-off mechanisms under Article 56 of the Bankruptcy Act, it would participate together with all other creditors in the distribution of funds that would eventually be made by the insolvency official.

A cash pooling agreement may also be used for fraudulent purposes, such as embezzling funds from the insolvent company before it is made subject to

128 See Article 96-*bis* of the Consolidated Banking Act.

129 The €100,000 insurance amount is available for each depositor with an institution as from May 7 2011, under Legislative Decree 49/2011 of March 24 2011 implementing EU Directive 2009/14/EC.

bankruptcy proceedings. In this scenario, although it is extremely unlikely where the insolvent company is the master account holder, the insolvency official would likely respond to all such transfers with claw-back actions.

If the master account holder's insolvency official is a foreign person, administering a foreign insolvency process opened in an EU member state, the EU Insolvency Regulation (1346/2000) would apply. Therefore, if the foreign process to which the master account holder is subject is the main process for the purposes of that regulation, the Italian courts should apply the law of the foreign jurisdiction where the insolvency has been opened. In certain cases, if necessary, the master account holder's insolvency official may need to start a secondary Italian insolvency process.[130] If the foreign country in which insolvency proceedings have been opened is not in the European Union, it will be necessary to assess on a case-by-case basis whether specific bilateral or multilateral treaties relating to the reciprocal recognition of insolvency processes are in place.[131]

Insolvency official's obligations to the operating bank and group companies: In the event of the master account holder's insolvency in Italy, the insolvency official is appointed by the competent court. The Italian insolvency official is a public official whose main duty is to manage the liquidation of the master account holder, protecting the interests of all creditors, under the supervision of the competent court and the designated judge appointed by that court.

The powers and duties of the insolvency official in the event of insolvency of the master account holder are the same as those outlined at section 2.3(a) above in connection with the insolvency of the operating bank.

The master account holder could be a debtor or a creditor of the operating bank and/or a group company, depending on the circumstances. Set-off mechanisms apply under Article 56 of the Bankruptcy Act; therefore, the operating bank and the group companies may be entitled to set off their reciprocal debit positions under the cash pooling agreement. The operating bank may also enforce guarantees if any were given by the group companies. Following all of the offset procedures, if the operating bank and/or a group company still has claims against the master account holder, they will participate along with the other creditors, according to the specific ranking of their claims in the distribution of funds made by the insolvency official.

If the operating bank and/or a group company's claims are secured by the master account holder and the relevant security is not challenged by the insolvency official, the operating bank and/or the group company will rank as secured creditors and will have a first claim over any funds before the unsecured creditors.

Often, in financing agreements between a group of companies and a bank, it is provided that any payment from the master account holder to a group company or from a group company to the master account holder is to be subordinated to the full

130 Secondary insolvency proceedings must be winding-up proceedings and their effects are restricted to the assets of the debtor situated within the territory of the member state in which they are opened (in this case, Italy).

131 Article 9 of the Bankruptcy Act provides that in the absence of any international treaty, a foreign debtor with an establishment in Italy may also be declared bankrupt in Italy if insolvency proceedings are pending abroad, in which case the process in Italy would be governed by the Italian Bankruptcy Act.

repayment of the credit facilities granted by the bank. In such circumstances, in the event of the master account holder's insolvency, if the insolvency official and the competent court recognise the enforceability of the subordination clause (which is not necessarily automatic or inevitable), then the group company will likely be excluded from any distribution, unless the operating bank has been paid in full.

Avoidance of transfers made to a group company before insolvency: In the case of a zero balancing cash pooling agreement (where actual transfers of funds are concerned), the relevant transfers may be subject to the claw-back provisions contained in the Bankruptcy Act.

That act sets out four types of claw-back actions:

- claw-back of gratuitous transactions executed by the debtor in the two-year period before the declaration of insolvency (Article 64);
- claw-back of payments of debts not yet due, or that become due on the date of the declaration of insolvency, made by the debtor in the two-year period before such declaration (Article 65);
- ordinary claw-back of any act or transaction intentionally executed by the debtor with the aim of defrauding creditors (Article 66);[132] and
- the special bankruptcy claw-back regulated by Article 67 of the Bankruptcy Act.

The most frequently used claw-back remedy in insolvency proceedings in Italy is that under Article 67 of the Bankruptcy Act. In particular, Paragraph 1 of Article 67 provides that the following acts and transactions executed by the debtor are subject to claw-back, unless the other party proves that it was not aware of the debtor's insolvency (ie, the burden of proof lies with the defendant):

- acts and transactions executed other than at a fair value in the year before the declaration of insolvency;
- payments of debts due and enforceable made by other than normal means of payment, if this occurred in the year before the declaration of insolvency;
- granting of security for pre-existing debts not yet due, if done in the year before the declaration of insolvency; and
- granting of security for debts due, if done in the six months period before the declaration of insolvency.

Paragraph 2 of Article 67 provides that the following acts and transactions executed by the insolvent debtor are subject to claw-back, if the insolvency official can prove that the other party had knowledge of the debtor's impending insolvency:

- payment of debts due and enforceable during the six months before the declaration of insolvency;
- transactions at a fair value, if executed during the six months before the declaration of insolvency; and
- granting of security for a new debt, if done during the six months before the declaration of insolvency.

132 This is the only claw-back action available to insolvency officials of Italian banks.

Finally, if the extraordinary administration procedure for large corporations under Italian Legislative Decree 270/99 of July 8 1999 or Legislative Decree 347/2003 of December 23 2003 applies, then for acts, payments or transactions identified in Article 67 between companies belonging to the same group (eg, between the master account holder and a group company), the relevant hardening periods (ie, the one-year or six-month period before the declaration of insolvency) are extended to five years and three years respectively.

(c) *Group company's insolvency*

The explanation provided above in connection with the master account holder is generally also applicable to the insolvency of a group company. A few additional words should be said in respect of this scenario, however, since the possible risks of liability for the parties involved may be significantly higher.

Under Italian law, shareholders' loans made to a company which is in a distressed situation are subordinated to any other claims of the company's creditors (ie, they cannot be repaid until all other current and future creditors of the company are repaid in full).[133] Also, if a shareholder loan is repaid by the company in the year before a declaration of bankruptcy, it will be clawed back. In light of these provisions, in the case of a zero balancing cash pooling agreement, if the sums are credited to the insolvent group company, the master account holder would face the risk of being subordinated to any of the group company's other creditors and any repayment from the group company to the master account holder in the year preceding the insolvency declaration may be set aside.

These provisions do not apply to upstream loans (ie, from the controlled entity to the parent company) and, therefore, would not apply in case of the master account holder's insolvency.

Furthermore, as already mentioned above in relation to insolvency of the master account holder, a cash pooling agreement may also be used for fraudulent purposes, such as embezzling funds from the insolvent company before it is made subject to bankruptcy proceedings. In this respect, inter-company transactions are normally subject to a higher degree of scrutiny by administrators and public prosecutors. In particularly, public prosecutors may want to examine in depth any payment made by the subsidiary to the parent company (or affiliates) to see whether any crime has been committed by the directors of the insolvent company or of the holding company (or affiliates), such as aggravating an insolvency, embezzling funds or aiding and abetting the aggravation of an insolvency.

---

133 These rules apply to any shareholders' loan made to limited liability companies under Article 2467 of the Civil Code. In the case of joint stock companies, these rules apply to loans made by shareholders that exercise direction and coordination activities under Article 2497 of the Civil Code. Under Article 2497-*sexies* of the Italian Civil Code, an entity is presumed to exercise direction and coordination activities over another company when it consolidates the relevant financial statements or controls the latter in the sense of Article 2359 of the Civil Code (ie, it owns the majority of the votes to be exercised at the shareholders' meeting, or in any case a number of votes sufficient to determine the outcome of the relevant resolution, or influences that company according to specific contractual provisions).

(d) ***Special rules as regards creditors of other parties to the cash pooling agreement***

In the event that the operating bank, the master account holder or a group company goes into liquidation, there are no special rules or obligations as regards creditors of the other parties to the cash pooling agreement. In Italy, an insolvency officialhas direct obligations and duties only towards the creditors of the insolvent company. Therefore, the insolvency official of the operating bank, for instance, would have no direct obligation to the creditors of the master account holder or the group company.

(e) ***Avoidance of payments made under a cash pooling agreement***

It should also be analysed whether the administrator in the insolvency of the master account holder or a group company is allowed to disregard or declare void transactions and claim the amounts as part of the bankruptcy estate if the bankrupt master account holder has transferred money to group companies prior to its bankruptcy, or the group company has transferred money to the master account prior to the bankruptcy of the group company. Such scenarios are similar to those described above in connection with the insolvency of the master account holder and the group company. To summarise:

- any transfer of money made by a bankrupt company to other companies of the group may be subject to the claw-back provisions contained in the Italian Bankruptcy Act (see section 2.3(b) above). Also, if the bankrupt company is eligible for extraordinary administration proceedings, the hardening period for any such transfer for the application of the relevant claw-back provisions would be extended;
- if the transfer is classified as a shareholders' loan, the relevant claim of the lender would be subordinated to all other creditors of the borrower. If, on the other hand, the transfer is classified as repayment of a shareholders' loan, such transfer would be subject to claw-back if made in the one-year period before the bankruptcy declaration (see section 2.3(c) above);
- if the insolvency administrator is administering foreign insolvency proceedings opened within another EU member state, the EU Insolvency Regulation would apply. In particular, any action aimed at voiding transfers detrimental to the other creditors would be governed by the law of the country where the insolvency proceedings have been opened, unless the entity which received the transfer proves that the transfer is subject to the law of a member state other than that of the state of the opening of the insolvency proceedings, and that law does not allow any means of challenging that transfer; and
- if the insolvency administrator is administering foreign insolvency proceedings that were opened in a jurisdiction that is not within the European Union, it will be necessary to assess on a case-by-case basis whether specific bilateral or multilateral treaties are in place concerning the reciprocal recognition of insolvency processes.

(f) ***Dissolution/termination of cash pooling agreement in the event of liquidation of the master account holder or a group company***

When insolvency proceedings are started in Italy, pending contracts are stayed until the insolvency official declares his intention to continue or terminate such contracts. The counterparty may force the decision of the administrator of the insolvent party, asking the court to set a term not exceeding 60 days for the administrator to express his position. If a response is not given, the contract is automatically terminated.

The Bankruptcy Act provides special rules for certain specific contracts, including bank account agreements and account agreements, which are automatically terminated upon an insolvency declaration in respect of one of the parties. Despite the fact that it is still debated whether a cash pooling agreement can be classified as an account agreement, most commentators hold that zero balancing cash pooling agreements should be treated as account agreements and, consequently, should be automatically terminated upon the insolvency of one of the parties under Article 78 of the Bankruptcy Act.

2.4 Perspective D: regulatory

One field in which Italy has introduced regulatory requirements regarding cash pooling agreements is in the regulation on transactions between related parties applicable to listed companies. As indicated above,[134] Italy has adopted stringent regulations on this matter, aimed at ensuring the transparency and procedural and substantial fairness of transactions between related parties (which may include a cash pooling agreement). In particular, listed companies must, among other things:

- adopt general procedures to be followed when the board of directors intends to adopt a transaction with a related party or parties (eg, a cash pooling agreement);
- form a special committee, composed entirely of independent directors, that shall express a favourable opinion on the procedures; and
- comply with certain continuing and periodic disclosure obligations.

If the company is subject to management and coordination, the opinion to be adopted in respect of a transaction with related parties must indicate the reasons for and the suitability of the transaction, where appropriate, in light of the intention of the supervision and coordination of transactions to eliminate potential damage resulting from transactions between related parties.[135]

Recently, an important cash pooling transaction was questioned by CONSOB in respect of the regulation of transactions between related parties.[136] In that case, CONSOB required the relevant Italian listed company to publish three supplements to the initial prospectus both in an Italian newspaper and on its website, as well as to clarify certain conditions of the cash pooling agreement for the benefit of minority shareholders.

---

134 Section 2.1(e) above.

135 See Article 14, first paragraph, of CONSOB Regulation 17221 of March 12 2010.

136 This was the cash pooling transaction carried out between Parmalat SpA and its French controlling company BSA Finances snc in late 2011/early 2012.

2.5 Perspective E: tax

As was briefly mentioned in section 1.3(d), under Italian law interest paid to companies resident in EU member states is not subject to tax,[137] provided that certain requirements are met.

In Circular 47/E of November 2 2005, and then again in Ruling 131/E of May 27 2009, the Revenues Agency set out the requirements that had to be fulfilled in order for a payment to be exempt.

Income arising from securities, bonds, loans and, of particular interest here, mortgage loans, deposits and bank accounts falls within the scope of the provision.

In terms of what entities qualify, the Revenues Agency has stated that an exemption applies to all companies and commercial entities that are resident in Italy and subject to corporation tax.

In addition, an exemption applies where:

- the company making the payment directly holds no less than 25% of the voting rights in the company receiving the payment;
- the company receiving the payment directly holds no less than 25% of the voting rights in the company making the payment; and
- a third company, resident in an EU member state, directly holds at least 25% of the voting rights in both the company making the payment and the receiving company.

The legislation in question provides that. for the purposes of exemption, investments in associates must be held without interruption for at least a year. In the event that, at the time of payment of interest, that requirement has yet to be satisfied, then the person withholding the tax at source must apply the ordinary rate of 20%. In the event that the requirement is subsequently fulfilled, the recipient of the interest payment may apply for the tax to be refunded.

137 Article 26-*quater* of Italian Presidential Decree 600/3.

Japan

Naoya Ariyoshi
Maya Ito
Shinsuke Ushirobira
Nishimura & Asahi

1. Introduction

1.1 Admissibility of cash pooling agreements

As long as the conditions outlined in this chapter are satisfied, it is permissible for corporations to execute a cash pooling agreement, and for holding companies to set up a cash pooling agreement and execute a cash pooling agreement with group members in Japan. Many Japanese corporate groups appear to have already adopted a cash pooling agreement.

It is also permissible to set up a cash pooling agreement when the master account holder, one or more group companies or the bank providing services for cash pooling is a foreign company. Furthermore, in practice, some companies have adopted a cash pooling agreement covering both accounts in Japan for Japanese companies and accounts in foreign countries for foreign companies.

However, master accounts are rarely located in Japan when adopting a global cash pooling agreement, due to the time difference (the business hours in Japan end before those in European and American countries), the high corporation tax rate in Japan and other reasons.

1.2 Types of cash pooling agreement

Cash pooling is not defined under Japanese laws and regulations; furthermore, neither physical cash pooling nor notional cash pooling agreements are referred to in Japanese laws and regulations. However, in practice, both physical cash pooling agreements and notional cash pooling agreements are used in Japan.

Below, we explain the types of cash pooling agreement used and provide an outline of the situation in which cash pooling agreements are used in Japan. In addition, we analyse the contractual relationships arising when a cash pooling agreement is adopted under Japanese laws and regulations.

(a) Physical cash pooling

Usage situation: Several Japanese banks provide services for physical cash pooling agreements, and many corporate groups have adopted such arrangements. The cash pooling services provided by Japanese banks enable corporate groups to determine the time and amounts for money transfers on a flexible basis.

Agreements between parties to set up a physical cash pooling agreement: A master agreement for a cash pooling agreement is often executed between the master account holder and each group company. Such master agreements often include provisions stipulating conditions for participation in the cash pooling agreement and conditions applicable when the arrangement is terminated.

Financial arrangements within a corporate group are then carried out under the provisions of the master agreement.

When a cash pooling agreement is operated, one party is considered to be lending or depositing funds to the other party; therefore, such a financial arrangement may be considered a form of money lending or deposit for consumption under the Civil Code.[1]

Moreover, a cash pooling agreement is generally executed between the bank providing cash pooling services and the master account holder (and sometimes also the bank and each of the group companies), in addition to the bank's standard agreement on bank transactions.

(b) *Notional cash pooling*

As far as we are aware, there is not currently high demand for notional cash pooling agreements in the Japanese business community; furthermore, such arrangements have rarely been adopted in Japan. One reason for this is that corporate groups in Japan do not find it so difficult to conduct physical cash pooling that they need to adopt notional cash pooling agreements instead. Another reason is that it may be very troublesome to manage two sets of books: the actual book and the notional book.

However, we have found no law or regulation that absolutely prohibits a notional cash pooling agreement. Therefore, corporate groups are – at least in principle – allowed to adopt such an arrangement in Japan with certain restrictions, outlined in section 2.5(b) below, should they desire to do so.

1.3 Specific legal requirements from various perspectives

(a) *Company law*

Resolution of board of directors: No special procedures – for example, the approval of a board of directors or a shareholders' meeting – are required to adopt a cash pooling agreement or to lend or deposit funds for such an arrangement under the Companies Act. However, if the transfer of funds contemplated in the cash pooling

---

1 Since the distinction between money lending and deposit for consumption is very vague (they are often distinguished by the purpose of the agreement between the parties (whether it is for deposit or consumption), and which side benefits from the agreement (if for the benefit of the person providing money, it is construed as a deposit for consumption; if for the receiving person, it is construed as money lending)), it is quite difficult to judge whether cash pooling agreements may be considered money lending or deposit for consumption.

2 Article 362, paragraph (4), item (ii) of the Companies Act. The precise meaning of 'substantial loans' is not clear under Japanese law; therefore, corporate groups have to consider whether the loans contemplated are 'substantial loans' on a case-by-case basis.

agreement falls under the notion of 'substantial loans', the board of directors is required to approve such a transfer.[2] Furthermore, if a person serving as the representative director of one party of a cash pooling agreement serves as a director of the other party, that person must disclose this conflict of interest at a meeting of the board of directors of the latter party[3] and obtain the board's approval before executing the cash pooling agreement or other related agreements as the representative of the former party.[4]

Such a person is considered to have a special interest in the resolution for the approval of the agreement. Therefore, he may not participate in the vote on that resolution and may not serve as the chairperson when the resolution is considered by the board. The board's resolution will be void if a person in that situation participates in the vote or serves as the chairperson.

Disclosure under the Companies Act: A company must disclose the principal terms and amounts of transactions that it has conducted with its affiliated companies, as a note regarding transactions with affiliated companies, in the company's financial statements. In addition, a company required to submit an annual securities report is required to specify the same information in its annual securities reports as in the financial statements under the Financial Instruments and Exchange Act.

2. Specific questions

2.1 Perspective A: corporate group

(a) Liability of group company and/or master account holder directors in the event of insolvency of the master account holder or a group company

We explain here the liability of directors, not only when the other party is no longer able to meet its payment obligations, but also as a result of executing a cash pooling agreement or operating a cash pooling agreement.

Liability of directors for breach of duty to exercise due care of a good manager: The relationship between a company and its directors is governed by the Civil Code provisions relating to mandates.[5] Therefore, directors of the company assume the duty to exercise due care of a good manager.[6]

Directors are also required to perform their duties for the company in a loyal manner in compliance with laws and regulations, the articles of incorporation and resolutions of shareholders' meetings.[7]

If directors neglect their duties as outlined above, they will be liable to the

---

3 Disclosure must be at a shareholders' meeting if the relevant company is a company without a board of directors.

4 Article 356, paragraph (1), item (i) and Article 365, paragraph (1) of the Companies Act.

5 Article 330 of the Companies Act.

6 Article 644 of the Civil Code.

7 Article 355 of the Companies Act. The meaning of a 'duty of loyalty' is controversial in Japan; however, the view that there is no real difference between the due of care of a good manager and the duty of loyalty is widely accepted.

company for damages arising as a result.[8] If the company does not file an action against its directors for their liabilities to the company within 60 days of the date of a request from a shareholder that has one or more shares to initiate such an action, the shareholder may file the action, which is called a 'derivative action'.[9]

Moreover, directors are also liable to third parties for damages suffered by them because of intentional misconduct or gross negligence in performing their duties.[10]

Regarding directors' liability, the business judgement rule accepted by the Japanese courts applies to judgements regarding the adoption of a cash pooling agreement or the conduct of a cash pooling agreement, unless it involves violations of laws or regulations or the articles of incorporation of the company. Under the business judgement rule, directors are given discretion as long as they are reasonably informed and the process of reaching their decision is reasonable. The fact that directors have recognised the benefit to be gained from a cash pooling agreement might be considered a ground for the reasonableness of the decision.

However, for example, if a company decides to lend or deposit funds without any mortgage or guarantee to a company in severe financial distress, the directors would have to show that their decision to do so on behalf of the company is based on reasonable grounds.

On February 28 2012 the Yokohama District Court dismissed an action from a shareholder of a group company participating in a cash pooling agreement seeking to impose liability on the directors and to make them cease their alleged misconduct, on the grounds that lending or depositing funds to a master account with low interest rates and without any mortgage or guarantee should be considered a breach of the duty to exercise due care of a good manager and the duty of loyalty. In that decision, the court found that there was no negligence on the part of the directors of the company. The court took into account the fact that the company benefited from the cash pooling agreement in which it was involved. As far as we are aware, this is the only Japanese court judgment concerning an action seeking to establish the liability of directors in relation to a cash pooling agreement. However, internal discipline within corporate groups has recently become of grave concern in Japan; therefore, further actions regarding the liability of directors in relation to cash pooling agreements may be filed.

The lender may incur losses equal to the balance of loans if the borrower is no longer able to meet its payment obligations. If any director of the lender is found to have neglected his duties in the decision to lend funds, or has not collected funds from the borrower, that director will be liable for both:

- damages incurred as a result of his negligence that would ordinarily arise from the negligent decision; and
- damages arising from special circumstances if the director did foresee, or should have foreseen, those circumstances.

---

8 Article 423, paragraph (1) of the Companies Act.
9 Article 847, paragraphs (1) to (3) of the Companies Act.
10 Article 429(1) of the Companies Act.

Other issues: If the subsidiary is conducting financial arrangements on terms which are unusually advantageous for the parent company and there is no rational reason for applying such terms, the financial arrangements may be considered to be:

- an infringement of shareholder equality;[11]
- the provision of benefits on the exercise of a shareholder's right;[12] or
- a circumvention of the restriction on the distribution of dividends under the Companies Act.

However, as long as the subsidiary is lending or depositing money to its parent company on usual terms, these problems will not occur.

In general, adopting or operating a cash pooling agreement would objectively serve company purposes and therefore would not be considered *ultra vires*.

Courts will not pierce the corporate veil if the businesses and properties of a company and its directors are managed separately.

There is no law or regulation expressly providing that directors of a listed company assume a greater duty of care than those of non-listed companies. However, for the two reasons mentioned below, directors of a listed company are factually required to give greater consideration to their duty of care:

- A company participating in a cash pooling agreement that is required to submit annual securities reports because it is a listed company or that has submitted an annual securities report for other reasons is required to specify the principal terms and amounts of transactions that the company has conducted with its affiliated companies in its annual securities reports. If the contents of such reports, including those regarding any cash pooling agreement, contain any false statement on important matters or omit either important matters that should be stated or a material fact that is necessary to avoid misunderstanding, the company that submitted the annual securities reports and directors and other officers of that company, or any person who can be regarded as equivalent thereto, will in principle be liable to compensate persons that have acquired the securities (including shares and bonds) for damages arising from the false statement or omission.
- In general, shareholders of a listed company are widely dispersed; therefore, directors of a listed company are factually exposed to a higher risk of derivative actions.

It does not matter under Japanese law whether the bank or the distressed group company is registered in a foreign jurisdiction.

(b) Liability of group companies in the event of insolvency of the master account holder

Even if the financial condition of the master account holder has deteriorated and its creditors have difficulty in collecting their claims, those creditors will be unable to hold the group companies liable for any losses suffered, except where the group

---

11 Article 109(1) of the Companies Act.
12 Article 120(1) of the Companies Act.

companies have guaranteed the debts of the master account holder. However, if the master account holder has a claim against a group company or holds shares in a group company, the creditors of the master account holder may file a petition for compulsory execution on any such claims or shares.

Under Japanese law, a creditor may request that a court rescind any transaction that a debtor (in this case, the master account holder) enters into knowing that it will prejudice the creditor (the right to demand the rescission of a fraudulent act).[13] Therefore, if the financially distressed master account holder repays a debt to the group companies under a cash pooling agreement, such performance might be rescinded on the basis of that right. However, we believe that such debt repayment will not be rescinded, except where a debtor repays a debt in collusion with a creditor to injure other creditors. In addition, we believe that normally a loan extended under a cash pooling agreement by a company participating in a cash pooling agreement cannot be rescinded under the right to demand rescission of a fraudulent act, because while that company will temporary lose an amount of funds, it will acquire exactly the same amount as the loan claim. Therefore, in general, extending a loan is not considered to prejudice creditors.

The above argument can be applied regardless of whether the master account holder, the claiming creditor or the group company is located in Japan or abroad, as long as Japanese law applies.

Regarding the possibility that the insolvency administrator may invalidate a repayment of debts or a loan under a cash pooling agreement when the master account holder is subject to insolvency proceedings, see section 2.3(a) below.

(c) Liability of the master account holder in the event of insolvency of a group company

The discussion in section 2.1(b) will similarly apply where a group company other than the master account holder is financially distressed. Creditors of that group company will be unable to hold the other group companies and/or the master account holder liable for losses suffered, except where they have guaranteed the debts of that group company. We believe that the repayment of a debt or a loan under a cash pooling agreement will not be rescinded on the basis of the right to demand rescission of a fraudulent act.

Regarding the power to invalidate in legal insolvency proceedings, see section 2.3(a) below.

2.2 Perspective B: bank

(a) Banking requirements

A bank entering into a cash pooling agreement with a corporate group will not be subject to any specific requirements in Japan merely because it enters into a cash pooling agreement.

---

13 Article 424 of the Civil Code.

(b) *Liability of the bank in the event of insolvency of the master account holder or a group company*

Creditors of either the master account holder or a group company that is financially distressed will be unable to hold the bank liable for losses suffered, except where the bank guarantees the debts of companies participating in a cash pooling agreement. We believe that repayment of a debt or a loan to the bank resulting from the cash pooling agreement cannot be rescinded on the basis of the right to request avoidance of a fraudulent act.

Regarding the right of avoidance in legal insolvency proceedings, see section 2.3(a) below.

2.3 Insolvency

(a) *Cash pooling agreements from the insolvency practitioner's perspective*

The major forms of insolvency proceedings in Japan are bankruptcy proceedings as liquidation proceedings, and civil rehabilitation proceedings and corporate reorganisation proceedings as rehabilitation proceedings. These proceedings are governed by, respectively, the Bankruptcy Act, the Civil Rehabilitation Act and the Corporate Reorganisation Act.

If any insolvency proceedings regarding a company participating in a cash pooling agreement have been commenced and that company has a claim against any other participating company under the cash pooling agreement (ie, deposit claims or loan claims), the insolvency administrator is authorised to administer and dispose of the debtor's property[14] so that it may claim the entire credit balance.

In the case where the insolvency administrator is appointed abroad (ie, foreign insolvency proceedings have been commenced), the proceedings will not take effect directly in Japan. However, if a Japanese court issues an order recognising such foreign insolvency proceedings[15], and orders that a recognition trustee administer the debtor's business and property in Japan,[16] then the recognition trustee is authorised to carry out the debtor's business and to administer and dispose of the debtor's property in Japan so that it may claim the entire credit balance.

With respect to the obligations of the insolvency administrator, first, if any insolvency proceedings regarding a company participating in a cash pooling agreement have been commenced, the claims against such a company are treated as bankruptcy claims (regarding bankruptcy), rehabilitation claims (regarding civil rehabilitation), or reorganisation claims (regarding corporate reorganisation).

Once such proceedings have been commenced, then with respect to the bankruptcy claims, rehabilitation claims or reorganisation claims, any actions to collect debts from a debtor by a creditor outside such proceedings are prohibited. Generally, these claims are subject to modification of rights, and payments or distributions from the assets to the creditors are made only through insolvency

---

14 Article 34 (1) of the Bankruptcy Act; Article 66 of the Civil Rehabilitation Act; Article 72 (1) of the Corporate Reorganisation Act.

15 Article 2 (1) (v) of the Act on Recognition and Assistance for Foreign Insolvency Proceedings.

16 Article 32 (1) of the Act on Recognition and Assistance for Foreign Insolvency Proceedings.

proceedings according to the order of priority prescribed by the applicable insolvency law. Therefore, the creditors may only receive reduced and delayed payments.[17]

The insolvency administrator shall perform its duties with the due care of a good manager,[18] irrespective of whether the creditors are located in another jurisdiction.[19]

If any insolvency proceedings regarding a financial institution such as a bank have been commenced in Japan, claims for the balance of any deposit with that institution are subject to insolvency proceedings in the same way as other general claims. However, in the event of the insolvency of a bank, there is a system providing insurance to depositors. More specifically, if a financial institution suspends repayment of deposits (a petition for commencement of insolvency proceedings is considered to fall under this category) or declares bankruptcy, then deposit claims are protected up to:

- Y10 million in respect of the principal and interest on the principal in general deposits;[20] and
- the full amount of chequable deposits, which are those in accounts which pay no interest, are payable on demand and offer a settlement service.[21]

This guarantee is fulfilled by the Deposit Insurance Corporation either by paying the protected amounts upon request[22] or by providing financial assistance to the bank.[23]

In practice, deposits of the master account holder or the group company participating in a cash pooling agreement may be general deposits or chequable deposits as required. In the event of the insolvency of the bank, such deposits are insured according to the type of account as described above. However, it should be noted that payment may be delayed because of deposit insurance proceedings even if the amount to be paid is preserved.

If bankruptcy proceedings regarding a company participating in a cash pooling agreement have been commenced and such company has deposit claims or loan claims under a cash pooling agreement against another participating company, the insolvency administrator has a duty to convert such claims into cash, irrespective of whether the other participating company is located in another jurisdiction.[24] However, if the other participating company is located abroad, it may actually be difficult to collect the claims.

When the insolvency administrator considers the possibility of disregarding transactions under a cash pooling agreement, two types of fund transfer should be noted: loans and performance of obligations. First, if the master account holder or a group company that has become insolvent had extended loans to the other

17 Article 100 of the Bankruptcy Act; Article 85 of the Civil Rehabilitation Act; Article 47 of the Corporate Reorganisation Act.
18 Article 85 (1) of the Bankruptcy Act; Article 78 of the Civil Rehabilitation Act; Article 80 (1) of the Corporate Reorganisation Act.
19 Article 3 of the Bankruptcy Act; Article 3 of the Civil Rehabilitation Act; Article 3 of the Corporate Reorganisation Act.
20 Article 54 (2) of the Deposit Insurance Act; Article 6-2 of the Order for Enforcement of the Deposit Insurance Act.
21 Article 54 (2) of the Deposit Insurance Act.
22 Article 53 of the Deposit Insurance Act.
23 Articles 59 to 69 of the Deposit Insurance Act.

participating company under a cash pooling agreement before the commencement of insolvency proceedings, then provisions regarding avoidance of acts prejudicial to creditors may come into play. These provisions allow the insolvency administrator to invalidate an action that reduces the debtor's assets.[25] However, extending loans is not subject to avoidance, except where the borrower is insolvent. This is because extending loans does not reduce the debtor's assets even if there is no security provided for repayment (nonetheless, as previously stated, the insolvency administrator has a duty to convert the claims of the debtor into cash during the bankruptcy proceedings; as a result of the insolvency administrator's collecting loan claims, the money will return to the bankruptcy estate).

Next, if the master account holder or a group company that has become insolvent had performed an obligation to another participating company under a cash pooling agreement before the commencement of insolvency proceedings, then provisions regarding avoidance of provision of security or repayment of a debt to specific creditors may apply.[26] These provisions allow the insolvency administrator to invalidate any payment or provision of security by a debtor to an existing creditor after becoming insolvent, because it causes unfairness among the creditors.

More specifically, after becoming unable to pay debts (ie, where a debtor is generally and continuously unable to pay its debts as they become due) or where a petition for commencement of insolvency proceedings has been filed, any payment or provision of security to an existing creditor by the debtor may be declared void if the creditor knew of the debtor's insolvency at the time of the payment or provision of the security.

In principle, if the insolvency administrator intends to execute its power to invalidate, the insolvency administrator has to prove that the creditor knew[27] of the debtor's insolvency at the time of the payment or provision of the security. However, if the creditor is the debtor's parent company, then as an exception to the general rule, the parent company must prove that it did not know of the debtor's insolvency at the time of the payment or provision of the security.[28]

If the insolvency administrator has been appointed abroad, whether such a foreign administrator may execute the power to invalidate is not expressly provided for in the Act on Recognition and Assistance for Foreign Insolvency Proceedings, which otherwise regulates the validity of foreign insolvency proceedings in Japan. Therefore, the position is still unclear as to:

- the governing law with which the foreign administrator must comply;
- the conditions required for the foreign administrator to execute the power to invalidate; and
- the effect of the avoidance.

---

24 Article 34 (1) of the Bankruptcy Act.

25 Article 160 of the Bankruptcy Act; Article 127 of the Civil Rehabilitation Act; Article 86 of the Corporate Reorganisation Act.

26 Article 162 of the Bankruptcy Act; Article 127-3 of the Civil Rehabilitation Act; Article 86-3 of the Corporate Reorganisation Act.

27 If the creditor should have known of the debtor's insolvency, but did not have actual knowledge thereof the insolvency administrator may not execute its power to invalidate.

28 Article 162 (2) (i) of the Bankruptcy Act; Article 127-3 (2) (i) of the Civil Rehabilitation Act; Article 86-3 (2) (i) of the Corporate Reorganisation Act.

Development of judicial precedent and theories with respect to these issues is expected.

(b) Special rules as regards creditors of other parties to the cash pooling agreement

Under insolvency law in Japan, an insolvency administrator must perform its duties to any interested person with the due care of a good manager.[29] However, a creditor of the insolvency creditor[30] or a creditor of the counterparty to any agreement with the insolvent company does not fall under the category of 'interested person'.

Furthermore, under insolvency law in Japan, there are no special rules relevant to cash pooling agreements.

(c) Dissolution/termination of cash pooling agreement in the event of liquidation of the master account holder or a group company

In practice, a cash pooling agreement entered into in Japan often contains a clause that stipulates that either of the parties can terminate the agreement unconditionally. In such cases, a participating company can terminate the cash pooling agreement if the counterparty becomes insolvent.

In addition, even if no such unconditional termination clause is provided, a cash pooling agreement may include a clause that gives either party the right to terminate where the counterparty files a petition for commencement of insolvency proceedings. However, the validity of such clause (known as an '*ipso facto* clause') is considered controversial. First of all, under Japanese insolvency law, the insolvency administrator may terminate executory contracts (bilateral or multilateral contracts under which the main obligations have not been completely performed by both the debtor and the creditor at the time the insolvency proceedings are commenced) or continue such contracts in order to request the counterparty to perform its obligation.[31] To protect the insolvency administrator's option in this regard, there is an argument that an *ipso facto* clause would be invalid. Furthermore, in the case of legal rehabilitation proceedings, if a contract necessary for the debtor's business is terminated pursuant to an *ipso facto* clause, it would make the restructuring more difficult. Therefore, there is an argument that an *ipso facto* clause should be considered to be invalid at least in the event of legal rehabilitation proceedings.[32] However, considering that a cash pooling agreement is an agreement involving credit being provided to the counterparty, it would be quite reasonable to consider an *ipso facto* clause in a cash pooling agreement to be valid.

Practically speaking, if a party to a cash pooling agreement becomes insolvent, it usually becomes difficult to execute the provisions of the agreement in whole or in part; furthermore, it may be deemed unreasonable to continue such an agreement.

---

29 Article 85 of the Bankruptcy Act; Article 78 of the Civil Rehabilitation Act; Article 80 of the Corporate Reorganisation Act.

30 In the case of cash pooling, for example, this would refer to a creditor of the master account holder where the bank goes into liquidation and the master account holder has claims against the bank.

31 Article 53 of the Bankruptcy Act; Article 49 of the Civil Rehabilitation Act; Article 61 of the Corporate Reorganisation Act.

32 For the interpretation of the validity of an *ipso facto* clause under the Japanese law, it makes no difference whether the relevant party is a Japanese entity or a foreign entity.

More precisely, if any insolvency proceedings regarding the master account holder have been commenced, the master account holder must obtain the court's permission under the applicable insolvency law in order to transfer any funds as contemplated in a cash pooling agreement. In such cases, it would become impossible to operate a cash pooling agreement under which the parties transferred funds daily and automatically. Therefore, it is expected that the parties would agree to terminate the cash pooling agreement.

In addition, a cash pooling agreement can be considered to be a mandate or quasi-mandate under the Civil Code as regards the relationship between the bank and the master account holder or the group companies. A mandate or quasi-mandate terminates automatically when the mandator or mandatary is subject to a ruling for the commencement of bankruptcy proceedings.[33] Therefore, in the above cases, if insolvency proceedings have been commenced in respect of a party to a cash pooling agreement, the cash pooling agreement will terminate automatically without requiring notice of termination from the counterparty.

2.4 Perspective D: regulatory

(a) Local cash pooling

Money Lending Business Act: If a cash pooling agreement is set up, other than between a parent company and its subsidiaries, the master account holder[34] must be registered by the prime minister or the prefectural governor under the Money Lending Business Act.

A person that intends to engage in 'money lending business' must be registered by the prime minister (when engaging in business within two or more prefectures) or the prefectural governor (when engaging in business within one prefecture).[35] 'Money lending business' is defined as "the business of loaning money or acting as an intermediary for the lending or borrowing of money ... on a regular basis".[36] The term 'on a regular basis' in this definition is interpreted in case precedents to mean that:

- only the intent to loan money regularly and continually, or to act as an intermediary regularly and continually, is required, and the intent to earn a reward or profit is not always required;[37] and
- numerous and unspecified counterparties are also not required.[38]

As mentioned in section 1.2 above, a cash pooling agreement might be considered a form of money lending,[39] in which case a cash pooling agreement will

33 Article 653 of the Civil Code.

34 At least logically speaking, a group company other than the master account holder might also be required to be registered under the Money Lending Business Act. However, in most cases in Japan, only the master account holder will be registered when a corporate group uses a cash pooling agreement.

35 Article 3 (1) of the Money Lending Business Act.

36 Article 2 (1) of the Money Lending Business Act.

37 Supreme Court judgment of November 11 1954; Supreme Court Reports (Criminal Cases) 8-11-1860.

38 Supreme Court judgment of July 22 1955; Supreme Court Reports (Criminal Cases) 9-9-1962.

be regarded as loaning money with an intent to loan money regularly and continually in line with the Supreme Court judgment referred to above. Thus, it will be a money lending business for the purposes of Article 3(1) of the Money Lending Business Act. However, the Financial Services Agency, which is the agency enforcing the Money Lending Business Act in Japan, released two no-action letters that state that money lending did not qualify as a money lending business:

- where two subsidiaries in Japan planned to lend money to their parent company in the United States;[40] and
- where a parent company and its 10 subsidiaries, all of which were in Japan, planned to use a cash pooling agreement.[41]

Based on these no-action letters, if a cash pooling agreement involves only a parent company and subsidiaries, more than 50% of whose voting rights are held directly or indirectly by the parent company (in other words, where funds are transferred only between a parent company and each of its subsidiaries, and between a subsidiary of a parent company and a subsidiary of such a subsidiary), then a cash pooling agreement is considered not to be a money lending business. Therefore, the master account holder need not be registered under the Money Lending Business Act.

On the other hand, another no-action letter stated that a money loan between subsidiaries of the same parent company (ie, fellow subsidiaries) did fall to be treated as a money lending business.[42] Therefore, the master account holder must be registered under the Money Lending Business Act when the cash pooling agreement is one in which funds are transferred between fellow subsidiaries.

As of March 2012, processing of applications for money lending business registrations is generally completed in two months, and registration is effective for three years.[43] The registration and licence tax is ¥150,000 for initial registration and subsequently for each renewal.[44] A person that engages in money lending business without registration may be punished by imprisonment with labour for up to 10 years, a fine of up to ¥30 million or both.[45]

Act Regulating the Receipt of Contributions, Receipt of Deposits and Interest Rates: When a company participating in a cash pooling agreement transfers surplus funds to another participating company, such a transfer of money might be considered a 'receipt of deposits of money' under Article 2 of the Act Regulating the Receipt of Contributions, Receipt of Deposits and Interest Rates.

---

39 On the other hand, if a cash pooling agreement is considered to be a deposit for consumption, registration under the Money Lending Business Act may not be necessary. However, as mentioned in section 1.2 above, the distinction between money lending and a deposit for consumption is very vague. Therefore, where a cash pooling agreement is planned, registration under the Money Lending Business Act is recommended in practice, because of the risk that such a financial arrangement may be considered money lending.

40 http://www.fsa.go.jp/common/noact/kaitou/024/024_01a.html.

41 http://www.fsa.go.jp/common/noact/kaitou/024/024_01a.pdf.

42 http://www.fsa.go.jp/common/noact/kaitou/024/024_04a.pdf.

43 Article 3 (2) of the Money Lending Business Act.

44 Appended Table 1-46(1) of the Registration and Licence Tax Act; Article 2 (1) of the Order for Enforcement of the Money Lending Business Act.

45 Article 47 (ii) and Article 11 (1) of the Money Lending Business Act.

Under that act, a 'receipt of deposits of money' is defined as "the receipt of money from numerous, unspecified persons";[46] furthermore, no person except an entity permitted under specific laws and regulations, such as a bank, may regularly receive deposits of money (Article 2(1) of the act). The purpose of this restriction is to avoid unexpected damage being incurred by the general public or by a person in a business relationship with the general public, where an entity conducting the business of receiving deposits of money goes bankrupt.[47] Considering this purpose, the phrase 'from numerous, unspecified persons' is interpreted to mean from the general public.

Accordingly, as long as it is not contemplated that funds are to be absorbed from the general public (eg, the cash pooling agreement to be conducted only within a corporate group with certain capital ties), transfers of surplus funds in a cash pooling agreement do not fall under the definition of 'receipt of deposits of money' prohibited under the Act Regulating the Receipt of Contributions, Receipt of Deposits and Interest Rates.

Banking Act: A person that has not obtained a Banking Act licence or a Payment Services Act registration may not engage in 'carrying out exchange transactions'.[48] The phrase 'carrying out exchange transactions'[49] is interpreted as referring to "an acceptance or an acceptance and fulfilment of a client's request to shift funds between persons at a distance using a nondirect mechanism of sending money".[50]

Although a transfer of funds in a cash pooling agreement might be considered, by definition, as carrying out exchange transactions, it would generally be considered that such a transfer is not the carrying out of exchange transactions for the purposes of the Banking Act. This is because it would be carried out solely as a consequence of a company performing its obligations under the cash pooling agreement.

(b) International cash pooling

International application of the Money Lending Business Act and Act Regulating the Receipt of Contributions, Receipt of Deposits and Interest Rates: Whether the Money Lending Business Act and the Act Regulating the Receipt of Contributions, Receipt of Deposits and Interest Rates are applicable is also an issue in the case of an international cash pooling agreement. There is no specific provision of any law ruling on the application of the Money Lending Business Act and the Act Regulating the Receipt of Contributions, Receipt of Deposits and Interest Rates in such circumstances. However, considering the territoriality principle,[51] the Money Lending Business Act and the Act Regulating the Receipt of Contributions, Receipt of Deposits and Interest Rates would be considered applicable if either lending or borrowing were made in Japan (ie, either the lender or the depositor was in Japan).

---

46 Article 2 (2) of the Act Regulating the Receipt of Contributions, Receipt of Deposits and Interest Rates.
47 Supreme Court judgment of April 26 1961; Supreme Court Reports (Criminal Cases) 15-4-732.
48 Article 4 (1) of the Banking Act and Article 37 of the Payment Services Act.
49 Article 2 (2) (ii) of the Banking Act.
50 Supreme Court judgment of March 12, 2001; Supreme Court Reports (Criminal Cases) 55-2-97.
51 Articles 1 and 8 of the Penal Code.

Foreign Exchange and Foreign Trade Act: When a Japanese resident has made a payment exceeding ¥30 million to a recipient in a foreign state, or has received a payment exceeding ¥30 million from a payor in a foreign state, that resident must report to the competent minister the content of the payment, the time the payment was made, and other detailed matters specified by Cabinet Order.[52] Therefore, a Japanese resident participant in a cash pooling agreement must report to the competent minister where the amount of a transfer made from or to such resident participant is more than ¥30 million.

2.5 Perspective E: tax

(a) *Physical cash pooling*

Transfer pricing: When a physical cash pooling agreement is adopted between domestic corporations and foreign affiliated persons, transfer pricing taxation applies regarding certain transactions – for example, the interest rate on loans between participating companies, the cost burden for constructing and operating a cash pooling system, and the distribution of pooling benefits.

Specifically, if there is any variation from an arm's-length price in respect of such transactions, and consequently Japanese taxable income is reduced, the taxable income will be calculated based on the transaction being deemed to have be made at an arm's-length price.[53]

Credit for foreign tax: With regard to the interest rate on loans between companies participating in a cash pooling agreement, when foreign income tax is withheld abroad, credit for foreign tax could be considered up to the equivalent of 50% of the amount for the tax base.[54]

(b) *Notional cash pooling*

Transfer pricing: When a notional cash pooling agreement is adopted that involves domestic corporations and foreign affiliated persons, as with a physical cash pooling agreement, transfer pricing taxation is applicable in respect of certain transactions, such as the cost burden of constructing and operating the cash pooling system, and the distribution of pooling benefits.

In addition, in a notional cash pooling agreement, with regard to the positive balance of a company participating in the cash pooling agreement – which

---

52 Article 55 (1) of the Foreign Exchange and Foreign Trade Act; Article 18-4 (1) (i) of the Foreign Exchange Order; Article 1 (1) of the Ministerial Ordinance concerning Reports on Foreign Exchange Transactions, etc.

53 Article 66-4 (1) of the Act on Special Measures Concerning Taxation. The effective corporate tax rate is approximately 40% in Japan.

54 Article 69 (1) of the Corporation Tax Act; Article 142-3 (1) of the Order for Enforcement of the Corporation Tax Act. This assumes that the domestic corporation is mainly engaged in business that is not finance business, life insurance business or non-life insurance business, and "the income ratio of its interest etc." in the last three fiscal years does not exceed 20% (Article 142-3 (2) (iv) of the Order for Enforcement of the Corporation Tax Act).

effectively functions as security for another participating company that intends to borrow from the bank – Japan's tax authority might deem that there is an security agreement between the companies from the tax aspect, and might apply transfer pricing taxation as regards the commission for such security.[55]

Credit for foreign tax: Credit for foreign taxes cannot be considered in a notional cash pooling agreement, because interest does not accrue without actual lending and borrowing.

Other possible forms of taxation: Because there is neither a contractual relationship nor claims and obligations between participating parties in a notional cash pooling agreement, essentially no other form of taxation will apply.

However, as mentioned in section 1.2 above, there have been few cases of a notional cash pooling agreements in Japan; therefore, the approach by Japan's tax authority to the taxation of notional cash pooling agreements remains unpredictable.

Masayuki Tani, Kotaro Fuji and Jun Akasakaya, all attorneys at Nishimura & Asahi, assisted in the preparation of this chapter.

55 If the provision of security is actually a gratuitous transaction, and no commission paid, it will be recognised as a 'contribution', but the company that has the surplus funds will not be allowed to include it in its deductible expenses (Article 66-4 (3) of the Act on Special Measures Concerning Taxation; Article 37 of the Corporation Tax Act). Such taxation of contributions (with the limitation of inclusion in deductible expense) can be an issue not only in a crossborder transaction, but also in a domestic one.

Luxembourg

Laurent Fisch
Molitor Avocats à la Cour

1. Introduction

1.1 Admissibility of cash pooling agreements

The laws of the Grand-Duchy of Luxembourg do not explicitly address cash pooling agreements. Agreeing and implementing either notional or physical cash pooling agreements (or any other agreement in the absence of a legal framework) is a basic citizens' right that is subject merely to the limitations arising from legal rules (see section 1.4 below).

1.2 Types of cash pooling agreement

There is no reliable source of information on the types, use and importance of cash pooling agreements in Luxembourg or by Luxembourg company groups. Notional and physical cash pooling agreements covering a number of denominations are known to exist, and several larger local company groups use cash pooling in a purely domestic context.

Local bankers tend to see cash pooling agreements as a banking product offered mainly by global competitors which have a presence in many jurisdictions and/or easy access to a group's head management and chief financial officer.

This view is, however, partially contradicted by the author's experience of notional cash pooling schemes operated by international company groups where the master account is held with the group's house bank, a local bank, and additional accounts are held with other banks rather than subsidiaries or branch offices of the house bank. It also seems to be a trend that large company groups identify the most appropriate host jurisdiction for their cash pooling agreements based on an international comparison of legal, accounting and tax issues.

The Luxembourg authorities promote cash pooling in and through Luxembourg alongside other bank industry products, as do the Luxembourg tax advisory community, lawyers and chartered accountants, despite the secondary role that tax planning usually plays in cash pooling schemes.

1.3 Legal requirements from various perspectives

Luxembourg law does not provide for specific rules in relation to cash pooling agreements, but there is an impressively large number of general legal requirements which need to be considered in relation to such agreements.

General legal rules from several sources might limit the possibilities for a Luxembourg company to enter into a cash pooling agreement, among which are rules concerning the group company's corporate purpose and its interest.

(a) General contract rules

Cash pooling agreements under Luxembourg law need to be agreed within the wide boundaries of Luxembourg civil law. Other than for evidence purposes, it is not even necessary that cash pooling agreements be agreed in writing (though this is advisable). If the cash pooling agreement provides for a security (eg, a set-off provision) that can be considered as financial collateral under the Financial Collateral Act of August 5 2005, it should be in writing. It would then also be advisable that each party to the agreement acknowledge receipt of an original copy of the agreement (particularly for filing reasons, which are discussed below) and, of course, actually receive a copy.

The legal basis for creating valid rights and commitments under Luxembourg law is the freely exercised joint intention of the parties. Flaws that may affect the validity of a contracts generally include violence, misrepresentation and sometimes a party's error. Additional validity issues may arise if it appears that the main reason for which some or all parties have entered into the cash pooling agreement is to harm a third party or a group company. It is, for instance, conceivable that a cash pooling agreement could provide for use of the cash or creditworthiness of a group member only or mainly in the interests of other group companies. This could then be seen as a misuse of corporate assets, a criminal offence, and the cash pooling agreement could be voided as a result. Another improper purpose would be to use a cash pooling agreement to strip a group company of its assets in anticipation of an insolvency event in the group.

Generally speaking, however, Luxembourg law allows the parties a lot of freedom to agree on such provisions as they wish. The courts are obliged by law to follow the joint intentions of the parties at the time of signing, rather than trying to consider a cash pooling agreement as a so-called 'named agreement' (ie, an agreement of a type that is specifically dealt with by Luxembourg law, such as a loan) and deriving the parties mutual obligations from it.

The use of English as the prevailing language of a cash pooling agreement is not a problem. In court, a translation of such an agreement into French or German might be needed.

There may be a need to file certain cash pooling agreements with the local indirect tax authorities (*Administration de l'Enregistrement et des Domaines*), which have the right and the obligation to levy a nominal registration duty or an *ad valorem* duty on a number of agreements and deeds entered into in Luxembourg, particularly agreements containing a reference to a claim (eg, a euro amount) in favour of one party (the rate of duty is 0.24% of the face value of the claim).

When filing an agreement, it is necessary to submit a copy together with an original version. Filing may be required for the agreement to be admissible as evidence in court, for it to be notified by a bailiff or for it to be referred to it in a notarial deed.

Luxembourg group companies are not prevented by law from entering into agreements governed by foreign laws, and Luxembourg courts generally recognise the choice of foreign law in accordance with domestic law rules and EU Regulation 593/2008 on the law applicable to contractual obligations.

Luxembourg courts may, however, refuse to apply the chosen governing law when all elements of the matter are situated in a country other than the jurisdiction of the chosen governing law (in which case Luxembourg courts may apply the imperative laws of that country); or when the agreement has a strong connection to another jurisdiction and certain laws of that jurisdiction are applicable regardless of the chosen governing law, in which case Luxembourg courts may apply those laws.

Submission by the parties to foreign judicial courts is also generally recognised and given effect by the Luxembourg courts, particularly in accordance with EU Regulation 44/2001 on jurisdiction and the recognition and enforcement of judgments in civil and commercial matters.

Notwithstanding a foreign jurisdiction clause, Luxembourg courts will, in principle, have jurisdiction for any conservatory or provisional action in connection with assets located in Luxembourg, and Luxembourg law will most likely govern any such action.

(b) Corporate purpose

A cash pooling agreement may contain a number of provisions and features which are not considered merely ancillary to the core provisions and should therefore be expressly permitted by the bylaws of any group company based in Luxembourg, including:

- the possibility of granting guarantees and security in favour of other members of the company group; and
- the possibility of granting advances and loans to group companies.

Any action taken by a corporation that does not fall within its corporate purpose may be rescinded if the third party knew or could not ignore that this action fell outside the corporate purpose. Any such action will also be a violation of the bylaws, which will trigger the increased joint civil liability of all directors to the company and to third parties (see section 2.1(a) below).

(c) Corporate interest

The corporate interest of a company is not a clear-cut concept and, depending on the context, matters which may be taken into consideration can include the financial, economic and commercial interests of the company itself, the interests of the shareholders, the interests of other group companies, the interests of the creditors and, sometimes, the interests of the employees in taking a particular action or entering into a specific transaction. Some authors put the emphasis on the long-term continuity and profitability of the company.

Directors of a Luxembourg company must exercise their functions in compliance with the corporate interest of the company. Failure to act in that way may result in civil management liability and also may amount to a criminal offence, such as the misuse of corporate assets (see section 2.1(a) below). Furthermore, in cases of fraudulent collusion, the validity of an arrangement, in terms of whether it is in the corporate interest of a Luxembourg company, could even be challenged on the basis of the principle that fraud negates everything (*'fraus omnia corrumpit'*). There is, however, no Luxembourg case-law publicly available in relation to this.

Luxembourg law puts the focus on the corporate interest of each company. Luxembourg directors would thus be well advised to ensure that the cash pooling agreement has sufficient benefit and interest for their company alone.

In a group context, the corporate interest of a group company needs to be put in perspective and be balanced with group interests. In this specific context, the Luxembourg courts tend to look at French court precedents and follow their findings.[1]

According to these court decisions as applied by Luxembourg courts, several conditions must be met before a transaction (eg, a cash pooling agreement beneficial to a group) is not considered a violation of the corporate interest of a (Luxembourg) group company:

- The agreement must be dictated by a common economical, social or financial interest, evaluated with regard to a group policy;
- The agreement must not be effected without consideration;
- It must not jeopardise the balance of the respective obligations of the various companies involved;
- The obligations arising out of the agreement must not exceed the financial capabilities of the group company; and
- The various group companies must have the same shareholders.

Therefore, it is important that a transaction entered into by several companies of the same group not only be in the interest of the group as a whole, but also benefit each of the companies involved proportionally to the obligations it assumes under such transaction.[2] As far as the liability of the directors is concerned, it is irrelevant whether other group companies benefit from the cash pooling agreements.

A cash pooling agreement will obviously not be in the corporate interest of a group company when the financial burden on that company largely exceeds the benefits deriving from it.

Furthermore, when a group company derives very little or no benefit from a cash pooling agreement, it is obvious that the management should not approve it. For example, in the context of a physical cash pooling agreement, it is likely that the cash transfers from the group company to the master account holder would be legally analysed as loans, although there is no case law available on this issue. Therefore, the management of the group company should make sure that the

---

1 French *Cour de cassation*, judgment of February 4 1985, *Rozenblum*, JCP 1986.II.20585; French Cour de cassation, judgment of February 1 2000, Dr sociétés 2000, n°50, p 12; Cass crim, February 13 1989; *Rev. sociétés* 1989, p 692, note B Bouloc; and Cass crim September 4 1996; *Rev sociétés* 1997, p 365, note Bouloc.

2 G Kolifrath, *"Les risques juridiques liés à la mise en place d'une centralisation de trésorerie au sein d'un groupe de societies"*, *Banque & Droit*, No 47, May-June 1996, p 5; Bernard Bouloc, talk entitled *"Abus de biens sociaux – le particularisme français à l'épreuve de l'Europe"*, meeting of April 2 2003, ESCP-EAP and *Centre de recherche sur le droit des affaires, Gaz Pal.* of 19-20 November 2004.

interest rates provided for by the cash pooling agreement are high enough and not under the legal rate of interest (which is revised each year; in 2012, the legal interest rate is 3.5%).

(d) *Bankruptcy*

If there are no specific contractual arrangements to the contrary, a group company participating in cash pooling does not have a direct right over the cash funds in the master account, but instead holds a receivable and has a claim against the master account holder. As a result, the group company has temporarily less cash available to pay its matured debts.

This may lead to a situation where the group company has ceased its payments and where its ability to raise credit is impaired, and, as a result a Luxembourg bankruptcy procedure can be launched against it. This may occur even if the group company's assets have a higher value than its liabilities.[3] Consequently, physical cash pooling increases the risk of a company being in a situation of cessation of payments and thus becoming bankrupt.

(e) *Management liability*

The possibility of liability arising for the company's management is discussed at section 2.1(a) below.

(f) *Conflict of interest*

The effect of rules on conflicts of interest is discussed at section 2.1(a) below.

2. Specific questions

2.1 Perspective A: corporate group

(a) *Liability of group company and/or master account holder directors in the event of insolvency of a group company*

From a company law perspective, it makes no difference if the troubled company is listed or is a private corporation. Directors are subject to the same management rules in either case.

However, listed companies are subject to specific information, public disclosure and group accounting rules which, in turn, require the management to take action, such as the obligation to disclose certain information in order to comply with the Market Abuse Act of May 9 2006 (as amended) or the Issuer Transparency Act of January 11 2008 (as amended).

Conflict of interest: In a Luxembourg *société anonyme* (joint stock company), a director who has a conflict between his personal interests and those of the company in any business or matter to be dealt with by a management meeting must promptly inform the meeting of the conflict, request that it be recorded in the minutes of the

3 Court of Appeal Decision 15508, January 28 1998.

meeting, and abstain from voting in relation to the matter in which there is a conflict.[4]

If a director sits on the board of several group companies, it may very well happen that the lawful interest of one group company conflicts with the interests of another group company. The director has similar duties to all companies to which he has been appointed and should therefore not prefer one company over another: he should declare a conflict of interest each time it is necessary. Failure to follow this procedure results in increased director liability (see below).

These rules apply only to directors of companies having their seat (ie, their true place of business) in Luxembourg.

Mismanagement: Directors of a Luxembourg company are agents of the company. As a general principle, when acting in the company's name, directors are not personally liable, but bind the company as regards third parties.

They can, however, be held liable in cases of misconduct. In that event, the trustee appointed in the context of bankruptcy of a Luxembourg group company could instigate several legal actions against the management, either on the basis of principles of ordinary management liability or on the basis of insolvency law.

These rules are applicable to both appointed and shadow management. A shadow or *de facto* director is defined by Luxembourg case law as "one who actually performs the management of the company in lieu of its statutory body or under its cover"[5] or as "he who appropriates the decisional power which rests with the directors and exercises it effectively, even with the consent of the latter, or who replaces the bodies of the company and freely makes decisions which are likely to bind it".[6]

A *de facto* manager is one who makes the decisions that affect the commercial and financial fate of companies.[7] This wide definition of a '*de facto* director' potentially covers other group companies and quite often the master account holder when it has a very strong influence over the management of another group company.

Ordinary management regulations: The Companies Act distinguishes between several types of civil management liability:[8]

- personal individual civil liability on the part of each director to the company for failure to manage some or all affairs of the company properly ('simple director liability'); and
- joint civil liability on the part of all directors to the company and to third parties for breaching the Companies Act or the bylaws of the company ('increased director liability').

---

4 Article 57 of the Law of August 10 1915 on Commercial Companies (as amended) (the Companies Act).

5 Court of Appeal, October 1 1997, List 12538, 12771, 12859, 12896 and 20243; Court of Appeal, July 10, 2002, BIJ 2004, p. 27.

6 Georges Ravarani, *"La responsabilité civile des personnes privées et publiques"*, 2e, *Pasicrisie*, 2006, No 561, p.456.

7 Rives-Lange, *La notion de dirigeant de fait*, Dalloz 1975, Chronique, page 43.

8 Articles 59 and 192 of the Companies Act.

Moreover, tort law is also applicable to management liability, including liability of the shadow management. The scope of liability of the management of a group company will be measured objectively against the average behaviour of a hypothetical normal director put in a similar situation. Civil liability rules generally apply to members of the management of companies having their effective place of business in Luxembourg.

Based on typical liability criteria considered by local courts, management liability in the context of a cash pooling agreement could, for instance, arise in the following situations if there is a loss to the group company:

- The cash pooling agreement in not in the company's corporate interest (see above);
- The cash pooling agreement is outside the company's corporate purpose (see above);
- The cash pooling agreement documentation is not valid, ineffective or voidable;
- The cash pooling agreement triggers unexpected legal, regulatory or tax consequences for the company;
- The cash pooling agreement has not been properly authorised;
- The obligations of the company under the cash pooling agreement result in limited cash availability in near-insolvency situations;
- Cross-guarantee obligations under the cash pooling agreement negatively impact on the company;
- The company is near insolvent but grants additional security to the bank or the master account holder;
- The cash pooling agreement increases the company's debts with no reasonable hope of rectifying the situation (eg, loans or advances are approved while the directors know that the company is virtually bankrupt); or
- The company is near insolvent but does not file a bankruptcy petition even though it has ceased payments (see above) and is unable to raise credit.

Appointed and shadow directors of a company can be further held criminally liable for misusing corporate assets when they have, in bad faith, used the corporate assets or the creditworthiness of the company in a way that they knew to be contrary to the company's interests, for personal use or for favouring another company or enterprise in which they had a direct or indirect interest.

Misuse of corporate assets is a criminal offence punishable by a jail term of one to five years and/or a fine from €500 to €25,000.[9] Luxembourg law will apply when the damaged company has its seat in Luxembourg or when the embezzlement itself has occurred in Luxembourg.

In a group context, an abuse of corporate assets will occur whenever the management of a group company has caused another group company to enter into a transaction that is to the management's own advantage and which they knew to be contrary to the second company's interests in that it jeopardises its assets or unnecessarily exposes the company to abnormal and serious risks.

9 Article 171-1 of the Companies Act.

Insolvency law: The following rules apply only to directors or the management of companies having their centre of main interest (as defined by the EU Insolvency Regulation (1346/2000)) in Luxembourg.

The court can decide that a company's directors should bear all or part of its debts if the directors' serious misconduct has led either to the company becoming insolvent or to the company's liabilities significantly increasing.

The so-called 'bankruptcy extension' is a court-ordered bankruptcy of the directors of an insolvent and bankrupt company. The liabilities of the bankrupt directors will include not only their personal liabilities, but also those of the insolvent company.

The court will order such a bankruptcy extension against each director (a person or a company) who personally meets both of the following conditions:[10]

- The director is bankrupt (ie, has suspended payments and is unable to raise credit); and
- The director has caused the company to act in his personal interest, has used the company's assets for his personal purposes or has carried on a loss-making business in his personal interest.

In practice, a bankruptcy extension is ordered when the director has mixed his assets and activities with those of the company.[11] A cash pooling agreement could, in specific circumstances, contribute to a so-called confusion of the assets of some or all of the group companies with those of the master account holder. In that case, the bankruptcy extension could apply.[12]

(b) Liability of group company and/or master account holder directors in the event of insolvency of the master account holder

The liability rules discussed at section 2.1(a) above could be generally applied to directors of the master account holder in the event of mismanagement of the company's affairs.

Should the master account holder get into financial difficulties, this may have an impact on the situation of group companies, and the directors of the group companies could be held liable unless they take particular precautions.

If the master account holder is near insolvent, its management should avoid:

- increasing their personal liabilities for no good reason;
- using the creditworthiness of group companies, by means of the cash pooling agreement, to delay an insolvency event;
- using funds belonging to group companies as collateral for existing or new creditors;
- creating artificial claims to the benefit of group companies, thus violating creditors' rights;
- not properly documenting management action;
- not informing shareholders of the problems;

---

10 Article 495, Code of Commerce.
11 TA Lux, January 25 1985, No 8/85.
12 TA Lux, July 9 1987, No 37623.

- not informing group companies of the problems; and
- not informing the bank of the near insolvency.

Also, in relation to *sociétés anonymes*, Luxembourg law provides that in the event of a loss of half the issued and paid-up corporate capital, the board of directors must convene a general meeting to be held within a period not exceeding two months from the time at which they became, or should have become, aware of the loss, and this meeting must pass a resolution on the possible dissolution of the company.[13] The general meeting remains free to dissolve the company.

Should management fail to comply with this provision, the directors may be declared personally and jointly and severally liable to the company for all or part of any increase in the loss.

In the context of physical cash pooling (where the group company's cash is replaced by a receivable against the master account holder), paying cash into the account of the master account holder does not, in itself, have any impact on the accounting situation of the group company. However, if the master account holder becomes less creditworthy, it will be necessary to create a reserve in the balance sheet of the group company, particularly when there is a risk that the master account holder will be unable to meet its payment obligations to the group company. These circumstances are likely to increase both the financial liability of the group company and its risk of potential loss, and could therefore trigger the requirement to call a general meeting to pass a resolution on the possible dissolution of the company[14] at the group company level.

(c) Liability of group companies in the event of insolvency of the master account holder

Luxembourg law will apply if the insolvent company has its place of business in Luxembourg.

Luxembourg law does not grant special protection to creditors of companies participating in cash pooling agreements.

Generally, the chances for a creditor of a company to have a direct and personal right against debtors of its debtor are very poor.

Indeed, under Luxembourg civil law, only direct and personal losses may give rise to damages. In other words, a creditor of the master account holder will not be entitled to claim any damages against a group company unless it shows that it has suffered a direct and personal loss, distinct from the loss incurred by the master account holder, because of misbehaviour by the group company.

As an exception, Luxembourg law allows creditors to take a legal actions in the place of a debtor by means of an indirect legal action.[15]

As an example, if the master account holder has a claim against a participant in a cash pooling scheme under an existing cash pooling agreement (eg, the group company owes money to the master account holder), and if the master account

13 Article 100 of the Companies Act.
14 Article 100 of the Companies Act.
15 Article 1166 of the Civil Code.

holder behaves in a passive manner (ie, does not enforce securities or take legal action against the group company), then the third party creditors of the master account holder can enforce the rights of the master account holder against the group company in place of the master account holder.

The indirect legal action is an option only as long as the master account holder has not been declared bankrupt. The indirect legal action by the creditor of the master account holder will be lodged on behalf of master account holder. Any proceeds recovered from the group company debtor belong to the master account holder (and not to its creditor). It is also conceivable that other participants in the cash pooling agreement (with a claim against the master account holder) can enforce the master account holder's rights against a group company debtor.

(d) Liability of master account holder in the event of insolvency of a group company

Luxembourg law does not set out a particular action for creditors of companies participating in cash pooling agreements.

Luxembourg law provides several actions that could be exercised by the creditors of a group company.

In the case of a group company that is in distress, but has not yet been declared bankrupt, there are two possible approaches:

- Indirect legal action – creditors could exercise the rights of the group company through an indirect legal action (as discussed in paragraph 2.1(c) above).
- Avoidance action – this action would enable the creditors to challenge, on their own behalf, transactions made by the group company defrauding them of their rights.[16] For example, in case of fraudulent collusion between the participants in the cash pooling agreements, creditors could act against that arrangement, which would obviously violate the obligation to observe the corporate interest of the group company In such case it would be irrelevant that the cash pooling agreement may have worked without a problem for many years prior to the avoidance action.

When a company is declared bankrupt under Luxembourg law, unsecured creditors are no longer entitled to take any legal action against the bankrupt company, or to take any indirect legal action against anyone owing something to the company. These restrictions apply from the time of the bankruptcy order.

Secured creditors are not in competition with unsecured creditors of the bankrupt company and may enforce their security interests under the Financial Collateral Act. The security interests that are preserved in the event of a bankruptcy under Luxembourg law include, in particular, pledges over cash, bank accounts, claims and securities, as well as set-off clauses and netting arrangements.

The court-appointed bankruptcy trustee acts against third parties, including other group companies, each time they appear to be responsible for losses suffered by the bankrupt company. This trustee could, in particular, ask for an extension of the group company's bankruptcy to the master account holder, or exercise a debt-

16 Article 1167 of the Civil Code.

contribution action, without prejudice to the other existing management liability actions, provided the relevant conditions are met (see section 2.1(a) above).

Furthermore, the bankruptcy trustee could also challenge a cash pooling agreement concluded during the suspect period or a transfer of cash made during this period (see section 2.3(a) below). If the arrangement or the transfer of cash is fraudulent, the trustee could seek to have them set aside even if they occurred before the suspect period.

2.2 Perspective B: bank

(a) Banking requirements

Luxembourg banks are subject to a prudential supervision of the Luxembourg financial sector watchdog, the *Commission de surveillance du secteur financier* (CSSF), and the Banking Act of April 5 1993 (as amended).

Luxembourg banks can freely enter into cash pooling agreements as part of their usual banking business activities (eg, taking deposits from the public), and no specific permits or authorisations are needed.

The Banking Act delegates the power to set a capital adequacy framework to the CSSF. The CSSF has issued a number of industry-binding circulars which may apply in the context of cash pooling, most notably Circular CSSF 06/273 (as amended), called 'the bible' by local bankers due to its impressive size.

Applicable international capital adequacy rules include the Basel standards as well as the large exposures rules created under EU Directive 2009/111 of September 16 2009, which were implemented by amendments to the Banking Act in 2011.

In the unlikely event that a bank is the parent company in a cash pooling set-up, the prudential supervision of the CSSF will apply to the financial situation of the bank and will cover its subsidiaries on a consolidated basis. Similarly, where a Luxembourg parent financial holding company has a subsidiary which is a regulated bank in Luxembourg, the prudential supervision of the CSSF applies to the entire group. Finally, where a parent financial holding company located in another EU member state has several subsidiaries in the European Union, including a regulated bank in Luxembourg, the CSSF may exercise its prudential supervision to the consolidated financial situation of the financial holding company if the Luxembourg regulated bank shows the largest balance sheet total.

(b) Liability of the bank in the event of insolvency of the master account holder or a group company

Luxembourg law does not have specific rules on the liability of the bank in the context of a cash pooling agreement.

Under the general law, liability on the part of the bank could arise in the event of mismanagement or misuse of corporate assets by the directors of a group company or the master account holder (see below).

Furthermore, if the bank was considered to be a shadow manager, liability rules described above could also be applied (see section 2.1(a)).

Civil liability for mismanagement: Luxembourg liability rules apply against a bank if the company in financial distress has its seat in Luxembourg. For example, creditors of a group company can sue the bank on the basis of tort law if the cash pooling agreement is not in the corporate interests of the group company and the bank was, or should have been, aware of this.

However, under the principle of non-interference, Luxembourg courts are not eager to hold a bank liable as long as the bank has duly fulfilled it duties to provide information and advice.[17]

Accomplice to misusing corporate assets: Luxembourg criminal law will always apply if the company suffering a loss has its effective place of business in Luxembourg or if the embezzlement has occurred in Luxembourg. Under Article 67 of the Criminal code, the following persons are generally regarded as accomplices to a criminal offence:

- anyone who has knowingly provided tools or any others means aiding commission of the offence;
- anyone who has knowingly helped or assisted the perpetrator in the course of the commission of the offence; and
- anyone who has helped or assisted the perpetrator by making the commission of the offence easier.

The criminal courts furthermore consider as perpetrators (rather than as accomplices) any persons or entities without whose assistance the offence could not have been perpetrated. Depending on the involvement of the bank in the context of cash pooling agreement being used for misusing corporate assets, the bank could be prosecuted as an accomplice or even as a perpetrator of the offence. There is, however, no Luxembourg case law publicly available on this point.

2.3 Insolvency

(a) Cash pooling agreements from the insolvency practitioner's perspective

Bank goes into liquidation – obligations of the administrator as regards the master account holder and group companies: Unless otherwise stated in the judgment ordering the judicial liquidation of a bank, the bank's administrator will not have any particular obligation towards the master account holder or the group companies, except to invite them to file a statement of claim, if they have one.

Creditors located abroad in principle have the same financial rights against a company declared bankrupt in Luxembourg as those residing in Luxembourg.

In the case of physical cash pooling agreements, only the master account holder is entitled to claim the credit balance of the master account through a statement of claim to be filed with the the bank's liquidator. As this claim is likely to be unsecured, even if its statement of claim is accepted, the master account holder will not receive

17 Luxembourg District Court, March 19 2008, No 101 588.

payment of the entire balance and will be in competition with other creditors.

In the case of notional cash pooling, the master account holder and group companies are in principle entitled to claim the balance of their respective accounts by filing a statement of claim with the bank's liquidator. These claims would both be unsecured.

Master account holder goes into liquidation – obligations of the administrator as regards the bank and group companies: Unless it is otherwise agreed in the cash pooling agreement, the master account holder's administrator will not have any particular obligation towards the bank and the group companies, except to collect any funds in the master account holder's bank account and to invite the group companies and bank to file statements of claim.

Group company goes into liquidation – obligations of the administrator as regards the master account holder and the bank: Again, unless it is otherwise stated in the cash pooling agreement, the group company's administrator will not have any special obligations towards the bank and the master account holder, except to collect the funds in the company's bank account and to invite the master account holder and the bank to file statements of claim.

Voidability of transactions: When declaring a company bankrupt, the Luxembourg courts define a so-called 'suspect period' of six months preceding the date of the opening of the bankruptcy. This period may theoretically be shorter, but in practice the court usually refers to six months.

If the bankrupt company made a transfer of money during the suspect period (or even during the 10 days before the beginning of the suspect period), the court-appointed bankruptcy trustee may petition for the setting aside of this transfer if:[18]

- the bankrupt company received no consideration for the payment or only consideration of a lower value;
- the transfer is payment of an unmatured debt;
- the recipient was aware of the cessation of payments by the bankrupt company and creditors' interests are at stake; or
- the transfer of money is a fraudulent payment (in which case the payment may be challenged even if it occurred before the suspect period).

For a payment to be fraudulent, the three following conditions need to be met:[19]

- The debtor paid fraudulently;
- The party receiving the fraudulent payment is an accomplice; and
- The loss suffered by creditors is due to the fraudulent payment.

Luxembourg courts recognise insolvency orders delivered by courts of other EU member states in accordance with EU Regulation 1346/2000 on insolvency

18 Articles 445, 446 and 448 of the Code of Commerce.
19 Court of Appeal, December 17 2008.

proceedings. In addition, Luxembourg recognises insolvency orders from non-EU jurisdictions, provided that all of the following conditions are met:

- The court that made the order had jurisdiction to hear the case;
- Proceedings were properly conducted;
- No fraud was involved in the context of the proceedings having started the insolvency;
- The order complies with Luxembourg international public policy rules; and
- The insolvency order has an extraterritorial impact.

Due to this recognition, the insolvency orders have the same effect as they would have in their original jurisdiction with the exception of those effects which would manifestly violate Luxembourg public policy rules, a concept that is not easy to define.

As a result, if the foreign insolvency order allows the foreign administrator to act abroad and to take all useful measures, a foreign administrator could challenge any suspect transfers of money in accordance with the law of his jurisdiction against a recipient located in Luxembourg.

(b) Special rules as regards creditors of other parties to the cash pooling agreement

In a context of bankruptcy or judicial liquidation, the administrator has no specific obligations in relation to creditors of the debtor's creditors. The administrator could, however, exercise an indirect action against the creditors of the debtor's obligors (see section 2.1(c) above).

(c) Dissolution/termination of the cash pooling agreement in the event of liquidation of the master account holder or a group company

Bankruptcy of master account holder: Upon the opening of a bankruptcy proceeding under Luxembourg law affecting the master account holder, the trustee in bankruptcy of the master account holder will play the key role in relation to the cash pooling agreement.

The trustee will typically review all agreements binding the bankrupt company as soon as possible after his appointment. Some agreements will have come to an automatic end because they contain provision for automatic termination in the event of bankruptcy of one or several parties (or because the law says so – for instance, for employment contracts). Other agreements may provide a procedure for terminating them.

Agreements that have not come to an automatic end essentially continue, and the trustee or the other parties to such an agreement must either terminate them in accordance with their provisions (notice period, written termination notice etc) or negotiate and agree an exit with the other parties.

Although the trustee has no extra powers of termination, he will effectively put an end to any physical cash pooling agreement, since the master account and the other bank accounts of the bankrupt company will, in practice, be blocked by and for the sole benefit of the trustee. Since the trustee has a legal mission to liquidate the master account holder, he would not want to continue the activities of the bankrupt entity, particularly when continuing agreements would mean increasing the liabilities of this entity. Trying to terminate all agreements would be a normal course of action.

Bankruptcy of a group company: Upon the opening of a bankruptcy proceeding in respect of a group company, the trustee in bankruptcy will also review all agreements as possible. If the cash pooling agreement contains no automatic termination clause or mechanism, the trustee will attempt to negotiate an exit – taking care, however, that existing rights of the bankrupt company are not jeopardised by this termination. The powers of the master account holder (to terminate or not) will be contained in the cash pooling agreement. Post-bankruptcy set-off is subject to limitations under Luxembourg law, unless the set-off provisions are considered a financial collateral arrangement under the Law on Financial Collateral.

Bankruptcy of the bank: The bank will not be put into bankruptcy under Luxembourg law, but placed under a special judicial liquidation proceeding provided for by Articles 61 to 61-22 of the Banking Act of April 5 1993 (as amended).

There are only minor differences in the way that judicial liquidations of banks are handled as compared to the bankruptcy proceedings applicable to non-banking (trade) companies.

The Banking Act empowers the courts to define the liquidation mode of a bank – that is, the way the liquidator will treat the creditors and their claims, the rights of the liquidator and so on. Legal provisions governing bankruptcy are not applicable to the judicial liquidation of banks unless otherwise stated in the liquidation order.

Typically, the banking licence is revoked by the local financial supervisory authority on the opening of the liquidation procedure. As a result, the bank cannot continue to carry out operations under a cash pooling agreement.

2.4 Perspective D: regulatory

In principle, no one other than a credit institution may carry on the business of taking deposits or other repayable funds from the public. As such, physical cash pooling will be considered as a banking activity and requires a banking licence in accordance with Article 2 of the Banking Act.

However, Article 1-1 of that act provides for an exemption for persons that provide a service exclusively to one or more undertakings forming part of the same group as the person providing the service. Therefore, cash pooling in intra-group structures is exempt from the licensing requirement.

2.5 Perspective E: tax authority

There is no specific Luxembourg tax impact with respect to notional cash pooling, since it does not involve cash movements. Normal taxation of profits will apply. Therefore, the analysis below deals only with physical cash pooling.

(a) Transfer pricing issues

Under Luxembourg administrative tax practice, it has been possible for several years to establish intra-group financing companies in Luxembourg. Typically, the tax base of these companies has been determined by applying a margin on the amount of the financing in advance tax clearances granted on a case-by-case basis.

The Luxembourg tax authorities have issued Circular 164/2 dated January 28 2011, taking into account the Organisation for Economic Cooperation and Development (OECD) transfer pricing guidelines, including developments on intra-group interest-bearing financing. This circular gives clear and specific rules regulating advanced tax clearances for intra-group financing activities.

The circular confirms that its scope covers 'group financing companies'. This term is defined as any company carrying out mainly intra-group financing activity disregarding activities in relation to the holding of participations. It is not entirely clear whether master account holders under a cash pooling agreements are group financing companies within the meaning of the circular.

Certain tax practitioners seem to consider that cash pooling agreements are generally not subject to the circular, unless these agreements provide the framework for intra-group financing. It is, however, advisable to seek informal input from the local tax authorities when setting up a cash pooling scheme, since physical cash movements between group companies and the master account holder could well be seen as intra-group loans. Indeed, from a Luxembourg accounting standpoint, physical cash movements are accounted as short or long-term debts.

Opposite is a simplified illustration of the accounting treatment for two group companies, one (Lux Co 2) having €100 of cash and one (Lux Co 1) having a deficit of €100.

In Luxembourg, the tax treatment follows the accounting treatment. Therefore, for tax purposes, the cash movements will also be treated as loans.

The circular requires that group financing companies (as defined in the circular) comply with the following conditions in order to obtain an advance pricing agreement from the Luxembourg tax authorities:

- The company must provide a transfer pricing analysis, including a risk analysis, comparability studies, market studies, a description of relevant transfer pricing methodologies used in the case at hand, and based on the OECD principles.
- The company must comply with certain so-called 'substance rules' showing that it is deeply rooted in Luxembourg (eg, the majority of board members, whether individuals or companies, must reside in Luxembourg for tax purposes or, if non-Luxembourg resident, be taxable for at least 50% of their professional income in Luxembourg; board meetings must be held in Luxembourg; at least one general meeting of shareholders must take place in Luxembourg; the company must have a bank account in Luxembourg).
- The group financing company must have equity (share capital and share premium) equivalent to at least 1% of the total financing or €2 million.

An advance pricing agreement is valid for five tax years and is binding on the tax authorities. After this period, an application for a new advance pricing agreement must be filed.

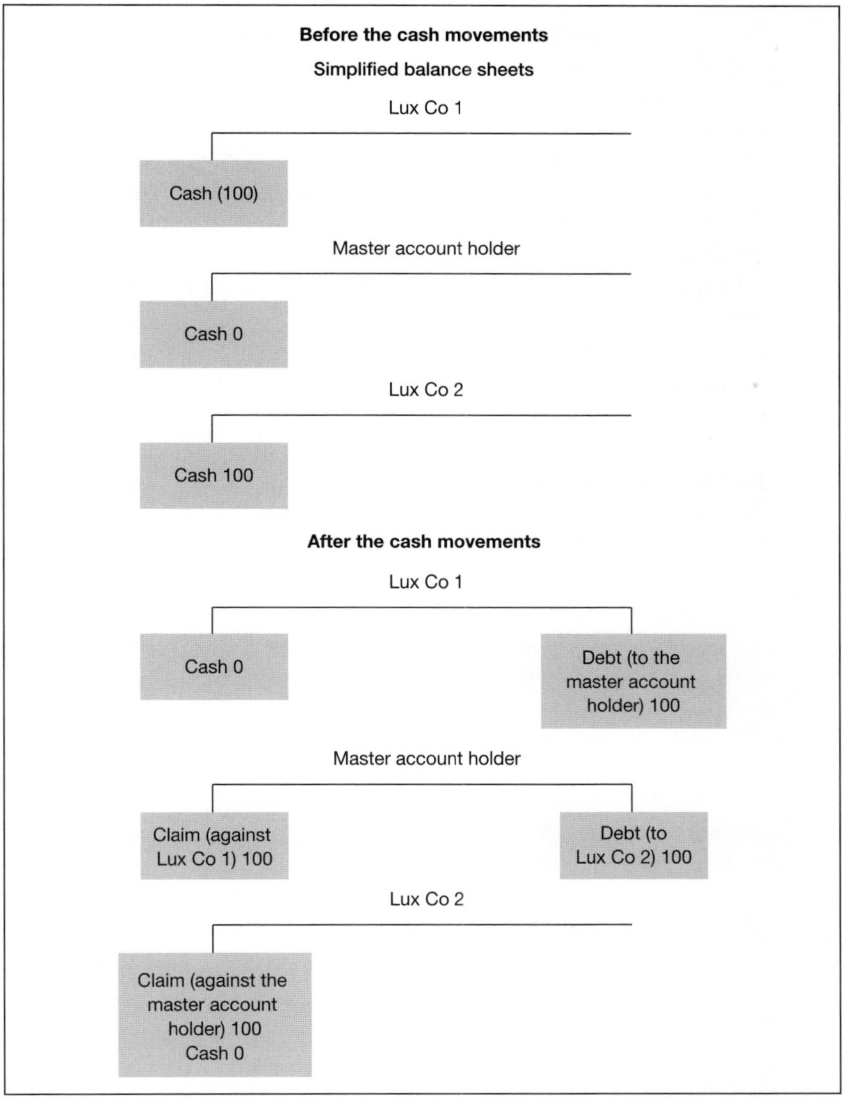

(b) *Luxembourg withholding tax*

In principle, there is no withholding tax on interest paid by a Luxembourg company to either a Luxembourg or a foreign company. Accordingly, a Luxembourg bank or a Luxembourg master account holder paying interest to a group member does not need to withhold taxes, and neither does a Luxembourg group member paying interest to another group member, to the master account holder or to the bank (regardless of its tax residency).

In addition, interest paid by a Luxembourg resident company can be deducted from its taxable basis (provided the interest does not relate to exempt income).

As an exception, there is a 35% withholding tax on interest paid to so-called 'residual entities' based outside Luxembourg in the European Union, in accordance with the EU Directive 2003/48/EEC.

A residual entity is basically a (non-Luxembourg) partnership without a legal personality and that is not taxed on its "profits under the general arrangements for business taxation" within the meaning of EU Directive 85/611/EEC.

In the context of a cash pooling agreement, there is a certain risk of re-characterisation of the interest paid by a Luxembourg resident company as dividend distributions. It may therefore be in the interest of the cash pooling agreement participants to seek an informal advance tax clearance from the Luxembourg tax authorities.

In the event of a re-characterisation, the payment will be subject to withholding tax at a rate of 15%, unless a double tax treaty provides for a reduced rate or an exemption, or the Luxembourg version of the parent-subsidiary exemption applies.

(c) *Luxembourg income taxes*

Interest received by a Luxembourg resident company is in principle fully subject to corporate income tax and municipal business tax at an aggregate rate of 28.8% in Luxembourg City.

Mexico

Darío U Oscós
Oscós Abogados

1. Introduction

1.1 Admissibility of cash pooling agreements

In Mexico, it is neither explicitly nor implicitly forbidden by law for corporations to enter into a cash pooling agreement or for holding companies to set up a cash pooling agreement with group members. A cash pooling agreement may be enter into on the basis of freedom of contract. Both notional pooling and physical cash pooling are permitted.

In Mexico, there is no provision or regulation explicitly recognising the concept of a corporate group. Accordingly, although there may be a group of companies as a fact, this group by itself has no individuality as a different legal entity separate from that of the member companies. That is, the group of companies does not constitute a new legal entity different from its members. In general, the corporate group is a factual economic group composed of holding and subsidiary companies, which from the point of view of Mexican corporate law are not consolidated. For tax purposes, there is optional consolidation for a group of companies. The Law of Financial Groups provides for some joint and several liabilities towards creditors on the part of the holding company and subsidiaries. In labour law there is a similar situation as to the joint and several obligations of the employer and what may be considered under labour law a 'substitute employer'. A substitute employer is an alternative employer that has equivalent labour links with the employees in question to those of the main employer, and may be jointly and severally liable to the employees.

1.2 Types of cash pooling agreement

The cash pooling agreements used in Mexico encompass both notional cash pooling and physical cash pooling.

The purpose of cash pooling is to bring together credit and debit balances. The two alternative approaches are notional pooling and cash concentration. With notional pooling, the actual funds do not move, but the bank will combine the balances of several accounts and pay or charge interest on the combined balance only. Cash concentration is where the funds are physically moved into a single combined account (the master account or concentration account). Zero balancing and flexible balancing are the two most commonly known methods of implementing cash concentration.

With notional pooling, the close-of-day balances across all participants' accounts are notionally netted. This can be technically implemented by establishing a parent-child relationship between the accounts, with the parent account being a dummy account which provides the notional balance entries.

In cash concentration, funds are physically moved from the accounts of the cash pooling participants to a single concentration account by means of account entry transfer. Zero balancing, the most traditional method of cash concentration, sweeps all credit balances of the source accounts to the concentration account. Debit balances are covered in the same way by a sweep from the concentration account.

Flexible balancing is an extension of zero balancing with the possibility of applying target balances (ie, a cap or floor) to each account in the cash pool. The caps and floors are used to keep group liquidity up to a certain level without manually transferring entries back from the concentration account, as would be necessary with zero balancing.

Technical methods and algorithms of account entry transfer are the basis of every cash concentration implementation. The task of the algorithm is to ensure that the sub-accounts have a constant/zero balance, and that all funds are transferred to the concentration account for the duration of the cash pooling agreement.[1]

1.3 Legal requirements from various perspectives

Under Mexican law, there are no specific legal requirements in respect of cash pooling agreements.

Banking transactions are governed by the Credit Institutions Law and banking regulations, which allow commercial banks to enter into a cash pooling agreement with a group of companies by means of a master banking account. The cash pooling agreement must be in writing, providing the terms and conditions of the agreement. In some instances, there may be a need for pre-authorisation from the Banking and Securities Commission. Public companies' involvement must comply with the Securities Market Law on capital maintenance provisions, corporate governance, risk management and reporting requirements. Public companies must periodically file with the Mexican Stock Exchange financial statements including details of inter-company transactions and cash pooling in order to show they are complying with the applicable regulations. These statements are available for public access through the Internet or from the Mexican Stock Exchange. Private companies must also comply with provisions of the General Law on Commercial Companies on capital maintenance, corporate governance, risk management and reporting requirements. Under the Commercial Insolvency Law, in the event of insolvency proceedings in respect of a group company, the cash pooling agreement remains in effect and will be enforced unless it is terminated by the insolvency trustee. Assets and obligations under the agreement are included in the insolvency estate. With regard to a cross-border cash pooling agreement, in the event of insolvency, only domestic assets and liabilities are brought into the insolvency estate of the domestic group company. The Income Tax Law is provisions on corporate tax consolidation must be followed, iby both domestic and foreign group companies.

---

1 Messner Wolfgang, "The Practice of Cash Pooling" *BIT Banking and Information Technology* 4/2001, p 25 (The Information Management Group, IMG Franfurt am Main).

2. Specific questions

2.1 Perspective A: corporate group

(a) Liability of group company and/or master account holder directors in the event of insolvency of a group company

Although an insolvent group company is no longer able to meet its payment obligations under the cash pooling agreement, there is no risk of liability on the part of directors of the group company or directors of the master account holder in the absence of fraud, default of fiduciary duties or mismanagement. If a company is in distress but nevertheless allows the periodic sweep of its bank accounts to continue, it may be grounds for directors' liability if such continued sweeping does not benefit the distressed company. In such case the cash pooling agreement will be terminated by the administrator (trustee). If termination is contractually forbidden or excluded in the event of insolvency proceedings, the Commercial Insolvency Law provides that that contractual provision will be void and the amounts swept will be returned to the estate.

In Mexico, filing for insolvency is optional, there is no mandatory requirement and it may be instigated by the insolvent debtor or its creditors.

Pre-existing obligations are suspended upon the initiation of insolvency proceedings and may not be paid. Pre-existing obligations under a cash pooling agreement are subject to the filing of proof of claim. Pre-existing obligations may not be offset against any rights to collect moneys that the insolvent company has under the cash pooling agreement, they belong to the insolvency estate.

Unlawful distributions may be revoked by set-aside or avoidance actions. Transactions involving *ultra vires*, conflict of interest or mismanagement may also be avoided by such actions. There is no piercing of the corporate veil with regard to the group company, since there is no consolidation of the corporate group under corporate law. Each legal group company keeps its own personality and independence from the corporate group. However, in cases of insolvency in which there is criminal fraud there may be piercing of the corporate veil of the group company and the corporate group in respect of liability on the part of their directors.

In that regard, it makes no difference whether the insolvent company is a listed corporation or a privately held corporation, although regulations as to governance of listed corporations may impose on the directors of such corporations particular fiduciary and reporting duties in respect of cash pooling agreements and insolvency issues.

The bank's being registered in a foreign jurisdiction will make no difference as to the treatment of the cash pooling agreement's master account. However, if the distressed group company is registered in a foreign jurisdiction and has a commercial establishment or branch in Mexico, only transactions performed by the branch will be subject to the domestic insolvency proceeding.

(b) ***Liability of group company and/or master account holder directors in the event of insolvency of the master account holder***

If the master account holder, rather than a group company, becomes insolvent, the legal situation is the same as described in paragraph (a) above, with the necessary changes being read in as to which party is which.

(c) ***Liability of group companies in the event of insolvency of the master account holder***

Mexican law does not give the creditors of an insolvent master account holder a legal right to hold other group companies liable for any losses suffered, except where a cross-guarantee or contractual joint and several liability has been agreed by a group company. Mexican law does not provide for or regulate corporate groups as a legal concept.

It is irrelevant whether the master account holder, the claiming creditor or the the group company is located in Mexico.

(d) ***Liability of the master account holder in the event of insolvency of a group company***

If a group company, rather than the master account holder, becomes insolvent, the situation is the same as described in paragraph (c) above, with the necessary changes being read in as to which party is which.

2.2 Perspective B: bank

(a) ***Banking requirements***

Banks are allowed to enter into a cash pooling agreement with a corporate group. A bank entering into a cash pooling agreement with a corporate group will not be subject to any specific local or global requirements in Mexico merely because it has entered into a cash pooling agreement. However, there are general legal and regulatory requirements governing banks' capital and security structures, as well as their liquidity. Basel standards also apply. Although commercial banks have standard formats for cash pooling agreements, any individual cash pooling agreement will be tailor made. Banks may require cross-guarantees and will have to make sure that each member is not acting *ultra vires* with regard to its legal authority to enter into the cash pooling agreement and the cross-guarantees. Issues of set-off between the bank and group companies will be reviewed, since under some circumstances set-off is not allowed. For instance, under Mexican law, financial institutions may not offset their accounts receivable against deposits held by their clients. When entering into a cash pooling agreement with a corporate group, banks should pay attention to general banking and financial regulations such as the Credit Institutions Law, the Law Regulating Financial Groups, the Securities Market Law, the Bank of Mexico Law, and associated regulations, as well as to financial regulators such as the National Banking and Securities Commission, the Bank of Mexico and the secretary of finance and public credit. Regard should also be given to the Commercial Insolvency Law. Describing the features of these laws and regulations would, however, be beyond the scope of this chapter, because of their general applicability which does not specifically focus on cash pooling agreements.

(b) Liability of the bank in the event of insolvency of the master account holder or a group company

The bank involved in the cash pooling agreement will not be liable for any losses due to the master account holder or a group company going into insolvency, unless the bank's failure in respect of its duties and obligations under the cash pooling agreement affects the insolvent company's rights or obligations, or the bank's failure in respect of its duties or obligations or fraud on its part under the cash pooling agreement causes or aggravates the insolvency.

Whether the master account holder, the claiming creditor or the group company is located in Mexico does not affect the liability of the bank involved in the cash pooling agreement.

2.3 Insolvency

(a) Cash pooling agreements from the insolvency practitioner's perspective

Under Mexican insolvency law, with regard to the enforcement of pre-insolvency contractual obligations under a cash pooling agreement, in the event that the agreement gives an entitlement to claim the entire credit balance, there will be grounds for the insolvency administrator of the bank, the master account holder or a group company to claim the entire credit balance or, that entity's part of the credit balance, as provided for in the agreement. Mexican law does not provide for corporate groups; therefore, enforcement of a cash pooling agreement will mostly be an issue of the terms and conditions agreed under it and applicable law (banking, commercial and civil).

If an administrator is appointed in Mexico, the administrator may take legal action seeking recovery of the credit balance. If an administrator is appointed abroad, then a Mexican administrator will also have to be appointed, who will enforce recovery actions in Mexico.

If the bank goes into liquidation, the administrator must pursue immediate collection of credit balances (even where there are protection measures), enforce the bank's rights under the cash pooling agreement and terminate the agreement if convenient.

Those obligations must also be observed if the master account holder or a group company has its seat in another jurisdiction.

The above also applies, subject to necessary changes, in the event that either the master account holder or a group company goes into liquidation.

If the bankrupt master account holder has transferred money to group companies prior to its bankruptcy or the group company has transferred money to its master account prior to the bankruptcy, such transfers qualify as fraudulent transfers and they fall within the voidable period (270 calendar days prior to the commencement of insolvency proceedings, or longer by court order), the administrator has legal standing to bring avoidance and set-aside actions before the court to recover the amounts as part as the bankruptcy estate.

Only a Mexican administrator may bring set-aside actions. If there is a foreign administrator, a Mexican administrator must be appointed, who in turn may enforce avoidance actions.

(b) Special rules as regards creditors of other parties to the cash pooling agreement

In Mexico, there are no special rules or obligations as regards the creditors of other parties to the cash pooling agreement. However, notice shall be given to the other parties of collection by the administrator of any credit balance in the master account that belongs to the insolvency estate, termination of the cash pooling agreement and related issues.

Other parties to the cash pooling agreement may enforce their rights in the liquidation by filing proof of claim and enforcing their rights under the agreement.

(c) Dissolution/termination of the cash pooling agreement in the event of liquidation of the master account holder or a group company

In the event of liquidation of the master account holder, the group companies may not terminate the cash pooling agreement. The Commercial Insolvency Law provides that any such contractual provision shall be void in event of the filing of an insolvency petition, and contractual obligations must be amended when they exacerbate the position of the insolvent; for instance, when a termination right is granted to a group company in the cash pooling agreement, but termination would have a material adverse effect on the insolvent company. On the other hand, if the cash pooling agreement does not benefit the insolvent company, the Mexican administrator may dissolve or terminate the agreement by giving notice to the other parties to the agreement. Under the Commercial Insolvency Law, other parties to the cash pooling agreement may ask the administrator whether he wishes to terminate the agreement. If the administrator decides that it will be enforced, then the administrator must guarantee fulfilment. In the event that the administrator does not oppose termination, or does not answer a request as to his intentions with regard to enforcement, the other party may terminate the cash pooling agreement. The same applies as regards liquidation of a group company or the bank.

2.4 Perspective D: regulatory

As noted in section 2.2(a), commercial banks are allowed to enter into a cash pooling agreement with a corporate group. There are specific legal and regulatory requirements governing banks' capital and security structures, as well as their liquidity. Basel standards may apply as well. Although commercial banks have standard formats for cash pooling agreements, an individual cash pooling agreement will be tailor made. Banks may require cross-guarantees and will have to make sure that each member is not acting *ultra vires* as to its legal authority to enter into the cash pooling agreement and the cross-guarantee. Issues of set-off between the bank and group companies should be reviewed, since under some circumstances set-off by a bank is not allowed. When entering into a cash pooling agreement with a corporate group, the bank should give consideration to banking and financial regulations such as the Credit Institutions Law, the Securities Market Law, the Law Regulating

Financial Groups, and the Bank of Mexico Law and associated regulations, as well as to financial regulators such as the National Banking and Securities Commission and the Bank of Mexico. Regard should also be had to the Commercial Insolvency Law as regards set-aside actions on fraudulent transfers, inter-company debt, financial and banking transactions pending execution and criminal law issues. Applicable corporate, securities, tax and insolvency law should be complied with as to dividends, loans, inter-company debt, tax and withholding tax related to the entering into and execution of cash pooling agreements. Describing the features of these laws and regulations would, however, be beyond the scope of this chapter, because of their general applicability which does not specifically focus on cash pooling agreements.

2.5 Perspective E: tax

In Mexico, the Income Tax Law and the Value Added Tax Law may have a tax impact on cash pooling agreements in relation to interest, fees, considerations, set-off, transfer pricing issues, dividends, equity, variations on exchange rates of foreign currency and withholding taxes. The Income Tax Law provides for the optional tax consolidation of a group of companies so long as specific standards are met, including when there are foreign group companies. In the case of foreign participants in a cash pooling agreement, issues relating to withholding taxes, cross-border tax treaties and deductions should also be considered. Describing the features of these laws and regulations would, however, be beyond the scope of this chapter, because of their general applicability which does not specifically focus on cash pooling agreements.

Netherlands

Joris van Horzen
Kennedy van der Laan NV

1. Introduction

1.1 Admissibility of cash pooling agreements

Under Dutch law, it is permissible for Dutch group companies to participate in a cash pooling agreement and for the treasury department of a Dutch parent company to set up a cash pooling agreement with (foreign) group companies.

1.2 Types of cash pooling agreement

Notional pooling is widely offered in the Netherlands. Banks also offer different options for physical cash pooling. The most commonly used options are:

- zero balancing;
- target balancing;
- constant balancing; and
- trigger balancing

For a description of zero and target balancing, reference is made to the introduction of this book. With constant balancing, the credit balances on the participating sub-accounts of the group companies are swept daily to the master account of the parent company, provided that the pre-agreed minimum constant balance always remains on the sub-accounts.[1] This means that only surplus balances are swept to the master account. If the balance of a sub-account drops below the constant balance level, it will be supplemented from the master account by means of a downstream sweep.

Under trigger balancing, the sub-accounts are swept only when their balances exceed a pre-determined level. As a result, the frequency of sweeping is irregular. The level of the trigger is set for both credit and debit balances.

Banks usually extend a credit facility related to the cash pooling agreement in the form of an overnight limit for the master account and an intra-day limit for the sub-accounts.[2] When a bank assigns intra-day limits to the sub-accounts, these sub-accounts may be overdrawn up to a certain amount during the day. This is generally needed when the sub-accounts are zero balanced. With an intra-day credit facility,

1 See *International Cash Management* by L van der Wielen in cooperation with W van Alphen, J Bergen and P Lindow.
2 See *International Cash Management.*

the group companies can make payments provided that the intra-day limit is not exceeded.

For reasons explained in section 2.2 below, it is common practice in the Netherlands that (a combination of) the following security rights be included in the cash pooling documentation:

- a right of pledge; and
- joint and several liability;
- a right to set-off; and/or
- a parent guarantee.

These security rights will in principle not be required with zero balancing, since the value balance on the sub-accounts will always be zero.

(a) Right of pledge

If the pool is located in the Netherlands, banks normally require that each group company grant a first ranking right of pledge on the credit balances of its sub-account(s) as security for the payment of all present and future obligations of any other group company to the bank under the cash pooling agreement. This is a form of cross-collaterisation. If the pool is located outside the Netherlands, banks will in general ensure joint and several liability of all group companies and the master account holder as an alternative.

(b) Joint and several liability

Under joint and several liability, each group company (and the parent company/master account holder) is jointly and severally liable for the secured liabilities. In order to prevent the group companies from exercising their right of recourse against another group company – which could potentially interfere with the bank's security rights – it is not unusual for this recourse rights to be subordinated to all rights of the bank as regards the group companies. Depending on the position of a group company within the group, joint and several liability is similar to an upstream, downstream or cross-stream guarantee.

(c) Right to set-off

In addition to a right of pledge or joint and several liability, banks often require a contractual right of set-off under which the bank may offset any amounts arising from the sub-accounts due from it to each group company (ie, any credit balances) against any amounts arising from the sub-accounts due to the bank by each group company (ie, any debit balances), regardless of the currencies in which the balances are held. As a result, the bank is entitled to offset, for example, the credit balance on the sub-account of group company A against the debit balance on the sub-account of group company B. This is an important contractual deviation from the statutory right of set-off,[3] under which claims to be set off must be between the same parties, acting in the same capacity, so that in the event of debts and rights between three or

3 As laid down in Article 6:127 of the Civil Code and Articles 53-54 and 234-235 of the Bankruptcy Act.

more parties, there is in principle no mutuality. It is generally accepted that these kinds of contractual set-off provisions will be effective if, and to the extent that, the effect will remain within the parameters established by the statutory set-off provisions of the Civil Code and the Bankruptcy Act.

As a result of the global financial crisis, numerous clients now demand a similar right of set-off from the bank. The rationale for a reciprocal right of set-off is that it would provide similar security to the client in the event that the bank becomes subject to insolvency proceedings. Another reason for a client to request a reciprocal right of set-off is to be able to comply with International Accounting Standard IAS 32.42. This is one of the requirements in order to be allowed to report various account balances on a net basis in the company's (consolidated) annual accounts. IAS 32.42 provides that:

> *A financial asset and a financial liability shall be offset and the net amount presented in the balance sheet when, and only when, an entity:*
>
> 1. *currently has a legally enforceable right to set off the recognized amounts; and*
> 2. *intends (i) either to settle on a net basis, or (ii) to realize the asset and settle the liability simultaneously.*

Most banks, however, are unwilling to agree to this. As a result of a reciprocal right of set-off, not only the bank but also the client may take the initiative to offset. This could potentially interfere with the bank's interests – for example, in the event of a restructuring of a distressed group in favour of the bank.[4] Apart from that, specific group companies may also be worse off if a reciprocal right of set-off is included. Whereas previously only the bank could decide to offset the rights of a group company against debt balances of other affiliates, now the parent company (or, depending on the wording of the reciprocal right of set-off, another affiliate) can also decide to exercise its set-off right.

(d) Parent guarantee

Under a parent guarantee, the parent company (being the master account holder) unconditionally and irrevocably guarantees to the bank the payment by other group companies of the secured liabilities and agrees to pay those liabilities to the bank on request.

1.3 Specific legal requirements from various perspectives

Apart from the regulatory requirements mentioned in section 2.2 below, there are no specific legal requirements with respect to cash pooling agreements in the Netherlands.

1.4 General legal requirements

When entering into a cash pooling agreement, the following general Dutch legal concepts could be relevant.

---

4 Think of a situation whereby a bank (in its capacity of security agent) ring fences the solvent group companies from the distressed group companies. If the distressed group companies were to have a reciprocal right of set-off, they would be entitled to offset their debit balances against the credit balances of the solvent group companies.

(a) Ultra vires

The validity and enforceability of a legal act (eg, a cash pooling agreement or the security rights) may be affected by the issue of *ultra vires* as laid down in Article 2:7 of the Civil Code. This provision gives a company the right to annul any legal act in relation to another party if:

- that legal act cannot serve the objects of that company; and
- the other party knew, or should have known, that the company's objects had been exceeded.

Only the company itself, which includes its trustee in bankruptcy, is entitled to invoke the *ultra vires* provision.

The question of whether entering into a legal act serves the objects of a company depends on all circumstances of the case. The most important circumstance is the wording of the objects clause in the company's articles of association. If the granting of security is not specifically allowed, there is an increased *ultra vires* risk. Accordingly, the objects clause of each group company's articles of association must always be verified before entering into a cash pooling agreement. If the wording of the objects clause does not allow for the granting of security, the articles of association will have to be amended. However, even in the event that the wording of the objects clause specifically allows for the granting of security, there is still no absolute certainty under Dutch law as to whether any particular transaction would be regarded to be in furtherance of the company's objects.

Another important circumstance is whether it is in the group company's own interests to participate in a cash pooling agreement – that is, whether and to what extent the group company derives benefits therefrom. In this context, the Supreme Court of the Netherlands has rendered an important decision. In the so-called *Rivier de Lek Case*,[5] the Supreme Court ruled that a facility granted to the parent company with the purpose of supporting the undertakings of the entire group should in principle be deemed to be in the interests of all group companies. This will be the case even if the group company has not directly received any loans under the facility.

One of the benefits of a cash pooling agreement is that it leads to an improvement of interest earnings and payments results. With zero balancing, it also gives the cash manager a better understanding of, and control over, the balances on the sub-accounts, and makes it possible, for example, to invest the credit balance on the master account in the money market. Obviously, the group companies will – indirectly at least – also derive benefits from such arrangements. One should also bear in mind, as mentioned in section 1.2 above, that banks usually also extend a credit facility related to the cash pooling agreement in the form of an intra-day limit for the sub-accounts. With an intra-day credit facility, the group companies can always make payments, provided that the intra-day limit is not exceeded.

In view of the above, there are good grounds to argue that all group companies can be deemed to benefit from a cash pooling agreement, even if:

---

5 HR April 18 2003, JOR 2003/160.

- with zero balancing, the group companies will lose their financial independence to the parent company; and
- with notional pooling, the group companies grant one or more security rights in favour of the bank.

As a result, a cash pooling agreement does not, in principle, conflict with the corporate objects of the relevant group companies. To date, there is no Dutch case law that would suggest otherwise.

(b) ***Fraudulent conveyance***

Under Article 42 of the Bankruptcy Act, a trustee in bankruptcy is entitled, for the benefit of the bankruptcy estate, to annul a legal act performed by the company if:

- the legal act was voluntary (ie, it was not a contractual or statutory obligation);
- the legal act adversely affects the company's creditors; and
- unless the legal act was performed for no consideration, both the company and the third party with which the company transacted knew, or should have known, that such an adverse effect would result from the legal act (the 'knowledge test').

These three criteria must all be met. This action is known as the *actio Pauliana*. A similar action is available for creditors outside a bankruptcy on the basis of Article 3:45 of the Civil Code (which does not substantially differ from Article 42 of the Bankruptcy Act).

The knowledge test is not satisfied by looking at the potential consequences of a legal act. According to consistent case law of the Supreme Court, the mere risk that an adverse effect may materialise is not sufficient. It must have been known by the parties, or they should have known, that the adverse effect would in fact materialise.[6] The rationale behind this is that there is obviously a need for legal certainty in commercial transactions.

However, Article 43 of the Bankruptcy Act[7] states that if the legal act which adversely affected one or more creditors was performed within one year prior to the bankruptcy, and if the company was not already legally bound to perform that act before the beginning of that period, the knowledge test is presumed to be satisfied on both sides, in the absence of evidence to the contrary:

- in the case of contracts in which the value of the companies' obligation considerably exceeds that of the other party's obligation;
- in the case of legal acts constituting payment of, or security for, a debt not yet due and payable; and
- in the case of legal acts performed between two group companies.

---

6 See, for example, the decisions of the Supreme Court of October 1 1993, NJ 1994,257(*Pellikaan*) and November 17 2000, NJ 2001,272 (*Bakker q.q./Katko*).

7 Which corresponds to Article 3:46 of the Civil Code.

In view of the above, this sort of action is a rather remote risk when setting up a cash pooling agreement, provided that a group company does not become bankrupt within a year of entering into the agreement. Obviously, banks will normally thoroughly verify the financial situation of each group company before it is allowed to participate in a cash pooling agreement. In order to prevent any future issues, it might be advisable to include a provision in the cash pooling documentation under which group companies are always obliged to grant (additional) security if the bank so desires. As a result of such a provision, the granting of any additional security, if it is required, would not qualify as a voluntary legal act.

(c) Conflict of interest

The concept of conflict of interest could be relevant where a (legal) person[8] is a director of more than one group company. Under Article 2:256[9] of the Civil Code, unless the articles of association provide otherwise, a company shall be represented by the members of its supervisory board in all matters in which it has a conflict of interest with one or more directors. Moreover, the general shareholders' meeting always has the power to appoint one or more other persons to represent the company in the event of a conflict of interest. If a director with a conflict of interest acts on behalf of the company, then the company or a trustee may annul the legal act if and to the extent that the other party knew or should have known that there was a conflict of interest.[10]

The concept of conflict of interest is especially relevant for trustees in bankruptcy wishing to set aside guarantees or other security rights. In order to avoid this risk, it is common practice in the Netherlands to demand a written resolution of the general shareholders' meeting appointing each member of the board of directors and/or an attorney to act as the company's representative in respect of the execution by the company of the relevant documents for a transaction. Accordingly, when setting up a cash pooling agreement, banks will in principle always require such a written resolution of the general shareholders' meeting of the parent company and of each group company.

2. Specific questions

2.1 Perspective A: corporate group

(a) Liability of group company and/or master account holder directors in the event of insolvency of a group company

In principle, directors are not personally liable for obligations that they have entered into on behalf of the company; nor are they liable to compensate damage arising from a tort committed by the company. In exceptional cases, however, it is possible to hold the directors personally liable.

8 Under Dutch law, a director can be a natural person or a legal entity.

9 Article 2:146 of the Civil Code applies to a private company with limited liability (a BV), whereas Article 2:256 of the Civil Code applies to a public company with limited liability (an NV).

10 According to a bill which will enter into force in 2012, violation of the conflicts of interest provision will have only internal effect – that is, the legal act itself cannot be annulled and is binding on the company.

The criteria for directors' liability mentioned below also apply to the liability of supervisory directors. However, given the (limited) scope of their duties (advising and supervising the board), it will be even more difficult to establish liability on the part of supervisory directors.

Internal liability: The term 'internal liability' refers to the situation in which a director is liable towards the company. On this ground, the company can recover the damage it has suffered as a result of the director's actions from the director personally. In practice, this ground is often used if a company has become bankrupt. The trustee then uses this ground to hold a director liable for the debts of the company not covered by the company's assets. A director can only be held personally liable if he can be seriously blamed for the improper management. Serious blame exists if the director has failed seriously in the performance of his obligations towards the company, in the sense that no reasonable director would have acted thus. The circumstances of the case determine whether this is the case. Circumstances that may play a role include the nature of the activities of the company, the risks inherent in those activities and the specific skills of the relevant director.

External liability: The term 'external liability' refers to a situation in which third parties have incurred damage as a result of a director's act or omission and hold him liable for that reason. External liability can be based on multiple grounds.

In the event of bankruptcy, if a trustee can demonstrate plausible grounds that the board has at any time during the three years preceding the bankruptcy performed its duties improperly, and that that impropriety is an important cause of the bankruptcy, the directors will be individually liable for the full deficit in the bankruptcy estate. The deficit in the bankruptcy estate is the amount that creditors can still claim from the company after all the assets have been liquidated (including general bankruptcy costs such as the trustee's fees). Whether the performance of duties has been improper is determined on the basis of the criteria mentioned above. This will particularly concern cases in which one or more creditors have been prejudiced by any acts on the part of directors.

If the company commits a tort, the directors are in general not personally liable. The only case in which they (as well as the company) are personally liable is if a tortious act or omission can be attributed to them personally on the basis of Article 6:162 of the Civil Code. This requires the existence of serious personal culpability. The circumstances of the case are decisive for the conclusion whether the director has personally committed a tortious act or omission. In general, the greater part of the cases in which a director is personally held liable on grounds of tort relate to one or more of the following actions:

- concluding or ratifying a legal act in the knowledge that the company will not, or not within a proper term, be able to fulfil its obligations or offer sufficient recourse for the damage the other party will suffer as a result;
- causing the company to commit a breach of contract, including non-performance of its payment obligations, even though it has or is able to acquire sufficient means to pay its debts – in other words in the case of refusal to pay; or

- withdrawing of assets from the reach of the company's creditors, or paying debts of persons having control over the company when there is a serious possibility that this would mean that the other creditors could not be paid in whole or in part.

To date, there is no specific Dutch case law whereby directors of a (bankrupt) group company have been held personally liable as a result of that company participating in a cash pooling agreement. An explanation for this may be that, as outlined in section 1.4 above, all group companies can be deemed to benefit from a cash pooling agreement. This may be different if the credit balances of a solvent group company are being swept under a zero balancing arrangement to a distressed parent company. Physical sweeping gives rise to inter-company loans between the parent company and the group companies. If the parent company were eventually to go bankrupt, a group company would then be an unsecured creditor in the bankruptcy. In such circumstances it could be argued that if the directors are to perform their duties properly, they should withdraw the group company from a physical cash pooling agreement if there is a risk of the parent company becoming insolvent, and that failing to do so could lead to personal liability on the part of the directors. However, if the cash pooling agreement does not contain a termination clause, a group company will in principle not be allowed to withdraw unilaterally from the pool under Dutch law. This may well be a strong defence against directors' liability. In view of all these considerations, directors' liability in connection with a cash pooling agreement is a somewhat remote risk under Dutch law.

Liability of the parent company: As a general rule under Dutch law, there is no liability for shareholders for the obligations of the company except for their obligation to pay up their part of the share capital. However, in certain very specific situations it is possible to pierce the corporate veil as a result of which an (indirect) shareholder could be held liable. The main situations are:

- liability for actions in tort affecting a third party; and
- liability for actions or omissions of a shareholder acting in its capacity as *de facto* director.

In both these cases, there must be a causal connection between the shareholder's act or omission and the damage suffered by a third party, such as a creditor of the company. Shareholders' liability based on *de facto* directorship applies mainly to situations relating to bankruptcy of the company.[11] Circumstances in which liability based on piercing the corporate veil has been established include the following:

- A parent company abused its position as shareholder by selling or

---

11 A party, including a shareholder, can be deemed to be a *de facto* director of a company where that party exercises factual management control or influence over the company. Factual management goes beyond the mere exercise of control as shareholder – for example, when a parent company issues promises directly to a creditor of its subsidiary. Whether a shareholder can be deemed to be a *de facto* director, will depend upon the specific circumstances of the case. The basis of such liability however, will be the same as that which applies to persons or entities appointed as directors, (ie, mismanagement).

transferring assets of the subsidiary for the sole benefit of the parent, while ignoring the rights of the subsidiary's creditors. The parent company was held liable for damages suffered by the creditors of the subsidiary, which, as result of the parent's actions, was no longer able to perform its obligations towards these creditors;

- A parent company created the reasonable expectation on the part of a subsidiary's creditors that it guaranteed or would otherwise ensure performance by the subsidiary of its (contractual) obligations; and
- A parent company has actual control over the management of the subsidiary due to the fact that the subsidiary is financially fully dependent on the parent company. In that case, the parent company is deemed to owe the subsidiary's creditors a duty of care as from the moment that there are indications that the subsidiary is no longer financially sound. In such a situation, if the parent company takes no action or refrains from certain actions in order to safeguard the position of the subsidiary's creditors, the parent company can be held liable to those creditors.

To date, however, there is no specific Dutch case law whereby a parent company of a (bankrupt) group company has been held liable in connection with a cash pooling agreement. Partly for the same reasons explained with respect to director's liability, the liability of a parent company in connection with a cash pooling agreement is a somewhat remote risk under Dutch law.

(b) Liability of group company and/or master account holder directors in the event of insolvency of the master account holder

Under Dutch law, there is no liability risk for the directors of a group company if the parent company is no longer able to meet its payment obligations. For the liability risks of the directors of the parent company, reference is made to paragraph (a) above.

(c) Liability of group companies in the event of insolvency of the master account holder

Under Dutch law, creditors of a distressed parent company do not have a legal right to hold another group company liable for any losses suffered, unless that company committed a tort itself as regards those creditors or acted as a *de facto* director of the distressed parent company.

(d) Liability of the master account holder in the event of insolvency of a group company

Under Dutch law, creditors of a distressed group company do not have a legal right to hold another group company liable for losses suffered, unless that company committed a tort itself as regards those creditors or acted as a *de facto* director of the distressed group company. As for the liability of the parent company, reference is made to paragraph (a) above.

2.2 Perspective B: bank

(a) Banking requirements

The Dutch Central Bank imposes solvency requirements on banks for outstanding debit balances on sub-accounts. Accordingly, banks must maintain a certain percentage of equity against these debit balances. Since equity is more expensive than debt financing, this requirement leads to higher costs for the banks, which they usually pass on to their clients through debit interest rates. Provided that a bank meets certain conditions, however, a bank is allowed, on its balance sheet, to net all debit and credit balances on the sub-accounts in a pool against each other.

The relevant conditions, which are laid down in Article 4:8 of the Regulation on Solvency Requirements for Credit Risk and Large Exposures 2010 are as follows:

- The credit balance is pledged to the bank pursuant to a separate pledge agreement as security for the debit balances;
- At all times the bank has the authority to satisfy its debts to a creditor by assigning its claim on the debtor to the creditor; or
- The following applies to the debit and credit balances:
  - The debit balance is for the account and risk of the creditor, the creditor stands surety for the debts of the debtor or the creditor is jointly and severally liable for such debts apart from the debtor itself; and
  - The credit balance is pledged to the debtor as security for the obligation of the creditor under the relevant arrangement set out the sub-paragraph above.

In order to comply with these conditions, (a combination of) security rights are in principle always included in an agreement regarding notional cash pooling. Apart from this, there are no specific legal requirements for a bank entering into a cash pooling agreement.

(b) Liability of the bank in the event of insolvency of the master account holder or of group company

Banks have a special duty of care when providing banking services to their clients. In its provision of services, a bank must take the client's interests into account to the best of its ability. Banks that do not comply with this principle could be held liable. In the context of a cash pooling agreement, this risk is highly remote. The fact that cash pooling agreements could have negative consequences for the creditors and group companies in insolvency situations does not change this. After all, a cash pooling agreement is a widely accepted banking product in the Netherlands.

2.3 Insolvency

(a) Cash pooling agreements from the insolvency practitioner's perspective

If a Dutch bank is declared bankrupt, any remaining debit balances will have to be paid by each relevant group company to the bankrupt estate. Any remaining credit balances must be filed with the trustee in bankruptcy. Depending on the total assets of the bankruptcy estate, group companies having a credit balance will eventually receive a (small) percentage of their total claim. This would be different if parties agreed on a reciprocal right of set-off for the benefit of the group (see section 1.2 above). In the case of zero balancing, there will in principle be a credit balance only on the master account. Again, this claim will also have to be filed with the trustee in bankruptcy. In most cases, the Dutch deposit guarantee scheme will not be relevant in the context of a cash pooling agreement, since it is available only to private individuals and small enterprises. Small enterprises are those that are permitted to publish a summary balance sheet.

If the parent company goes bankrupt and the bank has a right of set-off, it will be entitled to offset the credit balance on the master account against the relevant debit balances on the sub-accounts. If there is a right of pledge on the credit balance, the bank may also choose to execute that right. As mentioned above, physical sweeping gives rise to inter-company loans between the parent company and the group companies. If the parent company goes bankrupt, a group company will have to file its (unsecured) claim with the parent company's trustee in bankruptcy.

If a group company is declared bankrupt and the bank has a right of set-off, the bank will be entitled to offset any credit balances on the sub-account against any debit balances on sub-accounts of other group companies, or, in the alternative, any debit balance on the sub-account against any credit balances on sub-accounts of other group companies. If there is a right of pledge on the credit balance, the bank may also choose to execute that right. In the event of zero balancing, the bankrupt group company's trustee in bankruptcy will recover any inter-company loan against the parent company.

In situations whereby the bankrupt parent company has transferred moneys to certain group companies prior to its bankruptcy, or a bankrupt group company has transferred moneys to the master account prior to its bankruptcy, the trustee in bankruptcy, for the reasons explained in section 1.4 above, will in principle not be allowed to disregard or annul such transactions and claim the amounts as part of the bankruptcy estate.

(b) Special rules as regards creditors of other parties to the cash pooling agreement

The trustee in bankruptcy is charged with the administration and liquidation of the bankruptcy estate. In doing so, the trustee will have to act for the benefit of all creditors. In the event that any one of the bank, the master account holder or a group company goes bankrupt, Dutch law does not prescribe any specific rules or obligations which a trustee in bankruptcy must observe as regards the creditors of the other parties to the cash pooling agreement.

(c) Dissolution/termination of cash pooling agreement in the event of liquidation of the master account holder or a group company

A cash pooling agreement normally gives only the banks a right to terminate the agreement or exclude a group company from the cash pool. Certain cash pooling agreements, however, also allow each group company to withdraw itself or any of its sub-accounts from the cash pooling agreement upon reasonable prior written notice to the bank. If the cash pooling agreement does not contain such a provision, Dutch law does not allow a group company to terminate the agreement in the event that the parent company goes into liquidation. The same applies for the parent company in the event that a group company goes into liquidation. In view of the foregoing, it is advisable – especially when entering into a zero balancing pool – to make sure that group companies are allowed to withdraw from the pool under certain circumstances.

2.4 Perspective D: regulatory

The only regulatory requirements in respect of cash pooling agreements under Dutch law are those relating to banks, which are discussed at section 2.2 above.

2.5 Perspective E: tax

The main tax consequences of cash pooling in the Netherlands relate to transfer pricing, especially with regard to the allocation of the overall benefits of the cash pool among the participating companies and determining the arm's-length remuneration for the master account holder through which the administration and handling of the cash pool takes place.

In the Netherlands, no withholding tax is levied on interest payments (eg, to the master account holder). If a Dutch master account holder, receives interest payments, the question may arise whether foreign withholding tax, if any, can be credited against Dutch tax due on the interest income. In addition, the question could arise as to whether a Dutch company receiving interest would qualify as the beneficial owner, for instance, in cases where this company is the master account holder and would need to pay the interest forward to the participating bank. However, this would generally be dealt with in the country of the foreign group company paying the interest to the Dutch company.

Under certain conditions, interest income received and interest payments made by a Dutch master account holder may be excluded from its tax base, if that company effectively does not run any risks in relation to the activity giving rise to the interest.

Norway

Borge Grottjord
Kari Amalie Pettersen
Grette DA

1. Introduction

1. 1 Admissibility of cash pooling agreements

In Norway, cash pooling is permitted, but various laws and regulations will apply and must be taken into consideration before the parties enter into any cash pooling agreement. Both notional and physical cash pooling is permitted. This includes physical pooling only within the company group, where the holding company or parent company acts as the facilitator. Most Norwegian banks do offer cash pooling agreements to their customers. The types of cash pooling and the agreements that are offered in Norway vary.

A Norwegian public (publicly listed) or private limited company may generally participate in any type of cash pooling agreement with its corporate group, if all companies are based in Norway. Norwegian companies can enter into cash pooling agreements with foreign companies in their corporate group, but certain restrictions will apply.

In Norway, cash pooling agreements are commonly entered into by both private corporate groups and public entities in order to utilise total available liquidity more effectively. Norwegian legislation also allow for companies to enter into cash pooling agreements with other types of entity in their corporate group, such as partnerships. However, we have limited our review of Norwegian legislation to situations where the participating parties to the cash pooling agreement are limited companies, either public or private, which is the most frequently used form of company incorporation in Norway.

1.2 Types of cash pooling agreement

The most common form of cash pooling used is physical cash pooling in a single legal account. This type of cash pooling is sometimes also referred to as Nordic or Scandinavian cash pooling. As the name suggest, the cash pooling system is set up so that only one single legal account – the master account – is held with the bank. The cash pooling agreement will state that the master account holder is the only entity with which the bank has a relationship, and that the balance on the master account is the only balance relevant to the cash pooling agreement. The underlying group company sub-accounts will not constitute legally separate bank accounts in relation to the bank, which means that a group company having a credit balance in its own account does not have a claim on the bank, but only against the other company participants in the cash pooling agreement. The sub-accounts are therefore not real bank accounts, but show the different participating companies' balances in relation to each other (cost control accounts), thus keeping a register of the net debt or claim that has arisen towards the other companies in the corporate group since the opening of the single legal account. However, cash pooling agreements that commonly include terms that state a general right for the bank to offset any claim the bank might have against the corporate group against any account held by the corporate group within or outside the single legal account.

By the use of a single legal account, the corporate group will manage its liquidity through the use of a balance netting system, whereby funds from subsidiaries are moved to a parent account. However, where in zero balancing all accounts in the cash pool are legal accounts and the transfers occur at given intervals, with single legal account balance netting the debiting occurs in real time in the master account when it is registered in the cost control sub-account that is designated to each company in the group. Both zero balancing/target balancing cash pooling and single legal account cash pooling improve the net interest position by offsetting debit and credit balances. The main benefit of the single legal account model is that the corporate group will keep real-time track of total liquidity.

Since the single legal account constitutes the only legal account with the bank, it will be the responsibility of the corporate group to keep actual track of the funds lent between companies, and the single legal account agreement will typically state that this is an inter-company issue not concerning the bank. The company owning the single legal account master account will typically be the company within the group with the most cost-intensive business activities – not necessarily the parent company. If the parent of the group is only a holding company, this company will seldom be the account holder.

Even though the single legal account arrangement is the most common form of cash pooling in Norway, other types of cash pooling scheme are fully allowed – both notional cash pooling and physical cash pooling with traditional zero balancing or target balancing. However, zero balancing or notional pooling is virtually not offered by Norwegian banks. This is mainly due to the costs associated with such pooling. Sweeping funds under a zero balancing/target balancing system will incur costs. Notional pooling has costs associated with it due to capital requirements and fees associated with the deposit guarantee scheme.

In practice, zero balancing will typically be offered only when a Norwegian company participating in a cash pooling agreement has a bank account in a Norwegian bank which is then swept to another (foreign) bank. Notional pooling is in practice offered only if the corporate group is in need of a multi-currency cash pool. In a typical multi-currency cash pool scheme, the structure will be a combination of the single legal account system and a notional cash pool, where a different single legal account exists for each currency, and these single legal accounts have multiple cost control sub-accounts associated with them. In addition, the total coverage control will be held with a superior cost control account where all the balances of the different single legal accounts are calculated in a single currency, normally euros. This last account does not constitute a legal account and exists only to keep track of the corporate group's total coverage. The single legal account top accounts are in this manner notionally pooled against each other.

1.3 Legal requirements from various perspectives

With one distinct exception, Norwegian law does not explicitly regulate cash pooling. However, general restrictions in company law regarding capital management and equity capital maintenance apply.

When it comes to the areas of banking law, insolvency law, regulatory issues and tax law, there are no specific legal requirements directly regarding cash pooling agreements. However, rules pertaining to banks capital requirements, the seizing of assets in the event of insolvency and bankruptcy, and issues related to transfer pricing in transactions between companies will apply to cash pooling agreements. These issues are therefore dealt with later this chapter.

(a) Company law

In Norway, the Limited Liability Companies Act applies to privately owned companies, while the Public Limited Liability Companies Act applies to public limited companies (they are jointly referred to as the Companies Acts). These two acts are largely identical when it comes to the relevant clauses regarding cash pooling agreements.

Only one single provision in Norwegian law regulates the issue of cash pooling agreements directly. However, many provisions regarding inter-company loans and capital maintenance will apply with regard to a cash pooling scheme. These issues are discussed here.

Issues regarding a company's actual participation in a cash pooling agreement will be regulated by two different chapters in the Companies Acts. First, any issue related specifically to inter-company loans or security interests granted from one company within a corporate group to another is regulated in the Companies Acts Chapter 8, Part III, "Distribution of dividend and other allocation of company assets – Granting of credit and furnishing of security etc." Second, any agreement in general between companies in a corporate group is also regulated in both Companies Acts Chapter 3, Part IV, "Company capital – Transactions between the company and the shareholders etc." Both of these sets of rules lay out material limitations for a Norwegian company when it comes to the scope of a cash pooling agreement, formal conditions for entering into such an agreement, and also consequences if the conditions are not met. When entering into a cash pooling agreement, a Norwegian company must act in accordance with both sets of rules.

Limitations on giving credit and furnishing security for shareholders and their subsidiaries – Companies Acts Chapter 8: All forms of cash pooling usually require that the participating companies place their assets with another company for the disposal of the corporate group. In a physical cash pooling scheme, the movements of money through and from group company accounts will be treated as inter-company loans, both in a single legal account scheme and in a zero balancing scheme. Additionally, and also with notional pooling schemes, the companies are generally required by the bank to provide guarantees or another form of security for the credit risk associated with the cash pooling agreement both to the bank and to the other participating companies in the agreement.

Usually, there will be few or no restrictions on shareholders granting credit to, or providing security for, their respective companies (downstream). However, there are restrictions the other way around (upstream), in order to ensure that the companies are not bled out and maintain appropriate funding. Such a restriction follows from the Companies Acts Section 8-7, Subsections 1 and 2, stating that:

(1) The company may only grant credit to, or furnish security for the benefit of, a shareholder or any person connected with the shareholder within the limits of the assets which the company may use for the distribution of dividends and only if adequate security is furnished for the claim for repayment or recovery.

(2) The prohibition in subsection (1) shall apply correspondingly to any credit which is granted to, or any security which is furnished for the benefit of, a shareholder or owner of an interest in another company in the same group, or any person connected with such shareholder or owner of an interest.

However, there are two general exceptions from this rule, both of which apply to cash pooling agreements.

The first exception, in the Companies Acts Section 8-7, Subsection 3 states that:

(3) The prohibition in subsections (1) and (2) shall not apply to:

1. Credit with maturity which is standard in connection with business agreements;

2. Credit or security for the benefit of the parent company or another company in the same group.

Paragraph 1 of Subsection (3) is not applicable to cash pooling agreements. The exception in paragraph 2 applies only if the companies constitute companies within the same corporate group within the meaning of the Companies Acts. In order to be defined as a 'corporate group', the parent company must have decisive influence over the other companies in the corporate group. Decisive influence can be based on either ownership or agreement. Decisive influence is always established when the parent company has the right to choose the majority of the subsidiary company's board members, or holds a majority vote in the subsidiary. All companies where the parent company has such decisive influence are companies belonging to the same corporate group.

If all companies participating in the cash pooling agreement are Norwegian companies and part of the same corporate group, this exception applies fully, meaning that all companies may freely give credit or furnish security for each other, and therefore may enter into any type of cash pooling agreement that will require this.

If one or more companies are based in another jurisdiction, the exception stating that a subsidiary company may lend funds to companies within its corporate group still applies, but only with certain specific limitations. The Companies Acts Section 1-4, Subsection 2, states that the exception that gives subsidiaries a legal basis to grant credit to other companies within their corporate group also applies to the granting of credit and furnishing of security for the benefit of a parent company or other group company based in a state that is a party to the European Economic Area

Agreement and which is subject to corresponding or more stringent legislation than the Norwegian rules pertaining to credit to shareholders (and office holders).[1] Whether other EEA countries have as stringent or more stringent rules than Norway has in practice proved difficult to assess. This has led to most Norwegian companies entering into cash pooling agreements based on this exception with companies only based in other Nordic countries.

The Ministry of Justice is currently in the process of considering simplifications to the Limited Liability Companies Act. One of the recommendations from the initial report is to allow Norwegian companies to lend funds to, and provide guarantees for, any other member in the corporate group that is based within the European Economic Area, regardless of the specific rules that apply in those other jurisdictions with regard to providing credit or security interests to shareholders.[2] This would simplify matters for Norwegian companies, because a Norwegian company would not, under that recommendation, have to consider specifically the prevailing law in any other EEA jurisdictions before entering into a cash pooling agreement. For the time being, these recommendations have resulted in no specific proposed changes to the Limited Liability Companies Act, but the matter is still under consideration at the Ministry of Justice.

For corporate groups with companies outside the European Economic Area, or in cases where it is difficult to assess whether the rules of an EEA member state are as strict as or stricter than the Norwegian rules, a second exception to the main rule exists. The Companies Acts Section 8-7, Subsection 4 states that:

The prohibition in subsections (1) and (2) does not prevent a subsidiary from participating in a group account scheme together with other group companies (cf. Section 1-4 (2) first sentence), provided that the funds in the accounts are used within the group's operations only.

The Ministry of Justice has stated in a letter to a Norwegian bank that it considers that the situation where one group company undertakes joint liability for another group company's overdraft facilitiess would generally fall within the exception, given that the security furnished constitutes a reasonable condition within a cash pooling agreement.[3]

It is the responsibility of the Norwegian company and its directors to ensure that the funds are actually used for corporate business purposes. If the funds are used in a different manner, this constitutes a breach of Norwegian company law, and the directors of the Norwegian company may be held liable for prospective losses. Liability in general is discussed further below.

Because of the first exception, this second exception will have significance only

---

1 The Companies Acts Section 8-9, "Credit to officeholders etc.", Subsection 1 states that
The provisions in Section 8-7 shall apply correspondingly to the company's right to grant credit to or furnish security for the benefit of a memeber of the board of directors, the general manager or a member of the corporate assembly in the company or in another company in the same group or any of their connected persons.

2 See "Simplification and Modernisation of the Limited Liability Companies Act" by Gudmund Knudsen, January 7 2012.

3 Letter from the Ministry of Justice (Department of Legal Affairs) to DnB NOR Bankk ASA of April 9 2005, 2004/06494.

if one or more companies in the corporate group participating in the cash pooling agreement are based either outside the European Economic Area, or within an EEA country with less stringent rules pertaining to shareholder (and officeholder)[4] loans. If the companies in the corporate group that participate in the cash pooling agreement are all based in Norway or another EEA state with rules regarding shareholder (and officeholder)[5] loans as stringent as those in Norway, the Norwegian company may in general grant credits or furnish security for other companies in the corporate group without having to monitor whether the funds are actually used exclusively for corporate business activities.

In summary:

- a Norwegian company can enter into a cash pooling agreement with another Norwegian company when, under the Companies Acts, they constitute entities within the same corporate group;
- if other entities within the corporate group are based in the European Economic Area, the Norwegian group company may still enter into a cash pooling agreement, provided that the limitations on giving credit to shareholders in those other entities' jurisdictions are as strict as or stricter than the Norwegian rules on the matter; and
- when it comes to entities within the corporate group that are based outside the European Economic Area, or EEA-based companies which are subject to rules on giving credit to shareholders that are less strict than those in Norway (or where this proves to difficult to assess), a Norwegian company can enter into a cash pooling agreement with such corporate group entities provided that the funds in the cash pooling system are used exclusively for corporate business activities.

These conditions will apply fully to any physical cash pooling scheme, as it will involve credit being granted through inter-company loans. They will also apply fully to any notional cash pooling scheme if the Norwegian group company provides some sort of security in favour of the other participants.

If a cash pooling agreement that involves credit being granted, such as a physical cash pooling scheme, is entered into without these conditions being fulfilled, then the agreement is invalid and any funds transferred from the Norwegian group company shall be transferred back. If security has been provided under a cash pooling scheme for a group company or the parent company in favour of a third party (generally the bank), invalidity may not, however, be invoked against a third party which has shown due care and acted in good faith when the security was furnished. This follows explicitly from the Companies Acts.[6] In practice, these rules limit the Norwegian companies' legal capacity to act, meaning that they cannot enter into a cash pooling agreement under less stringent conditions by way of agreeing to a choice of law clause.

4 See footnote 1.
5 See footnote 1.
6 Companies Acts Section 8-11.

General company law requirements pertaining to company capital and transactions between the company and shareholders – Companies Acts Chapter 3: There are some additional requirements that any Norwegian company entering into a cash pooling agreement must take into consideration, irrespective of the jurisdictions in which other participating companies are based. These requirements are not only relevant when it comes to a cash pooling agreement, but will apply to any agreement between a Norwegian company and other companies within the corporate group.

First, any transaction or agreement between companies in the same corporate group must be governed by ordinary commercial principles and based on commercial terms and conditions. This implies an arm's-length principle when it comes to transactions within the corporate group.[7]

Second, any substantial agreement between companies in the corporate group must be entered into in writing.[8] The Ministry of Justice has stated in the preparatory works to the Limited Liability Companies Act that a cash pooling agreement involving physical cash pooling should be deemed to be a substantial agreement, which means that it must be in writing. Notional cash pooling schemes were not commented upon explicitly, but generally any agreement concerning financial issues of some importance would be deemed to be a substantial agreement. Both physical cash and notional pooling agreements should therefore be entered into in writing.

Third, for a private limited liability company to participate in a cash pooling agreement with its corporate group, the agreement must be formally approved by the general shareholders' meeting, if the consideration from the company has a real value of more than 10% of the registered share capital[9] at the time of the agreement, but not if the real value constitutes less than Nkr50,000.[10] For a publicly listed limited liability company, the limit is set at 5% of the registered share capital,[11] without a minimum threshold. What constitutes real value should be assessed as of the time when the agreement imposes an obligation on the company. The board of directors will have to evaluate the cash pooling agreement before entering into it.[12] The board of directors must ensure that a review of the agreement is prepared for the general meeting. Until these requirements of approval are met, the agreement is not formally valid and binding on the company. Any performance on the company's part prior to approval is not binding and must be reversed. Anyone that has participated in the

7 Companies Acts Section 3-9.

8 Companies Acts Section 3-9. This goes further than the general principle of Norwegian contract law, which states that any oral agreement is as binding as a written one.

9 The minimum share capital for Norwegian limited companies is currently Nkr30,000 – Limited Liability Companies Act Section 3-1.

10 Limited Liability Companies Act Section 3-8.

11 For a public company, the miminum share capital is Nkr11 million – the Public Limited Liability Companies Act Section 3-1. Effectively, a fair value of Nkr50,000 would therefore also be the threshold for public companies.

12 The law states that what constitutes real value should generally be assessed at the time of the agreement. However, in the case of a cash pooling agreement it might be difficult to estimate the total credit to be given under the agreement when the company enters into it. If it seems likely that the company's participation will go further than the limits given above, the company would be wise to enter into the agreement with a provision that sets a cap on its participation, or go to the general meeting even though it might not prove necessary.

company's performance of a non-binding agreement might be held liable for the funds being returned to the company.

Finally, a general requirement in Norwegian company law is that all rules pertaining to general and relevant administrative procedures[13] within the company be followed. However, notwithstanding the particular situations discussed above that can render an agreement non-binding for the company, not fulfilling the general rules on administrative procedures under Norwegian company law will not necessarily render an agreement non-binding between the parties. It may, however, constitute a legal basis for holding the involved persons liable for any loss that the company sustains.

1.4 General legal requirements

In addition to the specific rules discussed above, general principles of contract law will apply both when entering into a cash pooling agreement and throughout the lifespan of the agreement. This means that the courts, when seeking to determine the subject matter of a cash pooling agreement, may also place emphasis on these principles. Examples of general principles of Norwegian contract law include the principle of *pacta sunt servanda* (agreements must be kept), and the principle that any agreement should be interpreted in accordance with the intentions of the parties. However, a cash pooling agreement will generally be fairly exhaustive, and Norwegian courts are usually reluctant to stray from the contractual wording when the agreement is between two professional parties.

2. Specific questions

2.1 Perspective A: corporate group

(a) Concept of insolvency under Norwegian law – initial clarifications

Questions may arise for members of the corporate group in relation to liability in insolvency situations. Initially, a clarification of terms must be made. In the Norwegian law relating to bankruptcy, the term 'insolvency' is used only in situations where both cash-flow insolvency (illiquidity) and balance-sheet insolvency (insufficiency) are present. A Norwegian company that is insolvent will normally be liquidated by an administrator of the bankruptcy estate. A company that experiences only cash-flow illiquidity may seek debt settlement proceedings. In that case a committee will be appointed and the proceedings will eventually lead to either a voluntary composition of the estate with mutual acceptance from all creditors or, if no consensus can be reached, a compulsory composition. A compulsory composition will, for all intents and purposes, follow the same rules and principles as ordinary liquidation. The questions pertaining specifically to liquidation issues are discussed further below.

Under Norwegian law, in general, possible liability for persons or companies involved is not dependent on insolvency or illiquidity of one or more of the parties

---

13 As set out in, for example, the Companies Acts Chapter 6.

to the cash pooling agreement; it is sufficient that one of the companies have suffered a manifested loss. However, such a loss may commonly be caused by the insolvency or illiquidity of another party to the cash pooling agreement.

(b) ***Possible liability of persons or companies involved, in the event of insolvency of one or more of the parties to the cash pooling agreement***

Piercing the corporate veil: A general principle of Norwegian law is that each company with limited liability, being a separate legal entity, is solely responsible for the debts it incurs and any transactions and arrangement it enters into. This form of delimitation regarding limited liability companies is usually referred to as the corporate veil. The contrast would be a company with unlimited liability or a general partnership, where the company is formally a separate legal entity, but no distinction is made between the company's and its owners' financial commitments, meaning that a creditor that cannot obtain satisfaction of a claim from the company can subsequently advance the claim against the owners of the company.

There is virtually no basis in Norwegian law for piercing the corporate veil, for example by holding a parent company responsible for the debts of its subsidiary solely based on the relation between the two. The Supreme Court has discussed the question of piercing the corporate veil, but so far there have been no cases in which the corporate veil has been pierced. The Supreme Court has stated that if this is to be done, at least two circumstances must be present:

- It must appear directly unfair to the creditors to observe the limitation of liability that lies in the company structure; and
- There must have been a commingling of assets and debts between the companies rendering the benefits of the formal company structure unmerited.[14]

For all intents and purposes, under Norwegian law, any liability must therefore be based upon the principles of the law of damages (tort).

Legal grounds for possible liability under company law: Under the Norwegian law of damages, three conditions must be present to establish liability. First, the person involved must have acted with negligence. Second, an economic loss must be shown. Third, there must be a proximate causal relation between the negligence and the economic loss.

The possible types of liability that may occur under Norwegian company law are the following, and these are identical with regard to both private and public companies:

- Ordinary liability (liability on a primary basis) – when a person represents a company, such as a member of the board of directors,[15] the general manager,[16]

---

14 See Judgments Rt-1996-742 (*Minnor*) and Rt-1996-672 (*Kongeparken*).

15 In Norwegian company law the board of directors is generally the only relevant board. However, in companies (private or public) with more that 200 employees, a corporate assembly of at least 12 members must be elected, and the corporate assembly supervises the board of directors and the general manager.

16 The Companies Acts use the term 'general manager', which is generally the same as the director of a company, meaning the person hired to run the company's operations on a daily basis.

or a member of the corporate assembly, that person can be held directly liable for any losses caused by his own negligence.
- Contributory liability – this arises when someone else can be held liable for contributing to a situation referred to above.

The application of these two types of liability is regulated partly by the Companies Acts and partly by general principles of the law of damages.

Norwegian company law does not apply to companies that are based outside the Norwegian jurisdiction, meaning that Norwegian rules of ordinary liability cannot be used against persons representing foreign companies or against the foreign companies as such. However, the concept of contributory liability nonetheless opens up the possibility to hold any person contributing to another person's liability liable.

In certain cases a cash pooling agreement may constitute an *ultra vires* transaction on the Norwegian company's part, meaning that any funds transferred by the Norwegian company must be transferred back. Legally, however, this is not a question of liability, but rather the effect of an invalid transaction. These situations will be examined more thoroughly below.

Ordinary liability/directors' liability: The Companies Acts Section 17-1, Subsection (1) states that:

> *The company, a shareholder or others may demand that the general manager, a board member, member of the corporate assembly, person conducting an inquiry or shareholder compensate any damage which they, in the capacity mentioned, may have caused the party in question by intent or through negligence.*

This possibility of liability under the Companies Acts Section 17-1 applies to all functions in the company as listed, as long as the damage has been caused by the person having that role "in the capacity mentioned". However, for the purpose of simplifying the presentation of the concept, we will from now on refer only to board members (given that the board of directors will generally be the entity responsible for the company's entering into, and for the supervision of, a cash pooling agreement).

For a board member of either the group company or the master account holder to be held liable for someone else's loss, due to either the group company's or the master account holder's failure to meet its payment obligations under the cash pooling agreement, the loss must be traced back to that board member's negligence. Negligence can be present either through a negligent act or through failures to fulfil duties. Liability is determined on an individual basis, meaning that negligence must be established individually for each person held liable, and there is no collective liability for the board of directors as such.

As mentioned above, lending funds to, or providing credit for, shareholders is generally not allowed because of the issue with possible unlawful distributions, but may be permitted within the corporate group. Within the context of a cash pooling scheme, the question of liability will most typically arise if the cash pooling agreement is used in a manner that bleeds the subsidiary group company out, distributing its funds to the parent company, the master account holder or other companies in the group. If the other participating companies in the cash pooling agreement are unwilling or unable to pay these funds back, the result is a loss for the group company, and perhaps subsequently its creditors. Situations may also arise where either the group company or the master account holder simply cannot fulfil its obligations under the cash pooling agreement, either to the bank or to the other participating companies.

A director's liability due to negligence has to be traced back to one or more mandatory duties that the board members have to the company or others. For instance, the directors of any limited liability company have an overall responsibility for the management of the company, to ensure that the business activities are soundly organised and to keep themselves informed about the company's financial positions.[17] Furthermore, they must supervise the day-to-day management and the company's activities in general.[18] In a corporate group, the board of directors of a subsidiary is also obliged to provide the board of directors of the parent company with any information which is necessary for an evaluation of the group's position and the results of the group's activities. The parent company, for its part, must notify its subsidiary's board of directors of matters which may be of importance to the group as a whole, and also of decisions which may be of importance to the subsidiary before a final decision is made.[19] Within these general duties also lies the responsibility for ensuring compliance with specific provisions in company law, such as preventing unlawful distributions to shareholders[20] and ensuring that the company at all times maintains adequate equity.[21]

If a company's participation in a cash pooling agreement results in losses and the agreement is within a purely Norwegian corporate group, the question of liability for members of that company's board will normally be raised only if the losses suffered can be tracked back to mismanagement. This might, for example, be the case if the company, as a result of the cash pooling agreement, no longer has adequate equity and this was not sufficiently controlled or monitored by the board members. This also goes for Norwegian group companies participating in a cash pooling agreement with companies registered in other EEA countries that have as strict or stricter rules as the Norwegian rules when it comes to unlawful distributions.

One example of breach of a specific responsibility that may lead to liability is if a Norwegian group company has entered into a cash pooling agreement with companies in the corporate group outside the European Economic Area, or with companies based in EEA countries where the rules on giving credit to shareholders are not as strict as in Norway. As discussed above, in these situations a Norwegian company may participate in a cash pooling agreement with other companies within its corporate group (sisters or parents)[22] only insofar as the credit or security granted is used exclusively for the corporate group's business activities. If the credit is used

17 Companies Acts Section 6-12.
18 Companies Acts Section 6-13.
19 Companies Acts Section 6-16.
20 Companies Acts Chapter 8.
21 Companies Acts Section 3-4.
22 If the company at issue is the parent company and it is only lending funds to subsidiaries, there are no restrictions under Norwegian law.

for any other objective, the company's participation in the cash pooling agreement will effectively violate the relevant Companies Act and the credit is legally defined as an unlawful distribution.[23] This means, first, that the cash pooling scheme will be without binding effect for the Norwegian company as the agreement will be an *ultra vires* transaction.[24] Any transfers will have to be returned to the Norwegian company.[25] If the cash pooling agreement also includes an element of security furnished by the Norwegian group company, invalidity may not, however, be invoked against a contracting party that acted in good faith when the security was furnished. In these cases the legal theory states that the Norwegian company will be obliged immediately to seek to free itself from the security obligation, but this duty is imposed solely on the Norwegian company and is not related to the validity of the security insofar as the contracting party is concerned. Second, any person who has carried out or approved an unlawful distribution on behalf of the company can be held liable for the funds distributed being returned to the company.[26]

In relation to this form of liability, when it comes to international cash pooling agreements the board members have the same general duties as with purely Norwegian agreements: ensuring that the Norwegian company has sufficient own funds and adequate equity, and a general responsibility for assuring sound administration of the company, both of which are duties whose breach can result in possible liability should the company suffer a loss. These duties, and the possible liability they carry along with them, may therefore cause the Norwegian group company to be reluctant to enter into a cash pooling agreement with one or more foreign companies, especially if these companies are based outside the European Economic Area.

The wording of the Companies Acts Section 17-1, Subsection (1) also provides for liability on the part of a shareholder that in that capacity causes someone damage. Given that liability is determined on an individual basis, this is not practical where the shareholder is a parent company rather than a physical person. The question of holding a board member in the parent company – or, in a cash pooling scheme, the master account holder – liable for losses caused by the group company's insolvency or liquidation will therefore more typically be a question of contributory liability, discussed below.

Contributory liability: The Companies Acts Section 17-1, Subsection (2) states that:

The company, a shareholder, or others can also demand compensation from a party who, by intent or through negligence, has contributed to damage as mentioned in subsection (1). Compensation can be claimed from the contributor even if the person

---

23 Companies Acts Section 8-7.

24 Comapnies Act Section 8-11.

25 If the cash pooling scheme involves more companies in the corporate group that are not regulated under Norwegian law, this *ultra vires* effect will not concern their participation in the agreement, or the agreement between the bank and the master account holder, beyond the obligation to repay to the Norwegian company which follows directly from the invalidity of the agreement on only the part of the Norwegian company. However, as each group company participating in a cash pooling agreement is generally in a direct contractual relationship with the master account holder, the obligation to repay will normally concern only the master account holder.

26 Companies Act Section 8-11, with reference to Section 3-7 second paragraph.

who caused the damage cannot be held liable because he or she did not act with intent or negligence.

This second subsection provides for liability on the part of anyone who has contributed to a board member's, general manager's or shareholder's negligence (or the negligence of any other person mentioned in Subsection (1)), in their capacity as such. Contributory liability is therefore conditional upon the principal having acted in conflict with a duty under company law and this action having caused the damage or loss in question.

Two important clarifications apply. First, when it comes to contributory liability, only negligent actions – and not negligent omissions – from the contributor give rise to liability. Second, contributory liability may be established even though the principal wrongdoer cannot be held liable, for example on the grounds that the principal has not acted negligently. It is sufficient that the principal have acted in breach of a duty in the capacity it holds.

Contributory liability is not formally limited to persons involved with the parent company. Anyone with a relationship to the company that contributes to such damage may be held liable, including a bank or other financial institution. However, contributory liability seems most likely when it comes to corporate groups. In corporate groups it is common that most substantial decisions are made by the board of directors or another body at the top level of the corporation. Subsidiary companies and their boards of directors may have little or no say in the decisions being made, but they still have distinct duties related to the administration and management of the subsidiary. Contributory liability may in certain situations place liability where it belongs: in the hands of the actual decision makers.

In principle, contributory liability may therefore be applied to persons that are not subject to the duties of Norwegian company law directly (as board members of a Norwegian company), insofar as these persons have actively contributed to the Norwegian board members' breach of duty. In practice, this will be most relevant to board members or other persons belonging to a foreign parent company.

If a Norwegian company has entered into a cash pooling agreement and any of the board members or the general manager (director) of the Norwegian company acts in conflict with the duties outlined in the discussion on ordinary liability above, anyone that has contributed to that person's breach of Norwegian company law may be held liable on the basis of contributory liability.

The concept of contributory liability in company law has existed on a statutory basis only since 2006. As of yet, no case law exists where anyone has been held liable under these rules on a contributory basis.

If a person within the parent company can be held liable on the basis of contributory liability, the parent company itself could also be held liable for the actions of its legal representatives on the ground of vicarious liability. However, as mentioned above, if negligence cannot be established, there is no general basis in Norwegian law to hold one legal person, such as a parent company, responsible for the ordinary debts of another legal person, such as the subsidiary company, if the latter is no longer able to meet its payment obligations.

2.2 Perspective B: bank

(a) Banking requirements

There are no rules that apply specifically to a cash pooling scheme from the bank's point of view. Any bank or financial institution authorised to receive deposits from the general public may offer cash pooling agreements to customers. When it comes to credit institutions and payment services providers, as Norway is a member of the European Economic Area, Norwegian law is harmonised with EU law. Norwegian rules pertaining to capital requirements, risk coverage and management and liquidity ratio are identical to the requirements set out in the EU Directive 2006/48 /EC on credit institutions,[27] derived from the Basel II requirements.[28] No additional rules apply to banks having their primary establishment in Norway or to banks from other EEA countries that either establish themselves in Norway through a secondary establishment or offer services here.

One general requirement pertaining to the Norwegian guarantee deposit scheme will have a distinct effect when it comes to notional pooling schemes and may explain why this type of cash pooling is generally not offered by Norwegian banks. All Norwegian banks are compulsory members of the Norwegian deposit guarantee scheme, guaranteeing, in the event of a bank default, customers' deposits up to Nkr2 million (about €266,666). Through their membership they must pay a fee, calculated on the basis of the deposits in the bank. Since all accounts in a notional pooling scheme are legal accounts (never being swept), each account with a positive balance will be included in the basis of calculating this fee. At the same time, notional pooling will cause the bank to earn less money than it otherwise would from the accounts with a negative balance, since all balances of the companies involved are offset against each other. The bank will also have to maintain capital for risk associated with each account.

(b) Liability of the bank in the event of insolvency of the master account holder holder or a group company

As discussed above, Norwegian company law on contributory liability may be applied to banks if a bank has actively contributed to a board member's or general manager's breach of a duty under company legislation. The same conditions as are discussed above from the perspective of the corporate group will apply where a bank is concerned.

Additionally, under the general Norwegian law on damages, anyone who has acted with negligence, thereby causing economic loss, may in theory be held responsible for that loss. Within the general law of damages, as in company law, negligence is dependent on a breach of a duty of care. When providing payment services, all banks are required, among other things, to provide relevant information and ensure the transparency of the conditions in the agreement. Theoretically, it is

---

27 Directive 2006/48/EC of the European Parliament and of the Council relating to the taking up and pursuit of the business of credit institutions.

28 Basel II Accord: International Convergence of Capital Measurement and Capital Standards: a revised framework.

possible to imagine a breach of these duties resulting in liability for negligence, but this is highly improbable when it comes to agreements with non-consumers and virtually inconceivable when entering into a cash pooling agreement with a corporate group.

2.3 Insolvency

The master account holder and participating group members are companies and may be subject to liquidation proceedings under the Bankruptcy Act of 1984. Banks, however, may not be subject to ordinary liquidation proceedings, but may be put under public administration and possible winding up under the Guarantee Schemes Act of 1996. In ordinary bankruptcy proceedings, an insolvency administrator is appointed by the bankruptcy court, while in a public administration an administration board consisting of at least three members is appointed by the Norwegian Financial Surveillance Authority. However, the rules concerning which assets may be seized by the insolvency administrators and creditors' rights to satisfaction of claims are very much alike in the two situations, as the implementation of these in both situations is guided by the Satisfaction of Claims Act and the Financial Collateral Act.

What must be settled initially is where the bankruptcy proceedings should be opened in the first place. If it is clear that the bankruptcy proceedings or public administration proceedings are to be opened in Norway, the process thereafter is subject to Norwegian law. In principle, it does not matter whether any of the other parties to the arrangement, other than the debtor, are based in another jurisdiction.

When it comes to insolvency proceedings involving companies, Norway, not being a member of the European Union, has not implemented the EU Insolvency Regulation.[29] At this point in time, Norwegian law lacks satisfactory rules on international insolvency proceedings. The Bankruptcy Act, Section 146, states that bankruptcy shall be opened in Norway if the debtor's main interest is situated here. The Norwegian rule is therefore equivalent to that of the EU Insolvency Regulation, Article 3.

Under Norwegian law, once bankruptcy is opened in Norway, ordinary insolvency proceedings as such also follow Norwegian law, including which assets outside the Norwegian jurisdiction may be seized by the insolvency administrator. However, the practical implications will depend upon whether the Norwegian bankruptcy proceedings are recognised under the rules of the non-Norwegian jurisdiction.

When it comes to insolvency proceedings opened in another jurisdiction, according to the preparatory works of the Bankruptcy Act and legal theory, such proceedings generally do not apply to those of the debtor's belongings that are situated in Norway. At the present time, only a treaty between the Nordic counties provides for mutual recognition of bankruptcy proceedings under Norwegian legislation, meaning that the rules of the country where the bankruptcy is opened apply in full to the bankruptcy proceedings (with some exceptions relating in particular to real estate).

---

29 Council Regulation (EC) 1346/2000.

If the insolvency administrator is appointed abroad, meaning that the bankruptcy has been opened outside the Norwegian jurisdiction, and the bankrupt company has assets situated within the Norwegian jurisdiction, in principle that bankruptcy as such is not recognised in Norway. This effectively means that the insolvency administrator of a non-Norwegian master account holder cannot, on the basis of the foreign bankruptcy proceedings alone, seize the balance in the master account if this account is situated with a Norwegian bank. Any individual creditor may open separate debt recovery proceedings against the master account holder in Norway and claim fulfilment of the debt from the master account holder's assets situated in Norway (ie, its bank account). The preparatory works to the Satisfaction of Claims Act do, however, presume that the bankruptcy estate of a foreign company may also initiate debt recovery proceedings in Norway on behalf of the company's creditors as a whole, in respect of the debtor's assets situated in Norway.

The Ministry of Justice is in the process of reviewing Norwegian international insolvency law. The current recommendations suggest that Norwegian rules on this issue should be modelled after the EU Insolvency Regulation. The consultation procedure ended on March 1 2012, but it is unclear when legislation will be in place.

When it comes to insolvency proceedings in respect of credit institutions, Norway has implemented the EU Winding Up Directive.[30] This means that Norwegian authorities accept the effects of bankruptcy proceedings in respect of a foreign bank as regards its Norwegian branch. However, if in a liquidation situation the bank continues to honour its obligations in its home state, but does not do so in relation to its Norwegian branch, a Norwegian administrative regulation[31] states that that branch may be subject to a separate liquidation process in Norway.

The following discussion is based on the principles of Norwegian insolvency law.

(a) General principles of determining seizable assets

When it comes to seizing the credit balance, the Satisfaction of Claims Act Section 2-2 states that:

> *Except as otherwise provided by this statute or other valid provision, the creditors have the right to seek satisfaction in any property which belongs to the debtor at the time of attachment, and which can be sold, leased or otherwise converted into money.*

To what extent the insolvency administrator of the bank, the master account holder or group company can claim either the entire credit balance or its part of the credit balance in the cash pooling agreement account(s) will therefore generally depend upon whether that credit balance actually belongs to the debtor. In order to determine this, the parties' underlying contractual relationship as defined in the cash pooling agreement must be analysed.

In certain cases assets that are not in principle owned by the debtor may be deemed to be part of the seizable assets. This happens when someone else's assets are legally held by the debtor, but mixed in with debtor's own assets in such a manner

30 Directive 2001/24/EC of the European Parliament and of the Council on the reorganisation and winding up of credit institutions.

31 Administrative Regulation of December 12 2008 on the opening of public administration in respect of a Norwegian branch of a credit institution with its primary establishment in a foreign state.

that they cannot be clearly separated. Such a situation is typically the case with loans: the funds borrowed by the debtor go into an operating account together with all the other funds that belong to the debtor. The specific funds that were the subject of the loan can no longer be separated from the rest of the debtor's assets, and are therefore seized by the debtor's insolvency administrator.

In a cash pooling agreement that is either a zero balancing scheme or a single legal account,[32] all funds that go through the system are treated as inter-company loans. When funds flow to and from the different companies within the corporate group through inter-company loans, the money, once lent, cannot be specifically and clearly distinguished from the other funds in the account. In the case of insolvency of either the master account holder or a group company, the insolvency administrator will therefore most likely seize the positive balance held in the name of the legal account holder. Due to the difference between zero balancing, notional pooling and single legal account pooling in this respect, there is also a difference as to what may be seized.

When it comes to the relationship between the different legal account holders and the bank, the principle is the same. If a party puts money into a bank account in its name, the deposit is an asset belonging to the depositor. However, the deposit is really a non-secured claim on the bank. The actual money is mixed with the bank's funds in such a way that it cannot be specifically and clearly distinguished from the other funds. In the event of the bank's insolvency, the bank's insolvency administrator will therefore seize the positive balance held in the name of the legal account holder.

In addition, in a bankruptcy situation, any creditor might have the right to offset off any claim the debtor has against it with any claim it has against the debtor, and which is due at the time of the bankruptcy filing. For example, if in a single legal account scheme the single legal account has a positive balance, the bank can generally offset this against a claim it has against the master account holder when the latter goes into liquidation. However, if the parties to the cash pooling agreement have explicitly provided in the agreement that set-offs cannot be made, the contractual provisions of the cash pooling agreement take precedence over the general right to offset a claim in bankruptcy situations.

Below, we provide a quick walkthrough of the three different types of cash pooling schemes in event of insolvency of the bank, a group company or the master account holder. The right of set-off outlined above is additional to the considerations discussed below.

(b) *Single legal account schemes*

The nature of a single legal account scheme is that there is only one actual legal account held by one of the participants: the master account holder. From a legal perspective, the master account holder is the only counterparty to the bank in the cash pooling agreement. The sub-accounts are off-balance sheet, and their only function is to keep track of the debts and claims between the master account holder and the group companies. In these situations the following would apply:

32 As explained in section 1.2 above.

- The bank goes into liquidation –
  - A negative balance means that the bank has a money claim against the master account holder. This money claim will be seized by the insolvency administrator, meaning that the administrator will claim payment of the negative balance from the master account holder.
  - A positive balance means that the master account holder has a money claim against the bank. However, the funds are mixed with the bank's assets, meaning that the master account holder will be unable to claim the positive balance from the bank, but will have to make a claim against the insolvency estate. The balance is effectively seized by the bank's insolvency administrator. However, the master account holder will be able to recover deposits with the bank of up to Nkr2 million through the Norwegian deposit guarantee scheme.
  - Any sub-accounts in the hands of group companies – whether the balance is positive or negative – do not reflect debts to or claims against the bank, but debts to or claims against the master account holder. This means that the bank may not, based on the negative balance in a sub-account[33] itself or the cash pooling agreement as such, make an independent claim against any group company. Likewise, the group companies are not party to the agreement establishing the single legal account, and therefore have no contractual relationship with the bank and cannot make independent claims against the bank.
- The master account holder goes into liquidation –
  - If the master account has a negative balance, the master account holder will not have a claim against the bank – there is nothing to be seized in the master account holder's hand from the bank. The bank on its part will have to seek recovery of the loan (the negative balance) by making a claim against the master account holder's insolvency estate (or possibly using whatever security or guarantee the bank has received).
  - In a single legal account scheme, the bank will usually have reserved the right to offset any negative balance in the master account with any other bank account that any company in the corporate group has with the bank outside the cash pooling agreement. The bank might also have obtained guarantees from other companies in the corporate group.
  - If the master account has a positive balance, the master account holder's estate may generally seize the entire credit balance, because the positive balance in the master account is effectively a money claim against the bank. When it comes to the relationship between the master account holder and group companies, the money lent from any group company to the master account holder cannot be specifically and clearly distinguished from the other funds in the account, and these companies will have no grounds to claim their part of the positive balance from the master account holder.

---

33 Which is only a cost control account – see section 1.2 above.

- A group company goes into liquidation –
  - In a single legal account scheme, the group companies are not party to the actual cash pooling agreement between the bank and the master account holder, but only continuously lend and borrow money through inter-company loans. The balances in the sub-account merely reflect this inter-company loan relationship and have no legally direct implications towards the bank, only the company's position as regards the master account holder.
  - A positive balance on a cost control sub-account will mean that the master account holder owes the group company money, a money claim that is seized by the group company's insolvency administrator.
  - A negative balance on a cost control sub-account will mean that the group company owes the master account holder money – but again, this is not money in a separate account, but loans from the master account holder to the group company. The master account holder will have to make a claim against the group company's insolvency estate.

Physical pooling – zero balancing and target balancing schemes: In a physical pooling scheme with end-of-business-day zero balancing or periodic target balancing, the same general principles apply when it comes to seizing the money in the accounts. Once money has been lent, it is mixed with the debtor's assets in a non-distinguishable manner. The difference between this situation and a single legal account scheme, however, is that every sub-account is a legal account.

This means that before sweeping is done, the funds have not been mixed with other entities' assets. In the event of either the master account holder or a group company going into liquidation, this is a crucial difference from a single legal account scheme. It makes no difference whether the bank goes into liquidation, though, as any positive balance in any sub-account before a sweep is still mixed with the bank's assets in an indistinguishable manner.

This gives the following situations when one of the bank, the master account holder or a group company goes into liquidation:

- The bank goes into liquidation – given that each sub-account is an actual account, any positive balance in any sub-account that has not yet been swept will go into the bank's estate, as will the positive balance in the master account. At the same time, the bank's insolvency administrator may still claim the negative balance on each sub-account from the master account holder and each individual group company. This may put the bank's estate in a better situation than after a sweep has been done. If the claims and debts of that day (or period) are not offset against each other or against the balance of the master account, the bank could claim repayment of any negative balances in the sub-accounts, even though the total balance of the sub-accounts or the balance of the master account is positive.
- The same principles apply if the master account holder goes into liquidation. The individual group companies may claim that the balance on their sub-account before zero sweeping represents their debt to or claim against the

bank, and not the master account holder. Before the sweep, the money has not been mixed with the master account holder's assets and should therefore be held separate from its insolvency estate. This is only relevant if the balance on the sub-account is positive – to prevent it away from being seized by the master account holder's estate.

- If a group company goes into liquidation, the same principles apply. If a sweep has not been done, the insolvency administrator will claim the positive balance in the sub-account. If the balance is negative, he will make a claim against the master account holder for the money lent to it.

However, in any cash pooling agreement that is not a single legal account scheme, the agreement will usually contain terms that, for example, allow the bank to offset any claims against one participating group company against any deposit from another, and/or to include cross-guarantees giving one of the bank, the master account holder or the group company special rights to claim the balance in another account, should that account holder owe a debt to them.

Notional pooling: In a cash pooling agreement with notional pooling, only the interest positions are consolidated. All the accounts in the cash pool are legal accounts and no inter-company loans are registered as a consequence of the cash pooling agreement. In the event that the bank, the master account holder or a group company goes into liquidation, the situation will be identical to the example given above for zero balancing before a sweep. The bank's insolvency administrator will take any positive balance in any account; the master account holder's insolvency administrator will claim the positive balance of the master account holder's account; and a group company's administrator will claim the positive balance of that company's account.

Interest payments follow the same system. Before the positions are consolidated, the interest will belong to each account and follow the insolvency administrator's seizure of the balance in that account. However, in the event of bankruptcy of either the master account holder or a group company, the bank will have the right of set-off.

Close-out netting in zero balancing or notional pooling schemes: The situations reviewed above illustrate the general rules according to Norwegian insolvency law. In cash pooling agreements involving several legal accounts, however, and where all the companies are parties to the cash pooling agreement, they may agree to close-out netting in the agreement under the Financial Collateral Act. The Financial Collateral Act is the Norwegian implementation of the EU Directive on Financial Collateral arrangements.[34] In these cases, the bank obtains security in the form of any deposits from any of the participating companies for any outstanding debt – so-called financial collateral. The act applies to any agreement pertaining to financial

---

34 Directive 2002/47/EC of the European Parliament and of the Council on financial collateral arrangements.

collateral, and states that the parties to a financial collateral agreement may agree that financial obligations should be subject to close-out netting in case of certain events as defined in the agreement.[35] The agreement will then be terminated, all accounts are offset against each other and only the final balance is to be settled by whichever party owes the other. The parties are free to agree upon which netting events apply, for instance in the event of possible insolvency or liquidation. If the parties have entered into a financial collateral agreement, in a liquidation event the process will follow the principles of the agreement and not the general rules of the Satisfaction of Claims Act.

The principle that an agreement on financial collateral takes precedence over the rights of the insolvency estate applies in relation to all aspects of the agreement, including the parties' possibility of acceding to or terminating an agreement in the event of bankruptcy (see section 2.3(c) below).

Insolvency administrator's obligations as regards other parties to the cash pooling agreement: Generally, the insolvency administrator will have no particular obligations to any other party to a cash pooling agreement. One exception occurs if one of the other parties to the agreement specifically asks whether the bankruptcy estate wishes to accede to the agreement, in which case the insolvency administrator has a duty to answer without undue delay.[36] If the insolvency administrator does not respond without undue delay, the other party can generally consider itself no longer bound by the agreement. Furthermore, the insolvency administrator has, under the Bankruptcy Act, a general obligation to safeguard the common interest of the creditors as a group against individual creditors and against third parties.

Transfers made prior to bankruptcy: Under the Satisfaction of Claims Act, the transfer of funds or furnishing of security prior to a bankruptcy may be declared void in certain situations. The act provides for declaring a transaction void both on objective grounds and if a transaction has been made in bad faith. The insolvency administrator will have to challenge any individual transaction he deems to be voidable, and, if necessary, obtain a judgement in court.[37]

Under Section 5-5 of the act, any payment of debts made less than three months before the bankruptcy,[38] may be declared void by the insolvency administrator if:

- the transfer of funds has manifestly weakened the debtor's ability to meet its payments; and
- the transfer cannot be deemed to be an ordinary transaction.

---

35 Financial Collateral Act, Section 6.

36 Satisfation of Claims Act, Section 7-3.

37 If a transfer has been made under a cash pooling agreement that the insolvency administrator deems is of no further interest to the bankruptcy estate, he will generally choose to not accede to the agreement (effectively terminating it). Terminating the agreement as such from the time of the bankruptcy is a different issue from voiding an individual transaction made under the agreement before bankruptcy is declared, and termination is discussed in section 2.3 (c) below.

38 The Satisfaction of Claims Act uses the term 'time limit', which will usually be set at the date of filing for bankruptcy, however, the time limit may be pushed back if the contitions for backruptcy (combined cash-flow and balance-sheet insolvency) are shown to have manifested before the filing date.

Both of these conditions must be present in any individual case. In general, if funds are transferred under a cash pooling agreement in the course of the daily business activities of the corporate group and no bad faith has been shown, there is a high probability that the transfer will be deemed to be an ordinary transaction, even if the transfer represents a payment of debts from company A to company B that has manifestly weakened A's liquidity. However, this provision may be used only if the transfer represents a repayment of debts (repaying credit already provided to that company under the cash pooling agreement – that is, covering a negative balance) and cannot be used if the transfer represents new credit from the now- insolvent company.[39]

In addition, Section 5-9 of the act regulates invalidity where the other party has not acted in good faith. According to the wording, any:

> *transactions which improperly give preference to one creditor at the expense of the others, or prevent the debtor's assets from being used to pay off the creditors, or increase the debtor's liabilities in an manner detrimental to the creditors, may be voided if the debtor's financial situation was weak or was seriously weakened by the transaction, and the other party to the transaction knew or should have known of the debtor's financial difficulties and the circumstances that made the transaction improper.*

There are examples of cases where a company's insolvency administrator has brought actions against the company's bank or against other companies in the corporate group under both of these provisions – for example, if the bank has kept a revolving credit facility open in spite of the company's critical situation,[40] or if a transaction has been made between companies. These types of transactions may be held void under Section 5-5 of the act, particularly if the payment was made several months after the debt's maturity date, or held void under Section 5-9 of the act if the other company acted as set out in that provision.

If the insolvency administrator is appointed abroad, the bankruptcy proceedings will be based on the rules of that jurisdiction. There is no basis in Norwegian law for disregarding or declaring void any transactions if the proceedings as such are not subject to Norwegian law. Such a claim against a Norwegian company would potentially have to be settled under the relevant laws in the competent jurisdiction.

(b) Special rules as regards creditors of other parties to the cash pooling agreement

An insolvency administrator does not have to observe any special rules or obligations as regards the creditors of the other parties to the cash pooling agreement under Norwegian law. The insolvency administrator will deal only with the creditors of the debtor that is under his administration.

(c) Dissolution/termination of cash pooling agreement in the event of liquidation of the master account holder holder or a group company

The fate of the cash pooling agreement in a liquidation situation will depend both on the type of agreement and on which company goes into liquidation.

---

39 In these cases the party receiving the payment will owe the now-insolvent company money, for which the insolvency administrator will demand repayment from that receiving party as an ordinary claim. Therefore, there is no need to void the transaction.

40 See the Supreme Court's decision in Case Rt-2001-1136.

In principle, it follows from the Satisfaction of Claims Act Section 7-3 that the insolvency administrator can freely choose to accede to or terminate any agreement to which the debtor is party. However, Section 7-4 states that if the agreement is acceded to, this means that the estate is bound by the agreement on its existing terms, meaning that the fulfilment risk is now taken over by the estate. Effectively, all obligations under the agreement will then be deemed preferential claims in the estate. The consequence is that the insolvency administrator will generally not choose to accede to an agreement if there is a moderate to high risk associated with the potential obligations under the agreement. If the insolvency administrator does not choose to accede to the agreement, it is considered terminated between the parties. The insolvency administrator will generally give an explicit and immediate statement to any counterparty regarding an agreement to which the administrator does not wish to accede.

In addition, the other party to the agreement may in principle not terminate the agreement on grounds of the insolvency alone. However, if the insolvency administrator has acceded to the agreement, the other party may terminate the agreement under the terms of the agreement itself.

As mentioned, when it comes to a cash pooling agreement with a bank, the agreement will sometimes include a provision on financial collateral close-out netting under the Financial Collateral Act. If this is the case, then the agreement on financial collateral takes precedence over the general provisions of the Satisfaction of Claims Act. If the parties have agreed upon a default event that triggers the right to termination and close-out netting, this applies notwithstanding the general ban on cancelling agreements on the basis of a counterparty's insolvency or liquidation.

2.4 Perspective D: regulatory

Granting credit as a means to finance another party's business activities, as is done within a cash pooling agreement, falls within the scope of the Financial Enterprises Act. All financial institutions providing such credit must be licensed.

From the point of view of the participating companies in the cash pooling agreement, they will provide such credit, but the act states that granting credit within a corporate group is an activity that falls outside its regulatory scope. Under the act, the Norwegian Financial Supervisory Authority may decide that entities that fall outside the regulatory scope of the act are nonetheless subject to supervision. We are, however, unaware of any cases in which a master account holder has been subject to supervision from the Norwegian Financial Supervisory Authority because of cash pooling agreements.

2.5 Perspective E: tax

(a) General

Limited companies (and corporate partners of partnerships) are liable to 28% corporate income tax on their worldwide earnings. Companies where the effective management at board level is carried out in Norway and companies incorporated under Norwegian law and registered in the Norwegian Registry of Business

Enterprises are considered resident in Norway for tax purposes. In order for foreign incorporated companies[41] to avoid tax residency in Norway, the board meetings and other decisions, beyond the day-to-day management of the company, must take place outside Norway.

Each company within a corporate group is, as a general rule, treated as a separate entity, and assets, dividends, interest, income and deductions cannot be moved between companies.[42]

In a physical cash pooling scheme, the transfers between group companies are treated as inter-company loans for both accounting and tax purposes. In general, no tax issues should arise in relation to the loan amount itself, because taxation and deduction is relevant only when it comes to either profits (income) or losses. However, accrued interest in a physical or notional cash pooling scheme is taxable corporate income. Also, if a company's income (including income from interest on inter-company loans) is reduced because of a common interest with another entity – which, for example, might be the case in a notional pooling scheme if a company, by participating in the cash pooling agreement, receives less income from interest than it would if its balance were not netted against the balances of the other companies in the corporate group – it may be subject to tax assessment.

(b) Withholding tax

There is no withholding tax on outward-bound interest payments under domestic law. When it comes to taxation of receipts, interest payments are taxable corporate income.

(c) Transfer pricing issues

With regard to interest incurred in physical cash pooling schemes and in notional cash pooling schemes, all interest on business debts (and loans) is deductible (or taxable) whether paid periodically or discounted. The extent to which inter-company loans are deductible depends on whether the payments are based on the arm's-length principle (ie, the extent to which an independent lender would lend money to a company with the current debt-to-equity ratio). Normally, a debt-to-equity ratio of 85:15 will be considered a safe harbour.

If the loans are not based on an arm's-length principle, the companies involved that are resident in Norway may be subject to a discretionary tax assessment of their income by the Norwegian tax authorities. The tax authorities, in making the tax assessment, should take into account the principles for transfer pricing as adopted by Organisation for Economic Cooperation and Development.[43]

---

41 Companies registered outside the Norwegian jurisdiction.

42 If a resident company holds more than 90% of the capital and votes of another resident company they will constitute a tax group. However, this is relevant only when it comes to making tax-deductible group contributions and intra-group transfers of assets without immediate realisation of latent gains.

43 Report: "Transfer Pricing Guidelines for Multinational Enterprises and Tax Administrations" [C (95) 126/Final].

Portugal

Miguel de Avillez Pereira
João Ochôa
Abreu Advogados

1. Introduction

1.1 Admissibility of cash pooling agreements

Portuguese civil law provides for the principle of the autonomy of parties to choose and agree upon, within the limits of the law, the terms of a contract that they intend to enter into. Cash pooling arrangements are not specifically regulated by law, and consequently are admissible under this freedom of contract. Nevertheless, there are laws and regulations that apply to cash pooling agreements. For a company to enter successfully into a cash pool agreement it must take into account corporate, banking, insolvency and tax laws and regulations. In addition, there are certain limits on freedom of contract – imperative rules set out in the law, consisting mainly of core principles deemed to be essential for upholding the values of society, and which it is therefore not possible for the parties to set aside (known as public order rules). Any clauses within a cash pooling agreement not complying with these rules are deemed to be null and void, although the remaining part of the contract will remain enforceable where the severability of the offending clauses makes this possible. As regards particular liability issues (eg, allocations, exclusions, limitations), the law sets out some restrictions on the parties' freedom to agree on their terms.

1.2 Types of cash pooling agreement

The most common types of cash pooling used by Portuguese companies are notional cash pooling and zero balancing (also known as cash concentration).

In notional cash pooling, there is a fictitious consolidation of account balances, which means that there is no real movement of funds between the accounts. Credit and debit balances on the accounts are notional, and are brought together by the financial institution for the calculation of interest. In this situation all of the entities that are part of the cash pooling agreement hold current accounts at a financial institution. An overdraft facility can be available for all accounts, but the balances remain in the participants' accounts. The daily balances, however, are recorded and the computation of interest is made on a fictitious consolidated amount and computed via the master account. With this type of cash pooling there is no co-ownership, as the balance offset is purely virtual.

In cash concentration (or zero balancing), there is a bank account in which the balances of the various participants' accounts are physically combined. Generally, all the bank accounts participating in the operation are brought to zero (zero balancing) on the periodic transfer of the funds to the master account.

1.3 General legal requirements

One of the first issues to bear in mind concerns the power to enter into short-term financing agreements.

Unless otherwise provided in a company's bylaws, the decision to enter into short-term financing agreements falls within the general powers of management granted by law to the board of directors. Bearing in mind that directors are bound to act in the interests of the company, it is advisable that the cash pooling agreement be approved by a resolution of the board of directors that includes the reasoning behind the decision to enter into the agreement.

If it is expected that the master account holder or a group company, when entering into a cash pooling agreement, will not be serving its own financing needs, because it will be systematically putting its own cash surpluses at the disposal of other group companies, the agreement may serve as a means of investing those cash surpluses against the payment of interest. Such investment of cash surpluses is also within the powers of the board of directors.

Again, given the directors' duty to act in the interests of the company, the reason for using such cash surpluses by entering into the agreement should be explained in the resolution of the board of directors that approves it.

In that respect, the parties involved – particularly the master account holder and the group companies – should gather sufficient evidence that the decision to participate in the agreement has been taken in the best interests of each company, taking into account the parties' potential need for future financing (unlikely though it may be). However, other stakeholders (eg, suppliers, other creditors) may have an interest in the decision, particularly if they are adversely affected by it, in which case they have standing to challenge the cash pooling agreement and seek its nullity or annulment.

It is also necessary to verify whether the financing arrangement under the cash pooling agreement fulfils relevant banking laws and regulations.

According to the General Regime for Credit and Financial Institutions, legally permitted cash pooling agreements are not deemed to be the exercise of a financial activity or provision of credit, as long as the participating entities are part of a group of companies under common control. At first sight, the term 'legally permitted' may seem to imply that the credit facilities under a cash pooling agreement are lawful only where expressly permitted – and that possibility is expressly allowed only for a specific type of company group controlled by a holding company, the SGPS.[1] However, the benefits of a cash pooling agreement apply to the entire group and there is no reason to limit the possibility of a centralised cash management structure to a group controlled by an SGPS, particularly given that a bank is generally involved in the day-to-day management of the structure and in securing debit and credit movements between the different participating entities.

---

1 The SGPS, or *Sociedade Gestora de Participações Sociais*, is the form required by Portuguese law for holding companies.

It is generally accepted that in cash pooling agreements between a master account holder and other companies in the same group, the operations under the cash pooling agreement do not entail the exercise of a financial activity, and therefore there are no banking requirements that the company must comply with.

Another common practical question in connection with cash pooling agreements relates to the choice of law and the choice of jurisdiction in agreements between a domestic national group of companies and a foreign bank, between a transnational group and a national bank, or between a transnational group and a foreign bank. Portuguese law provides that the obligations arising from a contract and its substance are regulated by the law that the respective parties have chosen and indicated, provided that the law selected by the parties is genuinely in the interests of the parties or has a connection with some of the element of the contract. The Code of Civil Procedure also establishes freedom of choice of jurisdiction in cases that are not purely domestic situations.

If the parties to the agreement are residents in EU member states, freedom of choice of law is even broader, as under Article 3 of EU Regulation 593/2008 on the law applicable to contractual obligations (Rome I), no specific interest or connection to the law of choice is required. The choice of jurisdiction where one or all parties of the cash pooling agreement are resident in a EU member state may also be made freely under Article 23 of EU Regulation 44/2001 (Brussels I).

2. Specific questions

2.1 Perspective A: corporate group

(a) Liability of group company and/or master account holder in the event of insolvency of a group company

An insolvency procedure is an element which may bring additional risks and liabilities in a cash pooling scenario.

Under Portuguese law, in the event of the insolvency of a group company, all assets of the Portuguese group company would become part of the insolvency estate. These assets would include any amounts deposited in the master account.

Cash pooling arrangements may survive the insolvency proceedings. However, a cash pooling agreement may also provide that the start of insolvency proceedings will trigger its automatic termination. Even though such a provision could be deemed to be unenforceable under Portuguese insolvency law,[2] the cash pooling agreement should establish a termination right linked to the commencement of insolvency proceedings, in which case no amounts should be transferred to or from the master account after that event.

Portuguese law provides that contracts signed in the four years preceding the insolvency proceedings may be annulled by the judicial liquidator, meaning that amounts paid during that period might become part of the insolvency estate, if they have damaged the interests of the insolvent company. The judicial liquidator may

---

2 Article 119º of the Insolvency and Recovery Code.

decide on such termination at any time within a period of two years from the commencement of the insolvency proceedings.

Under Articles 17 and 25 of the EU Insolvency Regulation (1346/2000), insolvency proceedings commenced in Portugal shall, with no further formalities, produce the same effects in any other EU member state as under Portuguese law, thus extending to other EU member states the applicability of the Portuguese court's and liquidator's decisions.

The only scenario where such recognition would not come about is if the decision would breach public policy rules of the other EU member state in which enforcement is being sought.[3]

However, the local liquidator may not challenge:

- the rights of a creditor under a valid security interest created under a different law, provided that at the moment of commencement of the insolvency procedures, the asset is located in an EU member state (apart from Denmark) other than Portugal (a bank deposit is deemed to be located in the jurisdiction where the relevant account is held);[4] and
- set-off rights under the governing law applicable to the debtor's cross-claim.[5]

Portuguese companies are prevented from returning any assets to their shareholders if that action would have the effect of making the company's net shareholders' equity less than the combined sum of the company's share capital and general reserves (or any other reserves specified in the company's bylaws).

If, as a result of those payments, the Portuguese group company's net shareholders' equity becomes less than the combined sum of its share capital and general reserves, that payment may be deemed to have been made unlawfully.[6] The directors of a Portuguese company that has unlawfully reduced its capital are subject to a fine and liable in the event of insolvency. The directors' liability for any loss in the event of insolvency is joint and several.

An unlawful distribution of dividends, however, should not in itself affect the validity of the set-off, but only create an obligation for the parent company to return the assets.

As a general rule, which is not only applicable to cash pooling agreements, when companies are under total direct or indirect control, the holding company is liable in the event of the insolvency of a group company and also in the event of breach of contract.[7] This rule is also applicable to companies under subordination contracts, with the controlling company being liable where annual losses are not covered by reserves and where the subordinate company breaches a contract.[8]

(b) Liability of group company and/or master account holder directors in the event of insolvency of the master account holder and/or a group company

As a general rule, which is also applicable to cash pooling agreements, the directors

3 Article 26 of the EU Insolvency Regulation.
4 Article 5 of the EU Insolvency Regulation.
5 Article 286 of the Insolvency Law, which replicates Article 6 of the EU Insolvency Regulation.
6 Article 32 of the Companies Code.
7 Articles 501 and 491 and Articles 481 *et seq* of the Companies Code.

of the participating companies must act diligently and always in each company's best interests. If they can show that the best interests of the company they manage (whether a group company or the master account holder) is to enter into the cash pooling agreements, there will be no liability for the directors. If the directors do not comply with this rule, they will be liable. As an example, if the cash pooling agreement does not allow for automatic termination and the group company cannot finance itself by other means while the cash pooling agreement could affect its financial stability, the cash pooling agreement could be interpreted as displaying a lack of diligence on the directors' part and a lack of respect for the company's best interests, and therefore give grounds for the directors' having liability.

To avoid any directors' liabilities in the event of insolvency of the master account holder the liquidity of the group company must be assured and vice versa. In order to do that, the cash pooling agreement should permit the possibility to sweep its cash surpluses from the master account. If that is not possible, then the cash pooling agreements should specifically provide for alternative financing.

(c) Liability of group companies in the event of insolvency of the master account holder

No particular liabilities are foreseen for the group company in the event of insolvency of the master account holder. See the discussion in the previous paragraphs.

2.2 Perspective B: bank

(a) Banking requirements

In Portugal, there are no specific rules concerning calculation of the capital requirements for net exposure in respect of cash pooling agreements.

The rules applicable to capital requirements are governed by the general regime. Under this regime, for credit risk and dilution risk in respect of all business activities – with the exception of their trading book business and illiquid assets if these are deducted from own funds – credit institutions and investment firms are required to provide own funds which are at all times more than or equal to 8% of the total of their risk-weighted exposure amounts, calculated in accordance with Decree-Law 104/2007 and as defined in Central Bank Regulation 5/2007.

The rules are applicable only to banks incorporated in Portugal or subject to the prudential supervision of the Central Bank.[9]

(b) Liability of the bank in the event of insolvency of the master account holder or a group company

A bank involved in a cash pooling agreement cannot be held liable for any losses in the event that the master account holder or a group company goes into insolvency.

---

8 Articles 501 to 504 of the Companies Code.

9 Articles 3 and 4 of Decree-Law 104/2007, dated April 3 2007.

2.3 Insolvency

(a) *Cash pooling agreements from the insolvency practitioner's perspective*

As mentioned above, Portuguese law foresees that contracts signed in the four years preceding the insolvency proceedings may be terminated by the judicial liquidator, meaning that amounts paid during that period might become part of the insolvency estate if they are deemed to have damaged the interests of the insolvent company, whether the Portuguese master account holder or a Portuguese group company. The judicial liquidator may decide on such termination at any time within a period of two years following commencement of the insolvency proceedings.

Under Articles 17 and 25 of the EU Insolvency Regulation, insolvency proceedings commenced in Portugal shall, with no further formalities, produce the same effects in any other EU member state as under Portuguese law, thus extending to other EU member states the applicability of the Portuguese court's or liquidator's decisions.

The only scenario where such recognition come about is if the decision would breach the public policy rules of the EU member state in which enforcement is being sought.[10]

However, the local liquidator may not challenge:

- the rights of a creditor under a valid security interest created under a different law, provided that at the moment of commencement of the insolvency proceedings, the asset is located in an EU member state that is not Portugal (a bank deposit is deemed to be located in the jurisdiction where the relevant account is held);[11] or
- set-off rights under the governing law applicable to the debtor's cross-claim.[12]

In the event that either the master account holder or a group company goes into liquidation, any amounts owed to other members of the group are deemed to be unsecured credits and are therefore paid only after payment of secured creditors.

(b) *Dissolution/termination of the cash pooling agreement in the event of liquidation of the master account holder or a group company*

As mentioned above, no legal provision requires that cash pooling agreements be automatically terminated by the commencement of insolvency proceedings. However, the cash pooling documentation may provide that the commencement of insolvency proceedings will trigger automatic termination of the cash pooling agreement. Even though we have some reservations as to whether such a provision would be enforceable under Portuguese insolvency law,[13] it is advisable that the agreement establish a termination right linked to the commencement of insolvency proceedings, and no amounts should be transferred to or from the master account by the Portuguese group company once that event occurs.

Portuguese law foresees that contracts signed in the four years preceding the

---

10 Article 26 of the EU Insolvency Regulation.
11 Article 5 of the EU Insolvency Regulation.
12 Article 286 of the Insolvency Law, which replicates Article 6 of the EU Insolvency Regulation.
13 Article 119º of the Insolvency and Recovery Code.

insolvency proceedings may be terminated by the judicial liquidator, meaning that amounts paid during that period might become part of the insolvency estate if they are deemed to have damaged the interests of the insolvent company, whether that be a Portuguese group company or the master account holder. The judicial liquidator may decide on such termination at any time within a period of two years following commencement of the insolvency proceedings.

2.4 Perspective D: regulatory

In principle, cash pooling agreements within a group of companies under common control do not amount to the exercise of a financial business activity. As noted above, under the general regime for credit and financial institutions, legally permitted cash pooling agreements are not deemed to constitute the exercise of a financial activity. Thus, cash pooling agreements are not deemed to be the provision of credit for the purposes of Portuguese banking laws, provided that the participating entities are part of a group under common control.

There are no specific regulatory requirements with which a Portuguese company must comply when entering into a cash pooling agreement.

2.5 Perspective E: tax

Cash pooling agreements may be subject to stamp duties and withholding taxes. The agreement must also operate at arm's length.

(a) Stamp duties

Stamp duties are levied in respect of all transactions carried out within Portuguese jurisdiction of the types set out in the General Table of Stamp Duties, which includes the provision of credit. Even though it is questionable, the Portuguese tax authorities take the view that loans granted by Portuguese entities to foreign entities are also liable to stamp duties.

The General Table of Stamp Duties establishes, as a general rule, that financial operations (including loans and treasury operations, in general, which comprise short term financing agreement) are subject to stamp duties, computed as appears below.

Term of the credit	Tax rate
Less than 1 year	0.04% (per month or fraction)
1 year to 5 years	0.5%
5 years or more	0.6%
Undetermined (eg, current accounts, overdraft facilities and other loans where the term is not pre-determined)	0.04% per month, assessed on the monthly average debt, which is calculated by adding up the daily negative balances and dividing them by 30)

In addition, where a short-term financing agreement involves the granting of guarantees, additional stamp duties may become due, as follows.

Duration of the credit	Tax rate
Less than 1 year	0.04% (per month or part of the month)
1 year to 5 years	0.5%
5 years or more No time limit	0.6%

As treasury (short-term) operations, cash pooling agreements generally come within the 'undetermined' category, meaning that stamp duties, if and when due, are calculated at the end of each month, on the basis of the average daily balances accrued during that month.

The taxpayer – that is, the company responsible for levying the tax and delivering it to the tax authorities – is the participating company that lends the money (ie, that in any given month takes a creditor position in the cash pooling agreement). However, where the lender is a non-resident company, it is the borrower that is responsible.

That said, the company that should bear the economic burden of the tax is the company that borrows the money, meaning that the lending company should recover from the borrower (by reference to each month) the amount of stamp duties it delivers to the tax authorities.

In the case of the additional duty payable on the provision of guarantees, the economic burden of the tax should stay with the beneficiary of the guarantee (generally, the master account holder).

However, some financial operations are exempted from stamp duties:

- treasury operations (loans and interest payments) for periods not exceeding one year, made by one corporation in favour of a corporation in which it holds a direct participation of at least 10% (so it applies only to downstreamloans and is not available where the creditor is the subsidiary),[14] and provided that participation has been held for a minimum consecutive period of one year or since the company's incorporation (in this latter case, provided further that it remains at such level for a period of one year); and
- treasury operations (loans and interest payments), for periods not exceeding one year, made by an SGPS[15] in favour of controlled companies or companies in which the SGPS has a participation, or made by a controlled company or one in which the SGPS has a participation in favour of the SGPS.

14 To avoid taxation on upstream loans, such loans are usually structured via tax planning schemes using the issuance of commercial paper.

15 *Sociedade Gestora de Participações Sociais*, the form required by Portuguese law for holding companies – see section 1.3 above.

In the case of cash pooling agreements, the first exemption will be applicable whenever a participating company that is in the position of being a lender under the scheme owns 10% or more of the borrowing company. In other situations, stamp duties should be assessed and levied.

(b) ***Arm's-length pricing and withholding tax***

Related entities should carry on business between themselves on regular market conditions. This means that any transaction carried out between related entities should be priced at arm's length.

The arm's-length price is generally determined by reference to local transfer pricing rules and regulations. In cash pooling agreements, this affects two different types of transaction:

- services provided by the master account holder, generally related to the setting up and administration of the arrangements with the bank;
- loans provided by group companies and by the master account holder within the arrangements themselves.

Remuneration for services provided: The master account holder may be paid for its services if services are being provided by it.

Under the Corporate Income Tax Code, payments for services provided by a non-resident company to resident companies are subject to withholding tax at a rate of 15%. However, where a double tax treaty applies and the appropriate tax residence certificates are provided, such withholding tax may be waived.

Income derived by a resident company is subject to the general corporate income tax rates.

Interest on loans provided under the cash pooling agreement: The use of funds in the cash pool by a company participating in the cash pooling agreement should generate an interest payment in favour to the company that makes those funds available.

Interest payments are subject to corporate income tax in the hands of the recipient of the interest. If the beneficiary is a Portuguese company, the interest is subject to tax at the general domestic corporate income tax rates.

If the interest is paid by a Portuguese entity to a non-resident company, the interest may be subject to a withholding tax rate of 5%, in line with the EU Interest and Royalties Directive (provided that all other requirements are met) if both companies are deemed to be associated – that is

- the first company has a direct minimum holding of 25% in the capital of the second company;
- the second company has a direct minimum holding of 25% in the capital of the first company; or
- a third company has a direct minimum holding of 25% both in the capital of the first company and in the capital of the second company.

If these requirements are not met, one of the more than 50 double tax treaties to which Portugal is a party may apply.

If neither the Interest and Royalties Directive nor a double tax treaty is applicable, the Corporate Income Tax Code prescribes a domestic withholding tax of 25%.

Under Portuguese transfer pricing legislation, whenever a transaction with a related party is not conducted at arm's length, the tax authorities have the power to make the necessary adjustments in order to reassess the company profits that would have been accrued if the underlying transaction had been conducted on a commercial basis.

In our opinion, this regime is applicable to any transaction carried out between related parties and therefore will apply to a cash pooling agreement. Therefore, in drafting and implementing the cash pooling agreement, the group should draft clear and detailed cash pooling agreements, addressing the following aspects in such a way as to demonstrate that the transaction is being carried out at an arm's-length price and under commercial conditions:

- criteria for determining the appropriate interest rate to be applied to intragroup balances:
- consideration of the duration of the position – typically, the cash pool positions are short term, so a short-term interest rate is applied. However, often there are companies that are frequently cash positive (which will be regular lenders), while others are usually cash negative (which will be regular borrowers). Therefore, consideration should be given to the possibility that positions in a cash pool that start off as being short term end up as long-term loans. In these situations, the payment of short-term interest rates could be regarded by the tax authorities as not being made at arm's length;
- consideration of the functional risk profile – the interest rate should vary with the risk level among the pooling participants (in particular, risks associated with default, deficiency of funds and currency exchange);
- consideration of any underlying guarantee structure; and
- remuneration of the cash pool leader.

Under the current transfer pricing rules, taxpayers must maintain documentation relating to the transfer pricing policy adopted with regard to contracts and other legal documents concluded with entities with which they have special relationships.

This documentation must also include any changes that occur in and information about related parties, a functional analysis, a financial analysis and other information that may be considered relevant in determining the terms and conditions that would normally apply between independent entities, to support the transfer pricing method used.

Taxpayers are obliged to indicate, in an annex to the corporate income tax return, the existence or non-existence for the respective tax year of transactions with entities with which it has special relationships, and must:

- identify the related entities involved;
- identify the amount of the transactions realised with each of the related entities; and
- declare whether, at the date of the transactions, documentation about the transfer prices exists.

South Korea

Sang-Jin Ahn
Keum-Ho Lee
Steve Sunghwa Song
Kim and Chang

1. Introduction

1.1 Admissibility of cash pooling agreements

In 2005, the Korean Foreign Exchange Transaction Regulation was amended to introduce a Cash Pooling Management System that provides convenient and efficient fund management for multinational corporations. Under Article 1-2, Section 27 of the regulation, 'cash pooling management' is defined as management of surplus funds or deficits among participants by foreign currency lending or borrowing between a resident company or a foreign investment enterprise[1] under the Foreign Investment Promotion Act and an overseas subsidiary or overseas parent company (including affiliates of the overseas parent company), or by a resident company or a foreign investment enterprise borrowing foreign currency from, depositing foreign currency with or providing collateral to a domestic or overseas bank, under a cash pooling agreement between a resident company or a foreign investment enterprise and an overseas subsidiary or overseas parent company, by which the surplus cash of participants may be pooled and frequently loaned to other participants.

Normally, activities involving foreign currency deposit, foreign currency loans or borrowing or provision of collateral by a resident to a non-resident are subject to reporting or approval requirements under the Foreign Exchange Transaction Regulation. However, if such transactions occur between a resident and a non-resident affiliate under the Cash Pooling Management System, the company need only report once to the Bank of Korea with regard to its cash pooling management instead of reporting each and every transaction as they occur. The total balance of offshore deposit, foreign currency lending or borrowing, or the provision of collateral by a resident to a non-resident through its designated foreign exchange bank under cash pooling management, may not exceed $30 million at any one time.

The Foreign Exchange Transactions Regulation governs only capital transactions between residents and non-residents, and although the definition of 'cash pooling management' under the regulation appears to be limited to physical cash pooling, Korean regulators have considered cash pooling management to include notional cash pooling as well. In principle, Korean regulators have treated physical cash

1 A 'foreign investment enterprise' under the Foreign Investment Promotion Act is a resident (Korean) enterprise in which a non-resident has invested with the intention of establishing an economic relationship with that enterprise

pooling as inter-company loan among participants in a cash pooling management system, whereas notional cash pooling has been treated as separate deposits made by each participant.

Given the Foreign Exchange Transactions Regulation, cash pooling seems to be a recognised concept under Korean law, but because restrictions are imposed on transactions among affiliated entities (as explained in more detail below), corporations may be unable to enter into cash pooling agreements freely under Korean law and will be subject to the following restrictions.

(a) Monopoly Regulation and Fair Trade Act

The Monopoly Regulation and Fair Trade Act restricts transactions among affiliated entities, and cash pooling agreements will likely be subject to the same restrictions. Article 23 of the Fair Trade Act prohibits 'unfair trading practices', which includes an entrepreneur committing any act of unfairly assisting a person with a special interest or another company by providing advanced payment, loans, manpower, immovable assets, securities, goods, services or rights in intangible property under substantially favourable terms.

In several cases, the Fair Trade Commission has held that a company providing its bank deposit as collateral for its affiliate without any benefit in return constitutes unfair trading practices in violation of Article 23 of the Fair Trade Act. Therefore, if a party provides its bank deposit as collateral for the benefit of another participant under a cash pooling agreement, that party should receive fair value in return in order to prevent any penalty under the Fair Trade Act.

With regard to cross-border transactions, the Fair Trade Commission will also examine whether a given practice undermines competition within the Korean market before ultimately holding a company liable for unfair trading practice under the Fair Trade Act. Therefore, an overseas participant providing a benefit to a Korean participant under a cash pooling agreement will probably be considered as a violation of the Fair Trade Act by the Fair Trade Commission. If, on the other hand, a Korean participant provides a benefit to an overseas participant under a cash pooling agreement, the liability of the companies under the Fair Trade Act will depend on whether the Fair Trade Commission can find that that practice undermines competition within the Korean market. Such restrictions under the Fair Trade Act may also apply to notional cash pooling.

Unfair trading practices under the Fair Trade Act also include activities by which an undertaking unfairly coerces or induces the customers of competitors to deal with it instead. Therefore, if the cash pooling agreement prevents a participant from dealing with a bank other than that where the master account is held, the bank where the master account is held may also be committing unfair trading practices in violation of the Fair Trade Act.

(b) Commercial Code

Under Article 542-9, Paragraph 1 of the Commercial Code, a listed company is prohibited from granting credit to "entities that have a special interest" in the listed company. Under Article 542-8 Paragraph 2 of the Commercial Code and Article 13,

Paragraph 4 of the Enforcement Decree of the Commercial Code, "entities that have a special interest" in a listed company include, among others, directors, auditors, affiliated companies, directors or auditors of such affiliated companies, and shareholders with an equity interest of 30% or more (solely or combined with any of the aforementioned entities). A grant of credit relevant to this provision of the Commercial Code includes lending assets with an economic value to the affiliate, guaranteeing the affiliate's indebtedness, purchasing the affiliate's stock in connection with providing financial support to the affiliate and any other transaction that entails credit risk on the part of the listed company.

Therefore, given that cash pooling in Korea can lead to the extension of a loan or the provision of collateral to an affiliate, listed companies in Korea may be restricted from entering into a cash pooling agreement with affiliates that have a special interest in that listed company.

Despite the restrictions mentioned above, Article 542-9 Paragraph 2 of the Commercial Code provides that a listed company may nonetheless grant credit to entities that have a special interest if the grant of credit is necessary to accomplish the business purposes of the listed company. However, the meaning of "necessary to accomplish the business purposes of the listed company" is unclear because of the lack of case law relating to this matter. Even if the grant of credit to an entity with a special interest is permissible under Article 542-9 Paragraph 2, Paragraph 3 of the same article further requires approval of the board of directors where the listed company has total assets of KRW2 trillion or more and the total amount of transactions between the listed company and the entity with a special interest during the listed company's current fiscal year would exceed 5% of the value of the listed company's total assets or turnover as of the end of the most recent fiscal year. Therefore, it is difficult to determine the precise restrictions that may be imposed on listed companies wishing to enter into a cash pooling agreement.

1.2 Types of cash pooling agreement

Despite the 2005 amendment to the Foreign Exchange Transactions Regulation, very few cross-border cash pooling agreements have been established in Korea at the time of writing. Therefore, in the Korean market, it is rather premature to categorise cash pooling agreements into certain types. Most of the cash pooling agreements in which Korean companies are involved have their master accounts established in a foreign jurisdiction. There seem to be few, if any, cross-border cash pooling agreements with a master account established in Korea.

1.3 Legal requirements from various perspectives

Under Korean law, there seems to be no explicit guidance regarding a cash pooling agreement, except in certain provisions of the Foreign Exchange Transactions Regulation. However, please refer to the discussion at section 1.1 with regard to the general restrictions under the Fair Trade Act and the Commercial Code.

In addition to such general restrictions, the Foreign Exchange Transactions Regulation requires domestic participants to a cross-border cash pooling agreement to adhere to the following instructions:

- The cash pooling agreement must be reported to the Bank of Korea before it takes effect;
- The total balance of offshore deposit, foreign currency lending or borrowing, the provision of collateral by a resident to a non-resident through its designated foreign exchange bank or the provision of collateral by a resident to a foreign exchange bank must not exceed $30 million; and
- Funds must be in a foreign currency.

There are also certain periodic reporting requirements to the Bank of Korea under the Foreign Exchange Transactions Regulation.

With regard to tax law, if the cash pooling agreement is not entered into as an arm's-length transaction, there could be issues related to transfer pricing.

2. Specific questions

2.1 Perspective A: corporate group

(a) Liability of group company and/or master account holder directors in the event of insolvency of a group company

As there have been few cross-border cash pooling agreements in Korea, there seems to be no precedent with regard to liability issues in the event of insolvency of either a group company or of the master account holder in a cash pooling agreement. Therefore, it is difficult to gauge the significance of any legal doctrine in making a general analysis with regard to insolvency, although the most likely concerns related to directors in such an event will include mismanagement.

If a group company is no longer able to meet its payment obligations under the cash pooling agreement, directors of the group company are unlikely to be liable to the master account holder for such non-payment, so long as they have performed their duty with due care and in accordance with the cash pooling agreement. Under Article 401 of the Commercial Code, a director is liable, in an individual capacity, to a third party only if the loss suffered by that third party is due to the director's wilful misconduct or gross negligence. Therefore, so long as the non-payment is not due to the director's wilful misconduct or gross negligence, the director will not be exposed to any separate liability risk for such non-payment.

As for any director liability to the group company, Article 399 of the Commercial Code limits a director's liability to the company to wilful misconduct or negligence that results in violation of any laws, regulations or the company's articles of association, or non-performance of the director's duty. So long as there are no violations under the Commercial Code, including Article 399, failure to make payments because the group company is insolvent is unlikely to be considered as negligent non-performance of a director's duty, and therefore the director will not be subject to any separate liability.

Directors of the master account holder will also not be subject to separate liability, even if the group company fails to make payments according to its obligations under the cash pooling agreement. So long as the group company's failure to make payments under the cash pooling agreement is due to its insolvency and nothing else, and the director of the master account holder has acted with due care, under Articles 399 and 401of the Commercial Code, that director will not be subject to any separate liability.

Assuming that the cash pooling agreement complies with all rules and regulations under Korean law (including those mentioned in section 1.1 above), whether the troubled company is a listed company or a private company is unlikely to affect the liability of the directors. Any potential liability of directors of a Korean company is also unlikely to be affected by the location of the bank or the distressed company.

(b) Liability of group company and/or master account holder directors in the event of insolvency of the master account holder

If the master account holder is no longer able to repay deposits made by a group company under the cash pooling agreement, its directors will not likely be liable for such non-payment, so long as they have performed their duty with due care and in accordance with the cash pooling agreement prior to the insolvency of the master account holder. Under Article 401 of the Commercial Code, a director is liable, in an individual capacity, to a third party only if the loss suffered by that third party is due to the director's wilful misconduct or gross negligence. Therefore, so long as the non-payment is not due to the director's wilful misconduct or gross negligence, and is due merely to the insolvency of the master account holder, the director will not be exposed to any separate liability risk for such non-payment.

Although a director of the master account holder will not likely be liable for non-payment, the issue remains as to whether the director can be found liable for receiving the deposit in the first place while knowing that the master account holder is unable to repay the deposit. However, it is it unclear whether the Korean courts would hold that a director who knowingly receives a deposit from a group company despite the potential risk of default constitutes gross negligence or wilful misconduct under Article 401 of the Commercial Code. In principle, a director of the master account holder will not be liable in the absence of wilful misconduct or gross negligence.

As for any director liability to the master account holder, Article 399 of the Commercial Code limits a director's liability to the company to wilful misconduct or negligence that results in the violation of any laws, regulations or the company's articles of association, or non-performance of the director's duty. Failure to make payments only because of the master account holder's insolvency is unlikely to be considered as negligent non-performance of a director's duty and therefore the director will not be subject to any separate liability.

With regard to directors of a group company, so long as the master account holder's failure to make payments under the cash pooling agreement is due to its insolvency and nothing else, and they have acted with due care, under Article 399 of the Commercial Code, the directors of a group company will not be subject to any separate liability.

Assuming that the cash pooling agreement complies with all rules and regulations under Korean law (including those mentioned in section 1.1), whether the troubled company is a listed company or a private company is unlikely to affect the liability of the directors. In addition, any potential liability of directors of a Korean company is unlikely to be affected by the location of the bank or the distressed company.

(c) ***Liability of group companies in the event of insolvency of the master account holder***

In the absence of special circumstances, third-party creditors of the master account holder will not have a claim against other group companies for losses suffered. As mentioned earlier, in principle, any deposit made by a group company to the master account will be treated as an inter-company loan in the case of physical cash pooling; and in the case of notional cash pooling, it will be treated as separate deposits made by each group company. Therefore, unless there are any special circumstances, the cash pooling arrangement in and of itself will not provide third-party creditors with a claim against other group companies. If the master account holder, creditor or group company is located outside of Korea, then the location of master account holder, creditor or group company and the governing law of the cash pooling agreement will decide the outcome under the choice of law rules.

(d) ***Liability of the master account holder in the event of insolvency of a group company***

As with the situation outlined in section 2.1(c) above, barring any special circumstances, third-party creditors of a group company will not likely have a claim against other group companies or the master account holder for their losses. There seems to be no indication under Korean law that, by entering into a cash pooling agreement, a group company's liability can be passed on to other group companies or the master account holder, thereby expanding its creditor-debtor relationship to include a third-party creditor.

The location of the master account holder, the claiming creditor or the group company is unlikely to change the above analysis, so long as the issue is governed by Korean law. However, if applying the choice of law rules results in a different governing law, the rights of a third-party creditor may vary according to the applicable governing law.

2.2 Perspective B: bank

(a) ***Banking requirements***

There are no specific requirements under Korean law for banks that may enter into a cash pooling agreement. However, when reporting such agreements to the Bank of Korea,it prefers banks with a global reputation that have previously operated similar cash pooling services in other countries.

(b) ***Liability of the bank in the event of insolvency of the master account holder or of a group company***

Because cash is pooled according to the terms of the cash pooling agreement, the bank will not likely be held liable for losses arising from the insolvency of one of the participating companies, so long as it complies with the terms of the cash pooling agreement and applies the proper standard of care. The location of the master account holder, the claiming creditor or the group company will not affect the bank's liability, so long as the issue is governed by Korean law.

2.3 Perspective C: insolvency

(a) Cash pooling agreements from the insolvency practitioner's perspective

As a general matter, there are very few cash pooling agreements in Korea, let alone cases where insolvency administration has been an issue. Therefore, the outcomes to the situations discussed in this section may vary depending on the terms of the cash pooling agreement. Generally, Article 90 of the Debtor Rehabilitation and Bankruptcy Law (for rehabilitation proceedings comparable to those in Chapter 11 of the US Bankruptcy Code) and Article 382 of that law (for bankruptcy proceedings comparable to those in Chapter 7 of the US Bankruptcy Code) provide that all assets in the debtor's possession at the time of bankruptcy shall form the bankruptcy estate.

Therefore, if the bank goes into liquidation, the entire balance in the master account will be part of the bank's bankruptcy estate. The master account holder will have a right to the liquidated assets as an unsecured creditor when the proceeds are distributed according to the bankruptcy procedure. Depending on whether the cash pooling agreement is notional or physical, the group companies may be able to participate directly in the insolvency proceeding. If the agreement is physical cash pooling, then any contribution made by a group company will be treated as inter-company loan to the master account holder, which has in turn deposited the same amount in the master account. Therefore, the group company will not likely be able to participate directly in the bank's insolvency proceeding . On the other hand, in the case of notional cash pooling, because deposits made by group companies are treated as separate accounts, with the group companies each being the beneficiary of their own accounts, the group companies will be able to participate directly in the bank's insolvency proceeding as unsecured creditors.

If the master account holder goes into liquidation, the entire balance in the master account will be part of the holder's bankruptcy estate. The group companies will have a right to the liquidated assets as unsecured creditors when the proceeds are distributed according to the insolvency proceeding.

Similarly, if a group company goes into liquidation, only the amount that that company has contributed to the credit balance of the master account will become part of the company's bankruptcy estate.

If the administrator is appointed outside Korea (ie, the main insolvency proceeding is opened outside of Korea), the debtor's assets located in Korea will be affected by the foreign insolvency proceeding only when and to the extent that the foreign insolvency proceeding is recognised and enforced in Korea by a recognition decision and relief orders granted by a Korean court under the Debtor Rehabilitation and Bankruptcy Law. The petition for the recognition decision can be made only by a representative of the foreign insolvency proceeding. The Korean court is required to make a decision on whether to grant recognition to the foreign insolvency proceeding within one month of the petition being made. The court's recognition decision is merely a basis for subsequently granting relief orders, and therefore the foreign insolvency proceeding would affect the debtor's Korean business and assets only through relief orders issued by a Korean court upon the petition of an interested party (including the representative of the foreign insolvency proceeding) or at its discretion. The recognition decision and a relief order may be granted jointly or separately. The cross-border insolvency receiver appointed by such a relief order from the Korean court has the exclusive authority and power to control and dispose of the debtor's business and assets in Korea (including making any transfer of assets to a foreign country, disposition of assets and distribution) subject to the approval of the Korean court.

Bank goes into liquidation: In the case of physical cash pooling, the bank's administrator will owe the master account holder the entire credit balance in the master account. However, because the amounts deposited by the group companies are treated as inter-company loans to the master account holder (which has, in turn, deposited them with the bank), the bank will have no direct obligation to the group companies.

In the case of notional cash pooling, the bank's administrator will owe both the master account holder and the group companies their respective credit balances because they will be treated as having separate accounts.

Article 2 of the Debtor Rehabilitation and Bankruptcy Law provides that non-residents and non-resident corporations will be treated in the same manner as residents and resident corporations regarding application of the law. Therefore, the analysis set out above will probably be the same even if the master account holder and/or the group companies are seated in another jurisdiction outside Korea.

Master account holder goes into liquidation: In the case of physical cash pooling, the master account holder's administrator will owe the group companies because any deposits made by the group companies are treated as inter-company loans extended to the master account holder. The master account holder's administrator will have no obligation to the bank. Rather, the master account holder will have a right to any deposit that it has made to the master account set up with the bank.

In the case of notional cash pooling, the master account holder's administrator has no obligation to the group companies, because any deposit made by a company will be credited to that company alone, and is not deemed to be an inter-company loan. The master account holder will have no obligation to the bank, the same as in the case of physical cash pooling.

The foregoing analysis will probably be the same even if the bank and/or the group companies are seated in another jurisdiction outside Korea.

Group company goes into liquidation: In the case of physical cash pooling, the group company's administrator will have a right against the master account holder because any deposit made by the group company will be treated as an inter-company loan extended to the master account holder. The group company's administrator will have no obligation to, or claim against, the bank.

In the case of notional cash pooling, on the other hand, the group company's administrator will have a right against the bank regarding the amount deposited with it, but will have no obligation to, or claim against, the master account holder.

The foregoing analysis will probably be the same even if the master account holder and/or the bank is seated in another jurisdiction outside Korea.

Voidability of transactions made prior to insolvency: The exact scope for disregarding a transaction that occurred prior to bankruptcy differs depending on whether the proceeding is a rehabilitation proceeding (similar to a reorganisation proceeding under Chapter 11 of the US Bankruptcy Code) or a bankruptcy proceeding (similar to a liquidation proceeding under Chapter 7 of the US Bankruptcy Code).

Under Article 100 of the Debtor Rehabilitation and Bankruptcy Law, a court-appointed receiver may avoid the following kinds of transactions by a company undergoing corporate rehabilitation as avoidable transfers or preferences:

- any action performed by the company with the knowledge that it will cause harm or otherwise be adverse to the general and secured creditors, unless the beneficiary of that action was unaware at that time of the harmful nature of the action to creditors;
- any action performed by the company after the suspension of payments or the filing of an application for corporate rehabilitation or bankruptcy (either of which constitutes an 'insolvency event') that adversely affects rehabilitation claims or secured rehabilitation claims, creates a security interest or satisfies the company's debt obligations, unless the beneficiary of the action was unaware at that time of the harmful nature of the action to creditors or the existence of the insolvency event;
- any action performed by the company after, or in the 60 days immediately preceding, the occurrence of an insolvency event and which involves providing a security interest or satisfying the company's debt obligation where the company was not obliged to provide such security or to satisfy such obligation at such time or in such manner, unless the beneficiary of the action was unaware at that time that the company, by that action, was adversely affecting the right of all creditors to be treated equally and, if the action took place after the insolvency event, the beneficiary of the action was also unaware at that time of the occurrence of an insolvency event; and
- any action performed by the company after, or in the six months immediately preceding, the occurrence of an insolvency event and which conferred benefits on the beneficiary in exchange for no, or only nominal, consideration.

These avoidance rights are wider with regard to transactions between specially related persons, under Article 101 of the Debtor Rehabilitation and Bankruptcy Law. In cases of avoidance under the second and third points above, awareness on the part of a specially related person is presumed. The 60-day period under the third point above and the six-month period under the fourth point above are both extended to one year where the transaction is between specially related persons.

Returning to the likely outcomes in the event of insolvencies affecting cash pooling agreements, in cases of physical cash pooling, payment by a bankrupt master account holder to a group company prior to its bankruptcy could fall under any of the first three points above, depending on the circumstances. Under the first point, payment by the master account holder to a group company could be seen as the master account holder satisfying its inter-company loan obligations to the group company, thereby causing harm to general creditors. If the payment occurs after the suspension of payment or the application of bankruptcy, but before bankruptcy is adjudicated by the court, then the payment will fall under either of the second or third points and therefore may be voided. A common requirement for all three cases is that the group company have been aware of the harm or adverse effect such payment would have on the master account holder's creditors. Therefore, if the requirements under Article 100 of the Debtor Rehabilitation and Bankruptcy Law are met, the insolvency administrator of the master account holder in a cash pooling scheme may be able to declare the payment void.

In cases of notional cash pooling, the deposit is not an inter-company loan to the master account holder and there is therefore no debtor-creditor relationship between the master account holder and the group company.

A similar analysis will apply if a group company, prior to its bankruptcy, has made a deposit in the master account. The group company's insolvency administrator may be able to declare the transfer of funds to the master account holder void if the group company made the transfer of money with the intent to cause harm to its creditors or adversely affect its rehabilitation procedure.

In case of a bankruptcy (ie, liquidation) proceeding, under Articles 391 and 392 of the Debtor Rehabilitation and Bankruptcy Law, a bankruptcy trustee may avoid the following kinds of transactions as avoidable transfers or preferences:

- any action performed by the company with the knowledge that it will cause harm or otherwise be adverse to the general and secured creditors, unless the beneficiary of the action was unaware at that time that it would cause harm or otherwise be adverse to creditors;
- any action performed by the company after the suspension of payments or the filing for bankruptcy (either of which constitutes an 'insolvency event') which adversely affects creditors' claims, creates a security interest or satisfies the company's debt obligations, but only if the beneficiary of the action was aware at that time of existence of the insolvency event. If the beneficiary is an entity with a special relationship with the company, it will be presumed that it was aware of the insolvency event at that time;
- any action performed by the company after, or in the 60 days immediately preceding, the occurrence of an insolvency event that involves providing a security interest or satisfying the company's debt obligation where the company was not obliged to provide such security or to satisfy such obligation at such time or in such manner, unless the creditor was unaware of the insolvency event or harmful nature of the transaction at that time. If the beneficiary of the transaction is an entity with a special relationship, then the 60-day timeframe shall be extended to one year and it will be presumed

that the entity with the special relationship was aware of the insolvency event at that time and of the harmful nature of the transaction to creditors; and

- any action performed by the company after, or in the the six months immediately preceding, the occurrence of an insolvency event that conferred benefits on the beneficiary in exchange for no, or only nominal, consideration. If the beneficiary of the transaction is a specially related entity, then the six-month timeframe shall be extended to one year.

Despite the difference in scope, an analysis similar to that set out above in realtion to avoidance in rehabilitation proceedings should apply to cases where either the master account holder or a group company files for bankruptcy (ie, liquidation).

(b) Special rules as regards creditors of other parties to the cash pooling agreement

There are no rules or regulations under Korean law imposing on the administrator of either the bank, the master account holder or a group company particular obligations as regards creditors of the other parties to a cash pooling agreement.

(c) Dissolution/termination of the cash pooling agreement in the event of liquidation of the master account holder or a group company

Discussion of the dissolution or termination of a cash pooling agreement in the event of the insolvency of one of the parties can be provided only in general terms, because there is no precedent on this matter, and the outcome will vary depending on the terms and conditions of the particular cash pooling agreement. Generally, under Article 543 of the Civil Code, a party to a contract may terminate a contract by notifying the counterparty, provided that the terms of the contract or applicable laws allow the parties to do so. Furthermore, Articles 544 and 546 of the Civil Code provide that non-performance of the contract by the debtor allows the creditor to terminate the contract.

If one party goes into liquidation and is therefore unable to perform its part of the cash pooling agreement, it is unclear whether the non-liquidated party will be able to terminate the cash pooling agreement on that basis. Articles 119 and 335 of the Debtor Rehabilitation and Bankruptcy Law provide that if there is a "bilateral executory contract" to which the bankrupt company is a party, the bankruptcy trustee or the court-appointed receiver may either terminate the contract or continue to honour it. Therefore, under the liquidation proceedings, the counterparty may not terminate the contract, as such termination would infringe the rights of the bankruptcy trustee or the court-appointed receiver under Articles 119 and 335 of the Debtor Rehabilitation and Bankruptcy Law.

However, according to a Supreme Court case, a 'bilateral executory contract' is a contract under which both parties are obliged to each other for economically similar consideration, and therefore there is an economic and legal relationship with regard to the creation, performance and existence of the obligations under the contract so that both parties' obligations function as collateral. From this point of view, a cash pooling agreement is unlikely to be considered to be a bilateral executory contract, because the group company's obligations (making deposits to the master account) and the master account holder's obligations (later repaying the deposit previously made by the group company) may not be functioning as collateral. Rather, the group company's obligation is unilaterally to make deposits to the master account independent of the master account holder's obligation to repay that deposit back to the group company in the future.

Therefore, based on such reasoning, termination of the cash pooling agreement by the group company or the master account holder will not be restricted in the event that the bank, a group company or the master account holder goes into liquidation. This matter will depend on the terms and conditions of the cash pooling agreement.

2.4 Perspective D: regulatory

There seems to be no regulatory requirement for domestic cash pooling agreements. As for cross-border cash pooling agreement, the resident participating party must report to the Bank of Korea as previously mentioned in section 1.3.

2.5 Perspective E: tax

Other than tax issues that arise in the context of transactions among affiliates, there seems to be no apparent tax issue with regards to cash pooling agreements in Korea.

Spain

Luisa de Alarcón
Borja Pardo
Felipe Pineda
JAUSAS

---

1. Introduction

1.1 Admissibility of cash pooling agreements

Under Spanish law, there is no explicit or implicit prohibition on corporations entering into a cash pooling agreement, or on holding companies setting up a cash pooling agreement with their group members. This applies to both notional pooling and physical cash pooling. The fact that a group company is a foreign company does not make a difference for the purposes of entering into a cash pooling agreement, although it may have an impact from the point of view of reporting obligations, in particular.

1.2 Types of cash pooling agreement

In general, the same types of cash pooling agreement used in other European jurisdictions, such as physical cash pooling and notional cash pooling in their various forms, are used in Spain.

1.3 Legal requirements from various perspectives

There are no specific legal requirements under Spanish corporate, banking, regulatory and tax laws as regards cash pooling agreements.

From the standpoint of insolvency law, Spanish regulations governing insolvency proceedings are based on the principle of legal unity. Therefore, the country's provisions on the matter are concentrated into one single regulation, the Insolvency Act, which was recently modified by the Insolvency Act Reform Act (38/2011).

Although the Insolvency Act contains no specific provisions regarding the issue of cash pooling agreements, such agreements will be governed by its general provisions.

Thus, first, in the case of voluntary insolvency (when the debtor itself applies for judicial insolvency proceedings), the debtor retains the powers of administration and use of its assets, although the exercise of these powers is subject to the involvement of so-called 'insolvency administrators' – professionals appointed by the judge hearing the insolvency proceedings – in the form of a requirement for their authorisation or consent.

In the case of compulsory insolvency (when the party applying for judicial proceedings is a creditor of the insolvent debtor), exercise by the debtor of any powers of administration or use of its assets is suspended and placed in the hands of the insolvency administrators.

These effects apply to the debtor's assets, rights and duties as a whole. Therefore, any rights and duties arising from any possible cash pooling agreement signed by the debtor would fall under the supervision and control of the insolvency administrators. As a result, the first automatic and direct effect of the declaration of insolvency would be to give parties outside the group of companies the possibility of familiarising themselves with, and analysing, the specific arrangements arising from the cash pooling agreement – something that could be business-sensitive for the remaining group companies. In this regard, bearing in mind the insolvent company's duty to collaborate with the administrators and the court, in practice, the impact of the submission of all documentation that will be requested by them – which will be any documents useful to the insolvency proceedings or to understanding the company's net asset situation – is that the remaining group companies can do little or nothing to keep the cash pooling agreement confidential.

Additionally, Article 25 of the Insolvency Act allows any creditors to apply for a joint declaration of insolvency of the rest of the companies in the group. In this regard, any publicity given to the cash pooling agreement that may arise from the insolvency proceedings affecting one of the group companies may bring about a sensitive and awkward situation for the rest of the companies, and lead to a joint declaration of insolvency.

With regard to the above, Article 25 of the Insolvency Act provides that the court with jurisdiction to make a joint declaration of insolvency is that of the place in which the debtor with the greatest liabilities has its centre of interests and, in the case of a corporate group, that of the place where the parent company has its centre of interests, unless insolvency proceedings are not applied for with regard to the parent company, in which case it is again the court of the place where the company with the greatest liabilities has its centre of interests.

With regard to the impact of the international dimension on this matter, the EU Insolvency Regulation (1346/2000) is centred around the principle of the 'centre of main interests' as the cornerstone of both material and jurisdictional competence. With regard to this concept, in a judgment of May 2 2006 in *Eurofood IFSC Ltd* (C-341/2004), the European Court of Justice defined and clarified the concept of 'centre of main interests', thereby permitting, in the case of corporate groups, a declaration of insolvency in respect of companies domiciled in other EU member states on the basis of the actual location of its centre of main interests.

Following this and other case law it is apparent that a range of criteria should be taken into consideration in determining a company's centre of main interests, including:

- the place where strategic decisions are taken;
- the domicile of the directors and senior managers;
- the place where the company's activities are carried out;
- the place where the greatest percentage of liabilities are located;
- the place where the majority of workers are located;
- the place where agreements with third parties are made; and
- the place where the bank accounts are held.

Furthermore, the Insolvency Act also contains specific provisions regarding the impact of a declaration of insolvency on agreements signed by the debtor. As the cash pooling agreement is a bilateral agreement with reciprocal duties, the relevant provision is Article 61, which states that, as general rule "the declaration of insolvency shall not, in itself, affect the enforceability of agreements with reciprocal duties awaiting performance by both the insolvent and the other party". Any consideration that the insolvent party has a duty to provide under the agreement is provided by being charged to the pool of assets. Consequently, the insolvent debtor will continue to be subject to the provisions of the cash pooling agreement, with a duty to comply punctually with its obligations, without these being affected by the declaration of insolvency.

Nevertheless, the administrators or the debtor itself (depending on whether the powers over assets have been suspended or are subject to outside approval, as previously noted) may seek termination of the agreement if they deem that this would be in the insolvency proceedings' interests. Termination of the agreement would be carried out via summary and special proceedings, which are concluded by a ruling issued by the judge regarding the termination, ordering any applicable restitution and any indemnification to be paid.

Article 61 on the Insolvency Act provides that "any clauses establishing a power to dissolve or terminate the agreement for the sole cause of the declaration of insolvency of any of the parties shall be regarded as not existing".

While a declaration of insolvency therefore does not mean the automatic termination of agreements with reciprocal duties, such as cash pooling agreements, Article 62 of the Insolvency Act provides for cases in which one of the parties commits a breach of contract, which in practice frequently happens given the situation of the insolvent company.

Article 62 states that "the declaration of insolvency shall not affect the power to terminate agreements for subsequent breach by any of the parties". It further notes that "in the case of continuing-performance agreements a power of termination can also be exercised when the breach has been committed prior to the declaration of insolvency". A cash pooling agreement would qualify as a continuing performance agreement within this provision. An action for termination under Article 62 is carried out before the insolvency judge, after insolvency has been declared.

However, the Insolvency Act provides an exception to the right of termination for breach of contract in Section 3 of Article 62:

Even if there is cause for termination, the judge, in the interests of the insolvency proceedings, may find for continued compliance with the agreement, with the payments/ services due or to be performed by the insolvent party being charged to its pool of assets.

Therefore, although there may be cause for termination because of a breach by one of the parties, the judge may order that a cash pooling agreement remain in force if this is of benefit to the insolvency proceedings – in other words, if it helps to guarantee the viability of the insolvent company in the case of a continuation of the business and the adoption of an arrangement with creditors involving a degree of debt relief, or if it is beneficial for the creditors as a whole in the case a of liquidation of the insolvent company.

Additionally, the potential effect on cash pooling agreements of so-called 'actions for restitution', governed by Articles 71 and following of the Insolvency Act, should be considered. These actions can rescind "acts prejudicial to the pool of assets" carried out by the debtor in the two years prior to the declaration of insolvency, even if there was no fraudulent intent.

Cash pooling agreements signed in the two years prior to a declaration of insolvency may be object of such an action if it is demonstrated that these have reduced the debtor's assets. Indeed, the Insolvency Act itself establishes a series of presumptions for demonstrating that a transaction has been prejudicial to the pool of assets, which include the fact that the transaction has been carried out for the benefit of a person or entity related to the insolvent party, which would include a company in the same group.

If the action for restitution is upheld, the transaction (in this case, the cash pooling agreement) will be declared null and void from that point on, and the return of any consideration that passed as a result of the transaction will be ordered. The third party that is stripped of the asset or entitlements acquired as part of the transaction that has been declared null and void will be compensated out of the pool of assets if it acted in good faith. If it is deemed to have acted in bad faith, not only must it return the asset or entitlement acquired, but its right to compensation will be classified as a subordinated claim, thereby drastically reducing its likelihood of collecting it.

It is therefore particularly important to carry out a detailed study of the effects of any cash pooling agreement on an insolvent debtor, and to bear in mind the date of signature of the agreement before seeking voluntary insolvency, so as to avoid the prejudicial effects of any potential action for restitution.

Finally, among the effects of a declaration of insolvency on cash pooling agreements, note should be made of the provisions of the Insolvency Act on the ranking of claims, which is of key importance to a creditors' likelihood of collection.

Article 92 of the Insolvency Act classifies as subordinated claims "those credits title to which is held by persons especially related to the debtor", which include those companies forming part of the same group. Subordinated claims are the last to be settled and, in fact, are paid by the debtor only when the rest have been settled in full. This means that in practice, it is highly unusual for a subordinated creditor to collect its claim, even in part.

1.4 General legal requirements

As mentioned above, there are no specific rules or requirements provided for under Spanish law in respect of cash pooling agreements. In addition, there is very limited case law, and what there is mainly relates to the insolvency and tax aspects of such agreements.

As a consequence, the contents of a cash pooling agreement will depend primarily on the conditions agreed between the group companies (including the master account holder) and the bank. In practice, cash pooling agreements have developed in Spain under the principles of freedom of contract and free will of the parties.

Cash pooling arrangements will simultaneously comprise a number of legal transactions of a mercantile (eg, inter-company loans), financial or banking nature (eg, cash pooling agreement, current account agreements, electronic transfer agreements, deposit agreements). In some cases (eg, loans), these legal transactions are generally regulated by law (under the Civil Code and the Commercial Code). However, most of them – particularly those of a financial or banking nature – are not regulated and the rules that apply to them are the result of case law.

(a) *Company law*

For a group company governed by Spanish law, being a party to a cash pooling agreement (as with being a party to a loan agreement or granting a guarantee) is generally considered under Spanish law as an ancillary activity, aimed at the group company further pursuing its main corporate purpose. Therefore, the group company will have the capacity to enter into a cash pooling agreement even if doing so is not specifically foreseen in its articles of association (provided that it is not clearly forbidden in them).

However, the directors of a Spanish company have an obligation to act with the diligence of a responsible businessman (Article 225.1 of the Corporations Act) and in the best interests of the company itself (Article 226 of the Corporations Act), rather than in the best interests of the group. Accordingly, the directors would have to assess the merits of the proposed cash pooling agreement for the company alone, bearing in mind the contents of the agreement, the financial needs of the company and the financial status (and future evolution) of the other group companies.

If the cash pooling agreement is beneficial for the group as a whole, but not for the Spanish company that the directors act for, the directors can be held personally liable to the company, the shareholders and the company's creditors for any damage that they suffer as a consequence.

In either case, it is usual to pass a shareholders' resolution approving the cash pooling agreement and authorising the directors to sign and execute all necessary documents, with a view to limiting the directors' exposure to shareholder claims.

In addition, company directors can have personal liability in the event that they fail to observe their duties with regard to the rules on capital maintenance. Under Spanish law, if as a consequence of losses the net equity of a company falls to less than half of its issued capital, then the directors are legally required to call a general shareholders' meeting to remedy the situation or otherwise wind up the company. Failure to do so, or to apply for the insolvency of the company, in due time can give rise to the directors' joint and several liability for the company's debts accrued after the time at which they should have acted (Articles 360 and following of the Corporations Act).

Finally, the directors (including *de facto* directors) can also face criminal liability (under Articles 290 and following of the Criminal Code) under certain extreme circumstances, particularly if they willingly behave in a disloyal or wrongful way or falsify corporate information.

2. Specific questions

2.1 Perspective A: corporate group

(a) Liability of group company and/or master account holder directors in the event of insolvency of a group company

Directors' liability (and supervisory directors' liability in the case of *de facto* directors) in the event of insolvency of a group company is governed in Articles 163 to 173 of the Insolvency Act. One feature of the current Insolvency Act is its tougher provisions on directors' liability, compared with previous legislation.

Fundamentally, insolvency will result in liability for the directors when the company's position has been brought about or worsened by its or its directors' fraudulent or culpable action; although there are some cases in which the directors' liability is objective, with no requirement for serious culpability or fraud. These cases are set out in Articles 164 and 165.

Article 164.2 establishes a series of non-rebuttable presumptions that enable a finding of culpability in insolvency to be made:

- when a debtor with a legal duty to keep accounting records substantially breaches that duty, keeps two sets of accounts or has committed an irregularity that significantly distorts the net asset or financial situation of the company as it appears in the accounts that it keeps;
- when the debtor has committed a serious error in any of the documents accompanying the application for a declaration of insolvency or submitted during the handling of the proceedings, or has attached or submitted false documents;
- when the opening of liquidation proceedings has been agreed at the initiative of the judicial body itself, because the company has breached its arrangement with its creditors due to a cause attributable to the company;
- when the debtor has disposed of all or part of its assets to the detriment of the creditors, or has carried out any act that delays, obstructs or impedes attachment in any class of enforcement that has been or is likely to be sought;
- when, in the two years prior to the date of declaration of insolvency, assets or entitlements have been fraudulently removed from the debtor's estate; or
- when, prior to the date of the declaration of insolvency (the Insolvency Act does not indicate any minimum or maximum time period), the debtor has carried out any legal act designed to simulate a fictitious net-worth situation.

In addition, Article 165 establishes a series of rebuttable presumptions that also allow a situation of insolvency to be classified as culpable if no evidence is produced to show otherwise. The insolvency shall be presumed to be culpable when the debtor or, as the case may be, its legal representatives, directors or liquidators:

- have breached their duty to apply for a declaration of insolvency;
- have breached their duty to collaborate with the court and the administrators in the insolvency proceedings, have failed to supply information required or useful for the progress of the proceedings or have not attended, in person or

by means of a representative, the creditors' meeting; or

- where legally obliged to do so, have failed to draw up annual accounts, have not submitted them to audit, or, once approved, have not deposited them with the Mercantile Register, in any one of the three financial years prior to the declaration of insolvency.

The consequences of the insolvency being declared culpable could be serious for the company's directors, and include the following:

- In the case of liquidation of the insolvent company, the court may order that those who have held the office of director in the two years prior to the declaration of insolvency pay to the creditors the amount of their claims when these cannot be satisfied from the liquidation.
- The directors can be disqualified from administering the assets of others for a period of between two and 15 years, and from representing or administering any natural or legal person or legal entity during the same period.
- The directors can lose any entitlement that they may have had before the insolvency of the company and be ordered to restore to the pool of assets anything that they have improperly obtained from the insolvent company. Thus, the court could order the directors to restore to the pool of assets specific goods fraudulently obtained from the company, all without prejudice to any personal liability (their entire present and future wealth) that may arise from a ruling that they must repay the company's creditors.

(b) *Liability of group company and/or master account holder directors in the event of insolvency of the master account holder*

As noted in section 2.1(a) above, directors' liability in the event of declaration of insolvency is established by Articles 163 to 173 of the Insolvency Act.

If the company whose insolvency is declared is the master account holder, the provisions regarding the possible culpability of the insolvency and, particularly, the presumptions contained in the Insolvency Act in these circumstances (discussed above) shall be equally applicable. Also applicable are the possible consequences arising from the classification of the insolvency as culpable, as set out above.

(c) *Liability of group companies in the event of insolvency of the master account holder*

As regards the consequences for a group company of the insolvency of the master account holder, reference is made to the discussion in section 1.3 above.

As noted there, first, a declaration of insolvency of the master account holder would mean that the insolvency administrators – figures from outside the corporate group – would have access to the specific arrangements arising from the cash pooling agreement, which could be sensitive and awkward for the remaining group companies.

Additionally, Article 25 of the Insolvency Act allows any of the debtor's creditors to apply for a joint declaration of insolvency of the rest of the companies in the group. Any publicity given to the cash pooling agreement that may arise from the insolvency proceedings affecting one of the group companies may create a sensitive and awkward situation for the rest of the companies, and result in a joint declaration of insolvency.

As also noted in section 1.3, Article 25 also provides that the court with jurisdiction to make a joint declaration of insolvency is that of the place of the group's centre of main interests, which is determined by reference to the centre of main interest of the parent company or, should the parent company's insolvency not be requested, that of the company with the greatest liabilities.

Furthermore, the remaining group companies may be affected by any eventual exercise of an action for restitution with regard to any cash pooling agreement signed by the insolvent company, with the prejudicial effects noted in section 1.3.

Finally, the claims of companies against others in the same group are classified as subordinated, thereby drastically reducing any likelihood of them being satisfied.

(d) Liability of the master account holder in the event of insolvency of a group company

In general, the master account holder may face liability in the event of insolvency of a group company typically in three different scenarios:

- It is found to have cooperated in committing any act that caused the insolvency to be deemed culpable. In this case, the master account holder may have to satisfy the creditors' claims to the extent that they are not satisfied from the liquidation of the insolvent company;
- It is found to be a *de facto* director of the insolvent company; or
- It is subject to an action for restitution conducted by the insolvency administrators, particularly if the cash pooling agreement was entered into in the two years prior to the debtor's declaration of insolvency. In this regard, as both would be related companies, both the result of any potential action for restitution and any hypothetical credit that may arise in favour of the master account holder after termination of the cash pooling agreement would be a subordinated credit, which, as noted above, is very difficult to collect.

In addition, if the master account holder owns 100% of the capital of the insolvent group company (ie, the latter is a single shareholder company (*Sociedad Unipersona*), under Spanish corporate law all contracts (including cash pooling agreements) entered into between the companies must be in writing or in the form established by law (if other than in writing) for contracts of that type, and must be transcribed into an official registry book lodged with the Commercial Registry. In addition, all such contracts must be mentioned in the notes to the annual accounts, accounts must be deposited with the Commercial Registry. If these formalities are not observed and the subsidiary becomes insolvent:

- the relevant contract(s) may not be enforced by the debtor's estate; and
- the sole shareholder (in this hypothesis, the master account holder) will be liable to the subsidiary for any advantages that it may have obtained, either directly or indirectly, at the subsidiary's expense as a consequence of any of the relevant contracts.

This liability applies for two years from the date on which the contracts were entered into.

2.2 Perspective B: bank

(a) Banking requirements

As mentioned above, there are no specific banking requirements for cash pooling agreements. In the event, however, that a cash pooling agreement could be interpreted as the granting of loans or credit by the bank, the general banking rules concerning regulatory capital, solvency and security structure may be applicable.

(b) Liability of the bank in the event of insolvency of the master account holder or of a group company.

In general, the same scenarios described previously concerning the liability of the master account holder in the event of insolvency of a group company (see section 2.1(d)) would apply to the bank. If there is evidence that the bank was aware of the debtor's insolvency at the time of signing the cash pooling agreement, the bank's conduct could be regarded as being in bad faith, with the result that any credit arising from the operation in the bank's favour could be classified as subordinated (and thus practically impossible to collect, as noted above).

In addition, Act 38/2011 has modified the regulations on actions for restitution, protecting the position of banking institutions, although this protection is applicable to cases not resembling that of the signing of a cash pooling agreement.

2.3 Insolvency

(a) Cash pooling agreements from the insolvency practitioner's perspective

As mentioned in section 1.3, the declaration of insolvency of a group company or of the master account holder will trigger the appointment by the judge overseeing the insolvency proceedings of independent professionals known as insolvency administrators, who will exercise, to a greater or lesser extent, powers over the debtor's assets (depending on whether it is a compulsory or voluntary insolvency).

These insolvency administrators will have access to the specific details of any cash pooling agreements and the rights and duties arising from them, and therefore would become aware of information that may be sensitive for the rest of the group companies.

With regard to the actions that the insolvency administrators may carry out, the most important (as discussed in section 1.3) are:

- applying for a declaration of insolvency of the group of companies as a whole (providing that Spanish jurisdiction is applicable);
- terminating the cash pooling agreement if it is not favourable to the insolvency proceedings;
- classifying any credits arising from the cash pooling agreement in favour of group companies as subordinated; and
- initiating actions for restitution in respect of any cash pooling agreement signed in the two years prior to the declaration of insolvency.

There are two particularly significant articles in the Insolvency Act. Article 35 states that the insolvency administrators shall "carry out their office with the care of a well-organised director and of a legal representative". Article 43 states that: "in the exercise of the powers of administration and use of the pool of assets, their upkeep shall be organised in the manner that best suits the interests of the insolvency proceedings". Article 43 concludes: "To this end, the insolvency administrator may request from the court any assistance they deem necessary".

One can therefore observe how the Insolvency Act imposes upon insolvency administrators the duty to keep the pool of assets in the manner most favourable to the interests of the insolvency proceedings, and to do so with the care of "a well-organised director and of a legal representative".

Therefore, if the cash pooling agreement gives rise to a credit in favour of the insolvent company against any of the participating undertakings (whether the bank, the master account holder or a group company), before anything else the insolvency administrators must claim the amounts arising from the cash pooling agreement. If not, they become subject to the strict liability provisions provided for in the Insolvency Act.

In any case, the insolvency administrators' actions must, first and foremost, be in the interests of the insolvency proceedings, which requires a case-by-case examination of the specific circumstances in light of the regulations governing the termination of agreements as part of such proceedings, discussed in section 1.3.

Finally, in the event of an insolvency administrator appointed abroad, the nationality of the insolvent company is decisive since, should it be located within an EU member state, the EU Insolvency Regulation applies. If not, the provisions of any international treaties signed by Spain and the country in question would be applicable.

(b) Obligations in the event that a participant in a cash pooling agreement becomes insolvent

If the bank, the master account holder or a group company enters into insolvency proceedings, the duties of the insolvency administrators would be those already noted.

Therefore, the insolvency administrator of the bank or the master account holder, or a group company (depending on the entity declared insolvent) will have a duty to keep the pool of assets in the manner most favourable to the interests of the insolvency proceedings and to do so with the care of "a well-organised director and of a legal representative". Among other actions he may carry out the most significant (as noted above and in paragraph 1.3 are:

- applying for a declaration of insolvency of the group of companies as a whole (provided that Spanish jurisdiction is applicable);
- terminating the cash pooling agreement should it not be favourable to the insolvency proceedings;
- classifying as subordinated any credits arising from the cash pooling agreement in favour of group companies; and
- initiating actions for restitution in respect of any cash pooling agreement signed in the two years prior to the declaration of insolvency.

These actions could be undertaken by the insolvency administrator of any of the cash pooling participants in respect of the others.

The fact that any of the undertakings concerned is foreign registered is no impediment to the possibility of taking any of the actions mentioned above, provided that they do not affect property rights over the debtor's assets, assets sold with reservation of title, debtor entitlements subject to a duty to register, rights over negotiable instruments or agreements over property assets, which are governed by the legislation of the state in which assets concerned are situated or of the registry in which those assets are recorded.

This being the case, should the main proceedings be brought in Spain, two provisions are applicable that may be of key importance with regard to the impact of a declaration of insolvency on a cash pooling agreement.

Article 205 of the Insolvency Act states that:

1. *The declaration of insolvency shall not affect a creditor's right to offset its credit when the law governing the insolvent party's reciprocal credits so permits in situations of insolvency.*
2. *The provisions of the preceding paragraph are understood as being without prejudice to any actions for restitution that may, as the case may be, be applicable.*

Article 208 states that:

The exercise of actions for restitution by virtue of this Act shall not be permitted when the party benefiting from the act prejudicial to the pool of assets proves that said act is subject to the legislation of another State that does not permit it to be challenged under any circumstances.

This being so, in the specific case of cash pooling agreements, the law applicable to the specific agreement should be established taking into account any possible forum selection clauses agreed by the parties. This means that it could be advisable for the signatory parties to the cash pooling agreement to agree to submission to a legal system that permits compensation even in the situation of insolvency.

Actions for restitution, already discussed in sections 1.3, 2.1(a) and 2.1(b) above, are applicable if the bankrupt master account holder has transferred money to group companies prior to its bankruptcy or if a group company has transferred money to the master account prior to the bankruptcy of the group company. Reference should be made to paragraph (a) above, with regard to the impact of the international dimension.

(c) ***Special rules as regards creditors of other parties to the cash pooling agreement***

Article 49 of the Insolvency Act states that:

after the declaration of insolvency, all the debtor's creditors, ordinary or otherwise, whatever their nationality or domicile, shall by law form part of the insolvency's pool of liabilities, with no exceptions other than those established by law.

Therefore, the only parties to the insolvency that will form part of the proceedings' list of creditors, and therefore be considered by it, are the insolvent parties' creditors themselves. The insolvency administrators have no special duty of care in respect of the creditors of other parties to the cash pooling agreement. This is without prejudice to the possibility of a joint declaration of insolvency, as discussed in section 1.3 above, and the impact, of the fact that sensitive information regarding the the group of companies will be in the hands of outside parties (the insolvency administrators).

(d) *Dissolution/termination of the cash pooling agreement in the event of liquidation of the master account holder or a group company*

The Insolvency Act contains specific provisions on the impact of a declaration of insolvency on agreements signed by the debtor. Given that a cash pooling agreement is a bilateral agreement with reciprocal duties, the relevant provision is Article 61 of the Insolvency Act, which states that, as a general rule, "the declaration of insolvency shall not, in itself, affect the enforceability of agreements with reciprocal duties awaiting performance by both the insolvent and the other party". Any consideration that the insolvent party has an obligation to provide under the contract is to be provided "by a charge to the pool of assets". In other words, the insolvent debtor shall continue to be subject to the provisions of the cash pooling agreement, with a duty to comply punctually with its obligations, without these being affected by the declaration of insolvency.

Nevertheless, the administrator or the debtor itself (depending on whether the powers over assets have been suspended or are subject to outside approval) may seek termination of the agreement if it deems that this would be in the interests of the insolvency proceedings. Termination of the agreement would be carried out through summary and special proceedings, which are concluded by a court ruling on the termination, ordering, as appropriate, any applicable restitution and any indemnification to be paid.

Article 61 of the Insolvency Act provides that: "any clauses establishing a power to dissolve or terminate the agreement for the sole cause of the declaration of insolvency of any of the parties shall be regarded as not existing."

Therefore, as noted, a declaration of insolvency does not mean the automatic termination of agreements with reciprocal duties, such as cash pooling agreements, although Article 62 of the Insolvency Act does provide for termination when one of the parties commits a breach of contract – something that, in practice, happens frequently given the situation of the insolvent company.

Article 62 states that "the declaration of insolvency shall not affect the power to terminate agreements for subsequent breach by any of the parties". It further notes that "in the case of continuing-performance agreements a power of termination can also be exercised when the breach has been committed prior to the declaration of insolvency". A cash pooling agreement would qualify as a 'continuing-performance agreement' within the meaning of this provision. An action for termination is carried out before the insolvency judge.

The Insolvency Acy does, however, also provide for an exception to the right to termination due to breach of contract, in Section 3 of Article 62, which states:

> *Even if there is cause for termination, the judge, in the interests of the insolvency proceedings, may find for continued compliance with the agreement, with the payments/services due or to be performed by the insolvent party being charged to its pool of assets.*

Therefore, although there may be cause for termination due to breach by one of the parties, the judge may rule that the cash pooling agreement remain in force if this is of benefit to the insolvency proceedings – in other words, if it helps to guarantee the viability of the insolvent company in the case of continuation of the business and the adoption of an arrangement with creditors involving a degree of debt relief, or if it is beneficial for the creditors as a whole in the case of liquidation of the insolvent company.

2.4 Perspective D: regulatory

As stated previously, cash pooling agreements are not subject to any specific regulatory requirements in Spain.

Entering into cash pooling agreements is not included among the types of activity reserved by law to financial institutions, which are essentially those linked to the receipt of refundable funds from the public (by way of deposits, loans, temporary assignment of financial assets or similar) in order to allocate them to the provision of financing. As stated, though, in the event that a cash pooling agreement could be interpreted as the provision of loans or credit by the bank, the general banking rules concerning regulatory capital, solvency and security structure may be applicable.

In addition, Spanish regulations establish a number of formalities or information obligations that can apply in relation to cash pooling agreements, and which, more specifically, are regulated by means of Bank of Spain Circular 6/2000 of October 31 2000, 2/2001 of July 18 2001, and 3/2006 of July 28 2006. These regulations have recently experienced a major change as a result of the publishing of Bank of Spain Circular 4/2012 of April 25 2012.

Although Circular 4/2012 has already been published in the *Official Gazette*, it will not be in force until January 1 2013 and provides for a transitional period throughout 2013. As a consequence:

- until the end of 2012, the information obligations resulting from the regime prior to Circular 4/2012 (ie, Circulars 6/2000, 2/2001 and 3/2006) will apply exclusively;
- through 2013, both the new regime provided for in Circular 4/2012, and the former regime of Circulars 6/2000, 2/2001 and 3/2006 will apply simultaneously (in other words, if a person or company is required to fulfil information obligations under both sets of regulations, it will have to do so); and
- from January 1 2014 onwards, the new regime of Circular 4/2012 will apply exclusively, Circulars 6/2000, 2/2001 (partially) and 3/2006 being no longer in force.

The formalities and information obligations provided for in the set of regulations still in force (Circulars 6/2000, 2/2001 and 3/2006) is, in summary, as follows.

(a) *Opening and cancellation of accounts abroad (Circular 3/2006)*

The Bank of Spain must be informed if natural or legal persons residing in Spain:

- open or cancel accounts abroad, with either Spanish or foreign financial entities;

- open or cancel accounts abroad with non-resident persons which are not foreign financial institutions, if such accounts are used to make foreign collections and payments and offset reciprocal credits and debits; or
- make term deposits in branch offices abroad, if such offices belong to either Spanish or foreign financial entities.

In the first two cases above, the relevant notice must be served to the Bank of Spain within one month of the date of opening or cancelling of the account, by filing certain official forms (DD1). In addition, any modification of the details of the holder or the account must also be notified to the Bank of Spain within one month of the occurrence of such modifications. If a modification affects essential details (eg, the holder of the account, type of account, currency), then a notice of cancellation of the former account and opening of the new account (with the new details) must be made to the Bank of Spain.

In addition, upon cancellation of an account, notice shall be sent to the Bank of Spain to inform it of the operation of the account since the time the last notice of this nature was submitted (see further below).

In the third case listed above (deposits in branch offices), if the collections and payments resulting from the creation or withdrawal of the deposit are made through a branch office that belongs to a Spanish financial entity, the relevant notice will be sent to the Bank of Spain with the assistance of that entity. If the branch office belongs to a foreign financial entity, then the notice must be submitted using the mechanism foreseen for the operation of accounts abroad (see below).

(b) Operation of accounts abroad (Circular 3/2006)

Any changes occurring in the balance of any of the accounts held abroad by a resident natural or legal person, as well as the collections, payments and foreign transfers which cause such changes, must also be communicated to the Bank of Spain.

In principle, the above information must be communicated periodically, every month, by filing certain official forms (DD2, DD2*bis*). The deadline is the 20th day of the following month.

By way of exception, notice is not required in the event that, within a given month, neither the aggregate of the credits nor the aggregate of the debits made on the account, exceeds the amount of €3 million (or its equivalent in another currency). However, if that figure is reached in a later month, the relevant notice must include details of all transactions made in the previous months for which notice had not been submitted.

In addition, the holder of the account must submit a final yearly notice if during the year it was exempt (either for the whole year or just one or more months) from the above information obligations. This notice must be submitted by January 20 of the following year. However, if the aggregate amounts of the debits and credits made on the account during the year do not exceed €600,000 (or its equivalent in another currency), then the notice shall be submitted only upon request of the Bank of Spain, within a notice period of two months from the date of the request.

In principle, the information to be communicated must comprise all transactions made during the months which had been exempt from information. However, if the aggregate amounts of the debits and credits made on the account do not exceed €6 million (or its equivalent in another currency), then the information need only include the initial and final balance and the overall aggregate of debts and credits made on the account.

(c) ***Holding of securities deposited with non-resident entities (Circular 2/2001)***
The Bank of Spain must be informed if natural or legal persons residing in Spain hold assets in the form of securities that are deposited with non-resident entities. The contents of Circular 2/2001 are not described here, as it would typically not be relevant for the purposes of a cash pooling agreement.

(d) ***Opening and operation of non-resident accounts in Spain***
In general, financial institutions operating in Spain are authorised to open accounts to non-resident persons (Circular 1/1994). Nevertheless, in addition to other requirements, the financial institutions must identify and gather evidence that the holder is a non-resident person.

(e) ***Foreign loans, credit facilities and set-offs (Circular 6/2000)***
The Bank of Spain must be informed if natural or legal persons residing in Spain, other than financial institutions, grant or receive loans or credit facilities, either of a financial or commercial nature, or offset credit and debits with non-resident persons. To the extent that a cash pooling agreement may lead to these types of transaction, group companies residing in Spain may be subject to the reporting obligations summarised below.

In general, the Bank of Spain must be informed if natural or legal persons residing in Spain, other than financial institutions:

- receive loans or credit facilities from non-resident persons, whatever the type of instrument used, in an amount equal to or higher than €3 million (or its equivalent in another currency). If the amount is less than €6 million and the lender does not reside in a tax haven, the relevant notice, by means of the correct official form (PE-2), can be processed through the financial institution where the funds are received. That institution will itself assign a financial transaction number to the specific transaction. In any other case, the notice must be served to the Bank of Spain (on Form PE-1), which will then assign a financial transaction number. Until this number has been assigned, the funds will remain blocked and the financial institution may not make any debit or credit deriving from the disposal, repayment or payment of interest on the loan or financing obtained from the non-resident person;
- grant loans or credit facilities to non-resident persons, whatever the type of instrument, for an amount equal to or higher than €3 million (or its equivalent in another currency). If the amount is less than €6 million and the borrower does not reside in a tax haven, the relevant notice, by means of the correct official form (PE-4), can be processed through the financial institution

from which the funds are to be transferred. That institution will itself assign a financial transaction number to the specific transaction. In any other case, the notice must be served to the Bank of Spain (on Form PE-3), which will then assign a financial transaction number. Until such number has been assigned, the financial institution may not make any debit or credit deriving from the disposal, repayment or payment of interest on the loan or financing granted to the non-resident person; or

- offset collections and payments with non-resident persons, which originate from any type of transaction (eg, sales of goods, provision of services or transactions of a financial nature), for an amount equal to or higher than €600,000 (or its equivalent in another currency). In this case, the relevant communication, by means of the correct official form (CP-1) must be submitted within one month of the effective date of the offset. A set-off transaction number will be assigned to each offset for the purposes of identification. In the event that a set-off is partial and, as a consequence, there are net collections or payments to be settled through a financial institution, or through the debit or credit in an account held abroad, the collections and payments offset thereby must be communicated in their respective amounts and separately (ie, without grouping or consolidation) through the mechanism established for the communication of the operation of accounts held abroad.

In addition, if a particular transaction is exempt from the above information obligations because its amount does not reach the relevant thresholds, the Bank of Spain still retains the right to require the holder of the relevant account to notify it if a series of transactions is made that exceeds, in aggregate, those thresholds. The deadline for such notification is one month from the date of the request for notification. The notice must be addressed directly to the Bank of Spain.

(f) ***New regime (Circular 4/2012)***

The formalities and information obligations provided for by the new regulations (Circular 4/2012), which will come into force on January 1 2013, are as follows.

In general, Circular 4/2012 (once it comes into force) provides for information obligations to be imposed on natural and legal persons (both public and private) residing in Spain as regards:

- transactions with non-resident persons that may give rise to collections, payments and/or transfers abroad, or variations in accounts or financial positions (whether of a credit or a debit nature); and
- assets or liabilities that they hold with non-resident persons.

By way of exception, payment services providers that are duly recorded in the official register held by the Bank of Spain are exempt from this regime.

The resident persons mentioned in the previous paragraph will be required to inform the Bank of Spain of:

- transactions that they carry out (in their own interest) with non-resident

persons, whatever their nature and regardless of how they are settled, including settlement via electronic transfers abroad, or debits or credits made in bank accounts or inter-company accounts, though set-offs or by means of cash payments; and
- balances and variations of assets and liabilities held with non-resident persons, whatever the form (eg, bank accounts and accounts with other financial entities, inter-company accounts, cash or security deposits, corporate shares, debt instruments, derivative financial instruments, real estate).

The transactions and the balances and variations mentioned above must be communicated to the Bank of Spain:
- on a monthly basis, within 20 days of the end of each month, if the amount of the transactions made the previous year or the balance of the assets and liabilities on December 31 of the previous year is equal to or in excess of €300 million;
- on a quarterly basis, within 20 days of the end of each calendar quarter, if the amount of the transactions made the previous year or the balance of the assets and liabilities on December 31 of the previous year is equal to or in excess of €100 million, but less than €300 million; and
- on a yearly basis, by January 20 of the following year, if the amount of the transactions made the previous year or the balance of the assets and liabilities on December 31 of the previous year is less than €100 million. If the amount is less than €50 million, the information may be submitted in abridged form. If the amount is less than €1 million, the information must be sent to the Bank of Spain only if it expressly requests it, in which case the information must be provided within two months of such a request.

In addition, the Bank of Spain will have the authority to request that the above information be provided with a higher frequency, and to request the details of all the transactions and balances included in the annual information provided in abridged form. The information must be submitted online, using an application provided by the Bank of Spain.

2.2 Perspective E: tax

In Spain, there are no specific civil, commercial or tax regulations governing cash pooling agreements.

Therefore, with regard to tax matters, the aspects that should be borne in mind when designing a cash pooling agreement between group companies are as follows.

(a) VAT

Given that the transactions that take place under a cash pooling agreement are financial transactions, they are regarded as subject to, but exempt from, value added tax (VAT)[1]. That should be borne in mind for the purposes of the VAT-related prorating rule, if the master account holder is Spanish (or EU-resident, since European

Court of Justice case law, which is followed by Spain's Directorate-General of Taxation when answering queries, is consistent on this point).

A number of rulings have been given by the Directorate-General of Taxation in reply to queries on this point that analyse the activites concerned. These state that, depending upon how the cash pooling agreement is configured, one could be dealing with:

- the receipt on the part of the master account holder of the cash surpluses of other participating companies for their assignment in its own name to other entities; or
- an intermediary role on the part of the master account holder allowing participating companies with cash surpluses to assign those surpluses to participating companies with cash deficits.

The Directorate-General for Taxation has concluded that, in either case, these activities are subject to, but exempt from, VAT.

(b) Corporate income tax

In this area, given that Spanish tax legislation does not specifically contemplate cash pooling agreements, it is necessary to consider the nature of the agreement to assess the corporate income tax implications.

Cash pooling is merely a set of automatic inter-company loans made on a day-to-day basis for the purpose of optimising the global position of the company or group, securing a single balance with each bank with which it has dealings. It is also a way of optimising treasury surpluses of those companies or offices/branches with such surpluses, offsetting the needs of those offices/branches with a shortfall.

Whatever the type of cash pooling chosen, when choosing it, the following requirements must be met in order to comply with Spanish corporate income tax legislation:

- Accounting for the financial income/expense at the agreed interest rate – positive and negative transfers made to the parent company are regarded as inter-company loans. Consequently, interest accruing on such loans must be accounted for by the companies for the expense to be tax-deductible.
- Accounting in accordance with accruals and income/expenditure matching principles – for tax purposes, expenses are deductible after they have been recorded in the accounting records and assigned to their accrual period. This must be borne in mind in the case of interest on company loans.

  In any case, and regardless of this limitation, such expenses must be necessary in order to obtain income if they are to be regarded as tax deductible. To be deductible, they must be documented and meet the requirements set out in the Corporate Income Tax Act:

  - They must be for a service actually provided, which may be of advantage

1 Technically, under Spanish tax legislation, it is possible – and sometimes common – to be subject to a tax, but exempt (*exento*) from it. If a person is not subject to a tax it is not possible to be exempt from it.

  or utility to the group entity that is a beneficiary of the service; and
  - Consideration for the service must have been at market value, and made to the entity in question on an individual basis (and, if this is not possible, it must be allocated on a rational basis).
- Agreed interest rate must be at market value – these transactions are intra-group transactions and therefore made between related parties. For accounting and tax purposes, they must therefore be carried out at market value, if problems are to be avoided in Spain.
- Supporting documentation for expense – the financial expense must be documented. In the case of a cash pooling agreement, the documentation will be the relevant agreement, which may be categorised as one of the services to be provided by the parent company to subsidiaries. In such case it would be worthwhile submitting the proposals for valuing the transactions under such an agreement to the Spanish tax authorities before their implementation.
- Limitation of deductibility of net financial expenses to 30% of operating profit for the period – on March 31 2012, Royal Decree Act 12/2012 was passed. For tax periods commencing on or after January 1 2012, this act removes the undercapitalisation rule and replaces it with a system that limits the deductibility of financial expenses. This amendment is incorporated as the new Article 20 of the Corporate Income Tax Act. The main features of this limitation are as follows:
  - Net financial expenses are deductible up to a limit of 30% of the operating profit for the period. The act defines what is meant by 'net financial expenses' and 'operating profit for the period'.
    'Net financial expenses' are defined as the excess financial expenses with regard to the income arising from the assignment to third parties of own capital falling due in the tax period, excluding those financial expenses considered non-deductible.
  - In all cases, net financial expenses of up to €1 million in the financial period shall be deductible.
  - The limitations to the deductibility of financial expenses outlined above are not applicable either to credit institutions (although there are certain special provisions if they consolidate with other non-credit undertakings), nor to undertakings that do not form part of a trading group (unless those financial expenses arising from transactions with undertakings and persons that are related by holdings of at least 20%, exceed 10% of net financial expenses);
  - Amounts that are not deducted in the period they fall due because they exceed the limits set out above may be carried forward and deducted in the tax periods that conclude in the 18 immediately following years, together with those of the corresponding period, up to the 30% limit set out above.

  In the case of tax groups, the 30% limit refers to the whole group (although the act specifies certain exceptions).

In the case of involvement of companies that are resident in countries that do not belong to the European Union, it will also be necessary to analyse any withholding tax applicable to interest under any double tax treaty that may have been signed, and in the absence of any applicable treaty, under the provisions of Spanish legislation.

Should the foreign companies in question be based in EU member states, withholding tax would not be applicable (except in the case of countries regarded as tax havens).

Sweden

Kristina Einarsson
Odd Swarting
Setterwalls Law Firm

1. Introduction

1.1 Admissibility of cash pooling agreements

There are no prohibitions under Swedish law on corporations entering into a cash pooling agreement or on holding companies setting up a cash pooling agreement with group members. Both notional pooling and physical cash pooling are provided by most major banks in Sweden.

The legal framework surrounding cash pooling agreements is liberal.[1] However, a transfer by a Swedish company of liquid funds into a central cash management or cash pooling structure together with parent and affiliated companies must in each case be examined in light of certain restrictions and conditions imposed by general principles of Swedish corporate and tax law.

One of these principles is that Swedish corporate law does not recognise an overall legal concept of integrated groups of companies. As such, the board of directors of a Swedish group company may not take a consolidated view and fulfil its fiduciary duty by merely considering the overall interests of the entire group of companies. Instead, it must assess and secure the financial status of each corporation on an independent and standalone basis, focusing on what is beneficial to each individual corporation.

Loans made under a cash pooling agreement must therefore generally fulfil the following conditions:

- The lender company should, at the time of completion of the transaction, carefully consider the borrower's creditworthiness as well as its willingness and ability to repay the loan; and
- The loan should provide for market rate interest.

1.2 Types of cash pooling agreement

Most banks offer domestic cash pooling and certain of the larger banks also offer cross-border solutions with domestic cash pools connected to regional structures capable of handling multiple currencies. Physical cash pooling is offered in the form of zero or target balancing and single legal account pooling. Notional cash pools are allowed, but are not widely used, as the banks are not permitted to offset debit and credit balances.[2]

---

1 Danske Bank, *Country profile, Sweden*, s 22.
2 Danske Bank, *Country profile, Sweden*, s 22; SEB, *Country Summary Report, Sweden*, s 17.

1.3 Legal requirements from various perspectives

(a) *Company law*

As noted above, each loan made under a cash pooling scheme must be examined in each case in light of certain restrictions and conditions imposed by general principles of Swedish corporate law. Non-compliance may lead to the invalidity of a loan, as well as to personal liability for directors and officers.

Loan to be within the corporate purpose: As a general rule, a commitment entered into on behalf of a Swedish company is binding on the company, to the extent that it is within the company's business purpose, as set out in its articles of association. If that is not the case, the commitment in question could be deemed *ultra vires* and therefore null and void from the outset. However, providing financial assistance, including upstream loans, to other European group companies would not generally be considered to conflict with a Swedish company's articles of association.

Loan prohibition rule: A Swedish limited liability company may not lend money to, among others, an entity or person which owns shares either in the Swedish company or in another company within the same company group (as defined in the Companies Act).

There are, however, two exceptions to this rule. First, a Swedish company may lend money to a company within the same company group as the Swedish company.[3] A 'company group' in this context means, essentially, a company group (within certain ownership thresholds) in which the parent is obliged to maintain accounts under the Accounting Act or a corresponding foreign legal person domiciled within the European Economic Area. The implication of this is that loans can be made between a Swedish subsidiary and a non-EEA subsidiary if the parent company has its domicile in the European Economic Area, but that loans cannot be made between a parent company and a subsidiary or between two subsidiaries located in the European Economic Area if the parent company is outside the European Economic Area.[4] If there are several layers of parent companies, the dividing line will be immediately above the EEA parent which is highest in the group structure.

The second exception to the prohibition is if the loan is intended exclusively for the borrower's business operations and the company provides the loan for purely commercial reasons.[5] This exception applies only if the loan can be of benefit to the lender company.[6] This means that the loan must, directly or indirectly, further the lender's business.[7] The implication of this is that loans, including loans under a cash pooling agreement, can be possible even if the parent company does not have its domicile within the European Economic Area if the loan is deemed to be of commercial benefit for the Swedish company's business.

---

3 Companies Act Chapter 21, Section 2.2.
4 Legal commentaries to Companies Act Chapter 21, Section 1-2.
5 Companies Act Chapter 21, Section 2.3.
6 Prop. 2004/05:85 s. 431 f.
7 Legal commentaries to Companies Act Chapter 21, Section 2.

Should neither of these two exceptions apply, a company can, under the Companies Act, apply to the Swedish Tax Agency or the Swedish Financial Supervisory Authority for exemption from the prohibition on loans. However, exemption may be granted only where particular cause exists.[8]

Value transfers and constructive dividends: A loan, even if it does not fall under the loan prohibition rule, may be unlawful according to the Swedish rules restricting value transfers. If the benefit received from a Swedish company is clearly disproportionate to the consideration given, the transaction may be considered a value transfer.

A loan could be deemed to be a value transfer if it is made to an insolvent or near-insolvent borrower, or if it does not carry interest at market rates. In the latter case it would normally be regarded as such only with regard to the amount corresponding to the difference between the interest actually charged and the interest that would have been charged at a market rate. Such a loan is unlawful if the amount of the transferred value is not covered by distributable equity in the lender company.[9] If is the loan comprises an unlawful value transfer, the board of directors of the lender would be forced to demand immediate repayment, of the loan irrespective of its term. In the event of any loss, the directors and advisers of the lender can be held liable.[10] The characterisation of a loan as an unlawful value transfer would also lead to adverse tax consequences (see paragraph (e) below).

It is important that the terms of the cash pooling agreement include a possibility to exclude insolvent members of the cash pool and allow any Swedish member to refuse to extend funds to a group company that is considered unable to repay the loans made.

Prohibition of loans for acquisition of shares: Under Swedish law[11] a Swedish company may not grant an advance, provide loans or provide security for loans in order for the beneficiary or any natural or legal person connected to the beneficiary to acquire shares in the company or any parent company in the same group. The implication of this is that an acquiring company may be restricted from taking part in a cash pooling system with the acquired company until a certain time from the date of acquisition has elapsed. Normally, a period of 30 to 90 days is applied, but there is no court precedent to give guidance as to the time required.

(b) Banking law

There are no specific Swedish banking rules covering cash pooling agreements. Instead, general Swedish banking rules apply.

The Capital Adequacy and Large Exposures Act ensures that banks and credit market companies have sufficient capital to meet the risks in the business. The act, which implemented the revised Capital Requirements Directive (ie, the Basel II Accord), contains requirements on credit risks, market risks and operational risks.

---

8 Companies Act Chapter 21, Section 8.
9 Companies Act Chapter 17, Section 3.
10 Companies Act Chapter 17, Sections 6 and 7.
11 Companies Act Chapter 25, Section 5.

Cash pooling is, according to the Swedish Bankers Association, treated under these rules in the same way as a regular deposit account. In order to fulfil the capital requirement for credit risks, a capital base equivalent to at least 8% of the value of the assets and liabilities of an institution or a financial group must be held, calculated following the provisions of the the act.[12] The capital requirement will, however, be strengthened with the implementation of the proposed Basel III.

(c) ***Insolvency law***

The bankruptcy estate can generally decide whether to continue the cash pooling agreement. Under the Bankruptcy Act, a company that receives a repayment from another company through the cash pooling agreement may find itself obligated to return the cash if the repaying company (the debtor) was, or through the procedure became, insolvent. This might be the case if the debtor, for example, is considered to have favoured one creditor ahead of others, or if the debtor's assets were diverted from its creditors in an improper way. However, it is the other party must have known or should have known of the debtor's insolvency and the circumstances that made the transaction improper. In the case of cash pooling agreements, affiliated companies are presumed to have the required knowledge unless it is shown to be probable that the recipient neither knew or should have had such knowledge. Furthermore, with regard to affiliated companies, the obligation is not limited in time and therefore the time between the receipt of the cash and the date of the bankruptcy petition is insignificant.

(d) ***Regulatory law***

No regulatory requirements exist under Swedish law that impact on cash pooling agreements.

(e) ***Tax law***

There are no specific Swedish tax rules in respect of cash pooling agreements; instead, general Swedish tax rules apply

Withholding and income tax implications of upstream loans: Ordinary and deemed profit distributions by resident companies are subject to Swedish withholding tax (currently at 35%) at source. Subject to certain conditions and upon request, the tax may be fully or partially refunded to the recipient of the profit distribution. For non-Swedish recipients, such a refund may be granted only on the basis of a double tax treaty between Sweden and the country of residence of the recipient.

Furthermore, profit distributions are not income tax deductible, for which reason they are added back to the taxable profit of the distributing company and, therefore, become subject to corporate income tax.

From a tax standpoint, a deemed dividend is always assumed when a company executes transactions with related parties other than at arm's-length. This is also the

12 Act on Capital Adequacy and Large Exposures, Chapter 2, Section 2 and Chapter 3, Section 1.

case with regard to upstream loans, where the fulfilment of the arm's-length requirement is typically assessed based on the following three elements:

- Interest rate – if the upstream loan is granted at an interest rate that is lower than that accepted by the Swedish tax authorities for tax purposes, any difference in the interest amount qualifies as a deemed dividend. The accepted interest rates differ from currency to currency and are published periodically by the Swedish Tax Agency.
- Loan amount – under certain conditions, the tax authorities may even characterise the total loan amount as a deemed dividend subject to withholding tax and income tax. This will be the case if the upstream loan is fictitious, that is, if there is never any intention of repaying the loan. Furthermore, such a characterisation is possible if, at the time the loan was granted or renewed, the borrower was in such a bad financial situation that repayment of the loan could not reasonably be expected, or if at that time a third party would not have granted or renewed such a loan on substantially the same terms and conditions.
- Liquidation proceeds – if the upstream loan is not paid back and this leads to the bankruptcy or liquidation of the Swedish lender, the granting of the upstream loan may be retroactively characterised as the first step in the liquidation of the Swedish lender under the concept of factual liquidation. As a result, Swedish withholding tax will be assessed not only on the amount of the upstream loan in question, but on the total amount of the (deemed) liquidation proceeds, calculated on the basis of the fair market values of the Swedish lender's net assets at the time the upstream loan was granted.

Since the withholding tax of 35% must be withheld at source, the tax authorities consider the actual payment to be only 65% of the full constructive dividend amount. Hence, they first gross up the constructive dividend amount to 100% and then levy the 35% withholding tax on that basis. Consequently, the potential withholding tax liability of a Swedish lender (or of members of the board of directors or management) would amount to as much as 53.8% of the deemed dividend amount. Directors and officers may, according to the Withholding Tax Act, become personally as well as jointly and severally liable for the unpaid withholding tax obligations of a Swedish company that is liquidated or becomes bankrupt. This liability is stricter than the general directors' and officers' liability insofar as the officers and directors, in order to avoid liability, have to prove that they have done everything which could reasonably be expected of them to ascertain and fulfil the company's tax obligations.

Transfer pricing: Under the Income Tax Act, commercial and financial transactions between affiliated enterprises, established in different countries, shall be based on the same terms and conditions that would have been applied between independent enterprises. This internal rule on transfer pricing conforms to the arm's-length principle in the Organisation for Economic Cooperation and Development (OECD) model tax convention on income and on capital.

The OECD transfer pricing guidelines for multinational enterprises and tax administrations can, according to Swedish case law, serve as a guide when deciding whether a certain arrangement between affiliated parties is at arm's length.

The arm's-length principle should be taken into account when deciding what income and expenditure to attribute to a branch office. For instance, costs for the management of the company can to a certain extent be deductible for the company's foreign branch office.

Sweden also has rules regarding transfer pricing documentation. The rules have introduced a formal obligation for multinational enterprises to document in writing their intra-group transfer pricing for all cross-border transactions.

Limitation on interest deduction: Under Swedish tax law, a limitation applies to deduction of interest paid between affiliated companies if certain requirements are met. From January 1 2010, this limitation also applies to loans from a foreign entity that is deemed to be an affiliated company. Under these provisions, deduction of interest on intra-group loans is denied where the loans are related to the acquisition of a company from a related party. Furthermore, deductions of interest expenses can be denied in cases where companies, through certain arrangements, try to avoid these rules.

There are two exceptions to these rules under which the interest expense is still deductible:

- The corresponding interest income should have been taxed at a tax rate of at least 10% according to the provisions of the jurisdiction where the company which has a right to the interest income is resident, if the company alone should have had that interest income (the 10% rule); and
- If both the loan and the acquisition are primarily made for business purposes (the business purpose test).

The Swedish government has recently presented a proposal which would amend these rules. The government now proposes to extend the interest deduction limitation provisions to cover all debts to affiliated companies. Consequently, the provisions will be applicable toall intra-group loans, regardless of the purpose of the loan.

Furthermore, the government proposes to amend the 10% rule with the addition of a reverse business purpose test. If the Swedish Tax Agency can show that the debt has been taken out primarily to obtain a significant tax benefit, the interest will not be deductible despite the fact that the corresponding interest income has been subject to more than 10% tax.

Moreover, it is also proposed to limit the business purpose test to apply only where the recipient of the interest income is in an EEA member state or in a country with which Sweden has a double tax treaty. This will mainly exclude loans from tax havens from the business purpose test.

It is proposed that these adjustments will enter into force as of January 1 2013. According to the proposal, 'normal' cash pooling operations should, however, be covered by the business purpose test if the operations are conducted in a country where interest is subject to a tax at a rate of at least 10%. However, what are deemed to be 'normal' cash pooling operations is not discussed further in the proposal.

Controlled foreign companies rules: Swedish rules on controlled foreign companies may be applicable. Under the Swedish controlled foreign company rules, a resident company, as well as any non-resident company with a permanent establishment in Sweden, which maintains a holding in a foreign legal entity is liable to Swedish tax on its share of the foreign legal entity's worldwide net profit, provided that:

- the income of the foreign legal entity is deemed to be subject to low taxation; and
- at the end of the income year at least 25% of the capital or voting rights in the foreign legal entity is controlled, directly or indirectly, by the Swedish shareholder alone or together with persons who have a community of interests with the shareholder.

Under the general rule, the income of a controlled foreign entity is deemed to be subject to low taxation if it is not taxed at all or is subject to tax that is lower than 14.5% (55% of the current Swedish corporate tax rate of 26.3%). Income is not considered to be subject to low taxation, however, if the foreign legal entity is a tax resident, and liable to income tax, in one of the countries listed on a 'white list', provided that the income in question has not been expressly excluded. Income from cash pooling operations may in some low tax jurisdictions be excluded from the white list, and a Swedish parent company may be taxed on the cash pool leader's worldwide net income.

An exemption from these rules applies to income from a controlled foreign company that is resident in an EEA member state, if the shareholder can prove that the foreign entity is established in the other country for business reasons and is engaged in real economic activities.

If a foreign cash pool leader has no substance (eg, personnel) in the country of residence, it can be deemed to have a permanent establishment in Sweden if it is managed by a Swedish group company. The cash pool leader will then be subject to tax in Sweden on any income attributable to Sweden, and certain tax administration issues have to be addressed, such as tax registrations and the filing of an income tax return.

2. Specific questions

2.1 Perspective A: corporate group

(a) *Liability of group company and/or master account holder directors in the event of insolvency of a group company*

In general, the directors and the senior management of a Swedish company may become personally liable to the company and to its shareholders and creditors for any damage caused by an intentional or negligent violation of their duties. With regard to a director's liability in this situation, a company's status as listed or privately held is irrelevant.

A supervisory board does not constitute a corporate body under the Companies Act. The Swedish board system is instead one-tiered, with all directors forming one board. The potential liability of someone appointed as a member of a supervisory board will therefore depend on whether he is deemed to be a director of the company.

Liability of directors of a Swedish group company: Under the Companies Act, the board of directors in a Swedish company is under an obligation to take certain steps if there is reason to believe that the company's shareholders' equity is less than half of the registered share capital. Failure to take these steps will result in joint and several liabilities for the members of the board for any obligations incurred by the company following the point in time when the board failed to act. Personal liability may also occur for any other person who conducts business on the company's behalf with knowledge of the board of directors' failure to act. Exemption from liability is, however, possible if a person can prove that the failure was not caused by negligence on his part.

If the situation is caused by an unlawful value transfer, the directors of a Swedish group company must demand immediate repayment and the recipient (the master account holder in a cash pooling scenario) will be obligated under Swedish law to make the repayment regardless of its domicile. In the event of any loss, the directors for the group company and its advisers (eg, auditors, special examiners or lawyers) can be held personally liable if they participated in the decision regarding the value transfer.

However, the director of a Swedish group company will not be held liable under the conflict of interest rule in the Companies Act. Generally, a board member may not participate in a matter regarding an agreement between the company and another legal person that the board member is entitled to represent. Disregard of this rule may result in liability. However, the rule provides an exception for undertakings within the same company group (the parent company and its subsidiaries).[13]

If the situation is so severe that the company is insolvent, liability may also be incurred for new debts if the board members continue the business even though the company is insolvent and the board members are aware, or ought to be aware, of this.

It is also a crime subject to liability for damages under the Penal Code for a board member, when the company is insolvent or there is an evident danger of insolvency, to act in ways that harm the company with regard to the creditors – for example, by making a transaction below value or continuing the business despite the financial status of the company significantly deteriorating. In practice, these provisions are invoked only in the case of serious, usually intentional, misconduct on the part of the board members.

Liability of shareholders of a Swedish group company: The company's shareholder can in certain situations also be held liable to the company. First, a shareholder might be liable for damage which it caused to the company, intentionally or through gross negligence, in violation of the Companies Act. Second, a parent company may in exceptional circumstances be held liable

13 Companies Act Chapter 8, Section 23

according to the doctrine of piercing the corporate veil. The requirements for piercing the corporate veil are, however, unclear under Swedish law. It will probably be required that the subsidiary be undercapitalised and in a dependent relationship with the shareholder, that there be a dishonest purpose behind the shareholder's actions, and that the party claiming liability have acted in good faith.

Liability of directors of the master account holder: With regard to the directors of the master account holder, they may be held liable towards their company and its shareholders and creditors if the company (ie, the master account holder) has sustained damage as a result of the insolvency and the directors are deemed to have violated their duties intentionally or negligently. Directors may also be personally liable for unlawful value transfers if the value transferred cannot be recovered from the transferee, because either the transferee is insolvent or the transferee has received the value in good faith.

Naturally, liability under Swedish law for directors of either a group company or the master account holder will arise only if their respective companies are located in Sweden. The same principle applies with regard to liability for a shareholder – that is, the company must have its domicile in Sweden.

(b) Liability of group company and/or master account holder directors in the event of insolvency of the master account holder

The directors of the master account holder will have the same liability as the directors of a group company discussed in paragraph (a) above.

The director of a group company may be held liable towards their company and its creditors if they continue to conduct business with a company in the knowledge that that company was insolvent and the group company suffers damage as a result. If the company grants upstream loans, the lender's directors and officers are under an ongoing duty to verify carefully the creditworthiness of the borrower during the entire term of the upstream loan and immediately to take appropriate measures if the borrower ceases to be creditworthy. Downstream loans to financially unstable subsidiaries may in many cases be permitted as they can be considered to be of corporate benefit to the lending parent company, but the directors will have a duty to assess the commercial benefit on a case-by-case basis.

(c) Liability of group companies in the event of insolvency of the master account holder

Swedish corporate law does not recognise an overall legal concept of integrated groups of companies. Instead, each company is a legal entity separate from its shareholders. An exception to this may in extreme circumstances occur under the doctrine of piercing the corporate veil. In this situation, however, the question is whether a subsidiary (a group company) can be held liable for a parent corporation's (the master account holder's) losses. It is unlikely that any such legal liability exists under Swedish law; at the very least, such liability would require exceptional circumstances.

In the unlikely event that liability for a subsidiary is established, the location of the claiming creditor or the group company (subsidiary) is irrelevant to the question of liability, as long as the company that has suffered losses – the master account holder – has its domicile in Sweden.

However, in the event of liquidation, insolvency law will be applicable and consequently other companies that have received payments from the master account holder, regardless of a parent-subsidiary relationship, can be obligated to repay (see section 2.3 below).

(d) *Liability of the master account holder in the event of insolvency of a group company*

In extreme circumstances a creditor may be able to hold a parent company, the master account holder, liable for a Swedish company's losses according to the doctrine of piercing the corporate veil. As noted above, such liability is hard to establish as its requirements are unclear under Swedish law (see section 2.1(a)).

However, it is unlikely that there is any principle of liability between sister companies under Swedish law; at the very least, such liability would require exceptional circumstances.

In the event that liability in either case was established, the liability would not be affected by the location of the parent company, the claiming creditor or the group company, as long as the company that has suffered losses has its domicile in Sweden.

Another situation arises if liquidation occurs: a recipient of payments from the group company can then be obligated to repay them under insolvency law regardless of the parent-subsidiary relationship (see section 2.3 below).

2.2 Perspective B: bank

(a) *Banking requirements*

Requirements that need to be met by a bank offering cash pooling are discussed at section 1.3(b) above.

(b) *Liability of the bank in the event of insolvency of the master account holder or a group company*

As mention above, each company is a separate legal entity. Liability for another company's loss where there is no parent-subsidiary relationship is extremely unlikely under Swedish corporate law. Instead, liability between unrelated companies will generally require a contractual relationship and/or damages caused by one of the companies to the other. Consequently, in the situation in question the bank will be liable only if liability can be established under the cash pooling agreement.

With regard to the location of the relevant parties, the important factor is that the company that has suffered losses have its domicile in Sweden.

2.3 Insolvency

(a) *Cash pooling from the insolvency practitioner's perspective*

Bank goes into liquidation: An insolvency administrator in a Swedish liquidation (bankruptcy) of a bank party to cash pooling would claim the credit balance of the cash pool, and the other parties would normally have only an unsecured claim in the bankruptcy. If the liquidation were opened in another country, the law of that country would apply.

The administrator would have no particular obligations to the master account holder and the group companies other than those it has to all creditors. It does not matter where the creditor companies have their seats.

Master account holder goes into liquidation: An insolvency administrator in a Swedish liquidation (bankruptcy) of the master account holder would claim the credit balance of the cash pool since it is in the possession of the master account holder, provided that a group company cannot prove that its part of the cash pool is to be treated as, and handled as, property of the group company to be separated from the master account holder's assets. If the liquidation is opened in another country, the law of that country would apply.

The administrator in a Swedish liquidation has a duty to separate the property of a group company if any exists and it has been treated as such (ie, as property belonging to a third party) correctly, by being kept separate from the debtor's assets. It does not matter where the group company has its seat. However, this is unlikely in the case of a cash pooling agreement where all moneys transferred by group companies have been placed in the same (master) account, and therefore have probably not been kept in a way that makes it possible to treat such amounts as separated in a legally correct manner. The administrator will have no particular obligations to the bank other than those it has to all creditors.

An insolvency administrator in a Swedish liquidation (bankruptcy) of a group company participant in a cash pooling agreement would claim that company's part of the cash pool. If the liquidation were opened in another country, the law of that country would apply.

The administrator has a general duty to claim the group company's part of the credit balance and to initiate recovery for any other recoverable funds paid into the cash pool. This would also be the case as regards the bank if the bank had received money through the cash pooling agreement.

Voidability of transactions made prior to insolvency: A Swedish administrator in the insolvency of the master account holder or a group company has powers to take initiate court proceedings to disregard or declare void those transactions made at the time when the insolvent company was insolvent, even if it was obligated under the cash pooling agreement to make those transfers, and the administrator will claim the amounts involved as part of the bankruptcy estate.

(b) Special rules as regards creditors of other parties to the cash pooling agreement

The administrator in a Swedish liquidation has a duty to separate the property of a group company if any exists and has been treated as such (ie, as property belonging to a third party) correctly, by keeping it separate from the debtor's assets. However such treatment is probably unlikely in case of a cash pooling agreement where the funds are mixed in the master account.

(c) *Dissolution/termination of the cash pooling agreement in the event of liquidation of the master account holder or a group company*

In the event that the master account holder goes into liquidation, a group company may dissolve or terminate the cash pooling agreement unless the bankruptcy administrator assumes all of the master account holder's obligations, but the effect is uncertain as regards any claim on the account. If a group company goes into liquidation, its administrator is not obliged to continue to use the cash pooling agreement. In the event that the bank goes into liquidation, the master account holder may dissolve or terminate the cash pooling agreement unless the bankruptcy administrator assumes all of the bank's obligations, but the effect is uncertain as regards any claim on the account.

2.4 Perspective D: regulatory

No regulatory requirements exist under Swedish law that impact on cash pooling agreements.

2.5 Perspective E: tax

Swedish tax issues that will be of relevance to cash pooling agreements are discussed in section 1.3(e) above.

Switzerland

Benedict F Christ
David Jenny
Nadia Tarolli Schmidt
VISCHER Ltd

1. Introduction

1.1 Admissibility of cash pooling agreements

As a general rule, cash pooling agreements are permitted under Swiss law. Corporations may participate in cash pooling agreements and holding companies may set up cash pooling agreements with their group members, both notional and physical. As far as rules regarding the Swiss companies involved are concerned, the analysis does not change where foreign companies also participate in the cash pooling agreement (be it as the master account holder or as a group company).

1.2 Types of cash pooling agreement

Given that there are no specific legal restrictions and that many multinational companies either are headquartered in Switzerland or have a local subsidiary in Switzerland, all types of cash pooling agreement are used in Switzerland.

1.3 Legal requirements from various perspectives

Under Swiss law, there are no specific statutory rules governing cash pooling agreements.

However, while there is no specific statutory law governing cash pooling agreements, a number of general rules must be considered in connection with cash pooling agreements. Generally, purely notional cash pooling does not create legal issues, as it does not create material legal obligations. The typical issues arise in the case of physical cash pooling, which involves loans between group companies and the master account holder, or if securities are granted in connection with either physical or notional cash pooling.

Most of the following principles have been tested generally in the Swiss courts, though there is little case law specifically relating to cash pooling agreements. For the purposes of this chapter, we discuss what we perceive as the majority view in the legal doctrine and those theories most widely accepted that are reasonably likely to prevail in court. However, in most instances, the legal doctrine includes views that support both more restrictive and less restrictive positions.

(a) *Company law*

Most restrictions regarding cash pooling agreements under Swiss law are related to provisions of company law.

Directors' duties include their inalienable responsibility for the company's financial strategy, including its planning, implementation, management and monitoring. Financial transactions must be at arm's length, although terms of downstream loan to a subsidiary that are more beneficial to the subsidiary than the parent are generally not problematic. Therefore, before entering into a cash pooling agreement, the board (be it of a group company or the master account holder) has the duty to evaluate carefully whether participation in the cash pooling agreement is in the company's best interests and (in relation to up- or cross-stream counterparties) at arm's length. Generally, in the case of physical cash pooling target balancing will be easier to justify than zero balancing. After entering into the cash pooling agreement, the board has a permanent duty to monitor the cash pooling agreement, in particular, the creditworthiness of the master account holder and the other group companies and, if necessary, to take appropriate measures to reduce their company's exposure.

There is no strict definition of whether a transaction is at arm's length. A transaction is considered to be not at arm's length if there is a gross discrepancy between the parties' obligations. Not only the primary obligations such as the amount of the loan or interest rate, but all terms of the relationship need to be considered, including the term of the loan, termination provisions, securities, creditworthiness of the other party and so on. One test is whether the same terms could be obtained from a third party. As a general rule, the granting of security to parent or sister companies is considered to be almost impossible to be structured on arm's length terms in an intra-group set-up. To reduce the risk of liability, in particular, in case of security being granted to parent or sister companies, companies should typically amend their articles with a specific provision allowing the grant of such loans or security free of charge, as discussed below.

The directors of a company have a duty of loyalty. The directors must always act in the best interests of the company and not those of third parties, including those of a parent company or other group companies. While most of the time the interests of different group companies will be aligned, there is an increased risk of conflicts of interest in situations of financial distress. A cash pooling agreement is prone to such conflicts of interest if the same directors serve on the board of a group company and that of the master account holder. Generally, conflicts of interest cannot be excused. A company's share capital plus the statutory reserves (together, the protected equity) may not be distributed to the shareholders (be it as a dividend or otherwise, for instance, as a disguised or hidden distribution). Therefore, when dealing with a parent or a sister company, to the extent that the cash pooling agreement could affect the company's protected equity, a cash pooling agreement may only be entered into on arm's length conditions. It is standard practice for Swiss companies to include limitation language in the documentation regarding credit and, in particular, the documentation regarding security to prevent the company from having an obligation to violate its protected equity. If a cash pooling agreement is not at arm's length and the company's balance sheet is not strong enough to support a daily cash sweep, the parties should provide for appropriate safeguards. For instance, target balancing at an appropriate amount might limit the risk of undue distribution of protected equity.

Under the doctrine of *ultra vires*, any transaction outside the scope of the company's purpose (as defined in its articles of association) is void. Therefore, as regards payments to a parent or a sister company under a cash pooling agreement that are not on arm's-length conditions, there is a risk that they will be void unless approved as a formal dividend by the shareholders' meeting. To avoid such *ultra vires* issues, it is generally recommended that the articles of association of Swiss group companies participating in a cash pooling agreement include a specific provision allowing the grant of loans or security free of charge to parent or sister companies. A downstream loan to a subsidiary could, in particular circumstances, be treated as subordinated debt if such debt serves equity-like purposes, in particular where a subsidiary is undercapitalised. In an insolvency, such debt would be subordinated to other debt of the company.

If a group company is not 100% owned by the group that has set up the cash pooling agreement, but has outside shareholders, all terms of the cash pooling agreement must be at arm's length (or more favourable to the group company) to avoid a violation of the outside shareholders' right to equal treatment.

Not only the directors formally appointed and registered in the registry of commerce are subject to the duties of loyalty and care, but also any person (be it an individual or a corporation) that has an influence on the board's decisions as if such person were a board member. *De facto* directors are subject to the same liability as formal directors.

Swiss law recognises the concept of piercing the corporate veil in cases of abuse of law. Commingling of funds or a systematic undercapitalisation could be an indication of such abuse. The courts are usually reluctant to pierce the corporate veil in the absence of blatant abuse. If the corporate veil is pierced, the parent company becomes directly liable for the subsidiary's debt alongside the subsidiary.

(b) ***Bankruptcy law***

Swiss bankruptcy law provides for claw-back under certain circumstances. In an insolvency the following transactions can be challenged:

- any transactions made in the year prior to insolvency that were not at arm's length, to the detriment of the insolvent company;
- any transactions made in the year prior to insolvency while the company's debt plus equity exceeded its assets where the transaction involved the grant of supplemental security or the repayment of a debt not due; and
- any transactions made in the five years prior to insolvency that were made intentionally in violation of the principle of equal treatment of all creditors. The threshold for assuming such intention is very low. Accordingly, any repayments of debt, even if due, or the grant of security, other than upon grant of a loan, could become subject to scrutiny.

(c) ***Criminal law***

Prejudicing creditors prior to an insolvency is a criminal offence, where it is done intentionally or through gross negligence; as is violating directors' duties in certain circumstances.

2. Specific questions

2.1 Perspective A: corporate group

(a) *Liability of group company and/or master account holder directors in the event of insolvency of a group company*

The members of the board of directors of a Swiss company are liable for any damage caused by a breach (whether negligent or wilful) of their duties. Claims for damages can be made by the company and, in particular in an insolvency, by the shareholders and the company's creditors. The board of a Swiss company is a one-tier board. Therefore, the rules regarding directors' liability apply to all directors, be they executive (with management function) or non-executive (with supervisory function), independently of how the company has actually organised such functions. In addition, members of the senior management and any other person acting as a *de facto* director can become subject to directors' liability as discussed below. Liability of the directors of a group company will mostly be an issue if a group company becomes insolvent and there is a balance in the cash pooling agreement in favour of the group company that cannot be recovered (in the case of zero or target balancing), or if securities granted by the company have been executed to satisfy debt other than the company's debt. In this case, the directors of the insolvent company could become liable, as outlined below, depending on how the cash pooling agreement is structured and on the actual circumstances.

If a group company becomes insolvent and there is a balance in the cash pooling agreement in favour of the master account holder, typically there will be no liabilities on group company directors that are specific to the cash pooling agreement.

Liability of group company directors: Where the master account holder is downstream from the insolvent group company, as a general rule, any terms of the cash pooling agreement that are not at arm's length, but are in favour of the subsidiary, would not be considered to be an issue, as they can be understood as capital injections that are also for the benefit of the parent and therefore there is no liability on the part of the directors of the parent company specifically related to the cash pooling agreement. Therefore, the following assumes that the master account holder is a parent or sister company of the insolvent group company:

- Duty to safeguard the protected equity – if payments under the cash pooling agreement or the execution of securities have the effect of being made out of the group company's protected equity, then the directors are in breach of their duty to protect the company's protected equity and will be liable for any damages caused thereby. While such depletion of the protected equity will not be an issue if made as part of a transaction at arm's length, in practice it is likely that it will not be possible to show this in the intra-group context of a cash pooling agreement, in particular to the extent that security is concerned. So, unless the group company's balance sheet is strong enough to support the loss of the respective assets, participation in a cash pooling agreement carries the risk for the directors of violating their duty to safeguard the protected equity.

- Duty to treat shareholders equally – if the group company is not a 100% subsidiary of the group that set up the cash pooling agreement, and if its terms are not at arm's length in all respects, then the directors will be liable for damage to minority shareholders for having violated their duty to treat all shareholders equally.
- Duty to manage finances properly – the directors are liable for mismanagement if they entered into the cash pooling agreement other than at arm's-length conditions. Even if the terms of the cash pooling agreement were originally at arm's length, the directors could be liable for mismanagement if they did not properly monitor the cash pooling agreement – for instance, if they did not reduce the exposure under the cash pooling agreement or ask for security as the creditworthiness of the master account holder deteriorated. In addition, the directors could be liable for unlawful hidden profit distributions (unless there was a specific and formal authorisation by the shareholders' meeting of the respective payments).
- Duty of loyalty – directors appointed by the parent company could be in breach of their duty of loyalty if participation in the cash pooling agreement was not in the best interests of the group company, but was forced on the group company by instruction from the parent company.
- Duty not to act *ultra vires* – if a transaction under the cash pooling agreement was not made at arm's length, the directors may have acted *ultra vires* and might be in breach of their duty to act within the company's purpose. As a general rule, the purpose of a Swiss corporation includes making profits. This could be avoided if the group company's articles of association waived the profit-making purpose by specifically permitting the grant of loans and security to parent and sister companies. Such a provision in the articles of association may also alleviate the directors' liability for breaches of their duties of care (other than the duty to protect the protected equity, which is absolute) or duty of loyalty discussed above.
- Criminal liability – the directors may be subject to criminal liability if they intentionally, or through gross negligence, prejudice the company's general pool of creditors in connection with transactions contemplated under the cash pooling agreement.

Liability of master account holder directors: The directors of the master account holder may become personally liable in an insolvency of a group company if they acted as *de facto* directors of the group company other than as appointees on the board (in which case they would be directly liable as formal directors). The criteria that could lead to a person being treated as a *de facto* director are relatively narrow. Only if a person had a direct influence similar to a formal director and, for instance, coerced the group company into becoming a member of the cash pooling agreement, or had significant influence in determining the group company's financial policies, would that person be considered to be a *de facto* director. If such a person did not act on his own, but as a representative acting on instructions from his employer, it will depend on the circumstances of the case whether he can excuse himself or will be liable together with the company from which he received instructions or by which he was employed. If a person is considered to be a *de facto* director, then he is treated like a director of the company and personally liable like a proper director of the group company as discussed above (and unlike the master account holder's liability, discussed at section 2.1(c) below).

Listed companies: As a basic rule, the standards of directors' liability are the same for the directors of private and listed companies. However, a listed company is subject not only to general corporate law, but also to the regulations of the stock exchange where it is listed. Such regulations may have been violated by the cash pooling agreement (eg, capital maintenance requirements or obligations regarding publicity).

Cross-border issues: Swiss company law applies to all companies registered in Switzerland. Therefore, for the liability of the directors of a Swiss master account holder or a Swiss group company, it does not matter whether other parties such as the bank or other group companies are registered in other jurisdictions. Liability as a *de facto* director is determined by the law applicable to the company of which such a person is acting as a *de facto* director. Therefore, a foreign person could become liable as a *de facto* director of a Swiss group company under the rules outlined above, while it will depend on the rules of the relevant foreign law whether a director of the Swiss master account holder acting as a *de facto* director of a foreign group company will be liable.

(b) Liability of group company and/or master account holder directors in the event of insolvency of the master account holder

Liability of group company directors: If the master account holder becomes insolvent, the directors of a group company may become liable if the group company had a net claim against the master account holder that cannot be recovered. The directors' liability will be to the group company and, in particular in the event of the group company's insolvency, towards the group company's creditors and shareholders. In such case, the liability of the directors is as discussed in section 2.1(a) above. If the director of any group company acted as a *de facto* director of the master account holder, such a director will become liable as described in section 2.1(a) above as if it were a formal director of the master account holder.

Liability of master account holder directors: If the master account holder was not the parent of the group and granted its loans to a parent or sister companies and had outstanding net balances against group companies in its favour that cannot be recovered (in the case of zero or target balancing) or if security granted by the company has been executed to satisfy debt other than the company's debt, then the directors of the master account holder may become liable on the basis described in section 2.1(a) above in relation to directors of the group company. If the master account holder is the parent of the group, then typically this is not an issue, as described in section 2.1(a) above.

Listed companies and cross-border issues: It will not make a difference whether the group company is a listed corporation or a privately held corporation as discussed in section 2.1(a) above. There is also no difference in the event that the bank or its counterparty is registered in a foreign jurisdiction, as also discussed in section 2.1(a).

(c) Liability of group companies in the event of insolvency of the master account holder

As a general rule, the creditors of an insolvent company have a claim only against the estate, but no direct claims against third parties such as debtors of the insolvent company. Therefore, in the event of insolvency of the master account holder, its creditors have no claims against group companies. However, in the course of the insolvency proceedings, the administration may assign claims against debtors of the insolvent company to the extent that the administration does not enforce them itself. In connection with cash pooling agreements, such claims of the master account holder against group companies could include claims arising from *de facto* directorships, claw-back and unlawful distributions. In addition, the creditors of an insolvent company may have a direct claim against the parent company if there is a reason to pierce the corporate veil. Finally, equity-like debt may become subordinated.

***De facto* director:** Any group company that acted as a *de facto* director of the master account holder could become liable for breaches of care and loyalty, as discussed above in section 2.1(a). Typically, this would be the parent company if the master account holder was a special finance entity. The concept of *de facto* directorship applies not only to individuals, as discussed in section 2.1(a) above, but also to corporations. The corporation would become liable if it had an influence on the master account holder like that of a director, for instance by forcing the master account holder to enter into the cash pooling agreement and giving instructions on how to act. The group company could become liable exclusively or together with an individual that represented the group company when acting as a *de facto* director. If acting as a *de facto* director, the group company could become liable for breaches of its duties of care and loyalty, as discussed in section 2.1(a).

Claw-back: The estate or a creditor to which a claim has been assigned can challenge any transactions made up to five years prior to an insolvency in violation of the statutory claw-back provisions. Particularly susceptible to claw-back in connection with cash pooling agreements are the following situations:

- any repayments of outstanding loans, unless all creditors were treated equally;
- the provision of additional or new security under an existing arrangement; and
- any transactions that were not made at arm's length (for instance low interest rates).

If a company starts to discriminate among creditors by delaying payment for some creditors, automatic daily sweeps under the cash pooling agreement (qualifying as repayments of outstanding debts) may become subject to claw-back after the company has gone into insolvency.

Repayment of unlawful distributions: If the cash pooling agreements terms were not made at arm's length to the disadvantage of the master account holder, and the master account holder made payments to a parent or sister group company in violation of its protected equity, then the recipient group company would be liable to pay back any such distributions to the master account holder.

Piercing the corporate veil: The master account holder's parent company could become directly liable for the debt of the master account holder if there is a basis for piercing the corporate veil. This could be the case if the use of a separate corporate form for the master account holder was abusive – for instance, if there was a commingling of funds and functions.

Subordination of debt: While not a strict liability, a risk of loss arises where payments were made by a group company to the master account holder (assuming that the latter is a parent or sister company) if such payments could be considered to have been given in place of equity. Such debt could be treated like equity and would be subordinated to all other debt of the insolvent master account holder.

Cross-border issues: All of the above claims are linked to the location of the master account holder. If the master account holder is located in Switzerland, it is subject to Swiss corporate and bankruptcy law and, thus, the above claims are governed by Swiss law independently of where the claiming creditor or the group company is located.

(d) Liability of the master account holder in the event of insolvency of a group company

In terms of liability, there is no difference between that of the master account holder and that of any group company. So the liability applying to group companies in the event of the master account holder's insolvency, as discussed in section 2.1(c) above, would apply in the same way to the master account holder in the case of a group company's insolvency.

2.2 Perspective B: bank

(a) Banking requirements

Under Swiss law, no specific banking regulation applies to cash pooling agreements. Independently of whether the members of a group of companies have entered into a cash pooling agreement, the bank must treat such customers as a group for the determination of any concentration risks. The respective rules will not change with the gradual implementation of Basel III, which is starting in 2013.

(b) Liability of the bank in the event of insolvency of the master account holder or a group company

In the event of the insolvency of the master account holder or a group company, the bank could become liable as a *de facto* director and also be liable to claw-back claims as discussed in section 2.1(c). Therefore, potentially, liability for the bank could arise if the bank had a direct influence over the insolvent company, or if the bank had a direct banking relationship with the company. Any liability claims are linked to the location of the insolvent company; therefore, a foreign bank may also be subject to liability.

2.3 Insolvency

(a) Cash pooling agreements from the insolvency practitioner's perspective

Claims relating to a non-Swiss insolvent entity can be enforced in Switzerland only by way of recognition of the foreign main proceedings by either the competent court or the Swiss Financial Market Authority. One condition for recognition is reciprocity. Therefore, if Swiss insolvency proceedings are not recognised in the jurisdiction of the insolvent entity, then no recognition will be granted in Switzerland. If recognition is granted, then a so-called mini-bankruptcy procedure is conducted in Switzerland. The questions related to claw-back and void transactions have been addressed above (see sections 1.4(b) and 2.1(c)).

In the event of the insolvency of the bank, the bank's administrator will enforce all claims on the part of the bank against the master account holder or the group company, regardless of whether such companies are registered in Switzerland. In the event of the insolvency of master account holder, that company's administrator will enforce all claims on the part of the master account holder against the bank or the group company, regardless of whether such companies are registered in Switzerland.

In the event of the insolvency of the group company, that company's administrator will enforce all claims on the part of the group company against the bank or the master account holder, regardless of whether such companies are registered in Switzerland.

(b) Special rules as regards creditors of other parties to the cash pooling agreement

The administrator of the insolvent entity – be it the bank, the master account holder or a group company – has an obligation only to the creditors of the entity administered by him. There is no formal or substantive consolidation of insolvency proceedings of several insolvent entities in Switzerland. If more than one insolvent entity is a debtor of the same claim, then a creditor cannot receive payments from such entities exceeding the total claim notified and admitted in the insolvency proceedings (ie, a creditor can never receive more than 100% of its claim).

(c) Dissolution/termination of the cash pooling agreement in the event of liquidation of the master account holder, a group company or the bank

Generally speaking, the parties to a cash pooling agreement may agree contractually, within certain limits, on the consequences of the liquidation of a party. Under the

the Swiss Code of Obligations rules governing loans, the lender may withhold performance (and may also terminate the loan agreement) if the other party has become insolvent (which may occur prior to the opening of formal proceedings) after conclusion of the agreement, or even before its conclusion if the insolvency was unknown to the lender. Termination cannot be prevented by the borrower by granting security. Under bankruptcy law, an administrator can honour contracts containing reciprocal obligations. However, the counterparty may demand that security be furnished (to what extent parties to a contract may rule out the applicability of this provision of bankruptcy law is disputed). As performance by the administrator of a contract converts the claims of the counterparty into administrative expenses, it is extremely unlikely that the administrator of an insolvent bank (if the activity is permitted in liquidation) or administrator of the insolvent master account holder would invoke the right of performance.

2.4 Perspective D: regulatory

There are no regulatory requirements specifically applicable to cash pooling agreements in Switzerland.

2.5 Perspective E: tax

From a Swiss tax point of view, the following aspects should be considered in connection with cash pooling agreements. As a general rule, issues arise only in connection with physical cash pooling:

- The terms and conditions agreed between the master account holder and the group companies must be at arm's length. Terms that are not made at arm's length may trigger withholding taxes (where excessive interest rates are paid by the Swiss entity to a parent or sister company) or stamp duty (where too low interest rates are paid by the Swiss entity to a parent company, or excessive interest rates are paid by the parent company of the Swiss entity). The Federal Tax Administration issues a circular letter every year setting out accepted maximum and minimum interest rates as safe haven rules.
- As a general rule, a participation by a Swiss master account holder or group company in a cash pooling agreement is no longer considered to be an issuing of bonds by the Swiss entity and, therefore, there are no withholding tax and stamp duty consequences. This new exception does not apply if the Swiss master account holder or a Swiss group company has granted a downstream guarantee for a foreign bond. In this case, if located in Switzerland, the master account holder and the group companies may become subject to withholding tax and stamp duty depending on the number and type of outstanding credit obligations (the so called '10/20 Swiss non-banking rule').

United States

Judith Elkin
Kourtney P Lyda
Arsalan Muhammad
Kelli M Stephenson
Haynes and Boone, LLP

1. Introduction

In discussing the legal implications of cash pooling as a cash management methodology for related corporate entities in the United States, certain definitions must be clarified to fit into US practice and procedure. Neither 'cash pooling' nor 'cash pooling agreements' is a term of art in the United States, in either ordinary corporate or insolvency practice. Therefore, this chapter discusses the concepts of cash pooling using applicable US terms of art.

A cash pooling agreement between a bank and a group of related companies – usually a parent company and subsidiaries and/or affiliates – is called a 'centralised cash management system' or 'cash management account'. These types of account are not prohibited in any jurisdiction in the United States. Typically, cash management accounts are held either in the name of the parent corporation or in the name of an entity specifically created for the purpose of holding the account. At its most simplistic level, operating subsidiaries will have bank accounts in their own name for certain ordinary purposes and the balance of cash received by the subsidiary will be swept, sometimes daily, up to the cash management account. The parent or entity controlling the cash management account will use the funds in that account to pay costs and expenses of the entities covered by the cash management account. Inter-company books and records will be maintained showing deposits of any subsidiary into the cash management account and obligations of those same subsidiaries paid by the cash management account. Since cash management accounts are a matter of contract between the bank and its customers, the terms and types of cash management accounts are numerous and operate as agreed upon by and among the parties, taking into account the corporate purpose and operations of the entities involved.

Cash management accounts are ordinary and customary among large corporate enterprises. They are viewed as being both economically and operationally efficient. In many instances, cash management accounts are a requirement of a corporate group's senior lenders, and such accounts are often held at the bank that acts as agent for a corporate group's senior secured credit facility – thus becoming part of the lenders' collateral. A centralised cash management system has the advantage of creating uniform corporate policies on obligations incurred and paid, and also eliminates certain decision making at the subsidiary levels. It allows the parent entity to control inter-company cash balances and move funds where needed – from a subsidiary with a surplus to one with a shortage – without having to tap into other funds and reserves.

A centralised cash management system should be under the direct control and supervision of a corporate group's treasury or finance department, and ultimately under the control of the chief financial officer. The goal should be the optimisation of cash flow and the investment of any excess cash. These types of control are essential. They are especially so in the case of multinational corporate group cash management systems, where the system needs to account not only for the inter-company balances, but also for the risks of currency exchange fluctuations.

Insolvency does not necessarily change any of the above, but it may complicate matters depending on the facts of a specific case. In the event that a group of companies files for Chapter 7 liquidation in the United States, a trustee will be appointed. That trustee will take control of all bank accounts, including the cash management account, as well as the books and records of the companies. The trustee will be charged with determining which funds belong to which entity and are available to pay the creditors of that entity. Depending on the quality and accuracy of the group's books and records, making such a determination may be an easy task or a difficult one.

However, in the event that a group of companies files for Chapter 11 reorganisation in the United States, in most cases the cash management account stays in place. One of the most common 'first day' motions[1] in a Chapter 11 case is a motion by the debtors to maintain current bank accounts and cash management systems. These types of motion are almost always approved by the court with the consent of the creditors, although the order may require an accounting determination of the status of inter-company accounts payable and receivable as of the bankruptcy filing date. In many instances, especially those where the bankruptcy is not believed to have been precipitated by some type of accounting fraud, the pre-petition inter-company balances are resolved with little discussion as part of the plan process.

With these caveats in mind, we discuss below some of the legal, operational and regulatory issues involved with multi-corporate group centralised cash management systems in the United States.

2. Specific questions

2.1 Perspective A: corporate group

A corporate group structure generally consists of a parent entity, usually a holding company, and one or more subsidiaries. Depending upon the nature of the group's businesses, the affiliates may be both related to each other and dependent on each other, or they may be totally separate operational businesses that can exist separately. Where business operations of the affiliates or their debt structure are sufficiently interrelated, it is customary for all entities to file for bankruptcy together in the event of insolvency. Where business operations or debt structure is not interrelated, an insolvent subsidiary might file for bankruptcy while its affiliate entities, and even its parent, do not.

---

1 'First day' motions are requests by the debtor for relief from the court on an expedited basis during the first several days after the filing of a Chapter 11 case.

Thus, as a matter of practice, if one member of a corporate group that was part of a centralised cash management system files for bankruptcy, an accounting determination will be made as to inter-company payables and receivables as of the bankruptcy petition date, but the debtor will be required to establish its own bank account or accounts for use during the Chapter 11 case in conformity with the requirements of the Office of the United States Trustee.[2] If all members of the corporate group file for Chapter 11 relief, it is customary for existing bank accounts and accounting procedures to be maintained, so long as the US trustee determines that the procedures comply with its requirements or the Court authorises the waiver of such requirements for cause shown.

(a) Liability of group company and/or master account holder directors in the event of insolvency of a group company

Typically, the directors of a corporation are not liable for the debts of the corporation, even if the company becomes insolvent. The corporate law of every state has adopted some form of the business judgement rule. This rule protects a board of directors from being questioned or second-guessed on their conduct of corporate affairs.[3] The rule creates a rebuttable presumption that "in making a business decision the directors of a corporation acted on an informed basis, in good faith and in the honest belief that the action taken was in the best interests of the company".[4] The deferential business judgement rule is "primarily a process inquiry. Courts give deference to directors' decisions reached by a proper process, and do not apply an objective reasonableness test in such a case to examine the wisdom of the decision itself".[5] Participation in a centralised cash management system will be protected by this rule.

However, directors of a group company may face liability in the event of insolvency of the group company if they have breached duties they owe to the company or have acted in a manner that is improper under applicable law. As stated, the insolvency of a group company will not, in and of itself, result in liability for the directors of other members of the corporate group. Therefore, going further up the

---

2 The US Trustee Programme was established by the Bankruptcy Reform Act of 1978 to serve as a watchdog for the integrity of bankruptcy proceedings. It operates as an adjunct to the US Department of Justice. It has many duties in respect of Chapter 11 cases, which include monitoring monthly financial reports and insuring that a debtor's bank accounts are maintained in accordance with certain investment and reporting requirements. A further discussion of the duties of the US Trustee in regards to a debtor's bank accounts is included in Section 2.3, below.

3 See, for instance, *In re PSE & G Shareholder Litigation*, 173 NJ 258, 801 A2d 295, 306 (2002). There is some academic debate over whether the business judgement rule applies equally to officers and directors. Compare *Cinerama, Inc v Technicolor, Inc*, 663 A.2d 1156, 1162 (Del 1995) (indicating, in *obiter dicta*, that the business judgement rule applies to officers in their capacity as such to the same extent as directors) with *Rafool v Goldfarb Corp (In re Fleming Packaging Corp)*, 351 BR 626, 635 (Bankr ND Ill 2006):
Although the Delaware Supreme Court routinely states that the business judgement rule covers officers as well as directors when it recites the rule in actions involving only directors, the court has never held that the rule applies to officers acting in that capacity citing Lyman PQ Johnson, *Corporate Officers and the Business Judgment Rule*, 60 Bus Law 439 (2005) arguing, generally, that the business judgment rule should be applied more narrowly to officers than to directors.

4 *Aronson v Lewis*, 473 A2d 805, 811 (Del 1984); see also *Gantler v Stephens*, 965 A2d 695, 705-06 (Del. 2009); *In re Healthco International, Inc.*, 208 BR 288, 306 (Bankr D Mass 1997); *In re PSE & G*, 801 A2d at 306.

5 *Brazen v Bell Atlantic Corp* 695 A2d 43, 49 (Del 1997).

corporate chain, directors of the master account holder (the cash management account) typically will not face liability in the event of the insolvency of a group company because the directors of the holder of the cash management account typically will not owe any duties to the group company or have participated in any of the group company's actions. The existence of the centralised cash management system alone is insufficient to impose liability on directors of either the group company or the holder of the cash management account. Rather, liability can be imposed only under other theories, such as breach of fiduciary duty or malfeasance by the director. While a sweep of cash from the group company's bank account to the cash management account when the group company is insolvent may be evidence that could be used to impose liability on a director under other legal theories,[6] the existence and use of a cash management account itself does not create liability.

In the United States, the law of the state of incorporation governs the actions, duties and responsibilities of the corporation and its directors.[7] If a group company or the holder of the cash management account is located in a foreign jurisdiction, the law governing the duties of the corporation's directors will typically be the law of the foreign jurisdiction in which the corporation is incorporated. However, conflict of law principles may dictate in favour of applying the law of the US state rather than the law of the foreign jurisdiction where "the corporation does all, or nearly all, of its business and has most of its shareholders in this other state and has little contact, apart from the fact of its incorporation, with the state of incorporation".[8]

As stated previously, in order for liability to be imposed on the directors of a holder of a cash management account, they must have committed some type of bad acts towards or breached some duty to the insolvent company. While the existence of a cash management account may be a factor in the analysis of whether bad acts were done or the cash management account may be the tool used by the directors to commit the bad acts, this is totally divorced from the mere existence of a cash management account.

For example, if the holder of the cash management account is a shareholder of a group company (as would be the case if the cash management account were held by the parent which owned the stock of the now-insolvent subsidiary), a transfer by the insolvent group company to the holder of the cash management account under the centralised cash management system might be considered an illegal dividend or a fraudulent transfer. In the United States, many states have enacted statutes that prohibit a corporation's board of directors from declaring a dividend to the corporation's shareholders if the corporation would be insolvent after the

6 Liability of directors for actions of the corporation is generally governed by state law, and the law often varies from state to state. This chapter endeavours to discuss the majority rules in the United States, but the law of the corporation's state of incorporation should be reviewed in each particular case to determine the particular liability risks to that corporation and its directors.

7 See *Walton v Morgan Stanley & Co*, 623 F2d 796, 798 n 3 (2d Cir 1980).

8 Restatement (Second) of Conflict of Laws, § 309 cmt C; see also *Norlin Corp v Rooney, Pace Inc*, 744 F2d 255, 263-64 (2d Cir 1984) applying New York state law, rather than Panamanian law, to a corporation incorporated in Panama but conducting most of its business in New York.

distribution.[9] The transfer need not be formally declared as a dividend to be characterised as such.[10] The directors of the corporation who assented to an illegal dividend are jointly and severally liable to the corporation for the amount of the distribution that exceeds the amount that could have lawfully been paid.[11] Thus, the directors of the group company who assented to the centralised cash management system could be held liable for transfers of funds from the group company to the cash management account under the terms of the centralised cash management system while the group company was insolvent if the transfers can be characterised as illegal dividends. In that event, the holder of the cash management account could be required to repay those funds.[12]

A corporation may also be liable for acts it takes that are beyond the scope of its powers under applicable state law or its articles of incorporation or bylaws. Such acts are considered *ultra vires*. The directors of the corporation are typically not personally liable for the corporation's *ultra vires* act, unless the directors specifically authorised the act or negligently failed to perform their duties to the corporation.[13] Under state law, corporations are typically granted authority to make contracts, incur liabilities, borrow money and take other actions in furtherance of the business of the corporation.[14] A corporation would thus be authorised to enter into a centralised cash management system under applicable state law. Because transfers from a group company to the holder of the cash management account are typically reflected as inter-company loans, the group company should be mindful of any limitations in the group company's articles of incorporation or bylaws that would limit the group company's ability to incur indebtedness. A transfer under a centralised cash management system in violation of the group company's articles of incorporation or bylaws could be considered an *ultra vires* act, and the directors authorising such transfer could be liable for any damages caused by the transfer. This type of liability for use of a cash management account would be uncommon in the United States, however.

A director may be liable to the corporation for breach of certain duties, including the duty of care and the duty of loyalty. In general, the duties owed by directors that

---

9 See, for example, Louisiana Revised Statures, Annotated § 12:63; Mississippi Code, Annotated § 79-4-6.40; New York Business Corporation Law § 510; see also Delaware Code, Annotated, Title 8, § 170 requiring that dividends be paid only from a corporation's surplus, or if there is no surplus, out of the corporation's net profits for the fiscal year for which the dividend is declared or for the preceding fiscal year.

10 See, for example, *In re Musicland Holding Corp*, 398 BR 761, 783-84 (Bankr SDNY 2008); *Official Comm. of Unsecured Creditors of Buckhead America Corp v Reliance Capital Group, Inc (In re Buckhead America Corp)*, 178 BR 956, 970 (D Del 1994).

11 See, for example, Delaware Code, Annotated, Title 8, § 174; Texas Business Organizations Code § 21.316(a).

12 Because transfers under a centralised cash management system are typically characterised as inter-company loans, a party asserting that such a transfer is, in fact, an illegal dividend would likely also have to recharacterise the transfer as an equity contribution, rather than a debt. In evaluating whether a transfer was a loan or an equity contribution, courts typically analyse numerous factors that:

> *devolve to an overarching inquiry: the characterization as debt or equity is a court's attempt to discern whether the parties called an instrument one thing when in fact they intended it as something else. That intent may be inferred from what the parties say in their contracts, from what they do through their actions, and from the economic reality of the surrounding circumstances.*

(*Cohen v KB Mezzanine Fund II, LP (In re Submicron Systems Corp)*, 432 F 3d 448, 456 (3d Cir 2006)).

13 See, for instance, *Brown Leasing, Inc v Stone*, 673 NE 2d 430, 438-39 (Ill App Ct 1996); *Fulton Paper Co v Reeves*, 441 SE 2d 881, 884-85 (Ga Ct App 1994); *Holmes v Crane*, 191 AD 820, 826-27 (NY App Div 1920).

14 See, for instance, Delaware Code, Annotated, Title 8, § 122; New York Business Corporations Law § 202.

could give rise to liability are owed regardless of whether the corporation is publicly traded or privately held. The duty of care requires a director to exercise the care that a reasonably prudent person in a similar position would exercise under similar circumstances.[15] As stated earlier, courts typically defer to the business judgement of directors acting in good faith.[16] The duty of loyalty requires a director to act in the best interests of the corporation, and prohibits a director from engaging in self-dealing at the expense of the corporation.[17] A group company's participation in a centralised cash management system typically will not give rise to liability for breach of the duties of care and loyalty. However, if the group company's participation in the centralised cash management system in some way contributed to the group company's insolvency, the directors could be liable if it can also be proven that the directors breached their duties of care or loyalty in authorising the group company to participate in the centralised cash management system or allowed the funds in the cash management account to be used for improper purposes.

While the legal theories discussed above – *ultra vires* acts, unlawful dividends, breach of fiduciary duty or the duty of due care – can be used to create liability for corporate directors, the theory of piercing the corporate veil (alter ego) – and its equivalent in bankruptcy proceedings, substantive consolidation – generally are not used in the United States to create director liability, except in the rare instance where an individual really is the alter ego of the corporation. In such instances, such as cases involving closely held corporations with a family-run board, a creditor might be able to pierce the corporate veil and have personal liability imposed on a director.[18] However, this would be highly unusual in the case of large corporate groups. In that context, piercing the corporate veil is used to create liability on the part of one corporate entity for the obligations of a related corporate entity. Piercing the corporate veil is permitted where corporate formalities have been ignored, and courts typically consider whether the corporation is undercapitalised, whether adequate corporate records have been maintained and whether the directors have been performing their duties, among other factors.[19] Centralised cash management systems typically will not factor into an analysis of whether a court should pierce the corporate veil and impose liability on a group company's or a cash management account holder's directors, unless there is some showing of accounting abuse in connection with the cash management account, such as not properly recording inter-company debits and credits or using funds for improper or non-corporate purposes.

Similarly, in the event of a bankruptcy, the theory of substantive consolidation can be used to make one debtor liable for the debts of another. Substantive consolidation is not statutorily provided for in the US Bankruptcy Code, but it has

15 See *Norlin Corp v Rooney, Pace Inc*, 744 F 2d 255, 264 (2d Cir 1984).

16 *Norlin Corp v Rooney, Pace Inc*, 744 F 2d 255, 264 (2d Cir 1984), citing *Auerbach v Bennett*, 393 NE 2d 994, 1000 (NY 1979).

17 *Norlin Corp v Rooney, Pace Inc*, 744 F 2d 255, 264 (2d Cir 1984).

18 See *Mills v Polar Molecular Corp*, 12 F 3d 1170, 1177 (2d Cir 1993): "A director is not personally liable for his corporation's contractual breaches unless he assumed personal liability, acted in bad faith or committed a tort in connection with the performance of the contract."

19 See *Teitelbaum v Lin*, 423 Fed Appx 106, 107 (2d Cir 2011); *Platten v HG Bermuda Exempted Ltd*, 437 F 3d 118, 128 (1st Cir 2006); *Hystro Products, Inc v MNP Corp*, 18 F3d 1384, 1388-89 (7th Cir 1994).

been developed through case law using the standards similar to that for determining piercing of the corporate veil or alter ego. The substantive consolidation of two or more entities is an important tool available to a bankruptcy court overseeing the cases of related entities whose financial affairs are hopelessly entangled, or whose separate corporate identities otherwise have been disregarded by officers and directors. In order to consolidate two or more estates, a court must conduct a factually intensive inquiry and carefully balance the competing concerns of all interested parties, especially the interests of the creditors of the more solvent entity whose assets are going to be used to supplement the recovery of the creditors of the less solvent entity.

As with piercing the corporate veil, the factors that may be relevant include:

- fraud or other complete domination of the corporation that harms a third party;
- the absence of corporate formalities;
- inadequate capitalisation of the corporation;
- whether funds are put in and taken out of the corporation for personal rather than corporate purposes;
- overlap in ownership and management of affiliated corporations;
- whether affiliated corporations have dealt with one another at arm's length;
- the payment or guarantee of debts of the dominant corporation by other affiliated corporations;
- the commingling of affiliated corporations' funds; and
- the inability to separate affiliated corporations' assets and liabilities.

The Second Circuit – which includes the Southern District of New York, a popular venue for large complex reorganisation cases – established a simplified standard for substantive consolidation in *In re Augie/Restivo Baking Co, Ltd.*[20] There, the court concluded that the factual elements considered by the courts are merely variants on two critical factors:

- whether creditors dealt with the entities as a single economic unit and did not rely on their separateness in extending credit; or
- whether the affairs of the debtors are so hopelessly entangled that the cost of disentangling is outweighed by the benefit of consolidation for all creditors.

Here again, while the use of a centralised cash management system may be one evidentiary factor, the existence of the cash management account alone will not justify substantive consolidation or veil piercing.

(b) *Liability of group company and/or master account holder directors in the event of insolvency of the master account holder*

The considerations for liability of directors of the group company or the master account holder in the event of insolvency of the master account holder are similar

20 *Union Savings Bank v Augie/Restivo Baking Co, Ltd (In re Augie/Restivo Baking Co, Ltd)*, 860 F 2d 515 (2d Cir 1988).

to the liabilities of directors discussed in paragraph (a) above. The directors of the master account holder may be liable to the entity that holds the master account under theories of improperly authorising illegal dividends, breaches of fiduciary duties or duties of loyalty, or other acts of malfeasance, such as embezzlement. The directors of a group company typically will not face liability in the event of insolvency of the master account holder, because the directors of the group company typically will not owe any duties to the master account holder or have participated in the master account holder's actions.

(c) Liability of group companies in the event of insolvency of the master account holder

As a technical matter, in the event of insolvency of the master account holder, creditors of the master account holder typically cannot look to the group companies for satisfaction of their debts simply by virtue of the existence of a centralised cash management system. As indicated previously, centralised cash management accounts are held either by the parent corporation or by an entity specifically designated to hold the account. In the case of the latter, these designated bank account entities do not generally have any creditors, other than the inter-company obligations owed to and from the affiliate entities to the bank account entities and each other. They are created solely for the purpose of holding the bank accounts.

If the cash management account is held by the parent corporation, it is likely that the parent company will have debts distinct from the debts owed by its subsidiaries. A parent company may be the primary obligor on senior secured debt. The cash management system is likely to be a requirement of the senior lender, and part of its collateral. However, the senior lender is also likely to have guarantees from all subsidiaries. Assuming that the subsidiaries have received some type of consideration for these guarantees, such as access to the loan proceeds, the entire corporate enterprise will be liable for the senior secured debt. Complications arise when the parent company has unsecured debt, such as bond debt, that is not guaranteed by the subsidiaries. In such an event, the bondholders and other unsecured creditors of the parent may claim that the funds in the bank account, to the extent not needed to pay the senior secured lender, should be available to them. Such a determination would require a court to balance the interests of the group members' inter-company receivables from the parent and disregard the inter-company accounting that is the bulwark of any well-run cash management account, or disregard the legal presumption that a bank account belongs to the account holder.[21]

Creditors of the master account holder may be able to pierce the corporate veil and impose liability on the group companies where the creditors can show disregard for corporate formalities by the master account holder and group companies. Imposing liability on a subsidiary for the debts of a parent corporation is permitted where the subsidiary: "has in reality no separate existence, is not adequately capitalized and constitutes a mere instrumentality of the parent corporation or a mere 'corporate pocket' or department of its business".[22] Piercing the corporate veil permits creditors of a subsidiary to impose liability on the parent as well as permitting creditors of a parent to impose liability on a subsidiary for disregard of corporate formalities.[23] A cash management system negotiated and entered into at arm's length by the master account holder and group companies typically will not give rise to liability to the group companies. However, a cash management system that was not negotiated and entered into at arm's length may be a factor that a court will consider, among other factors such as lack of adequate records and undercapitalisation, in determining whether to allow the creditors of the master account holder to pierce the corporate veil and impose liability on the group companies.[24]

The ability of creditors to pierce the corporate veil may be complicated if one or more of the group companies is located in a foreign jurisdiction. Under applicable conflict of law principles, US courts may find that the laws of the place of incorporation of the group companies may apply.[25] If the laws of the place of incorporation of the group companies do not permit piercing the veil of a corporation to impose liability on an affiliated corporation, creditors of the master account holder will be unable to impose liability on the group companies for the master account holder's debts.[26]

(d) Liability of the master account holder in the event of insolvency of a group company

As with the insolvency of the master account holder discussed in paragraph (c) above, in the event of the insolvency of a group company, creditors of that group

21 In the bankruptcy case *In re Adelphia Communications Corp. et al* (Case 02-41729, US Bankruptcy Court for the Southern District of New York), this very scenario arose. Not only had interrelated debtors operated with one cash management system, but there had been massive accounting fraud perpetrated by the insider directors of the public companies and the same directors of the related privately held companies. The senior secured lenders had several credit facilities with different collateral and guarantees, and there were public debt holders at both the parent level and at some of the operating subsidiary and affiliate company levels. Which debtors' creditors were entitled to which funds and what assets was impossible to determine – the companies and their bank accounts and assets were so intertwined that the court established a procedure for resolving the issues that was to take place over four stages. All of this had to occur before the debtors' new management could effectively develop a plan of reorganisation. After months of evidentiary discovery and months of trial, as well as the expenditure of millions of dollars on legal and expert witness fees, it became apparent to the court that a true determination of which creditors should have access to which bank accounts and other assets was going to be nearly impossible. The court appointed a mediator and the parties were sent to try to work out a settlement. Ultimately, a settlement was reached which was incorporated into a plan of reorganisation.

22 *Stone v Eacho (In re Tip Top Tailors, Inc)*, 127 F 2d 284, 288 (4th Cir 1942); *Nichols & Co v Secretary of Agriculture*, 131 F 2d 651, 657 (1st Cir 1942).

23 *Tip Top Tailors*, 127 F 2d at 288.

24 In the context of a bankruptcy case, discussed above and in section 2.3 below, a bankruptcy court may substantively consolidate the assets and liabilities of two or more related corporate entities, such as a parent and its subsidiary. Upon substantive consolidation of the corporate entities, the creditors of all of the corporate entities will look to the common pool of assets of the corporate entities for recovery on their claims.

25 In addition to limitations imposed by conflict of law principles, a US court may not have jurisdiction over a foreign group company unless the foreign group company has sufficient contacts in the United States; see *World-Wide Volkswagen Corp v Woodson*, 444 US 286, 291-92 (1980) (citing *International Shoe Co v Washington*, 326 US 310 (1945)). If a foreign group company transfers funds to the master account holder, and the master account holder is located in the United States, such transfers may be evidence of contacts with the United States that would enable a US court to exercise jurisdiction over the foreign group company.

26 See *Bondi v Bank of America Corp (In re Parmalat Securities Litigation)*, 479 F Supp 2d 332, 341 (SDNY 2007) declining to hold subsidiaries liable for the debts of the parent where the subsidiaries were incorporated in Italy, the Netherlands and Luxembourg, which jurisdictions did not permit liability under a reverse veil-piercing theory.

company may be able to seek satisfaction of the group company's debts from the other group companies and/or the master account holder if the creditors can pierce the corporate veil by establishing that the group companies disregarded corporate formalities. The existence of the centralised cash management system does not give rise to such liability; rather, the relationships among the group companies and the master account holder will determine whether creditors can pierce the corporate veil. A cash management system that is not negotiated at arm's length may be evidence that a court would consider in evaluating whether the group companies and the master account holder disregarded corporate formalities.

As noted above, the ability of creditors to impose liability on other group companies and/or the master account holder may be complicated if the other group companies or the master account holder is located in a foreign jurisdiction. Both conflict of law principles and jurisdictional issues may prevent creditors of a group company from prevailing in a veil-piercing action in the United States against the foreign master account holder or foreign group companies.

2.2 Perspective B: bank

(a) Banking requirements

The United States does not have regulations aimed specifically at multi-corporate centralised cash management systems. However, federal regulations aimed at preventing money laundering do require banks to monitor their accounts and report suspicious activity to the US Department of the Treasury.[27] These regulations apply to all accounts, including accounts in a centralised cash management system.

The Bank Secrecy Act of 1970[28] was enacted to require financial institutions to monitor transactions and report any suspicious transactions to the US Department of the Treasury. The Bank Secrecy Act imposes civil and criminal penalties on financial institutions that fail to comply with the act's reporting requirements. The Bank Secrecy Act has been amended by several legislative amendments since its enactment in 1970, including the Annunzio-Wylie Anti-Money Laundering Act,[29] the Money Laundering Suppression Act of 1994[30] and the International Money Laundering Abatement Act and Anti-Terrorist Financing Act of 2001.[31]

In particular, financial institutions are required to file a report of "each deposit, withdrawal, exchange of currency or other payment or transfer, by, through, or to such financial institution which involves a transaction in currency of more than

27 In addition to anti-money laundering regulations, banks may be restricted by regulations designed to enforce US economic sanctions programmes against certain countries and groups, including terrorists and narcotics traffickers. Such economic sanctions programmes are administered by the Office of Foreign Assets Control (OFAC). The federal regulations promulgated by OFAC are located at 31 CFR subtit B, ch V Such regulations apply to banks regardless of their participation in centralised cash management systems with certain of their customers, and are beyond the scope of this chapter.

28 Currency and Foreign Transactions Reporting Act (Bank Secrecy Act), Pub L No 91-508, tit II, 84 Stat 1118 (1970).

29 Housing and Community Development Act of 1992, Pub L No 102-550, tit XV, 106 Stat 4044 (1992).

30 Riegle Community Development and Regulatory Improvement Act of 1994, Pub L No. 103-325, tit IV, 108 Stat 2243 (1994).

31 Pub L No 107-56, 115 Stat 272 (2001).

$10,000".[32] The report is known as a currency transaction report and must be filed with the Financial Crimes Enforcement Network (FinCEN), which is a bureau of the US Department of the Treasury.[33] The currency transaction report must be filed within 15 days of the day on which the reportable transaction occurred.[34] A 'transaction in currency' is defined as a physical transfer of currency from one person to another, but specifically excludes transfers by means of bank cheque or electronic transfer.[35] For purposes of cash management systems involving sweeps of funds from one account to another by means of electronic transfer, the bank is likely not to be subject to the reporting requirement discussed above for such sweeps. However, if a physical transfer of currency occurred as part of the cash management system, then the reporting obligations of the Bank Secrecy Act would apply.

In addition to filing currency transaction reports, financial institutions are required to report suspicious transactions to the US Department of the Treasury. A bank is required to file a suspicious activity report for any transaction aggregating at least $5,000 in funds or other assets and for which the bank knows, suspects or has reason to suspect that:

- "the transaction involves funds derived from illegal activities or is intended or conducted in order to hide or disguise funds or assets derived from illegal activities... as part of a plan to violate or evade any Federal law or regulation";
- the transaction is designed to evade the Bank Secrecy Act reporting requirements; or
- "the transaction has no business or apparent lawful purpose or is not the sort in which the particular customer would normally be expected to engage, and the bank knows of no reasonable explanation for the transaction after examining the available facts, including the background and possible purpose of the transaction".[36]

The bank must file a suspicious activity report with the FinCEN within 30 calendar days of "the date of initial detection by the bank of facts that may constitute a basis for filing a Suspicious Activity Report."[37] A bank that is party to a centralised cash management system would be required to monitor the accounts in the cash management system for any suspicious transactions and would be required to report any suspicious transactions to FinCEN.

(b) Liability of the bank in the event of insolvency of the master account holder or a group company

A bank typically will not be liable for any losses in the event of the insolvency of the master account holder or a group company simply by virtue of participating in the

32 31 CFR § 1010.311 (2011).

33 Form 104 is the form for filing Currency Transaction Reports with the FinCEN. Form 104 can be obtained from the network's website at www.fincen.gov/.

34 31 CFR. § 1010.306(a)(1) (2011).

35 31 CFR § 1010.100(bbb)(2) (2011).

36 31 CFR § 1020.320(a)(2) (2011).

37 31 CFR § 1020.320(a)(3).

cash management system. However, where a bank is also a lender to the master account holder or the group company, certain causes of action can be alleged to seek to impose liability on the bank in its capacity as lender, especially since the bank will most likely assert a lien on any and all accounts held at the bank, including the cash management account.

A lender may be liable for breach of a fiduciary duty if the creditor of the master account holder or group company can establish the lender owed a fiduciary duty to the master account holder or group company. A lender does not ordinarily owe a fiduciary duty to a borrower.[38] However, if a lender exercises significant control over a borrower, a fiduciary relationship between the lender and the borrower may be implied.[39] A lender exercises significant control over a borrower when the lender is involved in the day-to-day management of the borrower.[40]

Where it cannot be established that the lender owed a fiduciary duty to the borrower, the lender may be liable under the theory that the lender aided and abetted a breach of a fiduciary duty on the part of an officer or director. A claim for aiding and abetting a breach of a fiduciary duty requires proof of four elements:

- the existence of a fiduciary relationship;
- a breach of the fiduciary's duty;
- a knowing participation in the breach by a defendant that is not a fiduciary; and
- damages which are proximately caused by the breach.[41]

Therefore, in addition to proving that an officer or director of the corporate borrower breached a fiduciary duty owed to the borrower, a plaintiff must prove that the lender knowingly participated in the officer's or director's breach of the fiduciary duty. The lender typically must have actual, as opposed to constructive, knowledge of the officer's or director's breach of a fiduciary duty.[42] The lender must also participate in the breach, which typically takes one of two forms:

- providing substantial assistance, by affirmatively assisting, helping to conceal, or failing to act when required to do so;[43] or
- inducing or encouraging a fiduciary to breach his duties to the corporation.[44]

A lender may also be liable for fraud if the lender failed to disclose or materially

38 See *Adelphia Communications Corp v Bank of America, NA (In re Adelphia Communications Corp)*, 365 BR 24, 63 (Bankr SDNY 2007); see also *American Consolidated Transportation Companies v RBS Citizens NA (In re American Consolidated Transportation Companies)*, 433 BR 242, 253 (Bankr ND Ill 2010).

39 See *Adelphia*, 365 BR at 63.

40 See *Adelphia*, 365 BR at 63: "Control over the borrower is demonstrated when there is evidence that the lender was involved in the actual day-to-day management and operations of the borrower, or had the ability to compel the borrower to engage in unusual transactions"; see also *American Consolidated Transportation*, 433 BR at 253: "Control may be shown by the actual exercise of managerial discretion to such an extent that the lender usurps the power of the borrower's directors and officers to make business decisions."

41 *Official Committee of Unsecured Creditors v Credit Suisse First Boston (In re Exide Technologies, Inc)*, 299 BR 732, 749 (Bankr D Del 2003) citing *Malpiede v Townson*, 780 A 2d 1075, 1096 (Del 2001)); see also *Sharp International Corp v State Street Bank & Trust Co (In re Sharp International Corp)*, 302 BR 760, 769-70 (EDNY 2003).

42 *Sharp International Corp*, 302 BR at 770.

misrepresented the financial condition of the borrower. Asserting fraud against a lender for failure to disclose a material fact typically requires either that:

- there be a fiduciary relationship that would impose a duty on the lender to disclose information about the borrower; or
- that the lender has superior knowledge that is not readily available to the other party and the lender knew that the other party was acting on mistaken knowledge.[45]

In the absence of such circumstances, liability may be imposed on a lender for aiding and abetting a borrower's fraud. Aiding and abetting fraud "requires plaintiff to plead facts showing the existence of a fraud, defendant's knowledge of the fraud, and that the defendant provided substantial assistance to advance the fraud's commission".[46]

The recent spate of financial and brokerage institution insolvencies has added additional risks to financial institutions that both act as lender to a corporate group and hold multiple cash management accounts. In April 2012, JPMorgan Chase agreed to pay a $20 million fine to settle federal regulators' civil charges of illegally handling customer funds that the failed Lehman Brothers had deposited with the bank.[47] The settlement with the Commodity Futures Trading Commission involved JPMorgan's handling of customer funds from November 2006 to September 2008 when Lehman collapsed. Lehman's futures brokerage firm (LBI) deposited its customers' funds with JPMorgan, and Lehman had many other accounts with and obligations (both loans and trading obligations) to the bank.

The Commodity Futures Trading Commission alleged that JPMorgan had extended too much credit to LBI on a daily basis for its own trades because the bank included customer funds in calculating LBI's equity. The Commodity Futures Trading Commission also alleged that after Lehman Brothers filed for bankruptcy protection, JPMorgan refused to release the customer funds, which totalled approximately $330 million, until Commodity Futures Trading Commission officials ordered JPMorgan to release them. JPMorgan denied any culpability and indicated that it had made the miscalculations in error. JPMorgan further indicated that no customer funds had ever been used to satisfy any debts owed to JPMorgan; nor were any customer funds in the accounts. The handling of customer funds at futures brokerages has drawn more attention since the failure of MF Global in November 2011. About $1.6 billion in MF Global customer funds is still unaccounted for.

Therefore, while a bank holding a cash management account should generally not be liable for obligations of the account holder or its corporate group in the event

43 *Sharp International Corp*, 302 BR at 774, noting that "without an independent duty to disclose, mere inaction does not amount to substantial assistance for purposes of determining aider and abettor liability".

44 *Sharp International Corp*, 302 BR at 774-75.

45 See, for instance, *Aaron Ferer & Sons Ltd v Chase Manhattan Bank*, NA, 731 F2d 112, 123 (2d Cir 1984).

46 *Adelphia Recovery Trust v Bank of America, NA*, 624 F Supp 2d 292, 312 (SDNY 2009), citing *Wight v BankAmerica Corp*, 219 F3d 79, 91 (2d Cir 2000)).

47 See, for instance, www.businessweek.com/news/2012-04-04/jpmorgan-pays-20-million-to-settle-cftc-segregated-fund-claims.

of the insolvency of the holder of the cash management account or a group company, strict controls must be in place to make sure the lender is not abusing the privilege of holding the funds.

2.3 Insolvency

(a) *Cash management systems from the insolvency administrator's/debtor-in-possession's perspective*

US bankruptcy law does not have the concept of an 'insolvency administrator'. In regard to the bankruptcy of a corporation or corporate group, a company can file for liquidation under Chapter 7 of the US Bankruptcy Code (11 USC §§ 101, and following, as amended) or for reorganisation under Chapter 11 of the Bankruptcy Code. In the event of a Chapter 7 liquidation, a company ceases operations and all assets are taken over by a trustee. A cash management account would be included in those assets. In the event of a Chapter 11 reorganisation, in most instances, the debtor remains in possession of its assets (called a 'debtor-in-possession'), and existing management continues to run the company in the ordinary course, subject to certain restrictions set out in the Bankruptcy Code.[48] The filing of the bankruptcy creates the legal fiction of the company as debtor-in-possession as a distinct and new legal entity from the company prior to the bankruptcy petition date, in terms of determining claims and obligations.

Cash management systems create inter-company claims when a group company transfers cash to the master account holder. In solvent group companies, these claims are processed in an orderly way and are part of a corporate structure which is able to realise efficiencies by creating economies of scale within the group companies. Furthermore, in solvent group companies, excess cash may be used as dividends paid to the parent. However, when companies become insolvent and file for bankruptcy protection, the inter-company claims may have significant unintended implications.

First, pre-petition inter-company claims arising from cash management systems would typically be unsecured claims that group companies have against the master account holder. It is possible that these claims will not be paid in full if the master account holder is also insolvent. Furthermore, the inter-company claims may be considered fraudulent conveyances. Under the Bankruptcy Code, a debtor may, among other things, avoid a transfer made in the two years prior to the date of the bankruptcy filing, if the debtor received less than reasonably equivalent value in exchange for the transfer and was insolvent at the time of the transfer.[49] Thus, if a group company is insolvent and has its bank accounts swept by a cash management system, the group company may be able to avoid the transfers to the master account holder and recover that money, to the extent that it did not receive reasonably equivalent value for the transfers. The Bankruptcy Code also allows debtors to recover preferential transfers made to or for the benefit of a creditor, for or on

48 The Bankruptcy Code does authorise the court to appoint a trustee in place of the debtor-in-possession in certain circumstances, such as where there is proven fraud or mismanagement; see 11USC § 104(a), (b) and (c).

49 11 USC § 547(a)(1).

account of an antecedent debt owed by the debtor, while the debtor was insolvent and if the transfer was made within a prescribed amount of time prior to the petition date.[50] There may be scenarios when certain transfers between or on behalf of a group company and the holder of the cash management account are deemed to be preferential transfers subject to avoidance.

Substantive consolidation, briefly discussed above, is a non-statutory mechanism that is a part of a bankruptcy court's general equitable powers under Section 105(a) of the Bankruptcy Code.[51] Under the substantive consolidation doctrine, a bankruptcy court may deem a group of companies to be substantively consolidated as if the group of companies was really just one company and the assets and liabilities of the group of companies were the assets and liabilities of just one company. To determine whether substantive consolidation is appropriate, some courts use tests similar to those for piercing the corporate veil and focus on the companies' disregard for corporate formalities.[52] Another test focuses on whether there was commingling of assets and business functions and the degree of difficulty in segregating individual assets and liabilities.[53] The impact of substantive consolidation on centralised cash management systems is that substantive consolidation extinguishes inter-company claims.[54] Since the group is now treated as one company, there is no need to have the company pay itself on its previous debts. Thus, if a group company is a net creditor to the holder of the cash management account under a centralised cash management system, the claim is eliminated after substantive consolidation, and the group company's creditors may recover less than they would have recovered if the group company was able to recover on its inter-company claims and pay its creditors from its separate assets.

If a group of companies is not substantively consolidated in a bankruptcy case, a creditor of one group company typically will be able to seek recovery from any of the other group companies only if any such company owes it money. If the group company has transferred money to the master account holder under a cash management system, there is a presumption that the money belongs to the master account holder under applicable state law.[55] Thus, creditors of the group company may not recover as much on their claims unless the group company is able to recover the transferred funds under a fraudulent transfer or other theory.

There are a number of practical considerations that a company seeking to reorganise under Chapter 11 of the Bankruptcy Code should take into account in continuing its centralised cash management system after the bankruptcy filing. Prior to filing a petition for bankruptcy protection, counsel for the filing company must understand the operations of the centralised cash management system for the company and any affiliates that participate in the centralised cash management

---

50 11 USC § 546(b).
51 See *Moran v Hong Kong & Shanghai Banking Corp (In re Deltacorp, Inc)*, 179 BR 773, 777 (Bankr SDNY 1995).
52 See *In re Tureaud*, 45 BR 658, 662 (Bankr ND Okla 1985).
53 See *In re Vecco Construction Industries, Inc*, 4 BR 407, 410 (Bankr ED Va 1980).
54 See *Moran v Hong Kong & Shanghai Banking Corp*, 179 BR at 777.
55 See, for instance, *LFD Operating, Inc v Ames Department Stores, Inc (In re Ames Department Stores, Inc)*, 274 BR 600, 617 (Bankr SDNY 2002): "As a general rule, once funds are deposited in a bank account, the account holder is presumed to have title to and control over those funds."

system. This includes an understanding of the types of account that each entity maintains, how the accounts are connected to other accounts the location and identity of the corporation which controls such accounts, and the manner in which funds in the accounts are collected, concentrated and disbursed. A large company may have a highly automated and complex centralised cash management system, with a significant number of interconnected accounts. The centralised cash management system of many companies includes a network of accounts, including concentration accounts, investment accounts, disbursement accounts for payroll and other operating expenses, zero balance accounts, stand-alone petty cash accounts, lockbox accounts and other types of account.

Centralised cash management systems allow a company efficiently to collect and transfer cash generated by its business and pay financial obligations. Centralised cash management systems also enable companies to fund their investments and maintain control over their bank accounts. Because some companies generate revenue and expenses both in the United States and internationally, centralised cash management systems allow the companies to control their accounts in a more cost-effective and efficient manner.

When a company files for bankruptcy protection in the United States, it is prohibited by US bankruptcy law from taking certain actions and paying certain claims, including incurring secured debt, paying claims arising prior to the date the bankruptcy case was filed, using cash collateral without consent of the companies' lenders, paying tax claims and paying employees or others for pre-petition services. The funding needs of affiliates and subsidiaries, both domestic and international, are important if these entities are not included as debtors in a bankruptcy filing. Special authorisation from the bankruptcy court (and possibly lenders) may be necessary to continue funding these entities after the bankruptcy case is filed.

The US Trustee Programme is a component of the Department of Justice responsible for overseeing the administration of bankruptcy cases and private trustees under 28 USC § 586 and the Bankruptcy Code. It consists of 21 regional US trustee offices nationwide and an Executive Office for US trustees in Washington, DC. Section 586(a)(3) of Title 28 of the United States Code provides that the US trustee shall monitor the administration of Chapter 11 cases within the region for which the trustee is appointed. As such, the US trustee for each region generally adopts operating guidelines and reporting requirements, and corporations that file for bankruptcy must comply with those guidelines and requirements. The US trustee guidelines typically require debtors, among other things, to close all existing bank accounts and open new debtor-in-possession bank accounts, establish one debtor-in-possession account for all estate moneys required for the payment of taxes (including payroll taxes), maintain a separate debtor-in-possession account for cash collateral and obtain cheques for all debtor-in-possession accounts that bear the designation 'debtor-in-possession', the bankruptcy case number and the type of account. The guidelines also require the debtors to close their books and records as of the bankruptcy petition date and open new books and records. These requirements are designed to provide a clear line of demarcation between pre-petition and post-petition transactions and operations, and to prevent the inadvertent post-petition payment of pre-petition claims. The Bankruptcy Code precludes a debtor from making payments on account of pre-petition claims. The restrictions contained in the Bankruptcy Code, coupled with the US trustee requirements, may cause serious complications if companies utilise a centralised cash management system.

As a practical matter, it would be extremely burdensome and expensive to establish a separate cash management system for each debtor entity and non-debtor entity once a bankruptcy is filed. Requiring corporations to establish separate systems would create large administrative burdens and could be very disruptive to domestic and foreign operations, which could hinder any reorganisation efforts. Therefore, corporations will generally file a motion in the bankruptcy court and seek immediate relief from the bankruptcy court to allow them to continue operating their existing cash management systems. So-called 'first day' motions are filed immediately after filing a petition for bankruptcy relief, with the intention of having such motions heard on, or shortly after, the first day of the bankruptcy case. To provide as much due process as possible under the circumstances, a company should be prepared to send notice (usually by email or fax) of the filing of the bankruptcy petition and any first day motions to known key parties upon the filing of its bankruptcy petition. These parties include the US trustee, the company's secured lenders, other major parties-in-interest and the largest unsecured creditors listed in the company's bankruptcy petition.

The primary purpose of a motion to maintain existing bank accounts and procedures is to allow the debtor company to continue the use of its existing centralised cash management system. Forcing a company to close all of its bank accounts and establish a new cash management system would likely create administrative burdens and could seriously disrupt the company's receipts and disbursements while the replacement system is being established. Bankruptcy is enough of a disruption in the business operations of a company without such disruption being exacerbated by sudden modifications in the operations of its centralised cash management system.

A cash management motion should describe the company's existing cash management system in reasonable detail, including a description of all bank accounts (including location and account numbers). The motion should provide an explanation of how cash receipts and disbursements are traced through the company's centralised cash management system and how such transactions are reflected in the company's books and records. Additionally, the motion should describe any controls established on disbursements, the manner in which excess cash is held, and the manner in which cash is transferred between and among each debtor, as well as between and among any non-debtor affiliates. If a cash management system allows for the transfer of funds between debtor entities, and the debtors are not substantively consolidated, the motion should detail how such transactions are reflected in the company's books and records. Additionally, if non-debtor affiliates have anticipated funding needs during the course of the bankruptcy, court authority for such transactions should be requested. It would be unusual for a court to permit the continued operation of a debtor/non-debtor centralised cash management system without the consent of the US trustee, lenders and creditor representatives, and without a significant evidentiary showing of necessity.

Bankruptcy courts generally grant motions for authority to continue the use of a company's existing centralised cash management system. Section 105 of the Bankruptcy Code provides in its pertinent part that: "The court may issue any order, process, or judgment that is necessary or appropriate to carry out the provisions of this title."[56] Additionally, Section 363(c)(1) of the Bankruptcy Code authorises the debtor-in-possession to "use property of the estate in the ordinary course of business without notice or a hearing".[57] The purpose of Section 363(c)(1) of the Bankruptcy Code is to provide a debtor-in-possession with the flexibility to engage in the ordinary transactions required to operate its business without unneeded oversight by its creditors or the bankruptcy court. Included within the purview of Section 363(c) is a debtor's ability to continue "routine transactions" necessitated by a debtor's cash management system, including the collection, concentration, and disbursement of cash pursuant to a centralised cash management system.

Bankruptcy courts have recognised that strict enforcement of the US trustee requirements does not always serve the purposes of a bankruptcy case. Accordingly, bankruptcy courts have often exercised their equitable powers by waiving such requirements and replacing them with alternative procedures. Often, the US trustee and other parties-in-interest may agree to allow the debtor to continue using its existing cash management system if the debtor provides such parties with periodic reports of its bank accounts and investments (both foreign and domestic) in a form agreed upon by the parties.

(b) Dissolution/termination of the cash management system in the event of liquidation of the master account holder or a group company

The parties to a centralised cash management system can typically terminate the cash management system at will. Centralised cash management systems in the United States are typically governed by contract: an agreement among the parties to the cash management system. Termination of the centralised cash management system would therefore be governed by that agreement. In addition, as noted in paragraph (a) above, in the event of insolvency of the master account holder and/or the group companies, the US trustee guidelines typically require debtors to close their pre-petition accounts and open new debtor-in-possession accounts. If the holder of the cash management account and/or the group companies files for bankruptcy protection and is unable to obtain the bankruptcy court's approval to maintain the existing centralised cash management system, the master account holder and the group companies will be required to terminate their pre-petition centralised cash management system. At that time, determination would have to be made by the bankruptcy court, after notice and hearing, as to how funds in the centralised cash management system should be distributed among the former participants in the centralised cash management system.

The insolvency of the financial institution generally does not prevent a depositor from terminating its cash management account. While most large corporate cash

56 11 USC § 105(a).
57 11 USC § 363(c)(1).

management accounts will exceed the limits of insurance guaranteed by the Federal Deposit Insurance Corporation, the US governmental agency that regulates banks and controls their liquidation, as a practical matter, in most bank liquidations, ordinary bank depositors have not lost their funds.[58] Additionally, the US trustee guidelines include a list of approved depository institutions for debtors. These financial institutions must meet certain capital requirements and also provide a bond to the United States for accounts of debtors.[59]

2.4 Perspective D: regulatory

As noted in section 2.2(a) above, the United States does not have regulations aimed specifically at cash management systems. Rather, centralised cash management systems are typically treated as contracts, and the terms of any agreement between a bank, the master account holder and group companies will govern the cash management system. There are many federal regulations that govern the activities of banks and other financial institutions in the United States. A general, but not all-inclusive, discussion of banking regulations in the United States that may apply to bank accounts, including centralised cash management systems, is included in section 2.2 above.

2.5 Perspective E: tax

Many companies with multiple operating entities implement a centralised cash management system for ease of use, to reduce costs and to achieve certain tax advantages. It is important to consult with tax counsel when implementing a centralised cash management system in order to understand the tax implications that can occur when utilising a centralised cash management system.

Physical cash pooling is often referred to as cash concentration or zero balancing, and can be achieved on a single-country basis or on a cross-border basis. Physical cash pooling must be done on a currency-by-currency basis. Each company or subsidiary maintains its own bank account which is generally a sub-account linked to a main account. At the close of each business day, the net funds from these sub-accounts are physically transferred to the main account (which is generally maintained by the parent company or a regional subsidiary). The movement of money to and from the sub-accounts is generally treated as inter-company loans. Physical pooling is actually a form of cash sweeping or cash concentration with the addition of multiple divisions or subsidiaries. The separation of division or subsidiary activity is achieved through zero balance sub-accounts.

The taxation of income associated with a centralised cash management system can be complex. The type of interest being earned is important and will affect the allocation back to the cash management system participants and how each

---

58 This chapter deals with issues of centralised cash management systems and the bank accounts that are included in such systems. While it is possible that such systems might include brokerage accounts held with a financial institution related to the bank holding the cash management account, which could be used to invest excess funds, such accounts are not ordinarily the types of accounts used by companies to fund their day-to-day operations. A discussion of customer losses from the insolvency of a broker, as seen in cases such as *Lehman Brothers* and *MFGlobal*, is outside the scope of this chapter.

59 See 11 USC § 345.

participant is taxed in its respective jurisdiction. Tax authorities in cash management system participants' jurisdictions may treat interest that is actually or notionally paid in that jurisdiction as being subject to withholding tax.

The master account holder will generally have two sources of income or expense:

- interest income or expense with respect to a surplus or deficit in the master account; and
- interest income or expense with respect to the inter-company accounts with each of the sub-account holders (the cash pool participants, which are generally the operating affiliates) that are adding to or taking from the cash pool.

If the cash pooling system involves both US and non-US entities, planning for 'Subpart F' income generated by interest earned on global cash poolings is necessary to avoid US tax on such interest income.[60] Moreover, the net cash position of each entity should be monitored to minimise the risk of deemed dividend treatment under Subpart F that would apply when a US entity is a net borrower. Triggering of either of these rules (Subpart F interest income or a deemed dividend) would cause a current taxable inclusion with associated foreign tax credit implications, in the absence of an actual cash payment.

In addition, if a cash pool participant has a different functional currency, as determined for US federal income tax purposes, from the currency in which the cash pool is maintained, it is important to consult with tax counsel to monitor:

- the foreign currency gain or loss that the cash pool participant would recognise on contributions to or withdrawals from the cash pool; and
- the tax implications of any associated currency hedging transactions entered into by the master account holder or the cash pool participant (eg, potential mismatches in the timing and character of gain or loss on the offsetting positions).[61]

The level of interest rates on inter-company accounts is influenced by transfer pricing considerations. Cash pool participants that make cash deposits should earn remuneration on their cash deposits consistent with that which would have been earned if the cash pool operator were a third party. In other words, the cash pool depositor should earn an interest rate consistent with those prevailing in money markets or the banking industry in general. Cash pool participants that borrow from the cash pool should pay what would have been paid to a third-party cash pool operation. In other words, the cash pool borrower should pay an arm's-length interest rate. Depending on the functions performed, the risks assumed and the assets employed, the cash pool operator should be remunerated for the financial intermediary services that it performs.

Additionally, most countries have a network of tax treaties which provide

---

60 See § 954, *et seq* of the Internal Revenue Code of 1986, as amended, and the regulations thereunder.

61 For further operational analysis of multinational corporate group cash management systems in general, see Madura, Jeff, *International Financial Management*, Abridged 10th ed, Thomson South-Western (2011), Chapter 21: "International Cash Management".

different tax concessions for various international transactions depending on the country. These treaties may provide for low or no withholding tax on cross-border interest, dividends and capital gains payments. To take advantage of the tax benefits of these treaties, the master account holder must be a resident company (ie, it must have a substantial business presence) in each treaty country.

3. Conclusion

Centralised cash management systems as used by corporate groups are viewed as ordinary and customary in the United States and are not forbidden in any way. While the insolvency of the holder the cash management account or any of its group members can create issues and complications, in the absence of bad faith, fraud or self-dealing, the existence of a centralised cash management system will not, in and of itself, shift liability to the directors of the entity holding the cash management account or to any group entities, and will not create liability on the part of one entity for the debts of another.

The authors gratefully acknowledge the assistance of John Podvin, of counsel, Haynes and Boone finance section (banking regulation), and Sam Lichtman, of counsel, Haynes and Boone tax section.

About the authors

Flavio A Acerbi
Associate, Paul Hastings
flavioacerbi@paulhastings.com

Flavio A Acerbi is an associate in the corporate practice of Paul Hastings and is based in the firm's Milan office. Mr Acerbi focuses on general corporate law, corporate governance, mergers and acquisitions, restructuring and securities regulation.

Before joining Paul Hastings in 2011, he worked on transnational and domestic corporate acquisitions and joint ventures, capital markets transactions and general corporate law in large international and Italian law firms in Rome, Milan and Moscow.

Mr Acerbi graduated from the *Università Cattolica* (Milan) (*summa cum laude*) in 2003, earned a postgraduate diploma in stock exchanges and financial markets from the *Università Bocconi* (Milan) in 2004 and an LLM from the University of Michigan Law School in 2005. He was admitted to the Milan Bar in 2007.

Sang Jin Ahn
Attorney, Kim & Chang
sjahn@kimchang.com

Sang Jin Ahn is an attorney in the firm's banking, M&A, foreign direct investment, real estate and Japanese practice groups.

Mr Ahn has extensive experience in a wide range of domestic and cross-border transactions and regulatory matters, including banking, corporate financing, ship financing, structured financing, acquisition financing, mergers and acquisitions of financial institutions and real estate acquisitions, representing top Korean, Japanese and international corporations.

Tomás M Araya
Partner, M&M Bomchil
tomas.araya@bomchil.com

Tomás M Araya is a partner at M&M Bomchil and a member of the firm's financial services and financial restructuring practices.

Mr Araya graduated from *Universidad Nacional de Rosario* in 1994 and received a master's in business law with honours from *Universidad Austral* in 1996. In 2001 he received an LLM from New York University, after being granted a Fulbright scholarship. Mr Araya is admitted to the Santa Fe Bar, the City of Buenos Aires Bar and the New York Bar.

Mr Araya specialises in financing and debt restructuring transactions. He has also led several M&A cases involving the acquisition of local companies with subsidiaries in Argentina and in other Latin American countries.

Mr Araya serves as professor of corporate law at *Universidad de Buenos Aires* Law School and on the LLM programmes of *Universidad Austral* and *Universidad Di Tella* School of Law.

Venetia Argyropoulou
Senior lawyer, Pelaghias, Christodoulou, Vrachas LLC
v.argyropoulou@pelaghiaslaw.com

Venetia Argyropoulou was educated in Thessaloniki at the Law School of Aristoteleion University, where she graduated with honours. Subsequently, she obtained a JD from Northwestern California School of Law. She then completed her studies at the University of Oslo, where she acquired an LLM in maritime law and a master's in international economic and investments law.

Ms Argyropoulou is a practising attorney in both Cyprus and Greece, and has successfully passed the California Bar exam.

Ms Argyropoulou is fluent in Greek and English, and has a good command of Italian and German.

Naoya Ariyoshi
Associate, Nishimura & Asahi
n_ariyoshi@jurists.co.jp

Naoya Ariyoshi is an associate of Nishimura & Asahi and works mainly in the areas of structured finance, transactions related to trusts and financial regulations. He joined the firm in 2002 after graduating from the University of Tokyo (LLB) in 2001 and attending the Legal Training and Research Institute of the Supreme Court of Japan. Since then, he has been involved in various financial transactions, such as structured finance transactions. He is a member of the Financial Law Board. He was seconded to the Corporate Accounting and Disclosure Division of the Planning and Coordination Bureau, Financial Services Agency of Japan from 2010 to 2011.

Mary Arzoumanidis
Associate, Borden Ladner Gervais LLP
marzoumanidis@blg.com

Mary Arzoumanidis is an associate in the insolvency and restructuring group in the Toronto office of Borden Ladner Gervais LLP. She was admitted to the Ontario Bar in 2007. Ms Arzoumanidis completed her LLB at the University of Windsor in 2003. In 2004, she received her LLM from King's College London, University of London, specialising in corporate insolvency. Prior to her legal studies, she received her BA (honours) from York University in 2000, with a major in history and a minor in psychology.

Daniela A Bianchi
Associate, M&M Bomchil
daniela.bianchi@bomchil.com

Daniela A Bianchi graduated as a lawyer with honours from *Universidad de Buenos Aires* in 2009 and as a public translator from *Universidad Católica Argentina* in 2008. For her academic performance, she won the *Premio a la Excelencia Académica* award from the *Colegio de Abogados de la Ciudad Autónoma de Buenos Aires* and the *Mejores Promedios* award from *Universidad de Buenos Aires*.

She has been a member of the financial services and capital markets practice area since June 2009. She serves as professor of international private law at *Universidad de Buenos Aires* Law School and is currently pursuing a master's in the area.

She is admitted to the City of Buenos Aires Bar.

Daragh Bohan
Partner, Mason Hayes & Curran
dbohan@mhc.ie

Daragh Bohan is a partner in the financial services department of Irish law firm Mason Hayes & Curran. He advises domestic and international banks and other financial services industry organisations on a broad range of transactions, including from a regulatory perspective. Mr Bohan has also acted for many domestic and international borrowers, including large Irish plcs. He advises on a wide range of financing for domestic and international, corporate and commercial transactions, including public-private partnerships/projects, mergers and acquisitions, joint ventures, bond financings, structured finance transactions and asset and tax-based lending.

Arno Brauneis
Partner, bkp Rechtsanwälte/Attorneys at Law
a.brauneis@bkp.at

Arno Brauneis is the founding partner of bkp (Brauneis Klauser Prändl) Rechtsanwälte GmbH/ Attorneys at Law. His areas of specialisation are corporate law and mergers and acquisitions.

Publishing regularly, he is the author of, among other things, the Austrian reference work on the lease of enterprises as well as several articles and book chapters on company-related legal issues.

Carsten Ceutz
Partner, Bech-Bruun
cac@bechbruun.com

Carsten Ceutz, a partner in Bech-Bruun's restructuring department, represents financial creditors with exposure through financial and operational leasing, loans to and charges over cooperative housing associations in distress, possession and administration of receivable charges and floating company charges, as well as the initiation and administration of company restructuring procedures.

As supervisor, administrator or trustee of many restructured businesses and bankruptcy estates, Mr Ceutz employs his substantial professional expertise to safeguard the interests of bankruptcy estates and creditors. He has vast experience in administering the bankruptcy estates of travel agencies and in the management of information technology, rights and employees in connection with company restructurings and insolvency.

Mr Ceutz and his partners work with specialists in order to reach the best possible solutions for companies and creditors. They have developed a comprehensive national and international network of contacts, providing quick access to accountants, engineers, consultants and appraisers so that they can assemble a multi-disciplinary team of legal and business professionals at short notice.

Benedict F Christ
Partner, VISCHER Ltd
bfchrist@vischer.com

Benedict F Christ is a partner in the corporate department of VISCHER Ltd in Zurich. He is admitted in Switzerland and New York, and has specialised in M&A and finance transactions for over 10 years while based in Zurich and New York.

Mr Christ focuses on M&A, banking, finance, contracts and corporate law. He has a wealth of transactional experience, and advises regularly on real estate, private equity, structured finance and capital markets matters.

Maria Luisa de Alarcón
Partner JAUSAS
malarcon@jausaslegal.com

Over the more than 25 years of her professional career, and thanks to her combined legal and business background, Maria Luisa de Alarcón has focused on advising business groups and individuals on financial and tax law, company law and mergers and acquisitions; assisting with tax advice and planning for resident and non-resident businesses and individuals and preparing family agreements; and managing complex deals (eg, mergers, splits and acquisitions and partnership agreements). In recent years, she has also worked with the Securities Litigation Department on the preparation of extrajudicial claims and settlements with financial institutions regarding complex swap and forward-type instruments.

Miguel de Avillez Pereira
Partner, Abreu Advogados
miguel.avillez.pereira@abreuadvogados.com

Miguel de Avillez Pereira graduated from the University of Lisbon Law School in 1989 and has an LLM from the Europa Institute of the University of Edinburgh. He became an associate lawyer with Albuquerque & Avillez law firm in 1989.

Mr De Avillez Pereira is senior vice chair of the International Bar Association Insolvency, Restructuring and Creditors' Rights Section and a member of the council of the European Forum. He is also a member of the International Insolvency Institute and honorary president of the International Association of Young Lawyers.

As a lawyer, he assists clients primarily on matters related to corporate, mergers and acquisitions, private equity, insolvency and corporate restructuring.

He is the author of several publications.

Bart de Man
Partner, Kennedy Van der Laan NV
bart.de.man@kvdl.nl

Bart de Man is a partner and heads the banking and finance department of Kennedy Van der Laan in Amsterdam. He specialises in financing, security rights and insolvency.

Mr De Man advises on financing transactions as counsel to banks and multinationals. He also acts as counsel to all relevant parties in insolvency proceedings, with a particular focus on cross-border insolvencies. He is currently the administrator in major insolvency proceedings involving La Perla, a Dutch global luxury real estate developer with affiliates in Spain, Antigua, France, Austria, Vietnam and Panama.

Kristina Einarsson
Partner, Setterwalls Law Firm
kristina.einarsson@setterwalls.se

Kristina Einarsson is a dual-qualified Swedish advocate and English solicitor, and focuses on capital markets, corporate finance and public and private M&A transactions. Ms Einarsson also works extensively with bank financing, particularly acquisition finance.

Ms Einarsson was named a Leading Lawyer in the *IFLR1000* (capital markets), and listed under Other Specialists by *Chambers Europe* (capital markets) and *Chambers Global* (capital markets).

Judith Elkin
Partner, Haynes and Boone, LLP
judith.elkin@haynesboone.com

Judith Elkin is a partner in Haynes and Boone's bankruptcy and business restructuring section. For more than 30 years she has represented debtors, creditors, creditors' committees, lenders and other parties-in-interest in reorganisation and Chapter 15 proceedings, financial restructurings and related litigation. She has represented major constituencies in some of the largest and most complex US and multinational insolvency cases, including *GM, Enron, Mirant, SemCrude, Adelphia,* F*ederal-Mogul, Kodak, Mexicana, ASARCO* and *Delphi*. She speaks frequently on insolvency issues in the United States and internationally.

Ms Elkin is a member of the International Bar Association Insolvency, Restructuring and Creditors' Rights Section (co-chair 2011-12), the International Women's Insolvency and Restructuring Confederation (chair 2010-2012), the American Bar Association (co-chair of Litigation Section Bankruptcy and Insolvency Litigation Committee 1997-2001), the American Bankruptcy Institute and the International Insolvency Institute. She has been recognised in *Best Lawyers in America* – Bankruptcy and Creditor-Debtor Rights Law and as a *Super Lawyer* – Bankruptcy and Creditor/Debtor Rights Law.

Bill Finney
Associate, Giese & Partner, vos
finney@giese.cz

Bill Finney joined Giese & Partner and became a member of the Czech Bar in 2001.

Since then he has been active in real estate law, banking law and M&A. He has advised a number of international leading banks on acquisition sales and finance transactions. He is the author of several legal essays and articles published in Central Europe.

He received a BA in foreign affairs and a JD (1991) from the University of Virginia. He became a member of the Washington State Bar Association in 1991 and began practising commercial litigation at a large Seattle law firm. Mr Finney speaks English, Czech and French.

Laurent Fisch
Partner, Molitor Avocats à la Cour
laurent.fisch@molitorlegal.lu

Laurent Fisch is a partner and heads the insolvency and restructuring practice at Molitor Avocats à la Cour.

Mr Fisch specialises in corporate finance and real estate projects, and advises companies and creditors particularly with regard to the purchase and sale of companies during insolvency proceedings, cash pooling structures and related aspects such as licensing, insolvency and creditor rights. He regularly reviews proposed deal structures, including finance, facility and security documentation.

PLC's *Which Lawyer?* ranks Molitor as highly recommended in restructuring and insolvency, and Mr Fisch is referred to as "a renowned insolvency and restructuring expert who also acts as liquidator in major administrations" (*Legal 500*).

Mr Fisch is the division officer of the International Bar Association's Insolvency, Restructuring and Creditors' Rights Committee and a member of INSOL Europe. He is a regular speaker on insolvency matters and contributed the Luxembourg chapter of PLC's *Cross-border Restructuring and Insolvency Handbook* 2010/2011 and 2011/2012.

Mr Fisch speaks English, French, German and Luxembourgish.

Frank Flanagan
Senior associate, Mason Hayes & Curran
fflanagan@mhc.ie

Frank Flanagan is a senior associate practising dispute resolution, insolvency and telecoms regulatory law at Irish firm Mason Hayes & Curran. He regularly provides advice to insolvency practitioners and has advised in relation to the winding up of a number of Irish companies in multinational insolvencies and in relation to transactions involving the cross-border transfer of debt.

Mr Flanagan is also a chartered engineer and, prior to joining Mason Hayes & Curran, was a director of a number of technology companies, where he was responsible for the delivery of a diverse range of products, including internet security hardware, video conferencing systems and real-time systems for manufacturing and utilities.

Anja Droege Gagnier
Partner, BMH Avocats
adroege@bmhavocats.com

Anja Droege Gagnier is head of the corporate/restructuring group of BMH Avocats in Paris.

For more than 18 years, Ms Droege Gagnier has gained broad experience in international transactions (cross-border M&A, joint ventures and distressed M&A), as well as in corporate restructurings and reorganisations in various industries (including steel, aeronautic, automotive, nuclear, petrol, real estate and luxury goods). She advises mainly foreign investors, banks and administrators in French insolvency and pre-insolvency proceedings.

Admitted to the Paris Bar since 1994, Ms

Droege Gagnier holds law degrees from University Robert-Schuman, Strasbourg (DJCE/DESS *Droit des Affaires/Magistère des Juristes d'Affaires Franco-Allemands*). Before joining BMH Avocats, she practised at Stibbe Simont Monahan Duhot, Haarmann Hemmelrath and Marccus Partners, all in Paris. She is co-chair of the Enforcement of Creditors' Rights Sub-committee, which is part of the International Bar Association's Insolvency, Restructuring and Creditors' Rights Section.

Tom Geudens
Partner, Lydian
tom.geudens@lydian.be

Tom Geudens is a partner in the corporate and finance department, where he heads the banking and finance practice.

His practice covers international banking, project finance, business restructuring and insolvency, capital markets and regulatory issues. His client base represents a cross-section of banks, corporations and public sector bodies.

Ernst Giese
Partner, Giese & Partner, vos
giese@giese.cz

Ernst Giese is the managing partner of Giese & Partner. He is a well-known expert on the acquisition and financing of real estate. In the last 15 years he has advised leading real estate banks and investors from Germany, Austria and Israel on the acquisition and sale of office, retail and residential projects in the Czech and Slovak Republics. He has been the legal adviser on major financing projects, advising several of the leading German banks. As co-author of the standard work on securing loans, he has influenced the development of this specific field of law.

Dr Giese was admitted to the German Bar in 1995 and has been a member of the Czech Bar since 1999. He is also admitted to the Slovak Bar. He speaks German, English, Czech and French.

Domenico Gioia
Associate trainee, Paul Hastings
domenicogioia@paulhastings.com

Domenico Gioia is an associate trainee in the tax department of Paul Hastings in Milan.

Mr Gioia focuses his practice on tax planning and consulting, as well as general tax matters regarding disputes. He has been actively involved in corporate reorganisation and acquisition transactions, focusing on direct and indirect tax issues, structured and asset finance deals, investment funds transactions and international fiscal planning.

Before joining Paul Hastings in November 2010, Mr Gioia worked as an intern in the New York office of a major Italian law firm.

Mr Gioia graduated with full marks from Bocconi University in 2009.

Borge Grottjord
Partner, Grette DA
bogr@grette.no

Borge Grottjord is a partner and the head of Grette DA's banking and finance department. He regularly advises clients on matters related to syndicated loans, secured finance, leveraged finance, project finance and structured transactions. Mr Grottjord has extensive industry experience and advises Norwegian banks, investment banks and sovereign funds.

Maya Ito
Associate, Nishimura & Asahi
m_ito@jurists.co.jp

Maya Ito is an associate at Nishimura & Asahi and works mainly in the area of cross-border project finance. She joined the firm in 2002 after graduating from Keio University (LLB) in 1999 and attending the Legal Training and Research Institute of the Supreme Court of Japan. She graduated from Columbia University School of Law (LLM) in 2007. Since then she has gained extensive experience in project finance, structured finance, international finance and general corporate law, advising a range of clients, including multinational corporations, commercial banks, multilateral financing institutions, project developers and sponsors, and other parties on a range of international and cross-border matters.

Pekka Jaatinen
Senior partner, Castrén & Snellman
pekka.jaatinen@castren.fi

Throughout his long career Pekka Jaatinen has specialised in M&A, insolvency and corporate law. He has advised large financial institutions and other clients acting as a leading legal counsel in relation to both domestic and international transactions, restructurings and insolvency proceedings. He is well recognised for acting as a trustee and administrator for many of the largest Finnish bankruptcy estates and restructuring proceedings. Mr Jaatinen is also a board member of several domestic and international companies.

David Jenny
Partner, VISCHER Ltd
djenny@vischer.com

David Jenny is a partner of VISCHER Ltd, a major Swiss law firm with offices in Basel and Zurich. He has been advising and representing corporations since 1991 in transactions and corporate and commercial matters. In insolvency, he acts as a liquidator and advises governing bodies of corporations and creditors. Mr Jenny is one of the authors of the leading commentary on the Swiss Bankruptcy Code. He also acts as an arbitrator. He is a member of various boards of directors and foundation councils. At present, Mr Jenny is president of the Basel Bar Association and co-chair of the Insolvency, Restructuring and Creditors' Rights Section of the International Bar Association. He holds *lic iur* (1984) and *Dr iur* (1988) degrees from the University of Basel and an LLM (1989) from the University of Michigan Law School.

Constantinos N Klissouras
Partner and head of litigation, insolvency and restructuring, K I P lf
cklissouras@kp-lf.com

Constantinos Klissouras heads the firm's disputes and restructuring team, and specialises in complex commercial litigation and arbitration, banking and finance, and domestic and cross-border insolvency and restructuring.

He acts for domestic and foreign financial institutions and companies from a variety of sectors in cross-border and domestic litigation and arbitration, as well as in contentious and non-contentious matters involving distressed, leveraged and structured finance, insolvency and restructuring.

Mr Klissouras has written in English on Greek insolvency law. He is a vice chairman of the Insolvency, Restructuring and Creditors' Rights Section of the International Bar Association, an honorary fellow of the Centre for International Legal Studies, a Gerson Lehrman educator and a member of the Hellenic Commercial Lawyers Association. He is a member of the Athens Bar admitted to the Supreme Court.

Morten Krogsgaard
Partner, Bech-Bruun
mok@bechbruun.com

Morten Krogsgaard, a partner in Bech-Bruun's banking and finance department, specialises in international financial law and has extensive experience in all aspects of finance law, including acquisition financing, syndicated loan agreements, mezzanine financing, guarantees and collateral security, bond issues and structured products.

He assists Danish and international financial undertakings in their capacity as lenders and Danish and international companies and private equity funds in their capacity as borrowers in many high-profile transactions.

Mr Krogsgaard previously worked at the

Danish Financial Supervisory Authority and advises on the regulatory environment for financial undertakings and their products, as well as the setting up of financial undertakings and branches of foreign financial undertakings.

Keum Ho Lee
Attorney, Kim & Chang
khlee@kimchang.com

Keum Ho Lee is a foreign attorney in the firm's banking, derivatives, aircraft finance, structured finance and other financial institutions practice groups.

Mr Lee joined the firm in 2001, after a distinguished 17-year career as a banking and foreign exchange specialist. Before joining the firm, Mr Lee served in the Bank of Korea in the Foreign Exchange Control and International Finance Department. Mr Lee has extensive experience in a wide range of cross-border and domestic transactions and regulatory matters with a focus on foreign exchange and banking law and derivatives transactions.

Yves Lenders
Partner, Lydian
yves.lenders@lydian.be

Yves Lenders is a partner in the commercial and litigation department, where he heads the ports and logistics and insolvency practice.

His practice area includes complex and cross-border litigation, alternative dispute resolution, commercial law and insolvency matters. Assisting clients in corporate litigation and criminal law is also part of his work.

Graeme Levy
Partner, Squire Sanders (UK) LLP
graeme.levy@squiresanders.com

Graeme Levy is a partner in the restructuring and insolvency group at Squire Sanders, and is based in London. He is co-chair of the firm's cross-border restructuring and insolvency practice. He has 25 years' experience in restructuring and insolvency matters, acting for distressed corporates, lenders, insolvency practitioners and other stakeholders. Much of his work is international in nature. He is co-author of *Practical Insolvency Precedents* (FT Law and Tax, 1995) and is a former contributing editor to the *Butterworths Encyclopaedia of Forms and Precedents.*

Kourtney P Lyda
Senior attorney, Haynes and Boone, LLP
kourtney.lyda@haynesboone.com

Kourtney P Lyda is a senior attorney in the bankruptcy and business restructuring section of the Houston office of Haynes and Boone, LLP. Ms Lyda received her BS from Texas A&M University, her LLB from University of Tulsa College of Law and her LLM in taxation from University of Houston Law Center. Her practice is a multi-disciplined practice concentrated in the area of commercial insolvency and reorganisation, both in and out of court. Ms Lyda has represented both debtor and creditor entities in all aspects of the debt restructuring and work-out process. The companies she represents generally have sophisticated capital structures and are across a variety of industries, including financial services, energy, oil and gas, consumer loan origination, securitisation and servicing, telecommunications and passenger and cargo aviation.

Michael J MacNaughton
Partner, Borden Ladner Gervais LLP
mmacnaughton@blg.com

Michael J MacNaughton is a partner and one of the national leaders of Borden Ladner Gervais LLP's insolvency and restructuring group. He was admitted to the Ontario Bar in 1986. He has been recognised by *Chambers Global, The Best Lawyers in Canada*, PLC's *Which Lawyer?*, *Lexpert*, *Who's Who Legal* and *IFLR* for insolvency and restructuring.

Mr MacNaughton has been involved in many of Canada's major restructurings and insolvencies.

He has written and spoken on insolvency and restructuring topics for the *Annual Review of Insolvency Law*, the Law Society of Upper Canada, the Canadian Institute, Insight, Osgoode Professional Centre and others. He is a member of the Insolvency Institute of Canada, the American Bar Association (Business Bankruptcy), the American Bankruptcy Institute, INSOL, the Turnaround Management Association, the Ontario Bar Association (Insolvency Section) and the Canadian Insolvency Foundation.

Daniela Mader
Associate, GÖRG Partnerschaft von Rechtsanwälten
dmader@goerg.de

Daniela Mader is an associate in the corporate department of GÖRG Partnerschaft von Rechtsanwälten in Berlin. She provides legal advice to international and domestic clients regarding mergers and acquisitions, as well as private equity and venture capital transactions.

Paolo Manganelli
Senior associate, Paul Hastings
paolomanganelli@paulhastings.com

Paolo Manganelli is a senior associate in the corporate practice of Paul Hastings' Milan office.

Mr Manganelli focuses his practice on corporate, M&A and insolvency matters, to which he brings an extensive knowledge of Italian bankruptcy law and corporate restructurings. He has been involved in the majority of the Milan office's M&A and restructuring deals since his arrival. In 2010 Mr Manganelli was seconded to Paul Hastings' New York office for 12 months, where he was involved in a number of Chapter 11 procedures.

Before joining Paul Hastings, from 2004 to 2006 Mr Manganelli worked as the Parmalat Group's deputy head of litigation, advising on all litigation matters arising from Parmalat's insolvency and financial fraud, as well as on legal matters relating to the Parmalat restructuring plan. Mr Manganelli was also in-house counsel of the Fiat Group, where he was actively involved in a number of corporate transactions in the automotive and service sectors and also worked on mergers and acquisitions, joint ventures and commercial agreements.

Mr Manganelli graduated from the University of Turin, Italy in 2000 and has been a member of the Turin Bar since 2003.

Arsalan Muhammad
Associate, Haynes and Boone, LLP
arsalan.muhammad@haynesboone.com

Arsalan Muhammad is an associate in the bankruptcy and business restructuring section in the Houston office of Haynes and Boone. His practice focuses on bankruptcy and insolvency law and related litigation, including representations of Chapter 11 debtors, as well as secured and unsecured creditors. He received his JD from Georgetown University.

João Ochôa
Trainee lawyer, Abreu Advogados
Joao.ochoa@abreuadvogados.com

João Ochôa graduated from the University of Lisbon Law School, in 2009. He is a postgraduate student in tax law at the Institute for Economic, Financial and Tax Law of Lisbon University. He also studied intellectual property on behalf of the Portuguese Intellectual Property Association at Lisbon University Law School in 2008.

Mr Ochôa is registered as a trainee lawyer with the Portuguese Bar Association, and has been a trainee lawyer with Abreu Advogados since 2009. He works mainly in tax and corporate law.

Darío U Oscós
Senior partner, Oscos Abogados
doscos@oscosabogados.com.mx

Darío U Oscós is a legal counsel and practitioner specialising in restructuring, creditors' rights, insolvency, litigation and arbitration both internationally and domestically in the fields of financing, securities, commercial, corporate, intellectual property, torts, energy and complex civil and commercial litigation and arbitration. He obtained and has enforced the first two foreign bankruptcy proceedings worldwide recognised under the UNCITRAL Model Law on Cross-Border Insolvency. Mr Oscós focuses on out-of-court settlements, work-outs and pre-package reorganisation plans. He counsels and represents creditors, debtors and trustees.

Mr Oscós is founder and senior partner of Oscós Abogados. He is a professor of insolvency, alternative dispute resolution and procedural law. He is a member of the American Law Institute, the International Insolvency Institute, the International Bar Association, Insol International, NABT, *Barra Mexicana Colegio de Abogados and Ilustre y Nacional Colegio de Abogados de México.* Mr Oscós and Oscós Abogados have been named as Best Lawyer and Best Law Firm in Mexico by publications including *World Finance, IFLR 1000, Intercontinental Finance, CNBC Business, Corporate International, Who's Who Legal, Intercontinental Finance, Deal Makers* and *Lawyers World.*

Christina K Papachristopoulou
Partner, KP Law Firm
cpapachristopoulou@kp-lf.com

Christina Papachristopoulou is a finance, corporate and commercial and capital markets partner, specialising in complex cross-border corporate transactions, including M&A, consensual and court-assisted restructuring and privatisation transactions, and the entire spectrum of underlying finance structures and methodologies, ranging from simple equity and debt financing to complex money and capital markets syndicated or underwritten transactions.

She is a recognised expert in sovereign finance and regularly advises lenders, syndicate agents and portfolio managers on Greek government bond issues, sovereign default and restructuring. She has been involved in some of the most significant privatisations in Greece over the past decade, involving most known methodologies, including initial public and secondary offerings, accelerated book building and other over-the-counter transactions.

Ms Papachristopoulou is a Centre for Effective Dispute Resolution accredited mediator, and a member of the International Bar Association, the Hellenic Association for Financial Law, the Penn Law European Association and the Penn Alumni Association. She has also been sailing competitively for more than 12 years.

Borja Pardo
Associate, JAUSAS
bpardo@jausaslegal.com

Borja Pardo is an associate attorney in the insolvency and business restructuring department at JAUSAS.

He also has extensive experience in litigation and arbitration law, having actively participated in many civil and arbitrary proceedings, as well as in bankruptcy proceedings of all kinds, including those involving the restructuring of listed companies.

In addition to his law degree from the University of Barcelona, he has a journalism degree from the Autonomous University of Barcelona. He has published various articles in legal publications specialising in business restructuring and insolvency, and has been a guest lecturer for various courses, including the master's in insolvency law organised by the Barcelona Bar Association and the master's in corporate law organised by the University of Barcelona.

Alexandra Pelaghias-Christodoulou
Partner, Pelaghias, Christodoulou, Vrachas LLC
alexandra.pelaghias@pelaghiaslaw.com

Alexandra Pelaghias-Christodoulou attended De Montfort University in Leicester, United Kingdom, where she obtained a BA (hons) in law. She was admitted as a member of the Cyprus Bar Association in 1984 and started practising the same year.

She deals with ship finance, shipping, corporate, commercial law and international tax planning.

Ms Pelaghias-Christodoulou is fluent in Greek and English, and has a good command of French.

Ms Pelaghias-Christodoulou is a member of the Shipping Committee of the Cyprus Bar Association, the New York State Bar Association, the International Bar Association, the Propeller Club of the United States and the Legal Council of the Democratic Rally.

Cosimo Pennetta
Associate, Paul Hastings
cosimopennetta@paulhastings.com

Cosimo Pennetta is an associate in the corporate department of Paul Hastings and is based in the firm's Milan office.

Mr Pennetta focuses his practice on banking and finance matters. He has been involved in and has assisted with acquisition and real estate financing, corporate restructuring, residential and commercial mortgage-backed securitisation and non-performing loan transactions. He also advises on regulatory issues pertaining to financial institutions.

He joined Paul Hastings in 2009 and previously worked at a major Italian law firm in Milan.

Mr Pennetta graduated *magna cum laude* from Bocconi University in 2008 and was admitted to the Italian Bar in 2011.

Kari Amalie Pettersen
Lawyer, Grette DA
kape@grette.no

Kari Amalie Pettersen is an attorney at Grette DA and works primarily with regulatory and insolvency law. She regularly advises clients on matters related to the validity and enforceability of collateral and set-off arrangements. She holds a master of laws from the University of Oslo.

Maurice Phelan
Partner, Mason Hayes & Curran
mphelan@mhc.ie

Maurice Phelan is a partner practising corporate restructuring and insolvency in Irish firm Mason Hayes & Curran. His practice is primarily focused on advising domestic insolvency practitioners, banks and distressed companies, and he regularly represents parties in cross-border insolvencies with an Irish element. Mr Phelan has acted for companies, insolvency practitioners, banks and other creditors in most of the high-profile restructurings and corporate collapses in Ireland in recent years.

Felipe Pineda
Associate, JAUSAS
fpineda@jausaslegal.com

Felipe Pineda specialises in commercial law and acquisitions. In particular, he has spent more than 10 years advising both national and international companies linked to the aeronautical and tourism sectors, working on transactions of all kinds – both those occurring as part of their normal activities and those arising from strategic projects. His professional career has always been closely linked to international law due to his work with multinational companies with business dealings in Spain, and Spanish companies operating abroad.

Anna-Kaisa Remes
Associate, Castrén & Snellman
anna-kaisa.remes@castren.fi

Anna-Kaisa Remes advises clients on all aspects of insolvency and corporate law. Within the field of insolvency law, her expertise includes handling restructuring and bankruptcy proceedings, as well as advising clients with regard to impending insolvency proceedings. In addition, Ms Remes has broad expertise in corporate law and advises clients on general issues within that field.

Ms Remes's recent publications include articles on cash pooling and corporate governance.

Arne Riis
Partner, Bech-Bruun
ari@bechbruun.com

Arne Riis, a partner in Bech-Bruun's tax department, has a broad background in business tax law and represents Danish and international banks, private equity and venture funds, property investment funds, pension and life insurance business and listed companies concerning taxation matters.

His practice encompasses the national and international taxation aspects of mergers and acquisitions, corporate restructurings and refinancing, including tax issues related to corporate organisation, financial products, pension and life insurance business and incentive structures for management and key employees.

Mr Riis is a member of an extensive international network of tax lawyers and advisers. He speaks on tax law issues for private companies and in professional taxation forums in Denmark and abroad.

Nadia Tarolli Schmidt
Partner, VISCHER Ltd.
ntarolli@vischer.com

Nadia Tarolli Schmidt is a partner of VISCHER Ltd, a major Swiss law firm with offices in Basel and Zurich. She heads up the Basel office of VISCHER's tax team. She advises companies and private individuals on all matters pertaining to Swiss tax law – both in the national and international environment and in criminal tax law. Ms Tarolli can draw on over 10 years' experience of topics such as restructurings, relocations and succession planning. The know-how she gained from her previous work at the Swiss Bankers Association is regularly brought to bear in banking and finance issues and in the advice she provides to banking clients. With regard to the latter, clients particularly appreciate her experience of US tax law. As questions about occupational pensions are often related to tax issues, Ms Tarolli also heads up the occupational pension funds team. She holds a *lic iur* degree (1999) and is a Swiss-certified tax expert (2008).

Kirsten Schümann-Kleber
Partner, GÖRG Partnerschaft von Rechtsanwälten
kschuemann-kleber@goerg.de

Kirsten Schümann-Kleber is an insolvency and restructuring partner with GÖRG Partnerschaft von Rechtsanwälten, one of Germany's largest business law firms with a leading reputation in insolvency law and restructuring projects. Dr Schümann-Kleber is based in Görg's Berlin Office. Before joining Görg in 2005, she worked in the corporate finance/financial restructuring department of an international firm.

Dr Schümann-Kleber has particular expertise in the restructuring of German renewable energy and property projects. She has worked on numerous restructurings of German property portfolios and frequently advises foreign clients on restructurings and insolvency proceedings affecting their German subsidiaries.

Dr Schümann-Kleber is a member of the American Bar Association and an officer of the International Bar Association (Insolvency and Restructuring Section), and is also a member of the Committee for Restructuring and Insolvency of the German Lawyers' Association and the Berlin/Brandenburg Working Committee for Insolvency Law.

Steve Sunghwa Song
Attorney, Kim & Chang
steve.song@kimchang.com

Steve Sunghwa Song is a foreign attorney in the firm's banking practice group. He has worked with financial institutions and public companies on cross-border transactions including debt financing, acquisitions and renewable energy development projects.

Before entering the legal profession, Mr Song worked at the Korea Development Bank, where he focused on corporate banking, project finance and infrastructure development.

Kelli M Stephenson
Associate, Haynes and Boone, LLP
kelli.stephenson@haynesboone.com

Kelli M Stephenson is an associate in the bankruptcy and business restructuring section in the Houston office of Haynes and Boone, LLP. Her practice focuses on bankruptcy and insolvency law and related litigation. Ms Stephenson has represented debtors and creditors in Chapter 7 and Chapter 11 cases in a variety of industries in the United States. Ms Stephenson received her bachelor's degree from Texas A&M University and her law degree from American University Washington College of Law.

Odd Swarting
Partner, Setterwalls Law Firm
odd.swarting@setterwalls.se

Odd Swarting has a wide variety of experience in corporate insolvency and restructuring, beginning in 1985, including appointments as bankruptcy trustee for companies quoted on the Stockholm Stock Exchange and stockbroker companies under the supervision of the Swedish Financial Supervisory Authority, and restructuring work for various industrial, IT, property and development companies.

Mr Swarting also has particular experience of international insolvency questions and has been the Swedish representative at international seminars held by the American Bar Association, the International Bar Association and the International Insolvency Institute. He has been chairman of the Swedish Restructuring and Bankruptcy Trustees Association since 2003 and was an expert on the Swedish government committee reviewing Swedish insolvency laws (2009-2011).

Mr Swarting also advises commercial clients, particularly within the pharmaceutical and pulp and paper industries, on regulatory, commercial and corporate law.

Mario Benjamín Terán
Associate, M&M Bomchil
benjamin.teran@bomchil.com

Mario Benjamín Terán graduated as a lawyer from *Universidad de Buenos Aires* in 2008. He joined M&M Bomchil in 2008 as a member of the financial services and capital markets practices.

Between 2005 and 2007 he served as assistant professor of corporations and business associations at *Universidad de Buenos Aires* Law School, and is currently pursuing a master's in business law there.

He is admitted to the City of Buenos Aires Bar.

János Tóth
Partner, Wolf Theiss Budapest
janos.toth@wolftheiss.com

János Tóth is a partner in the Budapest office of Wolf Theiss, one of the leading law firms in Central and Southeastern Europe. He has been head of the corporate/M&A practice group, including competition/antitrust, since the launch of the Budapest office in 2007, and in recent years has participated in several significant M&A transactions in both Hungary and the region.

Mr Tóth's wide-ranging expertise in transactional and commercial matters, combined with his local market knowledge within Hungary, made him the perfect addition to Faludi Wolf Theiss's original team.

He lectures on international private law and international business law at the Károli Gáspár University in Budapest.

Shinsuke Ushirobira
Associate, Nishimura & Asahi
s_ushirobira@jurists.co.jp

Shinsuke Ushirobira is an associate at Nishimura & Asahi and works mainly in the area of restructuring/insolvency. He joined the firm in 2008 after graduating from the University of Tokyo School of Law (JD) in 2006 and attending the Legal Training and Research Institute of the Supreme Court of Japan. Since then, he has been involved in a number of bankruptcy proceedings, civil rehabilitation proceedings, corporate reorganisation proceedings and voluntary liquidations.

Joris van Horzen
Senior associate, Kennedy van der Laan NV
Joris.van.Horzen@kvdl.nl

Joris van Horzen is a senior associate in the banking and finance team of Kennedy Van der Laan. He specialises in cross-border finance transactions, security laws and financial regulatory laws. In particular, Mr van Horzen works for international banks and other financial institutions. He has also gained much experience in the field of payment transactions and has assisted a number of banks in implementing the EU Payment Services Directive. From 2007 to 2009 Mr Van Horzen was seconded to the legal departments of ABN Amro and Royal Bank of Scotland. He is recommended as "an associate to watch" in *Chambers Europe 2012* for banking and finance.

Ian Walker
Partner, Minter Ellison
ian.walker@minterellison.com

Ian Walker is a partner in the insolvency and reconstruction and dispute resolution groups of Minter Ellison in Melbourne.

Mr Walker holds degrees in law and commerce from the University of Melbourne. He has specialised in insolvency and reconstruction and work-outs, security enforcement, banking litigation and general commercial litigation for 28 years. He led the Minter Ellison team acting for the administrators of Pasminco Limited. He also advises secured lenders in relation to all aspects of enforcement of their securities.

Mr Walker advises directors on their duties when the company is facing financial distress. He acts for receivers and managers of trading businesses and for liquidators and administrators in connection with all aspects of their duties and the exercise of their powers. He is experienced in preparing and implementing deeds of company arrangement and other forms of solvent and insolvent restructuring.

Marcel Willems
Partner, Kennedy Van der Laan NV
marcel.willems@kvdl.nl

Marcel Willems started his professional career in 1988. In 1992 he co-founded Kennedy Van der Laan, now one of the leading firms in the Netherlands. Mr Willems has broad experience in insolvency, banking and finance and dispute resolution, mostly in a cross-border setting. He publishes and lectures regularly. Mr Willems has been active in the Insolvency, Restructuring and Creditors' Rights Section of the International Bar Association for a number of years, and is currently the secretary treasurer.

Celso Caldas Martins Xavier
Partner, Demarest e Almeida Advogados
cxavier@demarest.com.br

Celso Caldas Martins Xavier graduated from the Law School of *Pontifícia Universidade Católica de Sao Paulo* in 1999, and was the teaching assistant to former Chief Justice of the Supreme Court Cezar Peluso in that law school from 2000 to 2004. He earned his LLM from Stanford Law School in 2005, and worked as a foreign associate at Silicon Valley law firm Fenwick & West LLP in 2005. Mr Xavier has been a partner in the restructuring department of Demarest e Almeida Advogados, Brazil since 2008.

He was named by *Chambers Latin America 2011 and 2012* in the restructuring and product liability areas, and by *Best Lawyers* in 2010 and 2011 for litigation in Brazil. *Análise Advocacia 2010* and 2011 named him as a leading lawyer in the car manufacturing industry, while *Análise Advocacia 2011* listed him as one of the most admired lawyers for commercial litigation. Mr Xavier has written numerous articles on litigation, arbitration, restructuring and product liability, as well as participating in conferences on these topics. He is fluent in Portuguese and English, and speaks good Spanish and Italian.

Tian Xu
Resident partner, Eiger Law
xu.tian@eigerlaw.com

Tian Xu is the resident partner of Eiger Law's Shanghai office and leads its China practice. He is admitted to the People's Republic of China Bar, holds degrees in law and international relations and has specialised in foreign direct investment, corporate, M&A and employment law for nearly 10 years.

Mr Xu advises a number of the world's leading, European-based luxury goods, logistics and freight forwarding companies, as well as mechanical product manufacturers.

He speaks fluent Mandarin Chinese, English and German.

Hans Qizong Zhang
Associate, Eiger Law
hans.zhang@eigerlaw.com

Hans Qizong Zhang is an associate in the corporate and investment department of Eiger Law's Shanghai office. He holds an LLB from Shanghai University of Political Science and Law, and has specialised in several major foreign investment projects. Mr Zhang has also participated in a number of M&A, private equity and foreign investment projects, accumulating considerable theoretical and practical knowledge in those fields.

Belinda Danqing Zhou
Associate, Eiger Law
belinda.zhou@eigerlaw.com

Belinda Zhou is an associate in the corporate and investment department of Eiger Law's Shanghai office. She received her LLB from Tsinghua University and her LLM from the University of Munich. She specialises in foreign investment, labour law and general corporate practice. She has participated in several corporate and tax law matters, as well as M&A projects.